HANDBOOK OF PRINCIPLES OF ORGANIZATIONAL BEHAVIOR

INDISPENSABLE KNOWLEDGE FOR EVIDENCE-BASED MANAGEMENT

SECOND EDITION

Edited by

EDWIN A. LOCKE

A John Wiley and Sons, Ltd, Publication

Library of Congress Cataloging-in-Publication Data

Handbook of principles of organizational behavior/edited by Edwin Locke.
    p. cm.
    Previously published under title: The Blackwell handbook of principles of organizational
behavior/edited by Edwin A. Locke. Malden, MA: Blackwell Business, 2000.
    Includes bibliographical references and index.
    ISBN 978-0-470-74095-8 (cloth) — ISBN 978-0-470-74094-1 (pbk.)
    1. Organizational behavior.   I. Locke, Edwin A.   II. Blackwell handbook of principles of
organizational behavior
  HD58.7.B574   2009
  658—dc22

                                                  2009019335

A catalogue record for this book is available from the British Library.

Set in 10/12pt Baskerville by Macmillan Publishing Solutions, Chennai, India
Printed in Great Britain by CPI Antony Rowe, Chippenham, Wiltshire

Contents

Contributors and Editor

Maryam Alavi
Goizueta Business School, Emory University
Maryam_Alavi@bus.emory.edu

Teresa M. Amabile
Harvard Business School
tamabile@hbs.edu

Deborah Ancona
MIT Sloan School of Management
ancona@mit.edu

Boris B. Baltes
Department of Psychology, Wayne State University
b.baltes@wayne.edu

Albert Bandura
Department of Psychology, Stanford University
Bandura@psych.stanford.edu

Murray R. Barrick
Mays Business School, Texas A and M University
mbarrick@mays.tamu.edu

Kathryn M. Bartol
Robert H. Smith School of Business, University of Maryland
kbartol@rhsmith.umd.edu

J. Robert Baum
Robert H. Smith School of Business, University of Maryland
jrbaum@rhsmith.umd.edu

Beth A. Bechky
Graduate School of Management, University of California
babechky@ucdavis.edu

Michael Beer
Harvard Business School
Email: mbeer@hbs.ed

Deborah A. Cai
Department of Communication, University of Maryland
debcai@umd.edu

David Caldwell
Management Department, Santa Clara University
dcaldwell@scu.edu

Malissa A. Clark
Department of Psychology, Wayne State University
malissa@wayne.edu

Jason A. Colquitt
University of Florida
colquitt@ufl.edu

Jay A. Conger
Kravis Leadership Institute, Claremont McKenna College
jay.conger@cmc.edu

Lex Donaldson
Australian School of Business, University of New South Wales
lexd@agsm.edu.au

Cathy C. Durham
Director, Title V Grant, Glendale Community College
cdurham@glendale.edu

Marion B. Eberly
Michael G. Foster School of Business, University of Washington
marionb@.u.washington.edu

Miriam Erez
Faculty of Industrial Engineering and Management, Israel Institute of Technology
merez@ie.technion.ac.il

Ashley Fielbig
College of Behavioral and Social Sciences
afielbig@umd.edu

Edward L. Fink
Department of Communication, University of Maryland
elf@umd.edu

Colin M. Fisher
Morris Hall 103A, Harvard Business School
cfisher@hbs.edu

Jerald Greenberg
Institute for Civil Justice, RAND Corporation
jgreenbe@rand.org

J. Richard Hackman
Department of Psychology, Harvard University
hackman@fas.harvard.edu

Brooks C. Holtom
McDonough School of Business, Georgetown University
bch6@msb.edu

Karen A. Jehn
Department of Social and Organizational Psychology, Leiden University, The Netherlands
Jehnka@FSW.Leidenuniv.nl

Timothy A. Judge
Department of Management, Warrington College of Business, University of Florida
timothy.judge@cba.ufl.edu

Ryan Klinger
Warrington College of Business, University of Florida
ryan.klinger@cba.ufl.edu

Shelley A. Kirkpatrick
Director of Assessment Services, Management Concepts, Vienna, Virginia
skirkpatrick@managementconcepts.com

Richard P. Larrick
Fuqua School of Business, Duke University
larrick@duke.edu

Gary P. Latham
Rotman School of Management, University of Toronto
latham@rotman.utoronto.ca

Thomas W. Lee
Michael G. Foster School of Business, University of Washington
orcas@u.washington.edu

Edwin A. Locke
Robert H. Smith School of Business, Univeristy of Maryland (Emeritus)
elocke@rhsmith.umd.edu

Fred Luthans
Department of Management, University of Nebraska-Lincoln
fluthans1@unl.edu

Terence R. Mitchell
Michael G. Foster School of Business, University of Washington
trm@u.washington.edu

Michael K. Mount
Tippie College of Business, University of Iowa
michael-mount@uiowa.edu

Gerardo A. Okhuysen
David Eccles School of Business, University of Utah
gerardo@business.utah.edu

Craig L. Pearce
Peter F. Drucker and Masatoshi Ito School of Management
Craig.L.Pearce@gmail.com

Tabea Reuter
Freie Universität Berlin, Germany
tabea.reuter@fu-berlin.de

Maria Rotundo
Joseph L. Rotman School of Management, University of Toronto
rotundo@rotman.utoronto.ca

Sabrina C. Salam
Editor's note: I regret to announce that Sabrina Salam died tragically in a car accident on April 4, 2005

Eduardo Salas
Department of Psychology and Institute for Simulation and Training, University of Central Florida
esalas@ist.ucf.edu

Frank L. Schmidt
Tippie College of Business, University of Iowa
frank-schmidt@uiowa.edu

Professor Dr. Ralf Schwarzer
Freie Universität Berlin, Germany
health@zedat.fu-berlin.de

Kevin C. Stagl
Senior Talent Advisor and CEO, Talent Threshold LLC
kevin@talentthreshold.com

Alexander D. Stajkovic
Department of Management and Human Resources, University of Wisconsin-Madison
astajkovic@bus.wisc.edu

Cynthia Kay Stevens
Robert H. Smith School of Business, University of Maryland
cstevens@rhsmith.umd.edu

M. Susan Taylor
Robert H. Smith School of Business, University of Maryland
staylor@rhsmith.umd.edu

Ruth Wageman
Department of Psychology, Harvard University
rwageman@wjh.harvard.edu

John A. Wagner III
Department of Management, Michigan State University
wagner@msu.edu

Laurie R. Weingart
Tepper School of Business, Carnegie Mellon University
weingart@cmu.edu

Youngjin Yoo
Fox School of Business and Management, Temple University
Youngjin.yoo@temple.edu

Dr. Gary Yukl
Management Department, School of Business, University at Albany
G.yukl@albany.edu

Preface

The handbook, now in its second edition, fulfills a promise made when the first behavioral research in organizations began (Munsterberg, 1913) at the outset of the 20th century. It identifies general principles, validated by science, for managing people, work, and organizations well. Mastering these principles is the essential focus of high-caliber management education and effective workplace practice.

This book helps the reader to close the gap between the mass of scientific knowledge on organizational behavior and the day-to-day decisions made in organizations. Managers typically make decisions using the knowledge they already possess. Few base their professional decisions on systematic knowledge of organizations and human behavior. Even managers with advanced training often possess little knowledge of scientific facts about the work they do. Further, many management educators do not keep up with the ever-accumulating state of knowledge in management research (Rousseau, 2006). By helping to close the research–practice gap, this handbook offers both practitioners and educators the opportunity to bring their own professional practices up to speed, building on the best available scientific evidence.

Scientific evidence is acquired through direct experience, controlled observation, measurement, and experimentation. It is both an epitome of human knowledge and a project involving many thousands of people. The science in this book stands in contrast to the business hype and fads pushed by self-appointed gurus, who offer a good story and one-size-fits-all solutions, but not scientific evidence. Acting on unsubstantiated beliefs and trendy claims ultimately wastes an organization's time and money and the efforts of many well-meaning people. Failed efforts to improve the workplace take a toll on organizational well-being and performance and on the relationship between an organization's leaders and its members.

As Thomas Huxley said, "The deepest sin against the human mind is to believe things without evidence." Managing by evidence and fact means taking action based on core principles and fundamental truths developed through science and systematic observation. Decisions made on this sensible and reliable foundation, in turn, build employee trust that managers are competent and well informed (Colquitt and Salam, Chapter 21). The handbook provides this foundation.

SCIENCE YOU CAN USE

The handbook is chock-full of science-based facts about the human-made world of organizations. Massive amounts of data have been accumulated and integrated to develop the knowledge base on which each chapter is based. Chapter authors are the field's leading experts, who have pulled together the most important facts regarding each topic in a fashion both educators and practitioners can use. In doing so, the authors present much of the best replicated and most useful knowledge in organizational behavior. For example, did you know:

◆ In skilled jobs, top workers produce 15 times as much as the poorest performers. The single best predictor of this difference in productivity is general mental ability (intelligence, Schmidt, Chapter 1).

◆ Hiring people who are conscientious and emotionally stable has numerous benefits for organizations (Barrick and Mount, Chapter 2).

◆ Job satisfaction is an important predictor of life satisfaction – and mental challenge is a key factor in job satisfaction (Judge and Klinger, Chapter 6).

◆ Turnover has several different causes. Each requires a different approach by management (Eberly, Holtom, Lee, and Mitchell, Chapter 7).

◆ Setting specific challenging goals for employees is a very effective motivational technique but only if certain procedures are followed (Latham, Chapter 9).

◆ Money does motivate people, but pay systems have to be designed very carefully to avoid dysfunctional consequences (Durham and Bartol, Chapter 12).

◆ Effective team leadership does not depend on leader charisma but rather on performing certain key leadership functions (Hackman and Wageman, Chapter 15; Ancona and Caldwell, Chapter 16).

◆ Groups become skilled in interpersonal and task processes as they develop subconscious knowledge (often called collective intuition) that helps them cope with new situations (Okhuysen and Bechky, Chapter 17).

◆ Conflicts within teams can be effectively managed by implementing various coordination mechanisms (Weingart and Jehn, Chapter 18).

◆ To do their jobs well, managers need to utilize more types of power (e.g. expert power) than simply the authority that comes with their position (Yukl, Chapter 19).

◆ Top managers who set a clear vision for their organization and promote and enforce a rational code of values typically outperform executives who don't (Kirkpatrick, Chapter 20).

◆ The optimal organizational structure depends upon a variety of factors including size, strategy, and degree of specialization (Donaldson, Chapter 22).

◆ A key to effective decision making is broadening the decision framework. Doing so is enabled by using checklists, logic models, and other heuristics (Larrick, Chapter 25).

◆ Negotiation is most effective if specific, research-based procedures are followed (Taylor and Fielbig, Chapter 28).

◆ Swift action and experimentation are critical to entrepreneurial success, but one does not have to be the first mover to succeed (Baum, Chapter 30).

◆ Work/family balance requires both organizational supports and individual flexibility (Baltes and Clark, Chapter 31).

New scientific knowledge is discovered every day. Such knowledge is the product of many thousands of actively thinking individuals. Just consider what was required just to discover, validate, and apply germ theory in the field of medicine. Though its body of knowledge is much younger than the core fields of the natural sciences, the same is true in the field of organizational behavior. People are complicated, and the complexity multiplies a million-fold when you put hundreds or thousands of them together in organizations. People think, feel and make choices; genes, particles, atoms, and molecules do not. Nevertheless, through systematic study it is possible to understand both people and the organizations they create and belong to. The chapters in this book summarize much of what's been discovered about behavior in organizations. This provides both the educator and the practitioner a foundation to build on in their own work.

Have you ever heard these complaints?

◆ "The collective wisdom from research is being lost."
◆ "Practitioners do not read academic journals."
◆ "Academics, not practitioners, are driving the research agenda."
◆ "The relevance, quality, and applicability of research are questionable."
◆ "Practice is being driven more by fads and fashions than research."
◆ "Many practices are doing more harm than good."

These statements might remind you of conversations with faculty in schools of business or with practicing managers. From a management perspective, all of the statements basically ring true. Interestingly, however, the above statements were commonly voiced opinions quoted in a nearly two-decade-old *British Journal of Medicine* editorial (Smith, 1991) complaining that the practices of physicians and hospitals were failing to apply evidence from medical research in the ways they cared for patients. Today, evidence-based medicine is becoming the established mode of practice, with participants from over 90 countries. Management at the end of the 21st century's first decade is, on the other hand, in the same position medicine was 20 or more years ago. A tremendous store of useful evidence is available, but it awaits uptake by informed practitioners.

What changed in the field of medicine? A small percentage of physicians recognized that much more was known about good medical practice than they actually used in day-to-day patient care. These early adopters of evidence-based medicine led the way. They changed the health-care environment by creating new practices and routines. Later adopters accepted and employed these new routines once they became the "way it's done." This pattern of early use of evidence-informed practice by a small percentage of professionals has been observed repeatedly. It has been true throughout the many professions that today base their core practices on evidence, ranging from medicine and nursing to public health and criminology (Proctor, 2004; Rogers, 1995). Turning insights from research-based evidence into standard operating procedures is now a norm in many fields. From giving aspirin after a first heart attack in order to reduce the odds of a second, to criminal justice programs that keep inmates actively involved in their families, these routines all began with practitioners acting on an accumulation of scientific evidence.

This handbook positions you as an educator and/or practitioner to become an early adopter of evidence-based organizational and management practices. As an early adopter, you should experiment with ways of implementing this book's principles, take special efforts to learn from your experiences, and provide such opportunities to others. Doing so will further your understanding of how these principles work and how to use them well. The very fact that you have opened this book suggests a search for more knowledge. You are likely to believe that improving performance is both important and possible. Acting on evidence requires active thinking and reflection, indicators of a certain hunger for understanding. It is that hunger and the commitment to learning that can make you an effective user of evidence (cf. McAuliff and Kovera, 2008).

Not everyone is motivated to use evidence. Some people fail to learn new things because they don't want to bother exerting the effort. Others are overly optimistic about the quality of their own expertise and performance (Ehrlinger et al., 2008). Ironically, poor performers are the ones most likely to overestimate their expertise, because their very lack of competence makes it difficult for them to recognize how incompetent they are. This book was written for those in the remainder of the spectrum: those who are willing and able to expand their knowledge and expertise. It is intended for those who are prepared to work at deepening their understanding of what makes organizations effective, particularly in terms of managing people.

The most useful products of evidence-based research in management are *principles*, that is, general truths. For example, an important principle discovered in personnel selection is: *unstructured interviews are poor predictors of job performance*. Interviewers using their own idiosyncratic questions have low inter-interviewer agreement on applicants and virtually no reliable capacity to identify the candidate who is best able to do a job. Recruiters and personnel interviewers, and the people who manage them, are quite limited as well as biased in the information they gather about the selection interview's effectiveness (Highhouse, 2008). The other side of this principle in personnel selection is: *structured interviews are good predictors of job performance* (Stevens, Chapter 3). This second principle provides a basis for improving the way personnel decisions are made.

At the same time, there are several reasons why evidence *in itself* is not a solution. First, non-evidence-based practices are the norm – and most people are comfortable with the status quo. In the case of personnel decisions, most interviewers believe they are good judges of an applicant's qualifications. Interviewers do not realize how poor their choices really are because they seldom get systematic feedback on their actual success rates. Second, there are many institutional forces in place that keep invalid and ineffective practices like unstructured interviews from being discarded. Colleges spend a lot of money creating dedicated space for on-campus recruiters to interview students. Thousands of books give advice on the right way to answer interview questions. Abandoning the unstructured interview in favor of structured interviews or any other validated selection tool can generate surprise, resentment, and potential backlash. Finally, it is often not obvious, at least at first, exactly how to act on an evidence-based principle. Actually developing structured interviews requires special effort to learn new techniques; design and format structured, job-related questions; train interviewers in the new processes; and convince managers to support the change. It often takes several attempts to introduce an effective new selection system, requiring the political will to sustain the effort. (The results are worth it.)

In response to these challenges, encouraging the use of evidence-based principles requires that you as an educator or practitioner are aware of, develop, and foster two kinds of knowledge: declarative and procedural (Anderson, 1976). Principles are scientific facts or *declarative knowledge*. Facts include systematic observations (e.g. unstructured interviews are unreliable; structured interviews are reliable; it is important to have inter-rater agreement). Declarative knowledge is very flexible. It reflects general facts about the world and is readily adaptable to new environments. For this reason, all chapters in the book describe important declarative knowledge with broad applicability to both practitioners and educators.

The second basic kind of knowledge is *procedural knowledge*, how to apply the facts science has discovered. The book offers this type of knowledge too. Procedural knowledge is more grounded in context. It is discovered by learning what works and what doesn't in particular environments and conditions of use. One exemplar of procedural knowledge can be found in justice research. Over the past three decades, justice research has focused largely on strategies for promoting fairness in the workplace. Following the early research on equity theory in the 1960s, a newer generation of research addresses those features of organizational decision making and policies that influence justice beliefs. It offers action guides regarding procedural justice that are adaptable to a variety of settings, including acting consistently, suppressing bias, and providing opportunities for participation (Greenberg, Chapter 14).

The chapters in this book present a mixture of declarative and procedural knowledge. Cases in point include the characteristics and processes that make a performance appraisal system work (Rotundo, Chapter 5), the value and ways of giving workers recognition for good performance (Luthans and Stajkovic, Chapter 13), and the risks associated with stress and ways of managing it (Reuter and Schwarzer, Chapter 27). The actual skills required to apply this knowledge must still be developed through practice. Procedural knowledge is itself further deepened through action. Acting on the knowledge this book provides will involve you in the process of implementing, and sometimes inventing, practices that execute the essence of scientific principles.

We cannot assume others will take even the best evidence on faith. Helping people understand what works and what doesn't, and why, requires deepening your own understanding of the principles themselves. Having a good appreciation of why a principle works is important for developing critical judgment about why and when the principle should be applied and how to do so. This underlying knowledge is important to overcoming objections and resistance, making it easier for you to effectively demonstrate how a principle applies. The handbook provides a rich level of detail to help you carry on critical conversations with those whose support you need. In many cases, people react emotionally to acting on evidence-based principles, often because of their own subconsciously held ideas (Locke, Chapter 8). In the course of your own practice or teaching of evidence-informed management, you are in a position to help others change the assumptions underlying their emotions. By cultivating your passion for evidence, you can become more creative in how you use it (Amabile and Fisher, Chapter 26) and in the ways you model for others what it means to be an effective practitioner or evidence-informed educator.

USING THIS HANDBOOK

A wonderful feature of this book is that you can begin with any chapter of interest and pick and choose as you go. Every chapter contains references to other chapters, so you can follow your interests to related chapters if you want to learn more. Indeed, you may find that, as you come to apply ideas in a chapter, re-reading it can lead you to fresh insights.

Each chapter is intended to be a reliable and useful companion to your progression toward mastering key behavioral and organizational principles.

This handbook's usefulness to you depends on your efforts as a self-improving educator or manager. For readers to be evidence-based practitioners or effective evidence-informed educators, they need to design ways for themselves and others to act on the scientific facts provided here. Evidence-based practice means obtaining and using the best available evidence to inform decisions. It requires "decision awareness," that is, being aware of the many decisions and choices a practitioner might make each day, including those where the choice might be to take no action at all. There is more reflection and judgment to being an evidence-based manager than is the case for a shoot-from-the-hip counterpart.

This is not a cookbook. Evidence doesn't make decisions or solve specific problems. People do. This is done by critical reasoning, reflection on a principle's conditions of use, and learning by doing. Acting on this book's principles requires a mindful approach. In her eminently useful book on mindful learning, Langer (1997) illustrates the principles of mindfulness. Students learning physics (or management, psychology, or medicine) are better able to use principles to solve problems when they learn such principles conditionally. There is a world of difference between learning "X follows Y" and "*X often follows Y but only under specific conditions.*" A mindful approach where practitioners think conditionally creates openness to new information. Let's take a case in point. Latham (Chapter 9) presents a host of evidence-based principles that are predicated on a fundamental fact: challenging goals motivate higher performance than do general goals. If we apply this principle mindfully, we say "higher performance (X) often follows from setting challenging goals (Y)." Actively framing this principle in a mindful way prompts a set of questions. What else is going on in the situation which might make high performance occur (or not)? If high performance didn't occur, what might account for that? Did the individuals involved *accept* the goal? Did they have the *ability or knowledge* to achieve the goal? As you can see, a mindful approach to each principle fosters an implicit awareness of other possibilities and relevant facts in the situation. Avoiding overconfidence in any single answer encourages more attention to all of the possible answers. Entertaining greater possibilities ultimately means that more information relevant to the problem is considered in trying to solve it.

Overthinking or analysis paralysis is a less common dysfunction than some might think. Non-reflective action – acting mindlessly out of habit or impulse – is far more common. Once again, we can learn from the pursuit of evidence-based practice in medicine. Physicians understand the pressure to make a diagnosis quickly. Doctors in training learn to assess a patient's status in a deliberate fashion to avoid committing to a particular judgment prematurely (Groopman, 2007). They learn routines for questioning their own assumptions and re-reviewing information to avoid overlooking possible diagnoses. Using evidence-based practice, the physician strikes a balance between the extremes of overthinking and impulsiveness. In becoming a more mindful practitioner, you will learn to keep your mind open to possibilities as you develop deeper skill in diagnosing situations and applying evidence in flexible ways. As an educator, by emphasizing mindful learning you will help students use principles more effectively to solve problems and appreciate the myriad ways in which they might apply to various situations.

Mindful learning increases with practice over time. The more you apply the handbook's principles, the more effective you will be at knowing how and when to use them and how they connect to one another. Applying the same principle across different situations will create more flexible categories for interpreting your observations and deepen the base of knowledge on which you can draw. Let's look at how one might mindfully use one of the classic principles in change management: *people characteristically resist change in organizations* (Beer, Chapter 29). The dynamics of resistance are closely tied to the degree of attachment human beings usually have to the status quo. Appreciating this underlying dynamic of change resistance can generate a host of considerations to guide the actions of a would-be change manager. In particular, a mindful change manager, reading Beer's chapter, can discover that he or she typically has an array of alternative interventions that can be used to implement change. Changes undermining the status quo are, other things being equal, more likely to generate resistance than changes keeping the status quo basically intact. Similarly, an add-on to circumstances people already accept is a lot less threatening than wholesale change. Thus, for instance, it typically is easier to add profit sharing on top of a salary system than it is to completely replace salaries with profit sharing.

One important factor in designing a change strategy is to identify how necessary it is to disrupt the status quo. Categorizing change interventions in terms of the degree to which they challenge the status quo can give the change manager a variety of choices. Profit sharing could be installed as an add-on to an existing system, period. Alternatively, there can be a gradual phase-in of profit sharing and a revamping or elimination of the salary system over time. Further, by reflecting on why people might resist or accept change at various times, a practitioner who appreciates *why* a principle works can identify more effective ways of acting on it in light of the circumstances he or she faces. Some people might actually dislike the present status quo or prefer the benefits a change offers. Those people are likely to be early supporters, rather than resistors of change.

Getting Ready for the Journey

Developing your professional evidence-based practice is a life-long journey. Handbook editor Ed Locke makes a compelling case that the principles presented herein give practitioners new ways to think and to organize their world. It is important that you incorporate the essential gist of this handbook's principles into your habits of mind. Doing so means working with these principles on a day-to-day basis. This can be done one principle at a time, as circumstances warrant. In time, you will develop powerful ways of acting effectively and modeling to others what it means to be a competent, trustworthy manager.

Thoughtful use of this book moves you along the path to becoming an informed user of evidence. Beware of any claim you encounter based on a single study (or none at all). Know that evidence comes from a body of research, as assembled in this handbook. The chapters herein reflect findings accumulated from many and varied studies. The critical reader should scrutinize each chapter for information that aids in applying its principles. Two kinds of information are particularly helpful to watch for: *supports* and *counter-indicating factors*. Supports are co-occurring conditions not part of the phenomenon itself that influence its occurrence or consequences. Knowledge about effective workforce training – which involves many critical subprinciples and often modern technology – has made huge strides in recent years. Training builds self-efficacy (Bandura, Chapter 10). Training and efficacy foster successful empowerment (Conger and Pearce, Chapter 11; Salas and Stagl, Chapter 4). Information technology can support new ways of organizing and learning (Alavi and Yoo, Chapter 32). Participation and quality communication foster indispensible knowledge exchange (Cai and Fink, Chapter 23; Wagner, Chapter 24). Counter-indicating conditions can also exist that make principles inapplicable or difficult to apply (e.g. for participation to work there must be knowledge to exchange). In particular, Erez (Chapter 33) provides a basis for reflecting on how cross-cultural forces can influence the application of principles. She notes that directive leadership produces more positive responses in countries valuing authority than in more egalitarian nations. Although each situation will have differing supports and counter-indicating factors present, the research on which this book's principles are based demonstrates considerable generalizability across circumstances, when mindfully applied.

The environments we participate in can help or hinder learning. Shaping your environment in ways that promote learning begins with sharing your insights from this book and engaging others in the process of learning to act on evidence-based principles. This book's principles offer considerable guidance in learning-to-learn – particularly when you use several principles in combination. Here are some basic combinations of principles that can aid you in learning-to-learn. Seek feedback regarding the outcomes of your decisions, and set goals for improving these outcomes (Latham, Chapter 8; Larrick, Chapter 25). Choose your initial applications of this book's principles for the observability of their results, so you get feedback you can learn from – and so you can demonstrate the benefits from acting on evidence to others (Beer, Chapter 29). Using after-action reviews can help evaluate what works and what needs improvement. Doing so regularly allows you to model effective use of evidence to the people you work with, and makes it easier to recognize them for their contributions to that effort (Luthans and Stajkovic, Chapter 13). Colleagues and employees who are later adopters of evidence will find it easier to apply evidence themselves if evidence-based routines, guidelines, and checklists are developed to help them (see Larrick, Chapter 25, for decision supports to improve decision processes; and Beer, Chapter 29, for ways of promoting organizational and behavioral change).

You – the reflective practitioner or the educator developing that competency in others – can use the principles in this book in a host of ways. Experiment. Seek feedback on the impact of your interventions or teaching. Redesign your management practice or teaching based on this feedback. Update your knowledge as new scientific evidence continues to emerge. In doing so, you are on your way to mastering evidence-based management.

Denise M. Rousseau

REFERENCES

Anderson, J. R. (1976). *Language, Memory, and Thought*. Hillsdale, NJ: Erlbaum.

Ehrlinger, J., Johnson, K., Banner, M., Dunning, D., and Kruger, J. (2008). Why the unskilled are unaware: Further explorations of (absent) self-insight among the incompetent. *Organizational Behavior and Human Decision Processes*, 105, 98–121.

Groopman, J. (2008). *How do Doctors Think?* Boston: Mariner.

Highhouse, S. (2008). Facts are stubborn things. *Industrial and Organizational Psychology*, 1, 373–376.

Langer, E. J. (1997). *The Power of Mindful Learning*. Cambridge, MA: Perseus.

McAuliff, B. D., and Kovera, M. B. (2008). Juror need for cognition and sensitivity to methodological flaws in expert evidence. *Journal of Applied Social Psychology*, 38, 385–408.

Munsterberg, H. (1913). *Psychology and Industrial Efficiency*. Boston: Houghton-Mifflin.

Proctor, E. K. (2004). Leverage points for the implementation of evidence-based practice. *Brief Treatment and Crisis Intervention*, 4, 227–242.

Rogers, E. M. (1995). *Diffusion of Innovation*. New York: Simon and Schuster.

Rousseau, D. M. (2006). Is there such a thing as evidence-based management? *Academy of Management Review*, 31, 256–269.

Smith, R. (1991). Where is the wisdom? The poverty of medical evidence [editorial]. *British Medical Journal*, 303, 789–799.

Editor's Introduction[i]

This handbook is about management principles, each chapter written by an expert in the field – but why do we need principles?

To quote Ayn Rand (1982, p. 6):

> . . . abstract ideas are conceptual integrations which subsume an incalculable number of concretes – and without abstract ideas you would not be able to deal with concrete, particular, real-life problems. You would be in the position of a newborn infant, to whom every object is a unique, unprecedented phenomenon. The difference between his mental state and yours lies in the number of conceptual integrations your mind has performed.

> You have no choice about the necessity to integrate your observations, your experiences, your knowledge into abstract principles.

What, then, is a principle? A "principle" is a general truth on which other truths depend. Every science and every field of thought involves the discovery and application of principles . . . a principle may be described as a fundamental reach by induction (Peikoff, 1991, p. 218).

Examples of principles that we use (or should use) in everyday life are:

"Be honest" (a moral principle);
"Eat plenty of fruits and vegetables" (nutrition);
"Exercise regularly" (health);
"Save for the future" (personal finance);
"Do a conscientious job" (work and career); and
"Do not drive under the influence of alcohol" (personal safety).

It would be literally impossible to survive for long if one did not think in terms of principles, at least implicitly. In terms of concrete details, every situation is different from every other. Suppose, for example, that a child were told, "Do not run across that part of this street today." What is the child to do on other days? On other streets? On other parts of the same street? Such a dictum would be useless to the child after the day had passed or if he were in another location. Properly, the child would be taught a principle such as

---

[i]This introduction is adapted from Locke (2002). I thank Jean Binswanger, Paul Tesluk, Cathy Durham, and James Bailey for their helpful comments on the original article.

"Never cross any street without first looking twice in each direction." This could guide the child's actions for life and in every location in the world.

How are principles formulated? By integrating conceptual knowledge (for more on concept formation see Locke, 2002, and Peikoff, 1991). Principles, in turn, are integrated into theories, again by induction (Locke, 2007).

TEACHING

The use of principles is critical to both the teaching and practice of management. Let's begin with teaching. Most instructors would agree that management is a difficult subject to teach. First, it is very broad in scope. It entails scores if not hundreds of different aspects. The more one studies the field, the more complex and bewildering it seems to become. Second, there are no concrete rules or formulas to teach as in the case of accounting, finance, or management science. Management is as much an art as a science. Third, although there are theories pertaining to different aspects of management (e.g. leadership), many find these theories to be less than satisfactory (to put it tactfully), because they are too narrow, trivial, or esoteric and/or lack firm evidential support. Often they are based on deduction rather than induction (Locke, 2007). The potentially useful theories are mixed in with those that are not.

Traditionally, teaching has been done with either textbooks and/or the case method. Both methods contain the same epistemological limitation. Textbooks, because they try to be comprehensive, pile up detail after detail, but the details, even of subtopics, are very difficult to integrate. As noted above, any theories that are presented often have severe limitations. The result is that students routinely suffer from massive cognitive overload and a sense of mental chaos; thus little of the material is retained (once the final exam is over). This makes it unlikely that what was memorized will be applied to the students' jobs and career.

With regard to case studies, these allow for the possibility of induction but shockingly, it has been reported that some business schools openly *prohibit* connecting the cases to each other. This is very unfortunate. Each case is a unique, concrete instance. Suppose, for example, a business student concluded from analysis of a particular case study that a certain high technology firm in New Hampshire should replace the CEO, develop a top management team, and change to a matrix structure. What could the student take away from such an analysis that would help him be a better manager? Nothing at all, if the analysis were left in the above form. The case would only be useful if the student could formulate some general principles from studying a variety of cases. The best way to do this is by induction from a series of cases (see Locke, 2002, for a detailed example), though even this could be limited depending on the choice of cases. Faculty whom I knew who used cases have admitted to me that they have to use theoretical materials (e.g. principles) for the students to be able to even analyze the cases in the first place.

The value of this book for teaching, therefore, is two-fold. First, it is an alternative to a traditional textbook. The material in this book is *essentialized*. Only what the expert chapter writers consider important is included; thus there is far less to remember than in a text. This means the material can be more easily retained and more readily applied to the real world of work. Further, the principles are evidence based and thus tied firmly to reality.

Second, this book can be used as an adjunct to a course which uses cases. Here both deduction and induction can be used. The book's principles can help students to analyze the cases, yet new principles (or qualifications to principles) could be developed through induction from the cases used.

(There are other problems with the case method that I can only note briefly here, for example the emphasis on verbal glibness; the fact that all the information needed is already in the case; the fact that the case is taken out of a wider organizational context; the fact that real action is not possible; and the lack of face-to-face contact with actual employees. Primarily, these problems are inherent in the attempt to teach a practical skill in a classroom and so have no perfect solution, though student mini-projects within real businesses help.)

MANAGEMENT

This book can also help managers and executives be more effective. However, reading a book of evidence-based principles does not magically turn one into a good manager. Principles cannot be mastered overnight and cannot be applied mechanically. Regardless of the level of abstraction at which they are formulated, they are still abstractions, not concrete rules such as "turn off the lights when you leave the room." Principles, however, are used to guide specific actions in specific contexts.

Consider the principle: "Motivate performance through goal setting" (Chapter 9 of this book). This principle does not tell one what to set goals for (a very critical issue); who is to set them; what the time span will be; what strategy to use to reach them; how performance will be measured; how flexible the goals will be; or how performance will be rewarded. To some extent formulating subprinciples can be a help, because these would give some idea of how to implement the principles. For example, subprinciples for goals (given in Chapter 9) would include (a) make the goals clear and challenging; (b) give feedback showing progress in relation to the goals; (c) get commitment through building confidence; (d) insure that people have the needed knowledge; (e) provide needed resources and so forth. But these subprinciples do not tell one everything. There will always be judgment calls to be made, because one cannot teach every possible context factor that a future manager might face.

Furthermore, principles cannot be applied in a vacuum, or one at a time in some arbitrary order. Many – maybe dozens or possibly hundreds – of principles must be used to run a successful business. (The problem of cognitive overload is mitigated over time by gradually automatizing the principles in the subconscious.) Furthermore, the principles must be orchestrated so that they function in concert rather than working at cross-purposes. It is not known how effectively one can teach such orchestration, although one can make the student aware of the issue and give some examples. For example, the goal system must be integrated with the performance appraisal system and the reward system.

It is worth observing here how principles are used in the real world of management. I will use Jack Welch as an example in that he is considered among the greatest CEOs in history, the creator of $300–400 billion in stockholder wealth at General Electric (e.g. see Slater, 1999; Tichy and Sherman, 1993). Some principles that Welch used as his personal guides to action are as follows:

- ◆ Reality. Face reality as it really is, not as you want it to be. (I believe that the failure to practice this principle is a major cause of business failures, for example Enron. Such failures may involve flagrant dishonesty, but they also may involve simple evasion – the refusal to look at pertinent facts – or putting emotions ahead of facts.)
- ◆ Control your own destiny or someone else will.
- ◆ Change before you have to.
- ◆ Compete to win.

Welch also helped develop a code of values or guiding principles for GE as a whole:

- ◆ Show integrity.
- ◆ Hate bureaucracy.
- ◆ Be open to new ideas regardless of their source.
- ◆ Pursue high quality, low cost, and speed.
- ◆ Have self-confidence.
- ◆ Have a clear, reality-based vision.
- ◆ Possess energy and energize others.
- ◆ Use stretch goals and (differential) rewards.
- ◆ View change as an opportunity, not as a threat.
- ◆ Have a global focus.

Obviously, Welch was able not only to formulate but also to apply and orchestrate principles in a way that no one else had. It helped that he had ambition and energy, a brilliant business mind, an insatiable curiosity, the capacity to judge talent, and an uncanny ability to figure out what businesses GE should and should not be in.

It is interesting that Jacques Nasser was a great admirer of Welch and tried to emulate his principles at Ford but was unable to do so and ultimately lost his job. It is clear that there is a long road between knowing good principles and being able to implement them successfully in the context of a given organization.

Management principles need to be organized and integrated hierarchically so that the leader will know what to do first, second, and so forth. Except for facing reality as it is (not evading), which should be the primary axiom of every manager, the hierarchy may not be the same from business to business or in the same business at different times. Nor will they all be OB principles. For example, in one context the most critical factor may be to decide, as Welch did, what business or businesses a corporation should be in. This is an aspect of vision and strategic management. There is no point in trying to manage the wrong business or working hard to do the wrong thing. But in another context, the critical issue may be cash flow, for example how to avoid bankruptcy in the next six months (a finance issue). In a different context, the core problem might be getting the right people in the right jobs or revamping the incentive system (HR issues).

What factors would determine the hierarchy? Three are critical: (1) *Context.* What are the most important facts regarding the present situation of this company? Context means seeing the whole and the relationship of the parts to the whole. (2) *Urgency.* What has to be fixed right away if the company is to survive? (3) *Fundamentality.* What is the cause of most of the different problems the organization is faced with or what must be fixed before any other fixes will work (e.g. get good people in key jobs)?

The hierarchy can change over time. For example, when Welch took over at GE, he focused first on changing the business mix (selling and buying businesses) and cutting costs (increasing productivity) and layers of management. Later, he focused on better utilizing people (empowerment), and still later on improving quality (quality goals). Reversing the sequence would not have worked, because empowerment and quality would not help businesses that were not viable and would not "take" in a ponderous bureaucracy.

The foregoing is to make an important point for the second time: *business is an art as much as a science.* Having correct principles will not work unless the leader knows how and when to use them. Great leaders are rare because not many of them can effectively perform all the tasks that leadership requires (Locke, 2003).

The way to manage complexity is not to complexify it, as academics love to do. After reading some six books about and one book by Jack Welch, I was struck by how frequently he stressed the importance of simplicity. He said:

> Simplicity is a quality sneered at today in cultures that like their business concepts the way they like their wine, full of nuance, subtlety, complexity, hints of this and that . . . cultures like that will produce sophisticated decisions loaded with nuance and complexity that arrive at the station long after the train has gone . . . you can't believe how hard it is for people to be simple, how much they fear being simple. They worry that if they're simple, people will think they are simpleminded. In reality, of course, it's just the reverse. Clear, tough-minded people are the most simple. (Quoted in Lowe, 1998, p. 155)

I am reminded of a recent conversation with a consultant who works as a coach to top executives. He told me that one question he always asks in the first meeting is "By the way, how do you make money?" The ones who answered by wallowing in complexity usually did not make any. The ones who gave succinct, clear answers usually did.

For a business leader, achieving simplicity, as opposed to simplemindedness, is much harder than achieving complexity. To achieve simplicity one must look through the morass of complexity one is seemingly faced with, integrate the key observations, and come up with the *essential* ideas that will make one's business succeed. That is, one must bring order out of chaos. The way to do this is to think inductively and integrate one's observations into principles.

Notes Regarding the Second Edition

The second edition of this book includes the following changes: (1) there are four new chapters, a new introduction, a preface, and new authors for some of the original chapters; (2) all the chapters have been updated with respect to the latest research and nearly all present new cases examples; typically, however, the original principles have remained the same (or been slightly reformulated); (3) all the chapters now have exercises at the end to help students better understand the principles. Although authors were asked to title their chapters in terms of a single principle, a few have two or three related principles.

This last relates to the issue of what the appropriate level of abstraction should be for management principles. If they are formulated too broadly (e.g. "be rational"), it can be hard to connect them to specific actions without very extensive elaboration. On the other hand, if they are too narrow ("turn out the light when leaving the room"), they are not broadly applicable and one would need thousands of them – too many to retain – to cover the waterfront. Thus I encouraged mid-range principles and the authors thankfully complied.

In closing, I should note that the principles in this book do not include all possible management principles (e.g. none of the chapters discussed strategic management principles – that would be another book). I chose topics from I/O psychology, human resource management, and organizational behavior (fields which all overlap) that I thought would be of most interest and use to present and future managers. I hope these hopefully timeless principles will contribute to your success at work.

References

Locke, E. A. (2002). The epistemological side of teaching management: Teaching through principles. *Academy of Management Learning and Education*, 1, 195–205.

Locke, E. A. (2003). Foundations for a theory of leadership. In S. Murphy and R. Riggio (eds), *The Future of Leadership Development*. Mahwah, NJ: L. Erlbaum.

Locke, E. A. (2007). The case for inductive theory building. *Journal of Management*, 33, 867–890.

Lowe, J. (1998). *Jack Welch Speaks*. New York: Wiley.

Peikoff, L. (1991). *Objectivism: The Philosophy of Ayn Rand*. New York: Dutton.

Rand, A. (1982). *Philosophy: Who Needs It*. New York: Bobbs-Merrill.

Slater, R. (1999). *Jack Welch and the GE Way*. New York: McGraw Hill.

Tichy, N., and Sherman, S. (1993). *Control Your Own Destiny or Someone Else Will*. New York: Currency Doubleday.

Part I

SELECTION

1

Select on Intelligence

FRANK L. SCHMIDT

Other things equal, higher intelligence leads to better job performance on all jobs. Intelligence is the major determinant of job performance, and therefore hiring people based on intelligence leads to marked improvements in job performance – improvements that have high economic value to the firm. This principle is the subject of this chapter.

This principle is very broad: it applies to all types of jobs at all job levels. Until a couple of decades ago, most people believed that general principles of this sort were impossible in personnel selection and other social science areas. It was believed that each organization, work setting, and job was unique and that it was not possible to know which selection methods would work on any job without conducting a validation study on that job in that organization. This belief, called the theory of situational specificity, was based on the fact that different validity studies of the same selection procedure(s) in different jobs in the same organization and/or different organizations appeared to give different results. However, we now know that these "conflicting findings" were mostly due to statistical and measurement artifacts and that some selection procedures have high validity for predicting performance on all jobs (e.g. intelligence) and others do a poor job of predicting performance on *any* job (e.g. graphology) (Schmidt and Hunter, 1981, 1998). This discovery was made possible by new methods, called meta-analysis or validity generalization methods, that allow researchers to statistically combine results across many studies.

Meta-analysis has also made possible the development of general principles in many other areas beyond personnel selection (Hunter and Schmidt, 2004; Schmidt, 1992). For example, it has been used to calibrate the relationships between job satisfaction and job performance with precision (Judge, Thoresen, Bono, and Patton, 2001) and between organizational commitment and work-related outcomes including job performance (Cooper-Hakim and Viswesvaran, 2005).

WHAT IS INTELLIGENCE?

Intelligence is not the ability to adapt to one's environment; insects, mosses, and bacteria are well adapted to their environments, but they are not intelligent. There are many ways in which organisms can adapt well to their environments; use of intelligence is only one possible way. Intelligence is the ability to grasp and reason correctly with abstractions (concepts) and solve problems. However, perhaps a more useful definition is that intelligence is the ability to learn. Higher intelligence leads to more rapid learning, and the more complex the material to be learned, the more this is true. Intelligence is often referred to as general mental ability (GMA) and general cognitive ability, and we use all these terms interchangeably in this chapter.

Intelligence is the broadest of all human mental abilities. Narrower abilities include verbal ability, quantitative ability, and spatial ability. These narrower abilities are often referred to as special aptitudes. These special aptitudes do predict job performance (although less well than GMA), but only because special aptitude tests measure general intelligence as well as specific aptitudes (Brown, Le, and Schmidt, 2006; Schmidt, Ones, and Hunter, 1992). It is the GMA component in these specific aptitude tests that predicts job performance. For example, when a test of verbal ability predicts job or training performance, it is the GMA part of that test – not the specifically verbal part – that does the predicting (Brown et al., 2006).

Intelligence predicts many important life outcomes in addition to job performance: performance in school, amount of education obtained, rate of promotion on the job, ultimate job level attained, income, and many other things (Brody, 1992; Herrnstein and Murray, 1994; Gottfredson, 1996; Jensen, 1998). It is even involved in everyday activities such as shopping, driving, and paying bills (Gottfredson, 1996). No other trait – not even conscientiousness – predicts so many important real world outcomes so well. In this sense, intelligence is the most important trait or construct in all of psychology, and the most "successful" trait in applied psychology.

The thousands of studies showing the link between intelligence (GMA) and job performance have been combined into many different meta-analyses. Ree and co-workers have shown this for military jobs (Olea and Ree, 1994; Ree and Earles, 1991, 1992; Ree, Earles, and Teachout, 1994), as have McHenry, Hough, Toquam, Hanson, and Ashworth (1990) in the famous Project A military study. (With a budget of 24 million dollars, Project A is the largest test validity study ever conducted.) Hunter and Hunter (1984) have shown this link for a wide variety of civilian jobs, using the US Employment Service database of studies. Schmidt, Hunter, and Pearlman (1980) have shown it for both civilian and military jobs. Other large meta-analytic studies are described in Hunter and Schmidt (1996), Schmidt (2002), and Schmidt and Hunter (2004). Salgado and his colleagues (Salgado, Anderson, Moscoso, Bertua, and de Fruyt, 2003a, 2003b) demonstrated the link between GMA and job performance across settings in the European countries. The amount of empirical evidence supporting this principle is today so massive that it is hard to find anyone who questions the principle.

There has been an important development since the first edition of this book appeared in 2000: a new and more accurate method for correcting for the biases created by range restriction has been developed and applied (Hunter, Schmidt, and Le, 2006; Schmidt, Oh, and Le, 2006; Schmidt, Shaffer, and Oh, 2008). (Range restriction is the condition in which variability of the predictor (here intelligence) in one's sample of people (job incumbents) is artificially lower than in the population of people (job applicants) one wants to get estimates for.) Application of this procedure to existing data shows that previous estimates of the validity of GMA – including those in the 2000 version of this chapter – were underestimated by 25% to 30%. In this chapter, I present the updated, more accurate validity estimates. When performance is measured objectively using carefully constructed work sample tests (samples of actual job tasks), the correlation (validity) with intelligence measures is about .84–84% as large as the maximum possible value of 1.00, which represents *perfect* prediction. When performance is measured using ratings of job performance by supervisors, the correlation with intelligence measures is .66 for medium complexity jobs (over 60% of all jobs). For more complex jobs, this value is larger (e.g. .74 for professional and managerial jobs), and for simpler jobs this value is not as high (e.g. .56 for semi-skilled jobs). Another performance measure that is important is amount learned in job training programs (Hunter et al., 2006). Regardless of job level, intelligence measures predict amount learned in training with validity of about .74 (Schmidt, Shaffer, and Oh, 2008).

WHY DOES INTELLIGENCE PREDICT JOB PERFORMANCE?

It is one thing to have overwhelming empirical evidence showing a principle is true and quite another to explain *why* the principle is true. *Why* does GMA predict job performance? The primary reason is that people who are more intelligent learn more job knowledge and learn it faster. The major direct determinant of job performance is not GMA but job knowledge. People who do not know how to do a job cannot perform that job well. Research has shown that considerable job knowledge is required to perform even jobs most college students would think of as "simple jobs," such as truck driver or machine operator. More complex jobs require even more job knowledge. The simplest model of job performance is this: GMA causes job knowledge, which in turn causes job performance. But this model is a little too simple: there is also a causal path directly from GMA to job performance, independent of job knowledge. That is, even when workers have equal job knowledge, the more intelligent workers have higher job performance. This is because there are problems that come up on the job that are not covered by previous job knowledge, and GMA is used directly on the job to solve these problems. Many studies have tested and supported this causal model (Hunter, 1986; Ree, Earles, and Teachout, 1994; Schmidt, Hunter, and Outerbridge, 1986). This research is reviewed by Schmidt and Hunter (1992), Hunter and Schmidt (1996), and Schmidt and Hunter (2004). It has also been shown that over their careers people gradually move into jobs that are consistent with their level of GMA (Wilk, Desmariais, and Sackett, 1995; Wilk and Sackett, 1996). That is, a process that sorts people on GMA takes place gradually over time in everyday life. People whose GMA exceeds their job level tend to move up to more complex jobs; and people whose GMA is below their job level tend to move down.

There is a broader theory that explains these research results: the traditional psychological theory of human learning (Hunter and Schmidt, 1996; Schmidt and Hunter, 2004). This theory correctly predicted that the effect of GMA would be on the learning of job knowledge. The false theory of situational specificity became widely accepted during the first eight decades of the 20th century in considerable part because personnel psychologists mistakenly ignored the research on human learning.

Many lay people find it hard to believe that GMA is the dominant determinant of job performance. Often they have known people who were very intelligent but who were dismal failures on the job because of "bad behaviors" such as repeated absences from work, carelessness at work, hostility toward the supervisor, unwillingness to work overtime to meet a deadline, or stealing from the company. These are examples of so-called "counterproductive work behaviors" (CWBs). Integrity tests predict CWBs with a validity of about

.35 (Ones, Viswesvaran and Schmidt, 1993). People with lower scores on integrity tests show more CWBs. The personality trait of conscientiousness also predicts CWBs (again, negatively). However, a recent large-scale study ($N > 800$) found that GMA predicted CWBs with a validity of .47; when the more accurate correction for range restriction is applied, this figure becomes .57. So it is possible that the best predictor of CWBs is GMA. People who are more intelligent show fewer CWBs.

There is also a facet of job performance called "contextual performance" (CP). CP is just good citizenship behaviors, while CWB is bad citizenship behaviors as discussed above. CP behaviors include willingness to help train new employees, willingness to work late in an emergency or on a holiday, supporting the community relations and reputation of the company, and many other such behaviors. CP behaviors and CWBs are different from core job performance but are often confused with core job performance by lay observers. CP and CWB behaviors are predicted by measures of the personality traits of conscientiousness and to a lesser extent agreeableness (Dalal, 2005). We do not yet know whether GMA predicts CP behaviors; these studies have yet to be done. Low ability leads to an inability to perform well; low conscientiousness and low agreeableness lead, not primarily to low performance on core job tasks but to lack of CP and/or more displays of organizationally disruptive behaviors (CWBs). These disruptive behaviors are more visible to lay observers (and to many supervisors) than differences between employees in core job performance, probably because they appear so willful. On the other hand, a low ability employee has difficulty learning how to perform the job, but if he/she has a "good attitude," this employee often seems like less of a problem than one showing CWBs. This makes it difficult for some to clearly see the GMA–performance link in the real world (Hunter and Schmidt, 1996).

Of course, low conscientiousness can lead to less effective performance if it results in reduced effort (see Chapter 2, this volume). For objective measures of job performance, empirical evidence indicates that on typical jobs this effect is limited, probably because most jobs are fairly structured, reducing the scope for individual differences in effort to operate (Hunter, Schmidt, Rauschenberger and Jayne, 2000; Hunter and Schmidt, 1996). However, it is important to remember that when supervisors rate job performance, they incorporate into their ratings both CP behaviors and CWBs, in addition to core job performance (Orr, Sackett, and Mercer, 1989; Rotundo and Sackett, 2002). Hence supervisory ratings reflect a combination of core job performance and citizenship behaviors, both good and bad. In the case of ratings, low conscientiousness and low agreeableness lead to poorer citizenship behaviors, which lead to lower ratings of overall performance. For the typical job, the weight on conscientiousness in predicting objectively measured core job performance is only 20% as large as the weight on GMA. In predicting supervisory ratings of job performance, it is 40% as large (Schmidt, Shaffer, and Oh, 2008).

What is Required to Make This Principle Work?

There are three conditions that are required to make this principle work. That is, there are three conditions that are required for companies to improve job performance levels by using GMA in hiring and to reap the resulting economic benefits.

Selectivity

First, the company must be able to be selective in who it hires. For example, if the labor market is so tight that all who apply for jobs must be hired, then there can be no selection and hence no gain. The gain in job performance per person hired is greatest with low selection ratios. For example, if one company can afford to hire only the top scoring 10%, while another must hire the top scoring 90% of all applicants, then with other things equal the first company will have a much larger gain in job performance.

There is another way to look at this: companies must provide conditions of employment that are good enough to attract more applicants than they have jobs to fill. It is even better when they can go beyond that and attract not only a lot of applicants, but the higher ability ones that are in that applicant pool. In addition, to realize *maximum* value from GMA-based selection, employers must be able to *retain* the high performing employees they hire.

Measuring general mental ability

Second, the company must have some way of measuring GMA. The usual and best procedure is a standardized employment test of general intelligence, such as the Wonderlic Personnel Test. Such tests are readily available at modest cost. Less valid are proxy measures such as grade point average (GPA) or class rank. Such proxy measures are partial measures of intelligence. Also, intelligence can be assessed to some extent during the employment interview (Huffcutt, Roth, and McDaniel, 1996), although this is a much less valid measure of GMA than a standardized written test.

Variability in job performance

Third, the variability in job performance must be greater than zero. That is, if all applicants after being hired would have the same level of job performance anyway, then nothing can be gained by hiring "the best." This condition is always met. That is, on all jobs studied there have been large differences between different workers in quality and quantity of output. Hunter, Schmidt, and Judiesch (1990) meta-analyzed all available studies and found large differences between employees. In unskilled and semi-skilled jobs, they found workers in the top 1% of performance produced over three times as much output as those in the bottom 1%. In skilled jobs, top workers produced 15 times as much as bottom workers. In professional and managerial jobs, the differences were even larger. These are very large differences, and they are the reason it pays off so handsomely to hire the best workers.

There is another advantage to hiring the best workers: the pool of talent available for future promotion is greatly increased. This is of great value to employers, because it helps ensure high performance all the way up through the ranks of managers. When the right people are promoted, their value to the firm in their new jobs is even greater than in their original jobs. Thus selection of high ability people has implications not only for the job they are hired onto, but for other jobs in the organization, too.

ARE THERE EXCEPTIONS TO THIS PRINCIPLE?

As long as the three conditions described above are met, there are no known exceptions to this principle. That is, there are no known cases or situations in which it is inadvisable to select employees for general intelligence.

However, there are some people, particularly labor leaders, who believe there is an exception. These people believe that companies should not select on mental ability if they can select on job experience instead. That is, they believe that job experience is a better predictor of job performance than general intelligence. What does research show? For applicants with job experience of between none and five years, experience *is* a good predictor of job performance. But in the range of higher levels of experience, say from five to 30 years of job experience, job experience does not predict performance very well (Schmidt, Hunter, Outerbridge, and Goff, 1988; Hunter and Schmidt, 1996). On most jobs, once people have about five years of experience, further experience does not contribute much to higher performance. This is probably because experience beyond five years does not lead to further increases in job knowledge. This, in turn, may be due to the fact that after five years of on-the-job learning, people in the typical job are forgetting job knowledge about as fast as they are learning new job knowledge.

Another important fact is this: even for new hires in the one to five year range of job experience, where experience is a valid predictor of job performance, the validity declines over time. That is, experience predicts performance quite well for the first three years or so on the job and then starts to decline. By 12 years on the job, experience has low validity. But GMA continues to predict job performance quite well even after people have been on the job 12 years or more.

What this means is that job experience is *not* a *substitute* for GMA. In the long run, hiring on intelligence pays off much more than hiring on job experience (Hunter and Schmidt, 1996). So if you had to choose, you should choose GMA. However, typically, you do not have to choose; more than one procedure can be used. It may be desirable to use *both* experience and GMA in hiring; as discussed later, it is usually best to use multiple hiring methods. But in this case, the *weighting* given to GMA should be higher than the weighting given to job experience.

ISSUES IN IMPLEMENTING AN ABILITY-BASED HIRING SYSTEM

Can intelligence be too high?

One issue is whether an applicant can have too much intelligence for a job. Recently, an applicant was rejected for a job as a police officer in a New Jersey city on grounds that his intelligence test score was too high! This city believed something that many people believe: that intelligence leads to better job performance *but only up to a point*. After that, more intelligence leads to *lower* job performance. Hundreds of studies have shown that this is false. Higher intelligence leads to better job performance up to the highest levels of intelligence (Coward and Sackett, 1990). There is a straight line (linear) relationship between intelligence and job performance. Why do so many people believe otherwise? Probably because they imagine a university professor or a medical doctor working as a janitor, and they think "This person would be so bored with this job that he would do a poor job." They forget that the university professor or doctor would never apply for the janitor's job to begin with.

Among people who actually apply to get real jobs, there is a straight line relationship between intelligence and performance; the higher the intelligence, the better the job performance. Hence, we do not have to worry about hiring people who are too intelligent for the job.

Does only intelligence matter in jobs?

A second issue is the one alluded to earlier: Although intelligence is the best predictor of job performance, it does not follow that use of intelligence *alone* in hiring is the best way to select people. In fact, it is well known that other predictors can be used along with intelligence to produce better predictions of job performance than intelligence alone. For example, for most jobs an intelligence test combined with an integrity test (a composite personality of conscientiousness, emotional stability, and agreeableness) is 20% more valid than an intelligence test alone. Adding a structured employment interview to an intelligence test increases validity by 14% (Oh, Schmidt, and Shaffer, 2008). It is almost always possible to add supplementary measures that increase validity. Some of these measures are discussed in other chapters in this book (e.g. Barrick and Mount's chapter on selection of conscientiousness and emotional stability).

Are there legal risks in selecting for intelligence?

A third issue is the potential for legal risks. Members of some minority groups, particularly blacks and Hispanics, typically have lower average scores on GMA tests, leading to lower hiring rates. Government agencies such as the Equal Employment Opportunity Commission refer to these lower hiring rates as "adverse impact." The term adverse impact is deceptive, because it implies that the GMA tests *create* the difference in test scores, when in fact the tests only measure real pre-existing differences in mental skills. This is shown by the fact that minorities and non-minorities with the same test scores have the same level of later job performance. That is, the test scores predict equally accurately for all groups; they are predictively fair or unbiased (Schmidt, 1988; Wigdor and Garner, 1982).

Despite this fact, a lower hiring rate for minorities does sometimes lead to lawsuits. Employers can win these suits by demonstrating that the tests are valid predictors of job performance. Today, such demonstrations rely increasingly on summaries of the kinds of research findings discussed in this chapter, rather than on studies conducted by the employer. (This is part of the move away from the theory of situational specificity, discussed earlier.) Since around the mid 1980s, employers have been winning more and more such suits, and today they prevail in 80% or more of such suits. Research shows that the value of the increases in job performance from good selection overshadows any potential legal costs stemming from defending against such suits. But a key fact is that today there are far fewer such suits to begin with. Currently, less than 1% of employment-related lawsuits are challenges to selection tests or other hiring procedures. This is almost certainly due to the greatly reduced chances of winning such suits.

Political risks

However, this does not mean that all employers are willing to use intelligence tests in hiring. Although the percentage of employers using GMA tests has been increasing, some firms view even the possibility of a lawsuit as a public relations disaster. They feel that even if they win, they still lose on the public relations front. And they believe that public relations problems can reduce sales and profits. These firms – mostly larger companies that sell directly to consumers – are willing to tolerate lower levels of job performance to avoid even the possibility of such a problem. Unfortunately for such firms, not using GMA tests does not remove the possibility of lawsuits. Other selection procedures also produce "adverse impact." Employers have tried to reduce adverse impact by introducing various forms of minority preferences in hiring, but courts have recently begun to strike down many forms of minority preferences. For example, under the 1991 Civil Rights Act, it is illegal to adjust test scores or other scores to equalize minority and non-minority hiring rates. This issue is one that will probably remain unsettled for some time.

Many firms that rarely use written GMA tests build oral GMA tests into the interview process. For example, in many employment interviews at Microsoft, job applicants are asked to solve complex mental puzzles that require high GMA to answer correctly. In fact, even ordinary job interviews have been found to be correlated with GMA scores (Huffcutt et al., 1996). And, as would be expected from this fact, it has recently been found that even ordinary job interviews show larger minority–majority differences (and thus "adverse impact") than was previously believed to be the case (Roth, Bobko, Switzer, and Dean, 2001).

The effect of testing for intelligence on employee attitudes

A fifth issue is whether the use of mental ability tests turns off applicants. Some have argued that applicants do not like to take ability tests. However, surveys of applicant attitudes reveal that they view mental ability and GMA tests as generally relevant to job performance (more so than they do personality, bio-data, and integrity tests, for example), and that they do not have a negative attitude toward such tests (Hausknecht, Day, and Thomas, 2004). It also appears to be the case that when GMA or other ability tests are used, applicants view the selection requirements as being higher and this increases the status of the job and hence its attractiveness. That is, something that is harder to attain is viewed as being more valuable.

The economic value of hiring on intelligence

A final issue is whether the economic value of the job performance gains from GMA-based hiring is cancelled out by higher wages and salaries. The argument is that if a firm hires more intelligent people, they will have to pay them more and this will cancel out the gains from the increased job performance. However, in most cases it appears that there is no increase in compensation costs, at least initially. This is especially likely to be the case when few of the firm's competitors use GMA measures in their hiring. Typically, there is a pool of available applicants in the area for a particular type of job, and the higher GMA applicants have no immediate effective way to command higher initial wages.

However, after some time on the job, when higher GMA employees have developed high levels of performance, the employer can afford to share some of these gains with such employees in the form of higher wages or salaries. In some cases, this might be necessary to retain high performing employees. In any event, the payoff to the employer in terms of enhanced job performance is much greater than any increase in compensation cost.

Although most employers, for most jobs, do not pay different people in the same job at different rates, they do typically promote the top workers to higher level jobs, and this does result in higher pay. But at promotion the value of the worker's performance to the firm increases much more than the worker's pay, creating another large net benefit to the firm of good selection. On the other hand, employers that hire only mediocre or poor workers at entry level find that their higher level jobs also become filled with mediocre or poor performers. Again, as noted earlier, selection based on GMA improves performance not only in the job in question, but also later in higher level jobs in the firm.

CASE EXAMPLES

We will first look at two negative examples and then examine two positive examples of real world applications of GMA-based hiring.

US Steel plant at Fairless Hill, PA

Up until 1978, the US Steel plant at Fairless Hills, PA, selected applicants into their skilled trades apprentice programs based on the applicants' total scores of a battery of ability tests. These total scores were a good measure of GMA, and selection was from the top down. The plant maintained apprentice programs in the wide variety of skilled trades needed to run a steel mill: machinists, tool and die makers, electricians, sheet metal workers, etc. The local unit of the United Steelworkers Union, however, did not like this selection method. In negotiations with the union, the company agreed to modify the selection system. In the new system, all applicants who scored above a low cut-off on each test, set at about the 7th grade level, were considered equally qualified and eligible for hire. Only a few applicants were screened out by this procedure. Applicants in the passing group were selected based on plant seniority only. Hence, this plant went from a GMA-based hiring system to one in which GMA played only a very minor role.

The apprentice training center at Fairless Hills was a well-run facility that kept excellent records of apprentice performance from both before and after the change in the selection system. These records showed that after the new selection system was introduced, performance plummeted. Scores on the mastery tests of amount learned in training declined markedly. The flunk-out and drop-out rates increased dramatically. The training time and training costs of those who did make it through the program increased substantially – because many apprentices had to retake multiple units in the training. And finally, the ratings of later performance on the job out in the plant declined.

This was a well-controlled natural quasi-experiment. The only change made was the lowering of mental ability standards in selection. The training program and the tests given in the program remained the same. The decline in performance was clearly due to the lower intelligence of the new apprentices.

The Washington, DC police force

Up until the mid 1980s the Washington, DC police force was one of the best in the USA. Applicants were selected for Police Academy training based on a general intelligence test constructed for the District of Columbia by the US Office of Personnel Management (OPM), as required by then existing Congressional regulations. This test had been challenged legally and the case had gone all the way to the US Supreme Court, where it had been upheld. A background investigation was also part of the selection process. The mayor of Washington, Marion Barry, repeatedly voiced opposition to both the test and the background check on grounds that the failure rate on both was higher for blacks. In 1987, when Congress relinquished control over the selection process to the Mayor's office, Barry took responsibility for the selection process out of OPM's hands. He then eliminated both the GMA test and the background test. The replacement selection process was somewhat unclear, but reputedly involved fairly perfunctory interviews.

The first consequence was that the flunk-out rate in the Police Academy soared, with over 80% of the new hires being incapable of completing the required training. Failure rates that high were viewed as unacceptable, and so the content of academy training was "dumbed down." When this reduced the failure rate only slightly, the content was further dumbed down, and then dumbed down again. This process of successive adjustments ultimately "solved" the flunk-out problem.

However, the police officers being produced were incompetent. Large numbers of murder indictments had to be dismissed because the reports written by the officers on the scene were unintelligible, due to the low literacy levels. The solution rate for murder cases, formerly one of the highest in the USA, declined precipitously to one of the lowest. Firearms accidents soared because officers did not know how to use their sidearms properly. Complaints of police abuse and incompetence from citizens soared. In addition, crime on the police force became quite common. For example, a group of police officers was found to be selling handguns previously confiscated from criminals *back to criminals*! These changes and others are described by Carlson (1993a, 1993b).

In this example, unlike the US Steel example, *two* things are happening. First, people low in intelligence are being hired, resulting in plummeting job performance. Second, criminals are being hired because there was no background investigation to ensure that they were not, and the result was crime on the police force.

Employment in the federal government

We now turn to a more positive example – or at least a less negative one. For many jobs in the federal government, people can either be hired from the outside using a GMA test or they can be promoted from within. When they are promoted from within, GMA tests are usually not used – although they sometimes are. Instead, people are evaluated based on records of their education and training and on appraisals by their supervisors of their performance in their present jobs. These procedures do have some validity but would not be expected to be as valid as GMA-based hiring.

So we can ask the following question. After people have been on the job some time, is the job performance higher for those initially selected using a GMA test? Government researchers at OPM addressed this question in a detailed study of three representative mid-level government jobs: IRS auditor, social security claims examiner, and customs inspector. In each of these jobs, people hired both ways had been on the job from five to eight years.

The measure of job performance was unusually good: it was the sum of a hands-on work sample test, a job knowledge test, and supervisory ratings of job performance.

In all three jobs, those selected years earlier using GMA tests had higher job performance. The average job performance of the non-GMA-selected employees was at the 50th percentile, while that of the GMA-selected employees was at the 70th percentile. This is a large difference. If this difference is projected over the federal workforce as a whole, it amounts to *billions* of dollars per year in increased output (Schmidt, Hunter, Outerbridge, and Trattner, 1986). We can also look at this another way. Americans expect their federal government to perform a wide variety of socially important tasks (e.g. administer the social security program, protect homeland security, run the federal tax system fairly and accurately, catch people who commit federal crimes, etc.). To the extent that the federal government hires less competent people, these jobs are done less well. As shown in this research, failure to select on GMA results in the hiring of less competent people and produces lower job performance.

This study was a reasonably controlled quasi-experiment. During the study, the researchers did not know which employees had initially been selected using a GMA measure and which had not. The only relevant difference between the two groups of workers was the method by which they had been hired. This study provides strong evidence that GMA-based hiring pays off in higher job performance.

The Philip Morris plant in Cabarrus County, North Carolina

The US Employment Service began a new nationwide program of employment testing, operated through state employment offices, in the early 1980s. Like its earlier program, it was based on the General Aptitude Test Battery (GATB). One of the three abilities measured in that program was GMA (the other two were general perceptual ability and general psychomotor ability). This new program was based on the methods of meta-analysis or validity generalization that were mentioned at the beginning of this chapter.

The large Philip Morris plant in Cabarrus County, North Carolina, was one of the first employers to subscribe to this testing program. They signed an agreement under which the state employment service tested and referred the higher scoring applicants to Philip Morris for possible hire. For the jobs at Philip Morris, most of the weight was placed on GMA in determining who was hired.

The human resources department at Philip Morris decided to conduct a study to compare the performance of GATB–GMA-selected workers and workers hired without use of the test. They found that the GMA-selected workers were superior across a variety of performance measures. For example, there was a 35% gain in output. The GMA-selected workers learned 8% more skills during job training, had 25% fewer operator failures and 58% fewer disciplinary actions. The incidence of unsafe job behaviors was 35% less and the reduction in work days lost to accidents was *82%*.

These are large differences. The Philip Morris personnel researchers, Dennis Warmke and William Van Arnam, noted the employment interview used might have contributed somewhat to the performance superiority of these workers. However, they stated that because it was the GMA test that screened out most of the applicants who were not hired, the GMA test was the dominant influence producing the performance improvements. This research is described in McKinney (1984).

CONCLUSION

Higher intelligence leads to better job performance on all jobs, and the increases in job performance resulting from hiring on GMA have high economic value for organizations. Higher intelligence causes higher job performance primarily because it causes people to learn job knowledge faster and to learn more of it. However, intelligence is also used directly on the job to solve performance-related problems, independent of prior job knowledge. The primary requirement that an organization must meet to make GMA-based hiring work well is the ability to attract job applicants and to retain them once they are hired. Despite beliefs to the contrary, hiring on job experience is inferior to hiring on GMA. Although GMA is the most important determinant of job performance, it is not the only determinant. Therefore, firms should use other valid procedures along with GMA. Finally, we have seen four concrete, graphic, real world examples of the impact of GMA on job performance.

REFERENCES

Brody, N. (1992). *Intelligence* (2nd edition). San Diego, CA: Academic Press Inc.

Brown, K., Le, H., and Schmidt, F. L. (2006). Specific aptitude theory revisited: Is there incremental validity for training performance? *International Journal of Selection and Assessment*, 14, 87–100.

Carlson, T. (1993a). D.C. blues: The rap sheet on the Washington police. *Policy Review*, Winter, 27–33.

Carlson, T. (1993b). Washington's inept police force. *The Wall Street Journal*, November 3.

Coward, W. M., and Sackett, P. R. (1990). Linearity of ability–performance relationships: A re-confirmation. *Journal of Applied Psychology*, 75, 295–300.

Cooper-Hakim, A., and Visweswaran, C. (2005). The construct of work commitment: Testing an integrative framework. *Psychological Bulletin*, 131, 241–259.

Dalal, R. S. (2005). A meta-analysis of the relationship between organizational citizenship behavior and counterproductive work behavior. *Journal of Applied Psychology*, 90, 1241–1235.

Gottfredson, L. S. (1996). Why g matters: The complexity of everyday life. *Intelligence*, 24, 79–132.

Hausknecht, J. P., Day, D. V., and Thomas, S. C. (2004). Applicant reactions to selection procedures: An updated model and meta-analysis. *Personnel Psychology*, 57, 639–683.

Herrnstein, R. J., and Murray, C. (1994). *The Bell Curve: Intelligence and Class Structure in American Life*. New York: The Free Press.

Huffcutt, A. I., Roth, P. L., and McDaniel, M. A. (1996). A meta-analytic investigation of cognitive ability in employment interview evaluations: Moderating characteristics and implications for incremental validity. *Journal of Applied Psychology*, 81, 459–473.

Hunter, J. E. (1986). Cognitive ability, cognitive aptitudes, job knowledge, and job performance. *Journal of Vocational Behavior*, 29, 340–362.

Hunter, J. E., and Hunter, R. F. (1984). Validity and utility of alternate predictors of job performance. *Psychological Bulletin*, 96, 72–98.

Hunter, J. E., and Schmidt, F. L. (1996). Intelligence and job performance: Economic and social implications. *Psychology, Public Policy, and Law*, 2, 447–472.

Hunter, J. E., and Schmidt, F. L. (2004). *Methods of Meta-analysis: Correcting Error and Bias in Research Findings*. Thousand Oaks, CA: Sage.

Hunter, J. E., Schmidt, F. L., and Judiesch, M. K. (1990). Individual differences in output variability as a function of job complexity. *Journal of Applied Psychology*, 75, 28–42.

Hunter, J. E., Schmidt, F. L., and Le, H. (2006). Implications of direct and indirect range restriction for meta-analysis methods and findings. *Journal of Applied Psychology*, 91, 594–612.

Hunter, J. E., Schmidt, F. L., Rauschenberger, J. M., and Jayne, M. (2000). Intelligence, motivation, and job performance. Chapter in C. L. Cooper and E. A. Locke (eds), *I/O Psychology: What We Know about Theory and Practice*. Blackwell Publishers, pp. 278–303.

Jensen, A. R. (1998). *The g Factor: The Science of Mental Ability*. Westport, CT: Praeger.

Judge, T. A., Thoresen, C. J., Bono, J. E., and Patton, G. K. (2001). Another look at the relationship between job satisfaction and job performance. *Psychological Bulletin*, 127, 376–407.

McHenry, J. J., Hough, L. M., Toquam, J. L., Hanson, M. L., and Ashworth, S. (1990). Project A validity results: The relationship between predictor and criterion domains. *Personnel Psychology*, 43, 335–354.

McKinney, M. W. (1984). Final report: Validity generalization pilot study. Southern Test Development Field Center, US Employment Service, Raleigh, North Carolina.

Oh, I., Schmidt, F. L., and Shaffer, J. (2008). Comprehensive updating of the validity and incremental validity of selection procedures based on 95 years of research. Working paper, Department of Management, Tippie College of Business, University of Iowa, Iowa City, Iowa.

Olea, M. M., and Ree, M. J. (1994). Predicting pilot and navigator criteria: Not much more than g. *Journal of Applied Psychology*, 79, 845–851.

Ones, D. S., Viswesvaran, C., and Schmidt, F. L. (1993). Comprehensive meta-analysis of integrity test validities: Findings and implications for personnel selection and theories of job performance. *Journal of Applied Psychology*, 78, 679–703.

Orr, J. M., Sackett, P. R., and Mercer, M. (1989). The role of prescribed and nonprescribed behaviors in estimating the dollar value of performance. *Journal of Applied Psychology*, 74, 34–40.

Ree, M. J., and Earles, J. A. (1991). Predicting training success: Not much more than g. *Personnel Psychology*, 44, 321–332.

Ree, M. J., and Earles, J. A. (1992). Intelligence is the best predictor of job performance. *Current Directions in Psychological Science*, 1, 86–89.

Ree, M. J., Earles, J. A., and Teachout, M. (1994). Predicting job performance: Not much more than g. *Journal of Applied Psychology*, 79, 518–524.

Roth, P. I., Bobko, P., Switzer, F. S., and Dean, M. A. (2001). Prior selection causes biased estimates of standardized ethnic group differences: Simulation and analysis. *Personnel Psychology*, 54, 591–617.

Rotundo, M., and Sackett, P. R. (2002). The relative importance of task, citizenship, and counterproductive performance to global ratings of job performance: A policy-capturing approach. *Journal of Applied Psychology*, 87, 66–80.

Salgado, J. F., Anderson, N., Moscoso, S., Bertua, C., and de Fruyt, F. (2003b). International validity generalization of GMA and cognitive abilities: A European community meta-analysis. *Personnel Psychology*, 56, 573–605.

Salgado, J. F., Anderson, N., Moscoso, S., Bertua, C., de Fruyt, F., and Rolland, J. P. (2003a). A meta-analytic study of general mental ability validity for different occupations in the European community. *Journal of Applied Psychology*, 88, 1068–1081.

Schmidt, F. L. (1988). The problem of group differences in ability scores in employment selection. *Journal of Vocational Behavior*, 33, 272–292.

Schmidt, F. L. (1992). What do data really mean? Research findings, meta analysis, and cumulative knowledge in psychology. *American Psychologist*, 47, 1173–1181.

Schmidt, F. L. (2002). The role of general cognitive ability in job performance: Why there cannot be a debate. *Human Performance*, 15, 187–210.

Schmidt, F. L., and Hunter, J. E. (1981). Employment testing: Old theories and new research findings. *American Psychologist*, 36, 1128–1137.

Schmidt, F. L., and Hunter, J. E. (1992). Development of causal models of processes determining job performance. *Current Directions in Psychological Science*, 1, 89–92.

Schmidt, F. L., and Hunter, J. E. (1998). The validity and utility of selection methods in personnel psychology: Practical and theoretical implications of 85 years of research findings. *Psychological Bulletin*, 124(2), 262–274.

Schmidt, F. L., and Hunter, J. E. (2004). General mental ability in the world of work: Occupational attainment and job performance. *Journal of Personality and Social Psychology*, 86, 162–174.

Schmidt, F. L., Hunter, J. E., and Outerbridge, A. N. (1986). The impact of job experience and ability on job knowledge, work sample performance, and supervisory ratings of job performance. *Journal of Applied Psychology*, 71, 432–439.

Schmidt, F. L., Hunter, J. E., Outerbridge, A. N., and Goff, S. (1988). The joint relation of experience and ability with job performance: A test of three hypotheses. *Journal of Applied Psychology*, 73, 46–57.

Schmidt, F. L., Hunter, J. E., Outerbridge, A. N., and Trattner, M. H. (1986). The economic impact of job selection methods on the size, productivity, and payroll costs of the Federal work-force: An empirical demonstration. *Personnel Psychology*, 39, 1–29.

Schmidt, F. L., Hunter, J. E., and Pearlman, K. (1980). Task difference and validity of aptitude tests in selection: A red herring. *Journal of Applied Psychology*, 66, 166–185.

Schmidt, F. L., Oh, I., and Le, H. (2006). Increasing the accuracy of corrections for range restriction: Implications for selection procedure validity and other research findings. *Personnel Psychology*, 59, 281–305.

Schmidt, F. L., Shaffer, J. A., and Oh, I. (2008). Increased accuracy for range restriction corrections: Implications for the role of personality and general mental ability in job and training performance. *Personnel Psychology*, 61, 827–868.

Schmidt, F. L., Ones, D. S., and Hunter, J. E. (1992). Personnel selection. *Annual Review of Psychology*, 43, 627–670.

Wigdor, A. K., and Garner W. R. (eds) (1982). *Ability Testing: Uses, Consequences, and Controversies* (Report of the National Research Council Committee on Ability Testing). Washington, DC: National Academy of Sciences Press.

Wilk, S. L., Desmarais, L. B., and Sackett, P. R. (1995). Gravitation to jobs commensurate with ability: Longitudinal and cross-sectional tests. *Journal of Applied Psychology*, 80, 79–85.

Wilk, S. L., and Sackett, P. R. (1996). Longitudinal analysis of ability–job complexity fit and job change. *Personnel Psychology*, 49, 937–967.

EXERCISES

Hiring office workers

You are the human resources director at a large firm and you are faced with designing a system for hiring office workers. An office manager comes to you and says the firm should not use written GMA tests because of the danger of law suits. He says he knows GMA is important to job performance but maintains that you can use "GMA-loaded" interviews to measure GMA and thus get the benefit of using GMA without leaving a "paper trail" of test scores that could stimulate a law suit. Respond to this manager based on what you learned from this chapter. What would you tell him? What is the foundation for your response?

Educating the CEO

You are the human resources director in your organization. The CEO calls you to her office for a meeting and tells that she knows from 35 years of experience in dealing with people that the key determinant of high job performance is personal values and sense of responsibility. She says she would like to have all hiring in the company done using measures of values and sense of responsibility. Based on what you learned in this chapter, what would you tell her? What is the basis for the position you are taking?

2

Select on Conscientiousness and Emotional Stability

MURRAY R. BARRICK AND MICHAEL K. MOUNT

Chapter 1 of this volume showed that selecting people with higher intelligence leads to better job performance. However, job performance is not only a function of an individual's ability (i.e. what he or she can do); it is also a function of their motivation (i.e. what they will do). The two personality traits that best predict individuals' long-term, dispositional motivation levels and subsequent work behaviors are conscientiousness and emotional stability. The universal principle that we advocate in this chapter is that organizations should always select on the personality dimensions of conscientiousness and emotional stability. A subprinciple of the chapter is that organizations should also select on other personality dimensions, but such practices should be dictated by the specific requirements of the job or the particular criterion.

What behaviors do employers perceive that employees need in order to succeed in the 21st century? A collaborative study of over 400 employers across the USA conducted by The Conference Board, Partnership for 21st Century Skills, Corporate Voices for Working Families, and the Society for Human Resource Management (2006) examined the readiness of new entrants to the workforce. Although both basic and applied skills are important, survey responses revealed, when results were combined across education levels, that the two most important applied skills were professionalism/work ethic and teamwork/collaboration. These skills are influenced by "will do" factors and were viewed as more important than those skills associated with the "Three Rs." Similar findings were reported in a large study conducted in a Midwestern state that asked employers which employee behaviors were most important for workplace success (Michigan Employability Study, 1990). The seven top ranked items were: be free from substance abuse; demonstrate honesty and integrity; pay attention to the person speaking; follow directions given verbally; show respect for others; show pride; and be punctual in attendance. Employers clearly value "will do" characteristics in applicants. Many of these essential workplace behaviors that employers desire are largely influenced by an individual's motivation and are influenced less by general mental ability.

In this chapter we discuss the benefits that accrue to organizations when they select employees on the personality traits of conscientiousness and emotional stability.

WHAT BEHAVIORS DO CONSCIENTIOUSNESS AND EMOTIONAL STABILITY PREDICT?

Personality can be defined as an individual's relatively stable and enduring pattern of thoughts, feelings and actions. Although more than 15,000 trait terms in the English language can be used to describe personality, most researchers agree that the structure of personality consists of five broad dimensions, often called the Big Five or the Five Factor Model (FFM) of personality: conscientiousness (i.e. dependable, industrious, efficient and achievement oriented), emotional stability (i.e. calm, steady, self-confident, and secure), extraversion (i.e. gregarious, sociable, ambitious, and active), agreeableness (i.e. courteous, helpful, trusting, cooperative, and considerate), and openness to experience (i.e. cultured, intellectual, imaginative, and analytical).

Performance

Of the five major personality dimensions, conscientiousness and emotional stability are the most valid predictors of performance outcomes (such as those listed above) across different occupations. Other things being equal, individuals high on conscientiousness and emotional stability perform better on the job and this improved job performance has a substantial economic impact on the firm. Conscientious individuals are achievement oriented, hard working, dependable, persistent, responsible, organized, careful, and reliable. Such traits are fundamentally related to motivation at work because they lead to increased effort and following rules. Similarly, neurotic individuals (emotional stability is often referred to by the low end traits) are nervous, highly strung, stress prone, moody, lack self-esteem, and are insecure. Not surprisingly, such traits tend to inhibit positive motivational tendencies at work. That is, individuals who spend time worrying about their performance, doubt their abilities, require assurance from others, are depressed and stress prone are unable to develop adequate coping strategies and cannot focus attention on the tasks at hand. In short, traits associated with the low end of emotional stability (neuroticism) lead to poor performance.

The general principles that we advocate in this chapter have a strong foundation in research. They are derived from the results of several large-scale, meta-analytic studies that have demonstrated the relationship between personality traits and job performance (e.g. Barrick and Mount, 1991; Barrick, Mount, and Judge, 2001; Hough, 1992; Hurtz and Donovan, 2000; Salgado, 1997, 1998). For example, Barrick et al. (2001) reviewed eight meta-analyses conducted since 1990 involving hundreds of studies and thousands of employees and reported that both conscientiousness and emotional stability predicted overall job performance across a wide variety of jobs. Furthermore, because conscientiousness and emotional stability are only moderately correlated with each other and have small correlations with intelligence, each can add unique information to the prediction of job performance. Thus, hiring applicants with higher conscientiousness, emotional stability and intelligence will result in an increase in the number of employees who perform assigned job tasks effectively, which in turn will have substantial economic benefits to organizations.

A major reason to select employees on conscientiousness and emotional stability is the remarkable breadth of work behaviors they predict. Importantly, many of these work behaviors relate to overall organizational effectiveness yet are not typically included in measures of overall job performance; moreover, they are not predicted as well by intelligence. In order to understand the behaviors that conscientiousness and emotional stability predict, it is useful to distinguish among the three major components of job performance: task behaviors, citizenship behaviors and counterproductive behaviors (Rotundo and Sackett, 2002). Task performance refers to the core behaviors of a job and includes those that (directly or indirectly) contribute to the production of a good or the provision of a service. These behaviors are usually captured by overall performance ratings or by objective measures of performance such as total sales during the quarter or number of new accounts opened. Organizational citizenship performance, also called contextual performance (Borman, Penner, Allen, and Motowidlo, 2001), refers to behavior that contributes to the goals of the organization by contributing to its social and psychological environment (such as providing assistance to co-workers who need help). Counterproductive work performance consists of a broad array of voluntary behaviors that harm the well-being of the organization or its employees and includes behaviors such as violence on the job, racial slurs, theft, unsafe behavior, and misuse of information, time, or resources (Berry, Ones, and Sackett, 2007).

The studies discussed above clearly demonstrate that conscientiousness and emotional stability predict overall job performance and the results are quite robust and generalize to nearly all jobs. In fact, Hurtz and Donovan (2000) reported that of the Big Five personality traits, conscientiousness and emotional stability have the highest relationship with task performance. Thus, whether predicting overall job performance or a narrower definition of task performance, conscientiousness and emotional stability emerge as the two critical personality traits that determine the employees' technical proficiency and performance completing specific job duties.

Citizenship and (non-) counterproductive work behaviors

In addition to predicting the task performance component of jobs, conscientiousness and emotional stability also predict citizenship and counterproductive work behaviors. This represents a difference between intelligence on the one hand and conscientiousness and emotional stability on the other, as there is little evidence that intelligence predicts citizenship and counterproductive work behaviors. Citizenship behaviors include the willingness to pitch in and help during emergency or overload situations, to take on tasks no one else is willing to do, and to go beyond prescribed role requirements to get the job done. Borman et al. (2001) showed that conscientiousness (especially dependability) and to a lesser extent emotional stability predict citizenship behaviors and these correlations are higher than those typically reported for task behaviors. In another meta-analysis, Hurtz and Donovan (2000) found these same two traits relate to citizenship behavior through dedication to the job and interpersonal facilitation. Job dedication includes measures of persistence, reliability, and commitment to goals, while interpersonal facilitation refers to interpersonal relationships at work (e.g. in work teams), cooperation, being courteous and a team player. Thus conscientiousness and emotional stability influence citizenship behaviors at work through their relationship to job dedication and interpersonal facilitation.

There is considerable evidence that conscientiousness and emotional stability are also related to organizational citizenship behaviors through the broad set of helping behaviors associated with teamwork and customer service. For example, Mount, Barrick, and Stewart (1998) found conscientiousness and emotional stability were consistently related to being a team player across 11 different studies. Selecting on conscientiousness and emotional stability is also important to optimize team performance. Based on responses of employees in 51 work teams, Barrick, Stewart, Neubert, and Mount (1998) found that teams higher in conscientiousness and emotional stability (as well as general mental ability and extraversion) received higher supervisor ratings of team performance. Two recent meta-analyses (Bell, 2007; Peeters, Van Tujil, Rutte, and Reymen, 2006) of the relationship between Big Five traits and team performance found that higher team scores on conscientiousness and agreeableness were associated with high team performance. If the analyses were restricted to actual work settings, Peeters et al. (2006) also showed teams with higher mean levels of emotional stability obtained higher team performance. Furthermore, Frei and McDaniel (1998) reported that customer service measures are strong predictors of supervisory ratings of performance, and other research has shown that the two strongest personality correlates of customer service orientation are emotional stability and conscientiousness (Ones and Viswesvaran, 1996). These findings are noteworthy as they correspond to the survey results described earlier in the chapter that showed one of the two most important workplace skills that employers desire is teamwork/collaboration.

Another important reason to select on conscientiousness and emotional stability is they are centrally (and negatively) related to intentional harmful behaviors at work, i.e. counterproductive work behaviors. Evidence was presented at the beginning of the chapter that employers are very interested in hiring employees who are honest, demonstrate integrity, and follow workplace rules. Research demonstrates that personality-based integrity tests are valid predictors of such counterproductive behaviors (Ones, Viswesvaran, and Schmidt, 1993) as "badmouthing" the organization, being belligerent with customers or fellow co-workers, sabotaging equipment or products, stealing goods or money, and even engaging in excessive alcohol or drug abuse, as well as being able also to predict supervisory ratings of overall job performance. As noted above, integrity tests are related primarily to conscientiousness and emotional stability (along with agreeableness). Results of a study by Berry et al. (2007) clarified how emotional stability and conscientiousness predict counterproductive behavior: emotional stability predicts both interpersonal deviance and organizational deviance, whereas conscientiousness predicts organizational deviance. Consequently, the more conscientious and emotionally stable a firm's employees are, the less likely they are to engage in counterproductive behaviors at work.

Low turnover and absenteeism

In addition to positive "citizenship" behaviors, individuals high on conscientiousness and emotional stability are more likely to stay with the organization. Turnover is a major cost to employers; consequently, many employers strive to hire employees who not only perform well but also stay on the job for a long period of time, particularly in tight labor markets. Conscientiousness and emotional stability have been found to consistently (negatively) predict an individual's propensity to withdraw at work. For example, Barrick and Mount (1996) showed that voluntary turnover was predicted by both personality traits.

A recent meta-analysis conducted by Zimmerman (2008) showed that personality traits impact individuals' intentions to withdraw from work, as emotional stability best predicted (negatively) employees' intentions to quit, whereas conscientiousness (and agreeableness) best predicted (negatively) actual turnover decisions. Similarly, a meta-analysis by Ones, Viswesvaran, and Schmidt (2003) showed that personality-based integrity tests predicted voluntary absenteeism and the validity generalized across various predictor scales, organizations, and jobs. Ones (1993) examined more than 100 studies reporting correlations between integrity tests and personality measures and found that integrity tests were related primarily to conscientiousness and emotional stability (along with agreeableness). Thus selecting on conscientiousness and emotional stability will reduce workforce instability due to excessive absenteeism, tardiness, even turnover.

Leadership and entrepreneurship

In addition to predicting task, citizenship, and counterproductive behaviors, emotional stability and conscientiousness also predict many other important work outcomes that cannot be neatly categorized into one of these three performance categories. For example, Judge, Bono, Ilies, and Gerhardt (2002) conducted a meta-analysis of the relationship between the personality traits and leadership (using a criterion that consisted of both leader emergence and leader effectiveness). Their results showed that both conscientiousness and emotional stability were generalizable predictors of leadership (as were extraversion and openness to experience). Further, both conscientiousness and emotional stability have been shown to predict entrepreneurial status (Zhao and Seibert, 2005). Although entrepreneurial activity involves leadership, it is "unique" as the context differs by involving a start-up or rapidly growing firm.

Expatriate success

These two traits are also related to other aspects of work performance that affect organizational productivity and profits. For example, organizations spend hundreds of thousands of dollars preparing and transferring employees overseas for work assignments. Research shows that individuals who are higher on both conscientiousness and emotional stability perform better as expatriates (Mol, Orn, Willemsen, and Van Der Moler, 2005). Moreover, organizations spend billions of dollars each year on training-related activities. One trend is to select employees to participate in training programs who are likely to benefit most from the training. Research has shown that individuals who are higher on conscientiousness are not only more motivated to learn (Major, Turner, and Fletcher, 2006), but also perform better in the training program, although other traits like openness to experience, extraversion, and proactive personality also predict training performance (e.g. Barrick et al., 2001; Salgado, 1997).

Earnings

Higher conscientiousness and emotional stability is also rewarded in the labor market. Using a large Dutch sample, Nyhus and Pons (2005) showed that emotional stability was positively associated with wages among both men and women and conscientiousness is most highly rewarded at the beginning of the employment relationship. Mueller and Plug (2006) found

that among a large group of high school graduates in 1957 all of the Big Five traits significantly predicted earnings and collectively their effects are comparable to those reported for
GMA. Further, Roberts, Caspi, and Moffitt (2003) found that people who were more conscientious in terms of being more controlled and industrious at the age of 18 tended to be on
higher status work paths at 26 years of age, to feel more involved in their work, and to feel
more financially secure.

Safety

A meta-analysis by Clarke and Robertson (2005) showed that *low* conscientiousness and low
agreeableness were valid and generalizable predictors of accident involvement. Two other
traits, openness to experience and emotional stability, were also found to be (negatively)
correlated to accidents, though there was more variance in these estimates across studies.
Given the high costs associated with accidents and the potential harm to human lives, this
shows another way selecting employees on conscientiousness and emotional stability can
benefit organizations. Taken together, all of these results convincingly reveal that employees
with higher levels of these two traits are likely to be successful in a myriad of ways at work,
including by being a higher performer, a better citizen, a more effective team player or leader,
with greater integrity and a propensity to be committed to and stay with the firm.

Compliance

Another benefit to organizations when employees are selected on conscientiousness and
emotional stability is compliance with existing laws and legal precedents. A key question all
employers face in their hiring practice is whether a predictor unintentionally discriminates
by screening out a disproportionate number of minorities and women. To the extent
this happens, the predictor has adverse impact, which may trigger legal action. Research
consistently demonstrates a large mean difference of approximately one standard deviation
(*d*-values of 1) between African Americans and whites on intelligence (Ployhart and Holtz,
2008). In contrast, there are relatively small subgroup differences on conscientiousness
and emotional stability. For example, recent meta-analyses (Hough, 1995; Foldes, Duehr, and
Ones, 2008; Ployhart and Holtz, 2008) report that differences between African American,
Asian, and Hispanic subgroups versus white subgroups are quite small (*d*-values around
zero). Similar non-significant differences have also been found for gender (Feingold, 1994;
Ployhart and Holtz, 2008). Thus, from a legal perspective, selecting on conscientiousness
and emotional stability (and other contextually valid personality dimensions) is advantageous
because it does not appear to result in adverse impact.

Healthy behaviors and longevity

Conscientiousness and emotional stability also predict a number of important life outcomes.
Certainly, one of the most consequential outcomes in life is how long a person lives.
Simply stated – conscientious and emotionally stable people live longer (Friedman, Tucker,
Tomlinson-Keasey, Schwartz, Wingard, and Criqui, 1993; Ozer and Benet-Martinez, 2006).
For example, Roberts, Walton, and Bogg (2005) cite evidence that people tend to live longer

if, as eight-year-olds, they were rated as more conscientious by parents and teachers. To put this finding in context, the impact of conscientiousness on longevity has been shown to be equivalent to the effect (inversely) of cardiovascular disease on longevity (Bogg and Roberts, 2004). Although the evidence is not as compelling, emotional stability is also associated with longevity. For example, in a study of 285 centenarians, Martin, da Rosa, and Siegler (2006) found that higher levels of emotional stability, high competence (conscientiousness) and high extraversion were associated with longevity. It makes sense that emotional stability should matter for longevity as well, because high levels of neuroticism have been associated with increased probability of illness and behavior leading to more illness (Ozer and Benet-Martinez, 2006). Smith and MacKenzie (2006) showed that neuroticism is associated with physical health problems, such as cardiovascular disease, which in turn results in less longevity. Furthermore, neurotic individuals have been shown to have lower resistance to stress and spend more time ruminating about illnesses (Ozer and Benet-Martinez, 2006). In essence, those with lower levels of emotional stability experience higher rates of actual illness and are more vulnerable to illness due to how the trait shapes the person's reaction to illness. Goodwin and Friedman (2006) extended these findings by reporting both conscientiousness and emotional stability are related to significant reductions in the likelihood of a wide range of mental and physical disorders among adults in the general population.

Terracciano, Lockenhoff, Crum, Bienvenu, and Costa (2008) examined the relationship between the Big Five and drug use in a large community sample. Compared to a sample of "never" smokers, current cigarette smokers were lower on conscientiousness and higher on neuroticism; similar but more extreme results were obtained for cocaine/heroin users. In addition, marijuana users scored low on conscientiousness. Bogg and Roberts (2004) conducted a meta-analysis of conscientiousness-related traits and the leading behavioral contributors to mortality in the USA including tobacco use, diet and activity patterns, excessive alcohol use, violence, risky sexual behavior, risky driving, suicide, and drug use. Based on 194 studies, results showed that conscientiousness-related traits were negatively related to all risky health-related behaviors and positively related to all beneficial health-related behaviors. Conscientious people avoid potentially harmful/risky behaviors such as fighting or other violent activities, as well as tobacco and drug consumption; instead, they engage in activities that promote good health (e.g. exercise regularly, eat healthy diets, schedule regular medical check-ups), and invest in work, family, and community in ways that are known to contribute to longevity.

Collectively, these results demonstrate that conscientiousness and emotional stability play important roles in a person's physical condition, even how long they live, by predicting social environmental factors and health behaviors that have meaningful effects on longevity. Although these behaviors are not directly related to work performance, how one feels and how long one lives will have important indirect effects. By leading healthy lifestyles, people high on conscientiousness and emotional stability, collectively, save organizations billions of dollars because of increased productivity associated with lower absenteeism rates due to fewer sick days and being healthier when they are at work. People high on conscientiousness and emotional stability also have substantially lower health care costs due to fewer visits to the doctor and fewer and shorter hospital stays. Given the emphasis in most organizations on reducing health care costs, one relatively inexpensive practice that will help accomplish this is to select employees high on conscientiousness and emotional stability.

MEDIATORS: HOW DO CONSCIENTIOUSNESS AND EMOTIONAL STABILITY PREDICT PERFORMANCE?

Motivation

Clearly, there are numerous advantages to organizations when they select applicants based on conscientiousness and emotional stability. Another way to view their impact is to consider the likely negative consequences to organizations that do not select employees based on conscientiousness and emotional stability – but all of their competitors do. Many of the applicants that remain in the applicant pool have already been screened on these two traits and have been found undesirable. That is, the remaining applicants are more likely to describe themselves as lazy, irresponsible, undependable, careless, moody, lacking confidence, stress-prone, anxious, and depressed. Clearly, this is no way to build a productive workforce.

But *how* do conscientiousness and emotional stability affect performance? Earlier we made the distinction that personality traits influence what people will do whereas intelligence influences what they can do. Research clearly demonstrates that motivational or will-do factors play a central role in predicting job performance (e.g. Mitchell and Daniels, 2003). Although there are many ways to conceptualize motivation, the three most commonly studied approaches are goal-setting theory, expectancy theory, and self-efficacy theory. According to goal-setting theory, the process of setting goals leads to greater performance because it directs effort and attention, increases time on task, leads to greater persistence, and provides feedback about one's performance. It also helps people devise strategies for attaining the goals; and once the goals are achieved, people feel more satisfied due to a greater sense of accomplishment. Thousands of laboratory and field studies conducted in a wide variety of settings using many different tasks demonstrate that the effects of goal setting on performance are positive, potent, and robust (Locke and Latham, 2005; see Chapter 9, this volume). With respect to expectancy theory, higher performance will result when people believe that their effort leads to better performance and when they believe higher performance leads to rewards they value. Self-efficacy theory posits that individuals who see themselves as competent, worthy, and confident interpret their environment in positive ways that influence work performance. These positive perceptions influence a person's beliefs that he or she can successfully cope with work's (and life's) exigencies.

Judge and Ilies (2002) conducted a meta-analysis to investigate the relationships among the Big Five personality dimensions and these three central theories of motivation. They found that the two strongest and most consistent correlates of performance motivation across the three motivation approaches were emotional stability and conscientiousness (extraversion was also a consistent predictor but the relationships were weaker). These results are important because they show that conscientiousness and emotional stability predict performance by increasing individuals' motivation levels. These findings are consistent with what we would expect from findings pertaining to the validity of the two traits in predicting performance. Conscientiousness and emotional stability are the best predictors of performance and because motivation is a major determinant of performance, it would be expected that these two traits are also the best predictors of motivation. Thus conscientiousness and emotional stability affect performance directly and indirectly through their effects on motivation processes.

Results from other studies support these findings. For example, meta-analytic research conducted by Mount and Barrick (1995) showed that conscientiousness correlates highly with the amount of effort exerted. Although the amount of effort expended is related to high levels of motivation, they are not identical concepts. Effort is multifaceted and includes both the amount of time as well as the intensity of the time spent on the task, i.e. the cognitive effort expended to focus and concentrate on the task at hand. Conscientious people spend more time on task, which leads to greater quantity of output and higher performance (Barrick, Mount, and Strauss, 1993). Greater time on task also provides more opportunities to practice and provides more exposure to a wider variety of problems. Both of these increase job knowledge, which in turn increases performance because, as discussed in the previous chapter, job knowledge is highly correlated with job performance.

Conscientious people are also more dependable and this leads to higher perform-ance. They plan and organize their work and are careful, thorough, and detail oriented. Conscientious individuals are more likely to perform tasks correctly the first time and are more likely to spot problems and errors in processes and output. This leads to fewer errors and enables highly conscientious employees to produce better quality work (Mount and Barrick, 1995). These findings are especially relevant as they are consistent with the survey findings of 400 employers discussed earlier, which showed one of the two most important workplace skills that employers desire is work ethic/professionalism.

Generally speaking, similar motivational mechanisms apply to emotional stability. Viewed from the negative pole, neurotic people are not able to control their emotions and moods; consequently, they cannot maintain focus and concentration on the task at hand especially under stress or in crisis situations (e.g. Kanfer and Heggestad, 1997). This lack of attention can lead to less productivity, more errors, and hence lower performance. Those prone to greater anxiety and insecurity (low on emotional stability) tend to be fearful of novel situations, be more concerned about failure, and are more susceptible to feelings of dependence and helplessness (Judge and Ilies, 2002). Those who experience greater and more frequent negative emotions may choose to withhold effort rather than risk the potential affective consequences of failure. Researchers label this phenomenon the "self-handicapping" paradox (Rhodewalt, 1994). In addition, the tendency of people to behave in this way, particularly within the context of achievement (i.e. job) settings, is fundamental to the learned helplessness theory of depression (Seligman, 1978). Taken together, these findings suggest that the inability of neurotics to cope with fear of failure substantively impacts job performance through the inhibitory effects on motivational levels. In contrast, employees scoring high on emotional stability are likely to be steady, calm, and predictable, which helps them obtain more commendations and recognition at work. In turn, commendations along with fewer disciplinary actions and reprimands have been linked to higher performance ratings (Borman, White, Pulakos, and Oppler, 1991).

Job satisfaction

Motivation is only part of the explanation as to why these two traits lead to more successful behavior at work. Another reason to select on conscientiousness and emotional stability is that they are related to work-related attitudes, which in turn have been shown to affect performance. For example, conscientiousness and emotional stability are positively related to job and career satisfaction (Judge, Heller, and Mount, 2002; Ng, Eby, Sorensen, and Feldman, 2005). Judge, Higgins, Thoresen, and Barrick (1999) found that conscientiousness and emotional stability assessed at an early age (12–14) were strong predictors of overall job satisfaction in late adulthood, even after controlling for clinicians' ratings of extraversion, openness to experience, and agreeableness. Furthermore, Judge et al. (2002) conducted a meta-analysis of the relationship of traits from the FFM model of personality to overall job satisfaction. The two personality traits that correlated highest with job satisfaction were neuroticism (negatively) and conscientiousness. In turn, job satisfaction has been shown to be positively related to job performance, which shows that another way these two traits relate to performance is through their relationship to job satisfaction.

Commitment

Another attitudinal variable that is closely related to job satisfaction is organizational commitment, which is of interest to organizations because it predicts who is likely to leave the organization rather than help the organization reach its objectives. Organizational commitment refers to a person's involvement with the organization, feelings of obligation toward the organization and perceived costs associated with leaving the organization. One meta-analysis of the influence of affect on job attitudes reports results between organizational commitment and only two personality traits, extraversion and emotional stability (Thoresen, Kaplan, Barsley, Warren, and De Chermont, 2003). This study shows neurotic individuals are less satisfied, less committed to the organization, and have higher turnover intentions. Erdheim, Wang, and Zichar (2006) found that conscientiousness is also related to one component of organizational commitment, continuance commitment. They reasoned that conscientiousness relates to continuance commitment because it represents a general work-involvement tendency that provides increased opportunity for an employee to obtain formal (e.g. pay, promotion) and informal work rewards (e.g. recognition, respect). Conscientious employees earn more of these rewards, which leads to heightened levels of continuance commitment because of the costs of leaving an organization. Zimmerman (2008) supports this conclusion by showing that these two traits are the best predictors of intent to quit.

Life satisfaction

Conscientiousness and emotional stability are also among the strongest personality-based predictors of subjective well-being or life satisfaction (DeNeve and Cooper, 1998; Steel, Schmidt, and Schulz, 2008). It has been argued that conscientiousness plays a major role in both job and life satisfaction because conscientious behavior is instrumental in attaining outcomes such as career success that achievement-oriented people value (McCrae and Costa, 1991). Schmutte and Ryff (1997) concluded that those high in conscientiousness are more satisfied because they achieve a heightened sense of control and competence through their diligent and responsible behavior. Thus conscientiousness is instrumental in attaining desired outcomes and fostering control, which leads to greater life satisfaction.

The effects of emotional stability on satisfaction are complex and are best viewed from the negative pole (i.e. neuroticism). People who suffer from low emotional stability experience greater distress and reduced job and life satisfaction because they experience more adverse events, and react negatively and more strongly when such problems occur. Neurotic individuals are unable to effectively cope with stress due to their reliance on emotion- and avoidance-oriented coping styles. Higher levels of emotional stability result in greater satisfaction because stable people have more confidence to approach stressful work, have a more positive view of themselves, others, and the world around them, and do not let nega-tive emotions and dysfunctional thought processes distract them from the task at hand. Overall, these results show that conscientiousness and emotional stability are fundamentally important to success at work, but are also important to satisfaction and commitment at work as well as one's overall satisfaction in life. It is not an exaggeration to say that conscientious-ness and emotional stability are fundamentally important to overall life success.

EXCEPTIONS TO THE PRINCIPLE

The general principle in this chapter is that individuals should be selected on their level of conscientiousness and emotional stability. However, this does not mean that these are the only valid personality dimensions that predict performance. A subprinciple of this chapter is that individuals should be selected on other personality dimensions according to the specific requirements of the job and/or the nature of the criterion. Research has shown that the other three personality dimensions in the FFM model (agreeableness, extraversion, and openness to experience) are relevant in some jobs or for some specific types of criteria. To clearly identify when these relationships are likely to be non-zero, practitioners need to focus more on job requirements, demands, or what now are labeled competencies. This does not imply an extensive, time-consuming, content-specific job analysis. Rather, it suggests that the relevance of these personality traits depends on the requirements and competencies generally demanded by the job to achieve successful job performance. For example, if the job requires extensive interpersonal interaction of a cooperative nature, agreeableness would be expected to be an important predictor. In fact, recent research demonstrates that agreeableness is the single best predictor of teamwork and is also related to service orientation (Bell, 2007; Mount et al., 1998; Peeters et al., 2006). Those employees who are more cooperative, caring, tolerant, flexible, and trusting (i.e. high in agreeableness) are likely to be more successful in teams.

In contrast, in jobs where the nature of the interpersonal interaction is competitive or requires persuasion or negotiation, being assertive, ambitious, energetic, and gregarious (i.e. highly extraverted) is expected to be a highly relevant set of personality traits. Thus, extraversion has been found to be a valid predictor of success in sales and management jobs (Barrick et al., 2001). Hogan and Holland (2003) reported extraversion (measured using ambition) was an important predictor for criteria where "getting ahead" of others was an important outcome in the job. Finally, it would be expected that companies who are seeking employees who are flexible and highly adaptive to the rapid changes frequently encountered at work would select on openness to experience. There is some limited evidence to support this. For example, Pulakos, Schmitt, Dorsey, Arand, Hedge, and Borman (2002) and LePine, Colquitt, and Erez (2000) found that openness to experience is positively correlated with adaptive performance. Further, as one would expect, employees higher on openness to experience tend to have higher training performance than those low in openness (Barrick et al., 2001; Salgado, 1997). Thus, being imaginative, innovative, curious, intellectual, with broad interests (i.e. high on openness to experience) appears to make one "training ready," which is relevant for training success. It should also be noted that trainees scoring higher on extraversion have been found to be more successful during training. This has been attributed to extraverts' increased and more active participation during training.

Although we advocate that organizations should always select employees on conscientiousness and emotional stability, there are some circumstances where this general principle oversimplifies the relationships between these two personality traits and job performance. In reality, our behavior is influenced by a constellation of personality traits represented by the Big Five traits and these traits (and other attributes of individuals) may interact to predict performance. For example, in four different samples Witt and Ferris (2003) found that the relationship between conscientiousness and interpersonal job performance depended on workers' social skills. The relationship was stronger among workers who are higher rather than lower in social skill. Further, Witt, Burke, Barrick, and Mount (2002) found that in jobs with frequent, cooperative interpersonal interactions, the relationship between conscientiousness and job performance depended on the level of agreeableness. The relationship was stronger for persons high in agreeableness than for those low in agreeableness. Similarly, Barrick, Parks, and Mount (2005) found that among high self-monitors (i.e. individuals who monitor, adjust, and control their behavior to make a favorable impression on others), the relationships between emotional stability and supervisory ratings of interpersonal performance decreased, and these effects were replicated using peer ratings of interpersonal performance. Collectively, these results illustrate that the relationship of personality traits to performance can be influenced by other attributes of the individual. Thus, although conscientiousness and emotional stability predict job performance across jobs, the magnitude of the relationship may vary depending on other personality traits as well as the specific component of job performance being predicted. Accounting for interactions between personality variables may further enhance prediction from these personality variables.

IMPLEMENTING THE PRINCIPLE

The general principle that we have discussed is that employers should select applicants who are hardworking, dependable, achievement striving (i.e. conscientious) as well as calm, tolerant of stress, able to handle anxiety, and avoid excessively worrying or ruminating (i.e. emotionally stable). This is not a particularly surprising statement; however, a necessary first step before a principle can be implemented is that it must be well understood. In this vein, much progress has been made in the past decade in understanding how conscientiousness and emotional stability relate to job performance. Equally important to the implementation of these principles has been the contribution of industrial–organizational psychologists to the development of reliable and valid measures of these constructs.

The use of personality assessment to select applicants requires collecting "personal" data. To make sure that accurate data are collected in a fair manner, attention must be given to the relevance of various personality traits and some consideration of the "demands" of the applicant setting. Implementation requires that the organization accurately identifies and measures applicant qualifications relative to job requirements. Thus, before assessing personality traits, a job analysis should be conducted to identify critical competencies and job requirements. By understanding the critical requirements of the job, one will recognize which personality traits are relevant predictors, in addition to conscientiousness and emotional stability. However, some consideration must be given to the "job" itself. Today, organizations are moving away from the use of narrow, well-defined jobs and towards broader, less well-defined, more amorphous jobs, with constantly changing content. The changing structure of jobs implies there will be greater emphasis on those traits and qualities that are valid for all jobs (intelligence, conscientiousness, and emotional stability). Nevertheless, it will be desirable to select on the other three personality traits (extraversion, agreeableness, and openness to experience) when those traits are valid predictors of requirements for critical tasks likely to be encountered by people being hired.

Once it is known which specific traits will be assessed, consideration must also be given to the best means for assessing personality. Research illustrates that co-workers, customers, and supervisors at work can rate a person's personality, and those assessments have been found to predict job performance better than self-reports of personality. For example, Mount, Barrick, and Strauss (1994) found that the validity of co-worker and customer ratings of conscientiousness were nearly twice as large as self-ratings when predicting supervisor ratings of performance. These predictive validities have since been replicated by others (Small and Diefendorff, 2006; McCarthy and Goffin, 2001; Taylor, Pajo, Cheung, and Stringfield, 2004). Huffcutt, Conway, Roth, and Stone (2001) report that interviewers often assess basic personality during the employment interview and found interviewer ratings of traits, including conscientiousness and emotional stability, are meaningfully related to later job performance. Thus, observer ratings of personality, even after a relatively short interview, predict later job performance and are larger than those we have historically found with self-reports. The magnitude of these relationships approaches the predictive validity of general intelligence. Zimmerman, Triana, and Barrick (2007) found that when candidates are asked to nominate up to three referents during the application process, these observer ratings of conscientiousness and emotional stability significantly predict job performance and team performance. Hence, there is even evidence that observer ratings from referents can be used for hiring.

Nevertheless, the most common means of assessing personality is through self-report personality tests. There are several construct valid measures of the Big Five traits. For example, the Personal Characteristics Inventory (PCI by Mount, Barrick, Laffitte, and Callans, 1999) is a self-report measure of the Big Five that asks applicants to report their agreement or disagreement with 150 sentences. The measure takes about 30 minutes to complete and has a 5th- to 6th-grade reading level. Another commonly used measure of the Big Five is the Hogan Personality Inventory (HPI by Hogan and Hogan, 1995). Responses to the HPI can be scored to yield measures of occupational success as well as employee reliability and service orientation. A third alternative is the NEO Personality Inventory, which is also based on the Big Five typology (Costa and McCrae, 1992). There are several versions of the NEO and it has been translated into multiple languages.

An implementation concern in the use of personality inventories is that job applicants may inflate their personality scores, due to the "demands" of the applicant setting. This concern becomes apparent when one considers the nature of some personality items. For example, few applicants would agree with the statement that "others would describe me as lazy or irresponsible at work," if they desperately wanted the job. Given the near impossibility of verifying responses to some of these questions, the possibility that impression management influences responses is quite real. In fact, research suggests applicants do manage impressions, as scores are higher by one-half standard deviation between applicants versus non-applicant settings. Given that a job is on the line when applicants complete a personality test, the tendency to enhance their impression is undeniable. Nevertheless, research clearly shows (Barrick and Mount, 1996; Ellingson, Sackett, and Connelly, 2007; Hogan, Barrett, and

Hogan, 2007; Ones, Dilchert, Viswesvaran, and Judge, 2007; Schmitt and Oswald, 2006) that impression management does not significantly detract from the predictive validity of the tests in actual applicant settings. However, both criterion-related validity and construct validity are affected in those studies where participants (mostly students) are instructed to fake good. These findings create a paradox. With respect to employment decisions, the biggest problem is that the rank order of applicants on personality traits such as conscientiousness and emotional stability may change due to differences in faking; at the same time, faking does not substantially change the validity of the traits in predicting performance. Thus, even though it has yet to be shown that faking undermines the predictive validity of personality tests in selection, there continues to be considerable debate about this issue in the literature. One important implication from these findings is that practitioners should not rely on norms based on incumbent samples, as they will tend to be one-half standard deviation lower than norms derived from incumbent samples.

In sum, significant progress has been made in understanding the magnitude of the relationship between conscientiousness and emotional stability to job performance and the processes by which these constructs affect performance. Successful implementation of the principles we advocate requires reliable and valid measure of both conscientiousness and emotional stability. Over the past decade several construct valid measures of the five factor taxonomy of personality have been developed. Nonetheless, additional research is needed to further develop and refine these measures to overcome potential problems associated with impression management and socially desirable responding.

Case Examples

Relationship of conscientiousness and emotional stability to career success

A recent study (Judge et al., 1999) investigated the relationship between traits from the Big Five model of personality to success in careers spanning over 50 years. The ability to predict success 50 years after assessing personality provides a rigorous test of the utility of selecting applicants using conscientiousness and emotional stability. The data for this study were obtained from the Intergenerational Studies, administered by the Institute of Human Development, University of California at Berkeley. The sample was derived from children born in Berkeley, California, in 1928 and 1929. Many measurements were collected from participants over the 60-year course of the study. For example, there were two studies during later childhood (11–13 and again 16–18), as well as three major follow-up studies conducted when participants were in early adulthood (30–38), middle age (41–50), and in late adulthood (53–62). In addition to collecting personality and intelligence test data, the subject's job satisfaction, income, and occupational status were collected during each of these studies. Thus, the records were rich with personality and career data, and comparisons were made across data collected at five different points in time (ranging from childhood to late adulthood).

Both childhood and early adulthood assessments of personality revealed enduring relationships between personality traits and later career success. For example, childhood assessments of conscientiousness and emotional stability predicted job satisfaction, income, and occupational status, even in late adulthood. These results show that conscientiousness and emotional stability measured early in life were effective predictors of satisfaction and success in one's later career, even over a 50-year time span. Results also demonstrated that these two personality traits explained significant incremental variance in these measures of career success, even after controlling for the influence of intelligence. Taken together, these results show that highly conscientious and emotionally stable children earned higher salaries, were more satisfied with their work, and attained higher positions in the social hierarchy later in life. Obviously, organizations will be better off selecting individuals who are conscientious and emotionally adjusted, as they will be rewarded by those decisions with higher performance and more committed employees for years to come.

The generalizability of conscientiousness and emotional stability as predictors

The Army conducted a large-scale study spanning seven years (the Selection and Classification Project or Project A) to investigate how the contributions of selection could maximize performance within the constraints of one of the largest operational personnel systems in the world. The Army personnel system includes over 276 jobs and hires, almost exclusively, inexperienced and untrained persons to fill them. A major goal of Project A was to develop a battery of predictor measures that would best serve the needs of all the jobs in the entire selection system for entry-level enlisted personnel. Thus, this project examined all of the major domains of individual differences that had potential for generating useful predictor variables. Several versions of the test battery were developed and examined in an iterative sequence, with each round of testing involving thousands of recruits or enlisted personnel. Rather than review the extensive list of predictors examined, interested readers are referred to Peterson, Hough, Dunnette, Rosse, Houston, Toquam, and Wing (1990). Suffice it to say that the range of individual differences was extraordinarily comprehensive, ranging from administrative/archival records to training achievement tests.

The study also rigorously modeled job performance to better understand what these individual differences were predicting. Given the large number of jobs examined, Project A determined whether a single model of performance would be stable across these jobs. Multiple methods were used to generate over 200 performance indicators of a subsample of jobs. An iterative procedure resulted in the identification of five broad performance dimensions that were found in all jobs. Two of these performance measures focus on specific technical competence called core technical proficiency and general soldiering proficiency. While the former dimension appears to be a basic performance component for any job (core task proficiency), the latter dimension would almost surely be specific to the military. The analysis also identified three non-job-specific performance dimensions that are more under motivational control. These are called effort/leadership, maintaining personal discipline, and physical fitness/military bearing. Again, while military bearing is unique to the military, the other two dimensions are quite likely basic performance components of almost any job. Although job performance was found to be multidimensional, an overall decision could scale each performance measure by its relative importance for a particular personnel decision or job.

The findings (McHenry, Hough, Toquam, Hanson, and Ashworth, 1990) from this large-scale project were that intelligence tests provided the best prediction of job-specific and general task proficiency (core technical proficiency and general soldiering proficiency), whereas the personality composites, particularly those traits measuring conscientiousness and emotional stability, were the best predictors of giving extra effort and leadership, exhibiting personal discipline, and physical fitness and military bearing. The study also illustrated the incremental validity contributed by other predictors over intelligence. The greatest amount of incremental validity over intelligence was generated by the personality measures, especially when predicting effort and leadership, personal discipline, and physical fitness and military bearing. These results show the generalizable value of using conscientiousness and emotional stability for purposes of selection.

CONCLUSION

The general principle in this chapter is that organizations should select employees based on their conscientiousness and emotional stability. A subprinciple is that organizations should also select on agreeableness, extraversion, or openness to experience when they have been shown to be relevant for specific criteria or requirements of the job. Hiring applicants who are more intelligent (see Chapter 1) will result in employees who are capable of acquiring more work-related facts and principles as well as greater procedural knowledge and skill. This contributes to job success, particularly on the core substantive or technical tasks central to the job. But hiring smart people is not enough. Hiring applicants who are more conscientious and emotionally stable will result in employees who have a stronger work ethic – they are predisposed to exert greater effort at work, to persist at work for a longer period of time, and to cope more effectively. In addition, these employees are likely to be better team players and are more collaborative – they are better citizens, and are more responsible and helpful to others at work. Further, they are less likely to engage in counterproductive behaviors at work. They also have more positive attitudes about work and life in general and lead healthier lifestyles, which leads to increased work productivity and reduced health care costs. In conclusion, hiring people who work smarter (select on intelligence), and who work harder and cope better (select on conscientiousness and emotional stability), will lead to increased individual productivity which in turn will lead to increased organizational effectiveness every single day the person (reliably) shows up to work.

REFERENCES

Are they really ready to work? Employers' perspectives on the basic knowledge and applied skills of new entrants to the 21st century US workforce (2006). Collaborative study by The Conference Board, Partnership for 21st Century Skills, Corporate Voices for Working Families and the Society for Human Resource Management.

Barrick, M. R., and Mount, M. K. (1991). The Big Five personality dimensions and job performance: a meta-analysis. *Personnel Psychology*, 44, 1–26.

Barrick, M. R., and Mount, M. K. (1996). Effects of impression management and self-deception on the predictive validity of personality constructs. *Journal of Applied Psychology*, 81, 261–272.

Barrick, M. R., Mount, M. K., and Judge, T. A. (2001). The FFM personality dimensions and job performance: Meta-analysis of meta-analyses. *International Journal of Selection and Assessment*, 9, 9–30.

Barrick, M. R., Mount, M. K., and Strauss, J. P. (1993). Conscientiousness and performance of sales representatives: Test of the mediating effects of goal setting. *Journal of Applied Psychology*, 78, 715–722.

Barrick, M. R., Parks, L., and Mount, M. K. (2005). Self-monitoring as a moderator of the relationships between personality traits and performance. *Personnel Psychology*, 58, 745–768.

Barrick, M. R., Stewart, G. L., Neubert, M., and Mount, M. K. (1998). Relating member ability and personality to work team processes and team effectiveness. *Journal of Applied Psychology*, 83, 377–391.

Bell, S. T. (2007). Deep-level composition variables as predictors of team performance: A meta-analysis. *Journal of Applied Psychology*, 92, 595–615.

Berry, B. M., Ones, D. S., and Sackett, P. R. (2007). Interpersonal deviance, organizational deviance, and their common correlates: A review and meta-analysis. *Journal of Applied Psychology*, 92, 410–424.

Bogg, T., and Roberts. B. W. (2004). Conscientiousness and health-related behaviors: A meta-analysis of the leading behavioral contributors to mortality. *Psychological Bulletin*, 130, 887–919.

Borman, W. C., Penner, L. A., Allen, T. D., and Motowidlo, S. J. (2001). Personality predictors of citizenship performance. *International Journal of Selection and Assessment*, 9, 52–69.

Borman, W. C., White, L. A., Pulakos, E. D., and Oppler, S. H. (1991). Models of supervisor job performance ratings. *Journal of Applied Psychology*, 76, 863–872.

Clarke, S., and Robertson, I. T. (2005). A meta-analytic review of the Big Five personality factors and accident involvement in occupational and non-occupational settings. *Journal of Organizational and Occupational Psychology*, 78, 355–376.

Costa, P. T., Jr., and McCrae, R. R. (1992). *Revised NEO Personality Inventory and Five-Factor Model Inventory Professional Manual*. Odessa, FL: Psychological Assessment Resources.

DeNeve K. M., and Cooper H. (1998). The happy personality: A meta-analysis of 137 personality traits and subjective well-being. *Psychological Bulletin*, 124, 197–229.

Ellingson, J. E., Sackett, P. R., and Connelly, B. S. (2007). Personality assessment across selection and development contexts: insights into response distortion. *Journal of Applied Psychology*, 92, 386–395.

Erdheim, J., Wang, M., and Zichar, M. J. (2006). Linking the Big Five personality constructs to organization commitment. *Individual Differences*, 41, 959–970.

Feingold, A. (1994). Gender differences in personality – a meta-analysis. *Psychological Bulletin*, 116, 429–456.

Foldes, H. J., Duehr, E. E., and Ones, D. S. (2008). Group differences in personality: Meta-analyses comparing five racial groups. *Personnel Psychology*, 61, 579–616.

Frei, R. L., and McDaniel, M. A. (1998). Validity of customer service measures in personnel selection: A review of criterion and construct evidence. *Human Performance*, 11, 1–27.

Friedman, H. S., Tucker, J. S., Tomlinson-Keasey, C., Schwartz, J. E., Wingard, D. L., and Criqui, M. H. (1993). Does childhood personality predict longevity? *Journal of Personality and Social Psychology*, 65, 176–185.

Goodwin, R. D., and Friedman, H. S. (2006). Health status and the five-factor personality traits in a nationally representative sample. *Journal of Health Psychology*, 11, 643–654.

Hogan, J., Barrett, P., and Hogan, R. (2007). Personality measurement, faking, and employment selection. *Journal of Applied Psychology*, 92, 1270–1285.

Hogan, R., and Hogan, J. (1995). *Hogan Personality Inventory Manual.* Tulsa, OK: Hogan Assessment Systems.

Hogan, J., and Holland, B. (2003). Using theory to evaluate personality and job performance relations: A socioanalytic perspective. *Journal of Applied Psychology*, 88, 100–112.

Hough, L. M. (1992). The "Big-Five" personality variables – construct confusion: Description versus prediction. *Human Performance*, 5, 139–155.

Hough, L. M. (1995). Applicant self descriptions: Evaluating strategies for reducing distortion. Paper presented at the 10th Annual Convention of the Society of Industrial and Organizational Psychology, Orlando.

Huffcutt, A. I., Conway, J. M., Roth, P. L., and Stone, N. J. (2001). Identification and meta-analytic assessment of psychological constructs measured in employment interviews. *Journal of Applied Psychology*, 86, 897–913.

Hurtz, G. M., and Donovan, J. J. (2000). Personality and job performance: the "Big Five" revisited. *Journal of Applied Psychology*, 85, 869–879.

Judge, T. A., Bono, J. E., Ilies, R., and Gerhardt, M. W. (2002). Personality and leadership: A qualitative and quantitative review. *Journal of Applied Psychology*, 87, 765–780.

Judge, T. A., Heller, D., and Mount, M. K. (2002). Five-factor model of personality and job satisfactions: A meta-analysis. *Journal of Applied Psychology*, 87, 530–541.

Judge, T. J., Higgins, C. A., Thoresen, C. J., and Barrick, M. R. (1999). The Big Five personality traits, general mental ability, and career success across the life span. *Personnel Psychology*, 52, 621–652.

Judge, T. A., and Ilies, R. (2002). Relationship of personality to performance motivation: A meta-analytic review. *Journal of Applied Psychology*, 87, 797–807.

Kanfer, R., and Heggestad, E. D. (1997). Motivational traits and skills: A person-centered approach to work motivation. *Research in Organizational Behavior*, 19, 1–56.

LePine, J. A., Colquitt, J. A., and Erez, A. (2000). Adaptability to changing task contexts: Effects of general cognitive ability, conscientiousness, and openness to experience. *Personnel Psychology*, 53, 563–593.

Locke, E. A., and Latham, G. P. (2005). What should we do about motivation theory? Six recommendations for the twenty-first century. *Academy of Management Review*, 29, 388–404.

Major, D. A., Turner, J. E., and Fletcher, T. D. (2006). Linking proactive personality and the big five to motivation to learn and development activity. *Journal of Applied Psychology*, 91, 927–935.

Martin, P., da Rosa, G., and Siegler, I. C. (2006). Personality and longevity: Findings from the Georgia centenarian study. *Age*, 28, 343–352.

McCarthy, J. M., and Goffin, R. D. (2001). Improving the validity of letters of recommendation: An investigation of three standardized reference forms. *Military Psychology*, 13, 199–222.

McCrae, R. R., and Costa, P. T. (1991). The neo personality-inventory – using the 5-factor model in counseling. *Journal of Counseling Development*, 69, 637–372.

McHenry, J. J., Hough, L. M., Toquam, J. L., Hanson, M. A., and Ashworth, S. (1990). Project A validity results: The relationship between predictor and criterion domains. *Personnel Psychology*, 43, 335–354.

Michigan Employability Skills Employer Survey: Technical Report (1990). East Lansing: Michigan State University.

Mitchell, T. R., and Daniels, D. (2003). *Motivation*. In W. C. Borman, D. R. Ilgen, and R. J. Klimoski (eds), *Handbook of Psychology (Vol. 12): Industrial and Organizational Psychology*: pp. 225–254. New York: Wiley.

Mol, S. T., Orn, M. P., Willemsen, M. E., and Van Der Moler, H. T. (2005). Predicting expatriate job performance for selection purposes. *Journal of Cross-Cultural Psychology*, 36, 590–620.

Mount, M. K., and Barrick, M. R. (1995). The Big Five personality dimensions: Implications for research and practice in human resource management. *Research in Personnel and Human Resources Management*, 13, 153–200.

Mount, M. K., Barrick, M. R., Laffitte, L. R., and Callans, M. C. (1999). *The Personal Characteristics Inventory Manual*. Wonderlic, Inc.: Libertyville, IL.

Mount, M. K., Barrick, M. R., and Stewart, G. L. (1998). Five-factor model of personality and performance in jobs involving interpersonal interactions. *Human Performance*, 11, 145–165.

Mount, M. K., Barrick, M. R., and Strauss, J. P. (1994). Validity of observer ratings of the Big Five personality factors. *Journal of Applied Psychology*, 79, 272–280.

Mueller, G., and Plug, E. (2006). Estimating the effect of personality on male–female earnings. *IZA Discussion Paper No. 1254*.

Ng, T. W. H., Eby, L. T., Sorensen, K. L., and Feldman, D. C. (2005). Predictors of objective and subjective career success. a meta-analysis. *Personnel Psychology*, 58, 367–408.

Nyhus, E. K., and Pons, E. (2005). The effects of personality on earnings. *Journal of Economic Psychology*, 26, 363–384.

Ones, D. S. (1993). The construct validity of integrity tests. Unpublished doctoral dissertation, University of Iowa.

Ones, D. S., Dilchert, S., Viswesvaran, C., and Judge, T. A. (2007). In support of personality assessment in organizational settings. *Personnel Psychology*, 60(4), Winter, 995–1027.

Ones D. S., and Viswesvaran, C. (1996). Bandwidth-fidelity dilemma in personality measurement for personnel selection. *Journal of Organizational Behavior*, 17, 609–626.

Ones, D. S., Viswesvaran, C., and Schmidt, F. L. (1993). Meta-analysis of integrity test validities: Findings and implications for personnel selection and theories of job performance. *Journal of Applied Psychology Monograph*, 78, 679–703.

Ones, D. S., Viswesvaran, C., and Schmidt, F. L. (2003). Personality and absenteeism: A meta-analysis of integrity tests. *European Journal of Personality*, 17, 519–537.

Ozer, D. J., and Benet-Martinez, V. (2006). Personality and the prediction of consequential outcomes. *Annual Review of Psychology*, 57, 401–422.

Peeters, M. A. G., Van Tuijl, H. F. J. M., Rutte, C. G., and Reymen, I. M. M. J. (2006). Personality and team performance: A meta-analysis. *European Journal of Personality*, 20, 377–396.

Peterson, N. G., Hough, L. M., Dunnette, M. D., Rosse, R. L., Houston, J. S., Toquam, J. L., and Wing, H. (1990). Project A: Specification of the predictor domain and development of new selection/classification tests. *Personnel Psychology*, 43, 247–276.

Ployhart, R. E., and Holtz, B. S. (2008). The diversity-validity dilemma: Strategies for reducing racioethnic and sex subgroup differences and adverse impact in selection. *Personnel Psychology*, 61, 153–172.

Pulakos, E. D., Schmitt, N., Dorsey, D. W., Arand, S., Hedge, J. W., and Borman, W. C. (2002). Predicting adaptive performance: Further tests of a model of adaptability. *Human Performance*, 15, 299–323.

Rhodewalt, F. (1994). Conceptions of ability, achievement goals and individual-differences in self-handicapping behavior – on the application of implicit theories. *Journal of Personality*, 62, 67–85.

Roberts, B. W., Caspi, A., and Moffitt, T. E. (2003). Work experiences and personality development in young adulthood. *Journal of Personality and Social Psychology*, 84, 582–593.

Roberts, B. W., Walton, K. E., and Bogg, T. (2005). Conscientiousness and health across the life course. *Review of General Psychology*, 9, 156–168.

Rotundo, M., and Sackett, P. R. (2002). The relative importance of task, citizenship, and counterproductive performance to global ratings of job performance: A policy-capturing approach. *Journal of Applied Psychology*, 82, 66–80.

Salgado, J. F. (1997). The five factor model of personality and job performance in the European Community. *Journal of Applied Psychology*, 82, 30–43.

Salgado, J. F. (1998). Criterion validity of personality measures based and non-based on the five factor model. Paper presented at the 106th Annual Convention of the American Psychological Association, San Francisco.

Schmitt, N., and Oswald, F. L. (2006). The impact of corrections for faking on the validity of noncognitive measures in selection settings. *Journal of Applied Psychology*, 91, 613–621.

Schmutte P. S., and Ryff, C. D. (1997). Personality and well-being: Reexamining methods and meanings. *Journal of Personality and Social Psychology*, 73, 549–559.

Seligman, M. E. P. (1978). Learned helplessness in humans – critique and reformulation. *Journal of Abnormal Psychology*, 87, 49–74.

Small, E. E., and Diefendorff, J. M. (2006). The impact of contextual self-ratings and observer ratings of personality on the personality–performance relationship. *Journal of Applied Social Psychology*, 36, 297–321.

Smith, T. W., and MacKenzie, T. (2006). Personality and risk of physical illness. *Annual Review of Clinical Psychology*, 2, 435–467.

Steel, P., Schmidt, J., and Shultz, J. (2008). Refining the relationship between personality and subjective well-being. *Psychological Bulletin*, 134, 138–161.

Taylor, P. J., Pajo, K., Cheung, G. W., and Stringfield, P. (2004). Dimensionality and validity of a structured telephone reference check procedure. *Personnel Psychology*, 57, 745–772.

Terracciano, A., Lockenhoff, C. E., Crum, R. M., Bienvenu, O. J., and Costa, P. T., Jr. (2008). Five-Factor Model personality profiles of drug users. *BioMedicalCentral, Psychiatry*, 8, 22. http://www.biomedcentral.com/1471-244X/8/22

Thoresen, C.J., Kaplan, S.A., Barsley, A.P., Warren, C.R., and de Chermont, K. (2003). The affective underpinnings of job perceptions and attitudes: A meta-analytic review and integration. *Psychological Bulletin*, 129, 914–945.

Witt, L. A., Burke, L., Barrick, M. R., and Mount, M. K. (2002). The interactive effects of conscientiousness and agreeableness on job performance. *Journal of Applied Psychology*, 87, 164–169.

Witt, L. A., and Ferris, G. R. (2003). Social skill as moderator of the conscientiousness–performance relationship: Convergent results across four studies. *Journal of Applied Psychology*, 88, 809–821.

Zhao, H., and Seibert, S. E. (2006). The Big Five personality dimensions and entrepreneurial status: A meta-analytical review. *Journal of Applied Psychology*, 91, 259–271.

Zimmerman, R. D. (2008). Understanding the impact of personality traits on individuals' turnover decisions: A meta-analytic path model. *Personnel Psychology*, 61, 309–348.

Zimmerman, R. D., Triana, M. J., and Barrick, M. R. (2007). Predictive criterion-related validity of observer-ratings of personality and job-related competencies using multiple raters and multiple performance criteria. Paper presented at the Academy of Management Conference, Anaheim, CA.

EXERCISES

Selecting applicants for entry level bank teller positions

You are the human resource manager for a large financial institution. You have been asked to recommend methods for selecting applicants for entry level bank teller positions. It is especially important that tellers have a strong work ethic, display integrity, interact well with others and are accurate in their work. Consequently, you recommend that the foundation of the selection program should be the personality traits of conscientiousness and emotional stability. List and discuss five desirable employee behaviors that will likely result from selecting employees on conscientiousness and emotional stability. Here are some questions you may want to address in your answer:

(a) What skills do all new entrants to the workforce need in order to be successful in the workplace?
(b) Which of these skills are especially important for bank tellers to be successful?
(c) How do conscientiousness and emotional stability influence these critical behaviors?
(d) Are there personality traits other than conscientiousness and emotional stability (e.g., agreeableness, extraversion or openness) that may be useful when selecting for the entry level bank teller positions?

Convincing a high level executive

You are the human resources director at a large firm and you have been asked to design a system for selecting managers. An integral part of your recommended hiring plan is the use of personality tests. A high level executive in the firm hears about your plan and expresses concerns about the use of personality tests. He took a personality test once and he believes it did not accurately describe his personality. He also says that personality tests can't be accurate because "everybody knows you can fake these things." What would you tell him? What is the basis for your answer?

3

Structure Interviews to Recruit and Hire the Best People

Cynthia Kay Stevens

Organizations use employment interviews as a primary means for applicants and hiring managers to meet and gather information from each other for the purpose of making selection and job choice decisions. When applicants or employers have limited time and many alternatives, interviews offer a flexible, efficient format in which to exchange information. Unlike other selection devices (e.g. tests, biodata inventories), interviews don't require expert advice and large samples for development and implementation. They typically do not raise the legal challenges and equal employment opportunity concerns that standardized tests do. Moreover, interviews can be easily adapted to accomplish different goals: introducing applicants and employers, attracting applicant interest, screening out unsuitable candidates, clarifying the rank order of finalists. Such efficiency and flexibility may account for its popularity; interviews (along with reference checks) are the most common selection procedure used across a wide range of jobs and industries (BNA, 1988; see Dipboye, 1992).

Paradoxically, their flexibility also makes it difficult to use interviews effectively. Interviews can vary widely in terms of how many applicants and interviewers are present, question types and sequences, topics covered, how much training and information interviewers and applicants have beforehand, consistency of practices across applicants, and how interviewers' evaluations are used. Some interview formats are better than others at achieving selection and recruitment goals; mismatches between the format and interview goals can impair the quality of managers' and applicants' decisions.

Empirical research has focused on how well interview ratings predict actual job performance, as measured by the correlation coefficient between interviewers' ratings and hired applicants' job performances. Although this research has offered useful insight into the interview formats needed to make good hiring decisions, the use of interviews to achieve other organizational goals (such as attracting top applicants) suggests the need for a broader perspective on how to design effective interviews.

At issue is the need to make good *joint* decisions – that is, to exchange accurate information that enables both applicants and organizations to make the best decisions given the alternatives available to each. To do this, managers can *structure* interviews so that they both provide and collect valid information for use in making decisions.

The purpose of this chapter is to review and summarize what we know about improving decision making in employment interviews. A key theme of this chapter is that, by understanding the factors that impair information quality or exchanges, managers can structure interviews to improve both decision quality and hiring and recruitment outcomes. I begin by describing decision-making research and the factors that affect applicants' and interviewers' judgments and decisions. Then, I discuss nine subprinciples for designing interviews to improve decision making. Finally, I conclude with examples of how poorly designed interviews might be restructured to enable both applicants and interviewers to make better decisions.

DECISION-MAKING RESEARCH

Decision theorists (see Chapter 25, this volume) have converged on the idea that people use one of two processes for making decisions: a rapid, largely unconscious, implicit approach in which choices are made with minimal effort, or a slower, deliberative, controlled approach in which alternatives are consciously weighed and compared (Evans, 2008). Particularly when facing numerous alternatives, decision makers will use these processes sequentially – first automatically screening out candidates that fail to meet some possibly arbitrary criteria, then concentrating their efforts on a closer, more conscious, evaluation of those that remain (e.g. Payne, Bettman, and Johnson, 1988; Svenson, 1992). This two-stage approach is common in both hiring and application decisions, in which "unsuitable" choices are eliminated quickly and without much conscious thought, and conscious effort is focused on a smaller subset. For example, both applicants and hiring managers often make early decisions about whether to interview on the basis of limited information (e.g. presence of grammatical errors in résumés; company reputation or familiarity), and then use later information (including that gained from interviews) to evaluate each other more thoroughly.

Within this dual-process approach, researchers have identified many cognitive, motivational, and contextual factors that affect decisions. The *cognitive factors* include how decisions are framed (e.g. as the potential gain or possible loss of good employees; see Tversky and Kahneman, 1981), a number of heuristics or mental shortcuts used to evaluate alternatives (e.g. comparing the similarity of candidates to current employees to judge suitability – see Tversky and Kahneman, 1974; or considering résumé length to judge applicant quality – see Chinander and Schweitzer, 2003), and a tendency to look for information that confirms, rather than tests, one's expectations (e.g. seeking answers that "screen in" rather than rigorously evaluate a favored candidate; see Snyder and Swann, 1978). *Motivational factors* include decision makers' goals, such as the desire to grow and develop versus to maintain a steady state (e.g. to hire someone with potential versus an established performer; see Brockner and Higgins, 2001), a desire to experience happiness or avoid disappointment with the decision's outcome (see Mellers, 2000), or the desire to justify a preferred conclusion (see Boiney, Kennedy, and Nye, 1997). Finally, *contextual factors* include the conditions or circumstances under which people make decisions, such as how many alternatives are available, what their characteristics are relative to each other, and the timing of the decision (see Hsee, Blount, Loewenstein, and Bazerman, 1999). For example, evaluations shift depending on the set of alternatives available: an applicant with average qualifications will be evaluated quite differently depending on whether they are the only candidate available or one of several candidates all of whom have either strong or weak qualifications.

In summary, applicants and hiring managers will use a combination of rapid/low effort and slower/deliberative decision processes when evaluating their choices. An examination of how the interview context and both individuals' cognitive processes and motivations influence these types of decision making enables us to identify strategies for improving the quality of their decisions.

DECISION MAKING IN INTERVIEWS

Interviews enable applicants and employers to meet – either face to face or via technology – to exchange information that will allow them to make decisions about each other. As such, it is useful to explore what we know about the context, cognitive demands, and motivations of each party and how these factors affect their evaluations.

Interviewers' decisions

Available studies show that interviewers' judgments can be swayed by many of the cognitive, motivational, and contextual factors that affect other types of decisions. For example, interviewers often judge applicants' suitability using implicitly held stereotypes about race, gender, age, or disability status (e.g. Hitt and Barr, 1989; Reilly, Bockettie, Maser, and Wenet, 2005; Segrest Purkiss, Perrewé, Gillespie, Mayes, and Ferris, 2006), although the impact of some factors such as applicants' race may be less than that found for standardized tests (Huffcutt and Roth, 1998). Some evidence suggests that interviewers weigh negative information about applicants more heavily than they do positive information (Macan and Dipboye, 1988), but the role that negative versus positive information plays depends on what sorts of judgments must be made and how involved interviewers are in the decision process (see Posthuma, Morgeson, and Campion, 2002).

Several features of the interview context and its goals can also shift interviewers' motivation and thus their evaluations. Research shows that when determining applicant suitability, interviewers often unconsciously consider personal qualities (e.g. interpersonal skills or appearance; see Huffcutt, Conway, Roth, and Stone, 2001; Pingitore, Dugoni, Tindale, and Spring, 1994), how similar they are to applicants (e.g. Kristof-Brown, Barrick and Franke, 2002), and how well they think applicants would fit with their organization's culture (Cable and Judge, 1997), regardless of whether others in their organization would agree with their assessments or whether those qualities are important for successful job performance. This subjectivity leaves room for applicants to present themselves as likable or similar to interviewers as a strategy to obtain higher interviewer evaluations (Levashina and Campion, 2007). Further, some studies have suggested that interviewers may use résumé and background information about applicants to form preliminary impressions about their suitability, and then elicit information during interviews that confirms these early impressions (Dougherty, Turban, and Callender, 1994), although additional careful studies of this issue are needed. Contextual factors such as whether applicants are evaluated sequentially (versus compared to one another at the same time) and the number of openings (few versus many) also affect interviewers' judgments, such that applicants are held to higher standards when evaluated as part of a larger pool or when there are fewer openings available (Huber, Northcraft, and Neale, 1990).

Because interviewers' evaluations can be affected by so many extraneous factors, an important question is whether interviewers in general can do a reasonably accurate job of predicting which applicants will perform well if hired. One possibility is to use at least three or four interviewers to *independently* interview each applicant; averaging these ratings yields good prediction regarding likely job performance (Schmidt and Zimmerman, 2004). If it is not possible to arrange for multiple interviews for each applicant, other studies have suggested that there are individual differences in interviewer accuracy – that is, some interviewers consistently make better predictions than others (Dougherty, Ebert, and Callender, 1986; but see Pulakos, Schmitt, Whitney, and Smith, 1996).

Structured interviews

Several modifications have shown promise for improving interviewers' accuracy, including training interviewers (Dougherty et al., 1986), having them set goals to form accurate impressions (Neuberg, 1989), and holding them accountable for their decisions and recommendations (Motowidlo, Mero, and DeGroot, 1995). However, the largest and most consistent gains in predicting which applicants will perform well on the job seem to come from *structuring* interviews – that is, standardizing some aspects of the questions asked, delivery, and evaluation process. Across interviewers, the use of structured interview formats leads to better prediction of job performance (correlations range from .35 to .62) than does the use of unstructured interviews (correlations range from .14 to .33; see Huffcutt and Arthur, 1994; McDaniel, Whetzel, Schmidt, and Maurer, 1994).

Applicants' decisions

Although less research has examined applicants' decision, the existing studies do suggest that many cognitive, motivational, and contextual factors can sway applicants' judgments. For example, applicants are concerned with finding jobs and organizations whose attributes provide a good fit with their interests and needs (Judge and Cable, 1997). Given that they often have little information to determine whether a given job opportunity provides a good fit, applicants may rely on signals to infer these attributes, such as whether the organization has a good reputation (Highhouse, Zickar, Thorsteinson, Stierwalt, and Slaughter, 1999), their beliefs about the organization's personality (Slaughter, Zickar, Highhouse, and Mohr, 2004), and whether the interviewer was warm and personable during the interview (Chapman, Uggerslev, Carroll, Piasentin, and Jones, 2005). Some data suggest that applicants dislike structured interviews and report being less likely to accept job offers from organizations that use them (Chapman and Rowe, 2002) although the data are mixed on the latter point. Applicants also show evidence of biased judgments depending on how difficult they think it will be to obtain a job: they evaluate the opportunity more favorably following interviews if they think they may receive fewer job offers than if they expect to have many offers (Stevens, 1997).

Researchers have not examined whether applicants' decisions following interviews predicts their subsequent job satisfaction or tenure with organizations. Nonetheless, some data indicate that interviews providing structured, realistic job information may help applicants self-select out of jobs in which they might be unhappy, and among those who do accept jobs, exposure to realistic job information leads to longer tenure on the job (see Buckley, Mobbs, Mendoza, Novicevic, Carraher, and Beu, 2002). This effect may be limited to situations in which applicants have other job offers from which to choose, however (Saks, Wiesner, and Summers, 1994).

How to structure interviews

Although interview structure is an important means for improving joint decision making, some managers are unclear regarding what it means to structure an interview, and many fail to see the value of increasing interview structure (Van der Zee, Bakker, and Bakker, 2002). Campion, Palmer, and Campion (1997) identified 15 possible content and process dimensions on which interviews could be structured (e.g. using job analysis to determine question content, standardizing interview lengths, using statistical procedures to combine interviewers' ratings). To reduce this list, Chapman and Zweig (2005) surveyed applicants and interviewers and found three primary areas that increase structure and one that reduces it. Features that increase interview structure include *question sophistication*, or using question formats known to yield valid information (such as past behavior description or situational questions); *question consistency*, or asking the same questions in the same order to all applicants; and *evaluation standardization*, or using the same numeric scoring procedures for rating all answers. *Rapport-building*, or asking non-content-related questions and making light conversation, is thought to put applicants at ease and improve their attraction to the organization, although it may reduce interview structure and any information obtained from applicants may be unrelated to their job performance. Their study found that interviewer training increased interviewers' use of standardized evaluations and sophisticated question formats, but had no effect on increasing consistency in questions asked. Importantly, applicants found highly structured interviews to be more difficult, but this did not reduce their intent to accept job offers.

Structuring interviews has many benefits for organizations and applicants, particularly in terms of increasing the exchange of valid information to make decisions. Clearly, there may be some tradeoffs with interviewer and applicant discretion (Van der Zee et al., 2002), although the loss of control may not be as great as managers assume it will be. The next section describes how to improve interview structure.

IMPROVING DECISION MAKING BY INCREASING INTERVIEW STRUCTURE

Effectively structuring interviews to improve decision making is not difficult, but it does require advance preparation and critical analysis. Involving interviewers in the process of developing an interview structure can improve their job challenge and satisfaction (see Judge, this volume). Moreover, it can communicate a greater sense of professionalism to applicants. To assist managers in improving the quality of decisions following interviews, I offer the following nine subprinciples.

Subprinciple 1: Identify the primary goals for the interview: recruitment, selection, or a combined focus

Goals enable people to channel their efforts in appropriate directions and gauge their progress (see Chapter 9, this volume). They also affect interview decision making by orienting interviewers to accomplish important tasks. Thus, interviewers need to have clear guidance regarding the purpose of their interviews: recruiting and attracting a larger applicant pool, screening out unsuitable applicants, or a combined focus on recruitment and selection. Such knowledge helps them determine the appropriate structure for their interviews – in particular, how much time should be devoted to collecting or providing information.

Subprinciple 2: Develop a set of questions – based on job analysis – that ask about applicants' capacity to perform the job

All interviewers ask questions, and having a prepared set of questions with clear links to job performance can only help applicants and interviewers by signaling what attributes are important. To ensure that questions are relevant to the job, begin by reviewing available job descriptions or specifications, which should state the knowledge, skills, abilities and other characteristics (KSAOCs) needed for success, the tasks performed, and essential work conditions. (O*Net online is a good generic source of job analysis information if job descriptions or specifications are lacking.) Identify the KSAOCs, tasks, and work condition requirements that are best assessed in an interview (e.g. intelligence is most effectively and reliably measured through cognitive ability tests; see Chapter 1, this volume), and write questions that ask – in a non-transparent manner – whether applicants have or can demonstrate those capabilities.

Formats.   Two question formats have proven to be most effective for interviews: past behavior description and situational questions. *Past behavior description questions* ask for examples of past performance (e.g. "Tell me about a time when . . . "), *whereas situational questions* ask what applicants would do in a given situation (e.g. "How would you deal with a situation in which . . ."). As an example of assessing customer service orientation, a past behavior description question might be, "Tell me about a time when you had to deal with the concerns of an upset customer – what was the situation and how did you respond?" A corresponding situational question would be, "Imagine you had to deal with an upset customer who did not receive their order when it was promised. What specifically would you do to deal with their concerns?" Some research suggests that, all other factors equal, past behavior description questions may yield more useful information than situational questions (Taylor and Small, 2002), although both formats are superior to other types of questions that may be asked (e.g. applicants' opinions).

Subprinciple 3: Develop a set of scoring criteria for evaluating applicants' answers

Once a set of interview questions has been written, it is extremely useful to create a set of criteria for evaluating applicants' answers. Having a scoring guide ensures that, no matter who conducts the interview, all applicants will be held to the same standards. Managers can identify which responses are optimal and which are problematic by talking to job incumbents, reviewing the work behavior of current good and poor performers, and in some organizations examining the performance evaluations themselves to identify important indicators. Research shows that having and using scoring criteria provides a significant and independent contribution to accuracy when predicting applicants' job performance (Taylor and Small, 2002). To the extent that interviewers are inexperienced, providing scoring guidelines can also help to make the task of conducting interviews easier.

Subprinciple 4: When interviewing, ask all applicants the same questions in the same order

Asking all applicants the same questions in the same order helps to provide comparable information about each applicant. It is inherently fairer, in that all applicants are given the same opportunity to explain what they can do and why they are qualified for the position. Some managers may resist such consistency, in that it limits their spontaneity and can make the interviews seem more rote. However, to the extent that interviewers spend a portion of each interview answering applicants' questions about their organizations, this concern may be less problematic.

Subprinciple 5: Ask interviewers to take brief notes on each applicant and to review their notes before rating applicants

Data concerning this recommendation are mixed: interviewers who take detailed notes show better recall of information about applicants, but their judgments about applicants' performance potential are not necessarily more accurate than those of interviewers who do not take notes (Middendorf and Macan, 2002). However, asking interviewers to take some notes accomplishes several objectives: (a) it aids in holding interviewers accountable for their recommendations, which has been shown to improve the quality of their recommendations (Motowidlo et al., 1995), (b) it communicates an interest in what applicants have to say, which can help when recruiting applicants, and (c) it enables interviewers to recall applicants' answers when comparing or discussing job candidates.

Middendorf and Macan (2002) found that interviewers who wrote down key points were better able to differentiate between applicants, possibly because their attention was less divided between listening to applicants and writing. Moreover, they found that asking interviewers to review their notes *prior* to making ratings of applicants helped them to make more accurate ratings. Such an approach should help interviewers to focus on what applicants have to say, and to make ratings without the added pressure of responding to or shielding their evaluations from applicants who are seated nearby.

Subprinciple 6: Select or train interviewers to build rapport with applicants

Research indicates that most applicants have determined which organizations they prefer well before their interviews (Collins and Stevens, 2002), but it also consistently shows that exposure to warm, personable interviewers improves their intentions to pursue or accept job offers (see Chapman et al., 2005). Interviewers who are high in extraversion and agreeableness are likely to be more successful in establishing rapport than are introverts or those low in agreeableness. If it is not possible to select interviewers who are naturally skilled at putting others at ease, interviewers can also be trained to improve their rapport-building behavior. For example, open non-verbal behavior (e.g. eye contact, smiling, and open body posture), welcoming statements, and a willingness to fully answer questions can improve applicants' perceptions of interviewers' personableness.

Subprinciple 7: If interviews receive preinterview information about applicants, make sure that it is valid

Research shows that, when interviewers have access to preliminary information about applicants (e.g. from résumés or test scores), it may prompt them to form impressions about applicant suitability which then affects how they conduct the interview (Dougherty et al., 1994). This problem has led some experts to recommend that *all* preinterview information be withheld from interviewers (e.g. Dipboye, 1989). Although this recommendation may ensure that interviews are not biased, it may not always be practical. For example, this procedure would not enable interviewers to clarify incomplete or ambiguous résumé or application information, and it may make it more difficult for interviewers to understand fully the context for applicants' answers.

Thus, it is important to be aware of the problems associated with preinterview information and to take steps to ensure that it is accurate, valid, and used appropriately. For example, if interviews will be used for screening purposes, ensure that any preinterview information is valid – that is, it has a reliable, statistical relationship with job performance. It is also valuable to independently verify basic information from the résumé, such as degrees earned, prior employers and dates of employment, as a single phone call can quickly eliminate unscrupulous applicants. If interviews are being used to *recruit* applicants, access to preinterview information may help determine how best to describe the job and organization. If interviewers' preinterview expectations are based on valid, accurate information, behavioral confirmation tendencies during the interview should pose less of a problem and may enable interviewers to shift their emphasis to recruiting promising applicants (Posthuma et al., 2002).

Subprinciple 8: Ask applicants about their decision process and criteria, and share realistic information tailored to those processes and criteria

Just as managers are interested in applicants who fit with their organizations, applicants typically seek organizations that provide a good fit with their interests and needs (Rynes, Bretz, and Gerhart, 1991). Most applicants share similar concerns such as job type, location, pay level, and training opportunities. However, the specific type of information they want and how it will affect their decision process can vary across applicants as well as within applicants over time. Thus, interviewers can structure interviews to help applicants make good decisions by asking about the criteria that will be important in their decisions and the context in which their decisions will be made.

There are several benefits to this form of interview structure. First, interviewers can offer realistic information tailored to applicants' interests, rather than giving a standard "speech" about their organizations' positive attributes. To the extent that other firms do not provide such individualized approaches, this practice may help firms gain an advantage in attracting applicants' interest. A second benefit is that such information can help interviewers estimate the probability that an offer would be accepted if extended. Applicants for whom one's organization does not meet important criteria are less likely to accept offers, and firms that identify such mismatches early may focus their effort toward pursuing other attractive applicants who are likely to accept offers.

Interviewers may also find it helpful to inquire about applicants' decision process, particularly the number of offers they expect or have received. This contextual factor has dramatic effects on decision making in other contexts – decision makers may reverse their preference for the same option when it is presented by itself versus as one of multiple options from which to choose (Hsee et al., 1999). Consistent with this, recruitment research has shown that applicants who expect to receive fewer offers evaluate a given firm more favorably after their interviews than do applicants who expect to receive multiple job offers (Stevens, 1997). Interviewers thus may gain insight into how their recruitment information will be received by asking about applicants' expectations for success in their job searches.

Subprinciple 9: If it is not possible to structure interviews, then arrange for 3–4 independent interviewers to meet with each applicant

As suggested earlier, structured interviews consistently provide valid, predictive information about which applicants are likely to perform well on the job (e.g. Huffcutt and Arthur, 1994). Yet, Schmidt and Zimmerman (2004) found that averaging the ratings of three to four *independent* interviewers who used unstructured interviews also yielded good predictions about applicants' likely job performance. Thus, if it is not possible to structure interviews, hiring managers can approximate their accuracy by obtaining and averaging the ratings from a set of unstructured interviewers. Of course, the best situation would be to conduct structured interviews with three or four independent interviewers – organizations would obtain high-quality information about applicants' capabilities, and applicants would be able to hear multiple perspectives on what they could expect from the job and organization if hired.

CASE EXAMPLES

Structure helps interviewers gather and disseminate information useful for making decisions. To illustrate this process, I provide several examples from my research (Stevens, 1998). The first comes from the transcript of an untrained interviewer who was screening applicants for a large public accounting firm. Untrained interviewers ask fewer open-ended, follow-up, and performance-differentiating questions, and they tend to ask such questions in ways that are transparent – that is, phrased to indicate the desired response. This interviewer's questions are typical of this (the numbers represent turns at talk).

211. **INTERVIEWER:** What else have you done that ah, you feel would be helpful to you in public accounting?
212. **APPLICANT:** Oh, gee, as far as extracurricular? Well I was in a lot of service clubs and, you know, I've worked with people, done March of Dimes, things like that. Just dealing with people.
213. **INTERVIEWER:** How would you say your communication skills are?
214. **APPLICANT:** I think they're pretty good. I think I have pretty good communication skills. Listening is part of it, yeah, so –
215. **INTERVIEWER:** Okay.

To screen applicants effectively, this interviewer could improve the information obtained by rephrasing and following up on these questions. For example, the question about what the applicant has done that would be helpful in a career in public accounting would yield more helpful data if the interviewer asked follow-up questions about what roles the applicant had held in various service clubs, and what specific things she had done for the March of Dimes. Asking about specific instances in which the applicant had worked with other people in these roles would provide important indications about how the applicant would interact with clients and co-workers. Likewise, the question about communication skills would prompt most applicants to answer that they had good communication skills – the "correct" answer is transparent. Rather than asking applicants for an evaluation of their own skills and taking that information at face value, the interviewer might instead ask past behavior description questions about instances in which the applicant had misunderstandings with other students or co-workers, and what she did to address those problems. Answers to this type of question would provide more concrete data about the applicant's communication skills and would allow fewer opportunities for the applicant to manage the interviewer's impression.

In contrast, the following (edited) segment shows how interviewers using past behavior description questions can gather high quality information.

103. **INTERVIEWER:** . . . Now I'd like to spend a little bit of time talking about decision making and problem solving. Tell me about a particularly difficult decision you had to make.
104. **APPLICANT:** Um, well . . . that ah, decision on the design approach, it was very difficult for me. 'Cause I didn't want to – I had the authority to overrule the design team. But I didn't want to use that um, unless I was absolutely sure they were wrong. I didn't want to alienate either the architect–engineer or the design team. And that resulted in a lot of squabbles and a lot of running back and forth negotiating between people to find out what – what is the best way . . .
105. **INTERVIEWER:** Mmm. So what were the things, some things you just considered in your decision?
106. **APPLICANT:** Um, I had to consider the qualifications of the person. Ah, whether they really knew what they were talking about. Um, another factor was there was a definite bias between the design team and the architect–engineer. They all took many years of, of infighting. And I had to try to consider how much of this is just due to the fact that "This person's designing it so I know it's no good," as opposed to, "It's just . . . not going to work in our best interests."

107. **INTERVIEWER:** Okay. And so what do you ... see then you decided where you ended up going with . . .?

108. **APPLICANT:** Design team's modifications, even though it was more expensive. In the long run, it proved to be ah, a better, um more cost effective way of operating.

Recruitment goals can also be met by structuring interviews through training and use of standardized questions. Recruitment-oriented interviewers are less likely than screening-oriented interviewers to receive training; given that untrained interviewers are seen by applicants as less organized and less professional, this trend is unfortunate. Untrained interviewers tended to talk more, jumping between asking and answering questions, providing unrequested information, and digressing into non-job-related topics. This problem is illustrated in the next example, in which an untrained interviewer sought to recruit an applicant for an insurance sales position. Although this segment is edited, the dialog between this interviewer and applicant followed the same pattern in which the interviewer did most of the talking.

25.–31. **INTERVIEWER:** Here are some reasons why you would want to choose a career with [name of firm]. We guarantee your income while you start, develop your own image on being your own boss, getting, ah, getting into management career status, extra benefits, ah, and on the back here, are twelve good reasons ... why you would want to be an insurance agent. And, um, here is, ah, a brochure that explains ah, the training program in general ... terms. It's a lifelong training program. Um, we have, we feel, the finest training, uh, in the industry, ahh, as a company ... And I believe, in my district, we have ah, the finest training in America simply because we use the company training in the first six–twelve months or so, and after that we go into material, we make available to you material from the Insurance Institute of America. Now when I say make available to you, ah, we recruit and train people from all walks of life. Some people can't handle the material from the Insurance Institute of America because it's college level and/or they don't have the math background or they don't have the interest, study skills ... to do it. I put on six people in 19[...] and to date, ah, none of them have taken advantage of all the material that I could give them. Because, well, it's not all bad either. Some of them, three of them are college students and they're doing so well that they don't have the time, they won't take the time to, to attend the course. Ah, one of 'em has gone through a couple of 'em or attempted to go through a couple of 'em, but ah, nevertheless I've kept my end of the bargain and I would make it available to her and now in their second or third year, ah, they would take it a little more serious, ah the more advanced learning of insurance. Okay?

32. **APPLICANT:** Um-hmm.

33. **INTERVIEWER:** So we say we'll make it available to you, if you're good enough to take advantage of it, that's fine.

34. **APPLICANT:** Um-hmm.

This interviewer clearly had a lot of positive information about his company to convey to applicants. Yet, his approach – doing all the talking, without finding out the applicant's unique interests or criteria for making decisions – doesn't allow him to tailor his "pitch" to her as an individual. He may or may not cover information about his company that would be of interest to her. A smarter strategy would be to ask her questions about why she was exploring a career in insurance sales, what she is looking for in a job or company, and what other jobs and organizations she has considered. Not only would this approach be more efficient in assessing her interest and communicating the information of greatest value to her, it would also convey interest in and concern for her as an individual. This interviewer might also spend some time talking about the less attractive aspects of being in insurance sales as a way to make the rest of the information he provides appear more balanced and credible.

A good way to approach this issue is provided in a final example, which is too lengthy to reprint fully here. The opening was for a human resources internship rotation program in a large conglomerate, and the interviewer determined through the résumé and some preliminary questions that the applicant had excellent qualifications. She then shifted the focus of their discussion to the factors that would be important in the applicant's decision, and discovered that his wife was applying to medical schools across the country. This enabled the interviewer to pinpoint several divisions to which he could be assigned that were located near his wife's preferred medical schools. Note that, had she relied on a prepared speech about the company's programs and benefits, she would have neglected to provide this critical information about how her company could meet this applicant's needs.

CONCLUSION

Interviews are typically used as one in a set of selection/recruitment tools to make decisions about whom to hire and which job offers to accept. Because they are flexible, interviews can be used to accomplish multiple purposes, such as introductions, recruitment, screening out unsuitable candidates, and so on. However, this flexibility can also be a stumbling block, as research shows that decision processes are susceptible to many cognitive, motivational, and contextual influences that may degrade the quality of the final decision.

Increasing interview structure can help managers achieve their recruitment or selection goals by helping to minimize the impact of irrelevant factors on interviewers' and applicants' decision processes. Structuring interviews introduces some standardization in procedures to make the judgments that follow less idiosyncratic. Wisely structuring interviews to balance the need for standardization with the need for interviewer and applicant discretion can ensure that both organizations and applicants get the most out of the process.

REFERENCES

Boiney, L.G., Kennedy, J., and Nye, P. (1997). Instrumental bias in motivated reasoning: More when more is needed. *Organizational Behavior and Human Decision Processes*, 72, 1–24.

Brockner, J., and Higgins, E. T. (2001). Regulatory focus theory: Implications for the study of emotions at work. *Organizational Behavior and Human Decision Processes*, 86, 35–66.

Buckley, M. R., Mobbs, T. A., Mendoza, J. L., Novicevic, M. M., Carraher, S. M., and Beu, D. S. (2002). Implementing realistic job previews and expectation-lowering procedures: a field experiment. *Journal of Vocational Behavior*, 61, 263–278.

Bureau of National Affairs (1988). Recruiting and selection procedures. PPF Survey No. 146, May.

Cable, D. M., and Judge, T. A. (1997). Interviewers' perceptions of person–organization fit and organizational selection decisions. *Journal of Applied Psychology*, 82, 546–561.

Campion, M. A., Palmer, D. K., and Campion, J. E. (1997). A review of structure in the selection interview. *Personnel Psychology*, 50, 655–702.

Chapman, D. S., and Rowe, P. M. (2002). The influence of videoconference technology and interview structure on the recruiting function of the employment interview: A field experiment. *International Journal of Selection and Assessment*, 10, 185–197.

Chapman, D. S., Uggerslev, K. L., Carroll, S. A., Piasentin, K. A., and Jones, D. A. (2005). Applicant attraction to organizations and job choice: A meta-analytic review of the correlates of recruiting outcomes. *Journal of Applied Psychology*, 90, 928–944.

Chapman, D. S., and Zweig, D. I. (2005). Developing a nomological network for interview structure: Antecedents and consequences of the structured selection interview. *Personnel Psychology*, 58, 673–702.

Chinander, K. R., and Schweitzer, M. E. (2003). The input bias: the misuse of input information in judgments of outcomes. *Organizational Behavior and Human Decision Processes*, 91, 243–253.

Collins, C. J., and Stevens, C. K. (2002). The relationship between early recruitment-related activities and the application decisions of new labor-market entrants: A brand equity approach to recruitment. *Journal of Applied Psychology*, 87, 1121–1133.

Dipboye, R. L. (1989). Threats to the incremental validity of interviewer judgments. In R. W. Eder and G. R. Ferris (eds), *The Employment Interview: Theory, Research, and Practice* (pp. 45–60). Newbury Park, CA: Sage.

Dipboye, R. L. (1992). *Selection Interviews: Process Perspectives*. Cincinnati, OH: South-Western Publishing Co.

Dougherty, T. W., Ebert, R. J., and Callender, J. C. (1986). Policy capturing in the employment interview. *Journal of Applied Psychology*, 71, 9–15.

Dougherty, T. W., Turban, D. B., and Callender, J. C. (1994). Confirming first impressions in the employment interview: A field study of interviewer behavior. *Journal of Applied Psychology*, 79, 659–665.

Evans, J. St. B. T. (2008). Dual-processing accounts of reasoning, judgment, and social cognition. *Annual Review of Psychology*, 59, 255–278.

Highhouse, S., Zickar, M. J., Thorsteinson, T. J., Stierwalt, S. L., and Slaughter, J. (1999). Assessing company employment image: An example in the fast food industry. *Personnel Psychology*, 52, 151–172.

Hitt, M. A., and Barr, S. H. (1989). Managerial selection decision models: Examination of configural cue processing. *Journal of Applied Psychology*, 74, 53–61.

Hsee, C. K., Blount, S., Loewenstein, G. F., and Bazerman, M. H. (1999). Preference reversals between joint and separate evaluations of options: A review and theoretical analysis. *Psychological Bulletin*, 125, 576–590.

Huber, V. L., Northcraft, G. B., and Neale, M. A. (1990). Effects of decision strategy and number of openings on employment selection decisions. *Organizational Behavior and Human Decision Processes*, 45, 276–284.

Huffcutt, A. I., and Arthur, W., Jr. (1994). Hunter and Hunter (1984) revisited: Interview validity for entry-level jobs. *Journal of Applied Psychology*, 79, 184–190.

Huffcutt, A. I., and Roth, P. L. (1998). Racial group differences in employment interview evaluations. *Journal of Applied Psychology*, 83, 179–189.

Huffcutt, A. I., Conway, J. M., Roth, P. L., and Stone, N. J. (2001). Identification and meta-analytic assessment of psychological constructs measured in employment interviews. *Journal of Applied Psychology*, 86, 897–913.

Judge, T. A., and Cable, D. M. (1997). Applicant personality, organizational culture, and organization attraction. *Personnel Psychology*, 50, 359–395.

Kristof-Brown, A., Barrick, M. R., and Franke, M. (2002). Applicant impression management: Dispositional influences and consequences for recruiter perceptions of fit and similarity. *Journal of Management*, 28, 27–46.

Levashina, J., and Campion, M. A. (2007). Measuring faking in the employment interview: Development and validation of an interview faking behavior scale. *Journal of Applied Psychology*, 92, 1638–1656.

Macan, T. H., and Dipboye, R. L. (1988). The effects of interviewers' initial impressions on information gathering. *Organizational Behavior and Human Decision Processes*, 42, 364–387.

McDaniel, M. A., Whetzel, D. L., Schmidt, F. L., and Maurer, S. D. (1994). The validity of employment interviews: A comprehensive review and meta-analysis. *Journal of Applied Psychology*, 79, 599–616.

Mellers, B. A. (2000). Choice and the relative pleasure of consequences. *Psychological Bulletin*, 126, 910–924.

Middendorf, C. H., and Macan, T. H. (2002). Note-taking in the employment interview: Effects on recall and judgments. *Journal of Applied Psychology*, 87, 293–303.

Motowidlo, S. J., Mero, N. P., and DeGroot, T. (1995). Effects of interviewer accountability on interview validity. Paper presented at the Annual Conference of the Society for Industrial and Organizational Psychology, Orlando, FL.

Neuberg, S. L. (1989). The goal of forming accurate impressions during social interaction: Attenuating the impact of negative expectancies. *Journal of Personality and Social Psychology*, 56, 374–386.

Payne, J. W., Bettman, J. R., and Johnson, E. J. (1988). Adaptive strategy selection in decision making. *Journal of Experimental Psychology: Learning, Memory and Cognition*, 14, 534–552.

Pingitore, R., Dugoni, B. L., Tindale, R. S., and Spring, B. (1994). Bias against overweight job applicants in a simulated employment interview. *Journal of Applied Psychology*, 79, 909–917.

Posthuma, R. A., Morgeson, F. P., and Campion, M. A. (2002). Beyond employment interview validity: A comprehensive narrative review of recent research and trends over time. *Personnel Psychology*, 55, 1–81.

Pulakos, E. D., Schmitt, N., Whitney, D., and Smith, M. (1996). Individual differences in interviewer ratings: The impact of standardization, consensus discussion, and sampling error on the validity of a structured interview. *Personnel Psychology*, 49, 85–102.

Reilly, N. P., Bockettie, S. P., Maser, S. A., and Wenet, C. L. (2005). Benchmarks affect perceptions of prior disability in a structured interview. *Journal of Business and Psychology*, 20, 489–500.

Rynes, S. L., Bretz, R. D., and Gerhart, B. (1991). The importance of recruitment in job choice: a different way of looking. *Personnel Psychology*, 44, 487–521.

Saks, A. M., Wiesner, W. H., and Summers, R. J. (1994). Effects of job previews on self-selection and job choice. *Journal of Vocational Behavior*, 44, 297–316.

Schmidt, F. L., and Zimmerman, R. D. (2004). A counterintuitive hypothesis about employment interview validity and some supporting evidence. *Journal of Applied Psychology*, 89, 553–561.

Segrest Purkiss, L. S., Perrewé, P. L., Gillespie, T. L., Mayes, B. T., and Ferris, G. R. (2006). Implicit sources of bias in employment interview judgments and decisions. *Organizational Behavior and Human Decision Processes*, 101, 152–167.

Slaughter, J. E., Zickar, M. J., Highhouse, S., and Mohr, D. C. (2004). Personality trait inferences about organizations: Development of a measure and assessment of construct validity. *Journal of Applied Psychology*, 89, 85–103.

Snyder, M., and Swann, W. B. (1978). Hypothesis-testing processes in social interaction. *Journal of Personality and Social Psychology*, 36, 1202–1212.

Stevens, C. K. (1997). Effects of preinterview beliefs on applicants' reactions to campus interviews. *Academy of Management Journal*, 40, 947–966.

Stevens, C. K. (1998). Antecedents of interview interactions, interviewers' ratings, and applicants' reactions. *Personnel Psychology*, 51, 55–85.

Svenson, O. (1992). Differentiation and consolidation theory of human decision making: A frame of reference for the study of pre- and post-decision processes. *Acta Psychologica*, 80, 143–168.

Taylor, P. J., and Small, B. (2002). Asking applicants what they would do versus what they did do: a meta-analytic comparison of situation and past behaviour employment interview questions. *Journal of Occupational and Organizational Psychology*, 75, 277–294.

Tversky, A., and Kahneman, D. (1974). Judgment under uncertainty: Heuristics and biases. *Science*, 185, 1124–1130.

Tversky, A., and Kahneman, D. (1981). The framing of decisions and the psychology of choice. *Science*, 211, 453–458.

Van der Zee, K. I., Bakker, A. B., and Bakker, P. (2002). Why are structured interviews so rarely used in personnel selection? *Journal of Applied Psychology*, 87, 176–184.

EXERCISES

Interviewing applicants

Imagine that you are preparing to interview applicants for a junior management consultant – a position in which incumbents conduct organizational studies and evaluations, design systems and procedures, conduct work simplifications and measurement studies, and prepare operations and procedures manuals to assist management in operating more efficiently and effectively. First, look up the necessary KSAOCs (knowledge, skills, abilities, and other characteristics), required tasks, and common work environment conditions. You can find a wealth of information on O*Net (http://online.onetcenter.org). Using the information you find, choose three important requirements for the job and generate SIX structured interview questions (three using the behavior description format and three using the situational format).

Evaluating applicant answers

For each of the questions you listed above, come up with scoring criteria to evaluate applicants' answers. Using a scale that spans from 1 to 5, generate criteria that would help you differentiate very poor (1), low effectiveness (2), average (3), above average (4), and extremely effective (5) answers to your questions.

Part II

TRAINING AND PERFORMANCE
APPRAISAL

4

Design Training Systematically and Follow the Science of Training

Eduardo Salas and Kevin C. Stagl

A national education crisis, employment levels topping 94%, a growing retiree bubble, and the rapid rise of emerging market opportunities are draining an already shallow domestic talent pool. And the scarcity of workers with cultural competence, interpersonal savvy, and technological acumen is not just a US problem as 41% of 37,000 employers across 27 countries report experiencing human capital difficulties (Manpower, 2007).

In response, US employers invest over $126 billion annually on training and development initiatives (Paradise, 2007); more than double their $55 billion annual investment just a decade ago (Bassi and Van Buren, 1998). Employers make sizable investments in training because it is a powerful lever for structuring and guiding experiences that facilitate the acquisition of affective, behavioral, and cognitive (ABCs) learning outcomes by employees (Kraiger, Ford, and Salas, 1993). In turn, learning outcomes can horizontally transfer to the workplace and over time transfer vertically to impact key organizational outcomes (Kozlowski, Brown, Weissbein, Cannon-Bowers, and Salas, 2000). In fact, systematically designed training can even help improve entire national economies (Aguinis and Kraiger, in press).

While trillions are spent annually worldwide on training activities, 52% of employers still report struggling to rapidly develop skills and only 13% claim to have a very clear understanding of the capabilities they need in the next three to five years (IBM, 2008). Moreover, only 27% find web-based training, and a mere 17% virtual classroom training, to be effective at meeting their needs (IBM). Perhaps this is not surprising given that estimates suggest only 10% of training expenditures transfer to the job (Georgenson, 1982) and a meager 5% of solutions are evaluated in terms of organizational benefits (Swanson, 2001). It seems now, more than ever before, there is a need for actionable guidance on designing training systematically.

Fortunately, the science of training has benefited from an explosion of research activity since the late 1990s and has much to contribute to ensuring the vitality of organizations and the domestic and global economies they fuel. For example, Salas and Cannon-Bowers (2000) tapped the science of training to extract fundamental principles and advance targeted guidance for designing systematic training in the first edition of this book series.

Almost a decade later, this chapter continues the tradition by providing a translation mechanism for stakeholders charged with fostering more effective individuals, teams, and organizations via systematic training initiatives. Specifically, we advance a set of theories, principles, guidelines, best practice specifications, and lessons learned that address some of the many linkages among training problems, theories, techniques, and tools.

Our discussion follows a four phase process to designing blended training solutions. We use our own experiences facilitating learning, and draw heavily upon the science of training, to advance phase-specific guidelines for designing, developing, delivering, and evaluating training solutions (Table 4.1). We cannot overstate the contribution of colleagues, who represent many disciplines, to shaping our thinking on training issues. Next, we describe the success of team training in the aviation industry and discuss the lessons learned from a failure to develop a sales force. We conclude by presenting two scenario-based exercises crafted to impart knowledge about designing and evaluating learning solutions.

Analyze Training Needs

Training needs analysis can be the most important phase of training design because its success depends on an intensive collaborative partnership between key stakeholders. The charge of this partnership is to clarify the purposes of training, illuminate the organizational context, define effective performance and its drivers, and begin to cultivate a climate of learning. Essential activities conducted during the needs analysis phase include: (a) conducting training due diligence, (b) defining performance functions and processes, (c) defining affective and cognitive states, (d) defining an attribute model, and (e) delineating learning objectives. When executed with care, these activities can help ensure remaining phases yield a meaningful learning solution.

Conduct due diligence

Training methods and techniques are not interchangeable or universally applicable, as evidenced by recent meta-analytic findings (Klein, Stagl, Salas, Burke, DiazGranados, Goodwin, and Halpin, 2007). For example, the same learning solution may be differentially effective if it is implemented to address short-, mid- and/or long-term business objectives. Hence, effective instruction in one setting may prove counterproductive elsewhere. This is why it is critical to describe the specific challenges and opportunities training will address; and thereby defining what, and for whom, benefits will accrue.

Due diligence is a process for clarifying and quantifying the expected benefits from training for individuals, teams, and higher-level units (division, organization, society). The purpose of the process is to gather the information required to have an objective and dispassionate dialog about whether or when a particular solution should be institutionalized. And the conversation must encompass more than just performance, productivity, and

Table 4.1 Summary of training phases, principles and guidelines

Training phase	Guiding principle	Training guidelines
Analyze training needs	Conduct due diligence	Describe an organization's mission, strategy, structure, context, and desired outcomes
		Articulate the benefits for individuals, teams, and higher-level units (division, organization, society)
		Link solutions to specific organizational outcomes (performance, effectiveness, profitability)
		Consider the impact on organizational performance-related factors (satisfaction, reputation, social capital)
		Frame cross-level effects of contextual factors on motivation, learning, and transfer
		Specify how individual results emerge to impact unit- or organization-level outcomes (vertical transfer)
		Conduct a stakeholder analysis to identify and understand parties advocating for and against training
		Estimate the expected net present value of proposed training solutions
	Define performance requirements	Leverage established theories of performance and taxonomies of processes to guide criteria specification
		Disaggregate dependent variables to illuminate the specific aspects of performance targeted by training
		Use task inventories, cognitive task analysis, and critical incident interviews to nuance key factors
		Conduct probed protocol analysis to elicit the stimuli, goals, and actions of experts in natural situations

(continued)

Table 4.1 (continued)

Training phase	Guiding principle	Training guidelines
	Define cognitive and affective states	Map the trajectory of change from novice to expert performance
		Describe the relative importance of taskwork and teamwork processes during performance episodes
		Frame individual-level cognitive (mental models, situation awareness) and affective (self-efficacy) states
		Describe the types of mental models (equipment, task, team) targeted for development
		Use event-based knowledge-elicitation techniques with subject matter experts to describe shared states
		Model the compositional or compilational emergence of cognitive and affective states
		Determine the relative importance of sharedness and accuracy of cognitive and affective states
	Define KSA attributes	Specify the direct determinants of the processes and emergent states comprising effective performance
		Leverage knowledge and skill inventories, skill repositories, and performance records
		Describe the declarative, procedural, and strategic knowledge applied to enact performance processes
		Describe the attitudes that can be changed as a result of the learning process
		Identify short-, mid-, and long-term competency requirements given alternative performance requirements

Delineate learning objectives	Translate training needs into training objectives, learning objectives, and enabling objectives
	Contextualize task statements by describing appropriate performance standards
	Delineate behavior-, cognitive-, and affective-based learning objectives
	Ensure learning objectives are clear, concise, and link to measurable learning outcomes
Design learning architecture	Develop an intelligent scenario management system that allows instructors and users to author content
	Design a dashboard interface that can be used to control training content, sequence, and pace
	Program systems to provide tailored training features based on aptitude–treatment interactions
	Design the capacity to manipulate action tempo and compress the arrival time of events
	Design the capacity to vary the predictability and difficulty of contexts, tasks, events, and situations
	Program intelligent tutors to dynamically monitor, assess, diagnose, intervene, and remediate performance
	Create the capacity to compile performance records and for an on-demand lesson learned repository
Develop training content	Develop an instructional management plan, instructor guides, and scripts
Forge instructional experiences	Map the branching paths learners can take and forecast where trainees are likely to encounter difficulties
	Construct a chronological timeline of training events
	Craft instructional content that has psychological fidelity as well as physical fidelity

(continued)

Table 4.1 (continued)

Training phase	Guiding principle	Training guidelines
		Include opportunities for trainees to discover knowledge and relationships for themselves
		Develop lectures, exercises, games, reading lists, and illustrative case studies
		Leverage role plays, motion pictures, closed-circuit television, and interactive multimedia to display models
		Increase stimulus variability by manipulating the character and competence of models
		Ramp practice difficulty by including multiple levels and increasingly incongruent environments
		Incorporate routine obstacles, emergency situations, and crisis events trainees must navigate
	Develop assessment tools	Develop tools to assess multiple dimensions of trainee learning and performance
		Construct multiple-choice and situational judgment tests to assess knowledge and skill
		Develop concept maps, card sorts, and pair-wise comparison ratings to illuminate knowledge structures
		Assess the fragmentation, structure, and accessibility of knowledge chunks
		Triangulate measurement by leveraging multiple elicitation and representation techniques
		Create tools to dynamically capture trainee key strokes, communication, and perceptual movements

Implement training		
Set the stage for learning	Provide trainers with frame of reference and rater error training if ratings are used to evaluate trainees	
	Measure and take steps to increase motivation to learn	
	Prepare trainees to engage in meta-cognitive and self-regulatory processes	
	Provide advanced organizers of learning points	
	Prompt trainees to explore, experiment, and actively construct explanations in their training environment	
	Frame errors as a natural part of training that contribute to learning	
	Ask trainees to reflect over the informative aspects of errors when they occur	
Deliver blended solution	Use information presentation techniques such as reading assignments, lectures, and discussions	
	Prompt learners to generate knowledge and skills that are targeted for acquisition	
	Require trainees to integrate and associate various facts and actions into coherent mental models	
	Pose difficult and structured reflection questions after case studies	
	Ask trainees to integrate information and discern common themes provided in contrasting cases	
	Explore the lessons learned from case studies of effective and ineffective performance	
	Guide trainees through deliberate practice by asking them to repeat similar tasks with gradual modifications	
	Encourage trainees to persist in practice to the point of overlearning/automaticity	

(continued)

Table 4.1 (continued)

Training phase	Guiding principle	Training guidelines
	Support transfer and maintenance	Conduct training debriefings organized around key events and learning objectives
		Guide self-correction by keeping the debriefing discussion focused and modeling effective feedback skills
		Reserve instructor input for times when trainees cannot generate input or when clarifications are required
		Identify lessons learned and areas for continued improvement to guide self-development efforts
		Prompt trainees to set proximal and distal goals for applying new capabilities
		Identify and implement solutions to accelerate the cycle time required to realize training benefits
		Schedule shorter booster sessions after the main training initiative is complete
Evaluate training	Execute evaluation plan	Determine the purposes, needs, and sophistication of the consumers of training evaluation findings
		Identify an appropriate experimental, quasi-experimental, or passive-observational training design
		Consider alternatives when rigorous experimental designs are not feasible in a given setting
		Review controls for factors that affected the inferences drawn from training evaluation
		Compile subjective evaluations and objective indices of multiple training criteria

Gauge trainee learning	Ensure consistency between the level of focal variables, contextual factors, design, aggregation, and analysis
	Consider the relative efficacy of various approaches to measuring longitudinal change
	Measure the extent trainees' expectations were fulfilled as proximal indicators of reactions and learning
	Differentiate between affective and utility reactions
	Assess learning in terms of affective, behavioral, and cognitive outcomes
	Measure short-term retention immediately after training and long-term retention
	Gauge transfer by examining generalization to the job context and maintenance of learning over time
	Plot a maintenance curve and determine reasons for any decrements in maintenance over time
	Consider the interactions of work characteristics and time on the application of skills in the workplace
Gauge team learning	Model unit-level outcomes as the mean of individual-level change when vertical transfer is compositional
	Evaluate both individual-level and unit-level outcomes when vertical transfer is compilation based
	Use longitudinal designs when evaluating vertical transfer based on compilation emergence models
	Use techniques applicable to analyzing non-linear configural relationships when emergence is compilational

(continued)

Table 4.1 (*continued*)

Training phase	Guiding principle	Training guidelines
	Gauge organizational impact	Estimate the cross-level relationships of improved individual performance on organizational performance
		Determine whether the costs of training were recouped
		Estimate the return on investment from training
		Estimate the utility or economic impact of a training solution over time
	Disseminate training results	Provide trainees with a copy of training evaluation reports
		Ensure the information collected from the transfer context is available to other designated parties
		Ensure designated parties have a clear understanding of the implications of evaluation findings
		Implement solution process changes suggested by the findings of formative evaluations
		Implement changes in the talent management system suggested by summative evaluations

profitability concerns, as training can also be a powerful lever for enhancing performance-related factors such as employee satisfaction, team cohesion, social capital, and organizational reputation.

A core component of the due diligence process is a pretraining transfer analysis. The analysis helps describe the dimensions targeted for horizontal transfer, the emergent processes of vertical transfer, and the contextual factors that may promote or impinge on the transfer process. For example, the number, scope, and nature of the salient nesting arrangements in an organization must be mapped to determine their potential effects on nested variables (Mathieu, Maynard, Taylor, Gilson, and Ruddy, 2007). Designers should be careful to distinguish between objective situational characteristics and social–psychological perceptions of organizational factors as well as evaluate the embeddedness or bond strength of key dimensions (Kozlowski and Salas, 1997).

Organizational leaders can actively contribute to a climate for learning, or passively inhibit the replication of learned behaviors in the workplace. A thorough stakeholder analysis can identify champions of training and provides a forum for airing concerns. This is important because training, like all initiatives, involves the allocation of limited financial resources which some may feel are better routed to the production of goods or services, marketing campaigns, infrastructure improvements, and/or technology upgrades. Yet, in order for training to be successful there must be both sufficient financial and personal support for it. Hence, parties on both sides of the isle are best identified and, when appropriate, persuaded in advance. Favorable projections of the net present value of training relative to other capital investments can be particularly persuasive evidence when estimates are based on realistic and conservative inputs.

Define performance requirements

A second training needs analysis activity involves defining performance requirements. Established theories of performance, and taxonomies of performance processes, should be leveraged to precisely define the nature of performance (see Campbell and Kuncel, 2002; Marks, Mathieu, and Zaccaro, 2001; Salas, Stagl, Burke, and Goodwin, 2007). This involves describing, disaggregating, and contextualizing the taskwork and teamwork processes that are critical to overall performance. Behavioral- and cognitive-oriented task inventories, critical incident interviews, focus groups, and card sorts can each help nuance key factors. Protocol analysis whereby experts verbalize their thoughts during problem solving is also an especially useful technique for eliciting decision-making processes in natural settings (Ericsson, in press). Training designers should also take steps to model and minimize the systematic and random sources of error inherent to job analysis data.

Once key performance dimensions are defined they should be bracketed by mapping their antecedents and moderators within and outside the focal level of interest (Hackman, 1999). For example, the effectiveness of team coordination can be predicated upon motivated members at an individual level and investments in information technologies at an organizational level. The relative importance of these factors to alternative short-, mid-, and long-term business scenarios should also be illuminated so that specific criteria can be better targeted for improvement. It is also essential to map the projected trajectory of trainee change in these factors over time. Describing the transitional process from novice to expert provides insight into how training content should be developed, delivered, and evaluated.

Define cognitive and affective states

Taskwork and teamwork processes are not executed in isolation. As employees enact performance processes (e.g. situation assessment) they dynamically draw upon and revise their cognitive (e.g. mental models, situation awareness) and affective (e.g. self-efficacy, motivation) states. Designers charged with creating training solutions must describe and frame these states, specify why and how they enable effective performance, and forge instructional experiences that appropriately target them for development. For example, both the content (e.g. declarative knowledge, procedural knowledge) and types of mental models (e.g. situation, task, equipment) should be delineated. Subject matter experts asked to complete an event-based knowledge-elicitation process can provide information that helps identify the states that should be targeted for development by training (Fowlkes, Salas, Baker, Cannon-Bowers, and Stout, 2000).

Once essential states are identified, it is important to determine if, and the extent to which, cognition and affect must be shared or be complementary to enable effective performance in the workplace. This is a particularly acute concern in team training settings because scholars often invoke shared mental models and shared affect to explain how collectives execute both routine and adaptive team performance (Burke, Stagl, Salas, Pierce, and Kendall, 2006). Moreover, cultivating shared affect via training simulations can help prepare teams to navigate even unprecedented challenges (see Klein, Stagl, Salas, Parker, and Van Eynde, 2007).

The unfolding compositional or compilational process via which the content and structure of cognition and affect emerge to the unit level should be clearly specified because it provides insight about the kinds of instructional methods, features, and tools required to facilitate the development of team states. For example, recent meta-analytic evidence suggests that cross-training teams is particularly well suited for imparting shared taskwork and teamwork mental models by providing members with knowledge about their teammates' tasks, roles, and responsibilities (Stagl, Klein, Rosopa, DiazGranados, Salas, and Burke, unpublished manuscript).

Define KSA attributes

In addition to framing the core processes and cognitive and affective states that collectively comprise affective performance, training practitioners must also define an attribute model. Attribute models specify the direct determinants of performance such as knowledge, skills, and attitudes (KSAs). Training designers should leverage structured attribute inventories, skill repositories, and even performance records to shed light on the KSAs that should be targeted for development by a training solution. For example, the declarative (i.e. what), procedural (i.e. how), and strategic (i.e. why) knowledge required to effectively execute performance processes must be defined. Strategic knowledge is especially important because it allows trainees to understand why and when to apply declarative knowledge (Kozlowski, Gully, Brown, Salas, Smith, and Nason, 2001). This example illustrates that KSAs must first be identified and then ordered in a sequence from those that are more fundamental to those that are more complex in order to maximize the benefit of sequenced learning opportunities.

Training designers should be cognizant that not all of the myriad of characteristics and capabilities can be targeted for development via a single training solution; and that not all KSAs are best developed via training methods (Campbell and Kuncel, 2002). Rather, the needs analysis process should allow for the identification of those KSAs that are most essential to performance at multiple levels with greater emphasis given to dimensions that are most amenable to change via an instructional experience as it is projected to be introduced in a particular setting. The opinions and insights of subject matter experts and past trainees can help practitioners hone in on key attributes. Multiple perspectives should also be leveraged when defining which KSAs are most relevant to organizational success given alternative business models.

Delineate learning objectives

The final step in analyzing training needs involves delineating learning objectives. The information gathered from the prior steps of the need analysis process must be translated into training objectives, learning objectives, and enabling objectives. In practice, task statements are often transformed into learning objectives by supplementing them with contextual information and performance standards. It is important to remember, however, that designers should not force learning objectives into behaviorally based statements of employee actions; as cognitive and affective learning objectives are equally important to fostering effective performance (Kraiger, 2002). Suitable learning objectives are clear, concise, and measurable. To the extent that these three criteria are met, instructional content will be more targeted and ultimately more useful.

DEVELOP TRAINING CONTENT

The second phase of designing a training solution involves a series of activities undertaken in support of developing training content, including: (a) designing a learning architecture, (b) creating instructional experiences, and (c) developing assessment tools. For the purposes of the present discussion it is assumed training is not confined to classroom walls, in-house or otherwise, but rather is delivered via a blended learning solution that encompasses multiple mediums and locations. While blended learning solutions typically include a dedicated block of classroom time, they also include other instructional mediums such as desktop computer- or web-based learning modules and sometimes even full-task simulators. Interestingly, the findings of a recent survey of 400 human resource executives across 40 countries suggest blended learning solutions are considered the most effective approach for meeting training needs (IBM, 2008). The specific content of a given training solution will vary widely from setting to setting given organizational objectives, financial constraints, and needs.

Design learning architecture

A learning architecture is comprised of several integrated subsystems which collectively provide the capability to plan, select, author, sequence, push, evaluate, store and mine learning content, techniques, assessment algorithms, KSA profiles, and performance records. An intelligent scenario management system can be programmed to provide instructional designers, instructors, and trainees with the access, tools, and guidance required to create and change content to reflect operational challenges (Zachary, Bilazarian, Burns, and Cannon-Bowers, 1997).

An intuitive dashboard interface (a graphical user interface with dropdown menus) with simple navigation can be designed to control the content, sequence, and pace of training. For example, employees with limited time for training may occasionally need access to quick refresher tutorials rather than more intensive mastery learning driven lessons. This example hints at what has too long been the holy grail of learning architectures (namely, computer adaptive training). The computing power to fulfill this quest is both readily available and increasingly affordable; so learning architectures should be designed to account for learner differences in goals, competencies, and capabilities and adjust accordingly.

With sufficient development time and psychometric expertise, architectures can be programmed to capitalize on the exponential gains in learning that can result from accounting for aptitude–treatment interactions (Cronbach and Snow, 1977). Embedded tools can assess a trainee's expertise, abilities, self-efficacy, and goal orientation and tailor training structure, content, feedback, and guidance to maximize the benefits accrued by learners. While the costs of such an approach are front loaded, often requiring substantially more content to be generated, scaled and sequenced, the horizontal and vertical rewards of computer adaptive training will ultimately deliver the knockout blow to static, out-of-the-box solutions.

Learning architectures can also incorporate additional useful features like text-to-speech conversion, speech recognition, information visualization, perceptual contrasts, and playback. A system that is comprised of several subsystems can highlight important events and cues (Stout, Salas, and Fowlkes, 1997) and pose questions and hints to learners (Lajoie, in press), thereby prompting self-regulatory activities (Bell and Kozlowski, 2002). The encoding and storage capabilities of some architectures can also dynamically capture instructor ratings, comments, and debriefing markers (Smith-Jentsch, Zeisig, Acton, and McPherson, 1998). Systems can also capture and upload information on an intranet or the internet so learners can leverage on-demand tutors, chat rooms, forums, and lessons learned repositories.

Forge instructional experiences

The most important step of developing training content involves forging and blending instructional experiences. The process includes outlining an instructional management plan, instructor guides, and when necessary detailed scripts. This stage is another important juncture at which instructional designers can lean on and learn from present or past trainees to help illuminate the multiple branching paths trainees may take when pursuing the attainment of learning objectives (Lajoie, in press). Mapping the potential paths, including some of those less traveled by, is essential to accurately forecast when trainees are likely to falter, crafting meaningful learning experiences and tailoring appropriate guidance.

When a myriad of branching paths preclude precisely defining a single overarching chronology of experiences, the most effective alternative event timelines should be mapped to help inform scenario sequencing, assessment, and feedback. Content in even high learner control environments must be sequenced to some extent because the development of knowledge structures and complex performance processes are contingent on the prior acquisition and chunking of more fundamental knowledge and skills (Anderson,

1993). This means it is essential to impart the capabilities underlying component tasks prior to developing KSAs underpinning linking tasks (Goldstein and Ford, 2002). For example, materials presenting general rules and principles should precede those highlighting the structural, functional, and physical relationships among systems. Scenarios, and the experiences they impart, can be sequenced to reflect increasingly complex operational realities (Gagné, Briggs, and Wager, 1988).

When instructional content is integrated and orchestrated it serves to foster holistic, meaningful experiences for trainees. For example, contextually grounded scenarios help trainees better understand their learning experience by replicating a familiar workplace. Unfortunately, stakeholders are too often preoccupied with representing, to the greatest degree possible, the operational context via high fidelity technologies. This can be a mistake because physical fidelity is often a secondary concern to the psychological fidelity induced by instructional experiences. The primacy of psychological fidelity is seen in the effectiveness with which computer-based training solutions can supplement, and for some soldiers substitute, for the large-scale military exercises conducted at the US Army's National Training Center (Chatham, in press, A).

Forging effective instructional experiences requires a systematic consideration of the methods via which information is delivered in training settings. Three of the most common means of packaging training content are via information presentation, demonstration, and practice. For example, lectures, exercises, case studies, and games can be used to present information to trainees. In terms of demonstrating or modeling key skills, role-plays, motion pictures, closed-circuit television, and interactive multimedia displays can be used in conjunction or separately. Trainee attendance to models can be increased by matching models to the demographic characteristics of trainees and by varying model competence.

In terms of scheduling opportunities for trainees to practice, initially alloting time for massed practice followed by a variable practice schedule can be effective for developing the capabilities required to perform complex tasks. It has also been suggested that interleaving, or providing information, demonstration, and practice across multiple mediums, on a single or small cluster of similar tasks, is more effective than blocking practice on separate tasks (Bjork, in press). Instructional designers should also ensure that there is sufficient spacing between separate training modules and between lessons and learning assessment.

In terms of the types of practice scenarios that instructional developers should craft, novice learners should be exposed to routine obstacles that must be navigated. As trainees move along the trajectory of development, practice difficulty can be increased to simulate complex challenges in increasingly incongruent environments. This requires training designers to systematically specify the dimensions along which training scenarios will become more complex and fluid. Finally, emergency situations and crisis events should be designed so that trainees are forced to persevere through adversity as their expertise accrues (McKinney and Davis, 2003).

Develop assessment tools

Once meaningful instructional experiences have been forged, assessment tools and techniques must be developed to operationalize key learning constructs. A comprehensive treatment of the application of psychometric theory to creating assessment tools and assessing the process and outcomes of learning is beyond the scope of the present discussion. Rather, only broad prescriptions are presented. Training designers are strongly encouraged to seek the consultation of subject matter experts when designing assessment tools, as poorly designed or improperly timed metrics can make even good training appear bad and bad training turn ugly.

The most straightforward guidance is to develop standardized measures of unitary constructs; assess multiple learning outcomes and performance processes; and triangulate the measurement of outcomes via multiple assessment methods (Nunnally and Bernstein, 1994). Following these truisms helps yield the tools required to understand the effects of training. For instance, the findings of an evaluation study may suggest that trainees acquired a great deal of factual information (namely, declarative knowledge) but have no concept of why and when to apply specific facts in context (namely, strategic knowledge). Without reliable measures of different knowledge types, stakeholders evaluating the training solution would be left pondering why transfer failed.

Fortunately, comprehensive guidance for designing and applying assessment tools in training initiatives is available to interested readers. For example, recent reviews of assessing learning outcomes have discussed the use of concept maps, card sorts, and pair-wise comparisons for scaling trainee's knowledge structures (Stagl, Salas, and Day, 2007). The benefits of situational judgment tests for training needs assessment, content delivery, and evaluation have also been discussed at length elsewhere (Fritzsche, Stagl, Salas, and Burke, 2006).

IMPLEMENT TRAINING

Implementation is a key phase in the training process, in part because it is tightly bound to the organizational system in which training is conducted. More specifically, there are three major activities associated with training implementation, including: (a) setting the stage for learning, (b) delivering a blended learning solution, and (c) supporting transfer and maintenance. The former and latter activities involve actions taken to foster a climate for learning.

Set the stage for learning

Setting the stage for learning begins by ensuring trainers are properly prepared to facilitate the delivery of instruction, recognize and assess learning, and reinforce effective performance when it occurs. There are several approaches to preparing trainers to perform their duties such as rater error training, frame of reference training, and the mental simulation of instructor activities. For example, frame of reference training increases the awareness and skill of trainers to indentify and assess key competency and performance dimensions when they are displayed in training.

The second step in setting the stage for learning involves preparing the trainee for the acquisition of KSAs. This includes measuring and increasing a trainee's motivation to learn, self-efficacy, and self-regulatory skills (Colquitt, LePine, and Noe, 2000). It is also important to de-emphasize pre-existing power differences, engage less verbal learners, and display an individualized interest in the development of each employee when training in group settings.

Once trainers and trainees are adequately prepared to engage in learning, the purpose and objectives of training must be stated and explained. This is an opportunity to frame training as both a privilege and a necessity by describing why it is instrumental to securing valued outcomes for individuals and their employers. It is also a time to provide a realistic preview of training and advanced organizers of the instructional experience can help guide this conversation.

The next step in setting the stage for learning involves stating learning and performance standards so that trainees have appropriate benchmarks against which to gauge their development. In addition to setting standards, trainers should discuss how trainees should pursue goals. For example, performance goals are often sufficient when training is concerned with skill automaticity for simple tasks; however, mastery goals, which emphasize learning rather than the demonstration of ability, are typically more useful for facilitating proficiency in complex task domains (see Chapter 9, this volume). Trainees should also be engaged in helping to set their own proximal and distal training goals.

A final step involves providing trainees with learning tips. For example, attentional advice, strategies and preparatory information about stressors can alert trainees to important aspects of instruction. Learners should be encouraged to explore, experiment, and actively construct meaning from training events. For example, errors should be framed as opportunities to reflect and delineate lessons that can be transferred to the workplace (Keith and Freese, 2008). Sometimes, trainees may require instruction on how to learn from their failures (Argyris, 1992).

Deliver the blended learning solution

The second stage in implementing training involves delivering the blended learning solution. There are three mechanisms for delivering content including information presentation, modeling, and practice. Information can be presented via the use of lectures, reading assignments, case studies, and open discussions. The specific content of what is discussed is dictated by the particular KSAs targeted for development but should also include descriptions of effective and ineffective performance, common workplace errors, and tactics for meeting business challenges.

Trainees should be encouraged to actively construct, integrate, and associate various facts rather than be treated as passive recipients of instructional content (Schwartz and Bransford, 1998). For example, couching lessons in contrasting cases comprised of alternative, but equally compelling, explanations for some event or dilemma can be a powerful approach for motivating the active construction and acquisition of knowledge and skill (Fritzsche, Stagl, Burke, and Salas, in press). Similarly, perceptual contrasts, or alternative pictorial depictions, can be useful for helping trainees notice the subtle features of information that can be visualized (Bransford, Franks, Vye, and Sherwood, 1989).

Prior to practice, trainees should be asked to engage in symbolic rehearsals or mental simulations of the processes they intend to enact during training. During practice, trainees should be given ample opportunity to repeatedly engage in the cognitive and behavioral actions targeted for development to the point of overlearning. It is important to note, however, that repeated practice is often not sufficient to develop learning outcomes and may even be counterproductive to skill generalization. Rather, trainers should guide trainees through deliberate practice by requiring repetitions on gradually modified tasks (Ericsson, in press). For example, difficulties, obstacles, and equipment malfunctions can be gradually introduced to ramp training complexity as learners develop competence in navigating routine challenges.

When training content is delivered, instructors, an intelligent learning architecture, or a combination of the two, must assess the progress of learners and deliver timely, accurate, and actionable feedback. For example, evaluative and interpretative feedback can be used to provide trainees with adaptive guidance (Bell and Kozlowski, 2002). While novice learners may need more immediate feedback, over time diagnostic information should be faded and delivered more intermittently to gradually remove the scaffolding inherent to training solutions.

Support transfer and maintenance

Training is often concluded when practice and assessment are complete. This is unfortunate because the post-practice stage provides a window of opportunity to enhance learning transfer and maintenance. For example, after action reviews both debrief and educate. Trainers should empower trainees to drive this dialog by soliciting and reinforcing comments while withholding input for clarifications (Tannenbaum, Smith-Jentsch, and Behson, 1998). Asking trainees to generate explanations for their actions during training is critical to the process.

Once the debriefing session is complete, trainers should offer final guidance to learners. Trainees, in conjunction with their managers and leaders, should be prompted to set proximal and distal goals for applying newly acquired capabilities in the workplace (Taylor, Russ-Eft, and Chan, 2005). It is also important to advise trainees to reflect over their training experiences and to continually refresh their learning to avoid skill decay. For example, peer-to-peer rehearsals, communities of practice, and online discussion forums can each contribute to facilitating the long-run maintenance of learning.

The final step of training implementation involves intervening in the workplace to help ensure transfer. Engaging a trainee's managers and supervisors to encourage, recognize, and reward the display of newly acquired KSAs can help foster a climate for learning. Steps should also be taken to minimize the delay between training and operational use of new capabilities.

EVALUATE TRAINING

The final phase in designing systematic training involves evaluating whether training was effective, and more importantly, why it was effective (or ineffective) so that required improvements can be made. Unfortunately, many organizations do not evaluate training effectiveness because evaluation can be costly and resource intensive. It often requires specialized expertise and a team of people who can collect and interpret performance data. However, organizations often fail to consider that ineffective training can be far more costly in the long-term, in terms of poor performance, errors, and missed opportunities, than an investment in training evaluation. Therefore, it is imperative that organizations assess the effectiveness of training and use the information gathered as a means to improve training design.

The first step in evaluating training involves determining the purpose of evaluation as well as the sophistication of the consumers of evaluation study findings (Kraiger, 2002). Many different variables can be measured during training evaluation including affective and utility reactions, expectation fulfillment, the ABCs of learning, and performance on a host of teamwork and taskwork processes, just to name a few. For example, we mentioned earlier in our discussion the importance of assessing the type, amount, and structure of newly acquired knowledge. Moreover, the proceduralization, compilation, and automaticity of new skills can also be gauged.

It is also important to think through the likely results from training evaluation studies. For example, in some cases pretraining levels of performance do not increase as a result of training, as assessed during or immediately after practice, and yet workplace performance improves substantially during an entire fiscal year. This result can occur when errors and difficulties are systematically integrated into a blended learning solution (Bjork, in press). Of course, without an infusion of obstacles, trainers can face the obverse problem of maximizing change on the ABCs of learning without fostering subsequent performance transfer, maintenance, and generalization in the workplace. This scenario demonstrates the importance of having quality metrics but also speaks to the criticality of knowing why and when assessment tools should be applied.

A variety of rigorous experimental designs are available to evaluate training and the strengths and weaknesses of a particular approach should be identified and addressed before it is used to evaluate training (Shadish, Cook, and Campbell, 2002). There are also a number of non-experimental designs that are also very useful for evaluation, given that situational constraints preclude the use of formal experimentation (Sackett and Mullen, 1993). One of the key questions to deciding between evaluation designs is whether the purpose of training is to facilitate change or to help trainees achieve some standard of performance. Comprehensive guidance on analytic techniques for conceptualizing and gauging change is available in the former case (Day and Lance, 2004). In the latter case, less rigorous research designs can yield useful information.

In order for the findings of evaluation studies to be meaningful there must be consistency between the level of the focal variables and contextual factors, research design, aggregation rules, analysis, and result interpretation (Kozlowski et al., 2000). Consistency is essential to meaningfully estimate the impact of training on organizational performance as well as to yield useful inputs for return on investment, cost–benefit and net present value calculations.

CASE EXAMPLES

A success: the aviation experience

Teamwork improves performance in some jobs; in others it is imperative. For example, teamwork in the cockpit is essential – lives depend on it. We know that 60–80% of the accidents or mishaps in aviation are due to human error and a large percentage of those are caused by coordination and other teamwork problems in the cockpit.

Research on team training has developed many instructional methods and techniques to enhance teamwork in complex environments such as the cockpit. These approaches are pervasive in the aviation industry. In fact, both the military aviation community and the commercial airlines implement systematic team training (Weiner, Kanki, and Helmreich, 1993). The Navy has designed and delivered team training for its aviation platforms for many years. For example, engagement simulations, which provided a forum and format for group experiential learning, helped the US Navy increase its superiority in air-to-air combat by a factor of 12 in one year (Chatham, in press, B). This training continues to be refined and scaled to reach more people more often via personal computer-based flight simulators (Brannick, Prince, and Salas, 2005).

Training scientists and learning specialists, in partnership with subject matter experts, developed an approach that systematically helps instructional developers design and deliver Crew Resource Management (CRM) training in the Navy (Salas, Prince, Bowers, Stout, Oser, and Cannon-Bowers, 1999). This method illustrates how to apply the four phases outlined in this chapter. It begins with an identification of operational and mission requirements and the required competencies and performance processes (i.e. needs analysis). Extensive interviews and observations were conducted in order to ensure the required KSAs for coordination were identified. The literature was reviewed and a theory-based framework developed.

In parallel to this process, the scientists, sponsors, users, and industry representatives met on an ongoing basis to discuss organizational procedures and policies that needed to be in place as the methodology evolved. In the end, this proved to be a very valuable dialog – it prepared the Navy for the training. Specifically, it created a learning climate – before the training was implemented, during and after. Once training objectives were derived and validated by SMEs, the methodology called for designing and creating opportunities for practice and feedback, developing measurement tools for feedback, and implementing the training. The methodology ended with suggestions for ensuring that a multi-component evaluation protocol is built into training.

This methodology has been translated into a detailed set of specifications. These are a set of step-by-step instructions that can be used by instructional designers to develop curriculum and supporting materials. The evaluation of communities following this approach suggest crews react better to the instruction, learn more about teamwork, and exhibit more teamwork behaviors in the cockpit as a result of the training (Salas, Fowlkes, Stout, Milanovich, and Prince, 1999).

In sum, this methodology has been implemented and tested in several communities – and it works. It works because the approach uncovers the needed KSAs and performance processes, prepares the organization for the training, relies on theories of learning, and applies sound instructional principles to the design of team training. It works because the training seeks to diagnose and remedy-specific deficiencies. It works because the implementation process sets the right climate for learning and transfer and evaluates its impact. It works because the methodology guides the instructional developer through a systematic process incorporating all the phases outlined here, and utilizes the best information that the science of training can offer.

A failure: training the sales force

Sales at a large telecommunications company were down for the third quarter. Management reviewed several strategies to improve sales and concluded that one solution would be to improve training for the large, dispersed sales force. For the sake of expediency, the training department began using a needs analysis they conducted several years before as a basis to develop enhanced training. Their plan was first to update the original needs analysis and then to develop new training strategies on the basis of what they found. They also began investigating new training technologies as a possible means to reduce training delivery costs. However, management was so intent on doing something quickly that the training department was ultimately pressured into purchasing a generic, off-the-shelf training package by a local vendor. One of the features of the package that appealed to management was that the course could be delivered over the web, saving the time and expense of having the sales force travel to the main office to receive the training. Hence, even though the package was costly to purchase, the company believed that it was a bargain compared to the expense of developing a new package in-house and delivering it in person to the sales force.

Six months after the training had been delivered, sales were still declining. Management turned to the training department for answers. Because no measures of training performance had been designed, the training department had little information upon which to base its diagnosis. For lack of a better idea, members of the training department began questioning the sales force to see if they could determine why the training was not working. Among other things, the sales people reported that the training was slow and boring, and that it did not teach them any new sales techniques. They also complained that, without an instructor, it was impossible to get clarification on the things they did not understand. Moreover, they reported that they believed that sales were off not because they needed training in basic sales techniques, but because so many new products were being introduced that they could not keep up. In fact, several of the sales people requested meetings with design engineers just so they could get updated product information. The training department took these findings back to management and requested that they be allowed to design a new training package, beginning with an updated needs analysis to determine the real training deficiencies.

So how could this company have avoided this costly mistake? Our contention is, had they engaged in a systematic training design and delivery process, they would have provided effective training and not invested in a useless product. For example, a careful needs analysis would have revealed specific performance deficiencies. In addition, a better assessment of the training delivery – especially as it related to trainee motivation – would have indicated that the web-based course may not have been the best choice. Unfortunately, cases like this occur all too frequently, but can easily be avoided if a systematic process for training design and delivery is followed.

CONCLUSION

As recently as the 1990s, the transformative power of training was not appreciated in some circles, as typified by Jack Welch's statement "We want only A players. Don't spend time trying to get C's to be B's. Move them out early" (Slater, 1998, p. 157). Today, the mandate to gain competitive advantage via the people who make the place has never been stronger; and even Wall Street wonders like GE are aggressively developing talent. In fact, 75% of 400 HR executives across 40 countries view leader development as mission critical (IBM, 2008).

There was a time from World War II until the 1960s when the training literature was voluminous but largely ". . . nonempirical, nontheoretical, poorly written and dull (Campbell, 1971). Today, the science of training has much to contribute to facilitating the systematic development of individuals, teams, and organizations. In this chapter we offered a translation mechanism for stakeholders charged with designing systematic training. To the extent that the theories, principles, guidelines, and best practice specifications presented herein are diligently applied, training solutions will be better positioned to provide meaningful learning experiences.

References

Aguinis, H. and Kraiger, K. (in press). Benefits of training and development for individuals and teams, organizations, and society. To appear in *Annual Review of Psychology*.

Anderson, J. R. (1993). Problem solving and learning. *American Psychologist*, 48, 35–44.

Argyris, C. (1992). *On Organizational Learning*. Malden, MA: Blackwell.

Bassi, L. J., and Van Buren, M. E. (1998). *Leading-edge practices, industry facts and figures, and (at last!) evidence that investment in people pays off in better performance: The 1998 ASTD state of the industry report*. Alexandria, VA: ASTD.

Bell, B., and Kozlowski, S. W. (2002). Adaptive guidance: enhancing self-regulation, knowledge and performance in technology-based training. *Personnel Psychology*, 55, 267–306.

Bjork, R. A. (in press). Structuring the conditions of training to achieve elite performance. To appear in K. A. Ericsson (ed.), *The Development of Professional Performance: Approaches to Objective Measurement and Designed Learning Environments*. Cambridge University Press.

Brannick, M. T., Prince, C., and Salas, E. (2005). Can PC-based systems enhance teamwork in the cockpit? *The International Journal of Aviation Psychology*, 15, 173–187.

Bransford, J. D., Franks, J. J., Vye, N. J., and Sherwood, R. D. (1989). New approaches to instruction: Because wisdom can't be told. In S. Vosniadou and A. Ortony (eds), *Similarity and Analogical Reasoning* (pp. 470–497). Cambridge: Cambridge University Press.

Burke, S., Stagl, K. C., Salas, E., Pierce, L., and Kendall, D. (2006). Understanding team adaptation: A conceptual analysis and framework. *Journal of Applied Psychology*, 91, 1189–1207.

Campbell, J. P. (1971). Personnel training and development. *Annual Review of Psychology*, 22, 565–603.

Campbell, J. P., and Kuncel, N. R. (2002). Individual and team training. In N. Anderson, D. S. Ones, H. K. Sinangil, and C. Viswesvaran (eds), *Handbook of Industrial, Work and Organizational Psychology* (pp. 272–312). London, England: Sage.

Chatham, R. E. (in press, A). Toward a second training revolution: promise and pitfalls of digital exponential training. To appear in K. A. Ericsson (ed.), *The Development of Professional Performance: Approaches to Objective Measurement and Designed Learning Environments*. Cambridge University Press.

Chatham, R. E. (in press, B). The 20th century revolution in military training. To appear in K. A. Ericsson (ed.), *The Development of Professional Performance: Approaches to Objective Measurement and Designed Learning Environments*. Cambridge University Press.

Colquitt, J. A., LePine, J. A., and Noe, R. A. (2000). Toward an integrative theory of training motivation: A meta-analytic path analysis of 20 years of research. *Journal of Applied Psychology*, 85, 678–707.

Cronbach, L. J., and Snow, R. E. (1977). *Aptitudes and Instructional Methods: A Handbook for Research on Interactions*. New York: Irvington.

Day, D., and Lance, C. (2004). Understanding the development of leadership complexity through latent growth modeling. In D. Day, S. J. Zaccaro, and S. M. Halpin (eds), *Leader Development for Transforming Organizations*. Mahwah, NJ: Erlbaum Associates.

Ericsson, K. A. (in press). Enhancing the development of professional performance: Implications from the study of deliberate practice. To appear in K. A. Ericsson (ed.), *The Development of Professional Performance: Approaches to Objective Measurement and Designed Learning Environments*. Cambridge University Press.

Fowlkes, J. E., Salas, E., Baker, D. P., Cannon-Bowers, J. A., and Stout, R. J. (2000). The utility of event-based knowledge elicitation. *Human Factors*, 42, 24–35.

Fritzsche, B. A., Stagl, K. C., Salas, E., and Burke, C. S. (2006). Enhancing the design, delivery, and evaluation of scenario-based training: Can situational judgment tests contribute? In J. A. Weekley and R. E. Ployhart (eds), *Situational Judgment Tests*. Mahwah, NJ: Erlbaum.

Fritzsche, B. A., Stagl, K. C., Burke, C. S., and Salas, E. (in press). Developing team adaptability and adaptive team performance: The benefits of active learning. *Human Performance*.

Gagné, R. M., Briggs, L. J., and Wager, W. W. (1988). *Principles of Instructional Design* (3rd edition). New York. Holt, Rinehart and Winston.

Georgenson, D. L. (1982). The problem of transfer calls for partnership. *Training and Development Journal*, 36, 75–78.

Goldstein, I. L., and Ford, J. K. (2002). *Training in Organizations*. (4th edition). Belmont, CA: Wadsworth Thompson Learning.

Hackman, J. R. (1999). Thinking differently about context. In R. Wageman (ed.), *Research on Managing Groups and Teams: Groups in Context*. Stamford, Connecticut: JAI Press.

IBM (2008). *Unlocking the DNA of the Adaptable Workforce, the IBM Global Human Capital Study*. Milwaukee, WI: IBM.

Keith, N., and Freese, M. (2008). Effectiveness of error management training: A meta-analysis. *Journal of Applied Psychology*, 93, 59–69.

Klein, C., Stagl, K. C., Salas, E., Burke, C. S., DiazGranados, D., Goodwin, G. F., and Halpin, S. M. (2007). A meta-analytic examination of team development interventions. Poster presentation conducted at the Best Paper Proceedings of the 22nd annual conference of the Society for Industrial and Organizational Psychology. Manhattan, New York.

Klein, C., Stagl, K. C., Salas, E., Parker, C., and Van Eynde, D. (2007). Returning to flight: Simulation-based training for the US National Aeronautics and Space Administration's Mission Management Team. *International Journal of Training and Development*, 11, 132–138.

Kozlowski, S. W. J., Brown, K. G., Weissbein, D. A., Cannon-Bowers, J. A., and Salas, E. (2000). A multilevel perspective on training effectiveness: Enhancing horizontal and vertical transfer. In K. J. Klein and S. W. J. Kozlowski (eds), *Multilevel Theory, Research, and Methods in Organizations* (pp.157–210). San Francisco: Jossey-Bass.

Kozlowski, S. W. J., Gully, S. M., Brown, K., Salas, E., Smith, E., and Nason, E. (2001). Effects of training goals and goal orientation traits on multidimensional training outcomes and performance adaptability. *Organizational Behavior and Human Decision Processes*, 85, 1–31.

Kozlowski, S. W. J., and Salas, E. (1997). An organizational system approach for the implementation and transfer of training. In J. K. Ford and Associates (eds), *Improving Training Effectiveness in Work Organizations* (pp. 247–290). Hillsdale, NJ: LEA.

Kraiger, K. (2002). Decision-based evaluation. In K. Kraiger (ed.), *Creating, Implementing and Maintaining Effective Training and Development: State-of-the art Lessons for Practice* (pp. 331–375). San Francisco: Jossey-Bass.

Kraiger, K., Ford, J. K., and Salas, E. (1993). Application of cognitive, skill-based, and affective theories of learning outcomes to new methods of training evaluation. *Journal of Applied Psychology*, 78, 311–328.

Lajoie, S. P. (in press). Developing professional expertise with a cognitive apprenticeship model: Examples from avionics and medicine. To appear in K. A. Ericsson (ed.), *The Development of Professional Performance: Approaches to Objective Measurement and Designed Learning Environments*. Cambridge University Press.

Manpower (2007). Talent shortage study: 2007 global results. http://files.shareholder.com/downloads/MAN.

Marks, M. A., Mathieu, J. E., and Zaccaro, S. J. (2001). A temporally based framework and taxonomy of team process. *Academy of Management Review*, 26, 356–376.

Mathieu, J. E., Maynard, M. T., Taylor, S. R., Gilson, L. L., and Ruddy, T. M. (2007). An examination of the effects of organizational district and team contexts on team processes and performance: A meso-mediational model. *Journal of Organizational Behavior*, 28, 891–910.

McKinney, E. H., and Davis, K. J. (2003). Effects of deliberate practice on crisis decision performance. *Human Factors*, 45, 436–444.

Nunnally, J., and Bernstein, I. (1994). *Psychometric Theory*. New York: McGraw Hill.

Paradise, A. (2007). *State of the Industry: ASTD's Annual Review of Trends in Workplace Learning and Performance*. Alexandria, VA: ASTD.

Sackett, P. R., and Mullen, E. J. (1993). Beyond formal experimental design: Towards an expanded view of the training evaluation process. *Personnel Psychology*, 46, 613–627.

Salas, E., and Cannon-Bowers, J. A. (2000). Design training systematically. In E. A. Locke (ed.), *The Blackwell Handbook of Principles of Organizational Behavior* (pp. 43–59). Malden, MA: Blackwell.

Salas, E., Fowlkes, J. E., Stout, R. J., Milanovich, D. M., and Prince, C. (1999). Does CRM training improve teamwork skills in the cockpit? Two evaluation studies. *Human Factors*, 41, 327–343.

Salas, E., Prince, C., Bowers, C. A., Stout, R. J., Oser, R. L., and Cannon-Bowers, J. A. (1999). A methodology for enhancing crew resource management training. *Human Factors*, 41, 61–72.

Salas, E., Stagl, K. C., Burke, C. S., and Goodwin, G. F. (2007). Fostering team effectiveness in organizations: Toward an integrative theoretical framework of team performance. In J. W. Shuart, W. Spaulding, and J. Poland, (eds), *Modeling Complex Systems: Motivation, Cognition, and Social Processes* (pp. 185–243). Lincoln, NE: Nebraska Press.

Schwartz, D. L., and Bransford, J. D. (1998). A time for telling. *Cognition and Instruction*, 16, 475–522.

Shadish, W. R., Cook, T. D., and Campbell, D. T. (2002). *Experimental and quasi-experimental designs for generalized causal inference*. New York: Houghton Mifflin Company.

Slater, R. (1998). *Jack Welch and the GE Way: Management Insights and Leadership Secrets of the Legendary CEO*. Columbus, OH: McGraw-Hill.

Smith-Jentsch, K. A., Zeisig, R. L., Acton, B., and McPherson, J. A. (1998). Team dimensional training: A strategy for guided team self-correction. In J. A. Cannon-Bowers and E. Salas (eds), *Making Decisions Under Stress: Implications for Individual and Team Training*. Washington: APA Press.

Stagl, K. C., Klein, C., Rosopa, P. J., DiazGranados, D., Salas, E., and Burke, C. S. (unpublished manuscript). The effects of cross training teams: A meta-analytic path model.

Stagl, K. C., Salas, E., and Day, D. V. (2007). Assessing team learning outcomes: Improving team learning and performance. In V. I. Sessa and M. London (eds), *Work Group Learning: Understanding, Assessing, and Improving How Groups Learn in Organizations* (pp. 369–392). New York, NY: Taylor and Francis.

Stout, R. J., Salas, E., and Fowlkes, J. E. (1997). Enhancing teamwork in complex environments through team training. *Group Dynamics: Theory, Research and Practice*, 1, 169–182.

Swanson, R. A. (2001). *Assessing the Financial Benefits of Human Resource Development*. Cambridge, MA: Perseus.

Taylor, P. J., Russ-Eft, D. F., and Chan, D. W. L. (2005). A meta-analytic review of behavior modeling training. *Journal of Applied Psychology*, 90, 692–709.

Tannenbaum, S. I., Smith-Jentsch, K. A., and Behson, S. J. (1998). Training team leaders to facilitate team learning and performance. In J. A. Cannon-Bowers and E. Salas (eds), *Making Decisions Under Stress: Implications for Individual and Team Training*. Washington: APA.

Weiner, E. L., Kanki, B. J., and Helmreich, R. L. (1993). *Cockpit Resource Management*. San Francisco, CA: Academic.

Zachary, W., Bilazarian, P., Burns, J., and Cannon-Bowers, J. A. (1997). Advanced embedded training concepts for shipboard systems. *Proceedings of the 19th Annual Interservice/Industry Training, Simulation and Education Conference* (pp. 670–679). Orlando, FL: National Training Systems Association.

EXERCISES

Training planning

A large computer manufacturer experienced declining revenues during FY08. After careful analysis, the executive team determined that global competitors were squeezing their market share by offering a suite of comprehensive technical support services for their computers. A mandate was issued from the c-suite to recruit and develop the human capital required to offer similar services. As the chief learning officer it is your charge to ensure your organization has proficient people in place by the close of the second quarter 2009. To accomplish your objectives, develop a plan for what kinds of training will be conducted, why training will be conducted, and how proposed solutions will contribute to meeting the immediate, mid-range, and long-run needs of your organization. Be precise in specifying what internal and external resources and support are required to design and implement the process in a timely manner.

Training evaluation

A management consultancy was contracted by a medical supply firm to evaluate an in-house training solution for medical representatives. Discouraged by the findings that medical reps were apparently not learning during training (as measured by post-training reactions and declarative knowledge), yet seemed to be performing very effectively in the workplace, the consulting house turned to you as a subject matter expert to review their training evaluation study results. Describe the steps you will take to help the consultants uncover the true impact of the training solution. Think through training design, criterion identification, change measurement, and data analysis issues. State your recommendations for conducting a stronger evaluation.

5

Conduct Performance Appraisals to Improve Individual and Firm Performance

Maria Rotundo

A performance appraisal is an evaluation of how well an individual achieves job-related duties and responsibilities. It can be used to make administrative decisions about promotions, terminations, and monetary/non-monetary incentives. Strengths and weaknesses are assessed in the process, and this information can be used to establish training and development needs. Performance appraisals have been applied in the court of law to justify employee terminations and to validate selection methods. Given the important functions that a performance appraisal serves, it is not surprising to find that it is held to such high psychometric standards and is scrutinized repeatedly by employers, employees, researchers, the media, and even the courts when these standards are not met. This chapter outlines basic principles that can be followed to improve the effectiveness of performance appraisals, especially with respect to improving an employee's future performance.

The process of conducting a performance appraisal includes two main stages: obtaining accurate information about the individual's performance and communicating the performance appraisal to the individual in a manner that maintains a high-performance work culture. The chapter is organized according to these two stages. Key principles to follow during each stage are offered.

The quest for accurate job-related information about individuals has plagued researchers and managers for years, dating back to the early 1900s (Farr and Levy, 2007). The body of knowledge that has been generated from years of research on accuracy can be summarized by several key principles. It requires that performance in the workplace is clearly defined and aligned with the organization's strategy (Wright, Dunford, and Snell, 2001). Managers need to be cognizant of rater biases that distort performance ratings and to recognize the importance of observing and recording performance-related information on a continuous basis to reduce these errors. Multiple rating sources such as the self, peers, subordinates, or customers in some instances can provide additional performance-related information but are subject to the same information-processing limitations (e.g. biases) as ratings by managers. Behaviorally based performance appraisal instruments with clearly defined scale anchors and job-related dimensions can be useful tools for documenting performance appraisals. Training managers on the key principles involved in performance appraisal can increase the accuracy of these ratings.

Accurate performance information is necessary but not sufficient for maintaining and improving performance. The manner in which the performance appraisal is delivered to the individual is equally important for achieving desired outcomes. Key principles for managing the delivery process include goal setting, participative two-way communication, coaching, and managing terminations. Following these principles can result in improved performance and more favorable reactions to the appraisal and the appraisal process.

To Improve Accuracy

Define job performance

The strategic planning process establishes a firm's medium and long-term goals. The top management team must translate these goals into individual level actions, behaviors, and outputs that support the strategic plan (Wright et al., 2001). How job performance is conceptualized in the workplace stems in part from this planning process. Historically, job performance was defined by a series of task statements that were derived from job descriptions. Individuals were rated solely on the basis of the extent to which they carried out these tasks (Fleishman and Quaintance, 1984). The workplace was considered to be relatively static, and job descriptions were dusted off periodically, as they typically withstood the test of time. The workplace in this new millennium is characterized by constant change. Success requires communication, ongoing learning, teamwork, effective relationships, and sharing knowledge. Ethical standards discourage harmful behaviors and hold individuals and the firm even more accountable for their actions.

Consequently, job performance is more than completing task requirements. It incorporates organizational citizenship behaviors (OCB) and counterproductive work behaviors (CWB) (Rotundo and Sackett, 2002; Rotundo and Xie, 2008). Organizational citizenship behavior (also referred to as contextual performance, extra-role behavior, etc.) includes actions that go beyond task or technical performance. They facilitate the attainment of organizational goals by contributing in a positive way to its social and psychological environment (Organ, 1997). OCB includes helping, protecting the organization from undeserved harm, making constructive suggestions, and spreading goodwill (e.g. Podsakoff, MacKenzie, Paine, and Bachrach, 2000). Counterproductive work behavior is an intentional act that harms the well-being of the organization or its members (also referred to as deviance). It includes absenteeism, production deviance, workplace aggression, theft, sabotage, and fraud (Berry, Ones, and Sackett, 2007; Bennett and Robinson, 2000). OCB and CWB are not opposite ends of a continuum. They can vary independently of one another (Dalal, 2005).

Criterion deficiency occurs when a performance appraisal is based upon incomplete information. The appraisal does not take into consideration all job-relevant facets of a person's performance. Thus, defining performance is important for protecting against criterion deficiency. In addition, firms need to decide on the relative importance of these three sets of behaviors (Rotundo and Sackett, 2002). To what extent does a firm value OCBs in relation to task performance? To what extent are CWBs explicitly discouraged or penalized? A firm's values are useful here because they signal to the employees the preferred actions and behaviors, and they make clear *how* employees should perform their jobs. Examples of such values include acting with integrity, and producing quality products (or providing quality services) in an environment that respects diversity and teamwork. Hence, the first step in obtaining accurate performance information is to define job performance in line with a firm's strategy and values and to communicate this information to all stakeholders. The focus in this chapter is on a firm's subordinates.

Observe and record performance frequently

Ideally, managers form impressions about their employees based on the behaviors or outputs they observe. If someone asks you for your opinion about a movie, it is difficult to give an answer if you have not seen or heard the movie. Likewise, it should be difficult to give your appraisal of an individual if you have not observed a representative sample of the person's performance behaviors or outputs. Unfortunately, there are competing demands on managers' time. Their span of control is often quite large. Remote work is becoming increasingly common making it increasingly difficult for managers to obtain adequate performance samples for each employee. Thus, it becomes even more important for managers to adopt a mindset of observing performance whenever the opportunities arise.

Criterion contamination occurs when information other than performance is reflected in the performance appraisal. Raters' impressions about employee performance are frequently influenced by their biases (e.g. halo error). Raters' general beliefs and assumptions about an employee, their likeability for the individual, and stereotypes about an employee based on age, race and gender can contaminate a performance appraisal (Latham and Mann, 2006). Continuously observing and recording performance behaviors can reduce the extent to which these biases influence a rating.

Rating accuracy is affected by the delay between when an employee's behavior is observed and when performance is actually rated (DeNisi and Peters, 1996). Performance information is often acquired on an ad hoc basis, and in contexts not necessarily related to performance evaluation. Keeping track of this information and documenting is as important as frequent observations of an employee. Fortunately, there are tools that can help managers organize performance information in a manner that makes it more accessible. Performance categories help managers organize and structure their observations (Foti and Lord, 1987). Examples of performance categories can include the three broad groups of behaviors mentioned earlier (i.e. task performance, OCB, and CWB) as well as a firm's values (e.g. honesty). These category schemes can aid recognition and be recalled by managers when they observe an employee.

Raters who keep performance logs or diaries of critical incidents and events organized by a person can store and recall performance information more effectively and provide more accurate ratings (DeNisi, Robbins, and Cafferty, 1989). Only the pertinent information pertaining to who, what, where, when, and why needs to be recorded. There are numerous electronic means available to managers that can make this process easier (e.g. handheld devices).

Utilize multiple sources of feedback

A boss is not the only source of performance information. Other internal and external individuals who interact with and observe employees' performance from a different perspective can provide meaningful information. These individuals typically include peers, self, subordinates, and customers. Systems that use ratings from these additional sources are referred to as multisource systems or 360 degree feedback. Multisource feedback systems can be traced back to the 1950s. It has been estimated that today about 40% of organizations use some form of multisource feedback (Bracken, Timmreck, and Church, 2001).

Since raters from various perspectives have access to and observe diverse examples of performance behaviors, they accumulate different knowledge about the individual, and thus have the potential to contribute unique and valuable information to the performance appraisal. However, it is not always the case that this information is consistent with what is observed or reported by the manager. Raters observe an employee from different perspectives. Thus, they may not necessarily agree in their performance ratings (Harris and Schaubroeck, 1988). Peer and self raters typically emphasize different dimensions of performance when appraising an individual (Murphy, Cleveland, and Mohler, 2001; Smither, London, and Reilly, 2005). Furthermore, regardless of the perspective of the rater, variation in performance ratings is associated more strongly with explicit or implicit standards of the individual raters than with the perspective of the rater (Mount, Judge, Scullen, Sytsma, and Hezlett, 1998). In fact, 20 to 30% of the variation in performance ratings has been found to be specific to the individual rater (Viswesvaran, Ones, and Schmidt, 1996). All the more reason to have multiple raters.

Peers, subordinates, and customers should comment on only those dimensions of performance to which they have access, which is not necessarily all dimensions. Peers may have more opportunities to interact with co-workers in person or via email and to observe them working with customers than a supervisor. Thus, they may have a more representative sample of these types of behaviors to draw from when appraising interpersonal or communication skills compared to other dimensions of performance. In contrast, managers often have direct access to written reports that individuals have prepared as well as documents that summarize various objective outcomes (e.g. absenteeism, meeting deadlines, work quality). This information is not usually available to peers. Hence, managers may be in a better position to appraise certain dimensions of performance more accurately than peers.

For managers with a large span of control, there may be too many peers in the group from which to gather input. In these circumstances, a subsample of peers can be identified who work closely with the individual who is being rated. Nurses or retail sales staff who work on the same shift or sales agents who are on the same team are reasonable choices. They are able to comment on each other's performance more accurately than individuals who work in different shifts or on different teams. Sometimes the individual is asked to nominate two to three peers who are then later asked to provide appraisals. This approach has serious risks because of obvious concerns about selecting only those peers who will provide a favorable rating.

Customer feedback can uncover strengths and weaknesses in the product, service, or supply chain. Technological advancements make it easier and more cost effective to gather customer feedback electronically instead of relying on paper surveys (e.g. Atwater, Brett, and Charles, 2007). When the customer pool is large, feedback systems can be designed to select customers at random.

Regardless of the perspective that is sought, building trust and acceptance of the multisource feedback system is also important. Anonymity among raters can reduce concerns that the source of the rating might be revealed. This makes raters comfortable providing honest feedback instead of inflated ratings (Atwater et al., 2007). In groups where there are fewer than three raters, it is difficult to assure anonymity. Firms that are undergoing significant restructuring or change might hold off on implementing a multisource feedback system because concerns around job insecurity or other consequences of restructuring make it more difficult for individuals to trust the firm or its systems (Atwater et al., 2007). An organizational culture that supports learning and development is important for acceptance of a multisource feedback system (Atwater et al., 2007). Thus, information provided by alternative sources can provide useful information.

Incorporating ratings from these other sources can improve performance (Atwater et al., 2007; Smither et al., 2005). Individuals who either give or receive feedback from peers display effective team behavior more often than individuals who do not either give or receive peer feedback (Dominick, Reilly, and McGourty, 1997). Structured, face-to-face developmental peer appraisals can have a positive impact on group member perceptions of open communication, group task focus, group viability, and member relationships (Druskat and Wolff, 1999). Managers who receive feedback from subordinates and who meet with the subordinates to discuss the previous year's feedback improve more than managers who do not (Walker and Smither, 1999). Furthermore, managers who participate in a leadership development program and who received evaluations from superiors, peers, subordinates, and the self report that the most important rating sources were subordinates, peers, then self, respectively, rather than superiors (Brutus, London, and Martineau, 1999). In other research, managers showed improved performance six months after an upward feedback program was implemented and feedback about leaders' behavior from followers tended to promote generally positive changes in leaders' behaviors (Atwater, Roush, and Fischthal, 1995; Smither, London, Vasilopoulos, Reilly, Millsap, and Salvemini, 1995).

Develop behaviorally based performance appraisal instruments

The accuracy of a performance appraisal is influenced by the instrument that is used to make the appraisal. This section describes both less effective methods and, more importantly, highlights the features of those that are effective. These features include behaviorally based measurement, job-related performance dimensions, and clearly defined scale anchors. Although these features may appear straightforward and easy to implement, few things are that easy and no appraisal instrument is without its limitations.

The comparative approach requires the rater to judge each individual against all others in the group and then make an overall ranking across all individuals. This method is not only cumbersome, it does not facilitate feedback. Employees respond negatively because their ranking depends entirely on who else is in the group at the time of the rating instead of on an absolute standard of performance. It is not always clear what performance criteria managers use in their ranking, which can pose legal problems when a performance appraisal is challenged in the courts.

The Graphic Rating Scale consists of job-related traits (e.g. knowledge, teamwork, communication) listed next to a 5-point rating scale (for example), where a 5 represents excellent or superior performance and a 1 represents poor or unsatisfactory performance. Although this approach is popular and easy to develop, it does not indicate what the employee needs to do to improve performance (e.g. teamwork).

The behavioral approach has the greatest research support of all of the appraisal methods. The most well-known examples of a behaviorally based instrument are the Behaviorally Anchored Rating Scale (BARS) (Smith and Kendall, 1963) and the Behavioral Observation Scale (BOS) (Latham and Wexley, 1994) (see Tables 5.1 and 5.2 for examples). Typical characteristics of methods that fall under this approach include a clearly defined set of performance dimensions that are job related and linked to the firm's strategy. Managers, job incumbents, and experts participate in all stages of its development making users more comfortable with the terminology because they understand it. Any discrepancies in what is considered to be important, or in what the standards of performance are, can be resolved in the development stage. The rating scale includes information that brings meaning to the numbers ranging from 1 to 5 or 7 reflecting poor or exceptional performance. Rather, the scale anchors are defined in behavioral terms and represent critical incidents of effective or ineffective performance derived from a job analysis.

The behavioral approach minimizes concerns about criterion deficiency or contamination that were discussed earlier. The detailed job-related information in the instrument guides managers and increases their understanding of which behaviors are important and what the standards of performance are. Thus, there is greater standardization across raters and less ambiguity and inconsistency in their ratings. Furthermore, it is conducive to

Table 5.1   Example of a behavior-anchored rating scale for the job of a manager: the performance dimension is crisis management

Performance dimension: crisis management

5	Responds immediately. Is aware of the needs of relevant individuals and proactive in addressing the needs. Communication is ongoing and frequent. Provides vision, leadership, direction, and reassurance.
4	Response is quick. Takes charge of the situation. Ensures all necessary individuals are in place. Provides direction.
3	Response is well organized and thorough. Contacts relevant individuals immediately. Provides direction in some aspects of the crisis.
2	Response is adequate and within acceptable time frame. Contacts most individuals who need to be informed. Provides some direction but still relies heavily on others' leadership.
1	Fails to recognize the nature/magnitude of the crisis. Does not appreciate the potential implications of the crisis. Relies on others to show direction and leadership.

Table 5.2 Example of a behavior observation scale for the job of a manager: the performance dimension is problem solving

Performance dimension: problem solving

Almost Never 1 2 3 4 5 Almost Always

_____ Analyzes complex problems.

_____ Persists even when the solution is not clear or obvious.

_____ Develops new methods for solving problems.

_____ Implements innovative solutions.

_____ Takes responsibility for difficulties in the group.

_____ Addresses difficulties in the group.

_____ Seeks advice of team members and others when needed and appropriate.

providing feedback to individuals that they can understand because the feedback is about observable job behaviors. Hence, individuals react favorably to these instruments (Tziner and Kopelman, 2002). Given the prevalence of rater errors, the bias in observation, recall, and the evaluation of performance, the importance of features like these cannot be overemphasized.

One other approach that should be mentioned is the traditional results-based method of rating individuals. The emphasis here is on whether the individual achieves the objective output that is established at the onset of the rating period (e.g. total sales per month). Although results-based measures are objective indicators of an employee's performance, and are less susceptible to the rater biases noted above, they are not without their drawbacks. Individuals may fail to meet the objectives as a result of factors beyond their control (e.g. poor economy, organizational constraints). However, these constraints are not always apparent to all stakeholders, nor are they agreed upon. It can be demotivating to receive less favorable appraisals in these circumstances. This approach makes it difficult for a manager to provide developmental feedback because it is not always clear why the objective or target was not met and managers and employees may have different explanations.

Although some firms still use the results-based approach in performance appraisal, it is often combined with a behavioral component. Lincoln Electric has one of the most talked about piece rate systems where individuals are evaluated and paid on the basis of objective/ quantifiable output (Hastings, 1999). However, this system also includes a behavioral component in which individuals are rated on the job dimensions of dependability, quality, ideas, and cooperation in addition to output. A more recent example of a results-oriented appraisal system can be found at Best Buy's corporate headquarters, where it implemented a Results Oriented Work Environment in 2003 (Conlin, 2006). In this system, there are no schedules and very few mandatory meetings. Individuals are free to work wherever they want, whenever they want, as long as they achieve the results they agree to. Best Buy indicates that productivity has increased and voluntary turnover has decreased (Conlin, 2006).

Train raters

The effectiveness of any performance appraisal instrument also depends upon how well managers understand it, buy into it, and use it (Tziner, Murphy, and Cleveland, 2001). Rating employee performance is one of the most important responsibilities of managers. It is also among the most dreaded tasks. More often than not, this skill is developed by trial and error. Managers learn how to rate performance from the mistakes they make along the way rather than by any systematic attempt to improve their skill at observation, recall, and evaluation, and thus their self-efficacy as a rater. Even the courts recommend that raters receive training on the principles for conducting accurate and effective performance appraisals (Latham and Wexley, 1994).

Training managers can increase the accuracy of their ratings. But, the extent to which their accuracy increases depends on the content of the training and the characteristics of the training process. Highly structured and interactive workshops that provide participants with the opportunity for practice and feedback regarding their own rating patterns tend to be more effective than lecture-style information-only programs that simply describe how to rate performance more effectively (Latham and Wexley, 1994).

Programs in which norms for desired behaviors and effective performance are developed on site and used in the training to provide a common frame-of-reference have also shown favorable results (McIntyre, Smith, and Hassett, 1984). This style of training, labeled frame-of-reference, has the objective of standardizing raters' perceptions of the relevant job behaviors and standards of effective and ineffective performance (Bernardin and Buckley, 1981). Although most BARS and BOS instruments facilitate this standardization, it is also important to train the managers to be aware of these processes.

Training designed to improve raters' observational skills or decision-making skills related to performance appraisal has increased rater accuracy when delivered in the interactive workshop format (Hedge and Kavanagh, 1988). Training designed to reduce the classic rating errors (i.e. halo or leniency) has also been shown to be effective at decreasing these errors (Latham, Wexley, and Pursell, 1975).

In summary, the key elements of training programs that improve accuracy and reduce rater errors include (a) establish as part of the training job-relevant performance dimensions that are defined in behavioral terms, (b) establish examples of effective/ineffective performance with specific behaviors that reflect a 7 out of 7 compared to a 3 out of 7, etc., (c) provide an interactive session in which participants observe, evaluate, and discuss individuals who are presented on videotape performing at different levels, and (d) provide the participants with feedback on the accuracy of their ratings and provide them with additional opportunities to practice.

HOW TO IMPROVE PERFORMANCE

Accurate information is essential but not sufficient for appraising performance effectively. The manner in which the performance appraisal is communicated to the individual and how it is used for long-term planning are equally important for improving employee performance. The significance of this step is often underestimated. Hence, it can be the source of perceptions of unfairness, cause misunderstandings between the manager and employee, and lead to job dissatisfaction. This step is not the easiest part for managers especially when the performance appraisal that the manager has to communicate is negative, or when the employee has to be terminated (Tziner, 1999). However, the principles of goal setting, two-way communication, and coaching can make this process easier for both parties while maintaining the desired performance culture.

Goal setting

A performance appraisal, whether positive or negative, can be more effective when it is followed by goal setting (Locke and Latham, 1990). The body of research on the role of goal setting in improving performance, largely conducted by Latham and colleagues, can be summarized by several fundamentals. Goals that are specific and challenging yield greater improvement in performance than goals that are easy or moderate. These effects have been demonstrated in laboratory and field settings and in various jobs (Latham and Locke, 2007). Goals help individuals decide where to direct their effort or on which tasks to focus their attention. Setting specific goals can reduce ambiguity in what is expected from the individual and make something that seems abstract or unachievable more concrete. The amount of effort to exert on tasks and the persistence of that effort is guided by how challenging the goals are (Latham and Wexley, 1994). Challenging goals can be more motivating because they provide a sense of accomplishment when achieved. Goals that are defined in behavioral terms make it easier to provide action-oriented feedback when goals are not attained and to establish the reason why (Latham, Locke, and Fassina, 2002). A longitudinal study of executives revealed that leading firms develop specific action plans for individuals at all levels of performance regardless of whether they are high potential, average, or poor performing individuals (Michaels, Handfield-Jones, and Axelrod, 2001).

The motivating potential of goal setting depends upon how committed employees are to the goals. A large part of goal commitment rests upon basic principles of learning and coaching (Latham and Wexley, 1994). Employees need to believe that they can achieve the goals, even if they know that doing so will be difficult. Involving employees in the process and setting a reasonable number of goals (e.g. three to seven goals) can increase their self-efficacy, namely their belief that the goals are attainable. Individuals should perceive that goal achievement will lead to positive outcomes, that the positive outcomes will be realized after goal attainment, and that the outcomes are actually valued (Latham, 2001). The outcome can be a favorable performance appraisal, positive feedback, monetary rewards, or other intrinsic or extrinsic rewards. Regardless of the type of consequence, the employee needs to believe that the performance–outcome link exists. These conditions explain in part why setting goals can improve performance.

Two-way communication

One of the more difficult parts of the performance appraisal process is delivering the performance evaluation to the individual. Traditionally, managers filled out an appraisal form for each individual and shared the rating with the employee in a meeting. Rarely was the employee given any input or voice in the appraisal process. It is not surprising to find that this approach can lead to perceptions of bias and unfairness, and is unsuccessful when challenged in the courts.

Performance appraisals that are based upon elements of due process are perceived to be fairer (Taylor, Tracy, Renard, Harrison, and Carroll, 1995). These elements include knowledge of job-relevant performance dimensions (i.e. define job performance in line with the organization's strategy and values and train raters), judgment based on a representative sample of behaviors (i.e. observe and record performance frequently and document using a behavioral performance appraisal instrument), and meetings that invite input from the individual (Folger, Konovsky, Cropanzano, 1992). The first two elements were covered in the section on *accuracy* and the third element will be discussed below.

The performance appraisal meeting is an essential part of communicating the performance appraisal. However, the thought of having to convey a less than favorable evaluation face to face can leave managers feeling uncomfortable and preferring to schedule a phone or lunch conversation or combining it with a meeting about something else altogether. But, the meeting should take place in person. The manager should be attentive during the meeting. Answering telephone calls or checking email sends conflicting messages. Setting aside time to meet and discuss performance signals the importance the firm places on the performance appraisal process and how much the firm values that individual.

The manager should recognize employees for goal attainment and explain how the goal helps the group, the firm, and the individual's career development. Managers should focus the discussion around the individual's actions and behaviors and not their personality. In circumstances when the goals are not attained, the manager should solicit input from the individual as to why. The meeting should not be the first time that the individual or manager is learning about a performance problem. If an employee is repeatedly late, this problem should be addressed immediately instead of waiting until the formal performance appraisal interview. If this pattern of behavior continues, even after repeated attempts to correct it, the performance appraisal meeting can be used to provide quantitative information on lateness frequency. During the meeting, the manager is advised to focus on the act of being late rather than on labeling the individual unreliable or lazy. The manager should focus on trying to solve the problem and be supportive, as the two parties try to reach an agreement on a remedy. This process of two-way communication is central to the success of the meeting. Research indicates that when these steps are followed, individuals perceive the process to be fairer (Taylor et al., 1995).

Ask for self-assessment

Managers should ask the employee for a self-assessment prior to the performance meeting. The self-assessment helps individuals reflect on their performance throughout the year and to justify their self-rating. The self-appraisal can be completed with the same instrument and language that the manager uses to make the appraisal (e.g. job relevant performance dimensions and anchors defined in behavioral terms), thereby further reducing ambiguity in what behaviors are being evaluated. Both parties should be prepared to discuss any discrepancies between the two appraisals. Although research suggests that there isn't always agreement between self-appraisals and appraisals from other sources, when a behaviorally oriented appraisal instrument is used, there is greater agreement between the individual and supervisor (Schrader and Steiner, 1996). Furthermore, the exercise of going through a self-evaluation can pinpoint the sources of some misunderstandings and facilitate the discussion. When the individual's input is factored into the appraisal, they perceive that they have been treated fairer than when it is not and report higher motivation to improve performance and greater satisfaction with the process (e.g. Cawley, Keeping, and Levy, 1998; Erdogan, Kraimer, and Liden, 2001).

Coach employees

Coaching as discussed here refers to the role of a "manager as coach" and not the coach as a third party who has been hired by the firm to help the employee develop specific skills. The formal performance appraisal may take place once a year. However, a manager should be coaching employees and providing feedback on an ongoing basis throughout the year. Historically, the manager's role was perceived to be one of "command and control." The manager derived power from the knowledge or information that he or she possessed and control from deciding when to disseminate it to the group. This style has become outdated and replaced by the "manager as coach" model. Year-round coaching that includes goal setting, participative communication, and problem solving improves productivity (Olivero, Bane, and Kopelman, 1997).

The foundation to effective coaching is the working relationship that a manager establishes with each individual. Although a manager may interact with some individuals more often than others, and may even feel a more positive affect toward some of them (Varma, DeNisi, and Peters, 1996), it is the responsibility of the manager to know each person and to be as objective as possible in making assessments. Mutual trust and respect are an important part of the coaching relationship (see Chapter 21). Not only do subordinates need to trust their manager and believe that the manager wants them to succeed, managers also need to trust their subordinates' motivations and intentions. By focusing on common goals, both parties can learn to accept each other for who they are even though they may not always agree on an appraisal.

An essential part of the "manager as coach" is to address performance incidents directly and immediately (e.g. Campbell and Garfinkel, 1996). When a manager observes or learns that an employee has a performance problem, the manager should gather information from all the relevant parties about the specifics of an incident instead of assuming a set of circumstances, over-reacting, or laying blame. Their goal is to remedy the problem and remind the parties of the proper procedures/behaviors that are to be followed, why they matter, and then to ask for a justification as to why the procedures were not followed. Gathering input about "why" it happened is important because this information may reveal or uncover a flaw or breakdown in systems, a deeper problem, or training needs. As indicated earlier, managers should focus on the actions of individuals involved in the incident instead of criticizing the person. If managers ignore these incidents instead of addressing them directly when they occur or shortly after, employees may conclude that the incident did not represent a transgression, even if it was a transgression, that it is not that important or doesn't really matter. If managers wait until the formal performance appraisal to address the behavior, the causes of the problems may have escalated and become so severe or relationships may be permanently damaged.

Examples of exceptional performance should also be rewarded even if simply with "praise" or verbal recognition. Acknowledging good performance sends the message that good things also get noticed, not just the bad things. Regardless of the positive or negative circumstances, managers should follow up with the employees to see if performance has improved or if any problems persist.

Managers should use a common language around job performance when coaching individuals. The first half of the chapter detailed the importance of defining job performance and designing an instrument around job relevant performance dimensions. Managers should use the same language when coaching individuals. Ambiguity in what is expected is reduced when individuals hear and see managers using this performance language repeatedly in their daily or weekly interactions. This consistency in language also reinforces the performance and feedback culture of the department and more broadly of the firm.

Manage the separation process of poor performers

Not everyone succeeds. Even valid selection systems are imperfect. Some individuals are assessed as having a high likelihood of performing well when in fact they do not. There will be occasions when the requisite ability and motivation is lacking; hence, these individuals should be terminated. However, the separation process needs to be handled carefully because perceptions of injustice can have psychological, not to mention physiological, consequences on the individual and increase the risk of litigation for the firm (Latham and Wexley, 1994; Roehling and Wright, 2006).

The assumption is that employees want to perform their job at least to an average level. If they are not performing there must be an explanation. For example, it may be the case that an employee is unaware of the poor performance, has different standards for what is considered to be an acceptable level of performance, argues that the poor performance is beyond their control and due to on-the-job constraints such as defective equipment, argues that they did not receive adequate training, believes that the manager holds a grudge against the employee, or is experiencing personal problems outside of work that are impeding the performance.

Before it is decided that termination is the answer, the manager should gather information and work with the individual to determine the underlying cause of the poor performance. This approach seeks to remedy the problem if possible and gives the employee an opportunity to improve. All possible alternative explanations, other than the employee does not have the ability or motivation to perform, should be ruled out before it is concluded that the employee should be terminated. The firm will be expected to provide strong documented evidence of poor performance and that the performance deficiency is dimensionally related to the job. Some firms have a policy of progressive discipline that must be followed before terminations are made. This process typically includes verbal warnings followed by written warnings and then termination.

CASE EXAMPLES

The two cases described below are based upon true stories of employees' experiences with the performance appraisal processes at firms. The first case illustrates a less effective style of managing performance problems. The second case illustrates how a manager can help an employee improve on certain dimensions of performance by applying some of the principles outlined in this chapter.

The case of Peter

Tom Ross leads a group of electrical engineers who work in research and development. Although Tom is satisfied with the performance of the group, the behavior of one of its members, Peter, is posing problems for the team. Peter also happens to be one of the stars. Unfortunately, Tom has not spoken to Peter about the behavior because he is afraid that it will create tension and that Peter might threaten to leave the firm in the middle of the project. Tom prefers to ignore the problem and to focus on meeting the project deadlines.

Tom keeps written records of all team members' achievements and performance problems. He reviews his record of Peter:

◆ Is late or misses meetings and expects to be briefed when he arrives, disrupting the flow of the meeting (e.g. missed meetings in September and November and was 20 minutes late for all other meetings).
◆ Is often impatient and interrupts team members who take a little longer to get to the point (e.g. interrupts members repeatedly and has sighed when some members speak).
◆ Appears headstrong and inflexible in his opinion even when evidence supports an alternative (e.g. decision to switch suppliers and cost-cutting strategy).
◆ Says what comes to his mind even if it offends team members (e.g. told a member that her report was elementary and shouted at a member when he suggested an extension on the deadline).
◆ Helps team members prepare their presentations (e.g. spent all day one Saturday helping a member with his presentation).
◆ Has a wide network of contacts that he shares with the team.
◆ Introduces team members to potential mentors (e.g. had members contact Peter's former colleague about suppliers).

Tom lacks the self-efficacy to handle this problem and believes that if he just ignores Peter's quirks the group will finish the project on time without upsetting the flow. He tells the other team members to be patient and to focus on Peter's strengths. However, the problems intensify and two team members quit, leaving Tom short staffed and behind schedule.

The case of Sue

John Lee is a division engineer for a large aerospace firm. As division manager he is in charge of a staff of over 50 professional and technical personnel. Five of these professionals are designated as project engineers responsible for specific contracts. John has been busier than usual lately taking care of last minute details on a new contract and has left the project engineers on their own.

One of the project engineers is giving him reason to worry. John has heard rumors that Sue Wells (who joined the firm six months ago) is extremely aggressive with co-workers and difficult to work with. Others say that Sue does not always follow the rules and procedures but rather acts quickly before getting answers or consensus from her team. Sue is one of the strongest and most knowledgeable performers.

More specifically, John learned the following about Sue's performance over the last few months:

- Clients indicate that she is extremely knowledgeable about the project and willing to respond to their requests for modifications.
- Has good awareness of "problem clients" in the industry and has advised the firm wisely to avoid certain deals.
- Always blames others when things do not work out. A month ago a client backed down on a contract. Sue returned to the office and yelled at the administrator and team member who helped her manage the contract. She blamed them for the client's decision and accused them of sloppy and slow work. In reality, the client's decision had nothing to do with sloppy work. More recently, Sue noticed an error on a client report during the middle of her meeting with a client. She went back to the office and yelled at the team for their failure to notice the error. In reality, the team did notice the error and warned Sue about it but she did not respond.

John decided that he needs to meet with Sue to discuss these concerns and other things. It has been about two months since their last discussion. Below are the details of that meeting.

JOHN: Hi, Sue, how do you feel the last few months have been going for you here.

SUE: There have been ups and downs. I get frustrated by how slow people are in giving me the information that I need. If I wait for answers, I am afraid that the clients will get impatient and go elsewhere. We lost a client because of this.

JOHN: I remember that client. What happened?

SUE: I went to visit the client expecting that we were ready to close on the contract but the client pulled out. They told me that they received a better response and service from one of our competitors. I knew that this would happen. So, I went back to the office and made sure everyone on the team knew about this and that they could have prevented it from happening if they just listened to me and worked faster and better.

JOHN: I see – but I think everyone here is working really long hours just to keep up. With respect to that contract that we lost, most of the team worked overtime and took work home on weekends in an effort to turn it around quickly. I am not sure that we can expect more of them. The team felt very bad when they were blamed and told that they worked too slow and were sloppy. It is easy for us to get frustrated about a lot of things but we cannot take out these frustrations on the group. We are a team and need to work together on projects and respect each other. They know that you work hard too and want to help you.

SUE: Oh – I didn't mean to offend anyone – I was just so disappointed that we lost the contract and probably over-reacted. What bothers me is that if processing contracts quicker gives us an edge over competitors, I just don't see why people can't work faster so that we get the contracts done sooner or why there are so many steps in the process anyway. We could have a much quicker turnaround if we removed even just two steps.

JOHN: Times are changing and there are more checks and balances today than ever . . . we need to manage our own expectations around timing of contracts and the expectations of the clients. There are ways to do this. How about giving Pam in Division II a call – she has a few strategies that might help. Most firms face the same constraints and legal obligations as we do with respect to approving contracts. Perhaps we can revisit the approval process during our planning meeting next month. We can also review the workload of our support staff to see if we need to expand the group or if there are any redundancies in procedures. How about keeping track of the situations when you feel that things are going too slow and talking to me about them to see if/where we can modify things.

SUE: I can do that.

Sue learned a lot from that discussion. She apologized to the team and thanked them for all of their hard work. She explained her concerns and asked for their input on the procedures. Together they prepared a plan for modifying approval procedures that conformed to legal requirements. They presented the plan to the manager at the next planning meeting and he agreed to circulate it to managers in other departments for their input.

CONCLUSION

The performance appraisal process has been criticized by employees, managers, and the courts as being biased, unfair, difficult to conduct, and invalid. Despite these concerns, the performance appraisal serves a necessary function in the workplace, and is not likely to go away. The principles of effective performance appraisal discussed throughout this chapter alleviate the criticisms noted above and can help managers realize the positive outcomes that are possible with an effective performance appraisal system.

To summarize, one step to achieving performance gains from this process is to make sure that the appraisal is based upon accurate performance information. Adopting a mindset of observing and recording performance as frequently as possible provides managers with the opportunity to deliver feedback about effective or ineffective performance immediately (as opposed to waiting until the end of the performance cycle). It also supplies them with a representative sample of behaviors that they can refer to when conducting and delivering the formal appraisal. Training managers on the performance appraisal process and using a performance appraisal instrument in which job-related performance dimensions and anchors are clearly defined can facilitate the process of documenting accurate information and delivering feedback that is developmental. Gathering input from alternative sources such as peers or customers can supplement the manager's perspective.

Another important step involves how the performance appraisal is communicated to the employee and used to set objectives and employee development. Performance appraisal meetings that invite input from the individual and that focus on job-related behaviors create an environment that is supportive, where both parties can reach solutions to any potential problems. The process of setting challenging and specific goals that are to be achieved during the next performance cycle help the individuals know where they need to focus their effort. Although the formal appraisal meeting may take place once per year, ongoing feedback and coaching by the manager facilitates the learning and development process. The application of these principles has been shown to improve performance.

REFERENCES

Atwater, L. E., Brett, J. F., and Charles, A. C. (2007). Multisource feedback: Lessons learned and implications for practice. *Human Resource Management*, 46(2), 285–307.

Atwater, L., Roush, P., and Fischthal, A. (1995). The influence of upward feedback on self- and follower ratings of leadership. *Personnel Psychology*, 48(1), 35–59.

Bennett, R. J., and Robinson, S. L. (2000). Development of a measure of workplace deviance. *Journal of Applied Psychology*, 85(3), 349–360.

Bernardin, H. J., and Buckley, M. R. (1981). Strategies in rater training. *Academy of Management Review*, 6(2), 205–212.

Berry, C. M., Ones, D. S., and Sackett, P. R. (2007). Interpersonal deviance, organizational deviance, and their common correlates: A review and meta-analysis. *Journal of Applied Psychology*, 92(2), 410–424.

Bracken, D. W., Timmreck, C. W., and Church, A. H. (eds) (2001). *The Handbook of Multisource Feedback: The Comprehensive Resource for Designing and Implementing MSF Processes.* San Francisco: Jossey-Bass.

Brutus, S., London, M., and Martineau, J. (1999). The impact of 360-degree feedback on planning for career development. *Journal of Management Development*, 18(8), 676–693.

Campbell, R. B., and Garfinkel, L. M. (1996). 6 strategies for success in measuring performance. *HR Magazine*, 41(6), 98.

Cawley, B. D., Keeping, L. M., and Levy, P. E. (1998). Participation in the performance appraisal process and employee reactions: a meta-analytic review of field investigations. *Journal of Applied Psychology*, 83(4), 615–633.

Conlin, M. (2006). Smashing the clock. *Business Week*, (4013), 60.

Dalal, R. S. (2005). A meta-analysis of the relationship between organizational citizenship behavior and counterproductive work behavior. *Journal of Applied Psychology. Special Section: Theoretical Models and Conceptual Analyses – Second Installment*, 90(6), 1241–1255.

DeNisi, A. S., and Peters, L. H. (1996). Organization of information in memory and the performance appraisal process: Evidence from the field. *Journal of Applied Psychology*, 81(6), 717–737.

DeNisi, A. S., Robbins, T., and Cafferty, T. P. (1989). Organization of information used for performance appraisals: Role of diary-keeping. *Journal of Applied Psychology*, 74(1), 124–129.

Dominick, P. G., Reilly, R. R., and McGourty, J. W. (1997). The effects of peer feedback on team member behavior. *Group and Organization Management*, 22(4), 508–520.

Druskat, V. U., and Wolff, S. B. (1999). Effects and timing of developmental peer appraisals in self-managing work groups. *Journal of Applied Psychology*, 84(1), 58–74.

Erdogan, B., Kraimer, M. L., and Liden, R. C. (2001). Procedural justice as a two-dimensional construct: An examination in the performance appraisal account. *Journal of Applied Behavioral Science*, 37(2), 205–222.

Farr, J. L., and Levy, P. E. (2007). Performance appraisal. In L. L. Koppes (ed.), *Historical Perspectives in Industrial and Organizational Psychology* (pp. 311–327). Mahwah, NJ, US: Lawrence Erlbaum Associates Publishers.

Fleishman, E. A., and Quaintance, M. K. (1984). *Taxonomies of Human Performance: The Description of Human Tasks*. San Diego, CA, US: Academic Press.

Folger, R., Konovsky, M. A., and Cropanzano, R. (1992). A due process metaphor for performance appraisal. In B. M. Staw and L. L. Cummings (eds), *Research in Organziational Behavior* (vol. 13, pp. 129–177). Greenwhich, CT: JAI Press.

Foti, R. J., and Lord, R. G. (1987). Prototypes and scripts: the effects of alternative methods of processing information on rating accuracy. *Organizational Behavior and Human Decision Processes*, 39(3), 318–340.

Harris, M. M., and Schaubroeck, J. (1988). A meta-analysis of self-supervisor, self-peer, and peer-supervisor ratings. *Personnel Psychology*, 41(1), 43–62.

Hastings, D. F. (1999). Lincoln Electric's harsh lessons from international expansion. *Harvard Business Review*, 77(3), 162–178.

Hedge, J. W., and Kavanagh, M. J. (1988). Improving the accuracy of performance evaluations: comparison of three methods of performance appraiser training. *Journal of Applied Psychology*, 73(1), 68–73.

Latham, G. P. (2001). The importance of understanding and changing employee outcome expectancies for gaining commitment to an organizational goal. *Personnel Psychology*, 54(3), 707–716.

Latham, G. P., and Locke, E. A. (2007). New developments in and directions for goal-setting research. *European Psychologist*, 12(4), 290–300.

Latham, G. P., Locke, E. A., and Fassina, N. E. (2002). The high performance cycle: standing the test of time. In S. Sonnentag (ed.), *The Psychological Management of Individual Performance. A Handbook in the Psychology of Management in Organizations* (pp. 201–228). Chichester, UK: John Wiley and Sons Ltd.

Latham, G. P., and Mann, S. (2006). Advances in the science of performance appraisal: Implications for practice. In G. P. Hodgkinson, and J. K. Ford (eds), *International Review of Industrial and Organizational Psychology* 2006 (vol. 21, pp. 295–337). Hoboken, NJ, US: Wiley Publishing.

Latham, G. P., and Wexley, K. N. (1994). *Increasing Productivity through Performance Appraisal* (2nd edition). New York: Addison-Wesley.

Latham, G. P., Wexley, K. N., and Pursell, E. D. (1975). Training managers to minimize rating errors in the observation of behavior. *Journal of Applied Psychology*, 60(5), 550–555.

Locke, E. A., and Latham, G. P. (1990). *A Theory of Goal Setting and Task Performance*. Englewood Cliffs, NJ, US: Prentice-Hall, Inc.

McIntyre, R. M., Smith, D. E., and Hassett, C. E. (1984). Accuracy of performance ratings as affected by rater training and perceived purpose of rating. *Journal of Applied Psychology*, 69(1), 147–156.

Michaels, E., Handfield-Jones, H., and Axelrod, B. (2001). *The War for Talent*. Boston, MA: Harvard Business School Press.

Mount, M. K., Judge, T. A., Scullen, S. E., Sytsma, M. R., and Hezlett, S. A. (1998). Trait, rater and level effects in 360-degree performance ratings. *Personnel Psychology*, 51(3), 557–576.

Murphy, K. R., Cleveland, J. N., and Mohler, C. J. (2001). Reliability, validity, and mean-ingfulness of multisource ratings. In D. W. Bracken, C. W. Timmreck, and A. H. Church (eds), *The Handbook of Multisource Feedback: The Comprehensive Resource for Designing and Implementing MSF Processes* (pp. 130–148). San Francisco, CA, US: Jossey-Bass.

Olivero, G., Bane, K. D., and Kopelman, R. E. (1997). Executive coaching as a transfer of training tool: Effects on productivity in a public agency. *Public Personnel Management*, 26(4), 461–469.

Organ, D. W. (1997). Organizational citizenship behavior: It's construct clean-up time. *Human Performance*, 10(2), 85–97.

Podsakoff, P. M., MacKenzie, S. B., Paine, J. B., and Bachrach, D. G. (2000). Organizational citizenship behaviors: A critical review of the theoretical and empirical literature and suggestions for future research. *Journal of Management*, 26(3), 513–563.

Roehling, M. V., and Wright, P. M. (2006). Organizationally sensible versus legal-centric approaches to employment decisions. *Human Resource Management*, 45(4), 605–627.

Rotundo, M., and Sackett, P. R. (2002). The relative importance of task, citizenship, and counterproductive performance to global ratings of job performance: a policy-capturing approach. *Journal of Applied Psychology*, 87(1), 66–80.

Rotundo, M., and Xie, J. L. (2008). Understanding the domain of counterproductive work behaviour in China. *International Journal of Human Resource Management*, 19(5), 856–877.

Schrader, B. W., and Steiner, D. D. (1996). Common comparison standards: An approach to improving agreement between self and supervisory performance ratings. *Journal of Applied Psychology*, 81(6), 813–820.

Smith, P. C., and Kendall, L. M. (1963). Retranslation of expectations: An approach to the construction of unambiguous anchors for rating scales. *Journal of Applied Psychology*, 47(2), 149–155.

Smither, J. W., London, M., and Reilly, R. R. (2005). Does performance improve following multisource feedback? A theoretical model, meta-analysis, and review of empirical find-ings. *Personnel Psychology*, 58, 33–66.

Smither, J. W., London, M., Vasilopoulos, N. L., Reilly, R. R., Millsap, R. E., and Salvemini, N. (1995). An examination of the effects of an upward feedback program over time. *Personnel Psychology*, 48, 1–34.

Taylor, M. S., Tracy, K. B., Renard, M. K., Harrison, J. K., and Carroll, S. J. (1995). Due process in performance appraisal: A quasi-experiment in procedural justice. *Administrative Science Quarterly*, 40(3), 495–523.

Tziner, A. (1999). The relationship between distal and proximal factors and the use of political considerations in performance appraisal. *Journal of Business and Psychology*, 14, 217–231.

Tziner, A., and Kopelman, R. E. (2002). Is there a preferred performance rating format? A non-psychometric perspective. *Applied Psychology: An International Review*, 51, 479–503.

Tziner, A., Murphy, K. R., and Cleveland, J. N. (2001). Relationships between attitudes towards organizations and performance appraisal systems and rating behaviors. *International Journal of Selection and Assessment*, 9, 226–239.

Varma, A., Denisi, A. S., and Peters, L. H. (1996). Interpersonal affect and performance appraisal: A field study. *Personnel Psychology*, 49(2), 341–360.

Viswesvaran, C., Ones, D. S., and Schmidt, F. L. (1996). Comparative analysis of the reliability of job performance ratings. *Journal of Applied Psychology*, 81(5), 557–574.

Walker, A. G., and Smither, J. W. (1999). A five-year study of upward feedback: What managers do with their results matters. *Personnel Psychology*, 52(2), 393–423.

Wright, P. M., Dunford, B. B., and Snell, S. A. (2001). Human resources and the resource based view of the firm. *Journal of Management*, 27(6), 701–721.

EXERCISES

Develop a performance appraisal instrument

Individuals and/or groups can learn a lot from going through the process of developing a performance appraisal instrument for their current job or for one of their group projects (if they are taking a course). Individuals/groups can apply the principles described in the section on accuracy (summarized below).

1. Reach agreement on what the deliverable is. For example, if the assignment is to conduct a "case analysis of an assigned case," a deliverable can be a "written report that analyzes an assigned case." More specifically, it can be a written report that identifies the strengths and problems inherent in the case, analyzes the problems using theories and concepts covered in the course, and provides recommendations.

2. Establish the group's goal with respect to the quality and standards of the written report. For example, is the group's goal to obtain an A grade on the assignment or to learn from the project, both, or something else altogether.

3. Establish the major responsibilities of each group member and translate these responsibilities into specific goals or actions.

4. Establish dimensions of performance and define them in behavioral terms. Dimensions can be grouped according to task dimensions, OCBs, and CWBs. Task dimensions can include timely submission of material to group members, depth of analysis of problems indentified in the case, appropriate use of theories, etc. OCBs can include reviews team members' submission, respects team members, shares important information, etc. CWBs can include conforms to university policy and procedures regarding code of conduct, is not late or absent from meetings, etc.

5. Establish standards of performance for each dimension using clearly defined anchors on the rating scale. For example, on the job dimension "attendance" (7 = attends all meetings, 2 = missed half of the meetings).

Conduct a self-appraisal

Another useful exercise is to ask individuals to rate their own performance. Using the performance appraisal instrument at your current employer (or former place of employment, or the instrument developed in the above exercise), conduct a self-appraisal and be prepared to deliver your self-appraisal to your boss, a peer, or the group. Remember to keep in mind the principles outlined in this chapter when appraising your own performance and delivering the appraisal. This exercise can help individuals appreciate the difficulty of this process.

Evaluating a performance appraisal process

A valuable exercise is to ask individuals to evaluate a performance appraisal they experienced personally (or the performance appraisal process) at their current employer or their former place of employment against the principles outlined in this chapter. They are asked to consider the following information in their evaluation:

1. What are the dimensions of performance on which they were rated? Were these dimensions defined?
2. Were the standards of performance made clear to them and were they defined?
3. Did their boss only provide the appraisal or were alternative sources also considered?
4. Describe the performance appraisal instrument.
5. Describe the process of how the performance appraisal was communicated to them.

Part III

TURNOVER AND SATISFACTION

6

Promote Job Satisfaction through Mental Challenge

Timothy A. Judge and Ryan Klinger

The most popular definition of job satisfaction was supplied by Locke (1976), who defined it as ". . . a pleasurable or positive emotional state resulting from the appraisal of one's job or job experiences" (p. 1304). There are many possible influences on how favorably one appraises one's job, and numerous theories of job satisfaction have attempted to delineate these influences. Empirical evidence, however, has suggested only one clear attribute of the work itself that consistently influences job satisfaction – the cognitive challenge of the work. This leads to the general principle that will be the focus of this chapter – that mentally challenging work is the key to job satisfaction. Thus, the most effective way an organization can promote the job satisfaction of its employees is to enhance the mental challenge in their jobs, and the most consequential way most individuals can improve their own job satisfaction is to seek out mentally challenging work.

Before discussing this principle in more detail, however, it is important to demonstrate the importance of the principle. Scores on a valid measure of job satisfaction are the most important pieces of information organizations can collect, not only as one measure of management effectiveness, but because, as we will note, job satisfaction scores predict a wide range of job behaviors. Yet, many organizations openly question whether they need to be concerned with job satisfaction. One study of how job satisfaction is viewed by managers (Judge and Church, 2000) drew the following comments:

- ◆ "Job satisfaction is virtually never discussed in the senior staff meetings I attend within our business unit."
- ◆ "Job satisfaction is not measured. Because this is Wall Street, money talks. If people weren't happy, they could have moved their whole team elsewhere."
- ◆ "Job satisfaction is not measured or considered at all."
- ◆ "There is some questioning of whether job satisfaction is desirable anyway."

Organizations would be well advised to place more importance on job satisfaction. It is related to many outcomes that individuals and organizations find important. Some of the outcomes that job satisfaction has been linked to are:

◆ *Job performance.* The relationship between job satisfaction and performance has an interesting history. In 1985, a quantitative review of the literature suggested that the true correlation between job satisfaction and performance was quite small (Iaffaldano and Muchinsky, 1985). However, more recent evidence reveals that the relationship is larger than was previously thought. A comprehensive review of 300 studies determined that when the correlations are corrected for the effects of sampling error and measurement error, the average true score correlation between overall job satisfaction and job performance is .30 (Judge, Thoresen, Bono, and Patton, 2001). Thus, it does appear that a happy worker is more likely to be a productive one. Evidence also exists for a relationship at the work unit level – units whose average employees are satisfied with their jobs are more likely to perform at a higher level than business units whose employees are less satisfied, and to be more profitable as a result (Harter, Schmidt, and Hayes, 2002). Of course, the relationship between satisfaction and performance may be reciprocal. Not only may employees who are happy with their jobs be more productive, but performing a job well may lead to satisfaction with the job, especially if good performance is rewarded (see Chapters 12 and 13, this volume).
◆ *Withdrawal behaviors.* Job satisfaction displays relatively consistent, negative correlations with absenteeism and turnover. Job dissatisfaction also appears to display negative correlations with other specific withdrawal behaviors, including unionization, lateness, drug abuse, and retirement. Furthermore, Harrison, Newman, and Roth (2006) and Fisher and Locke (1992) have shown that when these specific behaviors are aggregated as indicators of a general withdrawal syndrome, job satisfaction is quite predictive.
◆ *Life satisfaction.* Evidence indicates that job satisfaction is also moderately to strongly related to one outcome that individuals find particularly important – life satisfaction (Tait, Padgett, and Baldwin, 1989). Since the job is a significant part of life, the correlation between job and life satisfaction makes sense – one's job experiences spill over onto life. Thus, people who have jobs that they like are more likely to lead happy lives.

Thus far, job satisfaction has been defined and it has been shown that job satisfaction matters. Thus, any principle that reveals how best to promote job satisfaction is important to understand. With this foundation, in the next section of the chapter, the model that best describes the principle – that job satisfaction is best achieved through mentally challenging work – will be reviewed.

JOB CHARACTERISTICS MODEL

The theory that best describes the role of the work environment in providing mentally challenging work is the Job Characteristics Model (JCM). The Job Characteristics Model argues that the intrinsic nature of work is the core underlying factor causing employees to be satisfied with their jobs. The model, in its full explication by Hackman and Oldham (1980), focuses on five core job characteristics that make one's work challenging and fulfilling: (1) task identity – degree to which one can see one's work from beginning to end; (2) task significance – degree to which one's work is seen as important and significant; (3) skill variety – degree to which the job allows employees to do different tasks; (4) autonomy – degree to which employees have control and discretion for how to conduct their job; (5) feedback – degree to which the work itself provides feedback for how the employee is performing the job. According to the theory, jobs that are enriched to provide these core characteristics are likely to meet individuals' needs for mental challenge and fulfillment in their work, and thus will be more satisfying and motivating to employees.

Measurement of job characteristics

There are various ways intrinsic job characteristics can be measured. Arguably the most common approach relies on the Job Diagnostic Survey (JDS) to measure the extent to which the five core intrinsic job characteristics are present in the job (for an alternative approach, see Morgeson and Humphrey's (2006) Work Design Questionnaire). Items from the JDS appear in Table 6.1. When responding to items in the table, individuals circle the number (from 1 to 7) that is the most accurate description of their job. The JDS can be used to rate almost any type of job. Ideally, one would give the JDS to a number of people in an organization within a job type to get a reliable measurement of the job characteristics. The JDS is not copyrighted and thus is free to use. However, care must be taken in administering the JDS. The reader interested in measuring intrinsic job characteristics should consult Hackman and Oldham (1980), who provide all of the JDS items, along with an excellent discussion of administrative issues.

Research support

There are several indirect pieces of evidence supporting Hackman and Oldham's model. First, when individuals are asked to evaluate different facets of their job such as pay, promotion opportunities, co-workers, and so forth, the nature of the work itself generally emerges as the most important job facet (Judge and Church, 2000; Jurgensen, 1978). Second, of the major job satisfaction facets – pay, promotion opportunities, co-workers, supervision, and the work itself – satisfaction with the work itself, far and away, best predicts overall job satisfaction (Rentsch and Steel, 1992). Thus, if we are interested in understanding what causes people to be satisfied with their jobs, the nature of the work (intrinsic job characteristics) is the first place to start. Unfortunately, managers often think employees are most desirous of pay to the exclusion of other job attributes such as challenging work. For example, a 1997 survey indicated that, out of 10 job attributes, employees ranked interesting work as the most important job attribute (good wages was ranked fifth), whereas when it came to what managers thought employees wanted, good wages ranked first while interesting work ranked fifth (Kovach, 1997).

Research directly testing the relationship between workers' reports of job characteristics and job satisfaction has produced consistently positive results. Humphrey, Nahrgang, and

Table 6.1   Measurement of intrinsic job characteristics: the Job Diagnostic Survey

1. How much *autonomy* is there in your job? That is, to what extent does your job permit you to decide *on your own* how to go about doing the work?

1----------------2----------------3----------------4----------------5----------------6----------------7

Very little; the job gives me almost no personal "say" about how and when the work is done.	Moderate autonomy: many things are standardized and not under my control, but I can make some decisions about work.	Very much; the job gives me almost complete responsibility for deciding how and when the work is done.

2. To what extent does your job involve doing a "*whole*" *and identifiable piece of work*? That is, is the job a complete piece of work that has an obvious beginning and end? Or is it only a small *part* of the overall piece of work, which is finished by other people or by automatic machines?

1----------------2----------------3----------------4----------------5----------------6----------------7

My job is only a tiny part of the overall piece of work; the results of my activities cannot be seen in the final product or service.	My job is a moderate-sized "chunk" of the overall piece of work; my own contributions can be seen in the final outcome.	My job involves doing the whole piece of work, from start to finish; the results of my activities are easily seen in the final product or service.

3. How much *variety* is there in your job? That is, to what extent does the job require you to do many different things at work, using a variety of your skills and talents?

1----------------2----------------3----------------4----------------5----------------6----------------7

Very little; the job requires me to do the same routine things over and over again.	Moderate variety.	Very much; the job requires me to do many different things, using a number of different skills and talents.

4. In general, how *significant or important* is your job? That is, are the results of your work likely to significantly affect the lives or well-being of other people?

1----------------2----------------3----------------4----------------5----------------6----------------7

Not very significant; the outcomes of my work are *not* likely to have important effects on other people.	Moderately significant.	Highly significant; the outcomes of my work can affect other people in very important ways.

5. To what extent does *doing the job itself* provide you with information about your work performance? That is, does the actual *work itself* provide clues about how well you are doing – aside from any "feedback" co-workers or supervisors may provide?

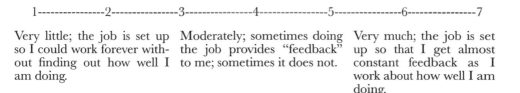

| 1---------------2---------------3---------------4---------------5---------------6---------------7 |

| Very little; the job is set up so I could work forever without finding out how well I am doing. | Moderately; sometimes doing the job provides "feedback" to me; sometimes it does not. | Very much; the job is set up so that I get almost constant feedback as I work about how well I am doing. |

From: Hackman, J. R., and Oldham, G. R. (1980). *Work Redesign*. Reading, MA: Addison-Wesley.

Morgeson (2007) meta-analyzed the results of over 250 studies of work characteristic – job outcome relationships. All five intrinsic job characteristics were strong predictors of employee job satisfaction. Moreover, these core characteristics were generally found to be significant predictors of other attitudinal criteria, such as organizational commitment and work motivation, as well as behavioral, job performance outcomes. The empirical data suggest that intrinsic job characteristics are the mostly consistently significant situational predictor of job satisfaction.

How to Increase Mental Challenge in Jobs

Ever been in a car accident? If you have, you probably remember picking up the phone to call your insurance company and, inevitably, talking to many different people, recounting the details of your accident several times. It may be weeks or even months before your claim is settled and, if you ever happen to call to inquire about the status of your claim, you may discover that your claim is buried somewhere in the system. As a customer in this situation, you probably feel irritated and poorly served being passed around like a hot potato. But have you ever wondered what the implications of such a system are for employees? When each employee specializes in processing one part of the claim, the mental challenge afforded by the job suffers. Over and over, the same person may answer the phone from customers, take down basic details of the accident, and then pass on the claim to someone else, never to see it again. Even the job of claims adjuster can be broken into segments that are very specialized. When individuals repeatedly perform narrow and specialized tasks, they are unlikely to see their work as very challenging or intrinsically motivating.

As an example of how to diagnose and change a work system in this situation, assume we have administered the JDS to several customer service representatives (CSRs) and managers of a local branch office of an insurance company. Assume the average JDS scores for each job characteristic are as depicted in Figure 6.1. From this figure, you can determine where the problems are and, if one is to improve CSR attitudes, where changes need to be made. Specifically, as compared to managers, CSRs report especially low levels of skill variety, task identity, and autonomy. Under such circumstances, you would expect the average CSR to report a low level of job satisfaction. But what can be done about it? How can the profile of a CSR job be made to look more like that of the manager? Before specifically addressing this question, let us consider some general ways of increasing intrinsic job characteristics:

- ◆ *Job rotation.* Job rotation entails employees perform different jobs; typically, rotation occurs once employees have mastered their present job and are no longer challenged

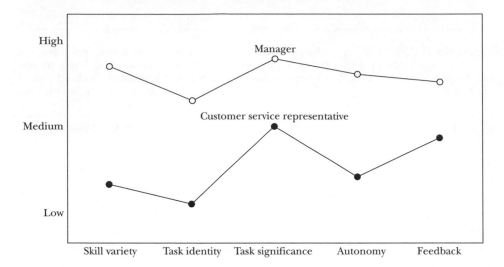

FIGURE 6.1 Job characteristics profiles for job of customer service representative and manager

by it. Many companies use job rotation to increase flexibility – i.e. having employees capable of performing a wide variety of jobs allows adjustments to be made due to absenteeism, injury, or changes in product demand. By allowing substitution, job rotation can be particularly useful when an employer faces skill shortages (Berry, 2008). However, there are also substantial satisfaction benefits. Many employees enjoy trying their hand at different jobs, and appreciate the broader perspective it provides (such as when Southwest Airlines ticket agents may try loading bags on the plane). Some companies even pay people for successfully rotating into new jobs; such pay systems are referred to as "skill-based pay."

◆ *Job enlargement*. Job enlargement, sometimes called horizontal loading, involves expanding the number of tasks associated with a particular job. The difference between job enlargement and job rotation may seem subtle. The difference is that with job rotation, jobs are not really redesigned. Employees simply systematically move from one job to another, but while they are performing a job, the nature of the work has not changed. Job enlargement is a more fundamental intervention because it involves actually changing the job. For example, an assembly line worker who formerly performed one discrete operation (bolting the seat to the floor of a car) may instead be part of a team that performs many phases of the assembly operation. Another example would be workers in a grocery store who may work at the checkout counter, stock shelves, or clean, depending on what needs to be done.

◆ *Job enrichment*. Job enrichment, sometimes referred to as vertical loading, involves increasing the *responsibilities* of the job. Compared to job enlargement, the increase in the variety in the work of an enriched job may be no more than of an enlarged job, but the responsibility (and often autonomy) of the job is increased. For example, self-managed work teams may take on responsibilities such as staffing, scheduling, and performance appraisal formerly assigned to the team's supervisor. One example of job enrichment occurred at the Duncan Hines angel food cake factory in Jackson,

Tennessee. Workers who combine the ingredients for the cake mix are given letters from customers who have had problems with the cake mix. Employees may call up customers to help them solve their problems and, in the meantime, perhaps learn how to make better mixes or provide clearer instructions (Johns, 1996). A similar job enrichment program was undertaken in a totally different industry. Saturn relies on enriched production work teams which are "self-directed and empowered with the authority, responsibility, and resources necessary to meet their day to day assignments and goals, including producing budget, quality, housekeeping, safety and health, maintenance, material and inventory control, training, job assignments, repairs, scrap control, vacation approvals, absenteeism, supplies, record keeping, personnel selection and hiring, work planning, and work scheduling" (Saturn Memorandum of Agreement, 1985).

Now let us return to our insurance company example. Having learned about the ways in which intrinsic job characteristics can be increased, how could we redesign the CSR job? Rotating CSRs through different specialties could increase skill variety. Providing CSRs with feedback on the resolution of each claim could raise task identity. Giving CSRs more latitude in servicing customers could increase autonomy. Though each of these piecemeal changes may have merit, a deeper approach would be to assign CSRs responsibility for entire claims. Although there are some aspects of the job that a CSR may not be able to accomplish on their own, these could be referred to a claims adjuster, or CSRs could be trained to take on some of the duties of a claims adjuster. By assigning an employee responsibility for the entire claim, both horizontal and vertical loading are increased. Horizontal loading is enhanced because the CSR may need to arrange a rental car for the customer, determine whether a check has been processed, or negotiate with another insurance company representative about payment on a claim. Vertical loading is increased by giving the CSR discretion to make decisions about various aspects of the claim (e.g. whether to provide a loaner car for a particular claim, prioritizing claims, etc.). The downsides of redesigns such as this come in the form of training costs and the recognition that there are some employees who do not welcome challenging work. In addition, more mentally challenging jobs may require more intelligent employees and, subsequently, higher compensation costs. However, research indicates that the benefits of job redesign generally outweigh these costs (Cascio, 1991).

CRITICISMS AND LIMITATIONS

The Job Characteristics Model has amassed a great deal of support in the research literature. Despite the support, there have been several criticisms of the model. Two of the most important concerns are reviewed below.

Measurement of job characteristics

The Job Characteristics Model assumes that job characteristics cause job satisfaction. It is important to remember that the measures of intrinsic job characteristics typically are perceptual. According to some researchers, perceptual measures are susceptible to biasing influences such as mood. If employees' mood at the time of rating their job characteristics and job satisfaction affects both ratings, the correlation between perceptions of job characteristics and job satisfaction would be inflated (i.e. the real relationship would be lower than it appears). Furthermore, there are concerns that the relationship is not solely from job characteristics to job satisfaction; job satisfaction may also (or instead) cause perceptions of job characteristics. Although some research has supported these criticisms, other research has shown that when these limitations are remedied (e.g. using objective measures of job characteristics), a relationship between job characteristics and job satisfaction still exists (Glick, Jenkins, and Gupta, 1986; Judge, Bono, and Locke, 2000). Thus, while these criticisms are important to keep in mind, they do not undermine the model.

Motivational vs. mechanistic work design approaches

Motivational approaches to work design, grounded in industrial and organizational psychology and exemplified by the Job Characteristics Model, aim to capitalize on the motivational and attitudinal benefits that accrue from a challenged and psychologically fulfilled workforce. In contrast, mechanistic approaches, as advocated by classical industrial engineers, emphasize increased efficiency through factors such as work skill simplification and task specialization. The mechanistic approach would seem to conflict with job design endorsed by the JCM: the former emphasizes efficiency in production (high output levels, low error rates, etc.), the latter emphasizes the advantages of a satisfied and motivated workforce (Campion, 1988; Edwards, Scully, and Brtek, 2000).

Subsequent research by Campion, Morgeson, and colleagues (Campion, Mumford, Morgeson, and Nahrgang, 2005; Morgeson and Campion, 2002), however, suggests that steps can be taken to minimize these efficiency-satisfaction tradeoffs. For instance, utilizing a *level-separation approach*, one might design organizational structures based on the mechanistic principles of standardization and simplification and still implement the core motivational characteristics within individual jobs. Thus, "basic efficiencies are built into the flow of the work, yet individual jobs are satisfying" (Campion et al., 2005, p. 371). Or, *a sequential approach* could be implemented in which both approaches are applied in succession. For instance, after tasks are specialized, management may take steps to increase autonomy and feedback.

MODERATORS

Employees with low Growth Need Strength

In considering the recommendation that organizations should increase the mental challenge of jobs, one might wonder whether everyone seeks mental challenge in their work. Indeed, the relationship between intrinsic job characteristics and job satisfaction depends on employees' Growth Need Strength (GNS). Growth Need Strength (GNS) is employees' desire for personal development, especially as it applies to work. High GNS employees want their jobs to contribute to their personal growth, and derive satisfaction from performing challenging and personally rewarding activities. One of the ways GNS is measured is by asking employees, with a survey, to choose between one job that is high on extrinsic rewards (such as pay) and one that is high on intrinsic rewards. For example, one item asks

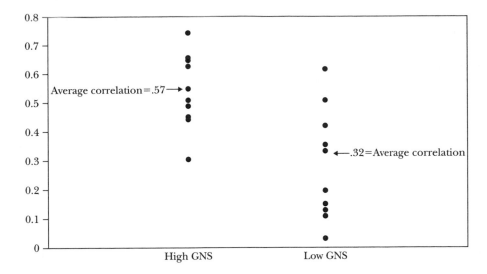

FIGURE 6.2 Studies of the correlation between intrinsic job characteristics and job satisfaction for individuals with high (High GNS) and low (Low GNS) Growth Need Strength

the employee to choose between "A job where the pay is very good" and "A job where there is considerable opportunity to be creative and innovative." Individuals who strongly prefer the latter job are likely to be high on GNS – all else equal, high GNS people prefer jobs that are challenging and interesting, which allow them to work autonomously and use a number of skills, over jobs that are otherwise rewarding (high pay, good supervision, pleasant co-workers, etc.). According to the model, intrinsic job characteristics are especially satisfying for individuals who score high on GNS. In fact, research supports this aspect of the theory. As is shown in Figure 6.2, across the 10 studies that have investigated the role of GNS in the relationship between intrinsic job characteristics and job satisfaction, the relationship tends to be stronger for employees with high GNS (average r = .57) than for those with low GNS (average r = .32). However, as the figure shows, it is important to note that intrinsic job characteristics are related to job satisfaction even for those who score low on GNS (Frye, 1996).

Employees who value other job attributes

Thus far we have established that job satisfaction is best promoted through intrinsically challenging work because most employees value the work itself more than other job attributes. One exception to this principle is that employees who do not care about intrinsic job characteristics (low GNS) will be less satisfied by challenging work. A more generalized means of considering this exception is through values. It may not be that only employees with low GNS will respond less favorably to intrinsic job characteristics, the exception would also apply to employees who value other job or organizational attributes. Following his definition of values as that which one desires or considers important, Locke (1976) argued that individuals' values would determine what satisfied them on the job. Only the unfulfilled job values that were important to the individual would be dissatisfying. Thus, value-percept theory predicts that discrepancies between what is desired and received are dissatisfying only if the job facet is important to the individual. Because as a general rule individuals value work more than other job attributes, Locke's argument is consistent with the general principle described in this chapter. Thus, if intrinsic job characteristics were the most important job facet to most individuals, then Locke's theory would predict that increasing the level of intrinsic job characteristics (thus reducing the have-want discrepancy with respect to intrinsic characteristics) would be the most effective means of raising employees' job satisfaction. However, it must be recognized that when an employee does not value challenging work, other values must be fulfilled to satisfy the person.

Personality

Implicit in Locke's definition of job satisfaction is the importance of both feeling and thinking. People's evaluation of their jobs is a process of rational thought (How is my pay relative to my peers? Is my work as challenging as I would like?), but it is also influenced by people's dispositional outlook. Research has shown that unhappy children become dissatisfied workers later in life (Staw, Bell, and Clausen, 1986). There is even evidence that job satisfaction is partly heritable (see Arvey, Carter, and Buerkley, 1991). Thus, part of the reason we like or dislike our jobs has nothing to do with the jobs. Rather, it is due to our dispositional outlook that derives from our genes and early childhood experiences. Judge, Locke, Durham, and Kluger (1998) have found that the key dispositional factor leading to job satisfaction is core self-evaluations – if we have a positive self-regard, we are likely to see our jobs positively and undertake jobs that are challenging. Evidence indicates that core self-evaluations are related to job satisfaction through various processes, including that those with positive core self-evaluations both attain more challenging work, and perceive their work as more challenging and interesting (Judge et al., 2000). Individuals with positive core self-evaluations are also more likely to work toward goals for reasons that are consistent with their values (Judge, Bono, Erez, and Locke, 2005).

Dispositions are important in understanding job satisfaction. To a large extent, they are what cause two people with the same job to be differentially satisfied by it. The main practical implication of the dispositional source of job satisfaction is that if employers wish to raise satisfaction levels of their workforce, they need to select applicants with positive dispositions. However, the dispositional source of job satisfaction does not invalidate the general principle presented in this chapter; it merely explains why the general principle does not account for all the variation in job satisfaction. Over and above dispositional factors and mental challenge, people also value pay and being treated fairly.

Other moderators

In addition to the boundary conditions mentioned above, management wishing to capitalize on the potential benefits of mentally challenging work should consider several moderators that impact the success of job redesign. For instance, any time new tasks or skill requirements are added to a job, one should consider issues such as:

◆ Do the employees possess excess cognitive capacity to handle the additional job demands (Phillips, 2008)? If not, then increasing the job demands might overload the employees.

◆ Do the employees believe they can successfully perform the new job? If not, the organization may consider techniques designed to increase employee self-efficacy (see Chapter 10, this volume) before or during the implementation of the new job.

◆ Are the employees intrinsically interested in the new demands or tasks? Employee satisfaction is unlikely to increase when the challenge comes from tasks or jobs which are not personally interesting, e.g. studying the law is mentally challenging but many people have no interest at all in it (Holland, 1997).

CASE EXAMPLES

Job redesign at Volvo's manufacturing plants

In the early 1990s, the Volvo corporation was experiencing high levels of employee absenteeism and turnover in their manufacturing facilities due to dissatisfaction with the "mass production environments dominated by . . . Tayloristic work practices" (Wallace, 2008, p. 113). In manufacturing plants across Sweden and the UK, Volvo attempted to combat these issues by experimenting with alternatives to the traditional assembly line-style manufacturing work design. As one production manager put it, a change was needed in order to "give all employees the chance to develop as a whole person, to take more responsibility for their work environment, to have more space to decide on what work they will do and to have more control on their working environment" (Wallace, 2008, p. 115).

Following the job redesign initiative, rather than being assigned one particular activity along an assembly line, employees were grouped into autonomous work teams and given responsibility for the overall production of the vehicles (*high task identity*). Employees were afforded the opportunity to utilize a *variety of skills* as they rotated job tasks, from foundry work to machine maintenance to painting and detailing, etc., depending on situational demands or personal preferences (Thompson and Wallace, 1996). For instance, at the Tuve plant, workers were allowed to rotate jobs as frequently as once ever four hours (Thompson and Wallace, 1996), with no approval from upper management necessary (*high autonomy*). Each team was also responsible for inspecting their finished products, providing members with *feedback* concerning the quality of their work. These changes resulted in significant perceptual adjustments as employees no longer felt that they were merely "machine operators" but rather "car manufacturers" (*increased task significance*).

Volvo's commitment to making automobile assembly a more intrinsically motivating occupation resulted in several positive work outcomes. In its Kalmar plant, turnover dropped from 24% to 5% following reorganization (Jones, 1991). Furthermore, in the Volvo Truck Corporation (VTC) plants, absenteeism fell from 15% to 12% and machine tool efficiency increased by 40–90% in some units (Thompson and Wallace, 1996). The time required to manufacture automobiles was reduced by 2–4 hours per vehicle and overall production costs decreased as well (Wallace, 2008).

Despite the overwhelmingly positive outcomes experienced across several Volvo plants, by 2004, nearly all had been reconfigured to more similarly reflect previous assembly line structures. Critics postulated that this move was "not totally based on logical overarching decisions or rational decision management" (Engstrom, Blomquist, and Holmstrom, 2004, p. 836), but rather reflected three shortcomings. First, Volvo's desire to seek more international ventures put pressure on the corporation to adopt the lean processing approach that had become the dominant paradigm in the automobile industry (Wallace, 2008; Womack, Jones, and Roos, 1991). Second, as pointed out by Wagner (see Chapter 24, this volume), efficient work techniques and other valuable information residing within the autonomous work teams were not being successfully distributed across the organization, thus hindering Volvo's ability to capitalize on team-level innovations and remain competitive in a global industry. Finally, although Volvo committed heavily in the technological aspects of the job redesign, experts point out that its commitment to the social/managerial aspects were inadequate (Engstrom et al., 2004). Human resource functions such as employee selection, training, compensation, and performance evaluation were never properly redesigned to reflect the changed nature of the work. For instance, many employees lacked the prerequisite skills to accomplish their new tasks, resulting in considerable variation in the effectiveness of the autonomous work teams. In sum, altering the nature of work to increase intrinsic satisfaction is one tool organizations can use to influence employee attitudes and behaviors. However, as the Volvo case illustrates, job redesign must be considered in terms of internal (e.g. human resource practices) and external (e.g. global competition) factors to capitalize on the potential benefits of mentally challenging work.

Tom Warner

Tom Warner owns a plumbing, heating, and air-conditioning business in the Annapolis, Maryland, area. Warner had observed over the past few years that his business had fallen off somewhat in his primary market – commercial property-management firms. In order to cut costs, these firms were hiring handymen to do work in-house. Thus, Warner decided to pursue the residential market. But how could his business, with more than 250 people, compete against little mom-and-pop operators who built personal relationships with many clients? Warner's answer was to expand the jobs of his plumbers, electricians, and technicians so that each operated like they owned their own business.

Warner divided the Annapolis territory into smaller territories of approximately 10,000 households. Each of his non-staff employees was given a territory. The employees were trained in how to run their territory as if it were their own business. They learned sales techniques, budgeting, negotiating, cost estimating, and how to handle customer complaints. Warner's vision was to run his business using a staff of technically superb, friendly, and ambitious mechanics who operate like small-town tradespeople despite the big-city reality.

The redesign of mechanics' jobs has been quite successful. Although turnover initially increased (perhaps because low GNS employees did not like the redesigned jobs), the remaining employees have developed a strong sense of pride and ownership in their territory. The average mechanic puts in 63 hours a week. They not only fix pipes and repair heaters, they generate referrals, schedule their own work, do their own estimates, handle their own equipment, develop their own advertising campaigns, and collect their own receivables. Warner provides training, trucks, tools, phones, pagers, dispatchers, and an all-night answering service. He also performs such chores as payroll and taxes. His mechanics are then free to run their businesses the best way they see fit.

CONCLUSION

Job satisfaction matters. Employees who are satisfied with their jobs tend to perform better, withdraw less, and lead happier and healthier lives. Organizations whose employees are satisfied with their jobs are more likely to be productive and profitable. The single most effective way organizations can achieve a satisfied workforce is to provide their employees with mentally challenging work.

REFERENCES

Arvey, R. D., Carter, G. W., and Buerkley, D. K. (1991). Job satisfaction: Dispositional and situational influences. *International Review of Industrial and Organizational Psychology*, 6, 359–383.

Berry, M. (2008). Skills commission to investigate how to maximise staff potential. *Personnel Today* (retrieved from http://www.personneltoday.com on Sept. 4, 2008).

Campion, M. A. (1988). Interdisciplinary approaches to job design: A constructive replication with extensions. *Journal of Applied Psychology*, 73, 467–481.

Campion, M. A., Mumford, T. V., Morgeson, F. P., and Nahrgang, J. D. (2005). Work redesign: Eight obstacles and opportunities. *Human Resource Management*, 44, 367–390.

Cascio, W. F. (1991). *Costing Human Resources: The Financial Impact of Behavior in Organizations*. Boston: PWS-Kent.

Edwards, J. R., Scully, J. A., and Brtek, M. D. (2000). The nature and outcomes of work: A replication and extension of interdisciplinary work design research. *Journal of Applied Psychology*, 85, 860–868.

Engstrom, T., Blomquist, B., and Holmstrom, O. (2004). Reconstructing the history of the main Volvo Tuve plant. *International Journal of Operations and Production Management*, 24, 820–839.

Fisher, C. D., and Locke, E. A. (1992). The new look in job satisfaction research and theory. In C. J. Cranny, P. C. Smith, and E. F. Stone (eds), *Job Satisfaction* (pp. 165–194). New York: Lexington.

Frye, C. M. (1996). New evidence for the Job Characteristics Model: A meta-analysis of the job characteristics–job satisfaction relationship using composite correlations. Paper presented at the Eleventh Annual Meeting of the Society for Industrial and Organizational Psychology, San Diego, CA.

Glick, W. H., Jenkins, G. D., Jr., and Gupta, N. (1986). Method versus substance: How strong are underlying relationships between job characteristics and attitudinal outcomes? *Academy of Management Journal*, 29, 441–464.

Hackman, J. R., and Oldham, G. R. (1980). *Work Redesign*. Reading, MA: Addison-Wesley.

Harrison, D. A., Newman, D. A., and Roth, P. L. (2006). How important are job attitudes? A meta-analytic comparison of integrative behavioral outcomes and time sequences. *Academy of Management Journal*, 49, 305–325.

Harter, J. K., Schmidt, F. L., and Hayes, T. L. (2002). Business-unit-level relationship between employee satisfaction, employee engagement, and business outcomes: A meta-analysis. *Journal of Applied Psychology*, 87, 268–279.

Holland, J. L. (1997). *Making Vocational Choices: A Theory of Vocational Personalities and Work Environments*. Odessa, FL: Psychological Assessment Resources.

Humphrey, S. E., Nahrgang, J. D., and Morgeson, F. P. (2007). Integrating motivational, social, and contextual work design features: A meta-analytic summary and theoretical extension of the work design literature. *Journal of Applied Psychology*, 92, 1332–1356.

Iaffaldano, M. R., and Muchinsky, P. M. (1985). Job satisfaction and job performance: A meta-analysis. *Psychological Bulletin*, 97, 251–273.

Johns, G. (1996). *Organizational Behavior*. New York: HarperCollins.

Jones, H. G. (1991). Motivation for higher performance at Volvo. *Long Range Planning*, 24, 92–104.

Judge, T. A., Bono, J. E., Erez, A., and Locke, E. A. (2005). Core self-evaluations and job and life satisfaction: The role of self-concordance and goal attainment. *Journal of Applied Psychology*, 90, 257–268.

Judge, T. A., Bono, J. E., and Locke, E. A. (2000). Personality and job satisfaction: The mediating role of job characteristics. *Journal of Applied Psychology*, 85, 237–249.

Judge, T. A., and Church, A. H. (2000). Job satisfaction: research and practice. In C. L. Cooper and E. A. Locke (eds), *Industrial and Organizational Psychology: Linking Theory with Practice* (pp. 166–174). Oxford, UK: Blackwell.

Judge, T. A., Locke, E. A., Durham, C. C., and Kluger, A. N. (1998). Dispositional effects on job and life satisfaction: The role of core evaluations. *Journal of Applied Psychology*, 83, 17–34.

Judge, T. A., Thoresen, C. J., Bono, J. E., and Patton, G. K. (2001). The job satisfaction – job performance relationship: A qualitative and quantitative review. *Psychological Bulletin*, 127, 376–407.

Jurgensen, C. E. (1978). Job preferences (what makes a job good or bad?). *Journal of Applied Psychology*, 50, 479–487.

Kovach, K. A. (1997). Do you know your staff? *Industry Trends*, September 26.

Locke, E. A. (1976). The nature and causes of job satisfaction. In M. D. Dunnette (ed.), *Handbook of Industrial and Organizational Psychology* (pp. 1297–1343). Chicago: Rand McNally.

Morgeson, F. P., and Campion, M. A. (2002). Minimizing tradeoffs when redesigning work: Evidence from a longitudinal quasi-experiment. *Personnel Psychology*, 55, 589–612.

Morgeson, F. P., and Humphrey, S. E. (2006). The Work Design Questionnaire (WDQ): developing and validating a comprehensive measure for assessing job design and the nature of work. *Journal of Applied Psychology*, 91, 1321–1339.

Phillips, J. M. (2008). The role of excess cognitive capacity in the relationship between job characteristics and cognitive task engagement. *Journal of Business and Psychology*, 23, 11–24.

Rentsch, J. R., and Steel, R. P. (1992). Construct and concurrent validation of the Andrews and Withey Job Satisfaction Questionnaire. *Educational and Psychological Measurement*, 52, 357–367.

Saturn Memorandum of Agreement (1985). Saturn Corporation, Detroit, MI.

Staw, B. M., Bell, N. E., and Clausen, J. A. (1986). The dispositional approach to job attitudes: A lifetime longitudinal test. *Administrative Science Quarterly*, 31, 437–453.

Tait, M., Padgett, M. Y., and Baldwin, T. T. (1989). Job and life satisfaction: A reevaluation of the strength of the relationship and gender effects as a function of the data of the study. *Journal of Applied Psychology*, 74, 502–507.

Thompson, P., and Wallace, T. (1996). Redesigning production through teamworking. *International Journal of Operations and Production Management*, 16, 103–118.

Wallace, T. (2008). Cycles of production: from assembly lines to cells to assembly lines in the Volvo Cab plant. *New Technology, Work, and Employment*, 23, 111–124.

Womack, J., Jones, D., and Roos, D. (1991). *The Machine that Changed the World*. New York: Harper-Perennial.

EXERCISES

Identifying factors related to job satisfaction

The National Opinion Research Center at the University of Chicago surveyed over 50,000 Americans to determine which occupations scored the highest and lowest in terms of overall job satisfaction. Whereas firefighters and physical therapists were generally very satisfied employees, roofers and cashiers were generally unsatisfied with their jobs.

Use the Department of Labor's Occupational Information Network (O*NET; http://online.onetcenter.org) to compare job descriptions and relevant knowledge, skills, abilities, and other characteristics of: (a) firefighters, (b) physical therapists, (c) roofers, and (d) cashiers. In terms of the core characteristics of the Job Characteristics Model, which occupations inherently have high levels of task identity, task significance, skill variety, autonomy, and feedback? Judging from these four jobs, do higher values of JCM core characteristics appear to correlate with higher job satisfaction? What other factors might impact the satisfaction scores?

Redesigning jobs to increase mental challenge

Identify three separate jobs. These can be current jobs, jobs you have had in the past, and/or jobs that you are familiar with. Use the Job Diagnostic Survey (Table 6.1) to assess each job's motivating potential. Formulate a plan to redesign the jobs that will increase their motivating potential. While working, think about the following issues:

1. How will redesigning your jobs impact other jobs within the organization?
2. What Human Resource (HR) functions (recruitment, selection, training, performance appraisal, compensation, etc.) will be impacted by the redesigned jobs? What can you do to realign HR functions with your new jobs?
3. Are some jobs easier to redesign than others? What factors make a job easy or hard to redesign?
4. Is it easier to increase some core JCM characteristics than others? What core JCM characteristics are easy or hard to adjust?
5. What are the costs associated with your job redesign plans? Given these costs, do you think an organization would benefit from implementing your changes?

7

Control Voluntary Turnover by Understanding its Causes

Marion B. Eberly, Brooks C. Holtom, Thomas W. Lee, and Terence R. Mitchell[*]

It's no secret, of course, that many people quit their jobs. Whether voluntary employee turnover is a problem, however, "depends." Sometimes, an individual's volitional quitting can be a *major* problem. In certain parts of the food and beverage industry, for example, turnover is routinely well over 100% annually, and many managers must often worry about simply having enough employees to keep their operations running. In segments of the software industry, moreover, losing a single key employee can not only decrease the likelihood of a project's success, but it can also reduce investors' confidence in the firm and thereby dramatically lower that firm's stock price. Sometimes, employee turnover can be far less of a problem, and in some cases it is even desired. If employees can be readily hired, trained, and integrated into the company's operations and culture, quitting might only be a minor nuisance. Relatedly, turnover may even be desirable because it serves as an immediate constraint on labor costs. Plus, the voluntary exit of a poor performer may be a welcome opportunity to strengthen the organization's human capital through selection. Thus, employee turnover is not necessarily bad or good. Instead, it is an ongoing organizational issue that needs to be managed. Thus, understanding how employees decide to leave is essential to gaining control.

Empirical research has established that there are four *complementary* approaches to understanding the turnover process. Two of these approaches focus on who quits and how they quit. In the first approach, leaving is traditionally described through a process initiated by an individual's feelings and beliefs. More specifically, job dissatisfaction is theorized to initiate a variety of job-search behaviors and corresponding comparative evaluations on the identified employment opportunities that, in turn, set the stage for an employee's quitting.

---

[*] All four authors contributed equally to this chapter and are listed in alphabetical order.

The second approach is called the "unfolding model of voluntary turnover." In contrast to traditional ideas, the unfolding model (a) describes multiple quitting processes, (b) includes non-cognitive and external-to-the-person factors, and (c) explains how *relative job satisfaction* can prompt an employee's departure. Rather than focusing on why people *leave*, the third approach examines the reasons why people *stay*. The broad influences that determine an employee's choice to remain within a job are represented by the job embeddedness concept. Job embeddedness captures the extent to which the employee is tied to the job, considering both on- and off-the-job factors. Finally, in the fourth approach, understanding focuses on the company's definition of the circumstances surrounding a person's leaving. Viewed from the manager's perspective, the questions are whether an employee's quitting is functional or dysfunctional as well as whether it is avoidable or unavoidable.

Based on these four approaches, we clarify in this chapter how turnover might best be understood and managed. First, we describe each of these four approaches and their corroborating evidence. Second, we summarize this body of evidence to identify the signals that management should monitor in order to predict future employee quitting. Third, we explain what to do after observing the signals of the enhanced likelihood of turnover. Fourth, we highlight notable exceptions. That is, we suggest conditions under which our recommended signs and actions may be more or less meaningful.

APPROACH 1: WHAT TRADITIONAL THEORIES ABOUT TURNOVER TELL US

Monitor job attitudes and withdrawal cognitions

The theorized linkages.   Based on the evidence to date, managers have *good* reason to expect links between job (dis)satisfaction and employee turnover. (See Hom and Griffeth (1995) for an excellent, comprehensive academic treatment of the major psychological theories of turnover using this perspective.) First, the lower the level of an employee's job satisfaction, the lower will be the level of his or her organizational commitment. Second, the lower these two job attitudes are, the stronger will be the initial thoughts, feelings, and expected positive outcomes of quitting. Third, according to this traditional approach, these thoughts, feelings, and expected outcomes lead most people to search for another job. The job opportunities found during this job search are then evaluated. Finally, actual quitting occurs when a "better" job opportunity is found. We hasten to note that "better" has rarely been fully defined. Most often, improved economic outcomes are implied (e.g. compensation and financial opportunities) but seldom explicitly stated.

The evidence.   Perhaps equally enlightening as the traditional dissatisfaction-induced leaving processes themselves, the statistical findings provide *compelling* reasons for a manager to expect the following stable and consistent relationships. The statistics that are provided in parentheses below are: (a) averaged across multiple studies; (b) weighted by large sample sizes; and (c) statistically significant. Furthermore, these values are taken from reports that quantitatively summarize the data from numerous empirical studies, by Griffeth, Hom, and Gaertner (2000), Meyer, Stanley, Herscovitch, and Topolnytsky (2002), and Spector (1997). Our description of a statistic's size (e.g. large, moderate, or small) derives from the common standards in the social sciences.

First, overall job satisfaction strongly correlates with affective organizational commitment (r = .65), and the intentions to search for another job (r = −.60) and intentions to leave (r = −.46). More specifically, lower scores on job attitude measures are consistently associated with more thoughts of leaving and job-search activities. Second, job satisfaction (r = −.19), organizational commitment (r = −.23), thoughts of quitting (r = .24), and intentions to search (r = .29) and intentions to leave (r = .38) correlate moderately well with *actual turnover behavior*. In other words, these variables are consistently associated with employee withdrawal. Third, until people quit, less satisfied employees are absent slightly more often (r's between −.10 and −.15), somewhat less helpful to co-workers (r's between .22 and .26), and perform their jobs more poorly (r = .25). Similarly, less affectively committed employees also perform fewer citizenship behaviors (r = .32), perform their jobs more poorly (r = .17), and have higher turnover intentions (r = −.51). Thus, employees with poor job attitudes often exhibit multiple negative behaviors and can be difficult to manage.

What to monitor first: job attitudes.   Every traditional theory on employee turnover includes job dissatisfaction as either the primary starting point or as an early stage in the turnover process. Moreover, the evidence indicates *consistent* and *large* correlations (cited above) between job satisfaction and the intermediate variables (e.g. organizational commitment, intention to search or to leave) before actual employee turnover occurs. In turn, the evidence reveals *consistent, moderate-sized, and predictive over time* correlations between the intermediate variables and actual quitting. When considered together, *job satisfaction* and *organizational commitment* should be monitored as clear and compelling indicators of future employees' quitting.

Merely analyzing employee job satisfaction and organizational commitment in a static manner is not enough. It is imperative to examine attitude trends over time. Employees may experience significant decreases in attitudes over time and these changes may lead to an increase in search and quit intentions and actual turnover. For example, employees who appear to be satisfied with their jobs may decide to quit because some aspect of their jobs changed over the past few weeks and made them be less satisfied than before. A static approach to monitoring job attitudes would miss these nuances, and managers might therefore inaccurately assume that these employees will most likely not leave. Eventual leavers will likely experience a decline in job satisfaction and organizational commitment over time, therefore rendering a dynamic monitoring of these attitudes essential to managers (Bentein, Vandenberg, Vandenberghe, and Stinglhamber, 2005; Kammeyer-Mueller, Wanberg, Glomb, and Ahlburg, 2005).

What to monitor second: global withdrawal cognitions.   These traditional approaches most often conceptualize factors such as thoughts of quitting, expected utility of job search, cost of quitting, intention to search, evaluation of alternative jobs, comparisons between current and alternative jobs, and intention to leave as separate entities. Correspondingly, organizational behavior researchers have sought to measure and study these variables separately. An enduring problem, however, is that these intermediate variables (between job satisfaction and turnover) are difficult to separate accurately (e.g. using various statistical methods). As a result, several turnover scholars have sought to simplify the meaning of these "intermediate steps." More specifically, these numerous factors have been reconceptualized and empirically measured as a global and broader-based variable labeled "withdrawal cognitions."

When measured directly, global withdrawal cognitions consistently correlate with actual turnover (r = .30). Thus, it is advisable to monitor employees' global withdrawal cognitions. Similar to job attitudes, managers will benefit from monitoring changes in withdrawal cognitions over time through surveys and questionnaires. Eventual leavers are likely to increase their withdrawal behaviors and cognitions under this traditional approach while stayers likely do not change (Kammeyer-Mueller et al., 2005). In short, the "evidence" informs us to dynamically monitor job attitudes and global withdrawal cognitions as leading indicators of potential turnover.

CASE EXAMPLE

According to hotel survey firm Market Metrix, on average, US hotels will replace two thirds of their workers every year. The annual costs of recruiting, selecting and training these replacements as well as the associated productivity losses range from $100,000 at a small property to more than $1,000,000 at a large hotel. In this competitive industry where labor costs account for nearly one half of total operating costs, expenses incurred because of high staff turnover can mean the difference between making a profit or loss in any given year. Given this context, consider the following example.

In just a few years, Joie de Vivre Hospitality has been able to drive staff turnover at the Hotel Carlton (San Francisco, California) from more than 50% a year to below 10% a year (Dvorak, 2007). While pay and benefits are largely unchanged, simple things that make a difference in morale have changed. The former management company at the hotel did not like to replace aging vacuums despite staff complaints. When Joie de Vivre took over in 2003, the new manager bought each of the 15 housekeepers a new vacuum – and he replaces them annually. A Hotel Carlton employee mentions this gesture as one of many that "seems to show that this company cares about us more." Other low-cost, high-impact changes include English as a second language and Microsoft Excel courses as well as regular dinners for employees and their bosses to communicate informally.

APPROACH 2: WHAT THE UNFOLDING MODEL OF TURNOVER TELLS US

Monitor shocks and paths as well as job attitudes and global withdrawal cognitions

The overall model.   By design, the unfolding model offers a broader perspective than the traditional theories of turnover. (See Lee and Mitchell (1994) for a detailed description of this model.) Based on the evolving evidence, managers should have confidence that the unfolding model broadly and accurately describes the leaving process. More specifically, the unfolding model informs us about *four* basic patterns of thoughts and actions (or psychological "paths") for leaving organizations. In one particular pattern, which is labeled "path 4," leaving is seen as *quite* similar to the traditional ideas of turnover described previously. Job dissatisfaction prompts thoughts of leaving that lead, in turn, to job search, evaluation of alternatives, and eventual departure from the job. Thus, much of the evidence on the traditional ideas about turnover *also* pertains to path 4 leaving. From an applied perspective, both traditional and path 4 approaches inform the manager to monitor employees' *negative* or *declining* job attitudes.

In paths 1, 2, and 3, a fundamentally different pattern is asserted. In contrast to dissatisfaction-induced quitting, the leaving process begins with a shock – an external-to-the-person event that causes him to think about leaving. Shocks serve to shake people out of their daily, habitual, ongoing patterns and routines. Although all shocks are mediated by an individual's perceptual processes, their jarring nature renders them easily identifiable, describable, and understandable by the employee and manager. Thus, shocks are a conceptual tool that keeps monitoring and observations firmly grounded on work behaviors and the employee's immediate situation. In our research, for example, people report that shocks can be: (a) positive (e.g. acceptance into graduate school) or negative (e.g. a nurse being forced into a life-threatening emergency surgery for which she was unprepared); (b) expected (e.g. a spouse's retirement) or unexpected (e.g. being denied a six-month leave of absence); and (c) organization related (e.g. the hospital shifts from individual-based to team-based nursing) or personal (e.g. becoming pregnant with one's third child). As a result, shocks *augment* job attitudes and global withdrawal cognitions as key antecedent signals to subsequent employee turnover and are easily identifiable by employees.

The unfolding model offers a unique lens through which to examine turnover, because it focuses on the *reasons* why people leave, and oftentimes these reasons are unrelated to attitudes such as job satisfaction and organizational commitment. Thus, exploring turnover *reasons* provides researchers and managers with a more complete and accurate picture of why employees leave, which in turn facilitates turnover management and control. Maertz and Griffeth (2004) developed a typology of turnover motives and argued that these motives capture the most proximal causes of turnover cognitions and therefore are the best predictors of actual turnover behavior. Combining these eight motives with the unfolding model, Maertz and Campion (2004) show that the reasons systematically relate to specific decision paths. Exploring turnover reasons therefore can tell us which paths employees will choose.

Monitor for specific paths.   Whereas monitoring for job attitudes, global withdrawal cognitions, and shocks is fairly straightforward, determining *which* specific path employees may take can be more complicated; but such monitoring offers the manager greater understanding of turnover. In path 1, a shock triggers a person to use a *pre-existing* action plan (or what social psychologists call a script). Minimal mental deliberations occur. A person leaves *without* considering his or her current attachment to the organization (e.g. organizational commitment) and *without* considering his or her current job alternatives. Unlike traditional ideas and path 4, job satisfaction is essentially *irrelevant*. In path 1, a satisfied person can appear to leave abruptly but is in fact following a pre-planned course of action. For example, an interviewee reported the following: "It was very simple; I am going to graduate school . . . It had nothing to do with my job. It had everything to do with my personal situation . . . Very quickly, as soon as I got the letter that I was accepted into graduate school, the decision was made" (Lee, Mitchell, Wise, and Fireman, 1996, p. 17). Note that path 1 involves a shock (e.g. the acceptance letter), script (e.g. return to graduate school), no job search, and no evaluation of alternatives.

In path 2, a shock prompts a person to reconsider his or her basic attachment to the organization because of *violations* to one's basic values, personal or professional goals, and/or plans for goal attainment ("images"). After completing these mental deliberations, a person leaves the organization *without* a search for work alternatives. Unlike traditional ideas and path 4 but like path 1, job satisfaction is also largely *irrelevant*. In path 2, a satisfied person can leave abruptly because she is reacting to the shock itself. For example, an employee recently left a bank where we were conducting research. In her words, she told us the following:

> I was working and minding my own business. Then, a new person was hired and she was pretty vocal. One day she was complaining about her pay. While that made me mad, what was worse is that I had been at the bank for over a year and she was making a dollar an hour more than me while doing the same job. I quit the next day.

Note that path 2 involves a shock (e.g. learning about the pay of a fellow employee), no script, violations (e.g. images of personal and professional goal attainment), no job search, and no evaluation of alternatives.

In path 3, a shock provokes a person to consider whether an attachment could form with another organization because of violations to one's basic values, personal or professional goals, and/or plans for goal attainment. The mental deliberations due to the shock and violations lead an individual to search for another job and to evaluate specific alternatives and one's current job. Unlike traditional ideas and paths 1 and 2, a reasonably job-satisfied person can leave for a *more* satisfying job. In path 3, job dissatisfaction may or may *not* be present. Previously, we reported the following example of path 3 leaving:

> Sammy Lew (a fictitious name) was a forty-five year old former electrical engineer who had worked for a major military-defense company. [Mr. Lew] . . . had worked for the same firm since graduation twenty-three years earlier. For the last ten years, Mr. Lew supervised a group of twelve engineers. When asked why he left his former company to become a real estate developer, Mr. Lew said that . . . it was the departure from the firm of another work group member. That departure left Mr. Lew as the work group's oldest and clearly most out-of-date engineer. [He realized that] he had minimal advancement prospects and that "it was time to move on." As such, he evaluated his interests, aspirations, and available opportunities. Although he had no particular connection to his new profession, real estate development appeared, on balance, his best choice. He quit the defense company upon finding an acceptable job in real estate. (Lee and Maurer, 1997, p. 249)

Note that path 3 involves a shock (e.g. co-worker's quitting), no script, violations (e.g. images of professional goal attainment), job search (e.g. finding real-estate work), and evaluation of alternatives (e.g. in comparison to his interests, aspirations, and available alternatives).

The evidence

ACCURATE CLASSIFICATIONS.   A fundamental test of the unfolding model is whether its four paths can accurately describe employees' actual leaving. In a set of initial studies, Lee et al. (1996) and Lee, Mitchell, Holtom, McDaniel, and Hill (1999) reported that 33 of 44 nurses (75%) and 212 of 229 former accountants from Big 6 public accounting firms (93%) could be accurately classified into paths 1–4. In independent tests of the model, 86% of public accountants (Donnelly and Quinn, 2006) and 77% of nurses were successfully classified (Morrell, Loan-Clarke, Arnold, and Wilkinson, in press). Holtom, Mitchell, Lee, and Inderrieden (2005) illustrated that precipitating events, or shocks, more often are the immediate cause of turnover than job dissatisfaction. Specifically, across 1200 "leavers" from a variety of industries, 60% reported that a shock precipitated their turnover, of which 59% were unexpected, 40% were personal, and 64% were positive. Similarly, Morrell, Loan-Clarke, and Wilkinson (2004) reported that 44.3% of the nurses in their sample considered a shock their primary reason for leaving while 43.8% of nurses did so in another study (Morrell, 2005).

PATH SPEED.   In addition to accurate classifications, a second testable attribute of the unfolding model involves the speed with which the four paths unfold. More specifically, paths vary by their levels of mental deliberation. For example, extensive evaluation of alternatives should take more time than doing no or minimal evaluations. Furthermore, paths differ by whether their basic features are readily available for mental deliberation. If job search is required, for instance, information about alternative employment is less readily available than if no job search is involved. Thus, the path speed should vary systematically. Among nurses, Lee et al. (1996) reported that the durations of paths 1 and 2 were significantly shorter than those of path 4. Among accountants, Lee et al. (1999) reported shorter durations for paths 1 and 2 than for 3 and 4, and a shorter duration for path 3 than for path 4.

SHOCK CHARACTERISTICS.   In their sample of 44 nurses, Lee et al. (1996) reported that: (a) path 1 was significantly associated with expected and personal shocks (e.g. your spouse relocates); (b) path 2 was significantly associated with organizational and negative shocks (e.g. you are passed over for promotion); and (c) path 3 was significantly associated with organizational shocks (e.g. you receive a competitive job offer). With the sample of 229 former Big 6 accountants, Lee et al. (1999) replicated two of the earlier findings. In particular, path 1 positively associated with personal shocks and path 3 positively associated with organizational shocks. When taken together, these two significant associations may be robust across industries, occupations, and gender. Key findings of the Morrell et al. (2004) study indicate that: (1) shocks that are expected are more likely to be positive, personal, and lead to unavoidable leaving, (2) shocks that are negative are more likely to be work related, associated with dissatisfaction, affect others, and lead to avoidable leaving, (3) shocks that are more work related are less potent, associated with dissatisfaction and search for alternatives, and lead to avoidable leaving, and (4) shocks tend to cluster into work and non-work domains. In another study, Morrell (2005) reported three distinct clusters of leavers. Cluster 1 (n = 103) leavers had a work-related shock that was unexpected, negative, and affected other workers. Cluster 2 (n = 50) leavers had a personal shock that was expected, positive and private. Cluster 3 (n = 196) leavers had no shock and followed a more traditional dissatisfaction-induced process.

In sum, monitoring for shocks is not enough. Managers must also analyze a shock's content. Different types of shocks will require different interventions. Rich information about shocks can help a manager decide how quickly to act (e.g. in paths 1 or 2) and what factors might inhibit leaving. In comparison to the traditional approach, the unfolding model identifies additional considerations and adds richness to our understanding of the turnover process.

CASE EXAMPLE

As the following example illustrates, not all turnover is job dissatisfaction induced. Indeed, we have seen many path 1 quits in the news. One involves Nirav Tolia, 27, who left Yahoo!

as a senior manager of its e-commerce marketing and $10 million in unvested options. The reason he left: upon hearing a "really interesting start-up idea from a friend" (the shock), he decided in only one day's time to pursue his dream (a script) of a net start-up e-commerce company. Joining Tolia, Ramanathan Guha, 34, left America Online as one of its senior ranking engineers and $4 million in unvested options also to pursue this shared dream (Bronson, 1999). In short, managers need to be prepared for the possibility that some turnover will be precipitated very quickly. Hence, potential responses need to be considered in advance for a variety of possible scenarios – especially those involving key employees.

APPROACH 3: WHAT A FOCUS ON STAYING RATHER THAN LEAVING CAN TELL US

Monitor the reasons for staying in addition to the reasons for leaving

The concept of job embeddedness. To avoid voluntary turnover, it is at first intuitive for managers to identify the reasons why employees are leaving and to attempt to eliminate or minimize the impact of those reasons. The first two approaches to turnover have taken this perspective. In contrast, a more recent approach focuses on why employees are *staying* and what might prevent them from leaving. The concept of job embeddedness is focused on the broad array of factors that influence a person's staying in a job. Mitchell, Holtom, Lee, Sablynski, and Erez (2001) identified three ways an employee might be embedded within an organization: links, fit, and sacrifice. (Sacrifice refers here to loss of a value or values, not necessarily to sacrifice to others as in the case of altruism.) Links refer to employees' formal and informal connections to other individuals or institutions (e.g. friendship ties to co-workers). Fit refers to the extent to which employees' jobs and communities are compatible with their personal values, goals, and plans (e.g. congruence with organizational culture, satisfaction with local amenities). Research on employee fit has established that it significantly lowers turnover (e.g. Hoffman and Woehr, 2006). Finally, sacrifice captures the perceived losses that individuals may suffer when leaving their job (e.g. loss of retirement benefits, loss of friendship support). Together, links, fit, and sacrifice reflect an employees' embeddedness within a job. The more embedded they are, the less likely they will quit. What is particularly novel about this approach to turnover is that job embeddedness considers not only links, fit, and sacrifice *on*-the-job, but also *off*-the-job – in employees' personal lives within the local community. For example, an employee with children in middle school and a wife who is engaged in local charities would have many close links to the community and therefore be less likely to leave – especially if getting a new job would entail relocation.

In addition to considering an *individual* employee's level of job embeddedness, recent research suggests that turnover might be "contagious" and that co-workers' job embeddedness may influence an individual's decision to leave (Felps, Mitchell, Hekman, Lee, Holtom, and Harman, in press). The less embedded one's immediate co-workers are, the more likely it is that they engage in job search behaviors. In an environment characterized by low job embeddedness, it may be more acceptable to discuss leaving or talk about other job opportunities. Thus, the salience and viability of leaving may increase when observing a number of co-workers looking for other jobs.

The evidence.   A fundamental test of the concept of job embeddedness is whether it can predict actual turnover. A variety of studies have shown that this is indeed the case (cf. Allen, 2006; Crossley, Bennett, Jex, and Burnfield, 2007). Specifically, Mitchell et al. (2001) reported that overall job embeddedness (on- and off-the-job) was negatively correlated with intention to leave and predicted subsequent voluntary turnover in two different samples. In a study with bank employees, Lee, Mitchell, Sablynski, Burton, and Holtom (2004) found that off-the-job embeddedness predicted volitional absenteeism and voluntary turnover. Mallol, Holtom, and Lee (2007) compared the relative strength of job embeddedness and its relationship to turnover among Hispanics and Caucasians and concluded that while job embeddedness may vary in strength across different demographic groups, it is nonetheless a robust predictor of employee retention. Tanova and Holtom (in press) further found that notwithstanding differences in labor laws, cultural factors, and unemployment rates between Europe and the USA, job embeddedness predicts turnover effectively on both continents. In summary, the diverse nature of the samples used in job embeddedness research so far suggests that the negative relationship between job embeddedness and turnover may generalize to many occupations, organizations and contexts.

In addition to establishing that job embeddedness predicts employee retention, it is important to show that it provides additional insights over and above the information the other two approaches offer. Only then would it be justified and meaningful to separately monitor embeddedness signals in addition to work attitudes, withdrawal cognitions, shocks, and paths. Mitchell et al. (2001) showed that job embeddedness predicted turnover even after taking into account the influence of gender, job satisfaction, organizational commitment, job search, and perceived alternatives. In an independent study with a diverse sample, Holtom and Inderrieden (2006) found that job embeddedness significantly improved the prediction of turnover above gender and job satisfaction. In addition, they showed that those employees who stayed on the job had the highest levels of job embeddedness followed by employees who left due to a shock followed by employees who left with no precipitating shock. Not only does job embeddedness supplement the traditional approach to turnover research, but it also complements the unfolding model by showing how job embeddedness may buffer the effects of shocks on turnover.

CASE EXAMPLES

Organizations do not have to be large to develop customized approaches for creating job embeddedness. Moreover, the benefits of such efforts not only include improved employee retention but also positive reputations as great employers that generate word-of-mouth advertising and favorable public relations. Following are a number of examples from the Wall Street Journal's Top Small Workplaces report (Spors, 2007).

Jere Cowden, chief executive of Cowden Associates, an actuarial and human resources consulting firm, keeps a running list of consultants he deems to be the best in the business. Then, when hiring, he draws from this list and evaluates how well each prospective hire would fit into the culture. Most also complete personality assessments to further assess *fit with the organization.*

FRCH Design Worldwide, an architectural and interior design company, works very hard to promote strong corporate culture in the face of rapid growth. A big part of the company's effort is devoted to giving employees many chances to have fun together and participate both at work and in their free time. It hosts an annual summer picnic for employees and their families, a trip to a Kentucky horse-racing track, a yearly anniversary party, and a Christmas party for families, along with some sporting events. Every other Friday evening, the company hosts hour-long "wing-dings," social gatherings at the office with food and drinks. While not all organizations will see the need to socialize so frequently, many would benefit from consciously considering how to increase the *links among people in the organization* as FRCH has.

At Exactech, an orthopedic device manufacturer, an employee's training regimen depends on his or her employee-development plan – a document updated at least twice a year by the employee and his or her supervisor that lays out the employee's key development area and "action plan." Sometimes the action plan includes reading a book on a particular topic. Other times it includes taking classes. For Anacielo Vale-Grogan, it meant going to weekly French lessons and a six-week language course in France so she could better communicate with representatives from the company's large French distributor. Such a tailored approach to employee development is relatively unique and represents a *sacrifice an employee would have to make if he or she were to leave Exactech.*

While not everyone would want to work in rural Vermont, employees of NRG Systems, a wind-measurement equipment maker, clearly do. Only one of 81 employees working there quit last year. Part of the appeal is the unique setting. The company is housed in a newly built solar-powered building replete with skylights, a commons area reminiscent of a ski lodge and an indoor swimming pool. Further, employees are eligible for as much as $2300 annually for purchases of items such as Toyota Priuses, backyard wind turbines, solar-powered water heaters and energy-efficient light bulbs. No doubt these benefits attract unique employees who *fit with the local culture* and want to be *linked in such a community.*

Finally, Corporate Ink Public Relations seeks to help its people reside in the local area. Employees buying a home within 20 miles of the office can get loans of as much as $10,000 at 2% interest, to help make the down payment – and the loans are forgiven after five more years of employment. This is clearly an example of creating *sacrifices related to the community* where employees live and work.

APPROACH 4: WHAT THE CIRCUMSTANCES SURROUNDING TURNOVER TELL US

Monitoring for signs of voluntary quitting may not be enough

Is turnover functional and avoidable?   A prevailing belief among many organizational behavior scholars and practicing managers is that employee turnover should be minimized. From the manager's perspective, turnover can substantially increase the costs of staffing, training, and general administration. More subtly, turnover can also often disrupt a business unit's operations and increase the workloads of remaining employees.

In contrast to this prevailing belief, a small body of empirical research indicates that turnover should be more carefully managed rather than minimized. (See Maertz and Campion (1998) for a thorough discussion of these issues.) Importantly, employee turnover can be beneficial to a company if marginal performers voluntarily leave. Whereas "truly bad" performers might be fired, having too many marginal performers (e.g. those persons who are not sufficiently bad to fire) can minimize a firm's productivity. Similarly, employees who may be labeled "bad apples" because they are chronically negative, do not do their fair share of the work, or bully their co-workers, may have a detrimental effect on how groups work together, and "spoil the barrel" (Felps, Mitchell, and Byington, 2006). The value accrued by encouraging these people to resign can often offset that individual's overall replacement costs. In a related vein, the new employees can oftentimes be a source of new ideas and mechanisms to shake remaining employees out of their inertia (i.e. "getting new blood"). In those situations where labor costs are substantial and salaries are expected to increase consistently over time, turnover can result in substantial savings and thereby enhance organizational profitability (e.g. replace higher-wage customer service agents with lower-paid new workers). In short, employee turnover should *not* simply be minimized nor dismissed as an unmanageable process.

The evidence. Two empirical studies directly address the functionality and avoidability of leaving. Based on termination records examined for a seven-month period, Dalton, Krackhardt, and Porter (1981) identified the volitional quitting of 1389 former tellers from 190 bank branches. Next, each former teller's immediate supervisor reported judgments about (a) their preference on rehiring that person, (b) the former employee's job performance, and (c) the ease of replacing that leaver. These voluntary leavers represented a 32% overall turnover rate. When voluntary leavers were classified into dysfunctional (e.g. good employees quit) versus functional (e.g. marginal employees quit) based on the supervisor's judgments on preference for rehire and job performance, the turnover rate of dysfunctional leaving dropped to 18%. When classified by ease of replacement, dysfunctional turnover (e.g. hard to replace) dropped to 9% of the overall turnover rate. These data indicate that the quitting of *some* people is actually functional or good for the company.

Using a sample of nurses, Abelson (1987) compared the job attitudes among 136 stayers, 30 avoidable leavers, and 16 unavoidable leavers over a one-year period. Levels of job satisfaction and organizational commitment were significantly *lower* for avoidable than unavoidable leavers and stayers. That is, people who left for unavoidable reasons (e.g. a spouse relocates) had satisfaction and commitment levels comparable to those who stayed. People who left for avoidable reasons (e.g. bad work schedules) had worse attitudes than those who stayed or those who left for unavoidable reasons. In addition, levels of thinking of quitting and intentions to search and to leave were significantly *higher* for avoidable leavers than unavoidable leavers and stayers.

Should Turnover be Encouraged or Discouraged?

When considered together, these data indicate the desirability of further classifying voluntary turnover by functionality and avoidability. Nevertheless, it remains the manager's decision as to: (a) whether dysfunctional turnover should be discouraged; (b) whether functional turnover should be encouraged; and (c) whether such turnover is also avoidable or unavoidable. These decisions focus the manager on differentiating between people he wants to keep or lose.

CASE EXAMPLE

As Lars Dalgaard, CEO of Successfactors, explains, organizations have an interest in not keeping nasty and demeaning people (Sutton, 2007). Companies that tolerate such malicious employees have trouble recruiting the best talent and have problems keeping clients. This may lead to damaged reputations and reduced investor confidence. Other aspects of a business may also suffer. For example, creativity and innovation may be impaired. And cooperation with others within and outside the organization may suffer. In short, the loss of a bad apple may be one of the best examples of *functional turnover*.

ACTION IMPLICATIONS

When all evidence is considered together, the results suggest value in monitoring for job attitudes, global withdrawal cognitions, shocks, paths, and job embeddedness as well as examining the functionality and avoidability of voluntary turnover. Although each manager's situation will be different, general action implications can be inferred from the four approaches reviewed. Initially, a company needs to determine the "value to the firm" of each employee. That is, managers need to decide – based on a sound definition of job performance and importance – which individual's leaving should be seen as a functional quit and which should be seen as a dysfunctional quit.

Job performance and the issue of functionality

To judge whether a particular employee's quitting would be functional, managers must have a solid definition of job performance. Job performance is commonly determined by a job analysis and often operationalized by the content of the firm's employee evaluation form. Historically, a host of traditional variables have been applied: observable work behaviors (e.g. cooperation), measurable employee actions (e.g. call time availability for telemarketers), supervisory judgments (e.g. quality, quantity, and overall performance), tangible work outputs (e.g. number of widgets produced each day), or revenues generated (e.g. total sales dollars).

An emergent issue among organizational behavior scholars is whether job performance has been too narrowly defined. Underlying these various and traditional performance variables is the standard job. More specifically, performance is often tied very closely to the job's formally required tasks. Scholars of organizational behavior have recently asked whether measuring performance based on a job's required tasks and behaviors is too restrictive.

Substantial research evidence shows that: what gets measured directs employee attention (e.g. dimensions of job performance); setting standards or goals directs employee efforts and behaviors (e.g. good versus bad job performance); and providing feedback allows for corrective actions toward the standard (e.g. the semiannual job performance evaluation meeting). We *know* that by focusing attention toward one's narrowly prescribed job tasks, work effort, behavior, and performance follow. It is not surprising then that focusing on one's own job can also distract such work effort, behavior, and performance *away* from other beneficial organizational actions. For a lower-level employee, for example, a focus on one's job may decrease the likelihood of helping another employee do his job. At the immediate cost of lost opportunity of doing one's own prescribed job, that lower-level employee may impose larger costs on organizational effectiveness by *not* helping another employee perform or learn to perform a job. For a higher-level manager, a focus on one's narrowly defined job may decrease the likelihood of meeting the larger organizational role of representing the company at industry and community events. At no cost to doing one's own job, for instance, this manager may voluntarily represent the company's commitment to community well-being or individual citizenship. Thus, employees may overly focus on the immediate job and thereby actually hurt larger organizational functioning.

Organizational behavior scholars have labeled our traditional focus on well-defined and prescribed job behaviors as task performance, in-role performance, or job performance. In contrast, the broader focus that includes non-job-specific effort, behavior, and performance but still benefits the larger firm is labeled extra-role performance, contextual performance, or organizational citizenship behavior. In making decisions about an employee's functional versus dysfunctional and avoidable versus unavoidable quitting, managers should also decide whether individual and organizational effectiveness can be enhanced by a traditional focus on the narrowly defined job functions or by a broader focus on task *and* contextual performance. In our judgment, the broader focus is typically better than the narrower view toward individual and organizational effectiveness.

The details of the unfolding model and avoidability

The unfolding model becomes particularly helpful in assessing avoidability because (a) path 4 captures much of the traditional approach, and shocks capture much of the avoidability issue. Because the speed of path 1 quitting can be unpredictable and the speed of path 2 quitting can be quite quick, managers may have minimal opportunity to respond to shocks that may initiate such leaving. Instead, they may need to have already in place a mechanism that allows for proactive and quick actions aimed at encouraging *or* discouraging an employee's leaving (e.g. quick counteroffers, rapid and informal grievance procedures, open-door policies by the firm's top executives). One technique that we've developed is to gather examples of (or stories about) actual shocks (e.g. specific events that initiate actual quitting) from leavers and other examples of events that prompted stayers to think about quitting. Managers can then simply list these examples and ask current employees (a) whether these events would prompt thoughts of leaving and (b) what scripts they might have in place and follow if the event were to occur. This information can help managers anticipate the events that likely prompt thoughts of quitting and scripted actions. As a result, the informed manager can elect to be proactive (or inactive) in discouraging (or encouraging) leaving.

In contrast, quitting in paths 3 and 4 is more predictable and slower. Because people search for alternatives and evaluate the located options, managers may have more opportunity to respond. Thus, they may have more opportunity to craft individualized actions that can encourage or discourage quitting (e.g. matching pay increases from external job offers, dealing with accumulated job dissatisfaction, restructuring one's job responsibilities, reassigning employees to other units within the company, loaning employees to external service organizations like the United Way).

Besides merely reacting to employees' withdrawal behaviors and cognitions, managers can also take a more proactive stance and reduce turnover by attempting to embed employees within their jobs. Managers may increase their employees' job embeddedness by hiring employees who already have established ties to the organization (e.g. peer referrals) or the community. Then, for all the newcomers, it is important to effectively integrate them into the social fabric of the organization. For example, training all newcomers together as a group, revealing the exact timing of the progression through the various socialization stages, and providing positive social support through organizational role models are all ways through which new employees may be embedded on the job during their first weeks in the organization (Allen, 2006). Once socialized, managers may continue to influence their employees' ties, fit, and sacrifices by, for example, designing work around teams, establishing mentoring programs, organizing social events, and identifying clear promotional paths through training and developmental activities.

How to monitor job attitudes, global withdrawal cognitions, shocks, paths, and job embeddedness

Surveys. Job satisfaction, organizational commitment, global withdrawal cognitions, and job embeddedness can be efficiently and validly measured via organizational surveys. In particular, they can be assessed with standard, professionally developed, and well-researched measures (e.g. validated scales). For several of the better-known scales, moreover, they are copyrighted and commercially available. Some of these validated scales measure *global* job satisfaction, organizational commitment, withdrawal cognitions, and job embeddedness whereas others measure *facets* of satisfaction, commitment, withdrawal cognitions, and embeddedness. Although valid, standard scales are often quite long. As a result, questionnaire length can discourage survey completion, and less information is actually obtained. Although less reliable and less valid than the longer standard scales, researchers and managers often must compose and use a smaller number of original questions (e.g. one to five items) to measure overall job satisfaction, organizational commitment, global withdrawal cognitions, and job embeddedness. Albeit less desirable, long-standing research practice and enduring empirical evidence indicate an *acceptable* tradeoff between shorter questionnaire length and lower (though adequate) strength in predicting voluntary turnover (e.g. Arnold and Feldman, 1982).

Management by wandering around (MBWA). Although shocks and paths can be measured with surveys, these concepts are relatively new. As a result, there are *no* standard and validated scales for their measurement. In addition to the technique of listing actual and potential shocks and scripts (described above), there are other useful techniques for identifying paths. In their delightful book, *In Search of Excellence*, Peters and Waterman (1982) initially recommended MBWA. The idea is simple and appealing. Managers should *prioritize* and *allocate* a certain portion of their day to watching, talking, and generally interacting with their employees. If done consistently and sincerely, understanding, empathy, and trust should develop. As a direct result, managers should readily learn: (a) what individuals interpret as shocks; (b) whether scripts exist; (c) the specific content of images and if image violations occur; (d) how embedded the employee is; and (d) whether job search cognitions and behaviors are engaged. Although performance appraisals may also generate some of this information (assuming managers have established an open and honest relationship with their employees), they are typically only conducted once or twice a year and would therefore miss out on crucial time-dependent information such as the occurrence of a shock. Consistently "wandering around," however, allows managers to collect data in real time and to intervene immediately as needed.

EXCEPTIONS

The research that we've reviewed offers some clear advice on managing (or controlling) employee turnover such as monitoring for signs or predictors of employees' quitting and assessing the functionality and avoidability of employee turnover. With that said, however, there are a number of considerations that should strengthen or weaken our recommended actions.

Importance of workforce stability

Selective retention is less important in situations where workforce stability is *less* critical; conversely stated, retention is more important in situations where stability is more critical. Four questions immediately arise. First, are replacement employees readily available? If replacement employees are readily available, selective retention should be less important to managers. An immediate indicator of availability is the unemployment rate in the "relevant labor market." Numerous studies indicate a consistently negative, substantial relationship between aggregate turnover and unemployment rates (r's commonly .80 and higher). In general, the higher the unemployment rate, the higher the availability of replacement employees.

Second, can the requisite job-specific knowledge, skills, and abilities (as well as broader needs for contextual, citizenship-based performance) be readily taught? If success in training is relatively quick and inexpensive, selective retention should also be less of an issue. Two immediate and related indicators of training success are the job's organizational level and whether advanced education is required. In general, lower-level (e.g. non-exempt) jobs that do not require advanced educational experiences (e.g. bachelor's or master's degrees) should lend themselves to quicker and less expensive training than higher-level (e.g. exempt) positions that require higher education. When considered together, lower-level jobs that are filled primarily with non-college-educated persons and that occur in labor markets with high unemployment rates strongly suggest far less attention might be devoted to selective retention.

Third, it is becoming increasingly clear that many employees are valued for their human and intellectual capital. More specifically, some employees may have specialized knowledge that is critical to organizational effectiveness. With the (incredible) pace of organizational change and the competitive nature of many industries, human and intellectual capital *should* become increasingly important in a manager's judgment about what is and what is not functional turnover.

Fourth, as an organization's success becomes more dependent on relationships, network connections, and interactions with others within and outside of the organization, an employee's social capital, independent of his or her skills, knowledge, and abilities, becomes a more critical asset. If employees with high social capital quit, they might leave behind a communication gap that cannot easily be filled. Unless other employees have worked closely with the quitter and developed a similar network of connections in both quantity and quality, such social capital losses may lead to immediate decrements in performance that, due to the inherently interdependent nature of today's work, may ripple throughout the organization (Dess and Shaw, 2001; Shaw, Duffy, Johnson, and Lockhart, 2005). In sum, managers need to consider the availability of replacement workers, the ease of training, and the leaver's human capital, intellectual property, *and* social capital in judging the functionality of an individual's turnover.

Finally, such analysis is not only important in operating an organization, but is also potentially vital to successful merger and acquisition activity. According to research done by partners at Bain Capital (Harding and Rouse, 2007), people issues are often at the root of failed deals. In analyzing 40 recent merger and acquisition deals, the 15 that were classified as successful, the acquirers had all identified key employees for retention during the due diligence phase or within 30 days of the announcement of the deal. This task was carried out in only one third of the unsuccessful deals.

Organizational types

Selective retention and workforce stability can be less critical in certain organizational types. In particular, turnover is likely *unimportant* in *temporary* organizations whose sole purpose is to create a given project or produce a certain service, and then, by design, disband. Common examples include independent motion picture productions (e.g. shooting a movie), political campaigns (e.g. winning an election), and joint ventures intended to spread risk across the multiple participants (e.g. oil exploration). Similarly, bureaucracies, which are relatively *buffered* from market forces (e.g. state and local governments, public universities), may have *limited concern* with retention and stability because, for example, of sufficient slack resources, adequate time to forecast accurately human resource requirements, or de facto monopoly position. Finally, those organizations where creativity and innovation are critical to survival might actually consider *encouraging* departures of less creative or innovative employees (e.g. think-tanks, innovation centers, and advertising firms).

"The more things change, the more things stay the same"

Given that people will and do quit firms, how have companies begun to control the leaving of these kinds of extraordinary and other less extraordinary (aka normal) people? Certainly, there is no single magic bullet that all firms should follow. With increasing frequency, however, many firms have (re)turned to the *old fashion* and followed the now *counterintuitive* idea of proactively building *loyalty* via mutual company and employee commitment (Bernstein, 1998). In other words, they seek to prevent the seeds of leaving (e.g. shock, image violations, and decline in job attitudes) *before* they get planted.

With these ideas in mind, Booz, Allen, and Hamilton implemented *job rotation* to help their consultants balance family and work stresses. During periods of unusual family turmoil, for example, consultants can be reassigned to jobs with stable hours and minimal travel; as a result, it is easier for their employees to deal with the work–family stresses. At International Paper (IP) and Citigroup, for instance, *career development programs* have been implemented. At IP, 13,000 white-collar workers must meet annually (and separately from their performance appraisal meetings) to map their long-term career strategies and their next specific job move. At Citigroup, 10,000 managers are reviewed twice a year to identify their next job placement. In short, labor market imperatives are driving firms to manage the quitting process proactively, and the research in organizational behavior provides strong and compelling managerial tactics.

CONCLUSION

In our view, this chapter mirrors a larger megapoint that underlies this entire volume. More specifically, the research on organizational behavior offers discernible, interpretable, logically consistent, and empirically verifiable foundation principles. With respect to controlling turnover, we *confidently* advise the following. First, consider whether selective retention and workforce security is sufficiently important in your particular firm's situation. If it is, then decide whether an employee's quitting is functional (versus dysfunctional) and avoidable (versus unavoidable). Third, anticipate an employee's leaving by monitoring job attitudes, global withdrawal cognitions, shocks, paths, and job embeddedness. Fourth, look at the shocks or levels (and reasons) of job dissatisfaction and embeddedness and decide whether there is anything the company can do (e.g. is this turnover avoidable?). Fifth, determine whether that employee is likely to leave more quickly (e.g. paths 1 and 2) or slowly (e.g. paths 3 and 4), which in turn advises a manager to be proactive (for path 1 and path 2 processes) or more reactive (for path 3 and path 4 processes). Finally, gather most or all of this information by routine employee surveys and/or "management by wandering around" (e.g. talk to people).

Simply put, our prescriptions say that turnover is a process that requires more active attention and management than it typically receives. Employee surveys are routinely administered, for example, but this information is infrequently used for specific and proactive interventions aimed at controlling turnover. Similarly, many companies designate their "key" employees whose leaving would be clearly dysfunctional but take little action to understand the events that prompt their thoughts of leaving. Also, companies can better anticipate employees' reactions to shocks by managing the information immediately before *and* after the occurrence of a particular jarring event. Job counseling can be made available, for instance, to deflect path 3 and 4 processes. Finally, companies can simply make it harder for employees to leave by "embedding" their key employees in the organization. For example, using teams, having people serve as mentors or having responsibilities for projects maintains attachments (or linkages) to firms. Generous perks and rewards contingent on continued tenure can also render turnover less appealing. In sum, controlling turnover requires substantial understanding of the phenomenon and the willingness to be proactive or reactive in managing the quitting process. Ultimately, appropriate management of turnover can increase organizational effectiveness and the bottom line.

REFERENCES

Abelson, M. (1987). Examination of avoidable and unavoidable turnover. *Journal of Applied Psychology*, 72, 382–386.

Allen, D. G. (2006). Do organizational socialization tactics influence newcomer embeddedness and turnover? *Journal of Management*, 32, 237–257.

Arnold, H. J., and Feldman, D. C. (1982). A multivariate analysis of the determinants of job turnover. *Journal of Applied Psychology*, 67, 350–360.

Bentein, K., Vandenberg, R., Vandenberghe, C., and Stinglhamber, F. (2005). The role of change in the relationship between commitment and turnover: A latent growth modeling approach. *Journal of Applied Psychology*, 90, 468–482.

Bernstein, A. (1998). We want you to stay. Really. *Business Week* (June 22), 67–72.

Bronson, P. (1999). Instant company. *The New York Times Magazine* (July 11), 44–47.

Crossley, C. D., Bennett, R. J., Jex, S. M., and Burnfield, J. L. (2007). Development of a global measure of job embeddedness and integration into a traditional model of voluntary turnover. *Journal of Applied Psychology*, 92, 1031–1042.

Dalton, D. R., Krackhardt, D. M., and Porter, L. W. (1981). Functional turnover: An empirical assessment. *Journal of Applied Psychology*, 66, 716–721.

Dess, G. G., and Shaw, J. D. (2001). Voluntary turnover, social capital, and organizational performance. *Academy of Management Review*, 26, 446–456.

Donnelly, D. P., and Quinn, J. J. (2006). An extension of Lee and Mitchell's unfolding model of voluntary turnover. *Journal of Organizational Behavior*, 27, 59–77.

Dvorak, P. (2007). Hotelier finds happiness keeps staff checked in. *Wall Street Journal* (December 17), B3.

Felps, W., Mitchell, T. R., and Byington, E. (2006). How, when, and why bad apples spoil the barrel: Negative group members and dysfunctional groups. *Research in Organizational Behavior*, 27, 181–230.

Felps, W., Mitchell, T., Hekman, D., Lee, T., Holtom, B., and Harman, W. (in press). When staying depends on others: Collective job embeddedness as a predictor of employee turnover. *Academy of Management Journal*.

Griffeth, R. W., Hom, P. W., and Gaertner, S. (2000). A meta-analysis of antecedents and correlates of employee turnover: update, moderator tests, and research implications for the millennium. *Journal of Management*, 26, 463–488.

Harding, D., and Rouse, T. (2007). Human due diligence. *Wall Street Journal* (October 2), A16.

Hoffman, B. J., and Woehr, D. J. (2006). A quantitative review of the relationship between person–organization fit and behavioral outcomes. *Journal of Vocational Behavior*, 68, 389–399.

Holtom, B. C., and Inderrieden, E. (2006). Integrating the unfolding model and job embeddedness to better understand voluntary turnover. *Journal of Managerial Issues*, 18, 435–452.

Holtom, B. C., Mitchell, T., Lee, T., and Inderrieden, E. (2005). Shocks as causes of turnover: What they are and how organizations can manage them. *Human Resource Management*, 44, 337–352.

Hom, P. W., and Griffeth, R. W. (1995). *Employee Turnover*. Cincinnati, OH: South-Western College Publishing.

Kammeyer-Mueller, J. D., Wanberg, C. R., Glomb, T. M., and Ahlburg, D. (2005). The role of temporal shifts in turnover processes: It's about time. *Journal of Applied Psychology*, 90, 644–658.

Lee, T. W., and Maurer, S. D. (1997). The retention of knowledge workers with the unfolding model of voluntary turnover. *Human Resource Management Review*, 7, 247–275.

Lee, T. W., and Mitchell, T. R. (1994). An alternative approach: the unfolding model of voluntary employee turnover. *Academy of Management Review*, 19, 51–89.

Lee, T. W., Mitchell, T. R., Holtom, B. C., McDaniel, L. S., and Hill, J. W. (1999). The unfolding model of turnover: a replication and extension. *Academy of Management Journal*, 42, 450–462.

Lee, T. W., Mitchell, T. R., Sablynski, C. J., Burton, J. P., and Holtom, B. C. (2004). The effects of job embeddedness on organizational citizenship, job performance, volitional absences, and voluntary turnover. *Academy of Management Journal*, 47, 711–722.

Lee, T. W., Mitchell, T. R., Wise, L., and Fireman, S. (1996). An unfolding model of voluntary employee turnover. *Academy of Management Journal*, 39, 5–36.

Maertz, C. P. Jr., and Campion, M. A. (1998). 25 years of voluntary turnover research: A review and critique. In C. L. Cooper and I. T. Robertson (eds), *International Review of Industrial and Organizational Psychology* (Vol. 13, pp. 49–81). New York: John Wiley and Sons.

Maertz, C. P. Jr., and Campion, M. A. (2004). Profiles in quitting: integrating process and content turnover theory. *Academy of Management Journal*, 47, 566–582.

Maertz, C. P. Jr., and Griffeth, R. W. (2004). Eight motivational forces and voluntary turnover: A theoretical synthesis with implications for research. *Journal of Management*, 30, 667–683.

Mallol, C., Holtom, B. C., and Lee, T. W. (2007). Job embeddedness in a culturally diverse environment. *Journal of Business and Psychology*, 22, 35–44.

Meyer, J. P., Stanley, D. J., Herscovitch, L., and Topolnytsky, L. (2002). Affective, continuance, and normative commitment to the organization: A meta-analysis of antecedents, correlates, and consequences. *Journal of Vocational Behavior*, 61, 20–52.

Mitchell, T. R., Holtom, B. C., Lee, T. W., Sablynski, C., and Erez, M. (2001). Why people stay: Using job embeddedness to predict voluntary turnover. *Academy of Management Journal*, 44, 1102–1121.

Morrell, K. (2005). Towards a typology of nursing turnover: The role of shocks in nurses' decision to leave. *Journal of Advanced Nursing*, 49, 315–322.

Morrell, K. Loan-Clarke, J., and Wilkinson, A. (2004). The role of shocks in employee turnover. *British Journal of Management*, 15, 335–349.

Morrell, K., Loan-Clarke, J., Arnold, J., and Wilkinson, A. (in press). Mapping the decision to quit: A refinement and test of the unfolding model of voluntary turnover. *Applied Psychology: An International Review*.

Peters, T. J., and Waterman, R. H. (1982). *In Search of Excellence.* New York: Harper and Row.

Shaw, J. D., Duffy, M. K., Johnson, J. L., and Lockhart, D. E. (2005). Turnover, social capital losses, and performance. *Academy of Management Journal*, 48, 594–606.

Spector, P. E. (1997). *Job Satisfaction.* Thousand Oaks, CA: Sage Publications.

Spors, K. (2007). Top Small Workplaces, 2007. *Wall Street Journal* (October 1), R1.

Sutton, R. I. (2007). *The No Asshole Rule: Building a Civilized Workplace and Surviving One that Isn't.* Warner Business Books.

Tanova, C., and Holtom, B. (in press). Using job embeddedness factors to explain voluntary turnover in 4 European countries. *International Journal of Human Resource Management*.

EXERCISES

Shock questionnaire

On a piece of paper, quickly provide answers to the following questions:

1. Have you ever left a job in response to a shock (a jarring event that caused you to reconsider your attachment to the organization)?

2. Do you know any people (e.g. friends, family, colleagues, former classmates) who have left a job in response to a shock?
3. What type of shocks did you or they experience?
4. Categorize the shocks according to the following criteria:
   (a) Personal vs organizational
   (b) Expected vs unexpected
   (c) Positive vs neutral vs. negative
5. What responses to the shocks were enacted by the organizations?
6. Were these responses effective in stemming turnover? If not, what should have been done?

Job embeddedness

Recently, a new theory has been designed to help organizations reduce voluntary turnover by increasing "job embeddedness." Empirical evidence suggests that such efforts are typically complementary to the traditional approach (e.g. increasing job satisfaction or organizational commitment) because job embeddedness focuses on different factors. Take a few minutes to think through the following issues with a small group of people from your organization.

How can your organization systematically increase each of the following aspects of job embeddedness among employees?

1. Fit in the organization (perceived congruence with the values, culture, etc.).
2. Links in the organization (number of people, groups and projects employees are meaningfully attached to).
3. Sacrifice related to leaving the organization (specific perks, benefits, or hardships incurred upon leaving).
4. Fit in the community (congruence with the values, amenities, offerings in an area).
5. Links in the community (number of institutions, friends, and family that employees are connected with).
6. Sacrifice related to the community (community-based issues that would arise if an individual leaves an organization; relocation to a new city is not required; for example, new commute patterns).

Part IV

MOTIVATION

8

Attain Emotional Control by Understanding What Emotions Are*

Edwin A. Locke

> *"Know thyself"*
> —Inscription above the Temple of Apollo at Delphi, Greece

There has been considerable interest in emotions in the workplace over the last 15 years, but strangely most discussions of emotion (even those outside the fields of organizational behavior and I/O psychology) have lacked one thing: a definition of emotion!

Why? Because one can only grasp the nature of emotions by introspection – by looking inwards at one's mental contents and processes – and introspection has been unofficially – and wrongly – banned (for reasons I need not go into here) from the field of psychology for close to 100 years (Locke, 2009).

WHAT EMOTIONS ARE

The nature of emotion

I will begin by defining what I am talking about: *emotions are the form in which one experiences automatic, subconscious value judgments* (value appraisals), Appraisal theory was first identified in psychology, to the author's knowledge, by Arnold (1960), but see Peikoff (1991) for a more complete statement. Every emotion involves a specific type of value appraisal. For example:

◆ Fear is the form in which one experiences a perceived threat to one's life or well-being (or that of a loved one).
◆ Anxiety is similar to fear but the nature of the threat is more uncertain and may involve one's self-esteem.

---

*Note: Because my examples in this chapter refer to people's internal states, usable reports from business people about their emotions are hard to come by. Thus some of the cases I use in this chapter are fictional (the real ones will be noted). Nevertheless, I believe they are realistic, that is, representative of real experiences.

- ◆ Sadness is the form in which one experiences the loss of a value. (Depression is a more intense form of sadness involving self-deprecation and a sense of hopelessness.)
- ◆ Anger is the form in which one experiences a perceived injustice or goal frustration.
- ◆ Guilt is the form in which one experiences the perception of violating one's moral values.
- ◆ Satisfaction is the form in which one experiences having gained or possessed a value.
- ◆ Love is the response to something appraised as a positive value. (It is a stronger emotion than satisfaction and the value does not necessarily have to be possessed (e.g., a work of art).
- ◆ Pride is the form in which one experiences an achievement, including the achievement of one's moral character, due to one's own efforts.
- ◆ Happiness is the state of non-contradictory joy (stronger and more all-encompassing than satisfaction).
- ◆ Admiration is the form in which one appraises the positive achievement(s) of another person.

The universal pattern of every emotion (excepting those caused by abnormal brain states or hormone imbalances) is: object→cognition→value appraisal→emotion. The object can be a thing, a person, an action, an event, an idea, a memory or a previous emotion. (In some cases people may not be aware or only peripherally aware of what the precipitating object is.) The cognition stage involves one's perception of the object and the present context plus all the stored knowledge which the subconscious automatically associates with the object. The value stage involves subconsciously "measuring" the object with respect to whether some value is perceived as being threatened or fulfilled in some form and to some degree. All emotions have either a positive or negative valence but to varying degrees, for example loving is stronger than liking, hating is stronger than disliking. (Emotions, of course, are accompanied by various physiological reactions. However, there is rarely any fixed, universal pattern of physiological reactions that is a unique indicator of one specific emotion for all people, though for certain basic emotions such as fear there may be broad similarities. Basic emotions, however, do have characteristic facial expressions.)

The crucial point here is that the two middle stages, cognition and value appraisal, are automatic (lightning fast and not chosen) rather than volitional, and subconscious rather than conscious. So what one consciously experiences is: object→emotion. In a waking state one is continually experiencing emotions, because the subconscious is always at work, although many emotions are mild and fleeting and thus not significant enough to notice or analyze.

A mood is an enduring emotional state

A mood is enduring because the object (such as an unpleasant boss) is omnipresent or because the subconscious causes endure based on memory (such as following the loss of a job one loved) or rumination (replaying the triggering event or one's thoughts about it). Some have argued that moods are defined by their having no known causes. Sometimes the cause of a mood is not known but that does not mean it cannot be identified. A good strategy is to identify exactly when the mood began and what was happening at the time, with respect to events or thoughts. For example, a spat with one's romantic partner could cause one to feel depressed all day (or longer). The emotional remnants of an unpleasant work experience (or a failed romance) could linger for days, months or even years. (Admittedly, some moods are caused by hormone imbalances.)

What's the proof that the causal, subconscious processes noted above really exist and cause the emotion? One has first to introspect backwards in time. Consider the following example.

Pat comes to a business meeting and is severely criticized by her boss for certain "mistakes" that caused the company to lose an important account. In reality, she was not to blame. It was the project leader who messed up the account, including acting against her advice in several important respects, and then told the boss that the outcome was Pat's fault.

The main, immediate, automatic emotion Pat will feel will be anger, because a grave injustice was committed towards her. The object was the attack. If asked what was upsetting after the fact, Pat could cognitively identify one key fact: the attack was based on false information. If asked what value was violated, Pat would say: the desire for just treatment (and/or honesty).

One can further validate the model by mental experiments in which the "script" is revised. "How," you ask Pat, "would you have felt if the boss had, instead of attacking you, attacked the project leader, after having gathered relevant information from reliable sources?" Pat's answer would probably be something like, "I would not feel anger. If the boss spoke factually without becoming enraged, I would have felt it was just but also a bit sad, because I wanted the project to succeed. If he had exploded with rage, I would have felt some fear, because it would mean the boss lacked self-control and could attack me next."

Next, one could ask, "What would you feel if deep down you considered justice to be an unobtainable value in this world and never expected to see it." Pat would probably reply that what she would have experienced is a kind of hopeless, cynical resignation, or sadness rather than anger.

(One can also validate the model with a simple pseudo-experiment. To show introductory psychology students the effect of ideas on emotions, I would suddenly state, in the middle of a class, that we were going to have an unannounced quiz right then, on the assigned reading which would count towards their final grade. The two emotions that automatically emerged every time were: anxiety and anger. The value standards involved are obvious. The emotions disappeared immediately when I said that I was just kidding in order to illustrate a point.).

The important point here is that the output, the emotion, is the result of three inputs: the object (event), the cognitive associations to the object and context, and the value appraisal(s). One input is usually (though not always) conscious and two are subconscious, but change any of these, and the emotion is changed. (I will have more to say about changing emotional responses later.)

The findings of neuropsychology do not invalidate the above model. Obviously, everything is stored in the brain and mental processes occur somewhere (e.g. the limbic system, or in several different places). But the brain is only the hardware. The ideas stored in the mind can be viewed as the software – they give the brain cognitive content. The concept of emotion would have no relevance or meaning to a totally unconscious being.

It is because people hold different ideas and values that the same object can cause different emotions in different people (and different emotions at different times in the same person, if their ideas change). A stern boss can be seen by one employee as businesslike and focused whereas another employee (with different beliefs and values) might see the same boss as cold and unfeeling. Even if the different emotions were processed in different parts of the brain, brain scans cannot identify the content of the person's ideas nor explain why different people process the same event differently.

Multiple emotions

It is possible to experience more than one emotion toward an object, especially a person, at the same time. Imagine an employee who cannot be located for three days. Then he comes into the office with a brilliant marketing plan that could save the company. The manager might experience three different emotions: anger because of being frustrated by the employee's mysterious disappearance; relief that the employee showed up; and elation about the marketing plan. One can also hold emotions at different levels. At one level an employee might admire a smart boss and at a deeper level feel jealous or inadequate. The human mind is a wonderfully complex instrument. (In romantic relationships things can get even more complicated – but that's another book).

Emotions and action

Every emotion has a built-in action tendency (Arnold, 1960), i.e. a felt impulse to action. (Again, such tendencies can be identified by introspection.) The survival value of, for example, lion→fear→run, etc. is obvious. The cave man who engaged in long, cognitive deliberation when confronted by a wild beast would not have many future opportunities to reproduce.

The action impulses for positive appraisals include wanting to keep, hold, or protect the valued objects. The impulses for negative emotions include wanting to avoid or harm (verbally or physically) the disvalued object.

It must be stressed that, although emotions automatically contain action impulses, everyone (this side of mental illness) has volitional choice as to what action to take in response to emotions. This too is validated by introspection. Consider this example.

Joe is called into the vice president's office and informed that he is being fired after 15 years with the company. Joe has long believed that he was unfairly treated and had all along been set up for failure by organizational politics. Joe is very angry at this perceived injustice. Joe's action impulse is to get even. Many possible actions might occur to him immediately. (Others might occur to him later.) One is to punch the boss on the nose. Another is to come back with a gun and kill some people. Another is to give the VP a tongue-lashing. Another is a blog attack on the company. Another is a lawsuit. Another is to pressure the company for a generous termination bonus.

Observe here that Joe may consider many action alternatives (which might or might not be similar to those of a different fired employee) but no overt actions are forced on Joe by his subconscious. Joe has the power, despite whatever impulses he might have, to consider different responses and to choose among them. Here is where, unlike the case of the lion menacing the cave man, he has time for deliberation, including the power to consider the pros and cons of various alternatives and to choose an appropriate course of action, including the choice of no action.

Which action Joe chooses will depend, in part, on his moral code. If he considers initiating physical force to be immoral, this will rule out all overtly aggressive acts. Of the remaining possibilities, the choice will depend on any number of personal factors such as knowledge, personality, and thinking.

(If Joe has spent his entire life acting impulsively, in which case he probably would never have held any job for very long and might even have a criminal record, self-control could be much more difficult because of the bad habits he had acquired.)

Emotions and reason

It has been treated as a virtual axiom from ancient Greek philosophers to the present day that emotions and reason are inherently at odds, i.e. in conflict. This is known in philosophy as the mind–body dichotomy. (There are other versions of the mind–body dichotomy but reason vs emotion is the most common version.) The belief is considered even more rock-solid today because the center for emotions is located in a different part of the brain than the center for thinking. However, this does not prove the case, because different parts of the brain are interconnected. The evidence from cognitive therapy is that you can change emotions by changing the thoughts underlying them (Butler, Chapman, Forman, and Beck, 2006; Clark and Beck, 1999). And, as noted, one can see that emotions are the product of (subconscious) ideas by introspection.

I believe the concept of a mind–body dichotomy to be profoundly mistaken (see Peikoff (1991), especially Chapters 1, 5, and 7, for a more detailed discussion). The cause of this error is, most fundamentally, the inability or failure to introspect.

What people experience as clashes between reason and emotion are actually clashes between consciously held and subconsciously held ideas.

Consider Sandra, a unit manager. When things go wrong, she gets angry and has the automatic urge to lash out at her subordinates; on the other hand, her reason tells her that this is a poor management practice. She thinks, "It's just reason versus emotion again. That's just the way people are." But are they? Why does Sandra feel angry? Perhaps because her subconscious premise is, "All my employees should do everything right all the time." Or, "I shouldn't have to be bothered by crises; I have other things I need to spend my time on." Or, "This will make me look bad and hurt my career."

Observe that the first two subconscious premises are mistaken; people do make mistakes and things just don't go perfectly all the time in any business. The third premise may be mistaken unless things go wrong constantly, but more relevant is what she learns from her mistakes so they are not repeated. If Sandra identifies her wrong premises through introspection, she has the power to correct them. Further, she can go deeper. She can ask herself why the problems that bother her arise in the first place, "Am I hiring capable, conscientious employees? Are they getting proper direction and training? Are crises occurring because there are issues I did not make an effort to foresee?"

(I will not go further into psychopathology in this chapter, but it is possible that Sandra is displacing her anger over something else – such as a troubled romantic relationship – onto her employees, or that she is feeling low self-efficacy (see Chapter 10, this volume) and is defending against her own self-doubts.)

Although emotions contain action impulses, they are, in a fundamental respect, the passive part of one's psychology. Given the perceived objects and one's premises at a given time, emotions are not chosen or willed; they just happen. Reason, on the other hand, is the locus of volition (Binswanger, 1991; Peikoff, 1991; this too is validated by introspection). One must choose whether to think or not to think. Reason is the active, self-caused part of one's psychology. Through reason we have the power to understand our emotions, to choose what action we will take in response to them and to reprogram them if needed. (Reprogramming can be very difficult in some cases, for example childhood abuse, post-traumatic stress disorder).

Consequences of emotion at work

It is interesting that studies of the consequences of subordinates' and leaders' emotions (or moods) at work, for example decision making, helping behaviors, absenteeism, subordinate performance in response to leader emotions, often lead to inconsistent or contradictory findings (Grandey, 2008; Humphrey, 2008). This would be expected if there was no deterministic relationship between emotions and specific actions (as contrasted with felt action tendencies). One of the most consistent findings in the literature is that low satisfaction is more likely to lead to turnover (quitting) than high satisfaction, but even here there are important exceptions (see Chapter 7, this volume). Since emotions in everyday life are not separate from cognitions (e.g. stored knowledge, interpretation of the current situation), one would need to know not only how a person feels but also how and what they think in order to predict and explain how they will act in the face of emotions.

Changing an emotion

Because emotions are automatic one cannot change them directly; one can only change them indirectly by modifying their causes.

Consider Peter who failed to get a much wanted promotion at XYZ Corp. He felt great disappointment, sadness, some anger, and considerable anxiety because he "failed" and now doubted his own competence. What can Peter do? The object is the failure to get a promotion. He cannot change that, but he can increase his chances for future success by seeking feedback regarding what his boss considers his weaknesses. He can then try to improve himself. What of his automatic cognitive appraisals? He may have subconsciously concluded that he was stupid and would always be a failure. These are clearly overgeneralizations that he can correct (cf. cognitive therapy). Finally, what of his value appraisal? He did not get what he wanted, thus the disappointment. And maybe he is not even capable of rising to the top of his industry. But if so, he can substitute new value standards, new aspirations that fit his capabilities. He might even change his career to something he likes more. Gradually, disappointment can be replaced by hope and self-doubt with self-efficacy.

I may have made this sound easier than it is, because there are always layers of value standards. Some may be tied to Peter's self-image or self-esteem, and people are often reluctant to give up the way they have viewed themselves. Sometimes changing this requires professional help. Also, deeply automatized premises that are tied to one's self-concept may take some time to change. Professional help may be required here as well. But the point is that one is not helpless in the face of emotions, because, as I noted, *they are not psychological primaries* (chemical imbalances aside).

Emotions and life

The psychological role of emotions is not simply survival for the cave man. The issue goes deeper. *The role of emotions is to make your values psychologically real* – as opposed to flat, cognitive abstractions. There is an enormous difference between saying "X is a good thing" and feeling an actual (and possibly burning) desire for it. Without desire, man is just an unmotivated robot. Emotions are not tools of actual knowledge (knowing requires reason); they are tools of motivation. They allow you to experience *wanting*, and thus be motivated to act.

Tragic errors are made by those who reverse these roles. Acting only on emotions without reason substitutes feelings for knowledge and thereby puts one's life out of control. An "emotionalist" will swing wildly from one impulse to the next with no sense of purpose or long range goal. On the other side of the coin, using reason but repressing emotions destroys one's capacity for joy and undermines one's motivation to pursue values. The issue is not reason or emotion but both together, *in harmony*. Harmony between reason and emotion is impossible without introspection. For example, a troublesome emotion can be caused by wanting the irrational, for example wanting a promotion one does not deserve.

To summarize the key points made so far:

1. Emotions are not unanalyzable primaries but the consequences of ideas stored in the subconscious.
2. Emotions are automatic but can be changed indirectly by changing the inputs (their causes).
3. There is no innate or inherent conflict between reason and emotion; such clashes are actually clashes between consciously held and subconsciously held ideas.
4. Emotions do not compel action; everyone (who is not suffering from severe mental illness) has the power to make choices in the face of emotional responses (including the choice of taking no action).
5. Both emotions and reason are critical to a successful and happy life. But it is critical to understand the proper function of each and to keep them in harmony.

MEDIATORS

The psychological mediators (causal mechanisms) of emotions are those noted earlier: the object that triggers the emotion, the subconscious cognitive associations to the object, and the subconscious value appraisals which follow.

MODERATORS

The key moderating factors in understanding emotion and in harmonizing reason and emotion are skill at introspection and the willingness to do it. People who won't or can't introspect will feel afraid of their emotions, because they will seem causeless, incomprehensible and uncontrollable.

Why don't people introspect? There are many reasons. One is that, in a way, it is not "natural." Extrospection is natural; every child starts life by looking outwards. Further, one gets immediate feedback if one fails to extrospect, like running into doors, or tripping over clothes or touching something hot on the stove. There is no such immediate, unequivocal feedback for not introspecting.

Second, most people don't know how to introspect. No one teaches it and psychologists have pretty much banned it from the literature for the past 100 years.

Third, most people do not see its value. The benefits are not immediately self-evident; it takes time to understand oneself and to see the payoff.

Fourth, introspection is hard work. Unlike extrospection (at the perceptual level) there is no special sense organ for looking inwards. It is a volitional process requiring the use of one's conceptual faculty. Many people do not want to expend the effort of actually thinking (reasoning) about either their own consciousness or the outside world.

Fifth, many people fear introspection. They fear what they might find or what they might have to face. They fear their emotions are primaries and are out of their control. They fear that understanding themselves might threaten their self-image or self-esteem which is built on various defenses which they do not want to acknowledge. This can become a vicious circle, because the more they rely on defenses, the more vulnerable they become and the more defenses they have to erect. Defenses are designed subconsciously to escape from reality, but, in the end, reality cannot be escaped. The more "well defended" an individual is, the more detached he is from reality. Of course, as implied earlier, people have the power to act against their fears.

Because most people are not very good at introspection, self-reports of emotion should be at least somewhat suspect (i.e. considered subject to error) unless the individual has some skill at introspection.

ACHIEVING EMOTIONAL CONTROL

What does it mean to achieve emotional control? It does not mean, in my view, to repress all emotion, that is, to give a standing order to one's subconscious not to allow any awareness of emotion to enter conscious awareness. This would be disastrous psychologically, as noted earlier.

Emotional control, as I view it, involves five elements:

1. Identifying, that is, *naming* your emotions – not every single one because that would occupy all your time but those which are most intense and/or enduring. This alone can enhance some feeling of control, because naming emotions makes them less mysterious.
2. Identifying their causes. This includes positive emotions. If you know what brings you pleasure or happiness, you can take steps to expose yourself to the same object (assuming it is not harmful like smoking). For example, if you know what parts of your job you like the most, you can try to build more of those tasks into your job. This helps control your mood in a positive way. But usually when people talk of emotional control, they refer to negative emotions. They mean things like not losing your temper or not being overwhelmed by panic or anxiety. Emotional responses can become habitual through repeated experiences (some going back to childhood). Nevertheless, their causes can be grasped.

3. Changing the causes when necessary. If the emotion is negative, you have three possible ways to intervene (object, cognition, values). You can change or avoid the objects, correct mistaken beliefs, and modify inappropriate values. As noted, the more strongly automatized they are and the more subconscious layers involved, the more difficult the change process.

4. Consciously and rationally choosing what action(s), if any, to take based on or regardless of your emotions.

5. Suppressing emotions, or actions based on them, *when necessary*. Suppression is different from repression. Repression is subconscious and based on an implicit standing order to the subconscious ("Don't let me feel X"). Suppression is conscious. It involves deliberately inhibiting an emotion (or an action based on it) because experiencing it or acting on it is not appropriate in a given context (e.g. it may be distracting or there may be conduct norms that it is important to honor). When analyzing emotions it can be very helpful to *write down* one's observations, for example what emotion(s) one is feeling, the causal elements, the action tendencies and action choices, the errors one's subconscious may have made, etc. This makes the emotion more objective and helps one to slow down one's mental processes so that one can understand what has happened.

CASE EXAMPLES

Mark

Let's begin with a negative example. Mark is a unit manager for a *Fortune* 1000 company. Since receiving his MBA from a high prestige school, Mark has received two promotions. Given his background he believes that he will surely become CEO of his company, or, if not, of another *Fortune* 1000 company. However, he is having a hard time mastering his present job which is highly technical – nothing like the cases he studied in his MBA classes. He is feeling self-doubt, a threat to his self-esteem, and he can't stand the feelings of anxiety that are the result of this doubt. Further, not being able to master something easily threatens his self-image as a brilliant person. He could study the technical aspects of his job more thoroughly, but this would imply that he cannot master things in a flash which his self-image requires. So he tries desperately to work "around" his ignorance. He delegates some of the work but to people who know less than he does. He tries to bluff his way through meetings. When glitches occur, he angrily blames others, even though at some subconscious level which he will not make conscious, he knows that he is the one to blame. When his boss inquires about problems, he evades giving straight answers and assures his boss that things will be taken care of. Eventually things get more and more out of control and Mark has to rely increasingly on outright lies and then more lies to cover up those lies. Gradually, his projects fall apart and he gets caught lying, because he can no longer recall which lies he told to which person. In the end he is fired; his career, for now, is in tatters.

Imagine the difference in the outcome if Mark had honestly and openly identified his initial self-doubt and its cause: "I don't know how to do this job, and I feel inadequate and scared. I am trying to live up to a self-image which maybe is not a rational one." Then he could have chosen what to do, for example seek therapy, consult experts, study on his own, get more training, ask his boss for advice, etc. The outcome could have been quite different if he had not evaded and let his unidentified emotions control him.

Sandra

Now let's consider a real case sent to me by an acquaintance (with details changed to preserve anonymity). Sandra works as a manager in the software industry. She finds that introspection "is indispensable for running effective meetings. For instance, I have often been in meetings where people 'admit to a certain deception' such as being much farther behind in a project than they have been letting on." Her immediate reaction in this situation is anger and she knows the source: "It is unjust that this person misled me. At this point it is necessary to first let go of the anger [suppression] and be able to have enough concentration to determine what is the correct response" (consciously choosing what action to take). She goes on, "I might even need to take into account future needs such as 'I need to set an example'" so that others don't explode in anger when things go wrong. "Then I must decide how much emotion I want to express. How will each person at the meeting react to my reaction? For a while I thought that this whole process was itself a deception, but I realized that a good manager needs to be in control of their emotions and needs to be cognizant of the emotional responses of the people who work for them."

A manager must show self-control or the employees will think they are living in an unpredictable, irrational universe. In addition to understanding her emotions, Sandra had to do two things in a situation like this: (1) make clear that dishonesty was unacceptable and (2) make it safe for people who have problems to admit them (but insist that it be done sooner).

Observe how many smart things Sandra did. First, she identified her emotional response (anger). Second, she identified its cause (injustice). Third, she thought about the proper response and realized that anger would be unwise and suppressed that impulse. Fourth, observe that her ability to introspect allowed her to empathize with others: she could foresee how others might react to her anger if it were extreme. That is why she suppressed it. Fifth, she used reason to decide exactly what she needed to communicate and how. (Incidentally, a precondition of empathy is understanding one's own emotions.)

AUXILIARY ISSUES IN EMOTION

Is there such a thing as emotional intelligence (EI)?

In short, no (see Locke, 2005). EI has been defined in so many ways and has so many components (on which advocates do not even agree) that it is literally unintelligible. Intelligence is the capacity to grasp abstractions, but you do not need a high IQ to introspect about your emotions. The best terms for what I have been talking about are skill at introspection and the willingness to use that skill. [In a recent article, Mayer, Salovey and Caruso (2008) admit the term has been defined too broadly, but I believe even their narrower definition is too broad. Furthermore, they end up characterizing EI as an ability, which is basically the same as skill, which means there is no need for the term intelligence here at all.] There is no doubt that introspective skill could be taught and that existing and would-be managers could benefit from such training. This is not to say that introspection is the most important managerial skill (I don't think it is), but it is a very useful one for reasons which I think I have made clear.

Emotional experience vs emotional expression

In the literature emotional expression is called emotional "display" but that sounds rather like making emotions into a peacock. As noted from the last case, sometimes it is best to suppress the overt expression of an emotion so as not to unduly upset others in the workplace. Here is the way to deal with justified anger without acting too angrily. From manager to work team (let's assume it is still Sandra speaking): "I have just learned that all the sub-tasks for our project X are behind schedule, even though I have been assured for the past several weeks that everything was on target. Let me say that this makes me quite angry for two reasons. First, I think I have been deceived. Maybe you were afraid I would blow up at you, but even if that were true (which it is not), how does it help to deny reality? It just makes the mess worse. From now on, I want you to tell me if you are having problems right away, and we will work to solve it. If you fail to do this in the future, I will assume you are lacking in moral integrity and will act accordingly. Second, because I was not kept informed, we may end up hurting our reputation with the customer and that reflects badly on us and our company. Now let's discuss how to insure better information exchange and then how to fix this project."

The proper tone here would be serious and stern but not enraged or intimidating. It is clear that the manager is angry, and she has identified but has not lost control of her anger. Further, she has explained the *reasons* for the anger and suggested specific actions that should be taken next.

What if the emotion is positive, for example the company or unit just got a new, much desired contract or other good news? Here is a real life example from Mickey Dresser, CEO of retailer J. Crew (and formerly of The Gap from which he was fired; Brodie, 2008, p. 56). Mickey likes to use a public address system to communicate with employees. One day in the middle of lunch he was patched through to the office PA system to give this message:

> Hi, everyone, it's Mickey. I'm at Koi [a restaurant], waiting to meet my son for lunch, and I'm seeing a woman wearing our Florentine-print dress. Her friend just asked her where she got it. She said, "J. Crew." It's going to be a great lunch!

Dresser was clearly expressing excitement and joy based on the anticipation of great sales and wanted to share his feelings with his employees. One can guess that most employees were pleased by this announcement. This brings us to another point.

The effect of the manager on the mood of the office

Because managers are in a position of power (see Chapter 19), they can influence the mood of the whole office, especially the mood of people they come into direct contact with (maybe through email too). An angry, condemning mood will incite anxiety and fear in others, because the manager will be seen as a threat (even without making specific threats). In contrast, a manager who projects a benevolent mood will create a happier atmosphere. Of course, a manager has to be businesslike but this is not incompatible with a pleasant demeanor. This issue brings up another one.

Should you fake emotions?

I agree with those who say: No (e.g. see Grandey, 2008). Employees can readily spot emotions which are not authentic. But how then can you set the mood of the office? Part of the answer lies in selection. Organizations should not choose people as managers who are not nice people (though obviously niceness is far from the only requirement). Some people are temperamentally (and ethically) unsuited to manage other people. But let's say you have personality problems and yet want to set a positive tone with your subordinates.

The first step would be to identify why your mood is predominantly negative; fixing this might require professional help. You may hold subconscious premises (e.g. no one can be trusted, people are out to get me) that could be changed. (In some cases medication may be called for as well.)

The next step would be to learn interpersonal skills – that is, appropriate ways of behaving with others regardless of your emotional impulses. For example, if you are angry that a subordinate has done a bad job, you can learn specific steps to follow to deal with the problem without blowing up, as noted in some earlier examples. Further, you can learn how to encourage subordinates and praise them for doing good work (Chapter 13). You can also learn how to listen, a skill that too many managers lack. You can apply these skills whether or not your emotions are pushing you in the right direction at a given time. (Many executives today have personal coaches who can help them learn these skills.)

Both these steps reflect aspects of emotional control.

In addition, you can make sure you are a person of outstanding moral character since character is within the realm of one's choice (see Chapter 20). This will build trust between you and your subordinates which helps foster high morale, providing you are also competent (see Chapter 21).

What about customer service personnel?

It is generally agreed that being a customer service representative is a stressful job, especially when it involves constantly dealing with complaints. The service reps get the brunt of the anger, because they are symbols of the whole company.

The first step is again selection: choose people who like this type of work. The second step involves a secret about emotions that 99% of customer service reps do not seem to know – it concerns how to deal with customers' anger. Most reps respond to anger or grumpiness (based on hundreds of examples from my personal experience) either by totally ignoring, i.e. by total silence, or by asking: "So what can I help you with?" or by defensiveness ("Don't blame me"). Usually, this simply increases the customer's anger.

Here is the secret: you have to *disarm the anger* by acknowledging it and even empathizing with it, namely: "I'm so sorry for the poor service (product, etc.). I don't blame you for feeling disappointed (frustrated, angry)." Because the customer feels *understood emotionally*, the result is that he or she virtually always calms down and becomes less moody.

Burnout

Burnout means that you no longer enjoy your job and lack enthusiasm for it. There can be many reasons for this which you can discover by introspection, for example you never really wanted to be in this type of job in the first place (you chose it based on status or pressures from others or because it was the "in" career at the time, for example law); the job does not allow you to grow in your knowledge and expertise (you are stagnating);

the job entails never-ending and unresolvable conflicts with others; the people you work with are mean, incompetent, and/or dishonest; the job was not what you expected and desired; stress on the job is unrelenting and you see no way to increase your self-efficacy enough to moderate it (Chapter 27), etc. The solution to burnout is usually a job or career change, ideally after you have had time off to reflect on what you want.

Defensiveness

Defensiveness involves trying to protect oneself against perceived attack or criticism. Specifically, what one is trying to protect is one's sense of self-esteem (which may be fragile). Common mechanisms of defense are rationalization (making excuses), denial (I didn't do it), and evasion (refusing to consider the issue). The danger of defensives is *that it detaches the mind from reality* and thereby makes the problem impossible to fix.

One of my business heroes in this respect is Ken Iverson, the late CEO of Nucor. Early in its history (after Iverson took over) the company was not doing well and a stockholder complained at the annual meeting. Iverson did not get defensive. His response was "What can I say? We're a lousy company." Of course, Iverson, unburdened by any desire to fake reality, went on to make Nucor one of the best steel companies in the world. Legendary investor Warren Buffett has the same attitude. When his company has a (rare) bad year, he simply says they did a poor job.

The key principle to sustain high self-esteem and prevent defensiveness is: *treat reality (facts) as an absolute*. Former GE CEO Jack Welch said that you must face reality as it is, rather than as you want it to be. If you want to change what is (e.g. poor past performance), you have first to acknowledge the facts in front of you, including your own mistakes. Then you are in a position to fix them.

Note that this policy eliminates the need for defensiveness, because your self-esteem is secure when reality rather than wishes come first. There is no illusion of self-esteem to protect.

Is the Core Role of the Leader Emotional or Rational?

A substantial segment of the leadership literature stresses or implies that the main role of the leader is that of motivator of employees. Although this is one role, I believe that it is not the main one and that focusing too heavily on the emotional aspect is very dangerous.

The most important trait of a great leader (over and above ability and integrity), I believe, is *rationality*. (Buffett says this is also the most important trait in a successful investor). Why rationality? Because virtually every decision a leader makes has to be based on looking at the facts, rationally integrating them and drawing conclusions. Many thousands (if not tens of thousands) of decisions have to be made (with or without others' input) in order to run a successful business (see Introduction, this volume). These include: what products (and product attributes) to make; where and how to make them; what people to hire and how to assign responsibilities; discovering a competitive strategy; financing the enterprise; managing risk; understanding the law and the economy; projecting trends into the future; anticipating threats; balancing the short term and the long term; constantly changing the organization to meet changing conditions, etc. And this only scratches the surface. Decision making is hard mental work (Chapter 25). Leading a company requires a never-ending process of thinking. Motivating people to work hard at doing the wrong thing only hastens the organization's destruction. Thus cognition must come before motivation.

Consider how many thousands of very hard working and emotionally passionate people were involved in America's current housing/financial crisis – but they were making a deluge of wrong decisions (the government's key role in starting the whole mess, for example the Fed's excessively low interest rates and the creation of Freddie Mac and Fannie Mae to push high risk loans and buy high risk securities notwithstanding).

One of the few top 20 banks that did not deal in subprime loans or invest in high risk securities was BB&T, a mid-Atlantic regional holding company (see Chapter 20, this volume). Its core value: rationality. Its CEO told me a long time before the blow-up that what the large banks were doing was irrational. They were making huge short-term profits, undoubtedly accompanied by soaring positive emotions, but the house of cards soon collapsed.

Emotion is no substitute for rationality.

Emotions about one's job and career as a source of life happiness

Most people spend a substantial part of their lives at work. Thus it is important that, if possible, they pick a job or career that they personally like, preferably love. In times of financial crisis, people can be forced to take jobs that are less than satisfactory but this should not stop them from looking for something better – even during mid-life or later. To do this they have to identify what they really like based on trying different things and then introspecting – and then acting. Pleasurable jobs entail mental challenge (Chapter 6), doing something one loves, and steady progress in building one's knowledge and expertise.

One of the most common tradeoffs people have to consider is money vs the job itself (i.e. the nature of the work). The work that you like the most may not be the type that pays the best. Another is career vs. family. Usually one cannot maximize everything. Again it is important to introspect to identify one's true value hierarchy. But existing value hierarchies don't have to be permanent. They can be chosen – and changed by a process of thought. By choosing and pursuing the right values (including those outside of work) and understanding their relationship to emotion, one can be the agent of one's own happiness.

CONCLUSION

In order not to be the helpless victim of one's emotions, one has to understand their causes. Even though emotions are automatic responses programmed by the subconscious, their causes can be identified and understood. Moreover, emotions can be changed by changing their causes. Further, one has a choice as to how one acts in the face of emotions. There is no innate conflict between reason and emotion. A key to happiness and the harmony of reason and emotion is good introspection.

REFERENCES

Arnold, M. B. (1960). *Emotion and Personality*, Vol. l. New York: Columbia University Press.

Binswanger, H. (1991). Volition as cognitive self-regulation. *Organizational Behavior and Human Performance*, 50, 154–178.

Brodie, J. (2008). King of Kool. *Fortune*, September 1, pp. 51–61.

Butler, A. C., Chapman, J. E., Forman, E. M., and Beck, A. T. (2006). The empirical status of cognitive-behavioral therapy: A review of meta-analyses. *Clinical Psychology Review*, 26, 17–31.

Clark, D. A., and Beck, A. T. (1999). *Scientific Foundations of Cognitive Theory of Therapy and Depression*. New York: Wiley.

Grandey, A. A. (2008). Emotions at work: a review and research agenda. To appear in C. Cooper and J. Barling (eds), *The SAGE Handbook of Organizational Behavior*, Vol. 1, pp. 234–261. Thousand Oaks, CA: Sage.

Humphrey, R. H. (2008). *Affect and Emotion*. Charlotte, NC: Information Age publishing.

Locke, E. A. (2005). Why emotional intelligence is an invalid concept. *Journal of Organizational Behavior*, 26, 425–431.

Locke, E. A. (2009). It's time we brought introspection out of the closet. *Perspectives in Psychological Science*, 24–25.

Mayer, J. D., Salovey, P., and Caruso, D. R. (2008). Emotional intelligence. *American Psychologist*, 63, 503–517.

Peikoff, L. (1991). *Objectivism: The Philosophy of Ayn Rand*. New York: Dutton.

EXERCISES

Analysis of personal emotions

Divide into small groups. Each group member, working alone at first, is to identify an emotion that he or she felt at one time on a job. Name the emotion. Identify the relevant object or objects, the relevant cognitions (beliefs, thoughts) and the nature of the value appraisal(s) that caused the emotion. Each member then presents his or her analysis to the other group members. One member from each group could be elected to present one example to the whole class, if they are willing.

Changing an emotion

Divide into groups. Each member, working alone, identifies a "problem emotion or emotions" – an inappropriate past emotion or a pattern that he or she would like to change. Each identifies ways in which they could change the object (in the future), correct erroneous beliefs, and/or modify value standards. Identify problems they might encounter doing this, for example defensiveness, discouragement, self-image, difficulty with introspection. Have each member perform mental experiments to anticipate how changing one or more of the three causes could change the emotion. If any member is willing, one example could be reported to the whole class. (*Instructor should strongly urge any member suffering from depression to seek professional help.*)

9

Motivate Employee Performance through Goal Setting

GARY P. LATHAM

Goal setting theory (Latham and Locke, 2007) provides a framework that specifies the most valid and practical ways of increasing employee motivation. This conclusion has been reached by multiple authors working independently (e.g. Earley and Lee, 1992; Miner, 1984; Pinder, 2008). The conclusion is based on the fact that the theory has been shown in more than 1000 studies to predict, influence, and explain the behavior of thousands of people in numerous countries (e.g. Australia, Canada, the Caribbean, England, Germany, Israel, Japan, and the USA), in both laboratory and field settings, involving more than 100 different tasks in occupations that included logging, word processing, engineering, and university scholarship (Locke and Latham, 1990; Mitchell and Daniels, 2003). Although developed as a theory of motivation in the workplace, it has been used effectively in sport psychology (Weinberg, 1994). The theory has even been found useful for promoting the motivational processes of brain-injured patients (Gauggel, 1999; Prigatano, Wong, Williams, and Plenge, 1997).

MAIN PRINCIPLE

The theory states that the simplest, most direct motivational explanation of why some people perform better than others is because they have different performance goals (Latham and Locke, 1991). The essence of the theory is four-fold (Locke and Latham, 1990). First, difficult specific goals lead to significantly higher performance than easy goals, no goals, or even the setting of an abstract goal such as urging people to do their best. Second, holding ability constant, as this is a theory of motivation, and given that there is goal commitment, the higher the goal the higher the performance. Third, personality traits and incentives influence an individual's behavior, at least in part, to the extent that they lead to the setting of and commitment to a specific difficult goal. Fourth, goal setting, in addition to affecting the three mechanisms of motivation, namely, choice, effort, and persistence, can also have a cognitive benefit. It can influence the motivation to discover ways to attain the goal (Seijts and Latham, 2005).

SUBPRINCIPLES

There are at least four subprinciples necessary for deriving the motivational benefits of goal setting. The goal must be challenging and specific, feedback must be provided on progress in relation to goal attainment, ways must be found to maintain goal commitment, and resources must be provided for and obstacles removed to goal attainment.

Set challenging specific goals

The goal must be both challenging and specific. Given adequate ability and commitment to the goal, the higher the goal the higher the performance. This is because people normally adjust their level of effort to the difficulty of the goal. In addition to being targets to attain, goals are the standards by which one judges one's adequacy or success. Challenging goals facilitate pride in accomplishment. People with low goals are minimally satisfied with low performance attainment, and become increasingly satisfied with every level of attainment that exceeds their goal. This is also true for individuals with a high goal. To be minimally satisfied, they must accomplish more than those who have a low goal. Consequently, they set a high goal to attain before they will be satisfied with their accomplishment. In short, to be satisfied, employees with high standards must accomplish more than those with low standards. In addition, an employee's outcome expectancies are typically higher for the attainment of high rather than low goals because the outcome one can expect from attaining a challenging goal usually includes such factors as an increase in feelings of self-efficacy, personal effectiveness, recognition from peers, a salary increase, a job promotion, etc. As a result people, in most instances, readily commit to a high goal if they believe they have the ability to attain it.

Goal specificity facilitates an employee's focus in that it makes explicit what it is the individual should choose to do or try to accomplish. If the goal specifies A, then B and C will be downplayed. Specificity also facilitates measurement or feedback on progress toward goal attainment. A drawback of an abstract goal such as "do your best" is that it allows people to give themselves the benefit of the doubt concerning the adequacy of their performance (Kernan and Lord, 1988). Thus their maximum effort is not aroused. For feedback to be used intelligently, it must be interpreted in relation to a specific goal. Goal specificity clarifies for employees what constitutes effective performance.

For goal setting to be maximally effective, the goal and the measure of performance effectiveness used must be aligned. Thus, if a logging crew wants to increase productivity by 15%, the performance measure must be the number of trees cut down divided by the hours worked. If the director of an organization's RandD division wishes to increase line managers' satisfaction with the unit, the goal set can be a specific increase in the frequency of behaviors emitted that have been identified through job analysis as necessary for line management's satisfaction. Goals and the measures of their attainment that have appeared in the scientific literature include physical effort, quantity and quality measures of production, costs, profits, and job behaviors.

Challenging, specific goals affect effort and persistence (Latham and Locke, 1991, 2007). When no time limits are imposed, a specific high goal induces people to work harder or longer than is the case when a low or abstract goal is set. Without time limits, a specific high goal induces people to work until the goal is attained. With time limits, difficult specific goals lead to more effort per unit of time. The American Pulpwood Association found that when paper companies impose quotas on the number of days that they will buy wood from pulpwood crews, the crews cut as much wood in the restricted number of days as they do in a normal five-day work week (Latham and Locke, 1975).

In summary, setting specific challenging goals is important for increasing both job performance and job satisfaction. Job satisfaction is the result of an appraisal of one's performance against one's goals. Job satisfaction is not a result of the person alone or the job alone, but of the person in relation to the job. To the extent that one's job performance is appraised as fulfilling or facilitating the attainment of one's goals, satisfaction is high (Latham and Brown, 2006; Latham, Locke, and Fassina, 2002). For example, in a study conducted in Germany, there were no data to suggest that those who had high goals experienced feelings of exhaustion. Only those employees who perceived their goals were difficult to attain experienced an increase in positive and a decrease in negative effect, an increase in job satisfaction, and perceptions of occupational success over a three-year timeframe. An unexpected finding was that lack of goal attainment in one's personal life was related to higher degrees of subjective well-being when the person experienced goal progress on the job (Wiese and Freund, 2005).

Provide feedback in relation to goals

A truism attributed to the late Mason Haire is "that which gets measured gets done." This is because the act of measurement conveys cogently what the organization truly values versus what it may state that it values. However, the accuracy of Haire's statement is improved through the insertion of the word goals: that which is measured in relation to goals is done. Both goal setting theory and empirical research indicate that in the absence of goal setting, feedback has no effect on performance. This is because feedback is only information; its effect on action depends on how it is appraised and what decisions are made with respect to it.

For example, the Weyerhaeuser Company found that engineers and scientists who were urged to do their best after receiving a performance appraisal performed no better than their counterparts in a control group. A significant increase in performance occurred only among those engineers and scientists who received feedback in relation to specific high goals (Latham, Mitchell, and Dossett, 1978).

Feedback moderates the effect of goal setting. Without feedback, the positive benefit of goal setting is minimized (Erez, 1977). This is because goals direct effort and persistence. Feedback allows people to discern what they should continue doing, stop doing, or start doing to attain the goal.

Gain goal commitment

Commitment is the sine qua non of goal setting. Without it, goal setting is a meaningless exercise. Two primary ways to gain commitment are to focus on an individual's *outcome expectancies and self-efficacy* (see Chapter 10, this volume).

A downside of setting challenging specific goals is that people may obtain tangible evidence that they did not attain them. A teenager may have test scores that provide strong evidence of failure in math. An employee in a consulting firm may have hours and hours of wasted effort, non-billable hours, on a potential client who subsequently took the business to a competitor. The result can be feelings of loss of control. People learn on the basis of evidence (e.g. revenue, client surveys, staff turnover) that they have failed to attain their goal no matter how much they truly tried to attain it. Through such repeated experiences they typically "learn" to give up; they learn helplessness. Thus there are employees who have learned that they cannot increase revenue from existing clients, they have learned that they are poor at bringing in new clients, and that they are not able to work effectively with staff. They have tangible evidence to support their conclusions that they should give up their attempts to attain their goal.

The solutions for maintaining goal commitment are at least two-fold. A first step, as noted above, is to focus on *outcome expectancies*. The role of a coach is to help people see the relationship between what they do and the outcome of their actions; to help people realize the outcomes that they can expect as a result of what they do. An early example of how outcome expectancies affect goal commitment can be found in a study by Lashley (1929). A man, after 900 repetitions, was still unable to master the alphabet. But after he was offered 100 cigarettes if he could learn the alphabet in a week, he proceeded to do so in only 10 trials.

Because the concept of outcome expectancies is as useful in one's personal life as it is in an organizational setting, allow me to share a personal example. I arrived home one day to discover my four children on the front step. They greeted me with the warning not to enter the house as Mom was in a horrific mood. As she had walked across the kitchen floor, her foot had come out of a shoe that had stuck to dried milk. As she fell, her hand braced her from injury as it slipped into an open dishwasher that oozed with leftover breakfast food.

To announce that I will solve the problem would not only have been lunacy on my part, it would have fostered dependence: "Let's wait until Dad gets here; he can fix anything." To look for blame would have been equally fool-hardy on my part: "So what did you do to get your mother in such a bad mood?" "I don't know." "It wasn't me." "She is always in a bad mood." I bet you did something, Dad."

The primary job of a coach is to improve performance rather than focus on blame. This is done through increasing the person's sense of control regarding the attainment of their goals. It is done by helping people to realize the outcomes they can expect from engaging in specific actions. Thus, I simply asked each of them: "What can you do within the next 30 seconds to improve Mom's mood?" Setting a goal focuses attention on discovering solutions to its attainment.

One son offered to clean the kitchen, another said he would get us both a drink, the third said he would make dinner. My daughter quietly ran off to prepare a bath for my wife. The outcome, as expected, was a dramatic upswing in my wife's affect and behavior.

A four cell empathy box can be used to understand: (1) the outcomes an employee expects from committing to a goal, (2) the negative outcomes expected from goal commitment, (3) the positive outcomes expected from sticking with the status quo, and (4) the negative outcomes expected from doing so. Understanding outcome expectancies enabled a forest products company to shift the dishonest (theft) to honest behavior in the workforce

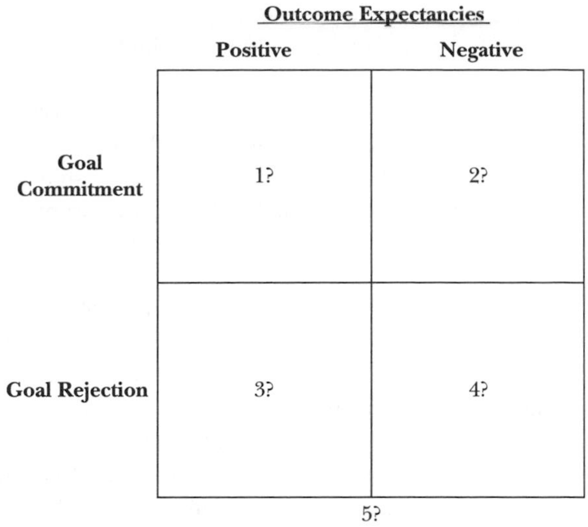

FIGURE 9.1 The empathy box

(Latham, 2001). The empathy box is shown in Figure 9.1. The five questions asked are as follows: (1) What positive outcomes do you expect from committing to and pursuing the goal? (2) What negative outcomes do you expect from committing to and pursuing the goal? (3) What positive outcomes do you expect from rejecting or ignoring the goal? (4) What negative outcomes do you expect from rejecting or ignoring the goal? (5) What would have to change for you to commit to the goal (look for answers in cells 2 and 3)?

This empathy box provides a systematic way to "walk in another person's shoes." To the extent that you understand the outcomes an individual or team expects, you will begin to understand their behavior. To the extent that you are able to change the outcomes they expect, you will be able to change their behavior – given the person or team has the confidence they can do so. This leads us to the second concept, self-efficacy.

A second step to maintaining goal commitment is to increase the person's *self-efficacy* (Bandura, 1997; 2001). Self-efficacy is the conviction that one can mobilize one's resources to attain a specific performance level. "I can cause . . ., I can bring about . . . I can make happen. . . ." Self-efficacy is different from self-esteem in that the latter refers to judgments of self worth: How much does Pat like Pat? Further, self-esteem is a general trait where as self-efficacy is task specific. The two are not necessarily directly related.

Pat may have low self-esteem due to a variety of events that have occurred in Pat's past. Pat has said and done things that are deeply regretted. For these reasons no one dislikes Pat today more than Pat. Nevertheless, Pat believes (high self-efficacy) that there is no one who is as effective in bringing in new business to the firm. Conversely, Pat may love Pat, yet she may have low self-efficacy in the ability to make a persuasive presentation to a potential client. Furthermore, because self-efficacy is task specific, an individual may have high self-efficacy on ability to work effectively with staff, low self-efficacy on working effectively with clients, and moderate self-efficacy on ability to work effectively within the firm.

People who have problems with self-esteem should be referred to a clinical psychologist. People who have low self-efficacy for attaining a specific, high goal can be coached by you in the workplace.

Bandura (2001) has shown that it is not just our ability that holds us back or propels us forward, it is also our perception of our ability. People with low self-efficacy look for tangible evidence to abandon a goal. A failure is confirmation that it is useless to persist in goal attainment. Conversely, people with high self-efficacy commit to high goals. They view obstacles and setbacks to goal attainment as challenges to overcome, as sources of excitement to be savored.

A possible indicator of low self-efficacy is self-denigration of one's ability. Statements such as "I can't deal with a personal computer" may indicate low self-efficacy.

High self-efficacy can be induced in the workplace in at least three ways, enactive mastery, modeling, and persuasion from a significant other. Enactive mastery involves sequencing a task in such a way that all but guarantees early successes for an individual. For example, to increase confidence in the use of a laptop, the following steps should be followed: (a) open/close, (b) on/off, (c) keyboard skills, (d) save. Early successes through "small wins" build confidence that "I can do this, my goal is indeed attainable."

An effective coach does not abandon an employee during the early stages of learning to attain a goal. To leave the employee to master keyboard skills before teaching the process of "save" is to provide the employee with a reason for abandoning the laptop in favor of pen and paper. All that was typed is lost forever when the laptop is turned off in the absence of knowledge of the necessity to "save."

The concepts of outcome expectancy and self-efficacy are often applied together. If the person hates the traditional "snail" mail system, show how hitting a key on the computer will send material any place in the world in seconds. In short, enable the person to see the relationship between mastery of the laptop and the desired outcome the person can expect. Then give the person confidence to do so through the sequencing of the tasks.

A second way to increase self-efficacy regarding goal attainment is through the use of models. The job of coach is to find people with whom the goal setter *identifies*, who have either mastered the task or are in the process of doing so. Note that the word identifies is italicized. Directing a manager who is struggling in the development of staff to another manager who has the "magic touch" with staff may not increase self-efficacy. It may even backfire as a coaching technique if this is all that is done. The person who is struggling may give up after concluding that "I will never acquire that 'magic touch'." Directing this manager to visit an additional colleague who has struggled recently in the past, and has subsequently improved the performance of staff, is more likely to increase the belief that "if she can, so can I."

For the same reason, visiting a benchmark company can sometimes be a demotivating experience. The idea underlying benchmarking is to minimize reinventing the wheel on the part of people in other organizations. Through benchmarking, the acquisition of knowledge is accelerated. But, the downside of benchmarking is that visitors can leave full of admiration for what they have witnessed, and demoralized because they are convinced that they do not have the ability to model it: "Their management system is different from ours. Their union contract is nothing like ours. There is no way that we can be like them." To increase their self-efficacy you must find an organization, in addition to the one that will be used as a benchmark, with whom employees can identify – an organization that has previously done poorly but has significantly improved its performance relative to that benchmark, or is in the process of doing so. Finding and visiting this additional organization increases the belief that "if they can, so can we."

The American Pulpwood Association found that *supervisory presence and support* is also a key to goal commitment and productivity (Ronan, Latham, and Kinne, 1973). When the goal is assigned by a supportive authority figure, goal commitment and performance are high (Latham and Saari, 1979a). These findings are supported by a meta-analysis that showed a 56% average gain in productivity when management commitment to a MBO program is high versus a 6% increase when their commitment is low (Rodgers and Hunter, 1991). Thus, it is not surprising that Bandura (see Chapter 10) found that a third way of increasing self-efficacy is through persuasion from a significant other. People tend to behave in accordance with the expectations of those people who are significant to them. Assigned goals themselves usually lead to high goal commitment because listening to the assignment without objection is in itself a form of consent (Salancik, 1977). Assigning the goal implies that the recipient is capable of attaining it, which in turn increases the person's self-efficacy regarding the task.

Bandura, a past president of the American Psychological Association, and a past honorary president of the Canadian Psychological Association, addressed a classroom of executives as follows:

> We know that intelligence is fixed. You either have it or you don't. We are going to put you through a simulation consisting of tasks that you typically confront as CEOs. I know you will find these tasks frustrating and seemingly impossible.

In an adjoining room, he addressed the other half of the class of executives as follows:

> We know that intelligence is not fixed. Intelligence is the ability to apply what you have learned on previous tasks to present ones. We are going to put you through a simulation consisting of tasks that you typically confront as CEOs. I know that you will find these tasks challenging and fun.

Several hours later he pushed back the dividing wall. The people in the second group were laughing among themselves as to how similar the simulation was to their daily work lives, and how much they had learned from their experiences that afternoon. The people in the first group were truly angry and frustrated. They demanded to be allowed to go through the same simulation as the second group before their four weeks of executive education at Stanford came to a close. The simulation that they had gone through, they claimed, was not similar at all to what they encountered on their jobs, and hence was a waste of their time.

In short, both groups behaved in accordance with Bandura's expectations of them, despite the fact that the simulation was identical for both groups. In less than a minute, Bandura's expectations of one group of executives ruined their afternoon and for the other group he had the opposite effect.

A coach may or may not be a significant other for the person who is being coached. Thus a role of you as a coach is to determine the identity of the person's significant other, and have that individual or individuals communicate, if true, why they believe the person can attain a specific high goal.

The most powerful significant other is one's self. *Verbal self-guidance* (VSG) or functional self-talk can increase or debilitate self-confidence in goal attainment. We are often our worst enemy. Millman and Latham (2001) trained displaced managers to systematically monitor their self-talk to exclude negative comments and increase positive ones with respect to job attainment. Within nine months, 48% of the people who were trained obtained a job that paid ±$10,000 of their previous job; only one person of eight in the control group was able to do so. The self-efficacy of the participants in the group who were trained in functional self-talk was significantly higher than those in the control group. Similar results have been obtained for Aboriginals in Canada (Latham and Budworth, 2006). Training in VSG also turned highly competitive MBA students into team players (Latham and Brown, 2006).

The order in which these two steps, outcome expectancies and self-efficacy, should be implemented varies by individual. If outcome expectancies are already high, this step may be skipped. Focus immediately on ways of increasing self-efficacy if the person lacks confidence that the goal is attainable.

Provide resources needed to attain the goal

Goals are unlikely to be attained if situational constraints blocking their attainment are not removed. Thus the organization needs to ensure that the time, money, people, and equipment necessary for goal attainment exist. Most importantly the measurement system must not only allow accurate tracking of goal progress, it must be aligned with and be supportive of goal attainment.

For example, a newly hired professor may set a goal to receive a mean score of 5 or higher on a 7-point scale of teaching effectiveness rated by students. If the measurement system for promotion and tenure focuses primarily on publications in mainstream academic journals, and resources are provided primarily for conducting research, commitment to this teaching goal may quickly wane.

Arguably, among the most important resources necessary for accruing the positive benefits of goal setting is the employee's ability. Organizations must provide the necessary training to give people the knowledge and skill to attain the goal. This is because the relation of goal difficulty to performance is curvilinear. Performance levels off after the limit of ability has been reached (Locke, Fredrick, Buckner, and Bobko, 1984).

Learning vs performance goals

Consistent with the above findings regarding an individual's ability are studies by Earley, Connolly, and Ekegren (1989) as well as Kanfer and Ackerman (1989). They found that when people lack the requisite knowledge to master a task, because they are in the early stages of learning, urging them to do their best results in higher performance than setting a specific difficult goal. The reasons are at least three-fold (Latham, Seijts, and Crim, 2008). First, such tasks are complex for people. Thus the direct goal mechanisms of effort, persistence, and choice are no longer sufficient to ensure high performance. This is because people have yet to learn the correct strategy for performing effectively. Second, such tasks require primarily learning rather than motivation. People have no problem-solving processes for these tasks to draw upon. Third, people with specific high goals feel pressure to perform well immediately. As a result, they focus more on their desire to get results than on learning the correct way of performing the task. In short, tasks that are straightforward as well as those that are complex for an individual require attentional resources, but the resource demands of the latter tasks are greater than those of the former (Kanfer, 1990). Where tasks fall within the problem-solving abilities of people, as in cases where they have had experience performing the tasks effectively, specific difficult performance goals readily lead to the development and execution of task-specific strategies. Truck drivers at Weyerhaeuser found ways to increase truck loads (Latham and Baldes, 1975) and to decrease truck turnaround time (Latham and Saari, 1982) after being assigned a specific difficult goal. They drew upon the knowledge they already possessed to attain the performance goal.

This was not the case in a study by Winters and Latham (1996) using a new (for them) complex class scheduling task developed by Earley (1985). Winters and Latham found a deleterious effect of a specific, difficult goal for performance because the wrong type of goal was set. When a high learning goal was set in terms of discovering a specific number of ways to solve the task, performance was significantly higher than it was when people were urged to do their best or had set a performance outcome goal. This is because a learning goal requires people to focus on understanding the task that is required of them and developing a plan for performing it correctly. As Oppenheimer noted during the development of the atomic bomb, determining how to get to one's destination is often more important than the critical target. Research on goal setting theory shows that high performance is not always the result of high effort or persistence, but rather high cognitive understanding of the task and strategy or plan necessary to complete it (Seijts and Latham, 2005). A learning goal is especially beneficial for people who score low on cognitive ability (Latham et al., 2008). As John D. Rockefeller said years ago, a goal of good management is to show average people how to do the work of superior people. A learning goal can raise the performance of people who score lower on cognitive ability to that of those who score higher on cognitive intelligence.

Environmental uncertainty

Among the biggest impediments to goal setting is environmental uncertainty (Locke and Latham, 1990). This is because the information required to set learning or outcome goals may be unavailable. And even when such information is available, it may become obsolete due to rapid changes in the environment. Thus as uncertainty increases, it becomes increasingly difficult to set and commit to a long-term goal.

In a simulation of such a situation, Latham and Seijts (1999) replicated the findings of Earley, Wojnaroski, and Prest (1987) and Kanfer and Ackerman (1989) using a business game where high school students were paid on a piece-rate basis to make toys, and the dollar amounts paid for the toys changed continuously without warning. Setting a specific high performance goal resulted in profits that were significantly worse than urging the students to do their best. But when *proximal performance goals* were set in addition to the distal goal, profit was significantly higher than in the other two conditions. This is because in highly dynamic situations, it is important to actively search for feedback and react quickly to it (Frese and Zapf, 1994). In addition, Dorner (1991) has found that performance errors on a dynamic task are often due to deficient decomposition of a goal into proximal goals.

Proximal goals can increase what Keith and Frese (2005) call error management. Errors provide information to employees as to whether their picture of reality is congruent with goal attainment. There is an increase in informative feedback when proximal or sub-goals are set relative to setting a distal goal only.

In addition to being informative, the setting of proximal goals can also be motivational relative to a distal goal that is far into the future. Moreover, the attainment of proximal goals can increase commitment, through enactive mastery, to attain the distal goal (Seijts and Latham, 2005).

Stretch goals

Don't expect people to willingly stretch themselves by committing to a very high goal if the outcome they expect is criticism for making an error. One or more errors are bound to occur in the active pursuit of a time-sensitive difficult goal. On tasks that are complex for people, Frese's research (Frese, 2005; Keith and Frese, 2005) shows that performance actually increases if errors are encouraged ("the more errors you initially make, the more you learn").

USE THE HIGH PERFORMANCE CYCLE

The usefulness of goal setting theory for everyday applications in work settings is shown in Figure 9.2. The high performance cycle (Locke and Latham, 1990; Latham et al., 2002) or HPC's usefulness for motivating employees in the public sector was demonstrated by Selden and Brewer (2000). It is a diagnostic tool or framework for understanding why employees are or are not motivated. For example:

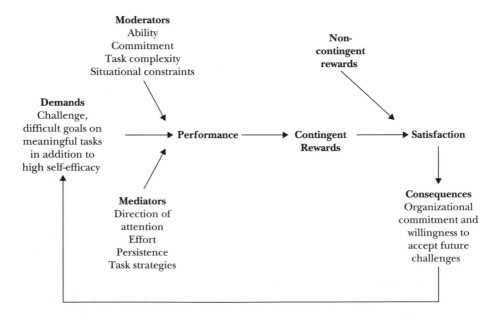

FIGURE 9.2 The high performance cycle

1. Demands
    (a) Do people have specific high goals?
    (b) Are the tasks "drudgery" or growth facilitating?
    (c) Do people have the confidence so that they can attain the goals set (self-efficacy)?
2. Moderators
    (a) Have people been trained adequately? Do they have the ability to perform the tasks required of them?
    (b) Are they committed to goal attainment?
    (c) Do they receive feedback on goal progress?
    (d) Do they have the resources to attain the goal or are there situational constraints?
3. Rewards
    (a) Are they rewarded for their accomplishments?
        (i) Intrinsically?
        (ii) Extrinsically?
    (b) Are they satisfied with their rewards?
4. Attitudes
    (a) Are they committed to their organization's effectiveness?
    (b) Are they willing to accept future challenges?

ISSUES IN IMPLEMENTATION

For what should goals be set?

As a theory of motivation, a goal refers to a desired outcome in terms of level of performance to be attained on a task. Goal content refers to the object or result that is sought after (Locke and Latham, 1990). Thus performance goals should be set for outcomes that are critical or valued by the individual or the organization in which the person is employed. An employee may have a career goal, a job goal, a financial goal, as well as psychological goals including job satisfaction and self-efficacy. A learning goal should be set for discovering the processes and strategies for reaching a desired outcome when the person lacks the knowledge to do so. Behavioral goals, identified through a job analysis, are more effective than a learning goal when the critical behaviors are known (Brown and Latham, 2002). To set a learning goal in this instance is to encourage paralysis through analysis. Behavioral goals are especially appropriate for job satisfaction and self-efficacy.

Because a goal is the object or aim of an action, the completion of a task can be a goal. As noted by Locke and Latham (1990), in most goal setting studies the term goal refers to attaining a specific standard of proficiency on a given task within a specific timeframe. This has resulted in practitioners of goal setting creating the acronym SMART, namely, goals that are *s*pecific, *m*easurable, *a*ttainable, *r*elevant, and have a *t*imeframe (Mealiea and Latham, 1996). The framing of a goal is especially important for implementation with regard to the stress that it can cause. Frame the goal positively, for example in terms of something a person can learn to perform well. Don't frame it negatively, as something a person may have difficulty attaining. A negatively framed goal ("Try not to miss answering 3 of these 15 anagrams") leads to worse performance than a positively framed one ("Try to make words from 12 or more of the 15 anagrams"; Drach-Zahavy and Erez, 2002; Roney, Griggs, and Shanks, 2003).

Who should set the goals?

A seminal study at the General Electric Company (Meyer, Kay, and French, 1965) revealed that it is not so important who sets the goal as it is that a specific challenging goal in fact be set. However, subsequent laboratory and field experiments revealed contradictory findings. Erez and her colleagues (e.g. Erez, 1986; Erez and Arad, 1986; Erez, Earley, and Hulin, 1985) found that goal commitment and subsequent performance are higher when employees participate in the setting of the goal than was the case when the goals were assigned. A series of 11 studies by Latham and his colleagues (e.g. Latham and Saari, 1979a, b; Latham and Steele, 1983) found that when goal difficulty is held constant, goal commitment and performance are the same regardless of whether the goal is assigned or set participatively.

In what is rare if not unique in science, the two antagonists, Erez and Latham, did a series of collaborative studies, with Locke as a mediator, to discover the basis for their conflicting findings (Latham, Erez, and Locke, 1988). They found that their methodology was highly similar in the way in which the goals were set participatively, yet highly different in the way in which the goals were assigned. In what would be expected, based on Greenberg's organizational justice principles (see Chapter 14, this volume), when the assigned goal was given tersely and without any rationale, it had a negative effect on performance relative to participatively set goals. When an assigned goal from an authority figure included a logic or rationale, it had the same positive effect on goal commitment and performance as did a participatively set goal. (For an overall summary of the research on the effects of participation, see Chapter 24, this volume.)

Subsequent research by Latham, Winters, and Locke (1994) revealed that Erez had been correct in arguing the benefit of participation in goal setting, but for the wrong reason. The benefit is primarily cognitive rather than motivational. Employee participation in decision making has a positive effect on performance to the extent that it increases self-efficacy and the discovery of task relevant strategies. When this does not occur, when these two variables are partialed out, participation in decision making has a negligible effect on performance.

Training self-regulation

The management of oneself lies at the core of goal setting theory. Setting a goal and taking action to attain it is a volitional process. Holding goal difficulty constant, self-set goals are as effective in increasing performance as are goals that are assigned or set participatively (Locke and Latham, 1990). This finding is the basis for training people skills in self-management.

CASE EXAMPLE

The University of Washington

The University of Washington trained their maintenance employees (carpenters, mechanics, electricians) in self-regulation to increase their job attendance (Frayne and Latham, 1987). The training took place in a group setting one hour a week for eight weeks. In the first session, the principles of goal setting were explained to the trainees. In Session 2, the trainees generated reasons for their low job attendance. The third session focused on the value of setting behavioral and outcome (days present) goals for attendance. In the fourth session, the importance of self-monitoring one's behavior was discussed. Specifically, the trainees were taught to use charts and diaries to record (a) their own attendance, (b) the reasons for missing one or more days of the week, and (c) the steps that were followed to subsequently return to work. The trainees identified rewards and punishers in the fifth session that they would self-administer contingent upon their attendance. In the sixth session the trainees wrote a behavioral contract with themselves. The contract specified writing the goal(s) to be attained, the timeframe for attaining the goal(s), the outcomes of attaining or failing to attain the goal(s), and the task strategies necessary for attaining the goal(s). The seventh session emphasized maintenance. That is, discussion focused on issues that might result in a relapse in absenteeism, planning for such situations should they occur, and developing strategies for dealing with such situations. During the final week of training, the trainer reviewed each technique presented in the program, answered questions from the trainees regarding these skills, and clarified expectations for self-management.

Observe that the training took explicit account of goal setting moderators and sub-principles discussed earlier in this chapter. Goal commitment was the focus of Sessions 5 and 6, where rewards and punishers were selected, and a behavioral contract was written. Feedback through self-monitoring was emphasized in Session 4. The complexity of the task and the situational constraints were the focus of Session 2 where employees specified in writing the behavior that they believed would enable them to get to work, and Session 7 where they outlined possibilities for a relapse and what could be done to overcome such issues.

Participatory group discussions occurred throughout the eight weeks of training. The main benefit of participation, as noted earlier, is cognitive; thus the training focused the attention of each person in the group on identifying effective strategies for overcoming obstacles to attaining the goal. In this way, self-efficacy was increased. Self-efficacy correlated significantly in the study with subsequent job attendance. Three months later employee attendance was significantly higher in the training than in the control group.

The University of Washington conducted a six-month and a nine-month follow-up study to determine the long-term effects of this training. Employees who had been trained in self-management continued to have higher job attendance than those in the control group. Moreover, when the people in the control group were subsequently given the same training in self-management, but by a different trainer, they too showed the same positive improvement in their self-efficacy with regard to coping with obstacles perceived by them as preventing them from coming to work. Moreover, their job attendance increased to the same level as that which the original training group had achieved three months after it had been trained (Latham and Frayne, 1989).

When are goals ineffective? The answer to this question is given throughout this chapter. For example, both the American Pulpwood Association and Weyerhaeuser found that when the goal is abstract such as urging loggers to do their best, productivity is lower than setting a specific difficult goal (Latham and Kinne, 1974; Latham and Yukl, 1975). They also found that when goals are set and supervisory supportiveness is lacking, turnover is high, people quit (Ronan, Latham, and Kinne, 1973). When specific challenging performance goals were set before people have acquired knowledge and skill to perform the task, the performance of Air Force cadets dropped (Kanfer and Ackerman, 1989). In short, goals do not work when the principles we have discussed are not applied.

FUTURE DIRECTIONS

A limitation of theories of consciously set goals is that they fail to take advantage of the subconscious, a storehouse of knowledge, and values beyond that which is found in awareness at any given point in time. This is a limitation because unlike the conscious mind, the subconscious has an enormous storage capacity. This storage capacity frees the conscious mind to focus on new facts and make new integrations. Priming may be a method for setting subconscious goals.

People were primed to diet through exposure to a room filled with exercise and dieting magazines. People in the control group entered a room filled with magazines about politics and economics. Participants in the primed condition subsequently chose an apple over a candy bar. They had no awareness of why they made that decision (Fishbach, Friedman, and Kruglanski, 2003). Employees in a call center were given written instructions over a backdrop photograph of a woman winning a race. They subsequently raised significantly more dollars than did employees whose instructions were written on an otherwise blank sheet of paper (Shantz and Latham, 2009).

CONCLUSION

Specific challenging goals are motivational regardless of whether they are self-set, set participatively, or assigned. If the person has the knowledge and skill necessary to perform the task, performance goals should be set. If the requisite knowledge or skill is lacking, learning goals should be set. If the moderators and subprinciples described in this chapter are taken into account by practitioners of goal setting, the probability that performance and satisfaction will increase is above .90 (Locke and Latham, 1990). No other theory of motivation has been found to be as consistently effective in the workplace as goal setting.

REFERENCES

Bandura, A. (1997). *Self Efficacy: The Exercise of Control*. New York: Freeman.

Bandura, A. (2001). Social cognitive theory: an agentic perspective. *Annual Review of Psychology*, 52, 1–26.

Brown, T. C., and Latham, G. P. (2002). The effects of behavioral outcome goals, learning goals, and urging people to do their best on an individual's teamwork behavior in a group problem-solving task. *Canadian Journal of Behavioural Science*, 34, 276–285.

Dorner, D. (1991). The investigation of action regulation in uncertain and complex situations. In J. Rasmussen, G. Brehmer, and J. Leplat (eds), *Distributed Decision Making: Cognitive Models for Cooperative Work* (pp. 349–356). New York: Wiley.

Drach-Zahavy, A., and Erez, M. (2002). Challenge versus threat effects on the goal–performance relationship. *Organizational Behavior and Human Decision Processes*, 88, 667–682.

Earley, P. C. (1985). Influence of information, choice and task complexity upon goal acceptance, performance, and personal goals. *Journal of Applied Psychology*, 70, 481–491.

Earley, P. C., and Lee, C. (1992). Comparative peer evaluations of organizational behavior theories. *Organizational Development Journal*, 10, 37–42.

Earley, P. C., Connolly, T., and Ekegren, G. (1989). Goals, strategy development and task performance: Some limits to the efficacy of goal setting. *Journal of Applied Psychology*, 74, 24–33.

Earley, P. C., Wojnaroski, P., and Prest, W. (1987). Task planning and energy expended: Exploration of how goals influence performance. *Journal of Applied Psychology*, 72, 107–114.

Erez, M. (1977). Feedback: a necessary condition for the goal setting–performance relationship. *Journal of Applied Psychology*, 62, 624–627.

Erez, M. (1986). The congruence of goal setting strategies with socio-cultural values, and its effect on performance. *Journal of Management*, 12, 83–90.

Erez, M., and Arad, R. (1986). Participative goal setting: Social, motivational, and cognitive factors. *Journal of Applied Psychology*, 71, 591–597.

Erez, M., Earley, P. C., and Hulin, C. L. (1985). The impact of participation on goal acceptance and performance: A two-step model. *Academy of Management Journal*, 28, 50–66.

Fishbach, A., Friedman, R. S., and Kruglanski, A. W. (2003). Leading us not unto temptation: Momentary allurements elicit overriding goal activation. *Journal of Personality and Social Psychology*, 84, 296–309.

Frayne, C. A., and Latham, G. P. (1987). The application of social learning theory to employee self-management of attendance. *Journal of Applied Psychology*, 72, 387–392.

Frese, M. (2005). Grand theories and midrange theories: Cultural effects on theorizing and the attempt to understand active approaches to work. In K. G. Smith and M. Hitt (eds), *The Oxford Handbook of Management Theory: The Process of Theory Development*. Oxford, UK: Oxford University Press.

Frese, M., and Zapf, D. (1994). Action as the core of work psychology: a German approach. In H. C. Triandis, M. D. Dunnette, and L. M. Hough (eds), *Handbook of Industrial and Organizational Psychology*: Vol. 4 (pp. 271–340). Palo Alto, CA: Consulting Psychologist Press. (Second edition.)

Gauggel, S. (1999). Goal-setting and its influence on the performance of brain-damaged patients. Unpublished doctoral dissertation, Philipps University of Marburg, Germany.

Kanfer, R. (1990). Motivation theory and industrial and organizational theory. In M. D. Dunnette and L. M. Hough (eds), *Handbook of Industrial and Organizational Psychology* (pp. 75–170). Palo Alto, CA: Consulting Psychologists Press.

Kanfer, R., and Ackerman, P. L. (1989). Motivation and cognitive abilities: An integrative/aptitude-treatment interaction approach to skill acquisition. *Journal of Applied Psychology*, 74, 657–690.

Keith, N., and Frese, M. (2005). Self-regulation error management training: Emotion control and metacognition as mediators of performance effects. *Journal of Applied Psychology*, 90, 677–691.

Kernan, M. C., and Lord, R. G. (1988). Effects of participative versus assigned goals and feedback in a multitrial task. *Motivation and Emotion*, 12, 75–86.

Lashley, K. S. (1929). *Brain Mechanisms and Intelligence*. Chicago: University of Chicago Press.

Latham, G. P. (2001). The importance of understanding and changing employee outcome expectancies for gaining commitment to an organizational goal. *Personnel Psychology*, 54, 707–716.

Latham, G. P., and Baldes, J. J. (1975). The "practical significance" of Locke's theory of goal setting. *Journal of Applied Psychology*, 60, 122–124.

Latham, G. P., and Brown, T. C. (2006). The effect of learning vs. outcome goals on self-efficacy and satisfaction in a MBA Program. *Applied Psychology: An International Review*, 55, 606–623.

Latham, G. P., and Budworth, M. (2006). The effect of training in verbal self-guidance on the self-efficacy and performance of Native North Americans in the selection interview. *Journal of Vocational Behavior*, 68, 516–523.

Latham, G. P., and Frayne, C. (1989). Self-management training for increasing job attendance: A follow-up and a replication. *Journal of Applied Psychology*, 74, 411–416.

Latham, G. P., and Kinne, S. B. (1974). Improving Job Performance through Training in Goal Setting. *Journal of Applied Psychology*, 59, 187–191.

Latham, G. P., and Locke, E. A. (1975). Increasing productivity with decreasing time limits: A field replication of Parkinson's law. *Journal of Applied Psychology*, 60, 524–526.

Latham, G. P., and Locke, E. A. (1991). Self regulation through goal setting. *Organizational Behavior and Human Decision Process*, 50, 212–247.

Latham, G. P., and Locke, E. A. (2007). New developments in and directions for goal setting. *European Psychologist*, 12, 290–300.

Latham, G. P., and Saari, L. M. (1979a). The effects of holding goal difficulty constant on assigned and participatively set goals. *Academy of Management Journal*, 22, 163–168.

Latham, G. P., and Saari, L. M. (1979b). The importance of supportive relationships in goal setting. *Journal of Applied Psychology*, 64, 151–156.

Latham, G. P., and Saari, L. M. (1982). The importance of union acceptance for productivity improvement through goal setting. *Personnel Psychology*, 35, 781–787.

Latham, G. P., and Seijts, G. H. (1999). The effects of proximal and distal goals on performance on a moderately complex task. *Journal of Organizational Behavior*, 20, 421–429.

Latham, G. P., and Steele, T. P. (1983). The motivational effects of participation versus goal setting on performance. *Academy of Management Journal*, 26, 406–417.

Latham, G. P., and Yukl, G. A. (1975). Assigned versus participative goal setting with educated and uneducated wood workers. *Journal of Applied Psychology*, 60, 299–302.

Latham, G. P., Erez, M., and Locke, E. A. (1988). Resolving scientific disputes by the joint design of crucial experiments by the antagonists: Application to the Erez–Latham dispute regarding participation in goal setting. *Journal of Applied Psychology*, 73, 753–772.

Latham, G. P., Locke, E. A., and Fassina, N. E. (2002). The high performance cycle: Standing the test of time. In S. Sonnentag (ed.), *The Psychological Management of Individual Performance: A Handbook in the Psychology of Management in Organizations* (pp. 201–228). Chichester: Wiley.

Latham, G. P., Mitchell, T. R., and Dossett, D. L. (1978). The importance of participative goal setting and anticipated rewards on goal difficulty and job performance. *Journal of Applied Psychology*, 63, 170–171.

Latham, G. P., Seijts, H., and Crim, D. (2008). The effects of learning goal difficulty level and cognitive ability on strategies and performance. *Canadian Journal of Behavioural Science*, 40, 220–229.

Latham, G. P., Winters, D. C., and Locke, E. A. (1994). Cognitive and motivational effects of participation: a mediator study. *Journal of Organizational Behavior*, 15, 49–63.

Locke, E. A., and Latham, G. P. (1990). *A Theory of Goal Setting and Task Performance*. Englewood Cliffs, NJ: Prentice Hall.

Locke, E. A., and Latham, G. P. (2002). Building a practically useful theory of goal setting and task motivation: A 35-year odyssey. *American Psychologist*, 57, 705–717.

Locke, E. A., Frederick, E., Buckner, E., and Bobko, P. (1984). Effect of previously assigned goals on self-set goals and performance. *Journal of Applied Psychology*, 69, 694–699.

Mealiea, L. W., and Latham, G. P. (1996). *Skills for Managerial Success: Theory, Experience, and Practice*. Toronto, ON: Irwin.

Meyer, H. H., Kay, E., and French, J. R. P., Jr. (1965). Split roles in performance appraisal. *Harvard Business Review*, 43, 123–129.

Millman, Z., and Latham, G. P. (2001). Increasing re-employment through training in verbal self guidance. In M. Erez, U. Kleinbeck, and H. K. Thierry (eds), *Work Motivation in the Context of a Globalizing Economy*. Lawrence Erlbaum.

Miner, J. B. (1984). The validity and usefulness of theories in an emerging organizational science. *Academy of Management Review*, 9, 296–306.

Mitchell, T. R., and Daniels, D. (2003). *Motivation*. In W. C. Borman, D. R. Ilgen, and R. J. Klimoski (eds), *Handbook of Psychology: Industrial Organizational Psychology*, Vol. 12 (pp. 225–254). New York: Wiley.

Pinder, C. C. (2008). *Work Motivation in Organizational Behavior* (2nd edition). Toronto, ON: Psychology Press.

Prigatano, G. P., Wong, J. L., Williams, C., and Plenge, K. L. (1997). Prescribed versus actual length of stay and impatient neurorehabilitation outcome for brain dysfunctional patients. *Archives of Physical Medicine and Rehabilitation*, 78, 621–629.

Rodgers, R., and Hunter, J. E. (1991). Impact of management by objectives on organizational productivity. *Journal of Applied Psychology*, 76, 322–336.

Ronan, W. W., Latham, G. P., and Kinne, S. B. (1973). The effects of goal setting and supervision on worker behavior in an industrial situation. *Journal of Applied Psychology*, 58, 302–307.

Roney, C. J. R., Griggs, M., and Shanks, B. (2003). The mediation and moderation of general motivational variables by specific goals that are negatively framed. Unpublished manuscript.

Salancik, G. (1977). Commitment and the control of organizational behavior and belief. In B. M. Staw and G. R. Salancik (eds), *New Directions in Organizational Behavior*. Chicago: St. Clair Press.

Seijts, G. H., and Latham, G. P. (2005). Learning versus performance goals: When should each be used? *Academy of Management Executive*, 19, 124–131.

Selden, S. C., and Brewer, G. A. (2000). Work motivation in the senior executive service: Testing the high performance cycle theory. *Journal of Public Administration Research and Theory*, 10, 531–550.

Shantz, A., and Latham, G. P. (2009). The effect of subconscious and conscious goals on employee performance. *Organizational Behavior and Human Decision Processes*, 109, 9–17.

Weinberg, R. S. (1994). Goal setting and performance in sport and exercise settings: A synthesis and critique. *Medicine and Science in Sports and Exercise*, 26, 469–477.

Wiese, B. S., and Freund, A. M. (2005). Goal progress makes one happy, or does it? longitudinal findings from the work domain. *Journal of Occupational and Organizational Psychology*, 78, 287–304.

Winters, D., and Latham, G. P. (1996). The effect of learning versus outcome goals on a simple versus a complex task. *Group and Organization Management*, 21, 236–250.

EXERCISES

Group exercise – goal setting

Randomly divide people into three groups. Tell one group (in writing in all cases), so no person will know the others' goals, to think of 14 ways to improve their business (UG or MBA) program or their business unit's effectiveness in two minutes. (Give all subjects actually three minutes to show the effects of persistence of the hard goal: the hard goal group will still be working.) Give a second group the goal of 4 and tell the third group to do their best. Calculate the mean score of each group at the end. (It is best to use lined sheets numbered 1 to 14 or 1 to 4) for the goal groups and a blank sheet for the do best group. (This helps prevent people from setting their own personal goals.)

Group exercise – subconscious priming

Give one group a photo of a woman winning a race and give the other group a blank sheet of paper. Ask both groups to come up with as many uses for a coat hanger as they can in two minutes. Count the scores of the two groups. This exercise is designed to measure the effects of subconscious priming.

10

Cultivate Self-efficacy for Personal and Organizational Effectiveness

Albert Bandura

Human behavior is extensively motivated and regulated through the exercise of self-influence. Among the mechanisms of self-influence, none is more focal or pervading than belief in one's personal efficacy. Unless people believe that they can produce desired effects and forestall undesired ones by their actions, they have little incentive to act or to persevere in the face of difficulties. Whatever other factors may serve as guides and motivators, they are rooted in the core belief that one has the power to produce desired results. That belief in one's capabilities is a vital personal resource and is amply documented by meta-analyses of findings from diverse spheres of functioning (Holden, 1991; Holden, Moncher, Schinke, and Barker, 1990; Multon, Brown, and Lent, 1991; Stajkovic, Lee, and Nyberg, in press, Stajkovic and Luthans, 1998). Perceived self-efficacy is founded on the agentic perspective of social cognitive theory (Bandura, 1997, 2006, 2008). To be an agent is to influence intentionally one's functioning and life conditions. In this view, people are contributors to their life circumstances not just products of them.

CORE FUNCTIONAL PROPERTIES OF PERCEIVED SELF-EFFICACY

Converging evidence from controlled experimental and field studies verifies that belief in one's capabilities contribute uniquely to motivation and action (Bandura, 1997, 2009; Bandura and Locke, 2003). Perceived self-efficacy occupies a pivotal role in causal structures because it affects human functioning not only directly, but through its impact on other important classes of determinants. These determinants include goal aspirations, incentives and disincentives rooted in outcome expectations, and perceived impediments and opportunity structures in social systems. Figure 10.1 presents the structure of the causal model. Diverse lines of research have verified the various paths in the structural model. Longitudinal research, evaluating the full set of determinants, confirms that the social cognitive model provides a good fit to the empirical evidence (Plotnikoff, Lippke, Courneya,

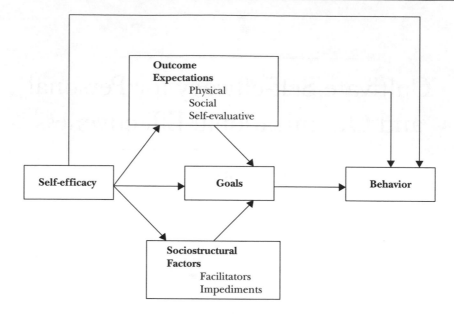

FIGURE 10.1 Structural paths of influence wherein perceived self-efficacy affects motivation and performance attainments both directly and through its impact on goals, outcome expectations, and perception of sociostructural facilitators and impediments

Birkett, and Sigal, 2008). Among the different determinants, self-efficacy emerges as the strongest predictor.

Efficacy beliefs affect self-motivation and action through their impact on goals and aspirations. It is partly on the basis of efficacy beliefs that people choose what goal challenges to undertake, how much effort to invest in the endeavor, and how long to persevere in the face of difficulties (Bandura, 1997; Locke and Latham, 1990). When faced with obstacles, setbacks and failures, those who doubt their capabilities slacken their efforts, give up prematurely, or settle for poorer solutions. Those who have a strong belief in their capabilities redouble their effort to master the challenges.

Perceived efficacy likewise plays an influential role in the incentive and disincentive potential of outcome expectations. The outcomes people anticipate depend largely on their beliefs of how well they can perform in given situations. Those of high efficacy expect to gain favorable outcomes through good performance, whereas those who expect poor performances of themselves conjure up negative outcomes. Anticipated outcomes may take the form of material costs and benefits, social commendation and reproof, and self-approving and self-censuring affective reactions.

In theories of motivation founded on the incentives operating through cognized outcomes, such as expectancy-value theories, motivation is governed by the expectation that a given behavior will produce certain outcomes and the value placed on those outcomes. This type of theory includes only one of the two belief systems governing motivation. People act on their beliefs about what they can do, as well as on their beliefs about the likely outcomes of performance. There are countless activities which, if done well, produce valued outcomes, but they are not pursued by those who doubt they can do what it takes to succeed.

They exclude entire classes of options rapidly on self-efficacy grounds without bothering to analyze their costs and benefits. Conversely, those of high efficacy expect their efforts to bring success and are not easily dissuaded by negative outcomes.

Rational models of motivation and decision making that exclude perceived self-efficacy sacrifice explanatory and predictive power. Perceived self-efficacy not only sets the slate of options for consideration, but also regulates their implementation. Having decided on a course of action, one cannot sit back and wait for the performances to appear. Making a decision does not ensure that individuals will mobilize the effort to execute the decided course of action successfully and stick to it in the face of difficulties. A psychology of decision making requires a psychology of action grounded in enabling and sustaining efficacy beliefs. One must add a performatory self to the decisional self, otherwise the decider is left stranded in thought.

Beliefs of personal efficacy shape whether people attend to the opportunities or to the impediments that their life circumstances present and how formidable the obstacles appear. People of high efficacy focus on the opportunities worth pursuing and view difficult obstacles as surmountable. (Krueger and Dickson, 1993, 1994). Through ingenuity and perseverance they figure out ways of exercising some measure of control even in environments of limited opportunities and many constraints. Those beset with self-doubts dwell on impediments which they view as obstacles over which they can exert little control. They easily convince themselves of the futility of effort so they achieve limited success even in environments that provide many opportunities.

Diverse Organizational Impact of Perceived Self-efficacy

The scope of the organizational applications of perceived self-efficacy will be summarized briefly before presenting the principles for altering efficacy belief systems. The brief review of its scope addresses the challenge of constructing a parsimonious theory of broad generalizability. To begin with, perceived self-efficacy is an influential determinant of career choice and development. The higher the people's perceived efficacy to fulfill educational requirements and occupational roles the wider the career options they seriously consider pursuing, the greater the interest they have in them, the better they prepare themselves educationally for different occupational careers, and the greater their staying power in challenging career pursuits (Lent, Brown, and Hackett, 1994).

New employees receive training designed to prepare them for the occupational roles they will be performing (see Chapter 4, this volume). Those of low perceived efficacy prefer prescriptive training that tells them how to perform the roles as traditionally structured (Jones, 1986; Saks, 1995). Employees of high perceived efficacy prefer training that enables them to restructure their roles innovatively by improving the customary practices and adding new elements and functions to them. Self-efficacious employees take greater initiative in their occupational self-development and generate ideas that help to improve work processes (Speier and Frese, 1997).

Organizations that provide their new employees with guided mastery experiences, effective co-workers as models, and enabling performance feedback enhance employees' self-efficacy, emotional well-being, job satisfaction, and level of productivity (Saks, 1994, 1995). Other organizational practices, such as job enrichment and mutually supportive communication, also build employees' perceived efficacy to take on broader functions and a proactive work role (Parker, 1998). Self-efficacy theory provides a conceptual framework within which to study the determinants of effective work design and the mechanisms through which they enhance organizational functioning.

Worklife is increasingly structured on a team-based model in which management and operational functions are assigned to the workers themselves (see Chapter 11). A self-management work structure changes the model of supervisory managership from hierarchical control to facilitative guidance that provides the necessary resources, instructive guidance, and the support that teams need to do their work effectively (Stewart and Manz, 1995). Enabling organizational structures builds managers' efficacy to operate as facilitators of productive team work (Laschruger and Shamian, 1994). The perceived collective efficacy of self-managed teams predicts the members' satisfaction and productivity (Lindsley, Mathieu, Heffner, and Brass, 1994, Little and Madigan, 1994).

Managers as enabling facilitators of team functioning (see Chapter 15) have also been studied in terms of empowering leadership. It is typically characterized as leading by example, participant decision making, enabling guidance, and receptivity to members' ideas (Arnold, Arad, Rhoades, and Drasgow, 2000). Empowering leadership has been found to be positively related to team performance, but the mechanisms through which it works have received little attention. Srivastava, Bartol, and Locke (2006) report that empowering leaderships is not directly linked to performance but operates through knowledge sharing and perceived team efficacy.

The development of new business ventures and the renewal of established ones depend heavily on innovativeness and entrepreneurship (see Chapter 30). With many resourceful competitors around, viability requires continual ingenuity. At the preparatory level, self-efficacy plays an influential role in the development of entrepreneurial intentions (Zhao, Seibert, and Hills, 2005). Learning experiences and risk propensity had no direct effect on intentions to pursue an entrepreneurial career. They had an impact only to the extent that they raised individuals' beliefs in their efficacy to identify new business opportunities, create new products, think creatively, and commercialize ideas. This is the structural pattern of relations after controlling for prior entrepreneurial intentions. Self-efficacy continues to play an influential role in the undertaking of new ventures.

Entrepreneurs have to be willing to take risks under uncertainty. Those of high efficacy focus on the opportunities worth pursuing, whereas the less self-efficacious dwell on the risks to be avoided (Kreuger and Dickson, 1993, 1994). Hence, perceived self-efficacy predicts entrepreneurship and which patent inventors are likely to start new business ventures (Chen, Greene, and Crick, 1998; Markman and Baron, 1999). Venturers who achieve high growth in companies they have founded or transformed, or those they have bought, have a vision of what they wish to achieve, a firm belief in their efficacy to realize it, set challenging growth goals, and come up with innovative production and marketing strategies (Baum, Locke, and Smith, 2001; Baum and Locke, 2004).

Effective leadership and workforces require receptivity to innovators that can improve the quality and productivity of organizations. Managers' perceived technical efficacy influences their readiness to adopt electronic technologies (Jorde-Bloom and Ford, 1988). Efficacy beliefs affect not only managers' receptivity to technological innovations, but also the readiness with which employees adopt them (Hill, Smith, and Mann, 1987; McDonald and Siegall, 1992). Efficacy-fostered adoption of new technologies, in turn, alters the organizational network structure and confers influence on early adopters within an organization over time (Burkardt, and Brass, 1990).

Perceived self-efficacy to fulfill occupational demands affects level of stress and physical health of employees (see Chapter 27). Those of low efficacy are stressed both emotionally and physiologically by perceived overload, in which task demands exceed their perceived coping capabilities; whereas those who hold a high belief in their efficacy and that of their group are unfazed by heavy workloads (Jex and Bliese, 1999). Perceived self-efficacy must be added to the demands–control model of occupational stress to improve its pre-dictability. It contends that being given control over work activities reduces the stressful-ness of worklife. High job demands with an opportunity to exercise control over various facets of the work environment is unperturbing to jobholders of high perceived efficacy, but stressful to those of low perceived efficacy to manage them (Schaubroeck and Merritt, 1997). Efforts to reduce occupational stressfulness by increasing job control without rais-ing self-efficacy to manage the increased responsibilities will do more harm than good. For the self-efficacious, job underload can be a stressor. Indeed, employees of high efficacy are stressed by perceived underload in which they feel thwarted and frustrated by organiz-ational constraints in developing and using their potentialities (Matsui and Onglatco, 1992). Exposure to chronic occupational stressors with a low sense of efficacy to manage job demands and to enlist social support in times of difficulty, increases vulnerability to burn-out (Brouwers and Tomic 1999, 2006; Leiter, 1992, Salanova, Grau, Cifre, and Llorens, 2000). This syndrome is characterized by physical and emotional exhaustion, depersonal-ization of clients, lack of any sense of personal accomplishment, and occupational disen-gagement with cynicism about one's work.

A resilient sense of efficacy provides the necessary staying power in the tortuous pursuit of innovation and excellence. Yet the very undaunted self-efficacy that breeds success in tough ventures may perpetuate adherence to courses of action that hold little prospect of even-tual success. Thus, for example, managers of high perceived efficacy are more prone than those of low efficacy to escalate commitment to unproductive ventures (Whyte and Saks, 2007; Whyte, Saks, and Hook, 1997), and to remain wedded to previously successful prac-tices despite altered realities that place them at competitive disadvantage (Audia, Locke, and Smith, 2000). The corrective for the perils of success is not deflation of personal efficacy. Such a disenabling remedy would undermine aspiration, innovation, and human accomplish-ments in endeavors presenting tough odds. Individuals who are highly assured in their cap-abilities and the effectiveness of their strategies are disinclined to seek discordant information that would suggest the need for corrective adjustments. The challenge is to preserve the con-siderable functional value of resilient self-efficacy, but to institute information monitoring and social feedback systems that can help to identify practices that are beyond the point of utility. Reliable risk analysis, when achievable, is essential in preventing irresponsible ventures that created a global financial crisis. However, one must distinguish between escalative commit-ment to a failing venture and engagement in deceptive and fraudulent corporate practices. Research on the exercise of moral agency attests to the influential role played by selective moral disengagement in corporate practices that spawn widespread harm (Bandura, 1999; Bandura, Caprara, and Zsolnai, 2002; White, Bandura, and Bero, 2009). As a trader in the midst of the growing financial crisis put it, "I leave my ethics at the door."

It is easy to achieve veridical judgment. Simply punish optimism. The motivational belief system that fosters accomplishments in difficult endeavors combines realism about tough odds, but optimism that through self-development and perseverant effort one can beat those odds. We study intensively the risks of overconfidence, but ignore the more pervasive personal and social costs of underconfidence. This bias probably stems from the fact that the costs of lost opportunities and underdeveloped potentialities are long delayed and less noticeable than those of venturesome missteps. The heavy selective focus on the risk of overconfidence stands in stark contrast to the entrepreneurial spirit driving the modern workplace in the rapidly changing world.

The functional value of veridical self-appraisal depends on the nature of the venture. In activities where the margins of error are narrow and missteps can produce costly or injurious consequences, one is best served by conservative appraisal of one's efficacy. It is a different matter when difficult accomplishments can produce substantial personal or social benefits and the personal costs involve time, effort, and expendable resources. People have to decide whether to invest their efforts and resources in ventures that are difficult to fulfill, and how much hardship they are willing to endure in formidable pursuits that may have huge payoffs but are strewn with obstacles and uncertainties. Turning visions into realities is an arduous process with uncertain outcomes. Societies enjoy the considerable benefits of the eventual accomplishments in the arts, sciences, and technologies of its persisters and risk takers. Realists trade on the merchandizable products that flow from the creations of innovative persisters. To paraphrase the discerning observation of George Bernard Shaw, reasonable people adapt to the world, unreasonable people try to change it, so human progress depends on the unreasonable ones.

Social cognitive theory distinguishes among three forms of perceived efficacy depending on the source of control over events. Direct individual efficacy pertains to belief in one's capability to exercise some measure of control over events within one's command. However, in many spheres of functioning, people do not have direct control over conditions that affect their lives. They exercise proxy efficacy through socially mediated influence. They do so by influencing others who have the resources, knowledge, and means to act on their behalf to secure the outcomes they desire. Many of the things people seek are achievable only by working collaboratively for common purpose through interdependent effort. In the exercise of collective efficacy, they pool their knowledge, skills, and resources, and act in concert to shape their future (Bandura, 2000; Gully, Incalcaterra, Joshi, and Beaubien, 2002, Stajkovic, Lee, and Nyberg, in press).

Given the generality and centrality of the self-efficacy mechanism in the causal structures governing diverse aspects of organizational functioning, programs aimed at developing a resilient sense of efficacy can yield significant dividends in performance accomplishments and personal well-being. The principles for developing and strengthening beliefs of personal efficacy are addressed in the sections that follow. Social cognitive theory lends itself readily to personal and social applications in diverse spheres of life. These applications are extensively reviewed elsewhere (Bandura, 1986, 1997, 2004, 2006). The present chapter summarizes the relevant principles for developing a resilient sense of efficacy and illustrates their application in the organizational field.

PRINCIPLES GOVERNING THE DEVELOPMENT OF PERSONAL AND COLLECTIVE EFFICACY

Self-efficacy beliefs are developed by four principal sources of information conveyed enactively, vicariously, persuasively, and somatically. The most effective way of instilling strong efficacy is through *enactive mastery experiences* structured through graduated attainments.

If people experience only easy successes they come to expect quick results and are easily discouraged by failure. Hence, resilient efficacy requires experience in overcoming obstacles through perseverant effort. The route to high attainments is strewn with failure and setbacks. Success is achieved by learning from mistakes. Resilience must also be built by training in how to manage failure so that it is informative rather than demoralizing.

The second way of developing personal and collective efficacy is by *social modeling*. Competent models convey knowledge, skills, and strategies for managing task demands. By their example in pursuing challenges, models foster aspirations and interest in activities. Seeing people similar to oneself succeed by perseverant effort raises observers' beliefs in their own abilities.

Social persuasion is the third mode of influence. If people are persuaded to believe in themselves they will exert more effort. This increases their chances of success. However, credible persuaders must be knowledgeable and practice what they preach. Effective efficacy builders do more than convey faith in others. They arrange situations for others in ways that bring success. They avoid placing them, prematurely, in situations where they are likely to fail. They measure success by self-improvement, rather than by triumphs over others. Pep talks, without enabling guidance, achieve little.

People rely partly on their physical and emotional states in judging their efficacy. They read their tension, anxiety, and weariness as signs of personal deficiencies. Mood also affects how people judge their efficacy. Positive mood enhances a sense of efficacy; depressed mood diminishes it. People often misread their fatigue, windedness, aches, and pains as evidence of declining physical efficacy. These physical conditions are often due to a sedentary lifestyle. Efficacy beliefs are strengthened by reducing anxiety and depression, building physical strength and stamina, and changing misrepresentations of bodily states.

As illustrated in the diverse organizational effects cited earlier, efficacy beliefs regulate human functioning through their impact on cognitive, motivational, affective, and decisional processes. They affect: whether people think productively, pessimistically, or optimistically and in self-enacting or self-debilitating ways; how well they motivate themselves and persevere in the face of difficulties; the quality of their emotional well-being they achieve and their vulnerability to stress and depression; and the life choices they make, which set the course of their life paths.

Information for judging personal efficacy, whether conveyed enactively, vicariously, persuasively, or somatically is not inherently informative. It is only raw data. Experiences become instructive through cognitive processing of efficacy information and reflective thought. One must distinguish between information conveyed by events and information as selected, interpreted, and integrated into self-efficacy judgments.

The cognitive processing of efficacy information involves two separate functions (Bandura, 1997). The first is the types of information people attend to and use as indicators of personal efficacy. Social cognitive theory specifies the set of efficacy indictors that are unique to each of the four major modes of influence. These are summarized in Table 10.1. For example, judgments of self-efficacy based on performance attainments will vary depending on people's interpretive biases, the perceived difficulty of the task, how hard they worked at it, how much help they received, the conditions under which they performed, their emotional and physical state at the time, their rate of improvement over time, and biases in how they monitor and recall their attainments.

Table 10.1   The distinctive sets of factors within each of four modes of efficacy influence
what can affect the construction of self efficacy beliefs

Enactive Efficacy Information	*Vicarious Efficacy Information*
Interpretive biases	Model attribute similarity
Perceived task difficulty and diagnosticity	Model performance similarity
Effort expenditure	Model historical similarity
Amount of external aid received	Multiplicity and diversity of modeling
Situational circumstances of performance	Mastery or coping modeling
Transient affective and physical states	Exemplification of strategies
Temporal pattern of successes and failures	Portrayal of task demands
Selective bias in self-monitoring of performance	
Selective bias in memory for performance attainments	
Persuasory Efficacy Information	*Somatic And Affective Information*
Credibility	Degree of attentional focus on somatic states
Expertness	Interpretive biases regarding somatic states
Consensus	Perceived source of affective arousal
Degree of appraisal disparity	Level of arousal
Familiarity with task demands	Situational circumstances of arousal

The indicators people single out provide the information base on which the self-appraisal
process operates. The second function in efficacy judgment involves the combination rules
or heuristics people use to weight and integrate efficacy information from the diverse sources
in forming their efficacy beliefs. The informativeness of the various efficacy indicants will
vary for different spheres of functioning. The various sources of efficacy information may
be integrated additively, multiplicatively, configurally, or heuristically. This judgmental process
is not entirely dispassionate. Strong preconceptions and affective proclivities can alter self-
efficacy appraisals positively or negatively.

The multiple benefits of a strong sense of personal efficacy do not arise simply from the
incantation of capability. Saying something should not be confused with believing it to be
so. A sense of personal efficacy is constructed through a complex process of self-persuasion
based on integrating constellations of efficacy information conveyed enactively, vicariously,
socially, and physiologically.

Enablement through guided mastery

Guided mastery provides one of the most effective ways of cultivating competencies.
However, a skill is only as good as its execution, which is heavily governed by self-regulatory
and motivational factors. Individuals may, therefore, perform poorly, adequately, or well
with the same set of skills depending on the beliefs they hold about their capabilities in

given situations (Bandura, 1997). Part of the power of guided mastery stems from its use of all four modes of efficacy development.

The method that produces the best gains in both self-efficacy and skill combines three components (Bandura, 1986). First, the appropriate skills are modeled to convey the basic rules and strategies. Second, the learners receive guided practice under simulated conditions to develop proficiency in the skills. Third, they are provided with a graduated transfer program that helps them to apply their newly learned skills in work situations in ways that will bring them success.

Enabling modeling.   Modeling is the first step in developing competencies. Complex skills are broken down into subskills, which can be modeled on videotape in easily mastered steps. Subdividing complex skills into subskills produces better learning than trying to teach everything at once. After the subskills are learned by this means, they can be combined into complex strategies to serve different purposes. Effective modeling teaches general rules and strategies for dealing with different situations rather than only specific responses or scripted routines. Voiceover narration of the rules and strategies as they are being modeled, and brief summaries of the rules, enhance development of generic competencies.

The execution of skills must be varied to suit changing circumstances. People who learn rules in the abstract usually do a poor job in applying them in particular situations. However, teaching abstract rules with varied brief examples promotes generalizability of the skills being taught by showing how the rules and strategies can be widely applied and adjusted to fit changing conditions. A single lengthy example teaches how to apply the rule in that particular situation but provides no instruction on how to adapt its application to varying situations.

People fail to apply what they have learned, or do so only half-heartedly, if they distrust their ability to do it successfully. Therefore, modeling influences must be designed to build a sense of personal efficacy as well as to convey knowledge about rules and strategies. The impact of modeling on beliefs about one's capabilities is greatly increased by perceived similarity to the models. Learners adopt modeled ways more readily if they see individuals similar to themselves solve problems successfully with the modeled strategies than if they regard the models as very different from themselves. The characteristics of models, the type of problems with which they cope, and the situations in which they apply their skills should be made to appear similar to the trainees' own circumstances.

Guided skill perfection.   Factual and strategic knowledge alone will not beget proficient performance. Knowledge structures are transformed into proficient action through a conception-matching process (Bandura, 1986). Enabling modeling provides the guiding conception for proficient management of one's worklife. The feedback accompanying enactments provides the information needed to detect and correct mismatches between the generic conception of requisite skills and action. This comparative process is repeated until a close match is achieved. Putting into practice what one has learned cognitively can also reveal gaps and flaws in the guiding conception. Recognizing what one does not know contributes to the refinement of cognitive representations by further modeling and verbal instruction regarding the problematic aspects of the representation.

In the transformational phase of competency development, learners test their newly acquired skills in simulated situations where they need not fear making mistakes or appearing inadequate. This is best achieved by role rehearsal in which they practice handling the types of situations they have to manage in their work environment. Mastery of skills can be facilitated by combining cognitive and behavioral rehearsal. In cognitive rehearsal, people rehearse mentally how they will translate strategies into what they say and do to manage given situations.

In perfecting their skills, people need informative feedback about how they are doing. A common problem is that they do not fully observe their own behavior. Informative feedback enables them to make corrective adjustments to get their behavior to fit their idea of how things should be done. Videotape replays are widely used for this purpose. However, simply being shown replays of one's own behavior usually has mixed effects (Hung and Rosenthal, 1981). To produce good results, the feedback must direct attention to the corrective changes that need to be made. It should call attention to successes and improvements and correct deficiencies in a supportive and enabling way so as to strengthen perceived efficacy. Some of the gains accompanying informative feedback result from raising people's beliefs in their efficacy rather than solely from further skill development. The feedback that is most informative and achieves the greatest improvements takes the form of corrective modeling. In this approach, the subskills that have not been adequately learned are further modeled and learners rehearse them until they master them.

Effective functioning requires more than learning how to apply rules and strategies for managing organizational demands. The transactions of occupational life are littered with impediments, discordances, and stressors. Many of the problems of occupational functioning reflect failures of self-management rather than deficiencies of knowledge and technical skills. Therefore, an important aspect of competency development includes training in resiliency to difficulties. As we shall see later, this requires skill in cognitive self-guidance, self-motivation, and strategies for counteracting self-debilitating reactions to troublesome situations that can easily unhinge one.

Gist, Bavetta, and Stevens (1990) augmented a guided model training in negotiation skills with a self-management component. In the latter phase, trainees were taught how to anticipate potential stressors, devise ways of overcoming them, monitor the adequacy of their coping approach, and use self-incentives to sustain their efforts. Trainees who had the benefit of the supplemental self-management training were better at applying learned negotiation skills in new contractual situations presenting conflictful and intimidating elements and negotiated more favorable outcomes than trainees who did not. The self-managers made flexible use of the wide range of strategies they had been taught, whereas their counterparts were more likely to persevere with only a few of the strategies when they encountered negative reactions.

Vinokur and his colleagues devised a multifaceted program to immunize laid-off workers against the debilitating effects of job loss and to restore their efficacy to secure employment in quality jobs (Vinokur, van Ryn, Gramlich, and Price, 1991). They were taught, via modeling and rehearsed role enactments, how to carry out effective job searches. They identified potential impediments and developed problem-solving strategies for generating alternative solutions. They received resilience training by anticipating potential problems and setbacks and developing coping strategies that enabled them to persist despite disappointments during their job search. In follow-up assessments conducted shortly after the program and several years later, the project participants had higher job-seeking efficacy, found jobs more quickly, got better quality jobs, and earned higher wages than did those who did not receive the program. In a meditational analysis, van Ryn and Vinokur (1992) found that the effect of the reemployment program on job search behavior was mediated by perceived self-efficacy.

Job searches in a competitive market require a lot of self-initiative and staying power in face of discouraging rejections. A resilient sense of efficacy is needed to sustain the effort. Yanar, Budworth, and Latham (2008) combined modeling, functional verbal self-guidance, role rehearsal, and proximal goal setting to hasten reemployment of women in an Islamic society. They face the added obstacle of gender discrimination in the workplace. Compared to women who received didactic instruction in job search, those who had the benefit of the enabling sociocognitive program were more persistent in their job search and more likely to find work in their area of interest. In accord with the findings of Vinokur et al. (1991), self-efficacy completely mediated the effect of the program on job search behaviors. This low cost/high benefit approach also enabled aboriginal youth to secure and maintain employment. The higher instilled self-efficacy the better their employment outcomes (Latham and Budworth, 2006). This research addresses a matter of growing import as societies continue to become more ethnically and culturally diverse.

Transfer training by self-directed success.   Modeling and simulated enactments are well suited for creating competencies. But new skills are unlikely to be used for long unless they prove useful when they are put into practice in work situations. People must experience sufficient success using what they have learned to believe in themselves and the value of the new ways. This is best achieved by a transfer program in which newly acquired skills are first tried on the job in situations likely to produce good results. Learners are assigned selected problems they often encounter in their everyday situations. After they try their hand at it, they discuss their successes and where they ran into difficulties for further instructive training. As learners gain skill and confidence in handling easier situations, they gradually take on more difficult problems. If people have not had sufficient practice to convince themselves of their new effectiveness, they apply the skills they have been taught weakly and inconsistently. They rapidly abandon their skills when they fail to get quick results or experience difficulties.

Mastery modeling is now increasingly used, especially in videotaped formats, to develop competencies. But its potential is not fully realized if training programs do not provide sufficient practice to achieve proficiency in the modeled skills or if they lack an adequate transfer program that provides success with the new skills in the natural environment. Such programs rarely include training in resiliency through practice on how to handle setbacks and failure. When instructive modeling is combined with guided role rehearsal and a guided transfer program, this mode of organizational training usually produces excellent results. Because trainees learn and perfect effective ways of managing task demands under lifelike conditions, problems of transferring the new skills to everyday life are markedly reduced.

A mastery modeling program devised by Latham and Saari (1979) to teach supervisors the interpersonal skills they need to work effectively through others is an excellent illustration of this type of approach to competency development. Supervisors have an important impact on the morale and productivity of an organization. But they are often selected for their technical competencies and job-related knowledge, whereas their success in the supervisory role depends largely on their interpersonal skills to guide, enable, and motivate those they supervise.

Latham and Saari (1979) used videotape modeling of prototypic work situations to teach supervisors how to manage the demands of their supervisory role. They were taught how to increase motivation, give recognition, correct poor work habits, discuss potential disciplinary problems, reduce absenteeism, handle employee complaints, and overcome resistance to changes in work practices (Goldstein and Sorcher, 1974). Summary guidelines defining key steps in the rules and strategies being modeled were provided to aid learning and memorability. The group of supervisors discussed and then practiced the skills in role-playing scenarios using incidents they had to manage in their work. They received enabling feedback to help them improve and perfect their skills.

To facilitate transfer of supervisory skills to their work environment, they were instructed to use the skills they had learned on the job during the next week. They then reviewed their successes and difficulties in applying the skills. If they encountered problems, the incidents were reenacted and the supervisors received further training through instructive modeling and role rehearsal on how to manage such situations. Supervisors who received the guided mastery training performed their supervisory role more skillfully both in role-playing situations and on the job assessed a year later than did supervisors who did not receive the training. Because the skills proved highly functional, the supervisors adhered to them. Weak training programs often rely heavily on platitudinous rules for success delivered in a hyped-up fashion. Any motivational effects rapidly dissipate as the initial burst of enthusiasm fades through failure to produce good results. Latham and Saari found that simply explaining to supervisors in the control group the rules and strategies for how to handle problems on the job without modeling and guided role rehearsal did not improve their supervisory skills. Because this approach provides supervisors with the tools for solving the problems they face, they expressed favorable reactions to it.

Supervisory skills instilled by guided mastery improve the morale and productivity of organizations (Porras and Anderson, 1981; Porras, Hargis, Patterson, Maxfield, Roberts, and Bies, 1982). Compared to the productivity of control plants, the one that received the guided mastery program improved supervisory problem-solving skills, had a significantly lower absentee rate, lower turnover of employees, and a 17% increase in the monthly level of productivity over a six-month period. This surpassed the productivity of the control plants. Mastery modeling produces multiple benefits in sales similar to those in production as reflected in enhanced productivity and a lower rate of turnover in personnel (Meyer and Raich, 1983).

There are no training shortcuts or quick fixes for perceived inefficacy, dysfunctional work habits, and deficient self-regulation and occupational competencies. As is true in other spheres of functioning (Miller, Brown, Simpson, Handmaker, Bien, Luckie, Montgomery, Hester, and Tonigan, 1995), the methods that are least effective are most widely used because they are easy to do, whereas enablement methods of proven value are used less often because they require greater investment of time and effort.

The application of guided mastery for markedly different purposes, such as the elimination of anxiety dysfunctions, further illustrates the power and generality of this approach (Bandura, 1997; Williams, 1992). Talk alone will not cure intractable problems. To overcome chronic anxiety people have to confront the perceived threats and gain mastery over them.

When people avoid what they fear, they lose touch with the reality they shun. Guided mastery provides a quick and effective way of restoring reality testing and disconfirming faulty beliefs. But even more important, mastery experiences that are structured to develop coping skills provide persuasive affirming tests that they can exercise control over what they fear. However, individuals are not about to do what they avoid. Therefore, one must create enabling environmental conditions so that individuals who are beset with profound self-doubt about their coping capabilities can perform successfully despite themselves. This is achieved by enlisting a variety of performance mastery aids (Bandura, 2004). This mode of treatment eliminates anxiety, biological stress reactions, and phobic behavior. It also transforms dream activity and wipes out recurrent nightmares of long standing. The changes endure.

Cognitive mastery modeling. A great deal of professional work involves making decisions and finding solutions to problems by drawing on one's knowledge, constructing new knowledge structures, and applying decision rules. Competency in problem solving requires the development of thinking skills for how to seek and construct reliable information and put it to good use. People can learn thinking skills and how to apply them by observing the decision rules and reasoning strategies models use as they seek solutions.

Over the years, organizational training relied almost exclusively on the traditional lecture format despite its limited effectiveness (but see Chapter 4). Mastery modeling works much better than lectures (Burke and Day, 1986). With the advent of the computer, talking heads are being replaced by self-paced instructional programs that provide step-by-step instruction, structured drills, and feedback of accuracy. Comparative tests indicate that cognitive modeling may provide a better approach to the development of higher-order cognitive competencies. In teaching reasoning skills through cognitive modeling, performers verbalize their strategies aloud as they engage in problem-solving activities (Meichenbaum, 1984). The thoughts guiding their decisions and actions are thus made observable. During cognitive modeling, the models verbalize their thoughts as they analyze the problem, seek information relevant to it, generate alternative solutions, judge the likely outcomes associated with each alternative, and select the best way of implementing the chosen solution. They also verbalize their strategies for handling difficulties, how to manage intrusive thoughts and disruptive emotional reactions, recover from mistakes, and motivate themselves. This enables them to remain task oriented under trying conditions.

Modeling thinking skills along with action strategies can aid development of reasoning skills in several ways. Watching models verbalize their thoughts as they solve problems commands attention. Hearing the rules verbalized as the action strategies are implemented produces faster learning than only being told the rules or seeing only the actions modeled. Modeling also provides an informative context in which to demonstrate how to go about solving problems. The rules and strategies of reasoning can be repeated in different forms as often as needed to develop generative thinking skills. Varied application of reasoning strategies to fit different circumstances increases their understanding and generalizability. Observing models verbalize how they use their cognitive skills to solve problems highlights the capacity to exercise control over one's thought processes, which has been shown to boost observers' sense of efficacy over and above the strategic information conveyed. Similarity to succeeding models boosts the instructional impact. And finally, modeling how to manage failures and setbacks fosters resilience to aversive experiences.

Gist (1989) taught managers how to generate ideas to improve the quality of organizational functioning and customer service by providing them with guidelines and practice in innovative problem solving. Cognitive modeling, in which models verbalized strategies for generating ideas, proved superior to presenting the same guidelines solely in the traditional lecture format. Managers who had the benefit of cognitive modeling expressed a higher sense of efficacy and generated considerably more ideas and ideas of greater variety. Regardless of format of instruction, the higher the instilled efficacy beliefs, the more abundant and varied were the generated ideas.

The advantages of cognitive mastery modeling are even more evident when the effectiveness of alternative instructional methods is examined as a function of trainees' preexisting level of perceived efficacy. Gist, Rosen, and Schwoerer (1988) taught managers with a computerized tutorial how to operate a spreadsheet program and use it to solve business problems. Cognitive modeling provided the same information and the same opportunities to practice the computer skills but used a videotape of a model demonstrating how to perform the activity. Videotaped cognitive modeling instilled a uniformly high sense of efficacy to acquire computer software skills regardless of whether managers began the training self-assured or self-doubting of their computer capabilities. A computerized tutorial had weaker effects on efficacy beliefs and was especially ineffective with managers who were insecure in their computer efficacy. Cognitive modeling also promoted a high level of computer skill development. The higher the preexisting and the instilled efficacy beliefs, the better the skill development. The benefits of mastery modeling extend beyond development of technical skills. Compared to the computer tutorial training, mastery modeling produced a more effective working style, less negative affect during training, and higher satisfaction with the training program. Mastery modeling provides an instructional vehicle that lends itself well for enlisting affective and motivational determinants of competency development.

We have entered a new era in which the construction and management of knowledge and development of expertise relies increasingly on electronic inquiry. Much information is currently available only in electronic rather than print form. The electronic network technologies greatly expand opportunities to attain expertise. Skill in electronic search is emerging as an essential competency. Knowledge construction through electronic inquiry is not simply a mechanical application of a set of cognitive operators to an existing knowledge base. Rather, it is a challenging process in which affective, motivational, and self-regulatory factors influence how information is gathered, evaluated, and integrated into knowledge structures.

Information seekers face an avalanche of information in diverse sources of varying value and reliability. It requires a robust sense of efficacy to find one's way around this mounting volume and complexity of information. People who doubt their efficacy to conduct productive inquiries, and to manage the electronic technology, can quickly become overwhelmed. In developing their cognitive skills for untangling the web, individuals were taught how to frame the electronic inquiry by selecting key constructs and finding reliable sources; how to broaden the scope and depth of inquiry by using appropriate connectors; and how to sequence the inquiry optimally (Debouski, Wood, and Bandura, 2001). Compared to a group that received a computer tutorial, those who had benefit of cognitive modeling that conveyed the same search rules gained higher perceived efficacy and satisfaction in knowledge construction. They spent less time in errors and redundancies, used better search and sequencing strategies, learned more, and were more successful in constructing new knowledge. Putting a human face with whom one can identify in electronic instructional systems substantially boosts their power.

Belief in one's efficacy to manage electronic technology influences not only how well individuals acquire knowledge by this means, but also their receptivity to electronic innovations, job satisfaction and productivity (Gist, Rosen, and Schwoerer, 1989; McDonald and Siegall, 1992). Many organizational activities are now performed by members of virtual teams working together from scattered locations through computer mediated collaboration. Working remotely with little direct supervision across time, space, and cultural orientations can be quite taxing. Those of high perceived efficacy for remotely conducted collaborative work have more positive job attitudes and achieve higher job performances than those of low perceived efficacy (Staples, Hulland, and Higgins, 1998).

Cultivation of Self-regulatory Competencies

The capacity for self-regulation through the exercise of self-influence is another core feature of an agentic theory of human motivation and action (Bandura, 2006). The accelerated growth of knowledge and rapid pace of social and technological change are placing a premium on capabilities for self-motivation and self-development (Bandura, 2002). Indeed, to keep up with a world that is rapidly changing, people have to develop, upgrade, and reform their competencies in continual self-renewal. To achieve this, they must develop skills in regulating the cognitive, motivational, affective, and social determinants of their functioning.

Self-management is exercised through a variety of interlinked self-referent processes including self-monitoring, self-efficacy appraisal, personal goal setting, and enlistment of motivating incentives (Bandura, 1986, 1991; Locke and Latham, 1990). Knowledge of how these various subfunctions of self-regulation operate provides particularized guides on how to develop and implement this capability.

People cannot influence their own motivation and actions if they do not keep track of their performances. Neither goals without knowing how one is doing nor knowing how one is doing without any goals is motivating (Bandura, 1991). Success in self-regulation partly depends on the fidelity, consistency, and temporal proximity of self-monitoring. Observing one's pattern of behavior is the first step toward doing something to affect it but, in itself, such information provides little basis for self-directed reactions.

Goals and aspirations play a pivotal role in the exercise of self-directedness. Goals motivate by enlisting self-evaluative investment in activities rather than directly. Once people commit themselves to goal challenges they care about how they do. Two types of affective motivators come into play – people seek *self-satisfaction* from fulfilling valued goals, and are prompted to intensify their efforts by *discontent* with substandard performances. The goals that are motivating are the type that activate self-investment in the activity. They include explicitness, level of challenge, and temporal proximity. Explicit goals motivate because they specify the type and amount of effort needed to attain them. Many of the goals people set for themselves result in failure because they are too general and personally non-committing. To create productive involvement in activities, goals must be explicit (see Chapter 9). The amount of effort enlisted and satisfaction that accompany different goal attainments depend on the level at which they are set. Strong interest and self-investment in activities are sparked by challenges. There is no self-satisfaction with easy successes. Nor do goals that are widely out of one's reach bring any satisfying accomplishments and, over time, they can weaken one's sense of efficacy.

The effectiveness of goals in regulating motivation and performance depends on how far into the future they are projected. Long range goals provide the vision and give direction to one's activities. But they are too distant to serve as current motivators. There are too many competing activities at hand for distant futures to exert much impact on current behavior. It is too easy to put off serious efforts in the present to the tomorrows of each day. Self-motivation is best sustained by attainable subgoal challenges that lead to distant aspirations. Short-term subgoals enlist the strategies and motivators in the here and now needed to get to where one is going. Difficult goal challenges are not achievable at once. Seemingly overwhelming activities are mastered by breaking them into smaller manageable steps. Concentrated effort in the short term brings success in the long term (Bandura and Schunk, 1981, Latham and Brown, 2006; Morgan, 1985).

Goal systems structured along the lines described above function as remarkably robust motivators across diverse activity domains, environmental settings, populations, and time spans (Bandura, 1997; Locke and Latham, 1990). The chapter by Latham (Chapter 9) provides further guidelines on how to structure and implement goal systems for productive engagement in personal and organizational pursuits.

Perceived self-efficacy plays an influential role in the self-regulation of motivation and actions through goal systems. It does so in part by its impact on goal setting. The stronger the people's belief in their capabilities the higher the goal challenges they set for themselves and the firmer their commitment to them. Graduated subgoals provide a means for building perceived self-efficacy and intrinsic interest where they are lacking (Bandura, 1991, 1997). There are several ways they achieve these effects (Bandura and Schunk, 1981). Sustained effort fostered by proximal goals builds competencies. Subgoal attainments provide clear markers of increasing mastery. Evidence of progress builds self-efficacy. Subgoal attainments also bring self-satisfaction. Satisfying experiences build intrinsic interest in activities.

Effective self-regulation is also central to personal management of emotional states and problem behaviors that have a negative spillover on work performance. Employee absenteeism costs US industries billions of dollars annually. It is a serious problem that disrupts work schedules, raises costs, and decreases productivity. Frayne and Latham (1987) provide the elements for an effective self-management system to reduce absenteeism. Employees who often missed work were taught in groups how to manage their motivation and behavior more effectively. They kept a record of their work attendance. They analyzed the personal and social problems that prevented them from getting to work, and were taught strategies for overcoming these obstacles. They set themselves short-term goals for work attendance, and rewarded themselves for meeting their goals. Training in self-regulation increased employees' beliefs in their efficacy to overcome the obstacles that led them to miss work. They improved their work attendance and maintained these changes over time (Latham and Frayne, 1989). The stronger they believed in their self-management capabilities, the better was their work attendance. A control group of employees who did not receive the program in self-regulation continued their absentee ways.

CONCLUSION

The guiding principles and applications reviewed in the preceding sections underscore the centrality of perceived self-efficacy as a personal resource that yields dividends in motivation, performance attainments, and emotional well-being. Social cognitive theory embeds perceived efficacy within a broad network of sociocognitive factors. There are several features of sociocognitive theory that lend themselves readily to widespread social applications. Its key sociocognitive factors are amenable to change, the theory specifies how to alter them, clarifies the mechanisms through which they work, and provides explicit guidelines on how to translate theory into effective practice for personal and social change.

A substantial body of evidence verifies that perceived self-efficacy operates as a common mechanism through which changes are achieved by diverse modes of influence, across markedly diverse spheres of functioning, with heterogeneous populations, and under differing life conditions. This widespread generalizability is in keeping with Occam's maxim advocating theoretical parsimony.

REFERENCES

Arnold, J. A., Arad, S., Rhoades, J. A., and Drasgow, F. (2000). The empowering leadership questionnaire: The construction and validation of a new scale for measuring leader behaviors. *Journal of Organizational Behavior*, 21, 249–269.

Audia, G., Locke, E. A., and Smith, K. G. (2000). The paradox of success: An archival and a laboratory study of strategic persistence following a radical environmental change. *Academy of Management Journal*, 43, 837–853.

Bandura, A. (1986). *Social Foundations of Thought and Action: A Social Cognitive Theory.* Englewood Cliffs, NJ: Prentice-Hall.

Bandura, A. (1991). Self-regulation of motivation through anticipatory and self-regulatory mechanisms. In R. A. Dienstbier (ed.), *Perspectives on Motivation: Nebraska Symposium on Motivation* (Vol. 38, pp. 69–164). Lincoln: University of Nebraska Press.

Bandura, A. (1997). *Self-efficacy: The Exercise of Control.* New York: Freeman.

Bandura, A. (1999). Moral disengagement in the perpetration of inhumanities. *Personality and Social Psychology Review*, 3, 193–209.

Bandura, A. (2000). Exercise of human agency through collective efficacy. *Current Directions in Psychological Science*, 9, 75–78

Bandura, A. (2002). Growing primacy of human agency in adaptation and change in the electronic era. *European Psychologist*, 7, 2–16.

Bandura, A. (2004). Swimming against the mainstream: The early years from chilly tributary to transformative mainstream. *Behavioral Research and Therapy*, 42, 613–630.

Bandura, A. (2006). Toward a psychology of human agency. *Perspectives on Psychological Science*, 1, 164–180.

Bandura, A. (2008). The reconstrual of "free will" from the agentic perspective of social cognitive theory. In J. Baer, J. C. Kaufman, and R. F. Baumeister (eds), *Are We Free? Psychology and Free Will* (pp. 86–127). Oxford: Oxford University Press.

Bandura, A. (2009). A dose of conditionality and scientific probity for the quest of negative self-efficacy effects. Submitted for publication.

Bandura, A., and Locke, E. (2003). Negative self-efficacy and goal effects revisited. *Journal of Applied Psychology*, 88, 87–99.

Bandura, A., and Schunk, D. H. (1981). Cultivating competence, self-efficacy, and intrinsic interest through proximal self-motivation. *Journal of Personality and Social Psychology*, 41, 586–598.

Bandura, A., Caprara, G. V., and Zsolnai, L. (2002). Corporate transgressions through moral disengagement. In L. Zsolnai (ed.), *Ethics in the economy: Handbook of business ethics* (pp. 151–164). Oxford: Peter Lang Publishers.

Baum, J. R., and Locke, E. A. (2004). The relationship of entrepreneurial traits, skill and motivation to subsequent venture growth. *Journal of Applied Psychology*, 89, 587–598.

Baum, J. R, Locke, E. A., and Smith, K. G. (2001). A multi-dimensional model of venture growth. *Academy of Management Journal*, 44, 292–303.

Brouwers, A., and Tomic, W. (1999). Teacher burnout, perceived self-efficacy in classroom management, and student disruptive behavior in secondary education. *Curriculum and Teaching*, 14, 7–26.

Brouwers, A., and Tomic, W. (2006). A longitudinal study of teacher burnout and perceived self-efficacy in classroom management. *Teaching and Teacher Education*, 16, 239–253.

Burke, M. J., and Day, R. R. (1986). A cumulative study of the effectiveness of management training. *Journal of Applied Psychology*, 71, 232–245.

Burkhardt, M. E., and Brass, D. J. (1990). Changing patterns or patterns of change: The effects of a change in technology on social network structure and power. *Administrative Science Quarterly*, 35, 104–127.

Chen, C. C., Greene, P. G., and Crick, A. (1998). Does entrepreneurial self-efficacy distinguish entrepreneurs from managers? *Journal of Business Venturing*, 13, 295–316.

Debouski, S., Wood, R. E., and Bandura, A. (2001). Impact of guided exploration and enactive exploration on self-regulatory mechanisms and information acquisition through electronic search. *Journal of Applied Psychology*, 86, 1129–1141.

Frayne, C. A., and Latham, G. P. (1987). Application of social learning theory to employee self-management of attendance. *Journal of Applied Psychology*, 72, 387–392.

Gist, M. E. (1989). The influence of training method on self-efficacy and idea generation among managers. *Personnel Psychology*, 42, 787–805.

Gist, M. E., Bavetta, A. G., and Stevens, C. K. (1990). Transfer training method: Its influence on skill generalization, skill repetition, and performance level. *Personnel Psychology*, 43, 501–523.

Gist, M., Rosen, B., and Schwoerer, C. (1988). The influence of training method and trainee age on the acquisition of computer skills. *Personnel Psychology*, 41, 255–265.

Goldstein, A. P., and Sorcher, M. (1974). *Changing Supervisor Behavior*. New York: Pergamon.

Gully, S. M., Incalcaterra, K. A., Joshi, A., and Beaubien, J. M. (2002). A meta-analysis of team-efficacy, potency, and performance: interdependence and level of analysis as moderators of observed relationships. *Journal of Applied Psychology*, 87, 819–832.

Hill, T., Smith, N. D., and Mann, M. F. (1987). Role of efficacy expectations in predicting the decision to use advanced technologies: the case of computers. *Journal of Applied Psychology*, 72, 307–313.

Holden, G. (1991). The relationship of self-efficacy appraisals to subsequent health related outcomes: A meta-analysis. *Social Work in Health Care*, 16, 53–93.

Holden, G., Moncher, M. S., Schinke, S. P., and Barker, K. M. (1990). Self-efficacy of children and adolescents: A meta-analysis. *Psychological Reports*, 66, 1044–1046.

Hung, J. H., and Rosenthal, T. L. (1981). Therapeutic videotaped playback. In J. L. Fryrear and R. Fleshman (eds), *Videotherapy in Mental Health* (pp. 5–46). Springfield, IL: Thomas.

Jex, S. M., and Bliese, P. D. (1999). Efficacy beliefs as a moderator of the impact of work-related stressors: A multilevel study. *Journal of Applied Psychology*, 84, 349–361.

Jones, G. R. (1986). Socialization tactics, self-efficacy, and newcomers' adjustment to organizations. *Academy of Management Journal*, 29, 262–279.

Jorde-Bloom, P., and Ford, M. (1988). Factors influencing early childhood administrators' decisions regarding the adoption of computer technology. *Journal of Educational Computing Research*, 4, 31–47.

Krueger, N. F., Jr., and Dickson, P. R. (1993). Self-efficacy and perceptions of opportunities and threats. *Psychological Reports*, 72, 1235–1240.

Krueger, N., Jr., and Dickson, P. R. (1994). How believing in ourselves increases risk taking: Perceived self-efficacy and opportunity recognition. *Decision Sciences*, 25, 385–400.

Laschruger, H. K. S., and Shamian, J. (1994). Staff nurses' and nurse managers' perceptions of job-related empowerment and managerial self-efficacy. *Journal of Nursing Administration*, 24, 38–47.

Latham, G. P., and Brown, T. C. (2006). The effect of learning vs. outcome goals on self-efficacy, satisfaction and performance in an MBA program. *Applied Psychology: An International Review*, 55, 606–623.

Latham, G. P., and Budworth, M. (2006). The effect of training in verbal self-guidance on the self-efficacy and performance of native Americans in the selection interview. *Journal of Vocational Behavior*, 68, 516–523.

Latham, G. P., and Frayne, C. A. (1989). Self-management training for increasing job attendance: A follow-up and a replication. *Journal of Applied Psychology*, 74, 411–416.

Latham, G. P., and Saari, L. M. (1979). Application of social learning theory to training supervisors through behavioral modeling. *Journal of Applied Psychology*, 64, 239–246.

Leiter, M. P. (1992). Burnout as a crisis in self-efficacy: conceptual and practical implications. *Work and Stress*, 6, 107–115.

Lent, R. W., Brown, S. D., and Hackett, G. (1994). Toward a unifying social cognitive theory of career and academic interest, choice, and performance. *Journal of Vocational Behavior*, 45, 79–122.

Lindsley, D. H., Mathieu, J. E., Heffner, T. S., and Brass, D. J. (1994). Team efficacy, potency, and performance: A longitudinal examination of reciprocal processes. Paper presented at the Society of Industrial-Organizational Psychology, Nashville, TN, April.

Little, B. L., and Madigan, R. M. (1994). Motivation in work teams: A test of the construct of collective efficacy. Paper presented at the annual meeting of the Academy of Management, Houston, TX, August.

Locke, E. A., and Latham, G. P. (1990). *A Theory of Goal Setting and Task Performance*. Englewood Cliffs, NJ: Prentice-Hall.

Markman, G. D., and Baron, R. A. (1999). Cognitive mechanisms: Potential differences between entrepreneurs and non-entrepreneurs. Paper presented at the Babson College/ Kauffman Foundation Entrepreneurship Conference, May.

Matsui, T., and Onglatco, M. L. (1992). Career self-efficacy as a moderator of the relation between occupational stress and strain. *Journal of Vocational Behavior*, 41, 79–88.

McDonald, T., and Siegall, M. (1992). The effects of technological self-efficacy and job focus on job performance, attitudes, and withdrawal behaviors. *The Journal of Psychology*, 126, 465–475.

Meichenbaum, D. (1984). Teaching thinking: a cognitive–behavioral perspective. In R. Glaser, S. Chipman, and J. Segal (eds), *Thinking and Learning Skills (Vol. 2): Research and Open Questions* (pp. 407–426). Hillsdale, NJ: Erlbaum.

Meyer, H. H., and Raich, M. S. (1983). An objective evaluation of a behavior modeling training program. *Personnel Psychology*, 36, 755–761.

Miller, W. R., Brown, J. M., Simpson, T. L., Handmaker, N. S., Bien, T. H., Luckie, L. F., Montgomery, H. A., Hester, R. K., and Tonigan, J. S. (1995). What works? A methodological analysis of the alcohol treatment outcome literature. In R. K. Hester and W. R. Miller (eds), *Handbook of Alcoholism Treatment Approaches: Effective Alternatives* (2nd edition). Boston: Allyn and Bacon.

Morgan, M. (1985). Self-monitoring of attained subgoals in private study. *Journal of Educational Psychology*, 77, 623–630.

Multon, K. D., Brown, S. D., and Lent, R. W. (1991). Relation of self-efficacy beliefs to academic outcomes: A meta-analytic investigation. *Journal of Counseling Psychology*, 38, 30–38.

Parker, S. K. (1998). Enhancing role breadth self-efficacy: the roles of job enrichment and other organizational interventions. *Journal of Applied Psychology*, 83, 835–852.

Plotnikoff, R. C., Lippke, S., Courneya, K. S., Birkett, N., and Sigal, R. J. (2008). Physical activity and social cognitive theory: A test in population sample of adults with type 1 or type 2 diabetes. *Applied Psychology: An International Review*, 57, 628–643.

Porras, J. I., and Anderson, B. (1981). Improving managerial effectiveness through modeling-based training. *Organizational Dynamics*, Spring, 60–77.

Porras, J. I., Hargis, K., Patterson, K. J., Maxfield, D. G., Roberts, N., and Bies, R. J. (1982). Modeling-based organizational development: A longitudinal assessment. *Journal of Applied Behavioral Science*, 18, 433–446.

Saks, A. M. (1994). Moderating effects of self-efficacy for the relationship between training method and anxiety and stress reactions of newcomers. *Journal of Organizational Behavior*, 15, 639–654.

Saks, A. M. (1995). Longitudinal field investigation of the moderating and mediating effects of self-efficacy on the relationship between training and newcomer adjustment. *Journal of Applied Psychology*, 80, 211–225.

Salanova, M., Grau, R., Cifre, E., and Llorens, S. (2000). Computer training, frequency of use and burnout: The moderating role of computer self-efficacy. *Computers in Human Behavior*, 16, 575–590.

Schaubroeck, J., and Merritt, D. E. (1997). Divergent effects of job control on coping with work stressors: the key role of self-efficacy. *Academy of Management Journal*, 40, 738–754.

Speier, C., and Frese, M. (1997). Generalized self-efficacy as a mediator and moderator between control and complexity at work and personal initiative: A longitudinal field study in East Germany. *Human Performance*, 10(2), 171–192.

Srivastava, A., Bartol, K. M., and Locke, E. A. (2006). Empowering leadership in management teams: Effects on knowledge sharing, efficacy, and performance. *Academy of Management Journal*, 49, 1239–1251.

Stajkovic, A. D., and Luthans, F. (1998). Self-efficacy and work-related performance: A meta-analysis. *Psychological Bulletin*, 124, 240–261.

Stajkovic, A. D., Lee, D., and Nyberg, A. J. (in press). Collective efficacy, group potency, and group performance: Meta-analysis of their relationships and test of a meditational model. *Journal of Applied Psychology*.

Staples, D. S., Hulland, J. S., and Higgins, C. A. (1998). A self-efficacy theory explanation for the management of remote workers in virtual organizations. *Journal of Computer-mediated Communication*, 3(4).

Stewart, G. L., and Manz, C. C. (1995). Leadership for self-managing work teams: A typology and integrative model. *Human Relations*, 48, 747–770.

van Ryn, M., and Vinokur, A. D. (1992). How did it work? An examination of the mechanisms through which an intervention for the unemployed promoted job-search behavior. *American Journal of Community Psychology*, 20, 577–597.

Vinokur, A. D., van Ryn, M., Gramlich, E. M., and Price, R. H. (1991). Long-term follow-up and benefit–cost analysis of the jobs program: A preventive intervention for the unemployed. *Journal of Applied Psychology*, 76, 213–219.

White, J., Bandura, A., and Bero, L. (2009). Moral disengagement in the corporate world. *Accountability in Research*, 16, 41–74.

Whyte, G., and Saks, A. (2007). The effects of self-efficacy on behavior in escalation situations. *Human Performance*, 20, 23–42.

Whyte, G., Saks, A., and Hook, S. (1997). When success breeds failure: the role of perceived self-efficacy in escalating commitment to a losing course of action. *Journal of Organizational Behavior*, 18, 415–432.

Williams, S. L. (1992). Perceived self-efficacy and phobic disability. In R. Schwarzer (ed.), *Self-efficacy: Thought Control of Action* (pp. 149–176). Washington, DC: Hemisphere.

Yanar, B., Budworth, M-H., and Latham, G. P. (2008). Training Islamic women in verbal self-guidance to overcome discrimination in Turkey. Submitted for publication.

Zhao, H., Seibert, S. E., and Hills, G. E. (2005). The mediating role of self-efficacy in the development of entrepreneurial intentions. *Journal of Applied Psychology*, 90, 1265–1272.

NOTE

Some sections of this chapter contain revised, updated, and expanded material from the book *Self-Efficacy: The Exercise of Control* (1997) New York, Freeman.

EXERCISES

Personal self-efficacy building

Identify a skill of competency that you lack but would like to have. Based on the material in this chapter, design a training program (others may be part of the program) which would increase your self-efficacy in this realm. Include both behavioral and cognitive aspects.

Building team efficacy

Based on your previous work experience in teams, identify a situation in which team efficacy was low.

What competencies did the team lack which undermined their effectiveness? How would you build the needed types of efficacy? What would you do to prevent overconfidence?

11

Using Empowerment to Motivate People to Engage in Effective Self- and Shared Leadership

Jay A. Conger and Craig L. Pearce

In recent decades there has been a steady increase in interest in empowerment as a motivational tool in both the academic (e.g. Conger and Kanungo, 1988; Houghton, Neck, and Manz, 2003; Liden and Arad, 1995; Mills and Ungson, 2003; Pearce and Sims, 2002; Thomas and Velthouse, 1990) and practitioner literature (e.g. Block, 1987; Conger, 1989; Manz and Sims, 1989, 2001; Pearce, 2008). The essence of empowerment, at the individual level of analysis, entails granting autonomy to individuals to perform tasks, while simultaneously enhancing their task-related self-efficacy (Bandura, 1986, 1997; see also Chapter 10). Naturally, empowerment needs to be founded on appropriately set goals (Locke and Latham, 1990; see also Chapter 9).

At the individual level of analysis, empowerment is ultimately experienced when followers engage in effective self-leadership (Manz and Sims, 1980; Houghton et al., 2003), where self-leadership is defined as "a process through which people influence themselves to achieve the self-direction and self-motivation needed to perform" (Houghton et al., 2003, p. 126). The empirical evidence on empowerment suggests that it has a powerful positive influence on individuals (e.g. Liden, Wayne, and Sparrowe, 2000; Spreitzer, 1995; Spreitzer, Kizilos, and Nason, 1994).

As we move to the group level of analysis, empowerment is experienced when the group effectively practices shared leadership (Pearce and Conger, 2003; Pearce, 2004, 2008), where shared leadership is defined as "a dynamic, interactive influence process among individuals in groups for which the objective is to lead one another to the achievement of group or organizational goals or both" (Pearce and Conger, 2003, p. 1). Here again, the empirical evidence is fairly robust regarding the positive influence of empowerment (e.g. Ensley, Hmieleski, and Pearce, 2006; Pearce and Sims, 2002; Pearce, Yoo, and Alavi, 2004). In the next section we explore the complex process of empowerment.

The Empowerment Process

The actual process of empowerment can be viewed along six stages that include the psychological state of an empowering experience, its antecedent conditions, and its behavioral consequences. The six stages are shown in Figure 11.1. The first stage is the diagnosis of conditions within individuals and their organizations that are responsible for feelings of disempowerment. Following the diagnosis of disempowerment, managers may employ certain strategies indicated in stage 2. The employment of these strategies is aimed at not only removing some of the conditions responsible for disempowerment; but also (and more importantly) at providing subordinates with empowerment information for stage 3. Individuals then interpret this information in stage 4 according to personal styles of assessment. If these styles assess the information as empowering, then an individual will feel empowered and the behavioral effects of empowerment will be observed in stage 5, where individuals become effective self-leaders (Manz and Sims, 1980). Beyond these five stages for the individual, empowerment can spread among group members and lead to group empowerment, whose result is the display of shared leadership in stage 6 (Bligh, Pearce, and Kohles, 2006).

Stage 1

Starting with the first stage (the context), there are specific individual and contextual factors that contribute to the lowering of empowerment feelings among organizational members (Block, 1987; Conger, 1989; Kanter, 1979, 1983; Thomas and Velthouse, 1990). From the standpoint of organizational factors, Table 11.1 identifies some of the principal factors that influence and hinder empowerment outcomes. These are organized into four categories: (a) organizational, (b) hierarchical leader behavior, (c) reward systems, and (d) job design.

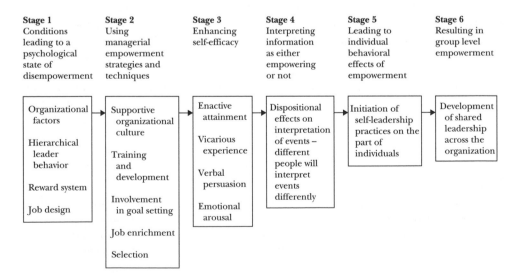

FIGURE 11.1 Stages of the empowerment process

Source: Adapted from Conger and Kanungo (1988)

Table 11.1 Context factors leading to potential lowering of empowerment beliefs

Organizational factors

- Significant organizational changes/transitions
- Competitive pressures
- Impersonal bureaucratic climate
- Poor communications/network-forming systems
- Highly centralized organizational resources

Hierarchical leader behavior

- Directive (high control)
- Aversive (emphasis on fear)
- Negativism (emphasis on failure)
- Lack of reason for actions/consequences

Reward systems

- Non-contingency (arbitrary reward allocation)
- Low incentive value of rewards
- Lack of competence-based rewards
- Lack of innovation-based rewards

Job design

- Lack of role clarity
- Lack of training and technical support
- Unrealistic goals
- Lack of appropriate authority/discretion
- Low task variety
- Limited participation in programs, meetings, decisions that have a direct impact on job performance
- Lack of appropriate/necessary resources
- Lack of network-forming opportunities
- Highly established work routines
- High rule structure
- Low advancement opportunities
- Lack of meaningful goals/tasks
- Limited contact with senior management

Source: Adapted from Conger and Kanungo (1988).

For instance, organizations with high levels of formalization and impersonal control systems can stifle member initiative (Chapter 22), meaningfulness, and a sense of responsibility. Aversive and directive hierarchical leader behavior can strip control and discretion from organizational members (Pearce, Sims, Cox, Ball, Schnell, Smith, and Trevino, 2003). Rewards may not be allocated on the basis of members' competence or innovative behavior, but rather on their blind compliance with formalized control from the top. When organizations do not provide rewards that are valued by members, and when the rewards are not based on member competence, initiative, and innovative job behavior, employees' sense of disempowerment increases (Sims, 1977; Szilagyi, 1980; see Chapter 12). Reward systems that emphasize innovative/unusual performance and high incentive values have a significant probability of fostering a greater sense of empowerment, while those that do not tend to disempower (Kanter, 1979; Kanungo, 1987; Lawler, 1971, 1977). Finally, when jobs provide very little challenge and meaning, and when they involve role ambiguity, role conflict, and role overload, employees can feel a crippling sense of disempowerment (Lawler and Finegold, 2000; see Chapter 6).

Stage 2

To address such conditions identified in stage 1, there are a number of management practices that can restore or heighten a sense of empowerment (stage 2). For example, at the organizational level, company policies and cultures can enhance empowerment by emphasizing self-determination, internal collaboration (Chapter 18), high performance standards, non-discrimination, and meritocracy. In addition, organizations that provide multiple sources of loosely committed resources at decentralized or local levels, that structure open communications systems (see Chapter 23), and that create extensive network-forming devices are more likely to be empowering (Kanter, 1983). Jobs that provide task variety, personal relevance, appropriate autonomy and control, low levels of established routines and rules, and high advancement prospects (Chapter 6) are more likely to empower subordinates (Block, 1987; Hackman, Oldham, Janson, and Purdy, 1975; Kanter, 1979; Oldham, 1976; Strauss, 1977).

The above practices can be viewed from the different perspectives of either formal/organizational mechanisms or individual/informal techniques. Organizations require both types to effectively instill a context of empowerment. For example, when organizations engage in participation programs, they establish formal systems that empower organizational members through the sharing of information (Chapter 24), formal power, and authority.

In order for this sharing of power to be effective at the individual level, however, employees must perceive it as increasing their sense of self-efficacy – which is accomplished largely through the more informal practices of individual managers and in their one-on-one interactions with subordinates and co-workers. Empowerment initiatives, which rely on a singular approach such as the delegation of decision making, usually prove to be ineffective. Rather, initiatives must be supported on multiple levels and by multiple interventions. In the ideal case, they would involve a highly supportive organizational culture; training and developmental experiences that heighten one's sense of competence; involvement in goal setting or, especially, in the means to achieve goals, job designs that are highly meaningful to employees; the selection of managers open to empowerment approaches and proactive in their use; and the selection and promotion of employees whose interpretative schemes are biased towards constructive and enabling self-assessments (Liden and Arad, 1995; Spreitzer et al., 1994).

Stage 3

In order to be effective, the empowerment practices outlined above must directly provide information to employees about personal efficacy, a sense of choice, meaningfulness of the task, and impact (stage 3). For example, on the dimension of competence or self-efficacy,

Bandura (1986, 1997) has identified four sources of such information (see Chapter 10): enactive attainment, vicarious experience, persuasion/feedback, and emotional arousal state. Personal efficacy gained through enactive attainment refers to an individual's authentic mastery experience directly related to the job. For example, a manager can allocate or structure tasks that provide an empowering experience for an individual. When subordinates are trained to perform complex tasks or are given more responsibility in their jobs, they have the opportunity to increase their efficacy and to receive positive feedback. Initial success experiences (through successively moderate increments in task complexity and responsibility along with training to acquire new skills) can make one feel more capable and, therefore, more empowered.

Empowerment information can also come from the vicarious experiences of observing similar others, i.e. co-workers, who perform successfully on the job. Very often, a manager's exemplary behaviors empower subordinates to believe that they can behave in a like manner or that they can at least achieve some improvement in their performance. In addition, words of encouragement, performance feedback, mentoring advice, and other forms of social persuasion are often used by leaders, managers, and group members to raise efficacy and provide empowerment information to subordinates and co-workers (Conger, 1989; Pearce and Sims, 2002). For instance, leaders may use annual meetings to provide empowering information in the form of praise and encouragement (Chapter 13) for exceptional performance. Through positive performance evaluations, managers may similarly foster an empowered state. Naturally, this does not imply that one should raise the performance evaluations of direct reports irrespective of their actual performance. Falseness breeds distrust (Chapter 21).

Leadership practices which have been identified as empowering include: (a) expressing confidence in subordinates accompanied by high performance expectations (Burke, 1986; Conger, 1989; House, 1977; Neilsen, 1986); (b) fostering opportunities for subordinates to participate in decision making and goal setting or to create their own jobs (Block, 1987; Burke, 1986; Conger, 1989; Erez and Arad, 1986; House, 1977; Kanter, 1979; Neilsen, 1986; Strauss, 1977); (c) providing autonomy from bureaucratic constraints and encouraging independent action (Block, 1987; Kanter, 1979; Ensley et al., 2006; Pearce and Sims, 2002); (d) setting inspirational and/or meaningful goals (Bennis and Nanus, 1985; Block, 1987; Conger and Kanungo, 1998; McClelland, 1975; Tichy and Devanna, 1986); and (e) encouraging self-development and opportunity thinking (Manz and Sims, 1989, 2001; Houghton et al., 2003).

Finally, personal competence expectations are affected by one's emotional arousal state. Individuals are more likely to feel competent when they are not experiencing strong negative arousal. Emotional arousal states that result from dysfunctional levels of stress, fear, anxiety, depression, and so forth, both on and off the job, can lower self-efficacy expectations (see Chapter 8 for a discussion of emotional control). Therefore empowerment strategies that provide information in the form of emotional support for subordinates and that create a supportive and trusting group atmosphere (Neilsen, 1986) can be effective in strengthening self-efficacy beliefs. For example, employees' stress, anxiety, and tension on the job can be reduced by managers clearly defining employees' roles, reducing information overload, and offering them technical assistance to accomplish job tasks. Similarly, the impact of depression and self-doubt on subordinates as a result of failures on the job could be lessened by their supervisor attributing such failures to external and unstable factors (assuming there are valid reasons for doing so) such as task difficulty, inadequate support systems, and so forth, rather than attributing it to the individual's efforts or abilities (Weiner, 1985). Employees, of course, must learn to take personal responsibility for what they can control.

Stages 4–6

As a result of receiving the above forms of information, employees will interpret this information according to their individual styles of assessment in stage 4. In other words, personal interpretations will determine whether the information is seen as empowering or not. Depressed individuals, for example, are less likely to see successes as indicative of their own competence (Abramson, Seligman, and Teasdale, 1978). Others may have irrational standards of perfection that in turn reduce perceptions of personal empowerment. For these very reasons, careful selection of employees is necessary (see Chapters 1–3). In the next section where we discuss exceptions, we will describe this assessment process in greater depth since it directly affects the success of any empowerment initiative.

If information is indeed interpreted as empowering, then the individual will enter a state of psychological empowerment – and the behavioral effects of empowerment will be noticed in stage five – followers becoming effective self-leaders (Manz and Sims, 1980). Beyond the behavioral effects of empowerment on individuals are the effects on groups. As individuals display effective self-leadership, the creation of shared leadership is the logical next step (stage 6): According to Bligh et al. (2006, p. 20), "the development of the self-leadership capabilities of team members sets into motion the meso-level processes that result in higher collective-levels of trust, potency, and commitment, which in turn facilitate the sustained sharing of mutual influence within the team that comprises shared leadership."

EXCEPTIONS

We do not advocate empowerment as a new panacea for all organizational woes. Clearly, there are limitations regarding the efficacy of empowerment. As Locke (2003) has indicated, there are certain tasks which are the responsibility of the top leader. For example, Locke (2003, p. 278) noted that "core values must be pushed from the top down." In fact, we believe there are situations in which empowerment is actually harmful (e.g. it could create anarchy with respect to core values). Further, empowerment could produce a state of overconfidence and, in turn, misjudgments on the part of followers. Because of a sense of false confidence in positive outcomes, employees might persist in efforts that, in actuality, are tactical or strategic errors.

Similarly, followers might overextend themselves through tasks which are largely impossible to accomplish. Leaders also might use such practices to garner commitment to tasks which are unethical. The positive personal effects that are felt by followers during empowering experiences may blind them to the leader's own pragmatic (whatever works for me today), non-value-driven agenda or the nefarious manipulation of others. (Self-interest is a good thing if it is tied to proper values.)

There may also be situations where managers and organizations have little latitude to increase a sense of empowerment. For example, some jobs are highly mechanistic and routine. No matter what attempts are made at redesign, the jobs remain essentially the same (but see Chapter 6). Serious economic downturns or intense competitive situations may limit an organization's ability to provide inspiring goals or appealing rewards other than simple job security. Trapped in autocratic cultures, managers wishing to empower may find themselves constrained by the larger system – their efforts at empowerment largely negated by the overriding culture or design elements of the organization.

Finally, there is the crucial issue of individual differences. For instance, some individuals may not have the requisite skills, ethical disposition, or conscientiousness necessary for empowerment. Further, during the process of empowerment, individuals are making subjective assessments about information and specific tasks. One individual may assess the same information quite differently from another. For example, some styles of assessment are properly self-enhancing and others are self-debilitating (Peale, 1954). As such, what might be an empowering experience for one individual may be a disempowering or non-empowering one for another. In the latter case, an individual may have set dysfunctional standards in the form of absolutistic "musts" concerning tasks. They may have the personal standard of "Perfection [outside of any rational context] is my goal on all dimensions of this task." Such standards tend to reduce a person's assessment of their success since anything short of perfection is seen as failure (Thomas and Velthouse, 1990). Followers can also get trapped in these self-reinforcing cycles. Low personal assessments of their competence can lead to low initiative and inactivity which further reinforces perceptions of low success and a sense of low competence (Thomas and Velthouse, 1990).

Followers' rational confidence in themselves clearly plays a central role. The motivation to undertake any new activity requires a measure of self-confidence on the part of individuals and a sense of potency (Bligh et al., 2006; Gully, Incalcaterra, Joshi, and Beaubien, 2002), or collective confidence, on the part of groups. If an individual has a strong foundation of belief in themselves, they are likely to be more optimistic than others when engaging in activities where information about task assessments are uncertain or cloudy (Thomas and Velthouse, 1990). In addition, followers vary to the degree in which they invest themselves psychologically in tasks. Termed global meaningfulness, this concept describes an individual's overall level of caring or commitment to tasks. People differ considerably along this dimension (Solomon and Patch, 1970). Individuals with low levels of global meaningfulness tend to experience alienation and are less likely to believe that new tasks will be meaningful (Thomas and Velthouse, 1990).

Given the above psychological dynamics, empowerment interventions must take into careful consideration the individuals, groups, and tasks involved. For some, their psychological outlook may prove a serious barrier to empowerment. Instead, it will be their capacity for self-reflection and learning that will determine, over the long term, whether they can at some point experience empowerment. At the same time, extended and persistent efforts at empowerment on the part of leaders will be required under such circumstances. With some individuals, there may be little that a manager or co-worker can, or should, do to empower them. This is especially true for followers who are in a psychologically unbalanced state. Outside professional help – for example, psychotherapy – may be the only possible option. For this very reason, careful selection and placement are critical factors.

CASE EXAMPLES

To understand how empowerment works in the real world, we will look first at two positive examples and one negative/positive example. Each will be drawn from case studies of actions undertaken by senior organizational leaders to empower their workforces.

Richard Branson, the Virgin Group

As chief executive officer of the Virgin Group (a diversified British company encompassing entertainment/communications businesses and an airline), Richard Branson employs a variety of means to empower members of the company. At an organizational level, he preserves an entrepreneurial atmosphere through a Japanese-style keiretsu structure whereby the 500 companies under the Virgin Group operate quasi-independently but collaboratively in a global network (Kets de Vries and Dick, 1995). Once a company reaches a certain size, it is split into several organizations so that employees retain their sense of identity with their organization and a small-company, entrepreneurial atmosphere is preserved. At the individual level, each unit is led by a managing director who has considerable freedom to lead the business as they see fit and who has an equity position in the company. Decision making within the company is therefore decentralized. At the same time, senior managers have access to Branson for advice and guidance and can reach him 24 hours a day (Kets de Vries and Dick, 1995).

To further promote individual entrepreneurship within the company, employees with attractive ideas for new ventures are provided with seed capital and ownership. As a result, many of the Virgin companies are the product of employee ideas. A bridal service division called Virgin Bride, for example, was the idea of a Virgin Airways stewardess to whom Branson provided "venture capital." The company's new ventures allow Branson to stretch and develop employees by creating more opportunities for upward mobility and greater responsibility (Kets de Vries and Dick, 1995).

A central tenet of the company's culture is the importance of employees. Branson's maxim is staff first, customers second, and shareholders third, and Branson clearly keeps an eye on these results. As a result, he has created a culture which is egalitarian, non-bureaucratic, friendly, and family-like in atmosphere. The culture is one where people enjoy their work and have fun. It is also one which emphasizes proactivity. As Branson likes to say, "We can decide on something in the morning and have it in operation by the afternoon" (Kets de Vries and Dick, 1995). Taken together, the corporate culture, the company's organizational design/reward systems, and Branson's leadership style work effectively to create a cadre of empowered managers.

Jack Welch, General Electric

An executive or manager can put in place mechanisms to promote an empowering organizational culture that values free information sharing through participation and feedback systems, meaningful jobs through enrichment and goal setting programs, and rewards for competence and initiative. Jack Welch, former chief executive officer of General Electric, began his tenure as CEO by delayering the entire corporate bureaucracy. This sent an impressive signal throughout the organization. He later implemented a program entitled Work Out throughout the corporation. Work Out addressed roadblocks to employee empowerment at lower levels of the organization (Bower and Dial, 1993; Tichy and Sherman, 1993). The program created forums for employees to speak candidly about unnecessary work in their jobs and the management of their business units without fear of retribution from senior managers. Its second objective was to stimulate immediate action on the issues that surfaced. In two- to three-day sessions of 50 to 100 people, these forums openly critiqued the management practices and processes in an operation, with a strong focus specifically on identifying bureaucracy and unproductive behaviors that impeded employees' effectiveness or efficacy. In essence, these forums tackled the barriers to empowerment. At the end of each session, the unit's manager received direct feedback from employees on their findings and recommendations for action. In response, the rules stipulated that the manager had to "on the spot" accept or reject recommendations at the meeting or else appoint a team to investigate and provide solutions by an agreed-upon date. As the process has evolved, issues have since moved on to address more complicated and structural barriers such as cross-functional processes and departmental boundaries. At the end of its first two years, some 2000 Work Out sessions were conducted with over 90% of the suggestions acted upon (Bowers and Dial, 1993; Tichy and Sherman, 1993).

As noted earlier in this chapter, one of the organizational barriers to empowerment centers on supervisors' needs to control. A principal objective behind Work Out was to redefine this relationship of control between a supervisor and their subordinates. Jack Welch explains: "Ultimately, we are talking about redefining the relationship between boss and subordinate. I want to get to the point where people challenge their bosses every day: 'Why do you require me to do these wasteful things? . . . Trust me to do my job, and don't waste all of my time trying to deal with you on the control issue'" (Tichy and Charan, 1989, p. 118). What is particularly interesting about this example is that it is an empowerment intervention instituted by an individual who demonstrates very directive and demanding leadership. Welch, for example, is known to routinely fire the bottom 5–10% of his senior managers for performance below his standards. He also sets well-defined goals for the organization. At the same time, he is a great believer in the ability of front-line individuals to address business problems and opportunities, that unnecessary bureaucracy is a major barrier to empowerment, and that individuals must have the freedom to choose the means necessary to reach set goals. It is therefore possible to have both strong leadership and empowerment.

To and from the depths of despair

Part A. This is the tale of an organization on the brink of disaster and of deep disempowerment. The company was known, for decades, as the standard bearer of quality in their industry. They were a commercial powerhouse in engineering and manufacturing. Under the rule of a dictatorial leader, however, the company systematically fell apart. This case is focused on just one of their facilities, located in the mid-Atlantic USA, which was an exemplar of the company's woes. This facility had approximately one million square feet under roof and employed approximately 5000 individuals. Then corporate leadership decided that payroll expenses were too high and that workforce reductions were an effective solution. First, they outsourced one of the main product lines of the facility. As a result, the remaining workers felt deep discontent and disempowerment. A byproduct was the decline in quality – the very dimension that differentiated the organization in the marketplace. Soon to follow was a downturn in profitability. According to the general manager of the facility, "We began to hemorrhage."

Following the outsourcing campaign, the corporate leaders decided that they wanted to break the union in order to lower wages and restore profitability. Accordingly, they transferred a third of the work to a different state, a right-to-work state. The union did not take that action lying down. They ultimately organized a union in the new location. According to the president of the union, "We took that action because the company had thrown down the gauntlet. And the fight began. The company was fighting their own workforce . . . and we won."

Soon on the heels of the transfer of work to the right-to-work state were contract negotiations with the union, and the company feared a walk-out. This precipitated what came to be known as "the strike bank incident." The strike bank incident involved the company ordering employees to work mandatory overtime in order to build up a reserve of parts to tide them through in the event of a strike. According to the general manager, "It was chaos. We had parts hanging from the ceiling. And of course quality went to hell, and we further alienated the workforce."

The upshot of all of these draconian management actions were several bomb threats, which caused the evacuation of the massive facility and continued disruption to the operations. Meanwhile, the organization continued to tally up record losses. The facility hit rock bottom when they experienced a murder and a suicide attempt.

Part B. Organizations, just like people, often need to hit rock bottom before they change, and this is exactly what happened in this case. Following the last incident the general manager and the president of the union got together and decided to bring in an outside consulting firm to help them get back on course. The general manager stated, "We decided to focus on quality as a way to rebuild our relationship with employees. Nobody can argue with quality." The president of the union was in complete agreement, stating, "We didn't want to fight. We never wanted to fight. We wanted to have pride in our work."

Thus they focused on workforce empowerment through several initiatives. It started with 20 hours of training for every single employee. The training focused on such things as problem solving, decision making, communication, and teamwork skills. The initial training was done by the consulting firm. From there on, the training was conducted by volunteers, from the shop floor.

Employees were formed into dozens of what they called Quality Action Teams. The teams were empowered to take on the quality problems facing the firm. Naturally, the transition was not easy for all of the managers (now called team leaders) involved. For example, the general manager recalled, "We had three guys who just couldn't make the transition. We told them 'No more hard ass, now you're a coach and a facilitator.' They just didn't want to make the adjustment. And lucky for them, we were able to give them early retirement."

Over time, the transition to an empowered workforce took hold. The plant saw steady rises in quality, productivity, and profitability. About a year into the process, one incident marked the turning point. The general manager recounted, "We started up a machine – it didn't work – it shut down our assembly plant. So we put together a team, and these guys were incredible. They were truly a super team. Every one of those guys showed real leadership, and in the end they had the machine back up and running. I put their success story up on the marquee, at the entrance to the plant to give them some recognition. That's when everybody realized what a little teamwork could do."

According to the union president, "In the past, common sense never entered into the picture. It was 'Do it the way we're telling you to do it because we're the managers and you're the employees.' Now each member of the team is expected to contribute to the leadership of the team. We've come a long way." One of the shop floor employees summarized the transition to empowerment the best by stating, "I finally feel liberated . . . yeah liberated, that's the word for it. For all these years I was just doing what I was told to do. Now Bob [the team leader] asks me what I think we should do. My ideas finally matter and it feels great!"

In the end, quality was improved by a factor of 10, the workforce was positively engaged, and the company returned to solid profitability. In fact, they ultimately, after about three years onto the road to empowerment, won their State Senate Productivity Award – analogous to the Malcolm Baldridge Award at the national level – an award the general manager and union president alike credit their success to the empowerment of the workforce.

This case is an excerpt from *Share the Lead* by Craig L. Pearce, Charles C. Manz and Henry P Sims Jr, reproduced with permission from Stanford University Press.

Conclusion

As readers will have realized by now, empowerment holds remarkable opportunities. We believe that we are in an era that is demanding far more empowerment, where power is truly shared across a greater number of individuals, as well as up and down the hierarchy. Only when we have achieved a greater appreciation for the positive outcomes associated with empowerment and a real understanding of how it works effectively, will we be able to harness its full potential to contribute to organizational performance. Only then will empowerment also stand as an equal to traditional notions of leadership, the solitary individual in a position of authority, where followers are simply interchangeable "parts."

References

Abramson, L., Seligman, M., and Teasdale, J. (1978). Learned helplessness in humans: Critique and reformulation. *Journal of Abnormal Psychology*, 87, 19–74.

Bandura, A. (1986). Social foundations of thought and action: A social-cognitive view. Englewood Cliffs, NJ: Prentice-Hall.

Bandura, A. (1997). *Self-efficacy: The Exercise of Control*. New York: W. H. Freeman.

Bennis, W., and Nanus, B. (1985). *Leaders*. New York: Harper & Row.

Bligh, M., Pearce, C. L., and Kohles, J. (2006). The importance of self and shared leadership in team based knowledge work: Toward a meso-level model of leadership dynamics. *Journal of Managerial Psychology*, 21(4), 296–318.

Block, P. (1987). *The Empowered Manager*. San Francisco: Jossey-Bass.

Bower, J. L., and Dial, J. (1993). *Jack Welch: General Electric's Revolutionary*. Boston: Harvard Business School.

Brooking, J. B., and Bolton, B. (2000). Confirmatory Factor Analysis of a Measure of Intrapersonal Empowerment. *Rehabilitation Psychology*, 45(3), 292–298.

Burke, W. (1986). Leadership as empowering others. In S. Srivastra (ed.), *Executive Power* (pp. 51–77). San Francisco: Jossey-Bass.

Conger, J. A. (1989). Leadership: The art of empowering others. *Academy of Management Executive*, 33, 17–24.

Conger, J. A., and Kanungo, R. N. (1988). The empowerment process: Integrating theory and practice. *Academy of Management Review*, 31, 471–482.

Conger, J. A., and Kanungo, R. N. (1998). *Charismatic Leadership in Organizations*. Thousand Oaks, CA: Sage Publications.

Ensley, M. D., Hmieleski, K. M., and Pearce, C. L. (2006). The importance of vertical and shared leadership within new venture top management teams: Implications for the performance of startups. *Leadership Quarterly*, 17(3), 217–231.

Erez, M., and Arad, R. (1986). Participative goal setting: social, motivational, and cognitive factors. *Journal of Applied Psychology*, 71(4), 591–597

Gully, S. M., Incalcaterra, K. A., Joshi, A., and Beaubien, J. M. (2002). A meta-analysis of team-efficacy, potency, and performance: Interdependence and level of analysis as moderators of observed relationships. *Journal of Applied Psychology*, 87(5).

Hackman, J. R., Oldham, G. R., Janson, R., and Purdy, K. (1975). New strategy for job enrichment. *California Management Review*, 17(4), 57–71.

Houghton, J. D., Neck, C. P., and Manz, C. C. (2003). Self-leadership and superleadership: The heart and art of creating shared leadership in teams. In C. L. Pearce and J. A. Conger (eds), *Shared Leadership: Reframing the Hows and Whys of Leadership* (pp. 123–135). Thousand Oaks, CA: Sage Publications.

House, R. J. (1977). A 1976 theory of charismatic leadership. In J. G. Hunt and L. L. Larson (eds), *Leadership: The Cutting Edge* (pp. 189–207). Carbondale: Southern Illinois University Press.

Kanter, R. M. (1979). Power failure in management circuits. *Harvard Business Review*, 57(4), 65–75.

Kanter, R. M. (1983). *The Change Masters*. New York: Simon & Schuster.

Kanungo, R. N. (1987). Reward management: a new look. In S. L. Dolan and R. S. Schuler (eds), *Canadian Readings in Personnel and Human Resource Management* (pp. 261–275). St. Paul: West.

Kets de Vries, M. F. R., and Dick, R. J. (1995). *Branson's Virgin: The Coming of Age of a Counter-cultural Enterprise*. Fontainebleau, France: INSEAD.

Lawler, E. E. (1971). *Pay and Organizational Effectiveness: A Psychological View*. New York: McGraw-Hill.

Lawler, E. E. (1977). Reward systems. In J. R. Hackman and L. J. Suttle (eds), *Improving Life at Work: Behavioral Science Approaches to Organizational Flange* (pp. 163–226). Santa Monica, CA: Goodyear.

Lawler, E. E., and Finegold, D. (2000). Individualizing the organization: Past, present and future. *Organizational Dynamics*, 29(1), 1–15.

Liden, R. C., and Arad, S. (1995). A power perspective of empowerment and work teams: Implications for human resource management research. *Research in Personnel and Human Resource Management*, 14.

Liden, R. C., Wayne, S. J., and Sparrowe, R. T. (2000). An examination of the mediating role of psychological empowerment on the relations between the job, interpersonal relationships, and workoutcomes. *Journal of Applied Psychology*, 85, 3, June, 407–416.

Locke, E. A. (2003). Leadership. In C. L. Pearce and J. A. Conger (eds), *Shared Leadership: Reframing the Hows and Whys of Leadership* (pp. 271–283). Thousand Oaks, CA: Sage Publications.

Locke, E. A., and Latham, G. (1990). *A Theory of Goal Setting and Task Performance*. New York: Prentice Hall.

Manz, C. C., and Sims, H. P., Jr. (1980). Self-management as a substitute for leadership: A social learning theory perspective. *Academy of Management Review*, 5(3), 361–367.

Manz, C. C., and Sims, H. P., Jr. (1989). *Superleadership: Leading Others to Lead Themselves*. New York: Prentice Hall Press.

Manz, C. C., and Sims, H. P., Jr. (2001). *The New Superleadership*. San Francisco: Berrett-Koehler.

McClelland, D. C. (1975). *Power: The Inner Experience*. New York: Irvington Press.

Mills, P. K., and Ungson, G. R. (2003). Reassessing the limits of structural empowerment: Organizational constitution and trust as controls. *Academy of Management Review*, 28, 143–153.

Neilsen, E. (1986). Empowerment strategies: balancing authority and responsibility. In S. Srivastra (ed.), *Executive Power* (pp. 78–110). San Francisco: Jossey-Bass.

Oldham, G. R. (1976). The motivational strategies used by supervisors' relationships to effectiveness indicators. *Organizational Behavior and Human Performance*, 15, 66–86.

Peale, N. V. (1954). *The Power of Positive Thinking*. New York: Prentice-Hall.

Pearce, C. L. (2004). The future of leadership: Combining vertical and shared leadership to transform knowledge work. *Academy of Management Executive*, 18(1), 47–57.

Pearce, C. L. (2008). Follow the leaders. *Wall Street Journal*, B8, 12, July 7.

Pearce, C. L., and Conger, J. A. (eds) (2003). *Shared Leadership: Reframing the Hows and Whys of Leadership*. Thousand Oaks, CA: Sage Publications.

Pearce, C. L., and Sims, H. P. (2002). Vertical versus shared leadership as predictors of the effectiveness of change management teams: An examination of aversive, directive, transactional, transformational, and empowering leader behaviors. *Group Dynamics: Theory, Research, and Practice*, 6(2), 172–197.

Pearce, C. L., Sims, H. P., Jr., Cox, J. F., Ball, G., Schnell, E., Smith, K. A., and Trevino, L. (2003). Transactors, transformers and beyond: A multi-method development of a theoretical typology of leadership. *Journal of Management Development*, 22(4), 273–307.

Pearce, C. L., Yoo, Y., and Alavi, M. (2004). Leadership, social work and virtual teams: The relative influence of vertical vs. shared leadership in the nonprofit sector. In R. E. Riggio and S. Smith-Orr (eds), *Improving Leadership in Nonprofit Organizations* (pp. 180–203). San Francisco: Jossey Bass.

Sims, H. P. (1977). The leader as a manager of reinforcement contingencies. In J. G. Hunt and L. L. Larson (eds), *Leadership: The Cutting Edge* (pp. 121–137). Carbondale: Southern Illinois University Press.

Solomon, P., and Patch, V. D. (1970). *Handbook of Psychiatry*, 2nd edition. Los Angeles: Lange Medical Publications.

Spreitzer, G. M. (1995). Individual empowerment in the workplace: Dimensions, measurement, and validation. *Academy of Management Journal*, 38, 1442–1465.

Spreitzer, G. M., Kizilos, M. A., and Nason, S. W. (1994). A dimensional analysis of the relationship between psychological empowerment and effectiveness, satisfaction, and strain. Paper presented at the Western Academy of Management Meetings.

Strauss, G. (1977). Managerial practices. In J. R. Hackman and L. J. Suttle (eds), *Improving Life at Work: Behavioral Science Approaches to Organizational Change* (pp. 297–363). Santa Monica, CA: Goodyear.

Szilagyi, A. D. (1980). Causal inferences between leader reward behavior and subordinate goal attainment, absenteeism, and work satisfaction. *Journal of Occupational Psychology*, 53, 195–204.

Thomas, K. W., and Velthouse, B. A. (1990). Cognitive elements of empowerment. *Academy of Management Review*, 15, 666–681.

Tichy, N. M., and Charan, R. (1989). Speed, simplicity, and self-confidence: An interview with Jack Welch. *Harvard Business Review*, Sept.–Oct., 112–120.

Tichy, N. M., and Devanna, M. A. (1986). *The Transformational Leader*. New York: Wiley.

Tichy, N. M., and Sherman, S. (1993). *Control Your Destiny or Someone Else Will*. New York: Currency Doubleday.

Weiner, B. (1985). An attributional theory of achievement motivation and emotion. *Psychological Review*, 92, 548–573.

EXERCISES

Your empowerment profile

Step 1: Complete the following questionnaire.

The following items ask you to assess how you experience your work setting. If you are not currently working, think back to a previous job, or internship. Circle the number that most accurately depicts your assessment where:

1 = Strongly disagree	3 = Neutral	7 = Strongly agree

1. The work I do is very important to me 1 2 3 4 5 6 7

2. I am confident about my ability to do my job 1 2 3 4 5 6 7

3. I have significant autonomy in determining how I do my job 1 2 3 4 5 6 7

4. My impact on what happens in my department is large 1 2 3 4 5 6 7

5. My job activities are personally meaningful to me 1 2 3 4 5 6 7

6. I am self-assured about my capabilities to perform my work activities 1 2 3 4 5 6 7

7. I can decide on my own how to go about doing my work 1 2 3 4 5 6 7

8. I have a great deal of control over what happens in my department.. 1 2 3 4 5 6 7

9. The work I do is meaningful to me 1 2 3 4 5 6 7

10. I have mastered the skills necessary for my job 1 2 3 4 5 6 7

11. I have considerable opportunity for independence and freedom
    in how I do my job... 1 2 3 4 5 6 7

12. I have significant influence over what happens in my
    department.. 1 2 3 4 5 6 7

Step 2: Add the totals of the following items:

1 + 5 + 9 = ———— ÷ 3 = ———— = Experienced meaningfulness score

2 + 6 + 10 = ———— ÷ 3 = ———— = Experienced competence score

3 + 7 + 11 = ———— ÷ 3 = ———— = Experienced self-determination score

4 + 8 + 12 = ———— ÷ 3 = ———— = Experienced impact score

Step 3: Compare your scores to the following averages:

Construct	Industrial company		Insurance company	
	Mean	Std. dev.	Mean	Std. dev.
Experienced meaningfulness	5.89	0.88	5.87	0.85
Experienced competence	5.69	0.98	6.05	0.79
Experienced self-determination	5.51	1.00	5.39	1.19
Experienced impact	5.52	1.02	3.80	1.50

Step 4: In small groups, or with the entire class, discuss how your scores compare. Also, explore good examples of how empowerment has been developed in your organization, as well as how your organizations could approach empowerment more effectively. As part of this discussion, explore both the appropriate applications of empowerment as well as its limits and potential liabilities. Finally, explore how empowering each of you want to be as a leader.

Analysis of the film "Dead Poets Society"

Instructions.   The film, ideally, should be assigned to be viewed outside of class time. During class the instructor will queue up several scenes to prompt discussion. Below is a list of discussion questions to guide the interpretation of the film:

- ◆ Under what conditions are individuals willing and motivated to accept empowerment?
- ◆ What is the effect of individual differences in empowerment?

◆ What are the effects of specific leader behaviors on followers, and do the effects differ by follower?

◆ What is the importance of background factors, such as the norms in place in the institution or the role of other influential individuals to the process?

◆ How does leadership come to be shared and how do the roles transition between various characters?

◆ How can empowerment go awry if followers do not have sufficient skills to make sound judgment, and how can you attempt to prevent this from happening?

◆ How do we apply the principles we have been discussing to organizations?

Film description.   The film *Dead Poets Society* is set at a private school – the Welton Academy for boys. During their first class with their English teacher, Mr. Keating, the boys are taken out into the hallway where he tells them they are bright individuals, with the power to choose their own path – to essentially become self-leaders. This is in stark contrast to the teaching norms at the academy. As such, Mr. Keating clearly demonstrates empowering leader behavior. As the movie progresses, we steadily see the boys take on this newfound empowerment and become effective self-leaders.

One day, one of the boys finds an old yearbook with Mr. Keating in it, where Mr. Keating listed the Dead Poets Society (DPS) as one of his important school activities. When questioned about it, Mr. Keating replies that the DPS was dedicated to finding meaning, that the members would sit in a cave near a pond and recite poetry. Subsequently, the boys decide to start up the DPS once again, ultimately demonstrating effective shared leadership in the process.

Unfortunately, we also get to witness empowerment gone awry, when the boys abuse their empowerment and begin drinking, smoking, going to parties, and otherwise running amok. Upon finding out about this, Mr. Keating counsels the boys to be wise, not foolish, with their empowerment.

In a plot twist, Mr. Keating is inappropriately made a scapegoat when one of the boys commits suicide, and he is terminated from his position. When Mr. Keating enters the classroom for the final time, several of the boys stand on their desks and call him O Captain!, My Captain!, as a way of demonstrating their sincere appreciation for how he empowered them to grow and expand their lives. The final message of the film is that people should think for themselves and be capable self-leaders, while empowering others in like kind.

12

Pay for Performance

CATHY C. DURHAM AND KATHRYN M. BARTOL

THE PRINCIPLE

Our principle is pay for performance. This principle involves providing monetary rewards through carefully designed compensation systems that base pay on measured performance within the control of participants. It also includes incorporating appropriate concerns for procedural and distributive justice. In most situations, properly designed pay-for-performance systems will lead to better performance results.

Well-designed pay-for-performance systems make major contributions to performance through two main mechanisms. First, they positively influence the motivation to perform. Second, they impact the attraction and retention patterns of organizations (i.e., who joins and who remains), thereby affecting the caliber of individuals available to perform.

A number of different pay delivery plans qualify as pay-for-performance systems, although they vary widely with respect to how closely they tie pay to performance. Pay-for-performance systems can deliver monetary rewards at the individual, small group, and/or division or organizational level. Evidence suggests that pay for performance at each of these levels can positively impact performance.

Individual level

At the individual level, there are three major types of pay-for-performance systems: *traditional incentive systems*, *variable pay configurations*, and *merit pay plans*. Traditional incentive plans include *piece-rate plans* and *sales commissions*. With piece-rate incentive plans, an employee is paid a specified rate for each unit produced or each service provided. Mitchell, Lewin, and Lawler (1990) estimate that proper use of piece-rate plans leads to performance gains in the 10–15% range. Based on their review of the literature, Locke, Feren, McCaleb, Shaw, and Denny (1980) concluded that the median productivity improvement from piece-rate plans is 30%. A meta-analysis involving mainly piece-rate pay found that financial incentives are associated with higher performance in terms of quantity and also found no detrimental impact on quality (Jenkins, Mitra, Gupta, and Shaw, 1998). The other traditional incentive, the commission, is a sales incentive that is typically expressed as a percentage of sales dollars, a percentage of gross profit margins, or some dollar amount for each unit sold (Colletti and Cichelli, 1993). The available research indicates that salespeople tend to prefer commissions over other forms of reward (Lopez, Hopkins, and Raymond, 2006) and can be effectively motivated by them (e.g., Banker, Lee, Potter, and Srinivasan, 1996; Ford, Walker, and Churchhill, 1985; Harrison, Virick, and William, 1996).

The second major type of individual level pay-for-performance plan, *variable pay*, is performance-related compensation that does not permanently increase base pay and that must be re-earned to be received again. Because base pay tends to move up more slowly with variable pay plans, the amount of bonus that can be earned needs to be substantial to make up for the fact that part of the pay is "at risk" (Schuster and Zingheim, 1996). The risk stems from the possibility that desired performance might not be achieved and therefore the pay not earned. The piece-rate and commission pay plans discussed above actually constitute forms of variable pay, albeit forms in which a greater proportion of pay is typically tied to performance than is the case with newer forms of variable pay. According to a Hewitt survey of Fortune 1000 companies, a growing number of employers are moving to variable pay: The portion of US companies offering one or more variable pay plans rose from 51% in 1991 to 78% in 2005 (Dean, 2006). Research suggests that variable pay plans are useful in boosting performance (e.g., Chung and Vickery, 1976; Lee, 1988; Smilko and Van Neck, 2004; Yukl and Latham, 1975).

A form of variable pay that is currently popular is a lump-sum bonus for achieving particular goals. Locke (2004) identifies four methods of linking bonuses to goals: assigning stretch goals and paying bonuses only if the goals are achieved, having multiple goal levels and corresponding bonuses that increase as higher goals are met, offering bonuses that grow incrementally as performance improves (with no upper limit), and setting specific, challenging goals but making decisions about bonuses after the fact so that contextual factors can be taken into account. Locke notes that each choice has its pros and cons. For example, bonuses paid only when stretch goals are met, although highly motivating, might also encourage employees to take shortcuts or cheat. Also, they could be discouraging for those who approach but do not reach the goals. Having either multiple or continuous goal and bonus levels (which are similar to piece-rate pay plus goals) may be less likely to result in cheating or gaming, but it is unclear whether such approaches can motivate the highest levels of performance. Setting goals but determining pay after the fact, while accounting for situational factors, requires bosses to understand the full context of employees' performance more than they often can do. Nonetheless, this method has been the approach of choice at both Microsoft (Shaw, 2004) and General Electric (Kerr and Landauer, 2004). Lacking comparative research to guide choices, Locke highlights the need for more experimental studies about how best to link bonuses to goals.

The third major type of individual level pay-for-performance plan, *merit pay*, rewards individuals for past work behaviors and outcomes by adding dollar amounts to their base pay. Merit pay is the most widely used pay system in US organizations (Bretz, Milkovich, and Read, 1992; O'Dell, 1987). Milkovich and Newman (2008) report that 90% of US firms reward employees through merit pay. Based on a review of 25 studies, Heneman (1992) concludes that merit pay plans appear to be moderately effective in influencing performance. Taking a longer-term view, Harris, Gilbreath, and Sunday

(1998) provide evidence that the connection between merit pay and performance may be greater than short-term studies can detect because the cumulative effects of various types of merit pay adjustments linked to performance, such as those related to promotions, can be substantial.

Team level

In addition to pay for performance at the individual level, there is considerable interest in pay-for-performance plans focused on small groups or teams (Parker, McAdams, and Zielinski, 2000). Such pay plans provide monetary rewards based on the measured performance of the group or team. Small work groups or teams are official (designated or recognized by management) multi-person work units composed of individuals who operate interdependently in the performance of tasks that affect others associated within the organization (Guzzo and Dickson, 1996; Hackman, 1987). One survey found that almost 70% of Fortune 1000 companies are using some type of work group or team incentives (Lawler, Mohrman, and Ledford, 1995). Usage in smaller organizations may be less, with one survey showing that 35% of the 140 companies responding, most of which had 2000 or less employees, reported using team rewards (McClurg, 2001). Evidence suggests that performance gains can be associated with the use of monetary rewards for groups (Cotton and Cook, 1982; Gomez-Mejia and Balkin, 1989; Quigley, Tesluk, Locke, and Bartol, 2007; Wageman and Baker, 1997), but that the results are likely to be heavily influenced by situational factors (Balkin and Montemayor, 2000; DeMatteo, Eby, and Sundstrom, 1998; Lawler, 2003). Increased interest in team pay is also emerging in the executive suite, particularly with respect to top management teams (Devers, Cannella, Reilly, and Yoder, 2007).

Organizational level

At the organizational level, three pay systems that potentially link pay and performance are *gainsharing, profit sharing*, and *stock options*. *Gainsharing* is a compensation plan in which an organization shares with employees a portion of the added earnings obtained through their collective increases in productivity (Henderson, 1997) or the achievement of other goals, such as customer satisfaction with quality (Gerhart and Rynes, 2003). Such plans usually involve a significant portion of an organization's employees and possibly all. In large organizations, plans may apply to plants, divisions, or other significant subsystems of the organization. In recent years, gainsharing has been growing in popularity, extending its reach beyond traditional industrial settings to other realms such as health care (Jain and Roble, 2008; Patel, 2006). The available evidence on gainsharing indicates that such plans have generally led to gains in productivity (Welbourne and Gomez-Mejia, 1995), as well as to other positive outcomes, such as decreases in absenteeism and the number of grievances (Arthur and Jelf, 1999).

The second type of organizational level pay system aimed at performance is *profit sharing*, which provides payments to employees based on the profitability of the business. Payments can be made through current distribution plans (paid in cash), deferred plans (paid toward retirement), or a combination of both, although most companies establish deferred plans because of the associated tax advantages. According to one estimate, more than 60% of Fortune 1000 companies have profit sharing plans (Lawler et al., 1995). Data supporting the performance effects of profit sharing plans is somewhat unclear. Kruse (1993) found that productivity growth in firms using profit sharing was 3.5–5.0% higher than in firms that did not use profit sharing. However, Kim (1998) found that profit sharing companies tend to have higher labor costs than other companies, thereby erasing any advantage of profit sharing. There are some weaknesses inherent in profit sharing plans as a direct means of boosting performance. One is that it can be somewhat difficult to establish a clear connection (sometimes referred to as "line of sight") between individual actions and impact on profits, especially in large organizations. Evidence for this is Kruse's (1993) finding that annual productivity growth was greater in smaller profit sharing companies than in larger ones (11–17% productivity growth in companies having fewer than 775 employees, versus 0.0–6.9% in companies having 775 or more). Another weakness is that accounting and financial management practices and other factors outside employees' control can also impact the bottom line. Finally, the deferred nature of many of these plans may not provide strong valence with respect to motivating performance. Indeed, Kruse (1993) found that productivity growth was higher for plans paying cash rewards than for those making deferred payments.

A third type of organizational level reward system is employee *stock ownership*. One study of Fortune 1000 companies showed that 71% had stock ownership programs of some type (Lawler et al., 1995). During the 1990s, the most rapidly growing approach was via stock options, which give employees the right to purchase a specific amount of stock at a designated price over a specified time period (Brandes, Dharwadkar, Lemesis, and Heisler, 2003). The basic rationale is that employees will be more concerned about the long-term success of the organization and increase their efforts if they can reap the benefits as reflected in the rising price of the organization's stock. Additionally, extending ownership can both attract new talent and enhance perceptions of fairness (and thus retention) in current employees. In 2000, a study of 490 organizations reported that companies with stock option plans that were broadly dispersed (beyond the executive level) performed better and had higher average compensation levels than companies without broad-based plans, and also that increases in productivity seemed to counterbalance any dilution of earnings per share that occurred when the options were exercised (Sesil, Kroumova, Kruse, and Blasi, 2000).

Since 2000, however, conditions have changed radically. In a much-debated ruling in 2005, the Financial Accounting Standards Board required companies to recognize stock options as a cost on their income statements in the year they were awarded rather than merely list them in the footnotes – a change that diluted earnings per share in the year options were granted and rendered options less attractive to many employers (Deshmukh, Howe, and Luft, 2008). Further, the value of options plummeted early in the decade and then again beginning in 2007, when a crisis in the mortgage markets ultimately led to the historic "Wall Street bailout" by the US government in 2008 and to widespread fear of a steep global recession. When an option is "underwater" (when its exercise price exceeds the current market price), the value is neutralized and employees' anticipated wealth – along with any motivational potential that might have existed in holding the option – evaporates (Delves, 2001). And, even in times of rising stock prices, the effect may be less than hoped for. One study found that when stock prices have risen above the option price, lower-level employees tend to exercise their options shortly after vesting, a factor that may truncate some of the longer-term motivational potential of the incentive (Huddart and Lang, 1996).

Overall effects

There is some debate regarding whether there are best practices that are applicable to most organizations (Gerhart, Trevor, and Graham, 1996; Huselid, 1995), or whether it is important to match pay systems to particular strategies (Montemayor, 1994; Youndt, Snell, Dean, and Lepak, 1996). The weight of evidence seems to be shifting toward the strategy argument (e.g., Shaw, Gupta, and Delery, 2001; Yanador and Marler, 2006), but more research needs to be done on how best to align pay systems with strategy to ultimately enhance organizational performance (Gerhart, 2000).

The direct impact of pay plans on performance is not the only effect to consider. Growing evidence suggests that there are indirect pay plan effects stemming from influences on *attraction and retention* patterns in organizations. For example, several studies support the notion that the level of compensation influences attraction to organizations (e.g., Saks, Wiesner, and Summers, 1996; Schwoerer and Rosen, 1989; Williams and Dreher, 1992). Moreover, individuals appear to be more attracted to organizations in which the pay system rewards individual rather than group performance and for job outcomes rather than acquiring new skills (Cable and Judge, 1994; Highhouse, Steierwalt, Bachiochi, Elder, and Fisher, 1999). Individuals may also be more attracted to organizations that offer fixed pay, rather than variable pay, unless there is sufficient upside potential to balance the pay risk (Bartol and Locke, 2000).

Pay for performance can also have a positive effect on retention. Research indicates positive relationships between employee perceptions of pay for performance and both pay satisfaction (Heneman, Greenberger, and Strasser, 1988; Huber, Seybolt, and Venemon, 1992; Williams, McDaniel, and Nguyen, 2006) and job satisfaction (Kopelman, 1976), factors that are related to intention to leave and turnover (Chapter 7). General level of pay is also a factor encouraging retention (Batt, 2002). There is some evidence that profit sharing is an important determinant of organizational commitment (Florkowski and Schuster, 1992; Coyle-Shapiro, Morrow, Richardson, and Dunn, 2002), which has been shown to be related to lower turnover. Based on a meta-analysis, Williams and Livingstone (1994) argue that pay-for-performance systems encourage better performers to remain with the organization while inducing poorer performers to leave. One caveat is that a high degree of pay dispersion, in which pay is much higher for relatively few employees at the top of the pay structure than for others, can lead to higher probabilities of turnover among managers (Bloom and Michel, 2002). These negative effects seem to be lessened when pay levels generally are high (Brown, Sturman, and Simmering, 2003).

Interestingly, due to the flexibility and control over labor costs that it provides, variable pay may also reduce turnover. By having more money allocated to bonuses or other forms of variable pay, an organization can shrink its payroll costs during downturns rather than downsize. Gerhart and Trevor (1996) provide evidence that variable pay plans lessen organizational employment variability, allowing for greater employment stability for employees and their organizations.

WHAT IS REQUIRED TO MAKE THE PRINCIPLE WORK?

Define performance

First, it is essential to identify explicitly what performance is desired. Clearly defining performance, however, requires looking beyond individual jobs and thinking strategically about the organization as a whole. It means developing a business model based on what drives the business (e.g., customer satisfaction), after which goals can be set at the various levels of the organization and determinations made about what will be rewarded. Without a business model (or with the wrong one), management risks setting goals and rewarding employees for the wrong things – and finding its employees doing those wrong things very efficiently, to the organization's detriment. Focusing on what drives the business leads to the setting of appropriate performance goals for individual employees at all organizational levels. Then, the act of tying incentives to the achievement of those goals will have not only motivational but also informational value, because people will receive a clear message about what specific behaviors and/or outcomes are expected via communications about the reward system. A temptation to resist is that of defining performance in terms of job aspects that are easily quantifiable, thereby ignoring job dimensions that may be critically important but difficult to measure. This can lead an organization to fall into the trap of "rewarding A while hoping for B" (Kerr, 1995). For pay for performance to be effective, strategically important job dimensions – even hard-to-measure ones – must be identified, communicated, assessed, and rewarded.

Communicate

Because it is impossible to be motivated by incentives one does not grasp, it is critically important not only to design a pay plan that is understandable but also to communicate both clearly and frequently how the program works and what employees must do to bring about the results that will trigger a payout. Communication also implies providing feedback along the way about progress toward targets (Smilko and Van Neck, 2004). Young, Burgess, and White (2007) describe the effects of a failure to communicate in a pay-for-quality project for physicians. Participants found the rules complicated, failed to fully understand the plan, and were not sufficiently engaged by meager attempts to explain it. Thus, although 75% of those eligible received a bonus payment in the first year, very few knew whether they had received their payment or, if they did, realized that it was for their performance on the program's quality measures. Some physicians were so unaware of the financial rewards available to them that they discarded, unopened, the mail that included their bonus checks.

Ensure competence

Employees must have the appropriate knowledge, skills and abilities (KSAs), and self-efficacy (Chapter 10) to perform at the desired level. Instituting pay for performance is a futile exercise if employees are unable to perform at the level required to receive the reward. Hiring people who are efficacious and who possess (or can readily obtain through training) the relevant KSAs is essential.

Make pay systems commensurate with employees' values

Pay for performance will only work if the rewards being offered are valued and the amount is viewed as sufficient, given what employees are being asked to accomplish. Employers can generally assume that money is a value to their employees, both practically and symbolically. Some employees, however, may not value the incremental gain being offered for high-level performance if the amount is viewed as paltry and thus not worth the additional effort. Further, a pay system can fail if it is perceived as undermining employees' other values. For example, individuals may be uninterested in obtaining even a substantial amount of additional pay if they believe that achieving performance goals means sacrificing greater personal values, such as time to pursue their own interests (e.g., family life), a low-stress work environment, or a commitment to high-quality work or to standards of ethical behavior.

Use non-financial motivators too

Most employers assume that money is an effective motivator because it enables employees to buy things that they want or need. Also, money is important from a justice standpoint, giving high performers what is due them for their exceptional contributions to the organization's success. Nonetheless, exclusive reliance on financial incentives would be an unwise policy because it would ignore other important sources of work motivation. Non-monetary motivators include a diverse assortment of activities, such as providing interesting and important work assignments (Chapter 6), engendering commitment to the realization of a vision (or to a visionary leader; Chapter 20), assigning challenging goals in conjunction with ongoing performance feedback (Chapter 9), granting autonomy regarding how a job is accomplished (Chapter 11), providing public and/or private recognition for outstanding contributions (Chapter 13), or simply enabling one to do work that one loves.

Use money in conjunction with intrinsic motivation

Amabile (1993) argues that it is possible to achieve "motivational synergy" by encouraging both intrinsic and extrinsic motivation (see Chapter 26). She posits that intrinsic motivation arises from the value of the work itself to the person. It can be fostered through such measures as matching employees to tasks on the basis of their skills and interests, designing work to be optimally challenging, and bringing together diverse individuals in high-performing work teams. Amabile further suggests that, when creativity is particularly important, it may be best to hold off heavily emphasizing extrinsic motivators during the problem presentation and idea generation stages when intrinsic motivation appears to be most important. Extrinsic factors may be particularly helpful during the sometimes-difficult validation and implementation stages. A meta-analytic study (Eisenberger and Cameron, 1996) and a set of laboratory and field studies (Eisenberger, Rhoades, and Cameron, 1999) also indicated that tangible rewards can enhance, rather than undermine, the effects of intrinsic motivation. Some (e.g., Ryan and Deci, 2000), however, contest this view.

Target the appropriate organizational level

Performance-based pay must be at the appropriate level. Increasingly, firms are rewarding performance at the group and/or organizational levels rather than at the individual level alone, in hopes of boosting organizational performance through enhanced information sharing, group decision making, and teamwork (Bartol and Hagmann, 1992; Parker et al., 2000). Lawler (1971) argues that the distinction between individual and group pay plans is important because individual and group plans are viewed differently by employees and have different effects. A key decision for management, then, concerns whether incentive pay should be based on individual or group performance. Further, if the organization chooses to reward group performance, decisions must be made about what constitutes a "group" for performance-measurement purposes. For example, will group-based pay be based on the performance of a team, a work unit, a division, or the entire organization?

There has been little actual research to offer guidance regarding the level of performance to which incentives should be tied, although several views have been advanced by compensation experts (e.g., Gomez-Mejia and Balkin, 1992; Mitchell et al., 1990; Montemayor, 1994). Key factors that should be considered when making this important decision include:

- ◆ *Nature of the task.* Pay for performance at the individual level is considered most appropriate when the work is designed for individuals, where the need for integration with others is negligible, where group performance means only the sum of members' individual performances, or where the work is simple, repetitive, and stable. For sequential teams that perform various tasks in a predetermined order, so that group performance cannot exceed that of the lowest individual member, it has been recommended that base pay be skill based, and team incentives be team bonuses with payouts distributed as a percentage of base pay. Alternatively, group-based incentive programs, through which all members receive equal shares of a team bonus, are generally considered appropriate when teams are composed of individuals from the same organizational level, when members have complementary roles and must depend upon each other and interact intensively to accomplish their work, so that group performance is enhanced by cooperation, and when the nature of the technology and workflows allow for the identification of distinct groups that are relatively independent of one another. Emerging research (Beersma, Hollenbeck, Humphrey, Moon, Conlon, and Ilgen, 2003) suggests that, when highly interdependent teams have members who are high in extraversion and high in agreeableness, they produce more accurate work under a cooperative reward system than teams with members who are relatively low on these personality dimensions. The increased accuracy, which was found to be due largely to the greater sharing of information (Chapters 17 and 18), came at the expense of speed. The decrement in speed was also related to a tendency for free riding by the lowest performer under the cooperative reward scheme. In contrast, a competitive reward system led to greater speed, but lower accuracy, regardless of the personalities of members. When the work is highly interdependent and a cooperative reward system is in place, it may be helpful to select individuals who are high on extraversion and agreeableness.

Some coaching of the team (Chapter 15) may help the group develop norms that discourage free riding (Hackman and Wageman, 2005), thus enabling accurate work with less decrement in speed.

◆ *Ability to measure performance.* Good performance measures are critically important in any pay-for-performance plan. Pfeffer (1998) argues that performance can often be more reliably assessed at aggregate than at individual levels. He concludes that individual incentive pay should be replaced by collective rewards based on organizational or subunit performance that highlight the interdependence among organizational members. Although many are unwilling to go as far as Pfeffer in discounting the potential value of individual incentives, most agree that group incentives are a suitable alternative when the identification of individual contributors is difficult due to the nature of the task. For gainsharing plans in particular, it is not only necessary that there be good performance measures for the unit or plant, but also that there be a reliable performance history in order to develop a gainsharing formula. When group performance is rewarded with gainsharing, however, it is nonetheless important, particularly in Western cultures, to provide a means for identifying individual contributions to the group effort (e.g., through peer evaluations), so that members keep in mind their accountability at both the individual and group levels.

◆ *Organizational culture.* Group incentive plans are best suited to situations in which the organizational culture emphasizes group achievements (Chapter 33). Group incentives work best when free riding is unlikely (e.g., because members hold each other accountable or because employees are professionals who possess high intrinsic motivation). If a corporate culture is strongly individualistic and competitive, group plans such as team incentives will likely encounter considerable resistance from organizational members accustomed to focusing on individual accomplishments and/or may lead to lower levels of cooperative behavior (Hill, Bartol, Tesluk, and Langa, 2009).

◆ *Management's purpose.* Group incentives are recommended in situations in which there is a need to align the interests of multiple individuals into a common goal, or when management wishes to foster entrepreneurship at the group level. At the organizational level, profit sharing is often used to communicate the importance of the firm's financial performance to employees, heightening their awareness of the overall financial performance of the organization by making a portion of their pay vary with it. This is thought to be most motivating when employees believe that they can substantially influence the profit measure, such as in smaller organizations and those in which the means by which profits are achieved are well understood.

Some have proposed mixed models, whereby incentive pay is based partially on individual measures of performance and partially on group measures. Wageman (1995), however, found that teams having mixed forms of reward (i.e., rewards based on both individual and group performance), mixed tasks (i.e., some tasks performed solely by individuals and some by interdependent groups), or both, had lower performance than those with task and pay designs that were clearly either individual level or team level. She proposes that mixed tasks and rewards may lead to inferior performance by adding a group element to what is primarily an individual task, thereby undermining attention to the task.

It also may be more difficult to develop supporting norms for cooperation in the team (Quigley et al., 2007). In addition, teams executing mixed tasks may need more time to adjust because of the greater complexity of tasks that have both individual and group performance components. In fact, one study (Johnson, Hollenbeck, Humphrey, Ilgen, Jundt, and Meyer, 2006) has shown that it even may be more difficult for a team to shift from a competitive to a cooperative reward structure than from cooperative to a competitive one. When a competitive reward structure was shifted to a cooperative one, team members seem to engage in "cutthroat cooperation" in which team members retained much of their competitive behavior within the new reward systems intended to foster cooperation. Another complicating factor is that some workers may prefer individual pay over team-based pay (Cable and Judge, 1994; Haines and Taggar, 2006; Shaw, Duffy, and Stark, 2001). The question remains, then, how best (or when) to mix individual- and group-based incentive plans.

Make pay commensurate with the level of risk employees are required to bear

Risk refers to uncertainty about outcomes (Sitkin and Pablo, 1992), and, by definition, pay-for-performance systems involve uncertain outcomes for employees. Employees tend to be risk-averse concerning pay because they have no way of minimizing their income risk through diversification, as investors are able to do with their stock portfolios.

At least four factors can affect employees' perceptions concerning the riskiness of a pay-for-performance plan. First is the proportion of employee pay that is performance based. Although the average percentage of variable pay in the USA is only 5%, the proportion ranges widely, from 0 to 70% (and even to 100% for salespersons; Gomez-Mejia and Balkin, 1992). The higher the proportion of variable pay, the more risk the employee must bear, in a tradeoff between income security and the potential for higher earnings (Gomez-Mejia, Balkin, and Cardy, 1998). At some point the level of risk may be perceived as so great that it would be unacceptable to the majority of employees, regardless of the potential for high pay. The second factor that influences employees' perceptions of risk is their self-efficacy (Chapter 10) that they can achieve the performance goals on which pay is contingent. Those who are confident of their ability to perform at a high level should perceive contingent pay as less risky than those who are less confident of their ability. Third, to the extent that the performance measure on which pay is based is influenced by factors outside individual employees' control (e.g., technology or macroeconomic factors affecting profits or stock prices), perceived risk for the employee is increased. For example, CEOs run the risk of losing income (and even employment) if the companies for which they are responsible are unsuccessful – whatever the cause. A fourth factor affecting employee perceptions of risk is the amount of time between performance and the receipt of rewards. Because the future is uncertain, deferred rewards involve more risk than immediate ones. For employees to accept a pay system offering long-term rewards, they must be willing to delay gratification in the hopes of greater (but uncertain) future returns. Research by Shelley (1993) indicates that managers may expect to be compensated for the loss of immediate compensation by the payment of a premium that is far in excess of the amount the time value of money would imply – a finding that is probably true of non-managerial employees as well.

POSSIBLE EXCEPTIONS TO THE PRINCIPLE OF PAYING FOR PERFORMANCE

It does not make sense for an employer to offer to pay employees more unless the employer will actually get more in the bargain. When, therefore, might it be unwise (or even counter-productive) to offer incentives?

When employees are learning

In learning situations, when employees are attempting to "get up to speed" on a new task, offering performance-based pay may frustrate more than it motivates. Performance fail-ures that are a natural part of learning may be exaggerated in the learner's mind because of failure not only to perform the task but also to obtain the monetary reward. Thus, it is unwise to pay for performance until employees are able to perform at the desired level.

When the employer can monitor

Agency theory (Jensen and Meckling, 1976) suggests that financial incentives are unnecess-ary when employers can easily monitor employees' behavior (e.g., by direct observation or through information systems) and give them ongoing direction and feedback. In such situations, employees' awareness that they are being monitored may obviate paying for performance.

When other motivators are sufficient or compensatory

Some people value other aspects of their jobs more than they value pay – factors such as interesting work, autonomy, desirable location, benefits that meet their needs, or having a boss they love working for. Such individuals will often accept lower pay in order to have what is more important to them in their jobs.

When the company is unionized

Union contracts constrain an employer's pay policies, and thus under collective bargain-ing agreements it may be impossible to pay for performance, especially at the individual level. When incentives are included in a union contract, they are usually group incentives, because group pay is viewed as encouraging cohesion rather than competition among members.

CASE EXAMPLES

Paying for individual performance

True Value Company.   Kelly and Hounsell (2007) provide an example of a highly success-ful individual level pay-for-performance plan at the True Value Company (previously TruServe Corporation), which since 2000 has offered a voluntary plan called "simplified gainsharing" (although not gainsharing in the traditional sense) at its regional distribution centers. The incentive relies on a comparison of the actual performance of individual warehouse workers against predetermined expectations based on historical averages and/ or engineered labor standards. Workers who perform above expectations are rewarded in the following month by an increase in their hourly pay rate for the entire month. As long as an employee's performance level is maintained (and there is no reduction in quality or safety), the rate increase continues. The addition to pay is funded from the savings resulting from productivity gains, the employee's share of which is approximately one third and the company's two thirds. Although there is no cap on savings to be shared, there is a provision under which management and employees can agree to increase performance expectation levels as processes become more refined (Kelley and Hounsell, 2007). Highly productive employees appreciate that their individual contributions are recognized, that rewards are immediate rather than deferred, and that the plan prevents poor performers from sharing the rewards of top performers (O'Reilly, 2006). Reported benefits to True Value have been a reduction in the number of employees needed to handle a consistent volume of warehouse activity, decreased turnover, increased quality, and savings of several millions of dollars annually (Kelly and Hounsell, 2007).

Countrywide Financial.   Countrywide Financial, rescued from financial ruin through acquisition by Bank of America in 2008, provides an example of the perils of rewarding the wrong things. Morgenson (2007) describes how Countrywide "effectively" used individual incentives to promote the strategic (albeit short-sighted, ethically problematic, and ultimately disastrous) goals of management during the recent mortgage lending boom. Because subprime loans were so lucrative, Countrywide's commission structure rewarded sales representatives for making extremely risky loans that imposed heavy burdens on borrowers. Incentives included: paying proportionately larger commissions for subprime loans (0.50%) than for loans of higher quality (0.20%), which led brokers and sales representatives to move borrowers possessing good credit (and thus qualified for prime loans) into the subprime category; adding an extra 1% of the loan's value to the sales commission when a three-year prepayment penalty was added, which encouraged locking borrowers into high-cost loans after the initial "teaser" interest rate was reset; and offering an additional 0.25% commission when the borrower added a home equity line of credit, which promoted more borrowing by cash-strapped mortgagees. Its commission plan supported Countrywide's position as one of the most aggressive home lenders in the USA and contributed to its role in triggering the global economic crisis of 2008.

Paying for team performance

Children's Hospital of Boston.   The accounts receivables (AR) department of Children's Hospital in Boston developed a team-based incentive program that led to a greatly reduced billing cycle and aided cash flow for the hospital (Cadrain, 2003). The department had installed a new billing system that was not working as intended, causing problems for employees and leading to low morale in the department. The time to receive payments after bills were sent out was stretching beyond 100 days and hospital officials were becoming concerned about cash flow. To help improve employee morale and shorten the billing cycle, hospital executives set up an incentive plan aimed at establishing a line of sight that allowed employees to focus on the connections between number of days a bill spends in AR and the quarterly cash flow of the hospital. Team members were provided with three possible goals stated in terms of number of days an unpaid bill remained in AR: threshold, target, and optimal. Each goal had a dollar amount attached to it with a provision for a quarterly payment of $500, $1000, or $1500, respectively. Within 30 days of the end of each quarter, each team member would receive a part of the payment prorated to reflect the number of scheduled hours the team member worked, and a progress celebration was held. Once the team members understood the connection between their work and the cash flow at the hospital as well as how their efforts could increase their personal cash flow, they began working closely as a team to follow up with patients, insurers, or the medical records people. By the end of the plan's first fiscal year, employees had succeeded in reducing the average number of days a bill was in AR from 100 to 75.8. Shortly after, they reached the middle 60s. The plan had an added bonus for the hospital because turnover in the AR department plummeted.

Hewlett-Packard. Beer and Cannon (2004) provide an example of team-based incentives having unforeseen negative consequences. With the intention of supporting a move to self-managed teams, managers at the San Diego site of Hewlett-Packard (HP) introduced a team pay-for-performance system. The purposes were to motivate teams to achieve specific goals related to improvement, production, and quality. There were three levels of team performance pay. Ninety percent of teams were expected to reach a Level 1 payout, with 50% at Level 2, and 10–15% at Level 3. For Level 3, members of the work team were given between $150 and $200 extra at the end of the following month. There was also a skill-based pay component, which allowed employees to achieve a higher base pay for increasing skill levels as certified by "subject matter experts;" this was instead of receiving merit raise increases. The program went well for the first six months as most teams reached Levels 2 and 3. However, the plan paid out more than expected and managers sought to raise the performance standards, much to the chagrin of the employees. It also became apparent that some factors, such as delays in shipments of parts or mechanical breakdowns, could interfere with teams meeting goals, but were beyond their control. Another unexpected outcome was that high performing teams did not want to allow anyone who might lower their performance to join the team, causing some teams to be composed of mainly low performers. Mobility between teams, which could help learning transfer, also became very limited. Finally, a majority of the employees did not like the additional pressure of taking tests for the skill-based pay. After about a year, one of the largest divisions at the site dropped the pay plan because managers grew weary of having to continually rework the pay plan, and because employee surveys indicated that employees preferred to change back to the standard pay system at HP. When the change back to the standard system was announced, the employees staged a party to convey their gratitude. The rest of the site eventually dropped the system when a major manufacturing reorganization was instituted.

Paying for organizational performance

Handelsbanken. Swedish-based Handelsbanken provides an example of profit sharing used effectively to reward performance and instill loyalty among employees (Hope and Fraser, 2003). The bank's stated goal has long been to consistently realize higher profitability than comparable banks, and in 1973 then-CEO Jan Wallander established Octogonen, a foundation through which Handelsbanken shares with employees the "extra profits" made possible through their efforts. Employees are rewarded when company profits exceed the average profits of comparable banks, and every year but one since 1973 the board has allocated a portion of profits to Octogonen. Each full-time employee in the bank's home markets receives an equal part of that year's allocated amount, regardless of position or salary. (As noted in Chapter 33, Sweden is an egalitarian culture, where equal allotments, regardless of rank, are likely to be more acceptable than in individualistic countries such as the USA, where formula-based allocations (e.g., a fixed percentage of salary) are more common.) Distributions are deferred until retirement at age 60. Since Octogonen's beginning, Handelsbanken has performed well, and the profit sharing system has paid out significant amounts of money. The plan, in conjunction with other employee-friendly human resource management practices, is thought to be an incentive for staff to remain with the company (Hammarström, 2007; Handelsbanken, 2007). In recent surveys, 82% of Handelsbanken staff reported believing they could make a valuable contribution to the bank's success (Times Online, 2007), and 86% reported that they would not leave, even if they had another job offer (Times Online, 2008).

American Federation of Government Employees. Miller and Schuster (1995) describe the failure of a gainsharing plan at a federally owned and operated industrial complex whose main mission was the maintenance, repair, and rebuilding of military equipment. The complex employed 4800 civilian workers, including several levels of management who ultimately reported to military offices. A local of the American Federation of Government Employees represented almost 60% of the hourly personnel. The gainsharing plan was developed in response to an order from an off-site military commander who wished to increase hourly productivity. The plan was designed by senior managers with no input from line personnel, union leadership, or gainsharing consultants. A total of 460 employees were involved in the gainsharing plan, which was initiated as a 15-month pilot program. The plan base and payout levels differed for various units and, although computed monthly, were distributed quarterly. The formula design apparently was flawed, and quickly caused feelings of inequity and dissatisfaction across units. The top departments in terms of monetary gain and payout earned did not register actual productivity gains, while several departments that did show productivity gains actually received lower payouts. Middle managers particularly were frustrated by their lack of input into the plan design. Both managers and production employees viewed the fact that the plan was labeled a pilot program as evidence that there was actually little commitment to it by upper management. Consensus also developed among participants that the quarterly period for payout was too long. Ultimately, few if any gains in productivity materialized and the plan was eventually discontinued, but not before it seriously damaged an effectively functioning quality program that it partially overlapped.

Global pay

Cisco Systems. Organizations with international operations are presented with some unique challenges when they attempt to pay for performance at the organizational (and thus global) level. Nonetheless, multinational firms are increasingly instituting global pay in an attempt to attract skilled workers and create organizational cultures in which employees feel part of the same company regardless of their location. Cisco Systems, a maker of Internet equipment, has 65,000 employees worldwide, with about one third operating outside of the USA (Cisco, 2008). The company sets base pay at the 65th percentile in every labor market and offers variable pay that brings total remuneration to the 75th percentile (Hansen, 2005). Cisco Systems' global strategy includes the use of stock options and a stock purchase plan, but its commitment to doing so has meant that the company has had to work hard to ensure that pay is understood, accepted, and deployed to the benefit rather than to the detriment of workers worldwide. Problems it has encountered include (Gross and Winterup, 1999): regulations in China and Russia that limit the ability of citizens to hold securities in foreign companies and differing tax regulations across countries within Europe, including taxing stock options when they are received rather than when they are exercised or severely taxing any profit if stock options are sold within the first five years. Differences in per capita income have also caused some adjustments in some countries to avoid having individuals receive such huge capital gains that they would be able to take early retirement in only a few years. These examples illustrate the importance of staying abreast of labor markets and changing laws wherever a company has operations, but Cisco Systems is convinced that doing so is worth the effort because it enables the firm to recruit and retain superior employees worldwide. The company considers its employees the company's best asset and, as a result, places heavy emphasis on a broad set of benefits and a culture that focuses on "nurturing and developing this talent to its full potential" (Cisco, 2004). Cisco frequently appears on various rankings of best places to work (Cisco, 2008; Gerdes, 2008).

Conclusion

Paying for performance works – when done right. It communicates what factors are most important to the company's success and focuses employees' attention and effort on those factors. It is fair, because it pays more to those who contribute more. In turn, it attracts individuals who can perform at high levels and, by recognizing and rewarding them for doing so, makes them want to remain.

References

Amabile, T. M. (1993). Motivational synergy: Toward new conceptualizations of intrinsic and extrinsic motivation in the workplace. *Human Resource Management Review*, 3, 185–201.

Arthur, J. B., and Jelf, G. S. (1999). The effects of gainsharing on grievance rates and absenteeism over time. *Journal of Labor Research*, 20, 133–145.

Balkin, D. B., and Montemayor, E. F. (2000). Explaining team-based pay: A contingency perspective based on the organizational life cycle, team design, and organizational learning literatures. *Human Resource Management Review*, 10, 249–269.

Bank of America (2008). Rewarding success. Retrieved October 4, 2008, from http://boa.stg.hodesiq.com/ada/rewarding.asp

Banker, R. D., Lee, S-Y., Potter, G., and Srinivasan, S. (1996). Contextual analysis of performance impacts of outcome-based incentive compensation. *Academy of Management Journal*, 39, 920–948.

Bartol, K. M., and Hagmann, L. L. (1992). Team-based pay plans: A key to effective teamwork. *Compensation and Benefits Review*, November–December, 24–29.

Bartol, K. M., and Locke, E. A. (2000). Incentives and motivation. In S. L. Rynes and B. Gerhart (eds), *Compensation in Organizations*. San Francisco: Jossey-Bass.

Batt, R. (2002). Managing customer services: human resource practices, quit rates, and sales growth. *Academy of Management Journal*, 45, 587–597.

Beer, M., and Cannon, M. D. (2004). Promise and peril in implementing pay-for-performance. *Human Resource Management*, 43(1), 3–48.

Beersma, B., Hollenbeck, J. R., Humphrey, S. E., Moon, H., Conlon, D. E., and Ilgen, D. R. (2003). Cooperation, competition, and team performance: Toward a contingency approach. *Academy of Management Journal*, 46, 572–590.

Bloom, M., and Michel, J. G. (2002). The relationships among organizational context, pay dispersion, and managerial turnover. *Academy of Management Journal*, 45, 33–42.

Brandes, P., Dharwadkar, R., Lemesis, G. V., and Heisler, W. J. (2003). Effective employee stock option design: Reconciling stakeholder, strategic, and motivational factors. *Academy of Management Executive*, 17(1), 77–93.

Bretz, R. D., Milkovich, G. T., and Read, W. (1992). The current state of performance appraisal research and practice: Concerns, directions, and implications. *Journal of Management*, 18, 321–352.

Brown, M. P., Sturman, M. C., and Simmering, M. J. (2003). Compensation policy and organizational performance: The efficiency, operational, and financial implications of pay levels and pay structure. *Academy of Management Journal*, 46, 752–762.

Cable, D. M., and Judge, T. A. (1994). Pay preferences and job search decisions: A person–organization fit perspective. *Personnel Psychology*, 47, 317–348.

Cadrain, D. (2003). Put success in sight. *HR Magazine*, 48(5), 84–92.

Chung, K. H., and Vickery, W. D. (1976). Relative effectiveness and joint effects of three selected reinforcements in a repetitive task situation. *Organizational Behavior and Human Decision Processes*, 16, 114–142.

Cisco (2004). On company's 20th anniversary, Cisco executives reflect on past success and look to the future. Retrieved on October 23, 2008, from http://newsroom.cisco.com/dlls/2004/ts_121004.html.

Cisco (2008). News@Cisco->Fact Sheet. Retrieved October 23, 2008, from http://newsroom.cisco.com/dlls/corpinfo/factsheet.html.

Colletti, J. A., and Cichelli, D. L. (1993). *Designing Sales Compensation Plans: An Approach to Developing and Implementing Incentive Plans for Salespeople*. Scottsdale: American Compensation Association.

Cotton, M. S., and Cook, J. L. (1982). Meta-analyses and the effects of various reward systems: Some different conclusions from Johnson et al. *Psychological Bulletin*, 92, 176–183.

Coyle-Shapiro, J. A-M., Morrow, P. C., Richardson, R. and Dunn, S. R. (2002). Using profit sharing to enhance employee attitudes: A longitudinal examination of the effects on trust and commitment. *Human Resource Management*, 41, 423–439.

Davis, P. (2005). B of A unveils profit-share program for 85% of staff. *American Banker*, 170(115), 1, 18.

Davis, P. (2008). No bonus under B of A profit program. *American Banker*, 173(37), 20.

Dean, S. (2006). Why companies are moving to variable pay. *Business and Legal Reports*. Retrieved September 19, 2008, from: http://comp.blr.com/display.cfm?id=155070.

Delves, D. P. (2001). Underwater stock options. *Strategic Finance*, 83(6), 26–32.

DeMatteo, J. S., Eby, L. T., and Sundstrom, E. (1998). Team-based rewards: Current empirical evidence and directions for future research. *Research in Organizational Behavior*, 20, 141–183.

Deshmukh, S., Howe, K. M., and Luft, C. (2008). Stock option expensing: The role of corporate governance. *Journal of Applied Corporate Finance*, 20(2), 122–129.

Devers, C. E., Cannella, Jr., A. A., Reilly, G. P., and Yoder, M. E. (2007). Executive compensation: A multidisciplinary review of recent development. *Journal of Management*, 33, 1016–1072.

Eisenberger, R., and Cameron, J. (1996). Detrimental effects of reward: Reality or myth? *American Psychologist*, 51, 1153–1166.

Eisenberger, R., Rhoades, R., and Cameron, J. (1999). Does pay for performance increase or decrease perceived self-determination and intrinsic motivation? *Journal of Personality and Social Psychology*, 75, 1026–1040.

Florkowski, G. W., and Schuster, M. H. (1992). Support for profit sharing and organizational commitment: A path analysis. *Human Relations*, 45, 507–523.

Ford, N. M., Walker, O. C., and Churchhill, G. A. (1985). Differences in the attractiveness of alternative rewards among industrial salespeople: Additional evidence. *Journal of Business Research*, 13, 123–138.

Gerdes, L. (2008). The best places to launch a career. *Business Week*, 36, September 15.

Gerhart, B. (2000). Compensation strategy and organizational performance. In S. L. Rynes and B. Gerhart (eds), *Compensation in Organizations* (pp. 151–194). San Francisco: Jossey-Bass.

Gerhart, G., and Rynes, S. L. (2003). *Compensation: Theory, Evidence, and Strategic Implications*. Thousand Oaks, CA: Sage.

Gerhart, G., and Trevor, C. O. (1996). Employment variability under different compensation systems. *Academy of Management Journal*, 39, 1692–1712.

Gerhart, G., Trevor, C. O., and Graham, M. E. (1996). New directions in compensation research: Synergies, risk, and survival. *Research in Personnel and Human Resources Management*, 14, 143–203.

Gomez-Mejia, L. R., and Balkin, D. B. (1989). Effectiveness of individual an aggregate compensation strategies. *Industrial Relations*, 28, 431–445.

Gomez-Mejia, L. R., and Balkin, D. B. (1992). *Compensation, Organizational Strategy, and Firm Performance*. Cincinnati, OH: South-Western.

Gomez-Mejia, L. R., Balkin, D. B., and Cardy, R. L. (1998). *Managing Human Resources* (2nd edition). Upper Saddle River, NJ: Prentice-Hall.

Gross, S. E., and Winterup, P. L. (1999). Global pay? Maybe not yet! *Compensation and Benefits Review*, 30(4), 25–34.

Guzzo, R. A., and Dickson, M. W. (1996). Teams in organizations: Recent research on performance and effectiveness. *Annual Review of Psychology*, 47, 307–338.

Hackman, J. R. (1987). The design of work teams. In J. W. Lorsch (ed.), *Handbook of Organizational Behavior* (pp. 315–342). Englewood Cliffs, NJ: Prentice Hall.

Hackman, J. R., and Wageman, R. (2005). A theory of team coaching. *Academy of Management Review*, 30, 269–287.

Haines, V. Y., and Taggar, S. (2006). Antecedents of team reward attitude. *Group Dynamics: Theory, Research, and Practice*, 10, 194–205.

Hammarström, H. (2007). Handelsbanken, Sweden: make work pay – make work attractive. Retrieved October 12, 2008, from http://www.eurofound.europa.eu/areas/qualityofwork/betterjobs/cases/se04handelsbanken.htm.

Handelsbanken (2007). *2007 Annual Report*. Retrieved October 12, 2008, from http://www.handelsbanken.com/us

Hansen, F. (2005). A new way to pay. *Workforce Management*, October 24, 33–40. Retrieved on October 23, 2008, from http://www.workforce.com/archive/feature/24/19/81/index.php?ht=

Harris, M. M., Gilbreath, B., and Sunday, J. A. (1998). A longitudinal examination of a merit pay system: Relationships among performance ratings, merit increases, and total pay increases. *Journal of Applied Psychology*, 83, 825–831.

Harrison, D. A., Virick, M., and William, S. (1996). Working without a net: Time, performance, and turnover under maximally contingent rewards. *Journal of Applied Psychology*, 81, 331–345.

Henderson, R. I. (1997). *Compensation Management in a Knowledge-based World* (7th edition). Upper Saddle River, NJ: Prentice Hall.

Heneman, R. L. (1992). *Merit Pay: Linking Pay Increases to Performance Ratings*. Reading, MA: Addison-Wesley.

Heneman, R. L., Greenberger, D. B., and Strasser, S. (1988). The relationship between pay-for-performance perceptions and pay satisfaction. *Academy of Management Journal*, 32, 466–476.

Highhouse, S., Stierwalt, S. L., Bachiochi, P., Elder, A. E., and Fisher, G. (1999). Effects of advertised human resource management practices on attraction of African American applicants. *Personnel Psychology*, 52, 425–442.

Hill, N. S., Bartol, K. M., Tesluk, P. E., and Langa, G. A. (2009). When time is not enough: the development of trust and cooperation in computer mediated teams. *Organizational Behavior and Human Decision Processes*, 108, 187–201.

Hope, J., and Fraser, R. (2003). New ways of setting rewards: the beyond budgeting model. *California Management Review*, 45(4), 104–119.

Huber, V. L., Seybolt, P. M., and Venemon, K. (1992). The relationship between individual inputs, perceptions, and multidimensional pay satisfaction. *Journal of Applied Social Psychology*, 22, 1356–1373.

Huddart, S., and Lang, M. (1996). Employee stock option exercises: An empirical analysis. *Journal of Accounting and Economics*, 21, 5–43.

Huselid, M. (1995). The impact of human resources management practices on turnover, productivity, and corporate financial performance. *Academy of Management Journal*, 38, 635–672.

Jain, S. H., and Roble, D. (2008). Gainsharing in health care: Meeting the quality-of-care challenge. *Healthcare Financial Management*, March, 72–78.

Jenkins, G. D., Jr., Mitra, A., Gupta, N., and Shaw, J. D. (1998). Are financial incentives related to performance? A meta-analytic review of empirical research. *Journal of Applied Psychology*, 83, 777–787.

Jensen, M., and Meckling, M. (1976). Theory of the firm: Managerial behavior, agency costs and ownership structure. *Journal of Financial Economics*, 3, 305–360.

Johnson, M. D., Hollenbeck, J. R., Humphrey, S. E., Ilgen, D. R., Jundt, D., and Meyer, C. J. (2006). Cutthroat cooperation: Asymmetrical adaptation to changes in team reward structures. *Academy of Management Journal*, 49, 103–119.

Kelley, P., and Hounsell, R. W. (2007). Engaging associates and unleashing productivity: The case for simplified gainsharing. *Performance Improvement*, 46(2), 30–34.

Kerr, S. (1995). On the folly of rewarding A, while hoping for B. *Academy of Management Executive*, 9, February, 7–14.

Kerr, S., and Landauer, S. (2004). Using stretch goals to promote organizational effectiveness and personal growth: General Electric and Goldman Sachs. *Academy of Management Executive*, 18, 134–138.

Kim, S. (1998). Does profit sharing increase firms' profits? *Journal of Labor Research*, 19, 351–370.

Kopelman, R. E. (1976). Organizational control system responsiveness, expectancy theory constructs, and work motivation: Some interrelations and causal connections. *Personnel Psychology*, 29, 205–220.

Kruse, D. L. (1993). *Profit sharing: does it make a difference?* Kalamazoo, MI: Upjohn Institute.

Lawler, E. E. III, (1971). *Pay and Organizational Effectiveness: A Psychological View.* New York: McGraw-Hill.

Lawler, E. E. III, (2003). Pay systems for virtual teams. In C. B. Gibson and S. G. Cohen (eds), *Virtual Teams that Work: Creating Conditions for Virtual Team Effectiveness.* San Francisco: Jossey-Bass.

Lawler, E. E., III, Mohrman, S., and Ledford, G. E., Jr. (1995). *Creating High Performance Organizations.* San Francisco: Jossey-Bass.

Lee, C. (1988). The effects of goal setting and monetary incentives on self-efficacy and performance. *Journal of Business and Psychology*, 2, 366–372.

Locke, E. A. (2004). Linking goals to monetary incentives. *Academy of Management Executive*, 18(4), 130–133.

Locke, E. A., Feren, D. B., McCaleb, V. M., Shaw, K. N., and Denny, A. T. (1980). The relative effectiveness of four methods of motivating employee performance. In K. D. Duncan, M. M. Gruneberg, and D. Wallis (eds), *Changes in Working Life* (pp. 363–388). London: Wiley Ltd.

Lopez, T. B., Hopkins, C. D., and Raymond, M. A. (2006). Reward preferences of salespeople: how do commissions rate? *Journal of Personal Selling and Sales*, 26(4), 381–390.

McClurg, L. N. (2001). Team rewards: how far have we come? *Human Resource Management*, 40(1), 73–86.

Milkovich, G. T., and Newman, J. M. (2008). *Compensation* (9th editon). New York: McGraw-Hill/Irwin.

Miller, C., and Schuster, M. H. (1995). The anatomy of a failure: A non-recommended application of gainsharing and its predictable effects on productivity in a public sector setting. *Public Administration Quarterly*, 19, 217–224.

Mitchell, D. J. B., Lewin, D., and Lawler, E. E. III, (1990). Alternative pay systems, firm performance, and productivity. In A. S. Blinder (ed.), *Paying for Productivity: A Look at the Evidence* (pp. 15–94). Washington, DC: The Brookings Institution.

Montemayor, E. F. (1994). A model for aligning teamwork and pay. *ACA Journal*, 3(2), 18–25.

Morgenson, G. (2007). Inside the Countrywide lending spree. *The New York Times*, August 26. Retrieved October 11, 2008, from http://www.nytimes.com/2007/08/26/business/yourmoney/26country.html?ex=1345780800&en=114a08fd2c6e219e&ei=5090&partner=rssuserland&emc=rss.

O'Dell, C. (1987). *People, Performance and Pay.* Houston: American Productivity Center.

O'Reilly, J. (2006). Gainsharing in the warehouse: Power from the people. Inboundlogistics. com, May. Retrieved October 12, 2008, from http://www.inboundlogistics.com/articles/ features/0506_feature02.shtml

Parker, G., McAdams, J., and Zielinski, D. (2000). Rewardings teams: Lessons from the trenches. San Fransciso: Jossey-Bass.

Patel, A. D. (2006, September). Gainsharing: Past, present, and future. *Healthcare Financial Management*, September, 124–130.

Pfeffer, J. (1998). Six dangerous myths about pay. *Harvard Business Review*, 76, May–June, 108–119.

Quigley, N., Tesluk, P. E., Locke, E. A., and Bartol, K. M. (2007). The effects of incentives and individual differences on knowledge sharing and performance effectiveness. *Organization Science*, 18, 71–88.

Ruiz, G. (2005). Bank of America ties bonuses to overall success, not individual achievement. *Workforce Management*, 84(10). Retrieved October 4, 2008, from http://www. workforce.com/section/00/article/24/18/27.html

Ryan, R. M., and Deci, E. L. (2000). Self-determination theory and the facilitation of intrinsic motivation, social development, and well-being. *American Psychologist*, 55, 68–78.

Saks, A. M., Wiesner, W. H., and Summers, R. J. (1996). Effects of job previews and compensation policy on applicant attraction and job choice. *Journal of Vocational Behavior*, 49, 68–85.

Schuster, J. R., and Zingheim, P. K. (1996). *The New Pay: Linking Employee and Organizational Performance*. San Francisco: Jossey-Bass.

Schwoerer, C., and Rosen, B. (1989). Effects of employment-at-will policies and compensation policies on corporate image and job pursuit intentions. *Journal of Applied Psychology*, 74, 653–656.

Sesil, J. C., Kroumova, M. A., Kruse, D. L., and Blasi, J. R. (2000). Broad-based employee stock options in the U.S.: Do they impact company performance? *Academy of Management Proceedings 2000 HR*, G1–G6.

Shaw, J. D., Duffy, M. K., and Stark, E. M. (2001). Team reward attitude: Construct development and initial validation. *Journal of Organizational Behavior*, 22, 903–917.

Shaw, J. D., Gupta, N., and Delery, J. E. (2001). Congruence between technology and compensation systems: Implications for strategy implementation. *Strategic Management Journal*, 22, 379–386.

Shaw, K. N. (2004). Changing the goal-setting process at Microsoft. *Academy of Management Executive*, 18, 139–142.

Shelley, M. (1993). Outcome signs, question frames, and discount rates. *Management Science*, 39(7), 806–815.

Sitkin, S. B., and Pablo, A. L. (1992). Reconceptualizing the determinants of risk behavior. *Academy of Management Review*, 17, 9–38.

Smilko, J., and Van Neck, K. (2004). Rewarding excellence through variable pay. *Benefits Quarterly*, 20(3), 21–25.

Times Online (2007). Best 100 Companies: 11. Handelsbanken. Retrieved October 12, 2008, from http://www.timesonline.co.uk/tol/life_and_style/career_and_jobs/best_ 100_companies/article1473616.ece

Times Online (2008). Best 100 Companies: 10. Handelsbanken. Retrieved October 12, 2008, from http://www.timesonline.co.uk/tol/life_and_style/career_and_jobs/best_ 100_companies/article3478984.ece

Wageman, R. (1995). Interdependence and group effectiveness. *Administrative Science Quarterly*, 40, 145–180.

Wageman, R., and Baker, G. (1997). Incentives and cooperation: The joint effects of task and reward interdependence on group performance. *Journal of Organizational Behavior*, 18, 139–158.

Welbourne, T. M., and Gomez-Mejia, L. R. (1995). Gainsharing: A critical review and a future research agenda. *Journal of Management*, 21, 559–609.

Williams, C. R., and Livingstone, L. P. (1994). Another look at the relationship between performance and voluntary turnover. *Academy of Management Journal*, 37, 269–298.

Williams, M. L., and Dreher, G. F. (1992). Compensation system attributes and applicant pool characterisitics. *Academy of Management Journal*, 35, 571–595.

Williams, M. L., McDaniel, M. A., and Nguyen, N. T. (2006). A meta-analysis of the antecedents and consequences of pay level satisfaction. *Journal of Applied Psychology*, 91, 392–413.

Yanador, Y., and Marler, J. H. (2006). Compensation strategy: does business strategy influence compensation in high-technology firms? *Strategic Management Journal*, 27, 559–570.

Young, G. J., Burgess, J. F., and White, B. (2007). Pioneering pay-for-quality: Lessons from the Rewarding Results demonstrations. *Health Care Financing Review*, 29(1), 59–70.

Youndt, M. A., Snell, S. A., Dean, J. W., Jr., and Lepak, D. P. (1996). Human resource management, manufacturing strategy, and firm performance. *Academy of Management Journal*, 39, 836–866.

Yukl, G. A., and Latham, G. P. (1975). Consequences of reinforcement schedules and incentive magnitude for employee performance: Problems encountered in an industrial setting. *Journal of Applied Psychology*, 60, 294–298.

Exercises

Analyzing the pay system at your job

1. Think about your current job (or a job you've held in the past). Circle the types of pay you receive in this job:

   Non-performance-based pay: Salary   Hourly pay

   Individual level: Piece-rate   Sales commission   Other variable pay   Merit pay

   Team level: Team-based pay

   Organizational level: Gainsharing   Profit sharing   Stock ownership (or options)

2. Use a scale from 0 to 4 to answer (a)–(c) below. *(Circle your ratings.)*

   (a) How well does the pay plan contribute to your *motivation to perform at a high level?*

       Performance: Not at all motivating   0 1 2 3 4   Extremely motivating

(b) How well does the pay plan contribute to your *motivation to collaborate with or help fellow employees accomplish their work goals?*

Collaboration: Not at all motivating   0 1 2 3 4   Extremely motivating

(c) How well does the pay plan contribute to your *motivation to remain with the organization?*

Retention: Not at all motivating   0 1 2 3 4   Extremely motivating

3. What (if any) aspects of the plan are demotivating or demoralizing to you?

4. (a) What is one change your employer could make to the pay system that would enhance your motivation to perform well and stay with the organization? (b) What potential pitfalls or risks (to you, your fellow employees, or the organization) would be associated with this proposed change?

Bank of America

In 2005, Bank of America unveiled a new profit sharing program, Rewarding Success, which links cash bonuses for 85% of its employees – those whose cash compensation is less than $100,000 and those not paid exclusively by commission or variable pay – to corporate performance goals. Aims of the program included: attracting and retaining employees, motivating performance, and creating a sense of shared destiny, especially after the bank's merger with FleetBoston in 2004 (Davis, 2005; Ruiz, 2005). When the company meets or exceeds annual business targets, all eligible employees receive equal bonuses, which they can take as cash or defer in whole or part to their 401(k) accounts (Bank of America, 2008). The minimum per-employee payout when the earnings trigger is reached is $500, and employee bonuses rise with bank earnings to a potential maximum of $3000. The bank originally considered offering equity as part of the new program, but a survey of employees showed that they preferred cash. Also, because companies would have to begin expensing stock options on their grant date beginning in 2006, the choice of cash over stock options was considered wise (Davis, 2005).

Davis (2008) reports that in 2006, eligible employees received bonuses of $1175, and in 2007 they received $1820. However, after lower-than-expected earnings in 2007 due to deteriorating credit quality and capital market difficulties, Bank of America informed employees that it would not pay bonuses under the program. Commented a company spokeswoman: "It's disappointing to all of us." Given the crisis in US financial markets in 2008, future bonus payments are uncertain at best. What is your assessment of the Rewarding Success program, from both the bank's and the employees' perspectives? What recommendations would you make to Bank of America?

13

Provide Recognition for Performance Improvement

Fred Luthans and Alexander D. Stajkovic

*It is difficult to conceive of a society populated with people who are completely
unmoved by the respect, approval, and reproof of others.* (Bandura, 1986,
p. 235)

The effect of positive reinforcement, contingently applied, on performance improvement
may be one of the most agreed upon principles in the field of organizational behavior, and
arguably psychology in general. In his pioneering work in organizational behavior, Vroom
(1964) noted that "without a doubt the law of effect or principle of reinforcement must
be included among the most substantiated findings of experimental psychology and is
at the same time among the most useful findings for an applied psychology concerned
with control of human behavior" (p. 13). Years later, in his classic work in psychology on
social foundations of thought and action, Bandura (1986) concludes that "human behavior cannot be fully understood without considering the regulatory influence of response
consequences" (p. 228). Recent work, synthesizing different subsets of this vast literature
over the years, has meta-analytically shown the positive effect that contingent reinforcers
have on performance outcomes (Stajkovic and Luthans, 1997, 2003).

We use the term "reinforcers" rather than "rewards" throughout this chapter to recognize that the more common term reward is used in the behavioral management literature
to refer to what managers think will have a positive impact, whereas a reinforcer is defined
as a consequence that, indeed, increases the frequency of the behavior that preceded it
(see Luthans and Kreitner, 1975; Luthans and Stajkovic, 1999). The three types of positive
reinforcers (treatment interventions) that have shown to increase the frequency of employee
behaviors, and that are most often used to improve performance in the behavioral management literature/research, are money, feedback, and recognition. Money (Chapter 12) and
feedback (e.g. see Chapters 9 and 10) are given attention in other places in this volume.
As reflected in the title, the principle described in this chapter is that providing contingent
(if-then) recognition for desired behaviors leads to improved performance.

In this chapter, beside using the term reinforcer rather than reward, we also make a distinction between formal and informal (sometimes referred to in the literature as "social", e.g.
see Luthans and Stajkovic, 1999; Stajkovic and Luthans, 2001, 2003) recognition. Formal

recognition refers to reinforcing employee accomplishments through *formal* company programs such as employee of the month or specific awards for attaining levels of performance. These formal recognition programs, if their psychological, reinforcing purpose is understood and taken seriously (e.g. by those who may be put in charge of administering these programs but may not necessarily be familiar with reinforcement theory), are typically accompanied by some form of tokens of visual acknowledgment (e.g. plaques) and are administered publicly (e.g. company banquet, some other formal ceremony). If these formal recognition programs are promoted by the company, but are not enacted fairly or consistently (e.g. played out differently for different employees, i.e. no plaques and/or ceremonies for you), they may be perceived as phony (or worse, discriminating) and not lead to performance improvement. Although this chapter does not focus on such formal recognition, we will provide some examples and guidelines to follow for successful programs.

This chapter is mostly concerned with social or informal recognition. We define this type of recognition as an individual and/or group (thus the use of the term social) providing contingently informal genuine acknowledgment, approval, and appreciation for work well done to another individual and/or group. This informal recognition is provided typically on a one-on-one personal level (thus the use of the term informal), verbally, and/or in writing/email. Besides social and informal, we also emphasize the qualifier "genuine" in this definition because it does not include phony praise, "attaboys" (or girls), a smiley face, or a pat on the back. This type of recognition is also given *contingent* upon exhibiting the desired/relevant behavior(s) that has a favorable impact on desired performance outcomes. In summary, though the term recognition as used in this chapter is social, genuine, and contingently administered, we will mostly refer to it as informal recognition to differentiate from formal recognition.

The broad appeal of informal recognition at work is that it applies to many (bottom to top in the hierarchy), few ever get too much of it (satiation principle mostly fails here), is readily available for use by everyone (i.e. anyone who can verbalize an appreciating sentence or two, and/or write such an email), and, to the potential disbelief of some economists (who, albeit, have increasingly been discovering the relevance of psychology to economics, e.g. Frey and Stutzer, 2002, 2007), it works but does not involve giving out money/monetary incentives. As noted by one employee:

> For me, receiving praise and recognition kind of sets off a little explosion inside. It's kind of like, "oh, that was good, but you know what? I can do better." It helps give you drive to want to continue achieving,. . . . (Wagner and Harter, 2006, p. 54)

To demonstrate the power of such recognition on a personal note, perhaps ask yourself this simple question: "Are you, or anyone else you know, suffering from too much *genuine* recognition?" We are not. For example, when Bob Hope, well into his eighties, was asked, "Why don't you retire?" he quickly answered, "Because the darn fish don't applaud!"

In addition to this common-sense appeal of providing informal recognition as a positive reinforcer to increase employee performance, there is also considerable theory and research in the field of organizational behavior supporting its effectiveness.

SOCIAL COGNITIVE THEORY ANALYSIS OF RECOGNITION

The use of recognition in behavioral management was initially based on reinforcement theory, which assumes that the causal agents of employee behaviors are found in the functional relationship between the environmental consequences and the behavior they effect (Komaki, 1986; Luthans and Stajkovic, 1999; Stajkovic and Luthans, 1997). However, the explanatory power of the reinforcement approach to human action has been questioned on the grounds that it falls short of providing the needed conceptual process-oriented analysis and understanding of the nature and underlying operating psychological mechanisms of recognition (i.e. how does it work) (Bandura, 1986; Locke, 1997; Stajkovic and Luthans, 1998a, 1998b, 2001, 2003).

Social cognitive theory (Bandura, 1986, 1999) has been offered as a more comprehensive analysis and understanding of organizational behavior in general (Stajkovic and Luthans, 1998b) and reinforcers such as recognition in particular than was provided by reinforcement theory (Luthans and Kreitner, 1985; Stajkovic and Luthans, 2001, 2003). Specifically, in our social cognitive analysis of the nature of recognition we offered three dimensions: (1) outcome utility; (2) informative content; and (3) psychological mechanisms through which it affects behavior (Stajkovic and Luthans, 2001, 2003). A conceptual process-oriented analysis of recognition along these three factors, we would argue, leads to a both deeper and more comprehensive understanding of its nature and underlying processes than is allowed by reinforcement theory's environmental determinism approach alone.

Outcome utility of social recognition

Bandura (1986) argues that recognition derives its outcome utility from its predictive value and not just from the social reactions themselves, as reinforcement theory would suggest. In other words, recognition (personal acknowledgment, approval, appreciation) precedes and could be perceived to lead to desired employee outcomes such as a promotion, raise, or an assignment to a desired project. Thus, in addition to the positive social reaction from the source of the recognition, it may also indicate to an employee a potentially upcoming desired outcome utility (and incentive value).

In terms of the magnitude of its effectiveness in affecting employee behavior, recognition given by those who have the power and resources to make desired outcomes a reality for the recipient (e.g. managers, supervisors) will arguably have a stronger effect than the recognition provided by those who may not have such power or resources (e.g. a staff member or an outside vendor). However, recognition provided by those who may not have financial resources and/or promotion power at their disposal, but have considerable respect/credibility (e.g. an admired peer, mentor), may also be powerful in affecting employee behavior for it may lead to desirable outcomes such as being included in the "in-group." In sum, the social cognitive approach predicts that employees will pursue behaviors that receive informal recognition, especially from those who can provide desired material and/or social outcomes, for it suggests that they may be on the "right track."

Informative content of informal recognition

Informal recognition, as we define it, has relatively less informative content than, for instance, specific performance feedback (e.g. you processed 10 applications and were supposed to process 15). Yet, because recognition is also a form of feedback that has been evaluated and the effective delivery of recognition should include a reasonable amount of specifics, there may be a different informative content value in what is expressed. It is important to note that the "scale" for the informative value of recognition focuses on the content value (i.e. the "quality") of what was said (e.g. the reason for the recognition) and not necessarily on the "quantity" of praise that was dispensed.

Showing employees how much their work is appreciated through informal recognition is not achieved by using non-contingent standardized phrases (e.g. good job!), but by conveying genuine personal appreciation for exhibiting desired behavior(s) and work well done. This is because indiscriminate approval that does not eventually result in tangible benefits becomes an "empty reward," thus lacking the potential to control or effectively manage employee behavior. It is the difference between indiscriminate approval and genuine appreciation (signaling future desired behaviors) that portrays the informative continuum of informal recognition. For example, instead of a generic phrase such as "good job," the recognition giver may provide specific information such as "I know that you stayed late last night to finish the presentation I gave you at the last minute. It was a great success in the meeting this morning." This reasonably detailed form of informal recognition not only conveys acknowledgment and appreciation, but also information for motivating subsequent desired behavior.

The regulatory mechanism: forethought

The third dimension of a social cognitive explanation of recognition focuses on the regulatory mechanism through which social recognition impacts human action. We have argued that the basic human capability of forethought (see Bandura, 1986) is the means to cognitively operationalize informal recognition as a reinforcer:

> Based on the recognition received and, thus, the perceived prediction of desired consequences to come, people will self-regulate their future behaviors by forethought. By using forethought, employees may plan courses of action for the near future, anticipate the likely consequences of their future actions, and set performance goals for themselves. Thus, people first anticipate certain outcomes based on recognition received, and then through forethought, they initiate and guide their actions in an anticipatory fashion. (Stajkovic and Luthans, 2001, p. 164)

Thus, forethought becomes a regulatory mechanism that permits perceived future desired outcomes based on the recognition to be transferred into current employee behaviors that lead to performance improvement. Overall, the above discussion of the three dimensions represents the nature and underlying conceptual mechanisms of recognition from the social cognitive perspective.

Empirical Research on the Use of Informal Recognition in Behavioral Management

In behavioral management research (Luthans and Kreitner, 1975, 1985; Stajkovic and Luthans, 1997, 2001, 2003), recognition plays a prominent role, i.e. there is considerable empirical evidence that recognition contingently provided to desired employee behaviors leads to performance improvement (i.e. recognition increases the measured frequency of desired behaviors). Examples from both manufacturing and service organizations can help illustrate this research.

In a manufacturing setting, a desired behavior identified to impact employee performance may be the productive use of idle time during preventive maintenance. The contingent recognition would be delivered by a supervisor perhaps saying to the worker in question, "I noticed that you helped out Joe while your equipment was being serviced by the maintenance crew." In this example, it is important to note that the recognition did not include a "gushy" "thanks a lot" or some phony praise for what this worker was doing. Instead, this employee simply "knew that his supervisor knew" that he had gone out of his way to help out a fellow worker. Because of the received positive reinforcer through contingent recognition from the supervisor, this employee would likely repeat (based on Thorndike's law of effect) the reinforced desired behavior in the future. In other words, instead of receiving no positive reinforcement for this work behavior (that would lead to extinction of such behavior in the future), the supervisor providing contingent recognition will likely repeat the worker's behavior, which in turn contributes to performance improvement. Multiply that by other employees and performance improves at no, at least direct, costs to the organization.

In a service setting such as a bank, an identified functional behavior targeted for improvement, say of tellers, may be providing customers information about various products the bank offers. As in the manufacturing example above, upon observing this behavior, the supervisor would provide contingent recognition by saying something like, "I overheard your explanation to that last customer about how to obtain, use, and the advantages of having a credit card. I think we may be adding her to our business." The positive reinforcement through the recognition provided, again, had the aim of increasing the desired employee behavior, which should subsequently help increase performance (of those reinforced employees).

A large number of studies over the years have verified that recognition is indeed a powerful reinforcer of employee behaviors leading to performance improvement. Meta-analysis of 19 reinforcement theory studies revealed (when all used Luthans and Kreitner's 1975, 1985 five step Organizational Behavior Modification or OB Mod. application model/ approach to behavioral management) an average effect of recognition on performance improvement of 15% (Stajkovic and Luthans, 1997). This was followed by a more comprehensive meta-analysis that examined 72 reinforcement theory studies in organizational settings that found (irrespective of a specific application model) an average effect size of social recognition on performance of 17% (Stajkovic and Luthans, 2003). Finally, in a recent field experiment, informal recognition increased performance of workers in the manufacturing setting by 24% (Stajkovic and Luthans, 2001).

Informal recognition has also been shown to have a strong performance impact at the business-unit level of analysis and in an international application. In a study of 21 stores in a fast-food franchise corporation, informal recognition as part of a non-financial (i.e. along with performance feedback) intervention in behavioral management significantly increased both unit profit performance and customer service measures and decreased turnover (Peterson and Luthans, 2006). Further analysis also indicated that these gains from the non-financial incentives were sustained over time and, when compared to financial incentives, had an equally significant impact except for employee turnover. Internationally, the application of social recognition in a modern Korean broadband internet service firm was found to have a significant impact on both the quality and quantity of performance (Luthans, Rhee, Luthans, and Avey, in press).

In addition to this research evidence, the practitioner-oriented, professional literature also contains some empirical support for the impact of informal recognition. For example, a nationwide survey of US workers found that about 70% report that non-monetary forms of recognition provide the best motivation (*HR Focus*, 1999). This same survey found that employees favor recognition from managers and supervisors by a margin of almost 2:1 over recognition from co-workers or other sources. Another survey conducted by the Council of Communication Management found that recognition for a job well done is the top motivator of employee performance. In the same survey, a third of the managers themselves report that they would rather work in an organization where they could receive more/better recognition (Nelson, 1994).

The Gallup Organization has also conducted an exploratory analysis on its database of 28 studies involving 105,680 employee responses to a large survey from a wide variety of firms. The survey item dealing with recognition ("In the last seven days, I have received recognition or praise for doing good work") was significantly and positively related to 2528 business units' outcome measures of customer satisfaction/loyalty, profitability, and productivity, but not turnover (Harter and Creglow, 1999). However, some other surveys (Nelson, 1996) indicate that recognition, along with the other desirable outcomes, may be a determinant of retention.

MODERATORS OF INFORMAL RECOGNITION

Based on reinforcement theory (which preceded social cognitive theory), it was generally implied that recognition had no moderators of its positive impact on performance. Unlike money and feedback, recognition, from a reinforcement theory perspective, was portrayed as always being a positive reinforcer (it always increases the preceding behavior). Even though, as the opening comments of this chapter indicate, recognition is still most often thought of as applying to everyone and no one (really) gets tired of it, the social cognitive conceptual analysis, as outlined above, and the recent meta-analyses of the literature pertaining to the effectiveness of different reinforcement interventions (Stajkovic and Luthans, 1997, 2003) seem to indicate that there may be moderators of the relationship between recognition and performance.

Type of organization

One moderator tested in our 1997 meta-analysis, which examined an impact of reinforcement interventions, was the type of organization. This analysis indicated that the average effect sizes for all the different interventions varied significantly between manufacturing and service applications (Stajkovic and Luthans, 1997); they all, including informal recognition, had a greater impact on performance in manufacturing than in the service organizations. A possible explanation of these findings may be that it is more difficult to identify critical performance-related behaviors to offer recognition in service than in manufacturing organizations, rather than to assume the lesser effect of recognition in service organizations. For example, in routine manufacturing even certain simple hand movements or procedures may impact performance, but in a service environment customer interactions typically may be highly individualized and unique.

Effects with money and feedback

In our 2003 meta-analysis, we found that not only recognition had a significant effect on performance (17% improvement), but it also produced a synergetic effect with money and feedback. The combined intervention of all three reinforcers produced the strongest effects on performance (45% improvement), with the theory being that money fosters effort, feedback clarifies the task, and social recognition is a desired outcome and predicts future outcomes. Another interesting aspect of these findings was that when social recognition and money alone were the two interventions examined, they did not seem to match well and produced the weakest impact, weaker than either one alone (we called this the "mismatch" cost). However, when feedback was added to the mix (apparently offering clarity to the recognition–money relationship), it fostered the strongest effect.

THE ROLE OF RECOGNITION IN BUILDING SELF-EFFICACY

Self-efficacy is a key variable in social cognitive theory (Bandura, 1997; Stajkovic and Luthans, 1998a, 1998b – see Chapter 10), and recognition may be an input into its development. Self-efficacy is defined as a belief in one's capabilities to organize cognitive and behavioral faculties and execute the courses of action required to produce desired outcomes in a specific context and on a specific task (Bandura, 1997; Stajkovic and Luthans, 1998a, 1998b). In performing a specific task, an employee's self-efficacy determines whether the necessary behavior will be initiated, how much effort will be expended and sustained, and how much persistence and resilience there will be in the face of obstacles, problems, or even failure (Bandura, 1997, 1999). Self-efficacy has been shown to be strongly related to work-related performance (a .38 weighted average correlation in our meta-analysis of 114 studies; Stajkovic and Luthans, 1998a).

Unlike personality traits, self-efficacy is generally recognized to be a state variable that can be developed and trained (Bandura, 1997; Luthans, Avey, and Patera, 2008; Stajkovic and Luthans, 1998a, 1998b). The key inputs into the development of self-efficacy are mastery experiences, modeling/vicarious learning, social persuasion, and physiological/psychological arousal (Bandura, 1997; Stajkovic and Luthans, 1998b). We suggest that recognition may have direct or at least indirect implications for each of these developmental dimensions of self-efficacy. For example: (1) recognition may be perceived as confirmation of success; (2) seeing others being recognized would be vicariously reinforcing; (3) recognition framed as social persuasion may enhance the receivers' beliefs as to what they can do with what they already have (without requiring new knowledge/skills); and (4) recognition would likely provide encouragement for employees to stay on the course of action and persist when meeting performance obstacles and problems. In other words, social recognition may help build self-efficacy, and those with higher self-efficacy perform better (Bandura, 1997).

FORMAL RECOGNITION PROGRAMS DRAWN FROM PRACTICAL EXPERIENCE

So far, the discussion has focused on the conceptual and empirical properties of informal recognition and its relationship to performance. As the introductory definitions indicated, another way to consider recognition is from the perspective of more formal programs used to recognize employees in real-world organizations. In that vein, largely based on experience and anecdotal evidence, Nelson (1994, 2005) gives practicing managers *1001 Ways to Reward Employees*. This best-selling handbook, according to the book jacket, is "A chock-full guide to rewards of every conceivable type of situation." Nelson (1994) provides the following guidelines for effective formal recognition programs:

◆ WHO (outstanding individual employees or teams/groups in terms of productivity, quality, suggestions, customer service, sales, attendance or safety);
◆ WHAT (time off, vacations, field trips, special events, educational classes, benefits, gift certificates, cash prizes, merchandise, trophies, pins or plaques);
◆ HOW (nomination procedures, representative committees, point systems, or contests); and
◆ WHERE (newsletters, regularly scheduled meetings or specific celebrations/banquets).

Nelson also provides specific company examples of recognition programs, such as at Home Depot, where each store picks an employee of the month (the criterion being someone who has given time to an area of the store that technically lies outside his or her responsibility). The recipient is given $100, a merit badge (five badges earn an extra $50), a special pin to wear on his or her apron, and the honoree's name engraved on a plaque displayed at the front of the store.

Our discussion of the theory and research points out *why* recognition should be used, and this practical handbook points out to managers that they no longer have the excuse of not using recognition because they do not know the pragmatics of who, what, how, or where. This book supports the use of both the informal/interpersonal and more formal recognition programs, offers a few featured quotes (e.g. Mary Kay Ash: "There are two things people want more than sex and money . . . recognition and praise"), and outlines guidelines for administering recognition (e.g. match the reward to the person, match the reward to the achievement, and be timely and specific).

IMPLEMENTATION GUIDELINES FROM THEORY AND RESEARCH

The principle of this chapter is drawn from both reinforcement and social cognitive theories, and is supported by the findings from the meta-analyses of research studies over the years (Stajkovic and Luthans, 1997, 2003). It says that managers providing recognition contingent upon individual employees' desired behaviors leads to performance improvement. Although the recognition that is inherent in formal reward systems and programs described above are included in the definitional domain of the principle, we suggest that informal recognition based on personal attention and appreciation has a relatively stronger impact on performance than the formal recognition programs. This is because the one-on-one contingently used recognition (of the form stated earlier "the employee knows that his or her supervisor/ manager knows") tends to be more valued and have more universal appeal than do formal recognition programs. Daniels and Daniels (2007) have recently noted that "Good personal relationships are the source of the best reinforcement such as positive comments . . . cost little or nothing and when done appropriately cannot be given too often" (p. 109).

The reason formal recognition programs may not have the desired effects, especially over time, is because they may easily turn into being phony, not valued by the recipient, or go against the cultural norms. For example, in employee of the month programs, the first few recipients may be deserving that everyone agrees with, but over time selections may become more and more subjective and controversial, often resulting in selecting less-qualified individuals (and potentially not agreed upon by their peers). At this point company politics too often come into play and those who deserve but do not receive the recognition feel betrayed. In this case, the program would most likely produce negative effects (i.e. "rewarding A while hoping for B") and the recognition is not given contingent upon exhibiting the desired behaviors. A formal recognition award such as the "Golden Banana" at Hewlett-Packard can initially be a reinforcer, but over time may become an empty reward (e.g. award or benefit tends to be valuable to the reward giver but not necessarily to the reward recipient) and be perceived even in a negative light. From a collectivistic cultural values standpoint, although many may like to be recognized for their efforts and achievements, not everyone likes to be singled out in a public way, which is usually the case with formal recognition programs.

The implementation guideline to get around problems associated with formal recognition would follow from the reinforcement and social cognitive theoretical frameworks. One suggestion would be to use formal recognition awards contingent upon objectively measured performance. The key is that everyone involved must perceive that the formal, public recognition is deserved. For example, formal awards based on sales performance (the famous pink Cadillac at Mary Kay Cosmetics or a plaque given for selling five million at a real-estate firm's banquet) would be appropriate and effective, but many outstanding performer of the month awards (or administrator-nominated, and not voted upon by students, teaching awards in academic institutions for that matter) may not be. The latter may be subjectively determined. To be effective as a reinforcer for performance improvement, they must be as objective as possible and be perceived by the recipient, and also by others, as being fairly and objectively selected (i.e. procedural and distributive justice – see Chapter 14). This guideline is compatible with both reinforcement theory applications (e.g. objective, contingent consequences) and the principle of justice.

Although the theory-based implementation guideline would be to depend on and provide relatively more informal recognition than formal recognition (as defined at the beginning of the chapter), it does not rule out the need for some formal recognition. Contingently given, informal, private recognition dominates the reinforcement-based behavioral management, and has been clearly demonstrated by empirical research to increase performance (Stajkovic and Luthans, 1997, 2001, 2003). As the more comprehensive social cognitive theory suggests, it is important to ground the informal, private recognition in the formal, public (symbolic) recognition domain. Also, the more objective and fair this formal recognition, the better. This example provided by a practicing consultant is indicative of such a symbolic application guideline:

> If people receive social reinforcement on the four-to-one ratio (a minimum of four socials to one tangible) and receive reinforcers for behaviors, not only results, they will view the tangible as a symbolic representation of appreciation. Then tangibles become items which serve as reminders of the social reinforcement they have already received. A tangible reinforcer carries the most impact when it symbolized the recognized behavior or result. (Allen, 1994, p. 25)

Again, reinforcement theory would say that recognition is reinforcing per se, but the social cognitive theory would suggest that the formal recognition is at least needed once in a while to provide outome utility (e.g. a raise, promotion, or special assignment), informative content (point to what the organization values), and regulatory mechanism (and symbolic value of recognized behavior, and forethought on developing strategies to obtain desired outcomes).

CASE EXAMPLES

Nelson's (1994) best selling book contains 1001 real-world examples, and a more recent version adds hundreds more (Nelson, 2005), many of which are short cases of mostly formal recognition programs in well-known firms such as Kodak, Honeywell, American Express, IBM, Procter and Gamble (but also in smaller organizations). Most of these are richly described with specific individuals and details regarding the form of recognition used to improve performance. However, only a very few of these provide any, even descriptive, evidence on the effectiveness of these formal recognition programs, and none uses research designs or statistical analysis to test hypotheses or draw causal conclusions. Thus, these examples are useful anecdotes, but we would argue that a more evidence-based analysis of recognition is needed for sustainable impact and justification. Thus, the examples described below are from our own empirical studies in manufacturing and service organizations using informal recognition. Most of these allow causal conclusions to be drawn on the effectiveness of informal recognition in improving performance. Largely summarized/drawn from Luthans' organizational behavior textbook and co-authored articles, these studies generally followed the five step OB Mod. model (identify, measure, functionally analyze, intervene with recognition, sometimes in combination with feedback, and evaluate) (Luthans and Kreitner, 1975, 1985; Luthans and Stajkovic, 1999; Stajkovic and Luthans, 1997).

Medium-size light manufacturing firm

This field study had two matched groups (experimental and control) of nine production supervisors each. The experimental group received training in behavioral management by the researchers. The intervention involved supervisors' providing recognition contingent upon their workers exhibiting the identified performance-related behaviors. On the charts kept by each trainee, it was clearly shown that in all cases they were able to change critical performance-related behaviors. Examples of behavioral changes accomplished by the supervisors included decreasing the number of complaints, reducing the group scrap rate, decreasing the number of overlooked defective pieces, and reducing the assembly reject rate. The most important result of the study, however, was the significant impact that the recognition intervention had on the performance of the supervisors' departments. It was found that the experimental group's departments (those in which the supervisors use the recognition intervention in their behavioral management) significantly outperformed the control group's departments.

Large-size manufacturing plant (supplier to the telecommunications industry)

This study started off as a replication of the study summarized above, but was disrupted by labor relations conflict and a strike at the national level preventing completion of the full analysis. However, the following summarizes some typical cases of behavioral change that occurred in the production unit of this manufacturing firm through contingent recognition:

1. *Use of idle time.* One supervisor had a worker with a lot of idle time. Instead of using this time productively by helping others, the worker would pretend to look busy and stretch out the day. The supervisor intervened by giving the worker recognition contingent upon the worker's helping out at other jobs during idle time. This approach notably increased the worker's productive use of idle time.

2. *Low performer.* A production worker in one of the supervisor's departments was producing below standard (80.3% of standard over a six-month period). The low performance was not deemed to be an ability, technical, training, or standards problem. After analyzing the situation, the supervisor used recognition to increase the types of behaviors that would lead to higher output. This intervention resulted in a 93% standard performance level, with no decrease in quality.

3. *Group quality.* One supervisor had a problem with the quality of work in his department. Objective measurement verified this problem. After analyzing the situation, the supervisor used recognition on the group as a whole. Shortly after its use, the group attained the quality standard for the first time in three years.

4. *Group attendance.* Another supervisor felt that he had an attendance problem in his department. Objective measurement revealed 92% attendance, which was not as big a problem as he had thought. However, he established the goal of 100%. After he used contingent recognition on the group, 100% attendance was attained rapidly. An interesting anecdote told by this supervisor was that one of his workers was riding to work from a small town in a car pool early one morning when they hit a deer. The car was disabled by the accident. Co-workers who worked in other departments in the plant and were also riding in the car pool called relatives and went back home for the day. This worker, however, did not want to ruin the 100% attendance record, so she hitchhiked to work by herself and made it on time.

5. *Problem with another department.* One supervisor felt that the performance of his department was adversely affected by the unrecoverable time of truck-lift operators who were not directly under his supervision. After obtaining objective measurement and conducting an analysis of the situation, the supervisor decided to use recognition with the informal group leader and the supervisor of the truck-lift operators. The intervention substantially reduced the unrecoverable time affecting the operational performance of his department.

These five examples are only representative of the types of behavior that the supervisors using a recognition intervention were able to change. Taken together, such individual behavioral projects contributed to improving the overall performance of these supervisors' departments.

Largest meat-packing plant in the world

This study was conducted in the labor-intensive meat-packing industry. In the largest packing plant in the world (in terms of employees and output), 135 production supervisors were trained by the researchers in behavioral management and used social recognition as the intervention. The recognition was contingently applied by the trained supervisors to identify employee-desired behaviors such as performing a particular operation more efficiently, and delivering a certain piece of material in a more timely manner.

This behavioral management with recognition as the intervention had a positive impact on all product areas in which it was applied. There was wide variation, but utility analysis indicated that although there was only a 2% gain in product #2, this still translated to an annual value of nearly $900,000 in this company, and the 1.4% gain in product #6 equated to an annual value of about $750,000. The projected values of the productivity gains in other product areas were estimated for this company as follows: product #1 $259,000; product #3 $510,000; product #4 $371,000; and product #5 an impressive overall $2.276 million gain.

Large comprehensive hospital

This study was conducted in the fast-growing, but much less structured than manufacturing, health care industry. As in the manufacturing application, 11 supervisors from medical service, business, and operations units in a large hospital were trained by the researchers in behavioral management and used contingent recognition as the intervention. The results showed that there was improvement in all the performance measures. For example, over the two months of the intervention, emergency room registration errors (per day) decreased by 76%; medical records errors (per person per audit) decreased by 97%; average output of transcriptionists increased by 2%; EKG procedures accomplished increased by 11%; drug output (doses) in pharmacy increased by 21% and waste decreased by 25%; retake rates (percent) in radiology decreased by 11% and in the admitting office time to admit decreased by 69% and average cost decreased by 22%. In other words, the recognition intervention was effective in modifying a broad range of performance-related behaviors in a hospital setting. This approach seemed to affect both the quality and the quantity performance measures. Moreover, the data indicate that each of the trained supervisors was successful in applying contingent recognition, despite the whole range of complex situations encountered on a daily basis in this complex industry.

The teller line in a bank

Unlike the manufacturing and even the hospital applications, which had specific performance outcome measures, this service application measured teller–customer quality service interactions as rated by customers. The experimental group in this study was the teller line at a branch of a medium-sized bank and the control group were the tellers at another branch of the same bank. The researchers gathered pre-intervention, intervention, and post-intervention data unobtrusively (around the corner from the teller line) from customers right after a service interaction between the tellers and customers in both the experimental and control groups. The customers rated the service they received according to six key dimensions that were identified from the service literature and this bank's management as being most important: greeting, eye contact, speed of service, degree of help offered, personal recognition of the customer, and appreciation for the customers' business. An overall perception of the quality service for the transaction was also obtained. These ratings were gathered randomly over a 10-day period in each phase of the experiment.

Since the data were collected out of sight of the tellers, they were unaware this was happening (follow-up checks indicated this was the case).

The intervention consisted of identifying, fully describing in behavioral terms, and emphasizing the importance to customer service of the six dimensions to the tellers and their supervisors in the experimental group. In particular, the supervisors were instructed by the researchers to provide contingent recognition when observing these six dimensions being exhibited by their tellers. This recognition was given throughout the intervention period, but then the recognition was withdrawn in the post-intervention (reversal) period. The researchers were frequently on site to assist the supervisors during both phases of the experiment, and manipulation checks verified the procedures were in effect.

The results indicated that four of the six dimensions (greeting, speed of service, personal recognition, and appreciation) were significantly higher in the experimental group. The overall measure of quality service was not different between the control and experimental groups during pre-intervention, significantly higher for the experimental group during intervention, and then not different during the post-intervention period when the recognition was deliberately withheld by the supervisors. In other words, like the manufacturing applications, a contingent recognition intervention seemed to have had a causal positive impact on customer service performance in this bank.

Largest credit card processing operation in the world

In this field study, Stajkovic and Luthans (2001) examined the relative differences in effects among monetary incentives, recognition, and performance feedback on a routine, low-task complexity job in the largest credit card processing operation in the world (58 million accounts outsourced from banks, retailers, and e-commerce firms). In terms of application procedures, the trained supervisors administered recognition contingent upon workers performing the specific behaviors identified in step 1 of the OB Mod. model. As we have emphasized throughout the chapter, supervisors were *explicitly* instructed that administering recognition and attention was not to be "sugary" praise or a "pat on the back." Rather, the intention was to let the employee know that their supervisor "knew" they were doing the behaviors previously communicated to be important to performance. For example, the trained supervisors said things such as, "When I was walking through your area on my way to the front office this morning, I saw you making a sequence check, that's what we're really concentrating on." Follow-up checks indicated this recognition intervention was indeed taking place.

The results of this study indicated: (a) the monetary incentives had a greater impact on performance improvement (31.7%) than the recognition (24%) and performance feedback (20%); (b) recognition produced relatively stronger effects on performance than performance feedback. These findings represent the first time that the most commonly used incentive motivators such as money, recognition, and performance feedback have been empirically shown to have different effect magnitudes on work performance when all three reinforcers are applied through the same, conceptually grounded, and empirically verified model of behavioral management. Although monetary incentives had a relatively bigger impact, recognition still held its own as being an important way to improve performance, especially when compared to a traditional pay for performance program (24% versus 11%) that did not use the above-mentioned OB Mod. application model.

CONCLUSION

The organizational behavior principle for this chapter is that providing recognition leads to performance improvement. Because of the broad appeal and common use (at work, at home, at play) of informal social recognition (and some more formal recognition programs), there are numerous examples (e.g. just think of how you express personal gratitude, appreciation, and recognition to co-workers, spouses, kids) and, thus, many guidelines for implementation. However, in the academic literature, except for those reviewed in this chapter, there are (still) surprisingly few studies that examine the impact of recognition on employee performance. Based on the studies summarized here, we would suggest that the principle of contingent application of informal recognition as an intervention to improve performance seems to hold, and recommend its use in both organizational behavior and life in general.

REFERENCES

Allen, J. (1994). In B. Nelson, *1001 Ways to Reward Employees* (p. 25). New York: Workman.

Bandura, A. (1986). *Social Foundations of Thought and Action*. Englewood Cliffs, NJ: Prentice.

Bandura, A. (1997). *Self-efficacy: The Exercise of Control*. New York: Freeman.

Bandura, A. (1999). Social cognitive theory: An agentic perspective. *Asian Journal of Social Psychology*, 2, 21–41.

Daniels, A. C., and Daniels, J. E. (2007). *Measure of a Leader*. New York: McGraw-Hill.

Frey, B. S., and Stutzer, A. (2002). *Happiness and Economics*. Princeton, NJ: Princeton University Press.

Frey, B. S., and Stutzer, A. (2007). *Economics and Psychology: A Promising New Cross-disciplinary Field*. The MIT Press.

Harter, J. K., and Creglow, A. (1999). A meta-analysis and utility analysis of the relationship between core employee opinions and business outcomes. In M. Buckingham and C. Coffman (eds), *First, Break all the Rules* (pp. 255–267). New York: Simon and Schuster.

HR Focus (1999). April 5.

Komaki, J. (1986). Toward effective supervision: An operant analysis and comparison of managers at work. *Journal of Applied Psychology*, 71, 270–279.

Locke, E. A. (1997). The motivation to work: What we know. *Advances in Motivation and Achievement*, 10, 375–412.

Luthans, F., Avey, J. B., and Patera, J. L. (2008). Experimental analysis of a web based training intervention to develop positive psychological capital. *Academy of Management Learning and Education*, 7, 209–221.

Luthans, F., and Kreitner, R. (1975). *Organizational Behavior Modification*. Glenview, IL: Scott, Foresman.

Luthans, F., and Kreitner, R. (1985). *Organizational Behavior Modification and Beyond*. Glenview, IL: Scott, Foresman.

Luthans, F., Rhee, S., Luthans, B. C., and Avey, J. B. (in press). Impact of behavioral performance management in a Korean application. *Leadership and Organizational Development Journal*.

Luthans, F., and Stajkovic, A. D. (1999). Reinforce for performance: the need to go beyond pay and even rewards. *Academy of Management Executive*, 13(2), 49–57.

Nelson, B. (1994). *1001 Ways to Reward Employees*. New York: Workman.

Nelson, B. (1996). Secrets of successful employee recognition. *Quality Digest*, August, 26–28.

Nelson, B. (2005). *1001 Ways to Reward Employees: 100's of New Ways to Praise!*, 2nd edition. New York: Workman.

Peterson, S. J., and Luthans, F. (2006). The impact of financial and nonfinancial incentives on business-unit outcomes over time. *Journal of Applied Psychology*, 91, 156–165.

Stajkovic, A. D., and Luthans, F. (1997). A meta-analysis of the effects of organizational behavior modification on task performance, 1975–95. *Academy of Management Journal*, 40, 1122–1149.

Stajkovic, A. D., and Luthans, F. (1998a). Self-efficacy and work-related performance: A meta-analysis. *Psychological Bulletin*, 124, 240–261.

Stajkovic, A. D., and Luthans, F. (1998b). Social cognitive theory and self-efficacy: Going beyond traditional motivational and behavioral approaches. *Organizational Dynamics*, 26, 62–74.

Stajkovic, A. D., and Luthans, F. (2001). The differential effects of incentive motivators on work performance. *Academy of Management Journal*, 4, 580–590.

Stajkovic, A. D., and Luthans, F. (2003). Behavioral management and task performance in organizations: Conceptual background, meta-analysis, and test of alternative models. *Personnel Psychology*, 56, 155–194.

Vroom, V. H. (1964). *Work Motivation*. New York: Wiley.

Wagner, R., and Harter, J. K. (2006). *12: The Elements of Great Managing*. New York: Gallup Press.

EXERCISES

1. Split into groups and, drawing from actual on-the-job or other relevant experiences, discuss examples of both informal recognition that was provided and informal recognition that you think should have been provided but was not. How did each affect the motivation of you personally and the others affected by this recognition (or lack of it)? Why do you think informal recognition may be motivating (list several specific reasons to be discussed in class with other groups). Why do you think it may be demotivating not to receive informal recognition (again, list several specific reasons to be discussed).

2. Split into groups and design a formal recognition program for your company (or a company one of the team members has worked for). After describing the type of work and culture of your company, draw from this chapter's theory, research and application guidelines, and discuss what you think this program would need to look like to work. Outline several specific steps you would take. Also, identify some potential pitfalls (e.g. what would you be sure not to do).

14

Promote Procedural and Interactional Justice to Enhance Individual and Organizational Outcomes

Jerald Greenberg

People in the workplace expect to be treated fairly and respond negatively when this expectation appears to have been violated. In fact, among employees asked to identify events that made them angriest, "being treated unfairly on the job" was found to be the most popular response (Fitness, 2000). Considering this concern, it is not surprising that the study of people's perceptions of fairness in organizations, known as *organizational justice* (Greenberg, 1987), has been of considerable interest to scholars in organizational behavior (OB) and related fields (Greenberg, 1996, 2007).

By examining several key aspects of this work here, I identify a general principle of organizational justice in addition to two more specific subprinciples. Following this, I discuss special cases and exceptions to these principles as well as issues regarding implementation of the principle. Finally, to illustrate the principles in action, I describe some case examples drawn from incidents in a variety of organizational settings. To set the stage for these discussions, I begin by providing some background material that will put the major concepts into perspective.

BACKGROUND: FORMS OF ORGANIZATIONAL JUSTICE

Organizational justice is widely regarded to be composed of at least three distinct forms – distributive justice, procedural justice, and interactional justice. I now describe these.

Distributive justice

For the two decades spanning the mid-1960s to the mid-1980s, Adams's *equity theory* (1965) was the prevailing approach to fairness in the workplace. Derived from Homans'

(1961) conceptualization of *distributive justice*, equity theory focused on people's perceptions of the fairness of the relative distribution of outcomes (i.e. rewards) and inputs (i.e. contributions) between themselves and others. The theory claims that people who perceive these conditions as being unequal experience the negative state of inequity distress, which they are motivated to redress by adjusting their own or the other's outcome or inputs either behaviorally or cognitively.

Equity theory has received good support from many of the early studies designed to test its basic tenets (for a review, see Greenberg, 1982). It also has been used to account for a wide variety of organizational phenomena. For example, equity theory has provided a useful basis for explaining why cuts in pay encourage factory workers to steal from their employers (Greenberg, 1990a) and why the performance of professional baseball players declines during seasons in which (as free agents) they are paid less than they were the previous season (Sturman and Thibodeau, 2001). Although it is not studied as much as it was during the 1970s, equity theory remains today's dominant conceptualization of distributive justice used by scientists in the field of OB (Mowday and Colwell, 2003).

Procedural justice

Some theorists have criticized equity theory on the grounds that its exclusive focus on distributions is overly narrow. This precludes it from accounting for many of the feelings of injustice people experience that cannot be captured in terms of relative outcomes and inputs. In a seminal article, Leventhal (1980) expressed this sentiment explicitly by posing the question, "What should be done with equity theory?" (p. 27). His answer called for supplementing our understanding of *distributive justice* – the perceived fairness of how outcomes are distributed – with a focus on *procedural justice* – the perceived fairness of the manner in which outcomes are determined.

The seminal work on procedural justice was Thibaut and Walker's (1975) monograph describing their program of research on fairness perceptions in legal disputes. Specifically, these researchers compared legal systems differing with respect to the amount of control disputants had over the procedures used to resolve disputes. Repeatedly, they found that the procedures disputants believed to be fairest were ones that granted them a *voice* in proceedings – that is, the capacity to influence outcomes (for an update, see Lind and Kulik, 2009).

Leventhal (1980; Leventhal, Karuza, and Fry, 1980) reinforced the importance of voice in fair procedures while also making two key claims: (1) that fair procedures are important to people in contexts other than dispute resolution and (2) that when people consider fair procedures in these contexts, they take into account factors in addition to voice. These factors – Leventhal's six "rules of fair procedure" – are as follows:

◆ *Consistency*. Procedures should be consistent across time and persons.
◆ *Bias suppression*. Procedures should not be affected by personal self-interest or blind allegiance to existing preconceptions.
◆ *Accuracy*. Procedures should be based on completely accurate and valid information.
◆ *Correctability*. Procedures should include opportunities to modify and reverse decisions (e.g. appeals and grievances).

◆ *Representativeness.* Procedures should reflect the basic concerns, values, and outlooks of the individuals who are affected by them.
◆ *Ethicality.* Procedures should be in keeping with the moral and ethical values held by the individuals involved.

The conceptualizations of Thibaut and Walker (1975) and of Leventhal (1980) received considerable support when, as recommended by Greenberg and Folger (1983; Folger and Greenberg, 1985), they were applied to studying organizations (Greenberg, 1990b). Research in this realm grew dramatically after some of the earliest studies revealed two important findings.

First, perceptions of the fairness of procedures used in organizations predicted key job outcomes (e.g. job satisfaction) independently of the effects of perceptions of the fairness of those distributions themselves. For example, whereas distributive justice was the primary predictor of workers' satisfaction with their raises, procedural justice was the primary predictor of people's feelings of commitment and trust (e.g. Folger and Konovsky, 1989; see Chapter 21, this volume). Taking a different approach, Greenberg (1986a) asked workers to indicate the factors that contributed to the fairness of their company's performance appraisal system (Chapter 5). Supporting the distinction between the two types of justice, participants' responses fell into two independent categories, distributive factors (e.g. pay as based on job performance) and procedural factors (e.g. performance rating is based on accurate information).

A second important finding from early studies (e.g. Alexander and Ruderman, 1987; Tyler and Caine, 1981) is that procedural justice accounted for significantly more variance than distributive justice in people's assessments of fairness in organizations. In other words, fairness of procedures carried greater weight than fairness of outcome distributions. Not surprisingly, researchers took this as a mandate to focus on procedural justice, which they have done ever since (for reviews, see Colquitt and Greenberg, 2003; Colquitt, Greenberg, and Zapata-Phelan, 2005).

Interactional justice

As organizational scholars were coming to appreciate the importance of procedural justice, Bies and Moag (1986) expanded our thinking about fair procedures from the realm of the structural into the realm of the interpersonal. They built upon procedural justice in the same way that procedural justice built upon distributive justice. Specifically, Bies and Moag (1986) introduced the highly influential notion of *interactional justice*: that people consider not only the fairness of outcome distributions and the procedures that led to them, but also the manner in which these outcomes and procedures are communicated. People expect to have things explained to them adequately and respectfully and when they believe that this has not occurred they feel that they have been unfairly treated. These feelings, in turn, frequently trigger feelings of moral outrage and righteous indignation (Bies, 2001), sometimes resulting in retaliation against the source of these feelings (Aquino, Tripp, and Bies, 2006). (Some may believe that interactional justice is just a matter of being nice, but this would be misleading. People who believe that the explanations they've received are inadequate report feeling injustice. And their responses often reflect this.)

The concept of interactional justice remains popular today (Bies, 2005) for two very practical reasons. First, procedural justice has a major effect on the way people respond to undesirable outcomes and procedures. As I describe later, research has found that high levels of interactional justice mitigate employees' negative reactions to distributive and/or procedural injustices (e.g. Greenberg, 1990a, 1994, 2006). A second reason for the widespread interest in interactional justice is that practicing managers are in a good position to bring about these beneficial effects by virtue of the way they treat others in the workplace. Although lower-level managers might be able to do very little about the distributions of reward in their organizations and the procedures used to determine them, the capacity to influence workers' feelings of interactional justice is under their control.

What, then, must managers do to demonstrate high levels of interactional justice? Two factors are key. The first, referred to as *interpersonal justice*, involves treating people with dignity and respect, showing that they care about the subordinate's personal feelings and welfare. When people believe that they have been treated in a way lacking in demonstrations of dignity and respect (i.e. when interpersonal justice has been violated), they feel unfairly treated. The second, referred to as *informational justice*, involves giving people clear and thorough explanations about the procedures used to determine outcomes. When people believe that they have been denied information they believe they should have (i.e. when informational justice has been violated), they feel unfairly treated.

Greenberg (1993a) first identified these two facets of interactional justice based on his post hoc analysis of research on interactional justice to that time. Subsequently, Colquitt (2001) established empirically that interactional justice and interpersonal justice are independent dimensions that are distinct from distributive justice and procedural justice. Although Colquitt (2001) developed separate measures of interpersonal and informational justice, the close conceptual relationship between the two often leads them to be combined in practice. I follow this approach here.

The main principle

The idea of using fair procedures (e.g. giving people voice) and communicating with them in a manner that shows dignity and respect may appear deceptively simple today, but in the 1980s, they represented new approaches to understanding people's perceptions of fairness in organizations (Greenberg, 1987, 1990b). Since that time, research and theory on procedural justice and interactional justice developed rapidly – so much so, in fact, that the broader umbrella concept under which they fall, organizational justice, is among the most popularly researched topics in OB and related fields (Colquitt, Conlon, Wesson, Porter, and Ng, 2001; Cropanzano and Greenberg, 1997; Greenberg, 2007).

Based on key findings of the research regarding procedural and interactional justice, it is possible to identify the following principle, which guides this chapter: *Using fair procedures (as defined by conceptualizations of procedural justice) and communicating them in a fair manner (i.e. by sharing information in a way that demonstrates dignity and respect) enhances individual and organizational outcomes.* Given that people generally embrace the concept of fairness in the workplace, this principle is unlikely to strike many as surprising. However, the many studies that have been conducted in this field reveal that it is actually quite complex and highly nuanced (Greenberg and Colquitt, 2005). I illustrate this here by breaking down this broad principle into two narrower subprinciples and describing research bearing on each.

Procedural and Interactional Subprinciples

The studies conducted to date make it possible to identify two distinct subprinciples. The first subprinciple focuses on the effects of procedural justice and the second subprinciple focuses on the effects of interactional justice. My discussion of these will focus on both their organizational and individual effects.

Effects of procedural justice

Consistent with Thibaut and Walker's (1975) work on voice, research has found that people respond positively to organizational decisions to the extent that they have a say in determining them, even if they cannot control the outcomes directly (Greenberg and Folger, 1983). Research also has supported Leventhal's (1980) idea that fairness is promoted by adhering to the six earlier-noted procedural rules. In other words, people respond positively to organizational decisions to the extent that they have been made using these criteria (Greenberg, 1986a).

Beneficial organizational effects of procedural justice. Several lines of research illustrate these subprinciples of procedural justice. For example, *employees' attitudes toward their companies' appraisal systems* are correlated positively to their beliefs about the opportunities they have to express their own viewpoints (Dipboye and de Pontbraind, 1981; Lissak, 1983), even when controlling for the outcomes of those systems (Landy, Barnes-Farrell, and Cleveland, 1980). Additional procedural factors, such as giving adequate notice, and basing judgments on sound evidence also enhance employees' perceptions of performance appraisal systems and the decisions resulting from them (Folger and Cropanzano, 1998; Greenberg, 1986a, 1986b).

Some of the earliest studies of organizational justice (e.g. Folger and Konovsky, 1989; Sweeney and McFarlin 1993) have established that procedural justice is predictive of *organizational commitment* whereas distributive justice is predictive of *job satisfaction* (for a review, see Greenberg, 1990b). Sweeney and McFarlin (1993) have referred to this as the "two-factor model," a term that reflects not only the statistical independence of distributive and procedural justice, but also the system-referenced nature of distributive justice and the person-referenced nature of procedural justice.

Research also has shown that procedural variables similar to those identified by Thibaut and Walker (1975) and by Leventhal (1980) also account for employees' reactions to other organizational phenomena. For example, Kim and Mauborgne (1993) have noted that employees' *acceptance of their companies' strategic plans* is enhanced to the extent that they are able to engage in bilateral communication and are given an opportunity to refute ideas. Similarly, personnel policies, such as the procedures used to screen employees for drug use (Konovsky and Cropanzano, 1993) and those used to make personnel selection decisions (Gilliland, 1994) are better accepted to the degree that they incorporate various procedural elements, such as accuracy, allowing for corrections, and providing opportunities for voice.

Several recent studies have focused on the association between procedural justice and various forms of extra-role behavior. A meta-analysis, for example, found that *organizational citizenship behavior* directed at both individuals and organizations (Organ and Ryan, 1995) was predicted strongly by perceptions of procedural justice (Fassina, Jones, and Uggerslev, 2008). Extending this idea to another form of extra-role behavior, Moon, Kamdar, Mayer, and Takeuchi (2008) found that procedural justice was also predictive of *"taking charge"* – *discretionary behavior aimed at bringing positive change to one's organiz-ation*, such as by making useful suggestions for innovation (Morrison and Phelps, 1999). Interestingly, employees' positive perceptions of procedural justice also have been linked to *extra-role behaviors aimed at customers*. Specifically, hotel workers who believe that their employers follow fair procedures have been found to deliver levels of service to guests that exceed standard role requirements (Moliner, Martinez-Tur, Ramos, Peiro, and Cropanzano, 2008). Together, these findings are consistent with the notion that employees who believe that their organizations have instituted fair procedures attempt to repay them by going above and beyond the call of duty to help them (and, by extrapolation, their customers).

Adverse health effects of procedural injustice. In contrast to the organizational outcomes discussed thus far, another line of research has focused on health risks associated with perceptions of injustice in the workplace. Such research has found that low levels of organizational justice are linked to prolonged negative emotional states, such as stress (Judge and Colquitt, 2004) and pathophysiological changes that are associated with health problems (Elovainio, Kivimäki, Vahtera, Keltikangas-Jjärvinen, and Virtanen, 2003).

Additional research has revealed that the adverse health effects are more negative when multiple sources of injustice are perceived instead of just a single source. Tepper (2001) reported evidence to this effect in a study assessing symptoms of clinical depression among residents of a Midwestern US city. Specifically, he found that participants reporting the highest levels of depression were those who experienced low levels of both procedural justice and distributive justice. Individuals who experience higher levels of either form of justice experienced significantly less depression. More recently, Spell and Arnold (2007) reported analogous findings. Instead of examining individual perceptions of injustice, these researchers studied shared perceptions of justice within work units (to which they refer as organizational justice climate). They found that workers' levels of depression were lowest when collective perceptions of distributive justice and procedural justice were lowest.

Effects of interactional justice

Greenberg (1990a) illustrated the effects of interactional justice in a study in which he examined *theft* by employees who felt underpaid due to a pay cut. These workers expressed their dissatisfaction by stealing twice as much from their companies when officials treated them in a vague and uncaring manner while announcing the pay cut (i.e. low interactional justice) as compared to when officials explained the reasoning for the pay cut thoroughly and in a sensitive, dignified, and respectful manner (i.e. high interactional justice) although they received the same exact pay cuts. This illustrates the subprinciple of interactional justice: *people better accept organizational outcomes to the extent that they have been treated with high levels of interactional justice in the course of explaining those outcomes.* I now describe this principle more closely by discussing studies revealing the adverse effects that follow when people perceive that they are experiencing low levels of interactional justice.

Adverse organizational effects of interactional injustice. The importance of both the inter-personal and informational facets of interactional justice has been demonstrated in several studies. For example, in a lab study, Greenberg (1993b) manipulated informational justice and interpersonal justice independently after paying participants less than expected.

Participants were then given an opportunity to retaliate anonymously by taking money back from the researcher. Retaliation was lower when the underpayment was explained using high levels of interpersonal justice and high levels of informational justice. These facets of interactional justice mitigated participants' beliefs about the unfairness of the same undesirable outcomes, leading them to accept those outcomes and diminishing their motivation to retaliate.

Another study by Greenberg (1994) demonstrated an identical effect in an organization that was about to introduce a smoking ban. This policy change (which is likely to be rejected by smokers) was introduced in a manner that systematically manipulated the amount of information about the need for the smoking ban (i.e. informational justice) as well as the level of sensitivity expressed regarding the difficulty the ban was likely to create for smokers (i.e. interpersonal justice). Employees who smoked expressed greater willingness to go along with the ban when it was thoroughly explained and when it was presented in a socially sensitive manner (i.e. when levels of both interpersonal and informational justice were high).

In yet another setting, Lind, Greenberg, Scott, and Welchans (2000) interviewed almost 1000 unemployed people about their reactions to being fired or laid off from their jobs. They found that individuals who believed they were treated in a dignified manner by company officials in the course of being terminated (high interpersonal justice) and who believed that the explanations they received about the termination decision were adequate (high informational justice) were significantly less inclined to bring suit against their former employers for wrongful termination than those who received more superficial explanations delivered in a less sensitive manner.

Adverse health effects of interactional injustice. Just as procedural injustice appears to take a toll on health, so too does interactional injustice. Indeed, high levels of stress were found to be associated with perceptions of interactional injustice (Judge and Colquitt, 2004). However, just as adverse reactions to procedural injustice are exacerbated when combined with distributive injustice, as noted earlier, so too are adverse reactions to procedural injustice exacerbated when combined with interactional injustice.

This is illustrated in a study of some 5300 Finnish hospital workers whose levels of stress were assessed along with their perceptions of procedural justice and interactional justice (Elovainio, Kivimäki, and Vahtera, 2002). Stress measures consisted of self-reports of physical and psychological health problems as well as the number of days absent from work due to certified medical reasons (a practice that is customary in Finland for absences in excess of three consecutive days). The researchers reported that all three measures of stress reached their highest levels among workers who perceived that they experienced low amounts of both interactional justice and procedural justice on their jobs. Low levels of each form of justice contributed somewhat to the signs of stress measured, but their combined effects were complementary, rather than redundant, in nature. More recently, additional evidence of complementary effects was reported in another study using a very large sample of Finnish workers from a variety of different occupations (Kivimäki, Vahetera, Elovainio, Virtanen, and Siegrist, 2007).

In sum, it's clear that low levels of interactional justice – both the interpersonal and informational forms – contribute to adverse organizational effects. And when combined with low levels of procedural justice, low levels of interactional justice also take their toll on the physical and mental well-being of employees.

SPECIAL CASES AND EXCEPTIONS

Having described the central principle of procedural and interactional justice and its major subprinciples, I now identify several key qualifying conditions under which these are likely to occur.

Outcome valence

Research has established that procedural justice's effects on the acceptance of organizational outcomes are qualified by the valence of the outcomes involved (Brockner and Weisenfeld, 1996). Specifically, fair procedures matter more to people when outcomes are negative than when they are positive – an effect known as the outcome × process interaction. Generally, employees receiving positive outcomes tend to be so pleased with what they got that they are unconcerned with how they got it. However, concerns about procedures become salient when outcomes are negative (for a detailed analysis of this effect, see Brockner, 2009). After all, people who don't receive what they want are likely to ask "why?" and the answers they seek are likely to be framed in terms of the procedures used to determine those outcomes. As I explained elsewhere (Greenberg, 1986b), people may feel that it is inappropriate to express their dissatisfaction with undesirable outcomes for fear of appearing to be "sore losers," but that it almost always is appropriate to ask questions about "how" outcomes were determined. Indeed, the basis for appealing grades in most universities and the verdicts of court cases is based not on dissatisfaction with the outcomes (although this may be the underlying motive for the appeal), but on the propriety of the procedures used to determine them. And, because procedures hold the key to understanding outcomes, their salience is heightened when outcomes are negative.

Although procedural justice might matter more when outcomes are negative than when positive, this applies to people's acceptance of organizational outcomes, but not to organizations themselves. Indeed, high levels of procedural justice can have beneficial effects on commitment to the organization in question even when outcomes are positive. For example, Greenberg (1994) found that a smoking ban that was explained fairly had stronger effects on smokers (for whom the impact was negative) than on non-smokers (for whom the impact was positive). However, both smokers and non-smokers expressed high levels of commitment to the organization when it used fair procedures. Apparently, organizations that use fair procedures send strong messages about their underlying commitment to fairness, which enhances employees' commitment to the organization regardless of the outcomes they receive from it.

The limits of voice

If the granting of voice enhances acceptance of outcomes, then it may be assumed that more voice promotes greater acceptance (see Chapter 24 for a discussion of participation in decision making). However, research suggests that such an assumption is fallacious. Specifically, two studies have shown that the benefits of the magnitude of voice are non-linear. For example, Hunton, Wall, and Price (1998) conducted an experiment in which they manipulated the number of supervisory decisions (0, 5, 10, 15, or 20) over which participants were given voice. Participants expressed greater satisfaction with decisions over which they had any degree of voice than decisions over which they had no voice at all. However, increasing levels of voice (from 5 through 20) had no effects whatsoever. These data suggest that the benefits associated with voice appear to be a simple binary function rather than a matter of degree.

Additional evidence suggests that under some conditions, at least, high levels of voice actually may reduce satisfaction with outcomes. For example, Peterson (1999) measured laboratory subjects' satisfaction with leaders in situations in which the parties were in conflict with each other over group decision problems. Corroborating earlier studies, Peterson (1999) found that satisfaction was greater among participants who were given an opportunity to explain their suggestions for solving a group problem (moderate voice condition) than those who were not given any such opportunity (no voice condition). However, he also found that when leaders gave participants surprisingly high levels of voice, participants believed that the leader was behaving inappropriately by relinquishing his or her power, and were less satisfied than they were in the moderate voice condition. In other words, Peterson (1999) found that satisfaction had an inverted-U relationship with magnitude of voice.

Because the findings of Hunton et al. (1998) and Peterson (1999) have not been replicated outside the laboratory, it is unclear how generalizable they are to other settings. However, they lead us to be cautious about the limits of the effects of voice that have been described in the literature to date.

Voice and social sensitivity must be sincere

In addition to qualifications regarding the amount of voice given, another qualification of the principle of procedural justice concerns the sincerity of voice. Specifically, granting employees a voice in the making of decisions leads them to believe that their voice will be listened to, enhancing the chances that their opinions will be accepted, even if they are not. Accordingly, employees who believe that the voice they are offered is insincere (such as would be the case if no one is listening to them) will not be satisfied with the resulting outcomes. In fact, insofar as employees' expectations about the outcomes first are raised, but later are dashed when confronted with a less positive reality, they may be more dissatisfied than they would be if their expectations were never raised in the first place – a phenomenon called the "frustration effect" (Greenberg and Folger, 1983). Not surprisingly, the practice of falsely creating the illusion of voice in the workplace is considered unwise insofar as it may backfire, leading employees to reject not only the outcomes, but the organization itself (Greenberg, 1990b).

The negative effects of insincerity also may be seen in the case of explanations for undesirable organizational outcomes. In other words, for perceptions of informational justice to be enhanced by the issuing of explanations for outcomes, it is necessary for those explanations to be not only accurate and thorough, but also to be perceived as genuine and sincere (Shapiro, Buttner, and Barry, 1994). Should employees suspect that the explanations they are receiving about outcomes are insincere – or worse, manipulative – the benefits of providing explanations are negated. In fact, under such circumstances, the organizational agent's manipulative intent is likely to reflect negatively on impressions of the organization itself, making matters worse (Greenberg, 1990b). In other words, unless employees are convinced that their superiors are "being straight" with them, the use of explanations is likely to backfire.

ISSUES IN IMPLEMENTATION

Having established what can be done to promote procedural justice in the workplace and the benefits of doing so, I now turn to the matter of implementation. In other words, we may ask if people actually do seek to establish procedural justice in organizations, and if so, how they go about doing so. I now will address these questions.

Training managers in procedural justice and interactional justice

Acknowledging that it is in their own best interest for managers to follow the principles of procedural and interactional justice outlined here, officials from several companies have allowed researchers to train supervisory personnel in ways of enhancing these forms justice. The effectiveness of these training efforts has been documented in the literature (for a review, see Skarlicki and Latham, 2005).

For example, Cole and Latham (1997) trained 71 unionized Canadian supervisors on six key aspects of procedural justice whose relevance to disciplinary settings had been established earlier (Ball, 1991): (1) an explanation of the performance problem, (2) the demeanor of the supervisor, (3) subordinates' control over the process, (4) arbitrariness, (5) employee counseling, and (6) privacy. The training consisted of role-playing exercises conducted in small groups held over five half-days. To assess the effectiveness of the training, two groups of expert judges evaluated the behavior of the supervisors who role-played supervisors administering discipline in various test scenarios. Not only did the judges agree that managers who were trained behaved more fairly than those in an untrained, control group, but they also predicted that the trained group would perform better as supervisors than the control group. Although Cole and Latham's (1997) findings do not assess the effectiveness of training on the job, they suggest that managers can be trained to emulate specific behaviors that enhance procedural justice.

However, two additional studies have shown that managers trained in various aspects of procedural justice do, in fact, behave in ways that yield beneficial organizational results. For example, Skarlicki and Latham (1996) trained managers in various aspects of procedural justice in an effort to enhance the level of organizational citizenship behavior (OCB) among a group of union laborers. The managers were trained on various determinants of procedural justice, including ways of providing voice, and techniques for facilitating the fairness of the social interaction between labor and management. Training consisted of lectures, case studies, role-playing exercises, and group discussions conducted in four three-hour sessions held over a three-week period. Three months after training, incidents of OCB were found to be higher among employees of the trained managers than the untrained ones, suggesting that OCB can be enhanced directly by training managers to behave fairly toward their employees.

More recently, Greenberg (2006) reported successfully training supervisors in ways of promoting interactional justice among their subordinates. In this study, nurses from four hospitals completed a scale indicating the extent to which they suffered symptoms of insomnia. Nurses in two of these hospitals experienced a cut in pay (resulting from a change in pay policy) whereas the pay of nurses in the other two hospitals was unchanged. The researcher trained nursing supervisors in one of the hospitals in each group in ways of promoting interactional justice among their subordinates but not the remaining hospitals (until after the study was over). The training consisted of two half-day sessions in which cases, role-playing exercises, and mini-lectures were used to train supervisors in three key skills associated with interpersonal justice (treating others with dignity and respect, demonstrating emotional support, and avoiding intimidation) and three key skills associated with informational justice (providing complete and accurate explanations, communicating details in a timely manner, and being assessable to others).

Reflecting the stressful nature of underpayment, insomnia was significantly greater among nurses whose pay was reduced than among those whose pay remained unchanged. However, the degree of insomnia was significantly lower among nurses whose supervisors were trained in interactional justice, when measured both immediately after training and again six months later. These findings demonstrate the buffering effects of interactionally fair treatment on reactions to underpayment. The study also establishes that the training technique was effective in this regard.

Taken together, these studies reveal that managers may be trained effectively in techniques for enhancing procedural justice and that such training is effective in improving various aspects of organizational functioning. Unfortunately, we cannot determine how long lasting the benefits may be. Also, because there have been so few investigations in this area, we do not know precisely what forms of training are most effective at improving specific dependent variables. Despite these uncertainties, it appears that the benefits of systematically attempting to promote procedural justice in organizations are very promising.

CASE EXAMPLES

The principles described here may be illustrated by cases demonstrating both the benefits that result from promoting procedural justice and/or interactional justice and the consequences of violating them.

New York City taxi drivers strike: the importance of voice

On May 12, 1998, most of New York City's 44,000 taxi drivers staged a one-day strike that all but paralyzed commuting within the USA's largest city (Allen, 1998). The action was in response to the imposition of new safety rules by the mayor at the time, Rudolph W. Giuliani. Among other things, the mayor required drivers to take a defensive driving class, raised the fines for smoking in a cab, and revoked drivers' taxi licenses for being convicted of too many moving violations. Most drivers did not oppose these rules. However, they were very threatened by the unilateral manner in which the mayor imposed them. Specifically a union official representing several thousand drivers explained that they favored the regulations, but were opposed to the mayor's disregard for the drivers by not consulting them on this matter.

Therein lies the problem. Because Mayor Giuliani failed to consult the drivers or seek their input in any way (i.e. denying them voice), they felt that they were unfairly treated. This led them to protest as they did, souring relations between cab drivers and city officials. Ironically, insofar as most drivers believed the mayor's plan was reasonable, the protest could have been avoided by simply consulting with the drivers beforehand. By not doing so, he demonstrated a level of arrogance and disrespect to which the drivers responded. Interestingly, only 40 months later, Mayor Giuliani was praised for the high level of compassion he demonstrated in the wake of the 9/11 terrorist attacks on his city. Might it be that his honor learned a lesson about interactional justice?

The new store manager: from injustice to justice

For many years, the manager of a large non-union supermarket in an affluent suburb of a large city, Mr. X, struggled to keep his employees. Turnover, already high in retail stores, was almost three times higher than the national average in this particular store. It was not unusual for some employees, mostly college students working part-time, to quit in their first week.

Several newly resigned workers consented to exit interviews by phone. In almost all cases, Mr. X was implicated as their primary reason for leaving. Some comments about Mr. X were particularly eye-opening. When making work assignments, he never asked anyone – except his friends – for their preferences and he never explained his decisions. He even punished his least favorite employees by giving them shifts he knew they didn't want. Almost none of his decisions were based on seniority or job performance, just personal bias. On top of all this, he was always rude and inconsiderate, calling people unflattering names and berating them in front of others.

No tears were shed when Mr. X was terminated after about two-and-a-half years. His replacement, Mr. A, could not have been more different. When it came time to make work schedules, he asked the crew for their preferences and did his best to accommodate them. When he couldn't, which was not unusual, he explained why by pointing to the rule he used to guide him. This rule gave higher priority to workers based on their seniority and their job performance and it was completely transparent. He showed no favoritism. If someone had a special occasion, such as a wedding, Mr. A checked with everyone to see if they wouldn't mind giving that individual higher scheduling priority than usual. So long as it wasn't abused, everyone went along with it, believing that they too would be able to get what they wanted when a need arose.

This is only one thing Mr. A did that came as a pleasant surprise to the store's employees. He also treated employees in ways that not only were much better than they were used to under Mr. X, but also much better than they had experienced in other jobs. He always smiled at the employees and asked them how they're doing. He took out time to talk to them and to make them feel like they really matter. The employees opened up to him and treated him as well as he treated them. Respect and trust was high and mutual.

After 10 months under Mr. A, turnover dropped to almost zero. Two people had to leave because they transferred schools and one left because she graduated and took a full-time job in another city. During goodbye parties for them, these people all expressed their sorrow at having to leave. Not only was turnover low at the store, but the good reputation Mr. A developed led to a stack of employees who wanted to work there. No recruiting or training problems for the store meant considerable savings, helping the store become more profitable. Today, the employees' only fear is that after Mr. A's successes come to the attention of officials at the chain's headquarters he will be promoted and leave them.

CONCLUSION

The research and cases reviewed here suggest that both procedural justice and interactional justice have beneficial effects on both individuals and organizations. Although policies may keep some managers from doing everything possible to promote procedural justice and interactional justice, it's likely that many managers will, in fact, have opportunities to promote fairness by doing several of the things described here. It's something managers can do. And, given the established benefits of promoting procedural justice and interactional justice, the effort required to do so would appear to be well worthwhile.

REFERENCES

Adams, J. S. (1965). *Inequity in social exchange*. In L. Berkowitz (ed.), *Advances in Experimental Social Psychology* (Vol. 2, pp. 267–299). New York: Academic Press.

Alexander, S., and Ruderman, M. (1987). The role of procedural and distributive justice in organizational behavior. *Social Justice Research*, 1, 177–198.

Allen, M. (1998). Giuliani threatens action if cabbies fail to cancel a protest. *New York Times*, May 15, p. C1.

Aquino, K., Tripp, T. M., and Bies, R. J. (2006). Getting even or moving on? Power, procedural justice, and types of offense as predictors of revenge, forgiveness, reconciliation, and avoidance in organizations. *Journal of Applied Psychology*, 91, 653–658.

Ball, G. A. (1991). Outcomes of punishment incidents: the role of subordinate perceptions, individual differences, and leader behavior. Unpublished doctoral dissertation, Pennsylvania State University.

Bies, R. J. (2001). Interactional (in)justice: The sacred and the profane. In J. Greenberg and R. Cropanzano (eds), *Advances in Organizational Justice* (pp. 89–118). Palo Alto, CA: Stanford University Press.

Bies, R. J. (2005). Are procedural justice and interactional justice conceptually distinct? In J. Greenberg and J. A. Colquitt (eds), *Handbook of Organizational Justice* (pp. 85–112). Mahwah, NJ: Erlbaum.

Bies, R. J., and Moag, J. S. (1986). Interactional justice: Communication criteria of fairness. In R. J. Lewicki, B. H. Sheppard, and M. Bazerman (eds), *Research on Negotiation in Organizations* (Vol. 1, pp. 43–55). Greenwich, CT: JAI Press.

Brockner, J. (2009). *Multiplying Insult Times Injury: The Interactive Relationships between Outcomes and Processes*. New York: Psychology Press.

Brockner, J., and Weisenfeld, B. M. (1996). The interactive impact of procedural and outcome fairness on reactions to a decision: The effects of what you do depend on how you do it. *Psychological Bulletin*, 120, 189–208.

Cole, N. D., and Latham, G. P. (1997). Effects of training in procedural justice on perceptions of disciplinary fairness by unionized employees and disciplinary subject matter experts. *Journal of Applied Psychology*, 82, 699–705.

Colquitt, J. A. (2001). On the dimensionality of organizational justice: A construct validation of a measure. *Journal of Applied Psychology*, 86, 386–400.

Colquitt, J. A., Conlon, D. E., Wesson, M. J., Porter, C. O. L. H., and Ng, K. Y. (2001). Justice at the millennium: A meta-analytic review of 25 years of organizational justice research. *Journal of Applied Psychology*, 86, 425–445.

Colquitt, J. A., and Greenberg, J. (2003). Organizational justice: A fair assessment of the state of the literature. In J. Greenberg (ed.), *Organizational Behavior: The State of the Science* (2nd edition). Mahwah, NJ: Erlbaum.

Colquitt, J. A., Greenberg, J., and Zapata-Phelan, C. P. (2005). What is organizational justice? An historical overview of the field. In J. Greenberg and J. A. Colquitt (eds), *Handbook of Organizational Justice* (pp. 3–56). Mahwah, NJ: Erlbaum.

Cropanzano, R., and Greenberg, J. (1997). Progress in organizational justice: Tunneling through the maze. In C. L. Cooper and I. T. Robertson (eds), *International Review of Industrial and Organizational Psychology* (Vol. 12, pp. 317–372). London: Wiley.

Dipboye, R. L., and de Pontbraind, R. (1981). Correlates of employee reactions to performance appraisals and appraisal systems. *Journal of Applied Psychology*, 66, 248–251.

Elovainio, M., Kivimäki, M., and Vahtera, J. (2002). Organizational justice: Evidence of a new psychosocial predictor of health. *American Journal of Public Health*, 92(11), 105–108.

Elovainio, M., Kivimäki, M., Vahtera, J., Keltikangas-Jjärvinen, L., and Virtanen, M. (2003). Sleeping problems and health behaviors as mediators between organizational justice and health. *Health Psychology*, 22, 287–293.

Fassina, N. E., Jones, D. A., and Uggerslev, K. L. (2008). Meta-analytic tests of relationships between organizational justice and citizenship behavior: Testing agent-system and shared-variance models. *Journal of Organizational Behavior*, 29, 805–828.

Fitness, J. (2000). Anger in the workplace: An emotion script approach to anger episodes between workers and their superiors, co-workers and subordinates. *Journal of Organizational Behavior*, 21, 147–162.

Folger, R., and Cropanzano, R. (1998). *Organizational Justice and Human Resource Management*. Thousand Oaks, CA: Sage.

Folger, R., and Greenberg, J. (1985). Procedural justice: An interpretive analysis of personnel systems. In K. Rowland and G. Ferris (eds), *Research in Personnel and Human Resources Management* (Vol. 3, pp. 141–183). Greenwich, CT: JAI Press.

Folger, R., and Konovsky, M. (1989). Effects of procedural and distributive justice on reactions to pay raise decisions. *Academy of Management Journal*, 32, 115–130.

Gilliland, S. W. (1994). The perceived fairness of selection systems: An organizational justice perspective. *Academy of Management Review*, 18, 694–734.

Greenberg, J. (1982). Approaching equity and avoiding inequity in groups and organizations. In J. Greenberg and R. L. Cohen (eds), *Equity and Justice in Social Behavior* (pp. 389–435). New York: Academic Press.

Greenberg, J. (1986a). Determinants of perceived fairness of performance evaluations. *Journal of Applied Psychology*, 71, 340–342.

Greenberg, J. (1986b). Organizational performance appraisal procedures: What makes them fair? In R. J. Lewicki, B. H. Sheppard, and M. H. Bazerman (eds), *Research on Negotiation in Organizations* (Vol. 1, pp. 25–41). Greenwich, CT: JAI Press.

Greenberg, J. (1987). A taxonomy of organizational justice theories. *Academy of Management Review*, 12, 9–22.

Greenberg, J. (1990a). Employee theft as a reaction to underpayment inequity: The hidden costs of pay cuts. *Journal of Applied Psychology*, 72, 55–61.

Greenberg, J. (1990b). Organizational justice: Yesterday, today, and tomorrow. *Journal of Management*, 16, 399–432.

Greenberg, J. (1993a). The social side of fairness: Interpersonal and informational classes of organizational justice. In R. Cropanzano (ed.), *Justice in the Workplace: Approaching Fairness in Human Resource Management* (pp. 79–103). Hillsdale, NJ: Erlbaum.

Greenberg, J. (1993b). Stealing in the name of justice: Informational and interpersonal moderators of theft reactions to underpayment inequity. *Organizational Behavior and Human Decision Processes*, 54, 81–103.

Greenberg, J. (1994). Using socially fair treatment to promote acceptance of a work site smoking ban. *Journal of Applied Psychology*, 79, 288–297.

Greenberg, J. (1996). *The Quest for Justice on the Job*. Thousand Oaks, CA: Sage.

Greenberg, J. (2006). Losing sleep over organizational injustice: Attenuating insomniac reactions to underpayment inequity with supervisory training in interactional justice. *Journal of Applied Psychology*, 91, 58–69.

Greenberg, J. (2007). Ten good reasons why everyone needs to know about and study organizational justice. In I. Glendon, B. Myors, and B. Thompson (eds), *Advances in Organizational Psychology: An Asia-Pacific Perspective* (pp. 181–297). Bowen Hills, Queensland, Australia: Australian Academic Press.

Greenberg, J., and Colquitt, J. A. (2005). *Handbook of Organizational Justice*. Mahwah, NJ: Erlbaum.

Greenberg, J., and Folger, R. (1983). Procedural justice, participation, and the fair process effect in groups and organizations. In P. B. Paulus (ed.), *Basic Group Processes* (pp. 235–256). New York: Springer-Verlag.

Homans, G. C. (1961). *Social Behavior: Its Elementary Forms*. New York: Harcourt.

Hunton, J. E., Wall, T. W., and Price, K. H. (1998). The value of voice in participative decision making. *Journal of Applied Psychology*, 83, 788–797.

Judge, T. A., and Colquitt, J. A. (2004). Organizational justice and stress: The mediating role of work-family conflict. *Journal of Applied Psychology*, 89, 395–404.

Kim, W. C, and Mauborgne, R. A. (1993). Procedural justice, attitudes, and subsidiary management compliance with multinationals' corporate strategic decisions. *Academy of Management Journal*, 36, 502–526.

Kivimäki, M., Vahetera, J., Elovainio, M., Virtanen, M., and Siegrist, J. (2007). Effort–reward imbalance, procedural injustice and relational injustice as psychosocial predictors of health: complementary or redundant models? *Occupational and Environmental Medicine*, 64, 428–434.

Konovsky, M. A., and Cropanzano, R. (1993). Justice considerations in employee drug testing. In R. Cropanzano (ed.), *Justice in the Workplace: Approaching Fairness in Human Resource Management* (pp. 171–192). Hillsdale, NJ: Erlbaum.

Landy, F. J., Barnes-Farrell, J., and Cleveland, J. (1980). Correlates of perceived fairness and accuracy of performance evaluation: A follow-up. *Journal of Applied Psychology*, 65, 355–356.

Leventhal, G. S. (1980). What should be done with equity theory? In K. J. Gergen, M. S. Greenberg, and R. H. Willis (eds), *Social Exchanges: Advances in Theory and Research* (pp. 27–55). New York: Plenum.

Leventhal, G. S., Karuza, J., and Fry, W. R. (1980). *Beyond fairness: A theory of allocation preferences*. In G. Mikula (ed.), *Justice and Social Interaction* (pp. 167–218). New York: Springer-Verlag.

Lind, E. A., Greenberg, J., Scott, K. S., and Welchans, T. D. (2000). The winding road from employee to complainant: Situational and psychological determinants of wrongful termination lawsuits. *Administrative Science Quarterly*, 45, 557–590.

Lind, E. A., and Kulik, C. T. (2009). Hear me out: voice and justice. In J. Greenberg and M. S. Edwards (eds), *Voice and Silence in Organizations* (pp. 135–156). Bingley, UK: Emerald.

Lissak, R. I. (1983). Procedural fairness: How employees evaluate procedures. Unpublished doctoral dissertation. University of Illinois, Urbana-Champaign.

Moliner, C., Martinez-Tur, V., Ramos, J., Peiro, H. M., and Cropanzano, R. (2008). Organizational justice and extra role customer service: The mediating role of well-being at work. *European Journal of Work and Organizational Psychology*, 17, 327–348.

Moon, H., Kamdar, D., Mayer, D. M., and Takeuchi, R. (2008). Me or we? The role of personality and justice as other-centered antecedents to innovative citizenship behavior within organizations. *Journal of Applied Psychology*, 93, 84–94.

Morrison, E. W., and Phelps, C. C. (1999). Taking charge at work: Extra role efforts to initiate workplace change. *Academy of Management Journal*, 42, 403–419.

Mowday, R. T., and Colwell, K. A. (2003). Employee reactions to unfair outcomes in the workplace: The contributions of Adams' equity theory to understanding work motivation. In L. Porter, G. Bigley, and R. Steers (eds). *Motivation and Work Behavior* (pp. 222–245). New York: McGraw-Hill.

Organ, D. W., and Ryan, K. (1995). A meta-analytic review of attitudinal and dispositional predictors of organizational citizenship behavior. *Personnel Psychology*, 48, 775–802.

Peterson, R. S. (1999). Can you have too much of a good thing? The limits of voice for improving satisfaction with leaders. *Personality and Social Psychology Bulletin*, 25, 313–324.

Shapiro, D. L., Buttner, H. B., and Barry, B. (1994). Explanations: What factors enhance their perceived adequacy? *Organizational Behavior and Human Decision Processes*, 58, 346–368.

Skarlicki, D. P., and Latham, G. P. (1996). Increasing citizenship behavior within a labor union: a test of organizational justice theory. *Journal of Applied Psychology*, 81, 161–169.

Skarlicki, D. P., and Latham, G. P. (2005). How can training be used to foster organizational justice? In J. Greenberg and J. A. Colquitt (eds), *Handbook of Organizational Justice* (pp. 499–522). Mahwah, NJ: Erlbaum.

Spell, C. S., and Arnold, T. J. (2007). A multi-level analysis of organizational justice: Climate, structure, and employee mental health. *Journal of Management*, 33, 724–751.

Sturman, T. S., and Thibodeau, R. (2001). Performance-undermining effects of baseball free agent contracts. *Journal of Sport and Exercise Psychology*, 23, 23–36.

Sweeney, D. P., and McFarlin, D. P. (1993). Workers' evaluations of the "ends" and the "means": An examination of four models of distributive and procedural justice. *Organizational Behavior and Human Decision Processes*, 55, 23–40.

Tepper, B. J. (2001). Health consequences of organizational injustice: Tests of main and interactive effects. *Organizational Behavior and Human Decision Processes*, 86, 197–215.

Thibaut, J., and Walker, L. (1975). *Procedural Justice: A Psychological Analysis.* Hillsdale, NJ: Erlbaum.

Tyler, T. R., and Caine, A. (1981). The influence of outcomes and procedures on satisfaction with formal leaders. *Journal of Personality and Social Psychology*, 41, 642–655.

EXERCISES

Unjust treatment

Recall in as much detail as possible a recent occasion on the job when you felt that a superior treated you in an especially unfair manner. Jot down the details so you can keep them straight in your mind when you answer the following questions about this experience.

1. Exactly what happened and how did you and other people involved in this incident respond?
2. What could have been done to avoid the injustice in this situation?
3. What particular forms of justice – distributive, procedural and/or interactional – were violated in this incident? Explain your reasons for this.
4. How did this incident make you feel?

A manager's problem

Imagine that you are the new manager of a team of software engineers in your department at a software development firm. You've been on the job for only two months, and things are not going well. Several of your most talented engineers have left the company and you hear grumblings that others are looking to leave as well. Morale is low and people are struggling to maintain the increased workload caused by the departure of their former colleagues. After mustering the courage to approach you, one of the engineers confessed that *you* are the problem: People think you've been treating them unfairly. This came as a shock to you, leaving you with lots of questions, but she didn't offer any details because she feared they might embarrass those who are implicated. As a result, you are now left ruminating about this situation.

1. Potentially, what might you have done to lead people to think of you as unfair? For each of these things, what specific changes in the company and/or your own behavior might you attempt to change so as to avoid these problems in the future?
2. In addition to people leaving the company, what other signs might you find to indicate that people are experiencing injustice?
3. Do you think that interactional justice training would help address this situation? If so, why. If not, why not?

Part V

TEAM DYNAMICS

15

Foster Team Effectiveness by Fulfilling Key Leadership Functions

J. RICHARD HACKMAN AND RUTH WAGEMAN

Observers commonly view team leaders as mainly responsible for how a team performs. An industrial team sets a new plant production record – and its supervisor subsequently receives an award and is promoted. All applaud the captain of an airline crew who finds a way to work around serious mechanical problems encountered in flight. An orchestra conductor accepts the audience's ovation for an outstanding ensemble performance. In each of these cases, the leader is viewed as the main cause of the team's success. It is the same when the outcome is negative: perhaps the most common response to a string of losses by an athletic team, for example, is to blame the coach. This attributional impulse is so pervasive and powerful that we have given it a name – the Leader Attribution Error (Hackman, 2002, Chap. 7; Hackman and Wageman, 2005b).[1]

The tendency to attribute responsibility for collective outcomes to the leader has its roots deep in the history of social science research. In the first experimental study of group leadership ever conducted, Kurt Lewin, Ronald Lippitt, and Ralph White (1939) compared the effects of three different leadership styles – democratic, autocratic, and laissez faire – on group behavior and performance. Since then, there has been a near-continuous outpouring of research to identify the best leadership traits and the behavioral styles that leaders should exhibit in various circumstances. As noted elsewhere (Hackman, 2002, Chap. 7; Hackman and Wageman, 2007), the record of that research is decidedly mixed – so much so that an alternative approach to thinking about team leadership is receiving increasing attention these days.

In the alternative approach, the leader is viewed not as the direct *cause* of team behavior. Instead, the team leadership role is viewed as having two components: first, identifying those functions that are most critical to the success of a team in its particular circumstances,

---

[1] This intense focus on the team leader is consistent with what Meindl and his colleagues (1990; Meindl, Erlich, and Dukerich, 1985) have described as the "romance" of leadership.

and then doing whatever may be needed to get those functions accomplished (Hackman and Walton, 1986; Wageman and Hackman, in press).

The functional approach to team leadership also has deep roots in social science history. At about the same time that Lewin, Lippitt, and White were conducting their experimental study of leader styles, Chester Barnard (1938) was writing a now-classic book called *The Functions of the Executive* which explained what senior leaders must do to help their organizations succeed. Barnard's core idea is encapsulated in the second word of the title: leadership is seeing to it that certain necessary *functions* – establishing direction, creating structures and systems, engaging external resources – are fulfilled so that organization members can work together well to accomplish shared purposes.

Some two decades after Barnard's book was published, Joseph McGrath (1962) picked up the same theme and applied it to groups. The leader's main job, McGrath proposed, "is to do, or get done, whatever is not being adequately handled for group needs" (p. 5). If a leader manages, by whatever means, to ensure that all functions critical to group performance are taken care of, then the leader has done well. This approach to team leadership leaves room for a wide range of ways to get key functions accomplished and, importantly, it avoids the impossibility of trying to specify all the particular behaviors or styles that a leader should exhibit in different circumstances.

For both Barnard and McGrath, the conceptual focus is identification of the core functions that must be accomplished to promote social system effectiveness – not who gets them accomplished or even how that is done. In this view, anyone who helps accomplish critical functions in any way they can is exercising leadership. Thus, at the most general level, the principle of team leadership is this:

> Effective team leadership is ensuring that the functions that are most critical for achieving team purposes are identified and fulfilled.

Research has identified four subprinciples that flow from this general principle. These subprinciples can be stated as four action imperatives and, as will be seen, they come in a particular order:

Subprinciple 1. Decide whether or not a team is appropriate for the work to be accomplished.

Subprinciple 2. Decide what *type* of team to create.

Subprinciple 3. Create structural and contextual conditions that facilitate teamwork.

Subprinciple 4. Coach the team to help members take full advantage of their favorable performance situation.

Before discussing these four subprinciples, we must first specify what distinguishes a work team from other organizational units, and clarify what is meant by "team effectiveness."

Effective Work Teams

The principles in this chapter apply only to work teams in organizations – that is, groups of people who work together to perform identifiable tasks in organizational contexts. Work teams generate outcomes for which members have collective responsibility and whose acceptability is potentially assessable. They also must manage relations with other individuals and groups. Usually, these entities also are part of the team's parent organization, but on occasion the salient context is outside the organization – such as the opposing team and spectators for an athletic team. Although many other kinds of units exist in organizations (e.g. departments, identity and reference groups, informal networks, and so on) the present discussion applies only to organizational work teams as just defined.

When someone says a work team is or is not "effective," that person necessarily (although perhaps implicitly) is making a value judgment. It can be helpful, therefore, to specify explicitly what is meant by "team effectiveness." The principles discussed here (and the research on which they are based) rely on the following three-dimensional conception of effectiveness.

1. *The team's product meets or exceeds the standards of quantity, quality, and timeliness of the people who receive, review, and/or use it.* It is clients' standards and assessments that count in assessing team products, not those of the team itself nor those of the team's manager (who rarely is the one who receives and uses what a work team produces).
2. *The team's work processes enhance members' capability to work together well.* Effective teams become adept at detecting and correcting errors before serious damage is done, and at noticing and exploiting emerging opportunities. They are more capable performing units when a piece of work is finished than they were when it began.
3. *The team contributes positively to the learning and personal well-being of individual members.* Teams can serve as sites for personal learning and can spawn satisfying interpersonal relationships – but they also can de-skill, frustrate, and alienate their members. Teams are fully effective only when their impact on members' personal learning and emotional well-being is more positive than negative.

It is important to consider social and personal criteria, the second and third dimensions, as well as task performance in assessing overall team effectiveness. And even task performance, the first dimension, can be challenging to assess since it depends as much on the values, standards, and perceptions of the people the group serves as on any simple objective indicator.

Subprinciple 1: Decide whether or not a team is appropriate for the work to be accomplished

Using teams to accomplish work can bring a number of advantages. For one thing, the task itself can be larger in scope and therefore more meaningful and consequential than would be the case for work carried out by any individual performer. Moreover, since the work is not parceled out in small pieces among multiple performers, it is easier to establish direct two-way communication between the team and its clients, which can generate prompt and trustworthy feedback about team performance. Tasks that require members to take on a whole piece of work rather than just one small subtask also require that teams be composed of diverse individuals who have different areas of expertise – and that, in turn, can foster cross-functional exchanges that generate unanticipated ideas and insights.

Some types of tasks, however, are inappropriate for teams, such as those that require sophisticated use of highly specialized individual knowledge or expertise. Another kind of task that often is assigned to a team but should not be is creative composition. Writing a group report would appear to have little in common with creating a novel, poem, or musical score – but both require bringing to the surface, organizing, and combining into an original and coherent whole thoughts and ideas that initially are but partially formed and that may even lie partly in one's unconscious. Such work is inherently more suitable for individual than for collective performance. Although the individual who does the writing can be helped greatly by the ideas, suggestions, and editing of other group members, the actual composition of even relatively straightforward group reports invariably is done better by one talented individual on behalf of the group rather than by the group as a whole writing in lockstep.

Unfortunately, managers sometimes form teams without giving the matter much informed or deliberate thought. Some managers, for example, assign work to a team because they believe that teams invariably produce higher quality products than individuals – a commonly held but erroneous assumption (Locke, Tirnauer, Roberson, Goldman, Latham, and Weldon, 2001). Others may decide to assign a controversial piece of work to a team in hopes of diluting, or at least distributing, their personal accountability for whatever is produced. Still others may use a team as a way to engage the attention and involvement of individual members and, they hope, thereby strengthen members' commitment to whatever is produced.

One of the first decisions a leader must make in creating a work team, then, is to ensure that the work actually is appropriate to be performed by a team and, if it is not, to find alternative means of accomplishing it. Those leaders who are not trapped by implicit cognitive models or emotional imperatives that are biased toward teamwork weigh carefully the advantages and disadvantages of creating work teams. They avoid assigning to a team tasks that actually would be better performed by individuals. And they never form a team that is a team in name only.

Subprinciple 2: Decide what type of team to create

If a leader decides that a piece of work should, in fact, be assigned to a team, what *kind* of team should it be[2] (see Chapter 16)? The choice most likely to be made by leaders who do not explicitly explore alternatives is the face-to-face interacting group. But there are others, each of which is appropriate in some circumstances but not in others. The right choice depends upon the answer to two questions:

1. Will responsibility and accountability for work outcomes lie primarily with the group as a whole or with individual members?
2. Will members need to interact synchronously in real time, or can the work be accomplished by members who work at their own paces and in their own places?

The answers to these two questions form the four-cell table shown Table 15.1. As will be seen, each of the four types of teams shown in the table is indicated for different types of work.

---

[2] This section draws on material developed by Hackman and Wageman (2005b) and Woolley and Hackman (2006).

Table 15.1   Common types of work teams

		Responsibility / accountability for outcomes	
		Individual members	Team as a whole
Level of synchronicity	Real-time interaction	Surgical teams	Face-to-face teams
	Asynchronous interaction	Coacting groups	Distributed teams

Note: Adapted from Hackman and Wageman (2005b).

Surgical teams.   Teams in the upper-left quadrant are what Frederick Brooks (1995) has termed surgical teams (see Chapter 17). Responsibility and accountability for outcomes lie primarily with one person, the surgeon, but accomplishing the work requires coordinated interaction among all members in real time. Brooks, who managed IBM's System 360 programming effort many years ago, argued that software development teams should be structured the same way.

Members of surgical-type teams provide the lead member, the person mainly responsible for team product, all the information and assistance that they can provide. This kind of team is indicated for work that requires a high level of individual insight, expertise, and/or creativity but that is too large or complex to be handled by any one member working alone.

Coacting groups.   Individual members also are primarily responsible for outcomes in coacting groups (the lower-left quadrant in the table). Each member's work does not depend upon what the others do, and the output of the group is simply the aggregation or assembly of members' individual contributions. Because members are performing independently there is no particular reason for them to coordinate their activities in real time.

Members of coacting groups typically have the same supervisor, and may or may not work in proximity to one another. A great deal of organizational work is performed by sets of people who are called "teams" but that really are coacting groups – perhaps because managers hope the benefits of teamwork can be obtained while continuing to directly manage the work behavior of individuals. Coacting groups are indicated when there is minimal need for interdependent work by group members who can, in effect, operate in parallel.

Face-to-face teams.   In these teams (the upper-right quadrant of the table) members are co-located and work together interdependently in real time to generate a product for which they are collectively accountable. Face-to-face teams are what people usually have in mind when they use the term *work team*, and the bulk of the existing research literature on team behavior and performance is about them. Such teams are indicated for a wide variety of tasks for which creating a high-quality product requires coordinated contributions in real time from a diversity of members who have complementary expertise, experience, and perspectives.

Distributed teams.   In the lower-right quadrant of the matrix are distributed teams (sometimes also called virtual teams – see Chapter 32). Although members of distributed teams are collectively responsible and accountable for work products, they are neither co-located nor are they required to interact in real time. Instead, members use information and communication technologies to exchange observations, ideas, and reactions at times of their own choosing.

Because members are not co-located, distributed teams can be larger, more diverse, and collectively more knowledgeable than face-to-face teams. Distributed teams are especially useful when it is logistically difficult or impossible for team members to meet regularly *and* the work does not require high levels of interdependence among them. When they function well, such teams can quickly and efficiently bring widely dispersed information and expertise to bear on the work.

As increasing numbers of organizations have logged experience with distributed teams; however, it has become clear that they are not a panacea. Although decision support systems can facilitate the performance of distributed teams, teamwork still tends to take more time, involve less exchange of information, make error detection and correction more difficult, and result in less participant satisfaction than is the case for face-to-face teams (for reviews of what is known about distributed and virtual teams, see Gibson and Cohen, 2003; Hertel, Geister, and Konradt, 2005; and Martins, Gilson, and Maynard, 2004).

Sand dune teams. Not included in Table 15.1 are "sand dune teams," a special kind of team that is not in any traditional sense a bounded work team at all. Instead, such teams are dynamic social systems that have fluid rather than fixed composition and boundaries. Just as sand dunes change in number and shape as winds change, teams of various sizes and kinds form and re-form within a larger organizational unit as external demands and requirements change. Sand dune teams may be especially well suited for managerial and professional work that does not lend itself to the formation of fixed teams whose members stay on the team for extended periods.

The organizational units within which sand dune teams operate typically are relatively small (perhaps fewer than 30 members) and have relatively stable membership, which makes possible the development of norms and routines that allow teams to form and re-form smoothly and efficiently. Dynamic teams of this type appear to have great potential, but considerable research is still needed to document the specific conditions needed to support them.

Subprinciple 3: Create structural and contextual conditions that facilitate teamwork

Two sets of conditions have been shown to foster the effectiveness of organizational work teams (Hackman, 2002; Wageman, Nunes, Burruss, and Hackman, 2008; Wageman and Hackman, in press). The first set, the *essentials*, are prerequisites for competent teamwork. If these essential conditions cannot be established, it is usually better not to create a team at all. The second set, the *enablers*, facilitate the work of the team. The enablers help a team take advantage of the full complement of both members' capabilities and external resources in accomplishing its work. These two sets of conditions are depicted in Figure 15.1.

The essentials. The three essential conditions are (1) creating a real team (not a group of people who are a team in name only) that is (2) composed of the right people for the work to be performed and that (3) has a clear and compelling purpose or direction. When present, these conditions provide a sturdy platform for teamwork.

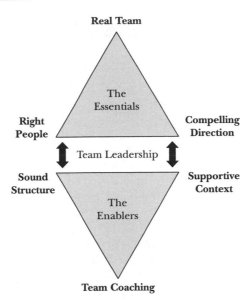

FIGURE 15.1 Essential and enabling conditions for team effectiveness

Real teams.   Real work teams are intact social systems whose members work together to achieve a common purpose. They have clear boundaries that distinguish members from non-members. They work interdependently to generate a product for which they have collective, rather than individual, accountability. And they have at least moderate stability of membership, which gives members time and opportunity to learn how to work together well.

Real work teams can be small or large, can have wide-ranging or restricted authority, can be temporary or long-lived, can have members who are geographically co-located or dispersed, and can perform many different kinds of work. But if a team is so large, or its life is so short, or its members are so dispersed that they cannot work together interdependently, then prospects for team effectiveness are poor.

Right people.   Well-composed teams consist of members who have ample task and interpersonal skills. In practice, however, work teams often are created simply by finding people who happen to be available, forming them into a group, and assigning them the work that needs doing. If members have the knowledge, skill, and experience that the work requires, so much the better. But no attempt is made to use what is known about the attributes of prospective team members, or about how well people with different attributes are likely to work together, in deciding who to put on a team.

That strategy of team composition, as common as it may be, is far more expedient than effective (Hackman, Kosslyn, and Woolley, 2008). A better strategy is to identify the knowledge and skill that the work requires and then to compose the team so that no critical area of expertise is left uncovered. But that is about as far as it goes in many organizations. At least these days, those who form teams may be disinclined to take into account "softer" individual differences, such as the interpersonal skills of prospective members, in selecting people for work teams – even though those softer attributes may be critical in enabling a team to actually *use* the full extent of members' task capabilities in carrying out the team's work.

Compelling direction.   A team's direction is the specification of its overall purposes. Direction is critical in energizing a team, in getting it properly oriented toward its major objectives, and in engaging members' talents. There are numerous choices to be made in the course of work on a task, and having a clear, concrete, and challenging direction almost always facilitates decision making about such matters. Purposes such as "serving our customers" or "staying on top of developments in our sector," or "increasing profitability," for example, are so vague and general that they are unlikely either to challenge members to give their best or to guide them in developing a good strategy for executing the work.

The most energizing statements of direction are those that are insistent about the *end-states* (see Chapter 9) the team is to achieve but that leaves open the *means* members can use in pursuing those ends. Those who create work teams should be unapologetic about exercising their authority to specify end-states, but equally insistent about not specifying the details of the procedures the team uses in carrying out the work (see Chapter 26). That state of affairs fosters energetic, task-focused work (in the jargon of the day, team empowerment). By contrast, specifying both ends and means mitigates the challenge to team members and underutilizes members' resources. Specifying neither ends nor means invites fragmentation rather than focused, purposive teamwork; and specifying means but not ends is the worst of all possible cases.

Direction is an essential condition because everything that follows depends upon it – how the team is structured, the kinds of organizational supports that are needed, and the type of coaching by team leaders that will be most helpful. Moreover, leaders who create a compelling direction for their teams reduce considerably the amount of attention that they must give to monitoring and managing team processes in real time.

The enablers.   Three additional conditions enhance the performance effectiveness of real work teams that have been well staffed and well purposed. These conditions are: (1) a sound team structure, (2) a supportive organizational context, and (3) competent team-focused coaching.

Sound structure.   A work team with a sound structure has a well-designed task, the right number and mix of members to accomplish that task, and norms of conduct that foster the development and use of task-appropriate performance strategies.

A well-designed team task is one that is both aligned with the team's purpose and high on what Hackman and Oldham (1980) call "motivating potential." This means that the task is a whole and meaningful piece of work for which members have ample autonomy to exercise judgment about work procedures, and that provides them with trustworthy data about how well the team is doing (see Chapter 6).

Well-designed team tasks foster high, task-focused effort by team members, but creating them can be a considerable challenge in traditionally structured organizations. It can take some doing to reassemble into a meaningful whole work that, in the interest of presumed efficiency, previously had been partitioned into small, easy-to-perform subtasks. Moreover, team autonomy is sometimes compromised by technical or procedural constraints that, perversely, originally were implemented to prevent errors or foster product quality. Finally, it can be difficult to arrange for teams to receive feedback from the clients of their work – perhaps because clients or customers are far removed from the team or because they are unaccustomed to giving feedback directly to those who serve them. In many cases, those who form work teams have to draw heavily on their persuasive and political skills to gain the cooperation of managerial colleagues in creating well-designed team tasks.

Well-composed teams consist of members who, collectively, have all the capabilities that the work requires – and, if that is not possible, who have links with people outside the group who *do* have the needed expertise. Well-composed teams also have a good *mix* of members, people who are neither so similar to one another that they duplicate one another's resources nor so different that they are unable to communicate or coordinate well. Moreover, they are as small as possible given the work to be accomplished. Members of large teams (for example, those with more than seven or eight members) can find it difficult to remain engaged in the team's work and to coordinate their activities efficiently. Managers often encounter serious obstacles, ranging from personnel regulations to political realities, in attempting to compose their teams well. And, as was the case for team task design, it can take considerable ingenuity and political skill to circumvent such obstacles.

Norms of conduct that are clear and explicit free team members from having to continuously monitor and manage member behavior – and thereby can help them work together in an efficient, orderly way in pursuing team objectives (see Chapter 18). All groups develop norms that specify what behaviors are expected of group members and what behaviors are out of bounds. These norms may be "imported" by members based on their previous team experiences, or they may be explicitly established early in a team's life, typically when the leader initially launches the team. In either case, norms tend to remain in place until and unless something fairly dramatic occurs to force members to reconsider what behaviors are and are not appropriate (Gersick and Hackman, 1990). Especially valuable in work teams are norms that actively promote continuous scanning of the performance situation and proactive planning of group performance strategies.

Supportive organizational context.   Team performance is facilitated when, in addition to the mundane material resources needed for actually carrying out the work, teams have the following three kinds of support.

◆ A *reward system* that provides recognition and positive consequences for excellent team performance. It is important that performance-contingent recognition be provided to the team as a whole, not to those individual members a manager thinks made the greatest contributions to the team product. Doing the latter risks introducing strong disincentives for task-oriented collaboration among members.

◆ An *information system* that provides the team with all available data and data processing tools which members need to competently plan and execute their work (see Chapter 32).

◆ An *educational system* that makes available to the team, at the team's initiative, technical or educational assistance for any aspects of the work for which members are not already knowledgeable, skilled, or experienced – including, if necessary, the honing of members' skills in working collaboratively on collective tasks.

Work team leaders sometimes find it difficult or impossible to obtain these kinds of support, especially in established organizations that have been fine-tuned over the years to support and recognize work performed by *individual* employees. State-of-the-art performance appraisal systems, for example, may provide reliable and valid measures of individual contributions but be wholly inappropriate for assessing and rewarding work done by teams. Compensation policies may make no provision for rewarding excellent collective performance and may even explicitly prohibit financial awards to teams. Human resource departments may be expert in identifying individuals' training needs and in providing courses to meet those needs, but training in team skills may not be available at all.

As was the case for the other aspects of team structure, aligning existing organizational policies and practices with the needs of task-performing teams can be a challenging undertaking, one that can require skilled negotiation with managerial colleagues to secure the needed resources and organizational changes.

Subprinciple 4: Coach the team to help members take full advantage of their favorable performance situation

The last of the three enabling conditions shown in Figure 15.1, team coaching, is the only one that relies mainly on direct, hands-on interaction between the leader and the team. It is addressed separately in this section.

The role of team coaching is not to dictate the one best way to proceed with the work. It is, instead, to help the team minimize its exposure to the dysfunctions that often are observed in task-performing teams (which Steiner (1972) calls "process losses"), and to maximize its chances of capturing the potential synergies that teamwork can bring ("process gains").

Teams that expend sufficient *effort* on the work, deploy *performance strategies* that are well aligned with task requirements, and bring ample *knowledge and skill* to bear on the work are quite likely to perform well. By contrast, teams that operate in ways that compromise their standing on these three performance processes are likely to underutilize their collective resources and turn in suboptimal performances. The specific process gains and losses that can develop for effort, strategy, and knowledge/skill are shown in Table 15.2. Competent coaching helps members work together in ways that foster process gains and minimize process losses for each of these three performance processes (Hackman and Wageman, 2005a).

Three caveats.   Coaching activities that focus on the three task processes just described can greatly facilitate teamwork. Moreover, task-focused coaching has been shown to be significantly more helpful to team performance than interventions that focus mainly on the quality of members' interpersonal relationships (Woolley, 1998). There are, however, three significant qualifications to this generalization.

The first caveat is that team leaders typically do not spend much time actually coaching their teams. This was seen both for leaders of analytic teams in the US intelligence

Table 15.2   Characteristic losses and gains for each of the three key performance processes

Effort
Process loss: "Social loafing" by team members
Process gain: Development of high shared commitment to the team and its work

Performance strategy
Process loss: Mindless reliance on habitual routines
Process gain: Invention of innovative, task-appropriate work procedures

Knowledge and skill
Process loss: Inappropriate weighting of member contributions
Process gain: Sharing of knowledge and development of member skills

community (Hackman and O'Connor, 2004) and for chief executive officers leading their senior management teams (Wageman et al., 2008). In both studies, team members were asked to report how their leaders spent their time. And in both settings they reported that their leaders gave most of their attention to getting the work itself structured properly. Next came running external interference – making sure that their teams had the resources they needed for the work and removing organizational roadblocks. Third came coaching individual members – dealing with personal issues and helping members overcome any performance difficulties they might be having. And last came coaching the team as a *team*.

Members reported that the team-focused coaching provided by their leaders was helpful, and research findings confirmed that it was significantly associated with measured team effectiveness. But most team leaders spent most of their time doing other things. For many teams, then, the issue is not whether coaching provided by the leader is helpful, it is whether the team actually is *getting* the degree of coaching that members want and need.[3]

The second caveat is that even highly competent coaching is likely to be futile when the other essential and enabling conditions for effectiveness are not in place. In a study of service-providing teams, for example, Wageman (2001) found that properly designed teams had fewer problems working together than did members of teams with unsound designs. Moreover, well-designed teams benefited substantially from competent coaching – and were not much hurt by bad coaching. Poorly designed teams, by contrast, experienced more performance problems, they were not much helped by competent coaching – and they were devastated by bad coaching. It is nearly impossible to coach a work team to greatness when structural and organizational conditions undermine rather than support teamwork.

The final caveat is that even competent coaching of well-designed teams is unlikely to be helpful if it is provided at a time when the team is not ready to receive it. Indeed, ill-timed interventions can actually do more harm than good by distracting or diverting members from other issues that *do* require their attention at that time. There are three times in a team's life when members are especially open to coaching interventions (for details, see Hackman and Wageman, 2005a).

- At the beginning, when a team is just starting its work, it is especially open to motivational interventions that focus on the *effort* members will apply to their work.
- At the midpoint, when a team has completed about half its work (or half the allotted time has elapsed), it is especially open to consultative interventions that help members reflect on and revise their *performance strategy*.
- At the end, or when a major segment of the work has been finished, a team is ready to entertain educational interventions aimed at helping members draw on their collective experiences to build the team's complement of *knowledge and skill*.

---

[3] In the study of analytic teams (Hackman and O'Connor, 2004), it turned out that *peer* coaching was an extraordinarily strong predictor of measured team performance (the correlation between peer coaching and team performance was .82). Members of these teams may have realized, perhaps implicitly, that some level of coaching was needed if they were to succeed in their interdependent work – and that they themselves were going to have to provide it since their team leaders were not.

In sum, competent team-focused coaching can significantly reduce a work team's vulnerability to process losses as well as increase the likelihood that members will generate substantial process gains. The efficacy of coaching interventions, however, depends on their being focused mainly on the three key performance processes discussed above. And it depends on their being provided at the proper time in the team lifecycle.

Potency of the conditions. How much of a difference do the conditions discussed above actually make in how well work teams perform? Three studies already cited provide some indication of their potency.[4] In her study of field service teams, Wageman (2001) found that team design features correlated far more highly with team self-management and team performance effectiveness than did team leaders' hands-on coaching. Design features correlated four times more highly with self-managing behavior than leaders' coaching activities; and team design correlated 37 times more highly with team performance than leaders' coaching activities.[5]

In the Hackman and O'Connor (2004) study of intelligence analysis teams, the degree to which all the essential and enabling conditions were present were correlated highly with an independent, multi-attribute measure of overall team effectiveness. Moreover, those teams in the research sample whose members were *collectively* responsible for work outcomes had a significantly higher standing on the enabling conditions than did coacting groups and, as would be expected, they performed significantly better.

Finally, in the cross-national study of 120 senior leadership teams (Wageman et al., 2008) the essential and enabling conditions together were also highly correlated with assessed team performance. Because these three studies did not experimentally manipulate the conditions investigated, it is not possible to make unambiguous attributions about causality from the findings. Even so, the three studies are consistent with the proposition that the presence of the essential conditions (a real team, the right people, and a compelling direction) and the enabling conditions (a sound structure, a supportive organizational context, and ample team-focused coaching) can substantially increase the chances that a team will perform effectively.

CASE EXAMPLES

The politics of supporting work teams

Team leaders rarely have much control over the work technologies, human resource policies, or organizational systems that affect the work of their teams. It sometimes is necessary, therefore, for leaders to engage in political behaviors to establish and sustain the conditions that foster team effectiveness. That was the situation in which Hank, a production manager

---

[4] The task and interpersonal skills of individual team members (the condition referred to earlier as "the right people") were not measured in these studies.

[5] Recall, however, that there was a substantial *interaction* between leader coaching and the design factors: the impact of competent coaching was greater for well-designed teams, and the impact of bad coaching was greater for poorly designed teams. The comparisons just reported are for coaching overall, without taking account of those interactions.

at a semiconductor plant, found himself (for details, see Hackman, 2002, Chap. 5, and Abramis, 1990).

Although Hank had not had formal training in semiconductor manufacturing, he came up with an innovative strategy for making memory chips. He converted existing serial production lines, the standard work design in that industry, into small teams, each with major responsibility for one part of the chip his unit produced. Team members learned one another's jobs, took on increasing responsibility for quality control, and were given substantial authority to improve their own work processes. Even though Hank had never read anything about the principles of team work design, he created a good one.

Results were encouraging: Yields increased, production workers were embracing their new responsibilities, and managers of other production units began to take an interest in what Hank was doing. But then he began to hear some worrisome rumblings from his teams, such as "*somebody* is making a lot more money these days than they used to – and it's sure not us!" Hank realized that he was going to have to provide more recognition and reinforcement for teams that performed well. But he had no control whatever over corporate reward and recognition systems.

His strategy was to invite two outsiders to visit the plant on the same day: a professor from a well-known university who had been tracking Hank's innovations, and the firm's corporate vice president for human resources. Over coffee, Hank described to the professor and the vice president what he had been hearing from his teams. The conversation then proceeded along the following lines:

PROFESSOR: This is serious. Unless you provide them some kind of rewards or recognition based on team performance, the whole thing could crater.

HANK: Can't do it. All I have to work with is my end-of-year bonus pool, and I can only use it to reward outstanding *individual* performers. Doing that could undermine the teams.

PROFESSOR: You're absolutely right, that would be the *worst* thing you could possibly do. It probably would kill your teams.

HANK: Well, then, I guess I'm just stuck.

VICE PRESIDENT: Well, just a minute now. Let's think some more about this, see if we can come up with any other possibilities. . . .

By the end of the meeting, Hank had obtained from the vice president an exception to corporate compensation policy that enabled him to use his end-of-year individual bonus funds to provide performance-contingent financial rewards to his teams. Because the corporation took its compensation policy quite seriously, the special arrangement Hank negotiated was an extraordinary accomplishment. But was his strategy in dealing with the vice president perhaps a bit unethical? Inspect his behavior a little more closely. Did he lie to anybody? No. Did he cheat anybody? No. Could he have made the decision to convert the individual bonus pool to team incentive funds on his own authority? Also no. Did he behave politically? Absolutely.

Hank's political behavior got him what he needed and did not have: the right to use corporate financial resources in a way that could promote, simultaneously, the interests of both the organization and his production teams. He could have used a different strategy to try to achieve the same outcome, of course. But given his organizational role (a low-level manager in a plant distant from headquarters), his corporate clout (none), and his expertise (unschooled in intervention strategies) what he did may have been about the most effective and appropriate thing he could have done. What would have happened if instead he had sent a reasoned memo to headquarters formally requesting permission to deviate from corporate compensation policy? He probably would still be waiting for a response. Fulfilling the leadership function of creating well-designed and well-supported work teams often requires both the ingenuity and the kind of political skill that Hank exhibited.

Launching a cockpit crew

In commercial aviation, cockpit technology, the regulatory environment, and the culture of flying significantly constrain the latitude that captains have to develop their crews into superb performing units (Hackman, 1993). For most flight deck crews, there exists a pre-existing "shell" for the team. That shell includes the properties of the aircraft to be flown, where it is to be flown, the roles of each crew member, basic work procedures such as checklists, the resources available to the crew, and more. All of these features are pre-specified and none of them are under the captain's direct control.

How that preexisting shell is brought to life, however, is very much under the captain's control. Research by Robert Ginnett has shown that what happens in the first few minutes of crewmembers' time together, when they first populate the shell and make it their own, carries forward throughout a crew's life (Ginnett, 1990, 1993). Crews led by captains who merely took the time in their preflight briefings to affirm the positive features of the crew shell – for example, by reviewing crewmembers' roles, emphasizing safety and timeliness goals, reviewing the organizational supports available to the crew, and so on – fared better than those that received no briefing at all or one in which the captain behaved in ways that undermined the standard shell. Best of all were crews whose captains went beyond mere affirmation and actively elaborated the shell by engaging their crews in discussion of the unique circumstances of the trip that was about to begin. These captains used the special opportunities always present when a group first comes together to transform a set of individual pilots into an actual flying *team*.

GETTING IT DONE

Although most work teams do not have structures as detailed and specific as those of cockpit crews just described, a leader's behavior at the launch of any work team can serve essentially the same function – namely, to breathe life into the team's basic design and thereby help the team start functioning on its own.

Good team beginnings are especially critical because the majority of key leadership functions are fulfilled, for better or for worse, by the time a team is only a few minutes old. Consider the list of functions we have discussed in this chapter, and when in the life of any given team each of them becomes relevant: deciding what kind of team is needed, designing an interdependent task, choosing the right people, imagining a compelling statement of purpose – all these are pre-work, cognitive tasks that are accomplished before members actually come together for the first time. The rest of the conditions for team effectiveness are brought to life when the team is launched.

Some leaders are fortunate in that they can draw on existing organizational processes that make team launch relatively straightforward. At PepsiCo, for example, we found that there were very strong norms about how people should operate both as team leaders and as team members (Wageman et al., 2008). A carefully scripted "on-boarding" process for teams was in place that showed leaders how to bring the main conditions for team effectiveness to life in the first meeting. That process included: (1) identifying and highlighting the core capabilities that each member brought to the team's work; (2) articulating the team purpose and inviting members to respond; (3) establishing team boundaries by creating a sense of shared identity, emphasizing what "we" share and "our accountablities"; (4) identifying the main resources the team would need and how to get them; and (5) putting the norms and expectations for members on the table for the group to revise and ratify. Collectively, these elements of the launch script animated all three essential conditions and all of the enablers except for ongoing coaching. And, collectively, they established a positive trajectory for teams that made later coaching interventions immeasurably easier.

If a team launch is successful, the team leader will have helped the team move from being just a list of names to a real, bounded social system. The official task that the team was assigned will have been examined, assessed, and then redefined to become the slightly different task that members actually perform. And the norms of conduct specified by those who created the team will have been assessed, tried out (sometimes explicitly but more often implicitly through members' behaviors), and gradually revised and made the team's own.

This picture of team leadership as cognitive pre-work combined with an animating launch stands in stark contrast to popular images of team leadership: the conductor waving his baton throughout a musical performance or the coach shouting from the sidelines during the game. This alternative view of team leadership requires giving exquisite attention to the actions that breathe life into a team right at its beginning. And when that is done well, many of the most important team leadership functions will have been completed before the team's actual work has even begun.

Imagine you soon will convene a new project team. How will you handle the first few minutes of that meeting? Should you begin by telling members the main objectives of the project? Or should you ease into the purposes of the project gradually, perhaps starting out by inviting each member to talk briefly about the contributions he or she has to make to it? Or should you prepare a read-ahead handout describing the project and open the meeting by asking members for reactions and questions? Should you strike a formal, task-oriented tone, or be more casual and interpersonally oriented?

There is no one best style to use in launching a team. In fact, your actual behavior at the first meeting will be significantly shaped by the circumstances of the moment: Is everybody present when the meeting is supposed to start? Do all members already know one another? How much enthusiasm do they seem to have for the project? Your behavior also will depend on your own preferred style of operating: Are you more comfortable taking an active, assertive leadership role, or do you prefer to solicit input from others and then summarize and integrate their ideas? Do you generally lead using a matter-of-fact style, or do you like to liven things up with humor? Are you someone who can describe a project in a way that engenders shared excitement in a group, or are you better at helping each member identify the particular aspects of the work that he or she personally finds most engaging? These and other considerations too numerous to mention – and certainly too complex to preprogram even with the most complicated decision tree – together will shape how you conduct your start-up meeting.

The great diversity of styles used by team leaders is seen not just when they launch a team, but also in how they establish and maintain the other conditions that foster team effectiveness – recruiting the right people for the team, clarifying its direction, getting its structure right, arranging for contextual supports, and ensuring that the team receives competent coaching at the appropriate times. The best team leaders use whatever styles and strategies that suit them best. There is no one best way to create the essential and enabling conditions for a work team.

There are, however, many *wrong* ways to go about leading a team – strategies and styles that backfire or whose short-term benefits are negated by long-term liabilities. One way to get it wrong is to mislead those who are in a position to provide teams with the structures, resources, or supports they need in their work. Beyond the moral problems of lying, disingenuous strategies destroy the credibility of those who use them when, inevitably, others discover that what is claimed cannot be believed.

Another way to get it wrong is to mimic someone else's style or to follow textbook prescriptions about how good leaders are supposed to act. It is always embarrassing to observe someone trying to enact a leadership style that is not the person's own – such as the junior manager who admiringly adopts the style of the charismatic chief executive but succeeds only in calling attention to the enormity of their differences. The junior manager would be better advised to cease practicing in front of a mirror and instead to spend that time and effort identifying and honing her or his *own* best style of leading.

The third way to get it wrong is to relentlessly enact one's preferred manner of leading, even in the face of data that it is not working very well, and rely on a comfortable style that is indeed one's own but that consistently yields unanticipated and unfavorable results. This problem becomes especially severe when a leader sees that things have not gone well but blames either the situation ("It was wired for failure") or team members ("They just wouldn't do what I told them"). In such cases, there is no opportunity for self-correction because the leader is not open to data that might suggest that his or her own actions contributed to the poor outcome.

Excellent team leaders, by contrast, are aware of their natural styles – they know what they like to do, what they can do easily and well, and what they can accomplish only with difficulty. They learn over time how to exploit their special strengths and preferences, and how to contain or circumvent their weaknesses. They attend carefully to the circumstances of the moment, and vary their behavior in real time to exploit unanticipated leadership opportunities and avoid obstacles that risk blunting their initiatives. Most importantly of all, they are continuously alert for signs that their actions may not be having their intended effects. And when they do discover a discrepancy between what they intended and what happened, they use those occasions to further expand and strengthen their repertoire of team leadership skills.

CONCLUSION

This chapter has explored the implications for practice of a *functional* approach to team leadership. In this view, the essence of team leadership is to ensure that those functions that are most critical for achieving team purposes are identified and fulfilled. Anyone who contributes to that – whether a formal team leader, a regular team member, or even an outside manager or consultant – is exhibiting team leadership.

Many leadership functions are best addressed before a team first convenes. Is a team an appropriate device for accomplishing the work to be performed, or is there a better way to get it done? What *type* of team should be created – a "surgical" team, a coacting group, a traditional face-to-face team, a distributed or virtual team, or even a fluid "sand dune" team? How can those structural and organizational conditions that are most critical to team effectiveness be created and sustained? And then, once the team does get under way, how should it be coached – what should be done to launch it well, what should be addressed when it nears the midpoint of the work, and what should be done when a significant piece of work has been completed? Finally, we have emphasized that there is no one best personality or style for getting key leadership functions fulfilled. Those who lead well do so by exploiting their preferred styles and their special capabilities rather than by following some textbook prescriptions or by mimicking how other successful leaders act. And, when a given leadership function requires knowledge or skill that is beyond one's own capabilities, the best team leaders do not hesitate to call on others to lend a hand in helping the team move forward. Team leadership is not a solo act. At its best, it too is a team activity.

REFERENCES

Abramis, D. J. (1990). Semiconductor manufacturing team. In J. R. Hackman (ed.), *Groups that Work (and Those that Don't)* (pp. 449–470). San Francisco: Jossey-Bass.

Barnard, C. I. (1938). *The Functions of the Executive*. Cambridge, MA: Harvard University Press.

Brooks, F. P. Jr., (1995). *The Mythical Man-Month* (2nd edition). Reading, MA: Addison-Wesley.

Gersick, C. J. G., and Hackman, J. R. (1990). Habitual routines in task-performing teams. *Organizational Behavior and Human Decision Processes*, 47, 65–97.

Gibson, C. B., and Cohen, S. G. (eds) (2003). *Creating Conditions for Effective Virtual Teams*. San Francisco: Jossey-Bass.

Ginnett, R. C. (1990). Airline cockpit crew. In J. R. Hackman (ed.), *Groups that Work (and Those that Don't)* (pp. 427–448). San Francisco: Jossey-Bass.

Ginnett, R. C. (1993). Crews as groups: their formation and their leadership. In E. L. Wiener, B. G. Kanki, and R. L. Helmreich (eds), *Cockpit Resource Management* (pp. 71–98). Orlando, FL: Academic Press.

Hackman, J. R. (1993). Teams, leaders, and organizations: New directions for crew-oriented flight training. In E. L. Wiener, B. G. Kanki, and R. L. Helmreich (eds), *Cockpit Resource Management* (pp. 47–69). Orlando, FL: Academic Press.

Hackman, J. R. (2002). *Leading Teams: Setting the Stage for Great Performances*. Boston: Harvard Business School Press.

Hackman, J. R., Kosslyn, S. M., and Woolley, A. W. (2008). The design and leadership of intelligence analysis teams. Technical Report No. 11, Project on Human Cognition and Collective Performance, Department of Psychology, Harvard University.

Hackman, J. R., and O'Connor, M. (2004). What makes for a great analytic team? Individual vs. team approaches to intelligence analysis. Washington, DC: Intelligence Science Board, Office of the Director of Central Intelligence.

Hackman, J. R., and Oldham, G. R. (1980). *Work Redesign*. Reading, MA: Addison-Wesley.

Hackman, J. R., and Wageman, R. (2005a). A theory of team coaching. *Academy of Management Review*, 30, 269–287.

Hackman, J. R., and Wageman, R. (2005b). When and how team leaders matter. *Research in Organizational Behavior*, 26, 37–74.

Hackman, J. R., and Wageman, R. (2007). Asking the right questions about leadership. *American Psychologist*, 62, 43–47.

Hackman, J. R., and Walton, R. E. (1986). Leading groups in organizations. In P. S. Goodman (ed.), *Designing Effective Work Groups* (pp. 72–119). San Francisco: Jossey-Bass.

Hertel, G., Geister, S., and Konradt, U. (2005). Managing virtual teams: A review of current empirical research. *Human Resource Management Review*, 15, 69–95.

Lewin, K., Lippitt, R., and White, R. K. (1939). Patterns of aggressive behaviors in experimentally created social climates. *Journal of Social Psychology*, 10, 271–299.

Locke, E. A., Tirnauer, D., Roberson, Q., Goldman, B., Latham, M. E., and Weldon, E. (2001). The importance of the individual in an age of groupism. In M. E. Turner (ed.), *Groups at Work: Theory and Research* (pp. 501–528). Mahwah, NJ: Erlbaum.

Martins, L. L., Gilson, L. L., and Maynard, M. T. (2004). Virtual teams: What do we know and where do we go from here? *Journal of Management*, 30, 805–836.

McGrath, J. E. (1962). *Leadership Behavior: Some Requirements for Leadership Training*. Washington, DC: US Civil Service Commission.

Meindl, J. R. (1990). On leadership: An alternative to the conventional wisdom. *Research in Organizational Behavior*, 12, 159–203.

Meindl, J. R., Erlich, S. B., and Dukerich, J. M. (1985). The romance of leadership. *Administrative Science Quarterly*, 30, 78–102.

Steiner, I. D. (1972). *Group Process and Productivity*. New York: Academic Press.

Wageman, R. (2001). How leaders foster self-managing team effectiveness: Design choices versus hands-on coaching. *Organization Science*, 12, 559–577.

Wageman, R., and Hackman, J. R. (in press). What makes teams of leaders leadable? In N. Nohria and R. Khurana (eds), *Advancing Leadership*. Boston: Harvard Business School Press.

Wageman, R., Hackman, J. R., and Lehman, E. V. (2005). The Team Diagnostic Survey: Development of an instrument. *Journal of Applied Behavioral Science*, 41, 373–398.

Wageman, R., Nunes, D. A., Burruss, J. A., and Hackman, J. R. (2008). *Senior Leadership Teams: What it Takes to Make Them Great*. Boston: Harvard Business School Press.

Woolley, A. W. (1998). Effects of intervention content and timing on group task performance. *Journal of Applied Behavioral Science*, 34, 30–49.

Woolley, A. W., and Hackman, J. R. (2006). Analytic zones in organizations. Technical Report No. 3, Project on Human Cognition and Collective Performance, Department of Psychology, Harvard University.

EXERCISES

Leader attribution error

Begin by asking students to recall (1) the best work team they have ever been on, and (2) the worst team they have ever been on. Then form them into three-person subgroups. Each subgroup is to draw on members' good and bad team experiences to identify the *one* factor that most powerfully explains the difference between the excellent and poor teams. Then the class reconvenes and subgroups give their reports. A large number of the explanations offered will have something to do with the personality or style of team leaders, which can be used to launch a discussion of the tendency of observers to over-attribute to leaders responsibility for team outcomes.

When that discussion has run its course, students are then asked to reconsider the examples they came up with at the beginning, this time focusing on the degree to which critical team functions had been fulfilled (whether by the leader or in other ways) for their "best" and "worst" teams. To prime their thinking, the following questions can be posed: (1) Was a team appropriate for accomplishing that particular piece of work? (2) Was the right *type* of team created? (3) Were the essential and enabling conditions for effectiveness in place? (4) Did the team have access to competent coaching to help members exploit the favorable aspects of their performance situation and overcome or circumvent obstacles to good performance? Discussion of these matters can provide a good review of both the functions that are most critical to team effectiveness and the variety of ways that they can be fulfilled by team leaders and members.

Team Diagnostic Survey (TDS)

The TDS is an instrument that assesses the standing of work teams on the conditions discussed in this chapter. A typical classroom project is to ask students to use the instrument as part of an analysis of the strengths and vulnerabilities of some team whose members are interested in learning about and improving their team.

The TDS is taken online and a graphical assessment report is also provided online. For a detailed description of the instrument and its psychometric properties, see Wageman, Hackman, and Lehman (2005). The TDS is freely available for educational, research, and government use; consulting and commercial users are asked to pay a fee to support programming and user services. The instrument can be accessed at: https://research.wjh.harvard.edu/TDS (educational, research, and government) or at: http://www.team-diagnostics.com (consulting and commercial).

16

Compose Teams to Assure Successful Boundary Activity

DEBORAH ANCONA AND DAVID CALDWELL

The basic principle we propose is that teams should be composed of individuals who can effectively carry out external boundary activity. The central argument is that teams need people who can bridge to the outside – people who can get resources, negotiate agreements, and know who to contact for expertise. A number of studies (cf. Ancona, 1990; Ancona and Caldwell, 1992; Gladstein, 1984; Hansen, 1999; Marrone, Tesluk, and Carson, 2007; Wong, 2004) have shown that external boundary activity is a key predictor of team performance. Therefore, an important element in a team's composition should be ensuring that such activity takes place.

This principle is very broad. In our view, it applies most directly to temporary teams or taskforces that are created for a particular purpose and then transfer their work product to others within the organization or the broader market. Typically, these teams draw on resources and information inside and outside the organization and often must gain the support of other entities within the organization if they are to be successful. The greater the complexity of the work and the higher the interdependence with other organization units, the more the team will need to engage in a complex web of external relationships to manage the coordination, knowledge transfer, and political maneuvering necessary to get its tasks accomplished (Cummings, 2004). As organizations get flatter, more global, and more cross-functional, fewer work groups can remain isolated and focus solely on internal activity and work. Thus, sensitivity to external issues is becoming increasingly important to a wide range of teams.

JUSTIFICATION OF THE PRINCIPLE

It is our assertion that the external activities of interdependent organization teams are related to their performance. Although relatively little research has directly addressed this issue – in part because many of our theories of group activities were developed using laboratory groups that do not have external links – the notion that groups require effective interaction with external systems has its roots in the writings of early social psychologists (cf. Homans, 1950; Lewin, 1951). This general idea was expanded throughout the 1970s and early 1980s by open systems theorists (Katz and Kahn, 1978), researchers studying boundary spanning behavior (Roberts and O'Reilly, 1979; Tushman, 1977), and writings on autonomous work groups (cf. Cummings, 1978). In addition, those studying innovation have written extensively about the transfer of technical information across boundaries (Allen, 1971, 1984; Aldrich and Herker, 1977; Katz and Tushman, 1979). In general, those results showed that in R and D teams with uncertain tasks, boundary-spanning activity was related to performance. More recently, similar results have been found for teams engaged in other types of development projects (cf. Scott, 1997).

We also assert that it is not just the frequency of external communication that is important but rather the content of that communication. Frequent communication with outsiders may be necessary for effective boundary management but it alone is not sufficient. The content and quality of interactions with outsiders will determine whether the team is able to tap into the power structure of the firm, understand and manage how the team's outputs fit into the broader workflow of the organization, and gain the information and the expertise from outside the team's boundaries that are necessary for success. In a study of 45 product development teams, we found that team members engaged in different activities in dealing with outside groups and it was the extent to which team members engaged in these activities that was related to team performance. We found that effectiveness in product development was most likely when team members engaged in two sets of activities: (1) those that were designed to promote the team and secure resources and (2) those that led to tighter links with other groups linked through the workflow. The frequency of communication with outsiders as such was unrelated to the performance of the teams. Interestingly, we also found that performance was negatively related to the frequency with which groups engaged in broad scanning of the environment, particularly when these activities were done late in the project (Ancona and Caldwell, 1992). Once the product idea was developed, the more successful teams cut down on broad, general communication and increased the number of exchanges aimed at acquiring specific information or coordinating distinct tasks. Less successful teams continued to seek out general information about markets and technologies.

Mechanisms for Meeting External Demands

How does one compose a team to meet external demands? Three aspects of team composition seem particularly relevant: (1) the background characteristics of individual team members, particularly the functional area to which the individuals are assigned; (2) the connections of team members to relevant networks inside and outside the organization; and (3) the configuration and nature of team members' assignments on the team. Although background characteristics have been studied extensively in prior research, we examine their effects on external linkages as well as internal dynamics. Network connections are the ties members have to individuals outside the group. Such ties represent the potential resources team members can access. The third component, team configuration, represents the level of involvement individual members have with the team.

The first step in designing a team to meet external demands is to develop an understanding of the key resources members must acquire from other groups, learn the expectations others have for the group, and understand how the group's product fits into broader strategic initiatives of the firm. In part, this means acquiring knowledge about the political "structure" of the organization as well as the location of information and resources that will benefit the group. Clearly, some individuals can "map" this network of information and resources better than others, and this mapping is a source of power for individuals who have it and teams that can harness it (Krackhardt, 1990).

Once the critical links between the team and outside groups have been identified, the team can be formed to create these critical connections. Three design variables can be used to manage these connections with other groups. We begin by describing the variables and then lay out some of the issues to be considered in applying these variables to team design.

Diversity in function

The first mechanism for designing a team that can effectively manage its boundaries is to select people for the team who can represent and have expertise in the functional areas that will contribute to the group's ultimate product. Based on a thorough review of studies of groups in organizations, Williams and O'Reilly (1998) conclude that teams made up of members from a variety of functional areas perform at a higher level than teams that do not have that diversity.

For example, functionally diverse top management teams are more successful in making administrative innovations (Bantel and Jackson, 1989) and in responding to environmental shocks (Keck and Tushman, 1993) than are less diverse teams. There seem to be both an internal and external rationale for the superior performance of functionally diverse teams. Internally, such teams have a greater range of viewpoints and more information exchange within the team (Glick, Miller, and Huber, 1993) than do less diverse teams. This broader range of shared knowledge and experience should allow the group to make more creative decisions than when the group has less information at its disposal. Functionally diverse teams are also likely to have greater communication with those outside the group and have more links to external resources than less diverse groups (Ancona and Caldwell, 1992). Studies of functional diversity have focused primarily on differences in the functional assignments of team members; however, functional diversity can also be intrapersonal. That is, individuals can vary in the number of different functions in which they have worked. Some research suggests that groups made up of individuals who have experience in different functions can have the same, or even greater, advantages of functionally diverse teams (Bunderson and Sutcliffe, 2002).

Members' connections to other groups and individuals

A second tool for managing team boundaries is including individuals on the team who have connections or relationships with others outside the group. The connections or ties between individuals in organizations can vary in strength. A strong tie describes a close relationship in which the individuals spend time together, know one another well and are likely to have helped each other in the past. A weak tie is a relationship that is more super-ficial. Individuals know one another but do not have the level of closeness as is present when there is a strong tie (Granovetter, 1973). There are a number of things to keep in mind about ties to understand how they can affect boundary activities. First, because strong ties require more time and effort to build and maintain than weak ties, individuals can have many more weak ties than strong ties (Burt, 1992). Second, individuals can vary in the pattern of ties they have with others. Some individuals will develop a large number of weak ties but few or no strong ties. Other people may concentrate on developing a few very strong ties but not have a large range of weak ties.

Both the strong and weak ties team members have with outsiders can help the team effec-tively manage its boundaries but they do so in different ways (Hansen, 1999). If team members have extensive networks of weak ties throughout the organization, it is relatively easy for the team to learn about developments in other areas, resources that might be available to the team, and who might have specialized expertise that could help the team. Simply picking up the telephone and calling an acquaintance in a different part of the company can help the team acquire valuable outside information.

However, sometimes a deeper involvement by an outsider is necessary in helping the team complete its job. For example, sharing detailed information or helping a team adopt a new technology for their project often requires a substantial amount of effort by the out-sider. Individuals are likely to be more willing to expend this effort to aid the team if they have a close, meaningful relationship with a team member – in other words, if there is a strong tie – than if the relationship is superficial. Thus, if extensive help is needed from some outsiders, having strong ties with those individuals can increase the chance that the team will get the help they need.

Team configuration

A third approach to composing a team that effectively manages its boundaries is through configuring the roles of team members. Most models of teams – particularly those based on laboratory research – assume equal involvement and commitment of all team members to the effort. We do not believe this assumption holds true for most teams in organizations. Composing teams with the assumption that individual members will make differential contributions to the team's effort provides an effective option for dealing with boundary management issues.

When teams must deal with a large number of external entities or draw information from many sources there are alternatives in how the team could be composed. The team could contain members who represent all these important groups. Doing so has the poten-tial to eliminate much of the need for boundary activity at the expense of creating a very large team. On the other hand, a smaller team would not have direct representation from all relevant groups and would therefore require greater boundary activity to guarantee success. An effective way of dealing with the need for including representation without expanding the size of the team is through configuring team member roles. That is, team members can be assigned limited roles on a team, yet still provide external information to the team or links to other groups.

There are a number of ways of doing this (Ancona and Bresman, 2007; Ancona and Caldwell, 1997). One approach is to bring experts into the team for a limited time or for a very specific aspect of the project. This allows the team to make use of critical information or expertise without having to integrate those individuals into the group. A second approach is to shift team membership over time. Individuals who have specific information or external contacts can temporarily join the team based on the boundary activities necessary at a particular time and then leave when their work is complete. A third approach is to have some members be part-time on the team. Individuals whose expertise or contacts are needed over the length of the project, but who may have other demands on their time or somewhat limited knowledge of broader project issues could serve on the team on a part-time basis. Finally, the decision-making roles of team members could be differentiated. For teams working on highly complex, interdependent projects, the need for information and coordination with other groups may be too high to be accomplished exclusively through boundary management or the part-time or part-cycle involvement of some members. Such situations may require the expansion of the team. However, as the team grows in size, difficulties in decision making and coordination may arise. One response to this is to develop a two-tiered membership made up of a relatively small number of core members – who play a major role in decision making – and a larger number of peripheral members – who play a more limited role – but are nonetheless fully fledged team members.

Applications of the Principle: Using Functional Diversity, Ties, and Team Configuration for Team Composition

Before deciding who to put on a team, it is important to identify the critical external contacts the team must rely on to be successful. In a real sense, this involves developing a "map" of the external environment, both inside and outside the organization. This map should not simply identify the direct contacts the team must have – for example, a process improvement team must coordinate with the information technology function – but also identify sources of general information that can help the team understand the issues it will face. Once a map has been developed, the tools we described can be applied.

First, the team should contain individuals from the range of functions that will be responsible for the product or process under development. In particular, if the team needs to engage in ongoing coordination around such things as specifications or schedules, including people from the affected functional areas on the team will make the coordination easier.

A second design principle is to include members on the team who have appropriate connections to others in the organization. Selecting team members based on their network connections may offer advantages over simply choosing people based on the function they are in. First, it may not always be possible to select on function given the need for individuals to have particular skills necessary for the project. Second, function may be a rough index of the person's network and considering the team members' connections may allow for a more precise ability to deal with specific external issues than simply selecting on the basis of function (Reagans, Zuckerman, and McEvily, 2004).

In our view, team members should collectively have a mix of strong and weak ties with other individuals. It is important to have individuals on the team who understand the knowledge and resources that may be spread out through the entire organization and even outside the organization. This implies that the team needs members who are connected to a wide range of different networks both inside and outside the organization. In other words, the team needs an extensive set of weak ties. However, it is at least as important that the team have deep connections with the groups with whom it must directly interface and work with to solve problems. This implies that the team includes members who have strong ties with other individuals who are in positions to provide resources or information to the group. Without a strong tie to a team member, an outsider may not be willing to expend effort in helping the team to meet its goals. Weak inter-unit ties help a project team search for useful knowledge in other subunits and organizations but may not facilitate the transfer of complex knowledge and large-scale assistance.

Finally, configuring individuals' roles is a valuable tool for enhancing other decisions. Effectively applying this concept requires understanding when and how individuals will make critical contributions to the team's work. This requires a detailed map of the environment and a clear understanding of the project. If a team needs extensive information, but only at a particular time, including individuals on the team, but in a limited way may allow the "external resources" of the team to be expanded without permanently increasing the size of the team. Individuals can be assigned to different roles on the team, whether it is by having a limited role in decision making or by serving on the team for a limited time. Team membership can also shift over time. This approach is taken by many research and development teams, which is to shift the team's membership as the technical challenges of the project evolve.

MODERATORS AND LIMITATIONS

Our central principle is that teams should be composed to maximize external boundary-spanning activity. Is this always the case? In answering this question, we think there are two things that must be considered. First, there are moderating factors that must be considered. Second, the principle must be applied appropriately.

An obvious moderating factor to our general principle is the assumption that the *team members are competent* to complete the task. Without competent and motivated people, no matter how boundaries are managed, the team is not likely to be successful. Making staffing decisions exclusively on the ability to bridge boundaries is likely to lead to failure. Drawing from a set of in-depth case studies, Ericksen and Dyer (2004) report that the leaders of low performing development teams selected team members primarily on "political" attributes such as the ability to represent the team to various stakeholders rather than on competencies and skills. In contrast, leaders of high performing teams consider skill and motivation as well as an ability to manage external boundaries.

A second important moderating factor is the nature of the *group's task*. Consider four types of team tasks that vary in the complexity of *both* the external or boundary activities and the internal or cooperative activities they must accomplish to be successful (see Figure 16.1). Along one axis are internal coordination demands that can be categorized as high or low. High demands require that team members interact frequently to exchange

Internal Coordination Demands

		Low	High
		Low	1. Minimal interaction	2. Internal work and relationship management
External Boundary Management Demands	High	3. External boundary management	4. Multi-process management

FIGURE 16.1 Critical processes for team performance*

*Based on a model found in Ancona and Nadler (1989).

information and coordinate work while low demands do not require such interaction. Along the other axis are external coordination and political demands that can also be high or low. High demands require that teams interact extensively with people external to the team to access information, coordinate work, and acquire resources and support. Low demands do not require this depth or complexity of external interaction.

Increasingly, as organizations become flatter and more flexible, as work becomes more complex, and knowledge workers take on complex tasks in teams, more teams will be found in cells 3 and 4, where external demands are higher than in the past. It is for these types of teams that our principle holds. Cell 1 is hardly even a team, but rather more of a set of people who have some aggregated output that is divorced from others in the organization. Cell 2 could represent teams that are configured to brainstorm creative ideas or solve a very circumscribed problem. Here all the necessary information resides in the team and there is little need to have others implement the team's ideas. In each of these two cases, external interactions are minimal and our principle would not apply. Instead, the team would need to be designed with internal demands being dominant. The focus would be to find the optimal number of people who have appropriate information and skills and the motivation to work together (cf. Campion, Medsker, and Higgs, 1993).

In contrast, cell 3 teams need to focus almost exclusively on external boundary management while cell 4 teams need to carry out multiprocess management – internal work management, relationship management, and external boundary management. Our principle holds for cell 3 while cell 4 requires that both internal and external demands be considered. In our view, more and more teams are moving toward cell 4 because organizations are increasingly using teams to replace formal structures and systems. Because of this, we believe that selecting team members on the basis of their abilities to bridge to outsiders while still being able to share information, handle conflict, and coordinate work with other team members will grow in importance.

The second issue has to do with applying these ideas appropriately. While the matrix presented above presents teams as having a single task, most teams have tasks that change over time so teams may move from one cell to another over their lives. For example, product development teams move from: (a) exploring product ideas to; (b) prototyping and exploiting technological achievements to; (c) exporting the product to others for manufacturing and marketing. Research has shown that while external boundary management is important throughout this process, it is more important for the exploration and exportation stages and less important during the prototyping and exploiting stage. At a more general level, the task demands at each stage of work need to be assessed and the team composition needs to shift accordingly. It is because of these changing task demands that team configuration is so important. It is through part-cycle membership, the use of experts, and shifting roles that shifting external demands can be met.

Although we argue that staffing a team to deal effectively with external groups is key to team success, it is important that the team be able to develop effective internal processes too. A team needs to create an identity that affords some separation from the larger organization (Yan and Louis, 1999). This may be a somewhat delicate balance. As Alderfer (1976) points out, teams that have too much boundary activity may find it hard to set and keep that "separateness" and to maintain the cohesion necessary to work as a team. On the other hand, a team with too much cohesion and too strong an identity may be less likely to productively engage external groups than are teams without such cohesiveness (Janis, 1982). Thus, composition needs to be based on external demands while assuring internal communication and cohesion. Designing a team to meet external demands may lead to a very heterogeneous group. This, in turn, may increase conflict among team members and make coordination problematic. Although different perspectives about the team's task may ultimately increase performance, if these are too great or lead to conflict that is "personal" in nature, performance may suffer (Pelled, Eisenhardt, and Xin, 1999; Reagans and Zuckerman, 2001). To prevent this, it may be useful to do things to enhance the ability of the team members to work together. This can be achieved by having some level of homogeneity or similarity among team members (e.g. having people with similar tenure to facilitate communication, ensuring that there is a shared goal among team members, etc.). It may also be facilitated by introducing management practices that create identity and facilitate conflict resolution (Jehn, 1995).

CASE EXAMPLES

The role of composition in the oil industry – alpha team

Two teams, in the same multinational integrated oil company illustrate the role of composition in managing external activities and in how the ultimate success of the projects were affected by decisions about composition.. One of the major problems faced by integrated oil companies is the depletion of reserves that can be obtained using traditional extraction techniques. Both teams were formed to address different aspects of this problem.

The alpha project team was created to develop new exploration methods for a specific geographic area. In addition, the team was to identify specific tracts in that area that the company should try to acquire because they showed the promise of large reserves.

The alpha project team consisted of 17 members from three different geographic-based organizations in the company who represented a number of departments based on different geological and geophysical disciplines. Traditionally, these discipline-based departments had worked sequentially on problems rather than as part of a team and our interviews indicated that many individuals were skeptical of this team approach. Team members were chosen for their technical expertise and were assigned to the project on a full-time basis. A group of three managers from one of the geographic organizations was created to oversee the team's efforts.

Although there was initial skepticism from some of the team members, the group quickly developed effective processes for working together. The team held several seminars and went on field excursions together to observe the geological area they were investigating. As is true of many large teams, alpha team members worked on different parts of the task in cross-functional subgroups and used a common database to track the status of the numerous activities. There was a great deal of informal communication between team members and although they had limited experience working in teams, they soon found that combining their knowledge led to solving key problems. Team members developed strong ties with one another.

Other than bi-weekly meetings with the steering committee and informal contacts with other experts in their respective fields, the team had little external contact. In fact, team members spent so much time with one another and so little with their functional departments that others outside the team commented that the team had a tendency to isolate itself from the rest of the company. The team leader took on nearly all the external activities of the team, particularly those with management. Team members primarily confined their external activities to exchanging technical information with others.

How successful was the alpha team? The two goals of the alpha team were to develop new exploration technologies and to apply these technologies to exploration of a new field. As might be expected, based on the points we have made previously, the team was very successful in finding new and effective ways to evaluate potential hydrocarbon prospects but was not as successful in getting their ideas accepted and utilized within the organization.

In the oil industry, companies may submit competitive applications to the government to obtain a license to further explore and develop a field. Once a license is obtained there is further exploration, and potentially, the development and the construction of a site. Deciding when to bid on a site and gaining government approval requires careful analysis of the site and accurate projections of the oil that can be extracted from it using various technologies. Once technology decisions were made, the alpha team left it to the steering committee to "transfer" the conclusions of their work to top management and the other groups who were responsible for developing and submitting competitive applications. Unfortunately, the transfer was problematic and it took a very long time for the results of the team to disseminate within the organization. Because of the delays and lack of broad support, the company was never able to obtain licenses for the areas the alpha team studied and for which they developed the technology. Some good did come out of the alpha team. Once the team was disbanded and members transferred to other teams, some consulted on a similar project. On this new assignment the old alpha team members were able to bring information and contacts into the new team that allowed the alpha technology to be successfully applied. The old alpha team members filled critical boundary roles in the new project.

The role of composition in the oil industry – beta team

At about the same time the alpha team was formed, a second team, the beta team, also came into being. Like the alpha team, the beta team was created to come up with innovative ways to explore new areas. The beta team differed from the alpha team in two important ways. First, it was responsible for both developing a new exploration technology and completing a bid on a specific project. In other words, it took on the next phase of work and had to implement their findings. Second, the beta team included members from two other firms with whom a joint application would be prepared. (In the oil industry, companies often partner with one another for competitive advantage or to undertake a large bid.)

The team was composed of 15 experts from the company and one from each of the partner companies. The beta team, like the alpha team, contained members with different areas of geological expertise. Like the alpha team, team members also worked full time on the project and shared common space. The team even used a similar process to the alpha team, dividing the task and working in cross-functional subgroups. Like alpha, the beta team was able to develop innovative technical solutions to problems in exploration.

Unlike the alpha team, this one added a new member six months after its formation. This new member was a field development expert who would eventually work on the application and developing the site that was chosen. Initially, he joined project meetings as an observer but later moved on to be an active contributor. Also, unlike the alpha team, this team did not have its external links handled by a manager, rather the team made numerous presentations to top management about project organization, cross-functional teams, alliances between oil companies, and their results. Despite its co-location, the beta team was not seen by others in the organization as isolated.

The beta team was able to move quickly from technical problems to the application phase. Although the first application bid prepared by the beta team was rejected, the team continued and prepared a new application that was accepted. The beta team was ultimately held up as a role model of collaboration between functions and across company boundaries.

How did composition contribute to outcomes of the alpha and beta teams? In both cases, the teams were composed of individuals from different functional areas. Both teams were co-located and had full-time members. There were substantial differences between the teams, however. The alpha team members were selected strictly on the basis of their technical expertise. Beta team members, especially those from the other companies, were selected both for their technical skills and for their connections to important networks throughout the organizations of which they were members. The beta team also shifted its membership by bringing in a specialized expert midway through its work and assigning this individual a specialized role. Perhaps most important, the beta team did not "delegate" boundary activity to one person as did the alpha team. Successfully completing the types of projects alpha and beta were assigned frequently requires more boundary management activity than can be accomplished by one or a small group of individuals. Finally, the internal processes of the two groups were somewhat different. The alpha group worked extensively with one another, usually to the exclusion of external activities. This was not the case in the beta team.

Conclusion

Compared to other areas of investigation of small groups, composition has been relatively neglected despite its obvious importance. Even the research that has been done has not led to systematic conclusions. In a summary of research on composition, Moreland, Levine and Wingert note that " . . . few researchers study group composition, and no general theory guides their work. Progress toward understanding group composition has thus been slow and sporadic" (1996, p. 11). Unfortunately, relatively little has changed in the last few years.

In our view, much of this lack of progress has come about because much of the research has been done with groups that do not have meaningful external connections. Such groups do not reflect the true nature of most organizational groups. For most groups in organizations, links with other groups and the external environment are critical for success. Information and resources must be imported if teams are to make effective decisions and the output of the group must be transferred to others. We propose that selecting group members on their ability to facilitate these boundary activities can be an important element in teams' success.

REFERENCES

Alderfer, C. P. (1976). Boundary relations and organizational diagnosis. In M. Meltzer and F. Wickham (eds), *Humanizing Organizational Behavior* (pp. 142–175). Springfield, IL: Charles Thomas.

Aldrich, H. E., and Herker, D. (1977). Boundary spanning roles and organization structure. *Academy of Management Review*, 2, 217–230.

Allen, T. J. (1971). Communications, technology transfer, and the role of the technical gatekeeper. *R and D Management*, 1, 14–21.

Allen, T. J. (1984). *Managing the Flow of Technology: Technology Transfer and the Dissemination of Technological information within the R and D Organization*. Cambridge, MA: MIT Press.

Ancona, D. G. (1990). Outward bound: strategies for team survival in an organization. *Academy of Management Journal*, 33, 334–365.

Ancona, D., and Bresman, H. (2007). *X-teams: How to Build Teams that Lead, Innovate, and Succeed*. Boston, MA: Harvard Business School Press.

Ancona, D. G., and Caldwell, D. F. (1992). Bridging the boundary: External activity and performance in organizational teams. *Administrative Science Quarterly*, 37, 634–665.

Ancona, D. G., and Caldwell, D. F. (1997). Rethinking team composition from the outside in. In M. E. Neale, E. A. Mannix, and D. H. Gruenfeld (eds), *Research on Managing Groups and Teams* 1 (pp. 21–37). Stamford, CT: JAI Press.

Ancona, D. G., and Nadler, D. A. (1989). Top hats and executive tales: Designing the senior team. *Sloan Management Review*, 31, 19–28.

Bantel, K., and Jackson, S. (1989). Top management and innovations in banking: Does the composition of the team make a difference? *Strategic Management Journal*, 10, 107–124.

Bunderson, J. S., and Sutcliffe, K.M. (2002). Comparing alternative conceptualizations of functional diversity in management teams: Process and performance effects. *Academy of Management Journal*, 45, 875–893.

Burt, R. (1992). *Structural Holes: The Social Structure of Competition*. Cambridge, MA: Harvard University Press.

Campion, M., Medsker, G., and Higgs, A. (1993). Relations between work group characteristics and effectiveness: Implications for designing effective work groups. *Personnel Psychology*, 46, 823–847.

Cummings, J. N. (2004). Work groups: structural diversity, and knowledge sharing in a global organization. *Management Science*, 50, 352–364.

Cummings, T. G. (1978). Self-regulating work groups: A socio-technical synthesis. *Academy of Management Review*, 3, 624–634.

Ericksen, J., and Dyer, L. (2004). Right from the start: Exploring the effects of early team events on subsequent project team development and performance. *Administrative Science Quarterly*, 49, 438–471.

Gladstein, D. (1984). Groups in context: A model of task group effectiveness. *Administrative Science Quarterly*, 29, 499–517.

Glick, W., Miller, C., and Huber, G. (1993). The impact of upper echelon diversity on organizational performance. In G. Huber and W. Glick (eds), *Organizational Change and Redesign* (pp. 176–224). New York: Oxford University Press.

Granovetter, M. S. (1973). The strength of weak ties. *American Journal of Sociology*, 78, 1360–1380.

Hansen, M. T. (1999). The search-transfer problem: The role of weak ties in sharing knowledge across organization subunits. *Administrative Science Quarterly*, 44, 82–111.

Homans, G. (1950). *The Human Group*. New York: Harcourt Brace Jovanovich.

Janis, I. (1982). *Victims of Groupthink: A Psychological Study of Foreign Policy Decisions and Fiascos*. Boston: Houghton-Mifflin.

Jehn, K. A. (1995). A multimethod examination of the benefits and detriments of intra-group conflict. *Administrative Science Quarterly*, 29, 499–518.

Katz, D., and Kahn, R. (1978). *The Social Psychology of Organizing*. New York, NY: Wiley.

Katz, R., and Tushman, M. (1979). Communication patterns, project performance, and task characteristics: An empirical evaluation and integration in a R and D setting. *Organizational Behavior and Human Performance*, 23, 139–162.

Keck, S., and Tushman, M. (1993). Environmental and organizational context and executive team structure. *Academy of Management Journal*, 36, 1314–1344.

Krackhardt, D. (1990). Assessing the political landscape: Structure, cognition, and power in organizations. *Administrative Science Quarterly*, 35, 342–369.

Lewin, K. (1951). *Field Theory in Social Science: Selected Theoretical Papers*. D. Cartwright (ed.). New York: Harper and Brothers Publishers.

Marrone, J. A., Tesluk, P. E., and Carson, J. B. (2007). A multilevel investigation of antecedents and consequences of team member boundary-spanning behavior. *Academy of Management Journal*, 50, 1423–1439.

Moreland, R., Levine, J., and Wingert, M. (1996). Creating the ideal group: Composition effects at work. In E. Witte and J. Davis (eds), *Understanding Group Behavior: Small Group Processes and Interpersonal Relations*, 2 (pp. 11–35). Hillsdale, NJ: Lawrence Erlbaum.

Pelled, L. H., Eisenhardt, K. M., and Xin, K. R. (1999). Exploring the black box: An analysis of work group diversity, conflict, and productivity. *Administrative Science Quarterly*, 44, 1–28.

Reagans, R., and Zuckerman, E. (2001). Networks, diversity and productivity: The social capital of corporate R and D teams. *Organization Science*, 12, 502–517.

Reagans, R., Zuckerman, E., and McEvily, B. (2004). How to make the team: Social networks vs. demography as criteria for designing effective teams. *Administrative Science Quarterly*, 49, 101–133.

Roberts, K., and O'Reilly, C. (1979). Some correlates of communication roles in organizations. *Academy of Management Journal*, 22, 42–57.

Scott, S. (1997). Social identification effects in product and process development teams. *Journal of Engineering and Technology Management*, 14, 97–127.

Tushman, M. (1977). Special boundary roles in the innovation process. *Administrative Science Quarterly*, 22, 587–605.

Williams, K., and O'Reilly, C. (1998). Demography and diversity in organizations: A review of 40 years of research. In B. Staw and R. Sutton (eds), *Research in Organizational Behavior*, 20 (pp. 77–144). Stamford, CT: JAI Press.

Wong, S. S. (2004). Distal and local group learning: Performance trade-offs and tensions. *Organization Science*, 15, 645–656.

Yan, A., and Louis, M. R. (1999). The migration of organizational functions to the work unit level: Buffering, spanning, and bringing up boundaries. *Human Relations*, 52, 25–47.

EXERCISES

The following exercises ask you to apply the concepts to a real team. The first exercise is most appropriate if you served on a "project" team. This could be at work or could be a committee you have served on at school (organizing a food drive, etc.). The second exercise is a tool for planning your next assignment. This could be a team project in a class or some project at work.

The "project" team

Think about a team that you are familiar with – perhaps a team you are now on or were on in the past. Try to identify the key external groups or individuals that could potentially help the team. For example, some groups might be able to provide information or resources to your team. Other groups or individuals might be able to help your team understand and respond to political or strategic issues within the organization. Still other groups might be responsible for either evaluating your team's work or integrating your work into their own. For each of these stakeholders, determine whether information, resources, political alignment, or task interdependence needs to be managed. Identify a team member who will interact with each stakeholder. If there are no team members with the skills or connections to manage these activities think about whom you might recruit from outside the team, whether as a full-time or part-time member, to help manage these interactions.

Planning your next assignment

Based on reading this chapter, think about how you might approach your next team assignment. What would you need to know to "map" the environment? How would you staff the team? What do you need to consider besides the functional competencies needed to do the task?

17

Making Group Process Work: Harnessing Collective Intuition, Task Conflict, and Pacing

GERARDO A. OKHUYSEN AND BETH A. BECHKY

Imagine, if you will, two groups with very similar members. Both have exceptionally talented individuals at the helm, committed participants, and compelling challenges that they must respond to. However, while in one group members actively share information, disagree with one another, and press ahead for action, in the other group members are passive, have little discussion of the challenges for the group, and adopt attitudes that make getting along more important than getting work done. The difference between these two groups is at the crux of this chapter and answers the question, does group process matter? By group process, we simply mean how group members go about interacting and making choices to get their work done.

The groups we discuss include shop floor teams that develop process improvements, surgery teams, cross-functional product development groups, police crisis teams, ongoing task forces, film project teams, and top management teams. In general, these are groups that demand active engagement and intense interaction among group members (Ashforth and Fried, 1988; Eisenhardt, Kahwajy, and Bourgeois, 1997a; Louis and Sutton, 1991).

Our central argument is straightforward. Although the membership of groups enables and constrains many of their activities, a central element that causes some groups to succeed and others to fail is group process. With a positive group process, a team of average individuals can perform better than a group of superstars with a bad group process. For us, group process opens the doors to the performance of individuals as part of a successful group. With poor group process, the doors to that performance remain closed.

Many people naively believe that effective group process requires group members to make difficult process tradeoffs: conflict comes at the expense of speed, speed sacrifices getting along, and getting along cannot happen with conflict. Yet we think that the reality of effective group process is different. After all, conflict is absolutely essential for effective groups, especially ones facing difficult choices in situations of high uncertainty (see Chapter 18, this volume). Timing and speed matter too. A decision made too late can cost money or leave an organization hopelessly behind the competition, leading to its failure. Group members also need to be able to work together in an ongoing way to complete their work. In our view, superior group process involves solving the classic tradeoffs of group process, not making them. That is, great group process is fast and responsive, with members acting under pressure. It is also conflictual and respectful, with group members who can disagree with one another and yet can walk away from meetings with mutual deference and the will to work together in the future. Importantly, not all groups adopt the same tactics to achieve great group process. Instead, groups adopt approaches that are ideally suited to their own circumstances.

In this chapter, we describe three principles that help create great group process. These are: creating collective intuition, stimulating task-related conflict, and driving the pace of action. We argue that each of these antecedents consists of a cluster of tactics that shape group process. These tactics are interrelated such that they work with one another, supporting each other and offering synergies in group process. We also describe the pivotal role of the leader in shaping the group process that emerges.

Building Collective Intuition

One of the myths of group process is that relying on extensive information is a problem. The argument goes like this: the cost of gathering information is very high, and large amounts of information are often ignored anyway due to the excessive demands on the time of group members (March and Simon, 1958; Simon, 1955). Therefore, it is not particularly useful to gather large amounts of information. In addition, since the perception and interpretation of information is fraught with personal and social biases, information must be treated with suspicion. As a consequence, group members should move ahead without spending too much time worrying about having all of the relevant information.

In contrast, recent research takes a different view (Dean and Sharfman, 1996; Eisenhardt and Bourgeois, 1988; Wally and Baum, 1994). Groups with great process rely on more, not less, information than less effective groups. The difference is in the kind of information that they use. Ineffective groups rely on either historical information about past performance or speculative information about how the world might unfold (Eisenhardt, 1989). In contrast, groups with superior process center their attention on real-time and fact-based information about current operations.

Gathering information: exploiting expertise and profiting from variety

For many groups, the involvement of individuals in the front lines of the action is critical to gather information. In film crews, individuals in every department are responsible for bringing potential problems to everyone else's attention (Bechky, 2006). Difficulties staffing a shooting crew, the absence of equipment, and the late arrival of actors or actresses are all communicated to those affected, providing critical and timely information on the performance of the crew. This intensity of information gathering is also evident in police crisis teams, with officers trying to understand "what's happening" in a moment-by-moment manner (Okhuysen, 2005). Each officer on the team plays an important role in gathering extensive real-time information. During missions, snipers double as observers, calling in information they glean from their observation perch about suspects, such as movement within an apartment or other activity. Perimeter team members cover the area surrounding the location, searching for possible escape routes for the suspects or places where adding officers might be useful. At the same time, detectives contact city building departments to get the blueprints for the apartments, homes, or businesses where suspects are holed up. The typical outcome of this team is an efficient and safe resolution of standoff situations, with suspects surrendering with no loss of life.

Further, research suggests that real-time information about the situation is particularly effective when different members of the group are responsible for specific pieces of it (Eisenhardt, 1989). In effect, members of groups with superior process adopt deliberately distinct information roles in the group. Often these roles are along the lines of functional expertise like engineering or marketing. This partitioning of responsibility for information cultivates a variety of different perspectives and provides depth of knowledge by focusing the attention of specific members on particular features of the situation. Not only is the information likely to be more accurate given that the group is leveraging the expertise of its members, but it is also likely to be obtained more quickly. This focus is not only effective for information that affects the internal operations of the crew, but also for external information that can lead members to a more effective group process by focusing their attention on important stakeholders (Ancona, 1990; Ancona and Bresman, 2007).

Of course, simply having knowledgeable individuals in a group paying attention is of little use if their information is not available to be used collectively by the group. Indeed, one of the main challenges of group process is to ensure that information is effectively exchanged with all other members of the group (Stasser, 1992; Stasser and Stewart, 1992). In order to share and use information effectively, groups with great process engage in frequent interactions. For example, some management groups set up "can't miss" meetings, police crisis teams engage in extensive information sharing during briefing meetings, and film crews continuously update one another using walkie-talkies on set. In general, these groups have a large number of regular interactions among members (Eisenhardt et al., 1997a; Bechky and Okhuysen, 2008).

The importance of real-time information, partitioned responsibility for that information, and frequent meetings appears in many organizational groups. For example, Eisenhardt (1989) examines group process among top management teams in start-up ventures in the computing industry. In particular, she describes how the members of one team, at a firm with the pseudonym Zap, operate. First of all, members of the management team at Zap claim to "over-MBA it" and to "measure everything." And they come close. They focus their attention on a wide variety of raw internal and external measures of current operations like bookings, backlog, revenue per employee, cash, and scrap in preference to refined, accounting-based indicators like profit.

Exploiting information: fostering positive interactions and dissimilarity of knowledge

Why does this combination of real-time information gathered and collectively shared by group members lead to effective group process? One reason is that this combination of tactics is fast. In particular, continual tracking of information acts as an early warning system that allows group members to spot problems and opportunities sooner. Groups that are mindful and attentive to such cues can respond more quickly (Levinthal and Rerup, 2006; Weick and Sutcliffe, 2001). This is especially true when group members have developed a routine for working together, either because they know each other well (Eisenhardt, 1989) or because they act on well-rehearsed roles (Bechky and Okhuysen, 2008; Edmondson, Bohmer, and Pisano, 2001). Therefore, when situations arise, members can go right to the problem, rather than groping about for relevant information. In addition, the development of distinct roles helps the information gathering process by ensuring that multiple perspectives are always represented (Eisenhardt, 1989), which in turn increases the potential range of action in the group (Schweiger, Sandberg, and Rechner, 1989).

For many teams concerned with fast performance, real-time information gathered by group members and shared together creates a collective intuition, a store of knowledge based on the experiences of the group that is related to the challenges they face over time. Through their experience, members develop an ability to build linkages among seemingly disparate pieces of information and to recognize and process information in blocks or patterns (Isenberg, 1986, 1988). Through repeated exposure to data, these patterns become recognizable, often subconsciously, even when there is only a small amount of current information available. This pattern processing is faster and more accurate than processing single pieces of information or waiting for additional information, and is a useful result of previous experience. Through the development of a collective knowledge base, all group members can also tap into relevant experiences when new situations appear (Thompson, Gentner, and Loewenstein, 2000), allowing them to make sense of complex situations quickly and elaborate responses to surprises (Bechky and Okhuysen, 2008). This "collective intuition" can help a group become faster and more effective in its work.

FOSTERING PRODUCTIVE TASK CONFLICT

A second reason that this combination of tactics builds effective group process is that the intense interaction creates groups whose members are more likely to disagree. Familiarity and friendship make such frank conversation easier because group members are less constrained by politeness and more willing to express diverse views (Okhuysen, 2001). In situations where developing this interpersonal familiarity is not possible, such as film crews where strangers come together for a few weeks to complete a shoot or emergency trauma teams in hospitals whose membership is constantly changing, the presence of strong roles can substitute for familiarity (Bechky, 2006; Klein, Ziegert, Knight, and Xiao, 2006). The presence of well-defined roles in these groups instantly achieves two objectives. First, it brings different perspectives to bear on a problem because each role represents a different point of view. Second, because each member is expected to be an expert in his or her role, bringing up problems or disagreements is a natural part of the role-based structure.

The familiarity that group members develop through their intense interactions is also one element that allows them to disagree in the short term, and yet still get along in the long term (Valley, Neale, and Mannix, 1995). Familiarity in a group develops as a consequence of the interactions among members and is constantly reinforced as members discover information regarding the expertise and preferences of their co-workers (Reagans, Argote, and Brooks, 2005). For groups where the deliberation of decisions is important, such as top management teams, the development of familiarity makes it easier for group members to separate task conflict from relationship or interpersonal conflict (Eisenhardt, 1989). Familiarity keeps task conflict from becoming relationship conflict through trust (Simons and Peterson, 2000). This trust comes from increased and intense interaction that allows the group to build common goals, ensuring the commitment and participation of all members. The familiarity that develops from intense and frequent interactions increases interpersonal knowledge regarding beliefs and norms, and makes work interactions easier (Jehn and Shah, 1997; Okhuysen, 2001; Shah and Jehn, 1993). In addition, groups that are successful in the long term distinguish themselves by having a proactive stand towards conflict, engaging conflict resolution strategies in a collective manner (Behfar, Peterson, Mannix, and Trochim, 2008). As individuals increase their knowledge about others and build trust in other members they are able to "agree to disagree" on substantive issues without engaging in personal attacks or recriminations.

The use of real-time information as part of the deliberations of the group also helps members engage in productive conflict and yet still get along (Eisenhardt et al., 1997a). The argument is as follows. In groups, disagreement can be viewed as personal or as issue based (Amason, 1996; Jehn, 1995, 1997; Schweiger et al., 1989). Personal conflict tends to create a dysfunctional process in which members listen poorly, fail to engage, and are distracted from the problem-solving task for the group. In contrast, issue-based conflict is related to superior group process (see Chapter 18). By relying on facts, people tend to attribute disagreement simply to issue-based differences among reasonable people. This attribution helps group members to avoid becoming sidetracked by personal agendas, to become task focused, and move more quickly to the central challenges facing the group. It also helps them to avoid becoming bogged down in arguments about what might be. Facts depersonalize discussion because they are not some member's fantasies, guesses, or self-serving desires. An emphasis on factual data creates a culture of problem solving, not personalities. The explicit anointing of individuals as experts adds to the effect, making it easier for the group to call on them to share their perspective on a given issue (Stasser, Stewart, and Wittenbaum, 1995). By providing specific areas of the organization that members represent and are responsible for, the use of group roles for information gathering helps to limit politicking by mitigating "turf" battles.

A key challenge for groups is developing interaction patterns that allow them to disagree, so that they can reach the best outcome possible. Consider the following story. On a hot and dusty August afternoon, a farming family was sitting on their front porch trying to get some relief from the heat of the Midwest summer. One family member suggested an outing to Abilene, about a two-hour drive away, to get some lemonade. Another member agreed. Before long, the whole family was in the car, on the way to Abilene. With the sun beating down on the roof, the trip in the crowded car was even more unpleasantly hot than sitting on the family porch. The lemonade was not particularly memorable either. In frustration, one member finally expressed regret at ever leaving the porch. With that, everyone chimed in that they had never really wanted to go to Abilene in the first place. They had all simply assumed that everyone else wanted to go to Abilene, and so they agreed to go too. The above story, dubbed the Abilene Paradox, has been told in a variety of ways and has become a classic parable in organizational behavior (Harvey, 1988). In the Abilene Paradox, every group member disagrees with the group choice, but does not express that disagreement. No one voices objections because each assumes that the other group members agree with the stated position and its underlying assumptions. Because no one expresses disagreement, no one realizes that conflict exists. This, in turn, leads to increased internal pressures to self-censor opinions. In its extreme form, the Abilene Paradox leads to a poor group process in which group members engage in activities or adopt directions that no one in the group agrees with simply because no one is willing to be the first voice of dissent.

The Abilene Paradox is only one example of many that showcase a common problem: not enough conflict in a group – although many people intuitively worry about the destructive effects that unimpeded conflict can have on groups. However, the reality is that the hazard is often the reverse, that a group will not have sufficient conflict and instead suffer from passivity and lack of energy. Groupthink (Janis, 1982), for example, is an extreme phenomenon where conflict is not only avoided, but actively suppressed by members. In situations where Groupthink emerges, a lack of critical thought and of realistic assessment of alternatives are consequences of too little conflict.

Groups with effective process have to exhibit extensive differences of opinion. In effective groups, members recognize that conflict is a natural feature of many organizational situations in which reasonable people should and often do disagree. Further, as research demonstrates, conflict stimulates innovative thinking, and creates better understanding of the options. This leads to better choices and implementation. Without sufficient conflict, group members have an impoverished process. They miss opportunities to question assumptions and overlook key elements of their situation. Given the value of conflict, groups with effective process make conflict part of that process.

Creating conflict: using devices to foster disagreement

One way that groups create conflict in their process is through *team composition*. For example, top management teams that are diverse in terms of age, gender, functional background, experience, and so forth are likely to see the world in different ways and so naturally create conflict. That is, the natural differences that exist across their areas of responsibility (e.g. marketing vs. logistics), focus of concern (e.g. labor unions vs. consumers), or other differences (e.g. gender) generate perspectives that disagree with one another. For example, it would not be unusual for a member representing manufacturing to be in conflict with the opinions of the marketing or R&D department.

Oppositional roles in a group may also develop through interaction, as group members naturally organize into antipodal roles such as short vs. long term, or status quo vs. change (Guetzkow and Gyr, 1954) in response to their perceptions of balancing the natural tensions within a group. In top management teams, one member who is particularly concerned with the current status of the organization may have major disagreements with someone whose focus is the future of the organization.

Another way in which conflict is introduced by members of a group is through the deliberate development of *multiple alternatives* for any given issue (Eisenhardt, 1989; Okhuysen, 2001). As different alternatives are explored, disagreements over assumptions, outcomes, and objectives are clarified. This clarification, while conflictive, can lead to the development of greater confidence among group members that they have adequately explored the issues as well as a higher-quality process overall. This, in turn, helps make sure that the best options, those that reflect the true underlying objectives of the group, are the ones selected. Effective decision-making groups highlight this diversity of knowledge and opinions and actively exploit it to uncover potential alternatives for the group (Schweiger and Finger, 1984; Schweiger, Sandberg, and Ragan, 1986).

Task conflict can also be generated by using *framebreaking* heuristics that lead to new perspectives and thinking. One such heuristic is *forecasting* (Eisenhardt et al., 1997a). Forecasting involves imagining future scenarios (i.e. assumptions about how the future will unfold) and then playing out various options in light of these scenarios. As a result, members can better grasp the range of possible futures and their options within them. A related heuristic is *backcasting*. Using this technique, the group builds alternative future scenarios. Having developed these different future scenarios, group members choose the most desirable ones and then reason backwards to figure out how to achieve those futures. For members of police crisis teams, these approaches are second nature (Okhuysen, 2005). During training sessions officers actively discuss different ways in which missions can unfold, always with an eye to be prepared for that eventual contingency. Similarly, during briefing meetings for missions officers discuss their preferences for the outcomes of the mission (e.g. capturing suspects, collecting evidence, using low levels of force), and work backward to develop approaches to the situation that will tip the odds in favor of achieving those objectives.

Framebreaking heuristics can also involve *members taking on particular roles* within the group. Sometimes the role-playing simply means taking the perspective of a key competitor or opponent or the point of view of an important constituent in the group's discussion. Group members may also take on a formal *devil's advocacy* role (Schweiger and Finger, 1984; Schweiger et al., 1989). The devil's advocate is a group member who is charged with questioning the assumptions and approaches of the group through critical evaluation. Since this role is formalized, it allows the devil's advocate to deeply explore issues and request clarification from other group members without the risk of censure that may come to an individual who pointedly disagrees with the group. Overall, role-playing heuristics allow members to argue and discuss alternatives with less risk of being reproached by other members of the group (Feldman, 1984; Murnighan and Conlon, 1991).

In other groups, differences of opinion and the value they bring to the group process take on different forms. For example, in surgery teams it is important that every group member feel safe raising his or her voice to highlight problems or unanticipated situations (Edmondson et al., 2001). However, the strong hierarchies that sometimes exist in these groups make it difficult, if not impossible, for low-status members to express their opinions. Here, the development of *psychological safety*, trusting the group to respect and support the individual who is raising his or her voice, is critical if the group is to perform well. Skillful leaders and group members are able to create psychological safety by valuing disagreement and giving voice to all members of the group (Edmondson et al., 2001). In film crews, in contrast, many of the concerns for things that can go wrong, such as safety for mechanical or electrical installations, are embodied in the roles of specific individuals. Any conflict that derives from fulfilling those roles in a proficient manner, such as by raising worries about things that could go wrong, is acceptable in the situation (Bechky, 2006).

Exploiting conflict: using conflict to achieve positive outcomes

Why do conflict-creating devices such as diverse groups, framebreaking heuristics, multiple alternatives, and role execution lead to more effective group process? Obviously, they hasten the emergence of conflict and so accelerate the entire group process. Rather than waiting or hoping that conflict will emerge, group members simply create that conflict. Less obviously, these tactics often give group members confidence that they are not overlooking key information and perspectives. Armed with such confidence, group members are likely to have a faster process. That confidence is especially crucial in situations where the barriers to group execution are as much emotional (i.e. fear of the unknown) as they are cognitive. More obviously, these tactics clearly improve group process by helping group members to come up with more varied viewpoints on their actions. They encourage group members to think over time, to reverse their usual path of thinking, and to assume new lenses for viewing the activities of the group. Through all of these tactics, group members are likely to develop a process that is more highly conflictual.

Finally, the combination of a diverse group, multiple alternatives, and especially frame-breaking heuristics and role structures affects group process by *legitimating* conflict. This helps group members to get along even as they disagree. For instance, when crew members on film sets voice their concerns about task accomplishments to other group members, they do so politely, often after first thanking their colleagues for things they are doing right (Bechky, 2006). These tactics normalize conflict by encouraging group members to frame conflict as less centered on personal differences and more centered on problem solving. That is, they put a cooperative, not competitive, perspective on the group process. For example, the use of a devil's advocate allows the group to formalize task conflict and use it as part of its work process. The artificial addition of such task conflict into the group allows members to capitalize on the group's problem-solving advantages, while at the same time providing legitimacy for the emergence of conflict within the group. The legitimacy of conflict that is afforded group members through the adoption of such tactics contributes to the prevention of premature and even false consensus.

PACING THE PROCESS

One of the striking features of the literature on group process is the lack of attention to time. Of course, there are some exceptions (including those noted below), but very often authors ignore or misunderstand time. Yet, in the world of real groups, time is critical. In fact, with the emergence of the Internet, the convergence of consumer electronics with computing and telecommunications, and the globalization of work, attention to time is becoming crucial for many groups. In places like Silicon Valley, quips like "snooze, you lose" or "the worst decision is no decision at all" underscore the importance of time. For other groups, such as police crisis teams, the timing of action is critical: acting too soon or not soon enough are both problematic. For film crews, pacing is central to maintaining control over the work. Pacing keeps group members moving forward, even as it gives them opportunities to adjust to unforeseen problems and unexpected opportunities, towards the completion of their work.

Setting the pace: adopting a rhythm of action

One way to drive the pace of the group is simply by developing a natural *rhythm* of action. For example, Eisenhardt (1999) describes how top management teams develop a sense of how long strategic decisions should take. Through the experience of decision making and the practice of self-reflection, they come to understand when a process is taking too long, which implies that the group is either tackling too large an issue or is simply slowing down. They also develop a sense of when the process is too fast, as in situations where management teams become overly ambitious and, in the process, develop increasingly fast spirals that lead to ineffective decision processes and outcomes (Perlow, Okhuysen, and Repenning, 2002). Similarly, Brown and Eisenhardt (1997) studied product development groups and found that the more successful ones developed a rhythm for their process around consistent lengths of their projects. This rhythm accelerated and focused the project teams. Overall, pacing in a group reflects the collective experience of individuals, and yields more effective outcomes (Eisenhardt, 1999).

For other groups the pacing of action is quicker and progress on the task is more immediate. Film crews, for example, place great value on making continuous progress – every minute of production add to the total cost of the film, because people and materials are in place to do the work. This ongoing pressure for progress is reflected in the actions of crew members, who are always ready to quickly move to the next task or to correct mistakes as the situation demands (Bechky, 2006). Similarly, for police crisis teams every second increases the danger in a situation since time gives suspects the opportunity to respond, sometimes violently, to the actions of officers. Officers are therefore prepared to take immediate action at every moment if the situation demands it, even when great uncertainty remains (Okhuysen, 2005).

For project groups, the use of *deadlines* is another way to set the pace of the group process (Gersick, 1989). Deadlines influence the group process by providing an easy measure of the progress that the group has made. For example, if a group is one third of the way to its deadline but has not completed one third of the work, members can easily conclude that an increase in activity is necessary. In a particularly interesting study, Gersick (1989) found that groups with deadlines often paused at the midpoint of their schedule in order to assess their progress towards their goals in light of the deadline. As a result of this pause, the groups often had an opportunity to assess their group process and to make major changes in that process in order to improve group performance.

More generally, *milestones* and even simple process interventions such as "watch your time" or "ask others about their information" can effectively alter the process of groups. Such milestones and simple group interventions often trigger group members to stop and think, to evaluate their work, and to discuss potential changes in group process or direction. During these interruptions, group members have an opportunity to focus critically on their process and look for better ways to accomplish the task (Okhuysen and Eisenhardt, 2002). That is, the group members are able to address accumulated problems, discuss future directions, and take action. The result is a group process with alternating periods of both full engagement on the task and opportunities to change the direction and process of the group.

Group members also set the pace of their work through the way in which they make choices or decisions. Police crisis teams and film crews often face unexpected events that can slow or stop their progress, and responding to them directs the pace of their work. Rather than looking for perfect solutions to these challenges given the time pressure, in these situations members "make do" with the materials and people they have at hand, and they develop improvised responses to the unexpected events. Police snipers, for example, will use armored vehicles, utility poles, or even trees as lookout posts if other locations, which could be better, safer, and more comfortable, cannot be found. Making do with what is immediately available, or *bricolage*, allows different types of teams to continue making progress on the task by overcoming the challenge that the unexpected situation represents (Bechky and Okhuysen, 2008).

For top management groups, using *consensus with qualification* as a decision rule is important in pacing their activity (Eisenhardt, Kahwajy, and Bourgeois, 1997b). Consensus with qualification is a two-step process. First, group members try to reach consensus. But, if they cannot do so, then group members make the choice by some sort of decision rule such as the most involved member chooses, the group votes, or the leader decides. By formally separating discussion and deliberation from the choice that has to be made, members of effective groups can ensure that everyone's ideas and opinions are heard, even if they are ultimately not part of the solution that is chosen. Consensus with qualification allows the group to move forward with its work rather than getting bogged down in endless discussions when agreement is hard to achieve.

Exploiting the pace: ensuring progress on the task

Why does the combination of rhythm, deadlines and milestones, simple interventions, improvisation and bricolage, and consensus with qualification lead to more effective group process? The obvious reason is that each of these tactics contributes to moving the group along more quickly. But more importantly, they can also drive a pace for the group, creating an internal process metronome that keeps the group moving forward. So, for example, milestones help group members to pace their activity (Okhuysen and Eisenhardt, 2002). Consensus with qualification provides a way for the group to stop an endless search for consensus that can waste time and energy as members pursue an objective that cannot realistically be achieved in a reasonable timeframe. Similarly, deadlines set pace and close group discussion.

This combination of tactics also helps group members to oscillate their attention from task execution to improvement of their problem-solving strategy and/or group process. Such opportunities to stop and think create greater self-reflection. For police crisis teams, these moments to stop and think occur away from their missions, during training and rehearsal sessions or mission briefing and debriefing sessions, where the group can collectively contribute to the reflective activity (Okhuysen, 2005). Self-reflection by these teams stimulates thinking and conflict within the group by often providing opportunities to examine and change group process and task strategy.

Finally, setting the pace through internal rhythms, deadlines and milestones, simple interventions, bricolage, and consensus with qualification helps group members to get along. Such tactics signal the need to focus on advancing the task, even when group members disagree. They also provide a legitimate platform for group members to address issues of ineffective group process including personal (as opposed to task) conflict. Consensus with qualification is particularly useful for helping group members to avoid the frustration of endless consensus seeking in decision-making groups. It helps them to take a realistic view of conflict as valuable and inevitable. At the same time, consensus with qualification lets group members resolve conflict (and maintain pace) in a way that is typically perceived as equitable (Eisenhardt, 1989). Most group members want a voice in their group's decisions, but rarely believe that they must always get their preferred choice.

Overall, tactics such as deadlines and milestones, rhythm, bricolage, consensus with qualification, and simple interventions set a pace for group process that keeps groups on track in terms of time while still offering opportunities for reflection and change in their process. In contrast, groups whose members do not use these tactics are prone to ineffective use of time. They may make decisions so quickly that they forget important information or miss sight of their broader objectives (Perlow et al., 2002). More likely, they will become bogged down in searches for consensus. These group members often stress the rarity of what they do, rather than recognizing its repetitive nature. They oscillate between letting critical issues languish and making "shotgun" moves with little thought.

LEADERSHIP

Thus far, we have argued that the tactics that are associated with creating collective intuition, stimulating quick task conflict, and setting the pace of the group all contribute to effective group process – that is, fast and high-conflict group process where members nonetheless get along. In this section, we focus briefly on the important role that the leader of the group plays in developing a great group process (see Chapter 15).

Guiding leadership: setting the tone for positive group processes

First of all, it is important to recognize that leaders have a disproportionate influence on group process. This influence is sometimes exerted in a negative, even if unintended, fashion. For example, surgeons can sometimes curtail the discussion of contrarian points of view during operations, limiting the opportunities for team members to contribute to the work of the group (Edmondson et al., 2001). But leaders can also use their asymmetrical influence on group process more positively. This is particularly the case when they provide legitimacy or "cover" to others in the group. In the same surgery teams (Edmondson et al., 2001), the surgeon in charge plays a disproportionate role in establishing the norms of the group. When the surgeon is *open to the opinions of others* and facilitates reflective practices in the team, members are more likely to point out problems and alternative solutions, especially if doing so requires side-stepping the hierarchy of the operating room. Similarly, junior members of trauma care teams such as interns are empowered to act by the "hands-off" approach of attending doctors, which puts pressure on interns but also gives them confidence to act to respond to the patients' needs (Klein et al., 2006). In decision-making teams, the leader can adopt framebreaking heuristics such as devil's advocacy more readily than can other members. By requesting multiple alternative approaches to a problem, the leader legitimates differences of opinion.

Leaders can also disproportionately influence the process of the group by stimulating explicit and even contrived attempts to have fun. *Humor* is effective within groups because it relieves tension and improves the cooperative outlook of team members as well as their listening skills (Eisenhardt, 1999). Humor bridges differences among group members as well (Kahn, 1989; Ziv and Gadish, 1990). Humor works as a defense mechanism to protect people from stressful situations that can arise in groups. Using humor, people can distance themselves from such situations by putting those situations into a broader life context, often through the use of irony. Humor, particularly given its ambiguity, can blunt the threatening edge of negative information. Group members can speak in jest about issues that might be threatening if said directly. Humor can convey serious messages in a less threatening way.

CASE EXAMPLES

Blockbuster

The crew of *Blockbuster*, a large studio-funded film, arrives on the set and each member receives a walkie-talkie, after which the head of each department reports for the kick-off production meeting. Here, the first assistant director takes everyone through the shooting schedule in detail, discussing potential problems with locations, equipment, effects, and costumes. After the meeting, each lead passes on the information to the members of his or her department, gathering ideas and suggestions on how to deal with the expected challenges and with potential problems. As production gets rolling over the next few hours and days, crew members bump into colleagues they recognize, saying things like, "Didn't we work together on *Talk to the Animals* in 2006?" The cinematographer and the first assistant camera operator reminisce about the *Rocky* sequel they worked on in Philadelphia, saying to a newcomer, "We've been working together for 20 years." They joke that in this business, it sometimes feels like you are married to your colleagues.

Over the course of the next six weeks of production, there is a constant chatter about what is going on, with up-to-the-minute updates on activities. There are constant conversations about what is going on among people, sometimes in person and sometimes simply over the walkie-talkies. On the grip channel, for example, the key grip informs his crew that they are shooting a different scene from the one they had planned, saying, "I'm sorry, guys, we need to reorganize. I need four of you over by the technocrane." When unusual incidents or concerns arise, crew members bring it to the attention of the person they think should know. For instance, when an actor in a minor role trips and falls during early morning filming and complains of a hurt wrist, five or six different crew members report this injury to the unit production manager later in the day, when he arrives on the set. Crew members also jump into action when they think they can help out, even if they are not asked. When a fire starts in a garbage can on set, two location assistants grab a cooler filled with water, run down the hill and extinguish the fire.

The heads of departments meet frequently over the course of the day, formally and informally. Particularly important are the meetings in the morning, when the work for the day is discussed, and the ones at the end of the day, when they check in on the progress of the shoot and talk over the scenes planned for the next day. When the executive producer, for instance, asks "What is going on with the aerial effects?" both the cinematographer and the unit production manager chime in. "We are having some trouble with the weather; it is too windy, and they are predicting more clouds and wind tomorrow. I don't think we can do it," says the cinematographer. But the unit production manager disagrees: "No, my weather service says it should clear up by tomorrow, and I think we should move ahead with it." The executive producer considers the two different opinions and decides the crew should prepare for the aerial shots the next day. Also at the end of every day, the executive producer or the unit production manager reports on their progress to the vice president of operations at the studio, on the other side of the country. She has them keeping very close track of the "hot costs," the daily tally of expenses the production incurs.

Reality Show

In contrast to the smooth operation of *Blockbuster*, *Reality Show* is having some trouble with its work. The production of this film is part of a reality television show. The crew members on this set are mostly unfamiliar to one another, because they were hired directly for the series and the heads of the departments did not get to select their own crew. Moreover, there are many novices on the crew. For example, the director of the film is a first-timer, chosen by a television audience vote, and knows nobody else on the set.

On this film set, you hear a lot of talking, but it is not about the tasks or the work on the project. Crew members are very worried about their careers, positioning themselves and posturing for the television cameras. "Why wasn't I in on that decision? That's part of my job," gripes one producer to the camera. There are repeated blow-ups on the set between the newbie director and the cinematographer, who have very different ideas about the tone of the film, and who continually point fingers at one another and develop an intense dislike of each other. "He thinks he's an auteur," complains the director, while the cinematographer rejoins, "He has no clue what he is doing!" After a few days, the cinematographer stops attending the morning meetings, and arrives only as the crew is ready to begin shooting.

One morning, the cinematographer looks through the camera and says, "Why wasn't that barn wall repainted? It is in the picture!" The set dressers, who were told by the director not to paint the wall when the cinematographer was not around, rush over and begin talking, while everyone else waits. Because key crew members are absent or arguing, key decisions are delayed. Information that is important also goes missing, causing even more problems. For instance, for the first three weeks of the shoot the director is not aware that the lead actor does not know how to ride a motorcycle, even though others on the set know this. Somehow, this bit of information falls through the cracks. Two days before the climactic bike chase scene is going to be shot the director talks to the actor about it and, delaying the shoot even more, the scene has to be pushed off for several days while they teach him to ride. The project continues to be plagued by these difficulties, and ends as a failure.

CONCLUSION

This chapter discussed some of the factors by which groups achieve a great process. A great group process is one that is responsive, that includes conflict, and where group members get along. The antecedent conditions that we discussed include sets of tactics around building collective intuition, stimulating quick conflict, and setting the pace of the group. We also indicated that the leader has a particularly powerful influence on the process of the group. Using research on groups, this chapter highlights some of the key ways to understand and improve group process. The result of such improvements can be high-quality and timely outcomes that improve the odds of the long-term survival of the group and its organization.

REFERENCES

Amason, A. C. (1996). Distinguishing the effects of functional and dysfunctional conflict on strategic decision making: Resolving a paradox for top management teams. *Academy of Management Journal*, 39, 123–148.

Ancona, D. G. (1990). Outward bound: Strategies for team survival in an organization. *Academy of Management Journal*, 33, 334–365.

Ancona, D. G., and Bresman, H. (2007). *X-Teams: How to Build Teams that Lead, Innovate, and Succeed*. Cambridge, MA: Harvard Business School Press.

Ashforth, B. E. F., and Fried, Y. (1988). The mindlessness of organizational behavior. *Human Relations*, 41, 305–329.

Bechky, B. A. (2006). Gaffers, gofers, and grips: role-based coordination in temporary projects. *Organization Science*, 17, 3–21.

Bechky, B. A., and Okhuysen, G. A. (2008). The element of surprise: Responding to the unexpected through organizational bricolage. Working paper.

Behfar, K. J., Peterson, R. S., Mannix, E. A., and Trochim, W. M. K. (2008). The critical role of conflict resolution in teams: A close look at the links between conflict type, conflict management strategies, and team outcomes. *Journal of Applied Psychology*, 93, 170–188.

Brown, S. L., and Eisenhardt, K. M. (1997). The art of continuous change: Linking complexity theory and time-paced evolution in relentlessly shifting organizations. *Administrative Science Quarterly*, 42, 1–34.

Dean, J. W., and Sharfman, M. P. (1996). Does decision process matter? A study of strategic decision-making effectiveness. *Academy of Management Journal*, 39, 368–396.

Edmondson, A. C., Bohmer, R. M., and Pisano, G. P. (2001). Disrupted routines: Team learning and new technology implementation in hospitals. *Administrative Science Quarterly*, 46, 685–716.

Eisenhardt, K. M. (1989). Making fast strategic decisions in high-velocity environments. *Academy of Management Journal*, 32, 543–576.

Eisenhardt, K. M. (1999). Strategy as strategic decision making. *Sloan Management Review*, 40(3), 65–72.

Eisenhardt, K. M., and Bourgeois, L. J. III (1988). Politics of strategic decision making in high velocity environments: Toward a midrange theory. *Academy of Management Journal*, 31, 737–770.

Eisenhardt, K. M., Kahwajy, J. L., and Bourgeois, L. J. III (1997a). Conflict and strategic choice: How top management teams disagree. *California Management Review*, 39, 42–62.

Eisenhardt, K. M., Kahwajy, J. L., and Bourgeois, L. J. III (1997b). How management teams can have a good fight. *Harvard Business Review*, 75, 77–85.

Feldman, D. C. (1984). The development and enforcement of group norms. *Academy of Management Review*, 9, 47–53.

Gersick, C. J. G. (1989). Marking time: predictable transitions in task groups. *Academy of Management Journal*, 32, 274–309.

Guetzkow, H., and Gyr, J. (1954). An analysis of conflict in decision-making groups. *Human Relations*, 7, 367–381.

Harvey, J. B. (1988). The Abiline paradox: The management of agreement. *Organizational Dynamics*, Summer, 17–43.

Isenberg, D. J (1986). Thinking and managing: A verbal protocol analysis of managerial problem solving. *Academy of Management Journal*, 29, 775–788.

Isenberg, D. J. (1988). How senior managers think. In D. E. Bell, H. Raifa, and A. Tversky (eds), *Decision Making: Descriptive, Normative, and Prescriptive Interactions*. New York: Cambridge University Press.

Janis, I. (1982). *Groupthink: Psychological Studies of Policy Decisions and Fiascoes*. Boston: Houghton-Mifflin.

Jehn, K. A (1995). A multimethod examination of the benefits and detriments of intra-group conflict. *Administrative Science Quarterly*, 40, 256–282.

Jehn, K. A (1997). A qualitative analysis of conflict types and dimensions in organizational groups. *Administrative Science Quarterly*, 42, 530–557.

Jehn, K. A., and Shah, P. P. (1997). Interpersonal relationships and task performance: An examination of mediating processes in friendship and acquaintance groups. *Journal of Personality and Social Psychology*, 72, 775–790.

Kahn, W. A. (1989). Toward a sense of organizational humor: Implications for organizational design and change. *The Journal of Applied Behavioral Science*, 25, 45–63.

Klein, K. J., Ziegert, J. C., Knight, A. P., and Xiao, Y. (2006). Dynamic delegation: Shared, hierarchical, and deindividualized leadership in extreme action teams. *Administrative Science Quarterly*, 51, 590–621.

Levinthal, D., and Rerup, C. (2006). Crossing an apparent chasm: Bridging mindful and less-mindful perspectives on organizational learning. *Organization Science*, 17, 502–513.

Louis, M. R., and Sutton, R. I. (1991). Switching cognitive gears: From habits of mind to active thinking. *Human Relations*, 44, 55–76.

March, J. G., and Simon, H. A. (1958). *Organizations*. New York: Wiley.

Murnighan, J. K., and Conlon, D. E. (1991). The dynamics of intense work groups: a study of British string quartets. *Administrative Science Quarterly*, 36, 165–186.

Okhuysen, G. A. (2001). Structuring change: Familiarity and formal interventions in problem solving groups. *Academy of Management Journal*, 44, 794–808.

Okhuysen, G. A. (2005). Understanding group behavior: How a police SWAT team creates, changes, and manages group routines. In K. D. Elsbach (ed.), *Qualitative Organizational Research* (pp. 139–168). Greenwich, CT: Information Age Publishing.

Okhuysen, G. A., and Eisenhardt, K. M. (2002). Integrating knowledge in groups: How simple formal interventions enable flexibility. *Organization Science*, 13, 370–386.

Perlow, L. A., Okhuysen, G. A., and Repenning, N. (2002). The speed trap: Exploring the relationship between decision making and the temporal context. *Academy of Management Journal*, 45, 931–955.

Reagans, R., Argote, L., and Brooks, D. (2005). Individual experience and experience working together: Predicting learning rates from knowing who knows what and knowing how to work together. *Management Science*, 51, 869–881.

Schweiger, D. M., and Finger, P. A. (1984). The comparative effectiveness of dialectical inquiry and Devil's Advocacy: The impact of task biases on previous research findings. *Strategic Management Journal*, 5, 335–350.

Schweiger, D. M., Sandberg, W. R., and Ragan, J. W. (1986). Group approaches for improving strategic decision making: A comparative analysis of dialectical inquiry, Devil's Advocacy, and consensus. *Academy of Management Journal*, 29, 51–71.

Schweiger, D. M., Sandberg, W. R., and Rechner, P. L. (1989). Experiential effects of dialectical inquiry, Devil's Advocacy, and consensus approaches to strategic decision making. *Academy of Management Journal*, 32, 745–772.

Shah, P. P., and Jehn, K. A. (1993). Do friends perform better than acquaintances? The interaction of friendship, conflict, and task. *Group Decision and Negotiation*, 2, 149–165.

Simon, H. A. (1955). A behavioral model of rational choice. *Quarterly Journal of Economics*, 69, 99–118.

Simons, T. L., and Peterson, R. S. (2000). Task conflict and relationship conflict in top management teams: The pivotal role of intragroup trust. *Journal of Applied Psychology*, 85, 102–111.

Stasser, G. (1992). Information salience and the discovery of hidden profiles by decision-making groups: a "thought experiment". *Organizational Behavior and Human Decision Processes*, 52, 156–181.

Stasser, G., and Stewart, D. (1992). Discovery of hidden profiles by decision-making groups: Solving a problem versus making a judgement. *Journal of Personality and Social Psychology*, 63, 426–434.

Stasser, G., Stewart, D. D., and Wittenbaum, G. M. (1995). Expert roles and information exchange during discussion: The importance of knowing who knows what. *Journal of Experimental and Social Psychology*, 31, 244–265.

Thompson, L., Gentner, D., and Loewenstein, J. (2000). Avoiding missed opportunities in managerial life: Analogical training more powerful than individual case training. *Organizational Behavior and Human Decision Processes*, 82, 60–75.

Valley, K. L., Neale, M. A., and Mannix, E. A. (1995). Friends, lovers, colleagues, strangers: The effects of relationships on the process and outcome of dyadic negotiations. *Research on Negotiation in Organizations*, 5, 65–93.

Wally, S., and Baum, J. R. (1994). Personal and structural determinants of the pace of strategic decision making. *Academy of Management Journal*, 37, 932–956.

Weick, K. E., and Sutcliffe, K. M. (2001). *Managing the Unexpected*. San Francisco: Jossey-Bass.

Ziv, A., and Gadish, O. (1990). The disinhibiting effects of humor: Aggressive and affective responses. *Humor*, 3, 247–257.

EXERCISES

Successful vs. unsuccessful groups

Briefly describe two groups that you have participated in, one that you consider was successful and one that was unsuccessful, explaining the work the groups were trying to accomplish. After you have described the groups, build a table in which you compare the two groups, noting similarities and differences in building collective intuition, the presence or absence of conflict in the group, and how pacing and timing affected the work process. Finally, describe the lessons you can draw from the successful group and describe how, in retrospect, you might have tried to change the dynamics in the unsuccessful group to improve its work process.

Improving group process

Describe a group that you are currently participating in where you would like to improve the group process. After describing the group and its work, indicate how well the group is performing with regards to building collective intuition, exploiting task conflict, and pacing the work. Which elements of group process do you feel need attention? What benefits do you think you could get from improving them? Lastly, describe in detail the actions that you can take to change or modify the group process to gain those benefits.

18

Manage Intra-team Conflict through Collaboration

LAURIE R. WEINGART AND KAREN A. JEHN

The basic principle we espouse in this chapter is that intra-team conflict should be managed using collaboration. Intra-team conflict occurs when team members hold discrepant views or have interpersonal incompatibilities. There has been a debate in organizational research regarding whether agreement or disagreement within teams is advantageous for overall performance. While a recent large-scale analysis of prior research on team conflict (i.e. a meta-analysis) found that on average, all types of conflict (task and relationship) can impede team performance (De Dreu and Weingart, 2003), conflict researchers have also found that while *relationship* conflicts based on personality clashes and interpersonal antagonism are detrimental to team performance and morale, *task* conflicts can be beneficial if managed collaboratively (Amason, 1996; Ensley and Hmieleski, 2005; Jehn, 1995, 1997; Liang, Liu, Lin, and Lin, 2007; Matsuo, 2006; Olson, Parayitam, and Bao, 2007). Our central argument is that collaboration can benefit both task and relationship conflict, but that task conflict should be actively managed (not necessarily eliminated) through collaboration in the work setting whereas relationship conflict should be collaboratively managed off-line, outside the work setting, (or avoided) to ensure high performance of teams.

Collaboration is a joint endeavor, involving two or more people working together to complete a task. Collaboration includes teamwork – the coordination of efforts of a group of people around a stated purpose. It involves constructive discussion among team members regarding the common workgroup goal. Different from negotiations (see Chapter 28), where parties often have divergent interests, teamwork, as we address it, is focused on groups in which members have common goals, thus making collaboration a key component to successful team outcomes. When embedded in the culture of an organization, this can be more than coordination and cooperation, but rather a continuous partnering of people based on shared values (Haskins, Liedtka, and Rosenblum, 1998).

There are three fundamental steps in managing team conflict through collaboration. The first step is to identify the type of intra-team conflict. The second is to identify appropriate collaboration strategies to resolve disputes. We argue that collaboration is a key strategy, but it needs to be applied differently, depending on the type of dispute. The third step is to cultivate conditions that increase the likelihood of collaboration. We address each step below.

IDENTIFYING THE TYPE OF INTRA-TEAM CONFLICT

The first major principle in dealing with intra-team conflict collaboratively is to determine the type of conflict. *Task conflict* involves disagreements among team members on performance-related activities. Some of these performance-related activities have to do with the actual task and others have to do with the process of doing the task or delegating resources and duties.

Task content conflicts are disagreements among group members regarding ideas and opinions about the task being performed, such as disagreement regarding an organization's current hiring strategies or determining the information to include in an annual report. Task content conflicts include debates over facts (driven by data, evidence) or opinions (De Dreu, Harinck, and Van Vianen, 1999). *Task process conflicts* are about logistical and delegation issues such as how task accomplishment should proceed in the work unit, who's responsible for what, and how things should be delegated (Jehn, 1997). They are often about the coordination of the task (e.g. three subtasks need to be completed) or coordination of the people (e.g. we should meet at 3 pm each day to update; Behfar, Mannix, Peterson, and Trochim, 2008). One important distinction about task conflict is that it often provides more useful information about the task, the process, or the people involved and their capabilities (Chapter 17). While the debate can be contentious, the differing views discussed will add to the group's overall store of knowledge. Relationship conflict is less likely to have this informational advantage (Cronin and Bezrukova, 2006).

Relationship conflicts are disagreements and incompatibilities among group members about personal issues that are not task related. Relationship conflicts frequently reported are about social events, gossip, clothing preferences, political views and hobbies (Jehn, 1997). Relationship conflicts are characterized by more personal and interpersonal concerns, can be driven by personality differences, and are more likely to affect group maintenance functions, such as cohesiveness, but can also interfere with task performance.

Take an R&D team: when the different researchers disagree about data interpretation and the meaning of the results, they are experiencing task content conflict. If they argue about who's responsible for writing up the final report and who will make the presentation, they are having a task process conflict. Disagreements about the fastest route to work, automobile gas mileage requirements by the government, politics, religion, and the intelligence level of anyone who would take the bus (which one member does) are relationship conflicts. Ongoing research on the distinction between task and relationship conflict is beginning to separate the content of the relationship conflict (on-task vs off-task) from the emotionality and source of that conflict (Cronin and Bezrukova, 2006; Jehn, Greer, Levine, and Szulanski, 2008; Weingart, Bear, and Todorova, 2008).

Relationship conflicts are characteristically more emotional than task conflicts – and those emotions tend to be negative ones – frustration, anger, stress (Greer and Jehn, 2007). Behavioral expressions of negative emotions include yelling, crying, banging fists, slamming doors, and having an angry tone and, when expressed in this way, are associated with conflict escalation. In contrast, a simple acknowledgment of emotion (e.g. "What you said about me makes me angry"; see Chapter 8) is less likely to elicit a heated exchange, but rather a discussion of causes and attempts to repair.

These negative emotions arise because relationship conflicts often involve threats to people's self-identity or self-esteem – the conflicts are often deeply value laden. For example, a conflict over whether a woman or minority could make a good US president taps into deeply held values and can be very personal both to men and women and majority and minority members. When negative emotions run high, collaboration between the disputants might not be possible. Collaboration requires a high level of interdependence and willingness to work together. Team members that feel animosity, frustration, anger, or distrust are not likely to be willing to rely on one another.

In contrast, task conflict tends not to be as deeply rooted in people's value systems. However, that's not to say that task conflict is never emotional. Debates of how to perform a task can get very heated – often because both sides believe they are right and have strong convictions to their opinions (Cronin and Bezrukova, 2006; Jehn, 1997).

People can also experience positive emotions in response to conflict. Consider a debate about an organization's strategy that is stimulating and energizing. Many positive emotions can accompany those task conflicts – happiness, elation, positive challenge. Ongoing research suggests that task conflict elicits more active positive emotions (e.g. active, interested, alert) as compared to other types of emotions (negative emotions and passive, positive emotions, e.g. content, at ease, quiet), whereas relationship conflict is more likely to elicit all types of emotions, but passive, positive emotions to a lesser extent.

Two other aspects of conflict that are important to consider are the dynamic nature of conflict and the different individual perspectives that members have. Conflicts can transform from task-oriented conflict to more relationship-focused conflicts over time. We consider this in the section on using collaboration to overcome the escalation of conflict. Thus, when considering the type of conflict, we also need to take into account the context within which it occurs and the origins of the conflict (Jehn and Mannix, 2001; Greer, Jehn, and Mannix, 2008). For example, what currently appears as an intense interpersonal conflict could have begun as a series of conflicts over task performance. On the other hand, relationship conflicts can also be disguised as, or turn into, task conflicts such that if a member has a personal issue with another member they may sabotage the group by undermining any opinion or suggestion the other member may have.

In addition, individuals within groups may have different perceptions about the level or type of conflict in the group (Jehn and Chatman, 2000; Jehn and Rispens, 2008). One member may perceive that there is a high level of conflict while others may think there is no problem. This can interfere with the process of resolution as it is difficult to find a collaborative solution when there is not even agreement as to whether there is a conflict or not. A first step, that we discuss in detail later, is to recognize the differences in perceptions and communicate openly regarding the existence (or lack) of conflict within the group.

IDENTIFYING APPROPRIATE COLLABORATION STRATEGIES

We assert that the detrimental effect of relationship conflict can be minimized if collaboratively managed *outside* of the task setting and the beneficial effect of task conflict can be maximized if collaboratively managed *within* the task setting. Thus, the appropriate collaborative strategy depends on the type of conflict experienced.

Task conflict

Although task conflict has been shown to have an overall negative impact on team performance (De Dreu and Weingart, 2003), it *can* improve decision quality, strategic planning, learning, and creativity (Amason and Schweiger, 1994; Cosier and Rose, 1977; De Dreu, 2006; Jehn and Rupert, 2008; see also Chapter 17). The cognitive, task-focused aspect of conflict can enhance the assessment of shared information and deliberate, careful assessment of alternatives. The useful give and take among members, the consultative interaction and problem solving, and the increased information exchanged enhance performance. Avoidance or suppression of conflict has been shown to interfere with team performance. When members agree with other group members about concepts or actions without presenting dissenting viewpoints, superior alternatives may be overlooked and thus performance may be suboptimal (Janis, 1982; see also Chapter 25). Putting pressure on dissenters, self-censorship, and collective justifications (all associated with groupthink) increase defective decision making (Chapter 17).

Relationship conflict

While *direct* collaboration is effective for task conflict, it is less so for relationship conflict. Collaboration (or contention) over non-task issues takes much time away from task performance, thus reducing functioning and effectiveness (De Dreu and Weingart, 2003; Murnighan and Conlon, 1991). However, collaboration *can* be used effectively to resolve many relationship conflicts when engaged offline. Offline discussions give team members opportunities to discuss relationship conflicts in a more private and personal forum. Without an audience, disputants should be less likely to posture and more likely to be open to the other party's point of view. Offline discussions can be engaged directly by the disputants or with the help of others. Sometimes facilitation might be necessary to bring the disputants together and dampen negative emotions.

However, some relationship conflicts are better avoided. Relationship conflicts that have their roots in deeply held values and assumptions are often impossible to resolve in the workplace where activities are primarily task focused. Thus, trying to get at true underlying interests for relationship conflicts may result in even more intractable disputes, distracting from task performance and escalating negativity. When relationship conflicts have a low potential for resolution they are sometimes better to avoid (De Dreu and Van Vianen, 2001; Druckman, 1994).

CULTIVATE CONDITIONS THAT PROMOTE COLLABORATION

Collaboration is effective in managing conflict, task or relationship, in that it sets a positive, team-oriented tone for the group (Mintzberg, Dougherty, Jorgensen, and Westley, 1996). However, collaboration doesn't just happen. Collaboration within teams must be fostered by promoting a team orientation, composing the team of members who are motivated to cooperate and think deeply, and reinforcing actions that promote problem solving (i.e. member behavior). Although we talk about team orientation, team member motives, and team member behavior as distinct categories, they are interrelated. For example, certain team member behaviors (e.g. information exchange) will influence a team orientation (e.g. open communication norms) and vice versa.

Create a team orientation

For a team to be collaborative, its atmosphere must support interdependence, reliance, respect, trust, open communication, and collective efficacy (Chapter 10). While a team orientation can be considered a precondition for effective collaboration, it will also improve as the group experiences successful collaborative events. In this way, norms are developed which perpetuate interdependence, reliance on, and respect for one another.

Framing. Creating a team orientation refers to framing the group's activities as belonging to the team rather than solely as a set of individual accomplishments. A common group goal and a superordinate team identity can promote this (see Chapters 9 and 17). With a team orientation, there is a sense that although we are *each* responsible for our individual contributions to the group, "we" are *jointly* responsible for the group's final product. Team-oriented members take personal pride in the team's performance and feel personally successful when the team is successful.

Team goals. When team goals and individual goals support one another, teams that focus on a meta-goal or team-goal are more likely to have constructive conflict management (Thatcher and Jehn, 1998). This is in contrast to the case where individuals focus *only* on their own contribution, claiming (or denying) responsibility for the overall group's performance.

Develop collective efficacy. Collective efficacy refers to a group's shared belief in its capabilities to perform a task (in this case, resolve a conflict) (Bandura, 1997; also see Chapter 10). Often what is most important in predicting high performance is that team members feel they have the capabilities to resolve the task and relationship conflicts at hand (Jehn et al., 2008). If members feel they, or others in the group, have the capabilities to constructively manage the conflict, they will engage in positive discussions with one another relying on the competence of the group to reach a satisfactory resolution consistent with the group goal.

Collective efficacy is driven both by the team's beliefs about its ability to work as a unit as well as team members' beliefs about their own and others' capabilities. Self-efficacy (held by an individual) can be raised using several mechanisms (Bandura, 1997; and, as noted, see Chapter 10), three of which also seem relevant to collective efficacy in teams. First, collective efficacy can be raised through "enactive mastery experience," in our case, prior successes at managing similar, challenging conflicts that required effort and perseverance to overcome (Jehn et al., 2008). Through experience, team members learn effective strategics for diagnosing and managing conflict, which increase their confidence for managing future conflicts that might arise. Second, collective efficacy can be raised through observing and modeling other teams' collaboration strategies. Teams that can observe similar teams' inner workings and subsequent performance can use that information as a comparator to determine where they stand relative to others. They can also learn from the other team's successes and failures. Third, collective efficacy can be raised via social persuasion – when others express confidence in the team's capabilities.

Affective integration.   A key component in collaborative approaches to conflict resolution is the attitudes members have toward one another. Affective integration is a group-level concept representing the feelings that team members hold for one another, specifically in terms of their interpersonal trust, respect, and liking (Cronin, Bezrukova, Weingart, and Tinsley, 2008; Weingart, Cronin, Houser, Cagan, and Vogel, 2005). These attitudes influence the beliefs about and behavioral inclinations members have toward each other. Trust evokes beliefs that others can be relied upon (Rotter, 1971). This is often called trustworthiness, and it leads to the willingness to be confident in another person's competence, integrity, and good will (Chapter 21). Respect, on the other hand, evokes beliefs about the intrinsic value of others and liking implies a general attraction to others (Chaiken, 1987) and at the group level this is often conceptualized as cohesion (Festinger, 1950).

Affective integration increases the likelihood that team members' assets (knowledge, skills, and abilities or KSAs) are actually used by the team while collaborating. Both trust and respect play a key role. Trust influences the willingness to share information and receive information as accurate (Carnevale and Lawler, 1986; Kimmel, Pruitt, Magenau, Konar-Goldband, and Carnevale, 1980). Without trust, team members will be unwilling to rely on the KSAs of others for fear that teammates might not follow through on their promises or work to undermine teammates' interests. Respect is what leads people to a priori assume potential utility in the ideas of others. People will devote more attention to these ideas in order to find the value that they assume exists.

Affective integration also buffers against the stresses and strains that often arise as a result of team conflict. Trust decreases the likelihood that task conflicts will be perceived as attacking or personal in nature (Simons and Peterson, 2000) because of the implied benevolence in those who are trusted. When people respect each other they take great care not to violate fairness norms regarding how people should behave toward one another (Bies and Moag, 1986). Respect has been shown to relate to (perceptions of) fair treatment as well as the inclination to acknowledge others' status and dignity (Tyler, Degoey, and Smith, 1996; Tyler and Lind, 1992). Finally, liking and its resultant cohesion can serve to prevent people from withdrawing from each other in the face of conflict.

Open and constructive conflict communication norms.   Collaboration requires norms for the expression of task-related conflict that support freedom to disagree and to constructively respond. Conflict communication norms can either be open to a free exchange of concerns and dissention, discouraging, or avoidant of those exchanges. If group members feel that it is appropriate and acceptable to discuss their differing opinions, disagreements are more likely to have a positive effect on group process and performance than if these disagreements are discouraged or avoided (Lovelace, Shapiro, and Weingart, 2001). However, openness must be accompanied by restraint and respect for others' contributions so that conflicts do not escalate and become more emotional, relationship conflicts. Openness can be communicated by using an inquiry approach to group decision making (Garvin and Roberto, 2001), for example allowing others to make their point without interruption, asking questions to improve your understanding, and engaging in active listening (i.e. repeating back what others have said in your own words to ensure that you heard and understood what they said) (Rogers and Farson, 1979). The ideal culture for a group is to have conflict norms that will allow constructive, open task-related debates but not critical, personal attacks detrimental to performance.

When task conflict is suppressed, the lines of communication will need to be opened for collaboration to be successful. Openness and trust must be nurtured within these teams (Simons and Peterson, 2000). Trust must be allowed to develop over time – through positive experiences group members will grow more comfortable engaging in collaboration. The team leader can play an important role in setting the norms for open conflict communication in the team (see Chapters 15 and 21). Research shows that teams with leaders who are rated to be effective experience more constructive conflict, more freedom to express doubts, and are more innovative (Lovelace et al., 2001; Manz, Barstein, Hostager, and Shapiro, 1989; Van de Ven and Chu, 1989). In addition, providing the team with the collaborative skills through training can aid in successful conflict management.

Identify team members with a propensity to collaborate

A team is more likely to engage in collaboration if its members are inclined to use collaboration. A team member's propensity to collaborate will be higher when he or she is motivated to work hard toward improving outcomes for oneself and for other members of the team. This requires a cooperative orientation (focus on self and others) (Van Lange, 1999) and epistemic motivation (the desire to develop and hold a rich and accurate understanding of the world) (Kruglanski, 1989). A cooperative orientation provides a focus on collaboration whereas epistemic motivation provides the drive (De Dreu and Carnevale, 2003). Both are needed for groups to be effective; for example, for win–win agreements to be achieved (De Dreu, Beersma, Stroebe, and Euwema, 2006).

Cooperative orientation.   Team members who are cooperatively oriented place value on maximizing outcomes for all team members and tend to engage in more collaboration as a means to this end (De Dreu, Weingart, and Kwon, 2000; Messick and McClintock, 1968). People who only care about themselves (individualistically oriented) have less interest in collaboration (Messick and McClintock, 1968). Since people who are solely interested in their own achievements will have little interest in teamwork, they may be better off working alone or having their ideas communicated to a group by a third party (Locke, Tirnauer, Roberson, Goldman, Latham, and Weldon, 2001). This is not to denigrate independent thinking which is the basis for constructive conflict (Chapter 17) – without independent thinking within groups (and the conflict that results), the group easily lapses into conformity and groupthink (Locke et al., 2001).

Cooperative orientations influence quality of agreements through their effect on group member behavior (De Dreu et al., 2000; Weingart, Bennett, and Brett, 1993). Cooperatively motivated team members tend to engage in more integrative/problem-solving tactics (e.g. truthful information exchange about preferences and priorities, multi-issue offers, tradeoffs) and fewer contentious tactics (e.g. threats, substantiation of position, power tactics) than do team members who are only individualistically motivated. Groups with mainly individualistic members, however, sometimes realize that disinterest in group collaboration will not allow them to reach an agreement and cooperation is necessary to reach their own goals (often referred to as "enlightened self-interest"; Rubin, 1991), resulting in a shift to team problem solving when they hit an impasse and are aware they are working with other people like themselves (Schei, Rognes, and De Dreu, 2008). As implied earlier, cooperative groups can become *too* cooperative, resulting in compromise (giving in rather than problem solving) and suboptimal agreements. This is most likely to occur when they do not have a strong reason to resist yielding, for example when they are under time pressure, have low aspirations, have bad alternatives, or are not accountable to others (De Dreu et al., 2000; Pruitt and Rubin, 1986).

To remedy the above, individualistically motivated group members can adopt problem solving to achieve their goals as a way to avoid impasse and cooperative group members may adopt more competitive strategies to protect themselves from being dominated by individualists who do not want to cooperate. However, the latter is more likely (Kelly and Stahelski, 1970). Faced with conflicting member motives, cooperative negotiators have been shown to become more competitive than individualists are to become more cooperative (Weingart, Brett, Olekalns, and Smith, 2007).

Although cooperatives will shift their overall approach toward competition as the number of individualists increases, they may also attempt to shift the interaction back to cooperation by strategically interjecting collaborative behaviors. For example, cooperatives who were in the minority in negotiating groups responded to attempts by individualists to claim value by providing information that could be used to find mutually beneficial agreements (i.e. integrative information). They also rewarded the individualists for providing integrative information by reciprocating with additional integrative information (Weingart et al., 2007).

Whereas these orientations (called "social value orientations" in the research literature) are treated as relatively stable individual differences, situational cues can also influence one's propensity to collaborate. As such, moving a group toward collaboration would require either changing the composition of the team to all cooperative members (via turnover and selection) or providing strong cues about the collaborative nature of the task and the cooperative motives of others. Team members can be instructed to adopt a cooperative approach or be incentivized, making cooperation in everyone's self-interest. Instructions from a supervisor or rewards for high joint value agreements have been shown to be effective. The expectation that team members will continue to interact on cooperative tasks in the future ("expected cooperative future interaction") has also been shown to increase cooperative motives (De Dreu et al., 2000). Finally, team members can adjust their motives in response to the behaviors of others in the group. Cooperative actions by others can serve as a signal of willingness to collaborate, but individualistically oriented members also need assurances that cooperation is in their own self-interest (Locke et al., 2001).

Epistemic motives.   People with high epistemic motivation have a desire to gain knowledge, think deeply, and more thoroughly process information. They engage in more deliberative and systematic processing (De Dreu and Carnevale, 2003). In that people with high epistemic motivation process information more thoroughly and are more likely to revise their view of a given situation (De Dreu, Koole, and Steinel, 2000), it is likely they would make strong contributions to collaborative teams.

People with low epistemic motivation are believed to solve problems and make decisions using heuristic processing, which is relatively quick and effortless. Low epistemic motivation has been shown to impede the quality of information processing and the collaborativeness of group decision making. Research on negotiation shows that low epistemic motivation increases reliance on stereotypes and irrelevant anchoring information

(De Dreu et al., 1999). Small groups composed of members with a high need for closure have been found to be less egalitarian in their decision making and more tolerant of an authoritarian leader (De Grada, Kruglanski, Pierro, and Mannetti, 1999), both of which run counter to collaboration.

Like a cooperative orientation, epistemic motivation is jointly determined by individual differences and situational cues. People with low epistemic motivation are likely to have a high need for closure (Webster and Kruglanski, 1994). The internal pressure to quickly complete the task at hand associated with a high need for closure tends to limit the motivation to deeply process information. Similarly, external time pressure has been shown to limit team members' epistemic motivation (De Dreu et al., 1999).

To increase the odds that a team includes epistemically motivated members, one could screen people in terms of their need for closure or for cognition. In addition, epistemic motivation can be induced by reducing time pressure (reducing the need for closure) or making them accountable for their process. Process accountability has been shown to increase epistemic motivation because when people expect to be observed and evaluated by others regarding the processes they engage they are more likely to use a more thorough process (Lerner and Tetlock, 1999).

Propensity to collaborate as a combination of cooperative orientations and epistemic motives.   The two dimensions, *cooperative orientations and epistemic motives*, are independent – cooperatives and individualists can hold high or low epistemic motivation. However, both a cooperative motive and high epistemic motivation are necessary for team members to effectively collaborate (De Dreu et al., 2006). Team members who hold the goal of maximizing joint (individual and group) gain *and* are motivated to process information thoroughly are most likely to engage in problem-solving behaviors and succeed in mixed-motive negotiations. The same should hold in teamwork contexts.

Team member behavior

Collaboration is enacted through group member behavior. Thus it is important to identify the behaviors that constitute collaboration. Although collaboration differs from negotiation, we can look to the negotiation literature to consider how to manage conflict in collaborative settings. The negotiation literature has identified *integration of interests* as a collaborative strategic approach for managing conflict (see Chapter 28). Integration of interests includes increasing the availability of resources (thus, "expanding the pie") as well as sharing in the distribution of those resources. The literature on integrative negotiation has identified a host of tactics that aid in the identification of opportunities for joint gain. We focus on three that are central to the process: exchange information, use packaging and tradeoffs, and work to break the chain of conflict escalation.

Exchange information.   A key mechanism for enacting an integrative strategic approach involves the exchange of accurate information. Exchanging information increases insight into the other party's preferences and priorities and the probability that negotiators will find integrative agreements, if a zone of agreement exists (Pruitt, 1981; Putnam and Jones, 1982). The benefit of sharing information varies depending on the type of information that is shared and how it is used. Sharing factual information, like constraints or costs, can be used to merely inform the other party (a collaborative application) or to substantiate one's position in an attempt to persuade the other party (a less collaborative approach). Sharing information about preferences for a given issue (i.e. what you want and why you should have it your way) can be more confrontational in nature and does not necessarily improve the quality of an agreement (Weingart, Hyder, and Prietula, 1996). In contrast, exchanging information about priorities across issues (i.e. the relative import-ance of the issues to a negotiator and why) represents an effective, collaborative type of information exchange as it involves multiple issues and can facilitate tradeoffs across issues (Pruitt and Lewis, 1975; Thompson, 1991).

Use packaging and tradeoffs.   It is not uncommon for discussions of multi-issue conflicts to progress one issue at a time – with the group resolving one issue before moving to the next. The problem with this approach is that tradeoffs cannot be made across issues. Tradeoffs occur when both parties make concessions on less important issues (to them-selves) to gain advantage on another (Pruitt, 1981). This tactic is effective at reconciling interests when parties have differing priorities on issues when each party gains more than they lose in the tradeoff.

When team members are unwilling to share this information (because they fear the other party might not reciprocate, putting themselves at an information disadvantage), effective tradeoffs can be identified by exchanging multi-issue offers (i.e. packaging). When issues are packaged together, instead of being considered independently and sequentially, it is easier to arrange trades or concessions as negotiators search for packages that are mutually beneficial (Thompson, Mannix, and Bazerman, 1988; Weingart et al., 1993). Discovering tradeoffs through the exchange of packaged offers is a more indirect method in that team members must infer other's priorities by stated package preferences (Adair, Weingart, and Brett, 2007).

Work to break the chain of conflict escalation.   One of the most difficult aspects of a successful negotiation is trying to balance the cooperative and competitive components of mixed-motive negotiations (Lax and Sebenius, 1986). Once a conflict takes on a competitive or personal tone (i.e. becomes a relationship conflict), it is very difficult to shift it to a more cooperative task-focused interaction, as the conflict can escalate into a destructive cycle. One way to break the chain of contentious behavior is to respond with integra-tive, collaborative responses (Brett, Shapiro, and Lytle, 1998; Putnam and Jones, 1982). Collaboration is then more likely to continue when that collaborative behavior is recip-rocated than when it is not (Weingart, Prietula, Hyder, and Genovese, 1999). Another method for breaking conflict spirals is explicitly labeling the contentious reciprocation as unproductive during the interaction. When a conflict is contentious and one party identi-fies the process as such, the other party would be hesitant to continue in a contentious manner without appearing irrational. Directly responding to a threat by identifying it ("Are you threatening me?") demonstrates that the threat was not effective and may cause the party making the threat to shift tactics or refocus onto the process (Brett et al., 1998).

Another component of conflict that encourages a negative escalation cycle is emotion (see Chapter 8). When people begin to take negative comments about their task perfor-mance or ideas personally, the conflict becomes more emotional and task conflict can escalate to become relationship conflict. Relationship conflict of this type is best handled by mediation by an outside party to sort through the negative emotions and ascribe more positive attributions to team members' behavior. Another option is that team members who are not emotionally inflamed might take the disputants off-site, such as into a social setting for drinks, or a walk, where they can reestablish their interpersonal bonds and discuss their concerns. If the negative emotions are so inflamed among two members that they are not willing to talk, we recommend having two members who are closest to each of the adversaries talk, collaboratively, with each of the parties. Then the two facilitators (i.e. 3rd and 4th parties) can talk and try to bring all four together. Finally, a trusted outsider to the team (e.g. manager or colleague) could help high negative emotion teams get to the point where they can engage in collaboration and constructive conflict without assuming the worst of others. When possible, irrational team members can be replaced.

CASE EXAMPLES

In order to illustrate the use of collaboration in teams, we present two case examples of team conflict: one managed ineffectively, the other effectively. These examples are compilations of conflicts we have observed in our research on teams in organizations. Both examples involve task conflict within cross-functional product development teams working to design a high-quality, low-cost automobile that will meet customers' preferences and desires. These teams are comprised of many parties (including marketing representatives and suppliers), but here we will focus on two central parties – designers and engineers. Each subgroup has its own concerns. The designers are responsible for the brand image and appearance of the car. The engineers are responsible for the functioning of the car and its components and have primary responsibility for keeping costs within budget. Unfortunately, these interests are not always in line with one another.

Dysfunctional cross-functional product development team

Consider a cross-functional product development team designing a subsystem of a new model of an automobile. This team is responsible for the design of the car's interior. They are at mid stage in the design process. Many decisions have been made about the design and functionality of the interior. Models have been developed and general layouts for components (e.g. the console, instrument panel, etc.) have been determined. Engineering feels it has worked out most of the major functionality issues and was able to remain within budget, but just barely. Then design comes in with a change in styling. In order to maintain brand identity, the shape and flow from the instrument panel to the console needs to change. Engineering is furious. Implications for this change are large. The changes will require a redesign of the placement of internal components within the instrument panel and console. To make these changes will be costly – it will require money that is not there. Design is indifferent to these concerns – they believe that the aesthetic component is what sells the car – and their job is to make sure the automobile sends a coherent message to the customer.

Each group sees the problem from its own perspective and neither is willing to give ground. Engineering tells design, "It can't be done." Design is tired of engineering's "no can do" attitude and continues to put pressure on engineering until engineering is willing to "make it work." Several meetings occur in which engineering and design try to convince the other on the merits of their positions. Arguments get heated, tempers flare. Little progress is made. After many heated discussions, a compromise solution is reached which moves away from the design intent, compromises functionality, and increases cost.

This conflict can be characterized as a task conflict with low resolution potential (i.e. team members have low collective efficacy). It involved an important aspect of their task performance and needed to be resolved, but neither side believed they had the ability to resolve the conflict. There was no sense of a shared fate – rather than focus on developing the best product, each side focused on its own concerns. Conflict norms were more toward blaming and attacking than listening and building. Negative emotions were evoked. What transpired was a contentious conflict, pitting "us" against "them," resulting in a solution that neither party was especially happy with. Was there another way out of this conflict? What could the team have done to find a better solution?

Collaborative integrated product development (IPD) team

Consider another design team working on the same component. This team faces the same change in styling. But this time, design presents the change in terms of a shared problem – they take responsibility for the change and are willing to consider its implications. Engineering is then willing to collaborate with design to try to make the change possible. The IPD team has a frank discussion about the implications of the change. Design tries to come up with less expensive and less disruptive ways to change the console and instrument panel while maintaining design intent. Engineering tries to develop innovative ways to fit the internal components in the new space. They also start looking for additional sources of funding for the change from the overall vehicle budget. Some discussions grow heated, but because frustration is focused on the problem rather than one another, tension is quickly dispersed. Several potential solutions are developed. A dominant option emerges which includes a slight design modification that provides adequate space for a key component and some additional funding is found.

This conflict situation differed in several ways from the previous example. While the conflict was just as important and difficult to resolve, collective efficacy was high. Both engineers and designers believed a solution was possible. They viewed themselves as a team tackling a common problem. As such, members were cooperatively oriented and epistemically motivated to work hard to find a mutually beneficial solution. Conflict norms supported open information exchange and constructive discussions. Emotions remained under control (Chapter 8). An integrative solution evolved because the entire IPD team "owned" the problem and worked together, collaboratively, to develop a solution. They trusted one another's expertise, motives, and information in a way that allowed them to reach a mutually satisfactory solution. A team orientation, trust in one another, and a belief that a jointly beneficial solution was possible motivated the team to search together for a solution. This search involved sharing information, creativity, some tradeoffs, and an effort to avoid turning task frustration into personal attacks. In addition to a high-quality agreement, this successful conflict resolution process reinforced the team's belief in its ability to solve problems and will make the team more willing to tackle similar problems in the future.

Summary of cases

The first team's conflict was very contentious, plagued by low affective integration and individualistic orientations – an "us versus them" framing of the problem. In contrast, the collaborative team shared ownership of the problem and developed solutions that recognized the concerns and interests of all parties involved. The first team was not willing to openly share information nor did they trust the information that was received. The information exchange that did occur served the purpose of bolstering a priori positions. In contrast, the collaborative team used information to develop understanding and potential solutions. Because motives were cooperative, it was easier to trust the information provided. In addition, they worked hard at processing the information made available to them, signaling high epistemic motivation. Finally, where the first team was very positional in making demands ("my way is the only way") resulting in a stalemate, the collaborative team used creativity and tradeoffs to develop potential solutions. What resulted for the non-collaborative team was a time-consuming, contentious, and sometimes emotional and personal conflict and an unsatisfactory solution. The collaborative team was able to succeed because it managed the conflict by focusing on team goals, exchanging truthful information, developing trust, and using tradeoffs and creativity to find integrative solutions that satisfied both engineering and design's concerns.

Conclusion

The literature on teamwork, negotiation, and conflict provided the foundation for this chapter. The principles gleaned from this prior research demonstrate that the broad set of activities associated with collaboration can be used to effectively manage team conflict. Managing task conflict via collaboration can improve the quality of team decision making and performance. Collaboration is fostered when there is a strong team orientation, team members are both cooperatively and epistemically motivated, and team members engage in problem-solving behaviors. Yet, the management of conflict is often difficult because negative emotions are easily evoked – defensiveness, anger, frustration. Collaboration provides a way to focus more objectively on the task at hand and integrate conflicting perspectives.

References

Adair, W., Weingart, L.R., and Brett, J. (2007). The timing and function of offers in U.S. and Japanese negotiations. *Journal of Applied Psychology*, 92, 1056–1068.

Amason, A. (1996). Distinguishing effects of functional and dysfunctional conflict on strategic decision making: Resolving a paradox for top management teams. *Academy of Management Journal*, 39, 123–148.

Amason, A., and Schweiger, D.M. (1994). Resolving the paradox of conflict, strategic decision making, and organizational performance. *International Journal of Conflict Management*, 5, 239–253.

Bandura, A. (1997). *Self-efficacy: The Exercise of Control*. NY: W. H. Freeman.

Behfar, K., Mannix, E., Peterson, R., and Trochim, W. (2008). Coordinating both people and task: Revisiting and explicating the process conflict construct. Paper presented at the Academy of Management, Anaheim, CA, August.

Bies, R. J., and Moag, J. S. (1986). Interactional justice: Communication criteria of fairness. In R. J. Lewicki, B. H. Sheppard, and M. H. Bazerman (eds), *Research on Negotiation in Organizations* (Vol. 1, pp. 43–55). Greenwich, CT: JAI Press.

Brett, J., Shapiro, D., and Lytle, A. (1998). Breaking the bonds of reciprocity in negotiations. *Academy of Management Journal*, 41, 410–424.

Carnevale, P., and Lawler, E. (1986). Time pressure and the development of integrative agreements in bilateral negotiations. *Journal of Conflict Resolution*, 30, 639–659.

Chaiken, S. (1987). The heuristic model of persuasion. In M. P. Zanna and J. M. Olson (eds), *Social Influence: The Ontario Symposium* (Vol. 5, pp. 3–39). Hillsdale, NJ: Lawrence Erlbaum Assoc., Inc.

Cosier, R., and Rose, G. (1977). Cognitive conflict and goal conflict effects on task performance. *Organizational Behavior and Human Performance*, 19, 378–391.

Cronin, M. A., and Bezrukova, K. (2006). Sweet and sour conflict: Information and affront as active ingredients of disagreements. Presented at International Association of Conflict Management Conference, June 2006, Montreal, Canada.

Cronin, M. A., Bezrukova, K., Weingart, L. R., and Tinsley, C. (2008). Subgroups within a team: the role of cognitive and affective states. Manuscript under review.

De Dreu, C. K. W. (2006). When too little or too much hurts: evidence for a curvilinear relationship between task conflict and innovation in teams. *Journal of Management*, 32, 83–107.

De Dreu, C. K. W., Beersma, B., Stroebe, K., and Euwema, M. C. (2006). Motivated information processing, strategic choice, and the quality of negotiated agreement. *Journal of Personality and Social Psychology*, 90, 927–943.

De Dreu, C. K. W., and Carnevale, P. J. D. (2003). Motivational bases for information processing and strategic choice in conflict and negotiation. In M. P. Zanna (ed.), *Advances in Experimental Social Psychology* (Vol. 35, pp. 235–291). New York, Academic Press.

De Dreu, C. K. W., Evers, A., Beersma, B., Kluwer, E. S., and Nauta, A. (2001). A theory based measure of conflict management strategies in the workplace. *Journal of Organizational Behavior*, 22, 645–668.

De Dreu, C. K. W., Harinck, F., and Van Vianen, A. E. M. (1999). Conflict and performance in groups and organizations. *International Review of Industrial and Organizational Psychology*, 14, 369–414.

De Dreu, C. K. W., Koole, S., and Steinel, W. (2000). Unfixing the fixed pie: A motivated information-processing account of integrative negotiation. *Journal of Personality and Social Psychology*, 79, 975–987.

De Dreu, C. K. W., and Van Vianen, E. M. (2001). Managing relationship conflict and the effectiveness of organizational teams. *Journal of Organizational Behavior*, 22, 309–328.

De Dreu, C. K. W., and Weingart, L. R. (2003). Task versus relationship conflict, team performance, and team member satisfaction: A meta-analysis. *Journal of Applied Psychology*, 88, 741–749.

De Dreu, C. K. W., Weingart, L. R., and Kwon, S. (2000). Influence of social motives on integrative negotiations: A meta-analytic review and test of two theories. *Journal of Personality and Social Psychology*, 78, 889–905.

De Grada, E., Kruglanski, A. W., Pierro, A., and Mannetti, L. (1999). Motivated cognition and group interaction: Need for closure affects the contents and processes of collective negotiations. *Journal of Experimental Social Psychology*, 35, 346–365.

Druckman, D. (1994). Determinants of compromising behavior in negotiation. *Journal of Conflict Resolution*, 38, 507–556.

Ensley, M. D., and Hmieleski, K. A. (2005). A comparative study of new venture top management team composition, dynamics and performance between university-based and independent start-ups. *Research Policy*, 34, 1091–1105.

Festinger, L. (1950). Informal social communication. *Psychological Review*, Unpublished doctoral dissertation, University of California, Santa Barbara, 57, 271–282.

Garvin, D. A., and Roberto, M. A. (2001). What you don't know about making decisions. *Harvard Business Review*, September, 108–116.

Greer, L., and Jehn, K. (2007). The pivotal role of emotion in intragroup process conflict. In M. Neale, E., Mannix, and C. Anderson (eds), *Research on Managing Groups and Teams* (pp. 21–43). Greenwich, CT: JAI Press.

Greer, L. L., Jehn, K. A., and Mannix, E. A. (2008). Conflict transformation: An exploration of the relationships between task, relationship, and process conflict and the moderating role of resolution potential. *Small Group Research*, 39(3), 278–302.

Haskins, M. E., Liedtka, J., and Rosenblum, J. (1998). Beyond teams: Toward an ethic of collaboration. *Organizational Dynamics*, Spring, 34–50.

Janis, I. L. (1982). *Victims of Groupthink* (2nd edition). Boston: Houghton-Mifflin.

Jehn, K. (1995). A multimethod examination of the benefits and detriments of intragroup conflict. *Administrative Science Quarterly*, 40, 256–282.

Jehn, K. (1997). A qualitative analysis of conflict types and dimensions in organizational groups. *Administrative Science Quarterly*, 42, 530–557.

Jehn, K. A., and Chatman, J. (2000). The influence of proportional and perceptual conflict composition on team performance. *International Journal of Conflict Management*, 11(1), 56–73.

Jehn, K. A., and Mannix, E. (2001). The dynamic nature of conflict: A longitudinal study of intragroup conflict and group performance. *Academy of Management Journal*, 44(2), 238–251.

Jehn, K., Greer, L., Levine, S., and Szulanski, G. (2008). The effects of conflict types, dimensions, and emergent states on group outcomes. *Group Decision and Negotiation*, 17(6), 465–495.

Jehn, K., and Rispens, S. (2008). Conflict in workgroups. In C. L. Cooper and J. Barling (eds), *Handbook in Organizational Behavior*. Sage Publications Ltd.

Jehn, K., and Rupert, J. (2008). Group faultlines and team learning: How to benefit from different perspectives. In V. Sessa and M. London (eds), *Continuous Learning in Organizations: Individual, Group, and Organizational Perspectives* (pp. 119–148). Lawrence Erlbaum Press.

Kelley, H. H., and Stahelski, A. J. (1970). Social interaction basis of cooperators' and competitors' beliefs about others. *Journal of Personality and Social Psychology*, 16, 66–91.

Kimmel, M. J., Pruitt, D. G., Magenau, J. M., Konar-Goldband, E., and Carnevale, P. J. D. (1980). Effects of trust, aspiration, and gender on negotiation tactics. *Journal of Personality and Social Psychology*, 38, 9–23.

Kruglanski, A. W. (1989). The psychology of being "right": The problem of accuracy in social perception and cognition. *Psychological Bulletin*, 106, 395–409.

Lax, D. A., and Sebenius, J. K. (1986). *The Manager as Negotiator: Bargaining for Cooperation and Competitive Gain*. New York: Free Press.

Lerner, J. S., and Tetlock, P.E. (1999). Accounting for the effects of accountability. *Psychological Bulletin*, 125, 255–275.

Liang, T. P., Liu, C. C., Lin, T. M., and Lin, B. (2007). Effect of team diversity on software project performance. *Industrial Management and Data Systems*, 107, 636–653.

Locke, E. A., Tirnauer, D., Roberson, Q., Goldman, B., Latham, M. E., and Weldon, E. (2001). The importance of the individual in an age of groupism. In. M. E. Turner (ed.), *Groups at Work: Theory and Research* (pp. 501–528). Mahwah, NJ: Lawrence Erlbaum.

Lovelace, K., Shapiro, D. L., and Weingart, L. R. (2001). Maximizing crossfunctional new product teams' innovativeness and constraint adherence: A conflict communications perspective. *Academy of Management Journal*, 44, 779–783.

Manz, C. C., Barstein, D. T., Hostager, T. J., and Shapiro, G. L. (1989). Leadership and innovation: a longitudinal process view. In A. Van de Ven, H. L. Angle, and M. S. Poole (eds), *Research on the Management of Innovation: The Minnesota Studies* (pp. 613–636). New York: Harper and Row.

Matsuo, M. (2006). Customer orientation, conflict, and innovativeness in Japanese sales departments. *Journal of Business Research*, 59, 242–250.

Messick, D. M., and McClintock, C. G. (1968). Motivational basis of choice in experimental games. *Journal of Experimental Social Psychology*, 4, 1–25.

Mintzberg, H., Dougherty, D., Jorgensen, J., and Westley F. (1996). Some surprising things about collaboration – knowing how people connect makes it work better. *Organizational Dynamics*, Spring, 60–71.

Murnighan, J., and Conlon, D. (1991). The dynamics of intense work groups: A study of British string quartets. *Administrative Science Quarterly*, 36, 165–186.

Olson, B. J., Parayitam, S., and Bao, Y. (2007). Strategic decision making: the effects of cognitive diversity, conflict, and trust on decision outcomes. *Journal of Management*, 33, 196–222.

Pruitt, D. (1981). *Negotiation Behavior*. New York: Academic Press.

Pruitt, D., and Lewis, S. A. (1975). Development of integrative solutions in bilateral negotiation. *Journal of Personality and Social Psychology*, 31, 621–633.

Pruitt, D. G., and Rubin, J. Z. (1986). *Social Conflict: Escalation, Stalemate, and Settlement*. New York: McGraw-Hill.

Putnam, L. L., and Jones, T. S. (1982). Reciprocity in negotiations: An analysis of bargaining interaction. *Communication Monographs*, 49, 171–191.

Rogers, C., and Farson, R. (1979). Active listening. In D. Kolb, I. Rubin, and J. MacIntyre (eds), *Organizational Psychology* (3rd edition). New Jersey: Prentice Hall.

Rotter, J. B. (1971). Generalized expectations for interpersonal trust. *American Psychologist*, 26, 443–452.

Rubin, J. (1991). Some wise and mistaken assumptions about conflict and negotiation. *Journal of Social Issues*, 45, 195–209.

Schei, V., Rognes, J. K., and De Dreu, C. K. W. (2008). Are individualistic orientations collectively valuable in group negotiations? *Group Processes and Intergroup Relations*, 11, 371–385.

Simons, T., L., and Peterson, R. S. (2000). Task conflict and relationship conflict in top management teams: The pivotal role of intragroup trust. *Journal of Applied Psychology*, 85, 102–111.

Thatcher, S., and Jehn, K. (1998). A model of group diversity profiles and categorization processes in bicultural organizational teams. In M. A. Neale, E. A. Mannix, and D. H. Gruenfeld (eds), *Research on Managing Groups and Teams: Vol. 1. Composition* (pp. 1–20). Stamford, CT: JAI Press.

Thompson, L. L. (1991). Information exchange in negotiation. *Journal of Experimental Social Psychology*, 27, 161–179.

Thompson, L. L., Mannix, E. A., and Bazerman, M. H. (1988). Group negotiation: Effects of decision rule, agenda, and aspiration. *Journal of Personality and Social Psychology*, 54, 86–95.

Tyler, T., Degoey, P., and Smith, H. (1996). Understanding why the justice of group procedures matters. *Journal of Personality and Social Psychology*, 70, 913–930.

Tyler, T., and Lind, E. (1992). A relational model of authority in groups. In M. Zanna
(ed.), *Advances in Experimental Social Psychology*, 25, 115–191.

Van de Ven, A. H., and Chu, Y. (1989). A psychometric assessment of the Minnesota
Innovation Survey. In A. H. Van de Ven, H. L. Angle, and M. S. Poole (eds), *Research on the
Management of Innovation: The Minnesota Studies* (pp. 55–103). New York: Harper and Row.

Van Lange, P. A. M. (1999). The pursuit of joint outcomes and equality in outcomes: An
integrative model of social value orientation. *Journal of Personality and Social Psychology*, 2,
337–349.

Webster, D., and Kruglanski, A. W. (1994). Individual differences in need for cognitive
closure. *Journal of Personality and Social Psychology*, 67, 1049–1062.

Weingart, L., R., Bear, J., and Todorova, G. (2008). Reconceptualizing relationship conflict: Interpersonal attitudes, emotions, and behavior. Work in progress.

Weingart, L. R., Bennett, R. J., and Brett, J. M. (1993). The impact of consideration of
issues and motivational orientation on group negotiation process and outcome. *Journal
of Applied Psychology*, 78, 504–517.

Weingart, L. R., Brett, J. M., Olekalns, M., and Smith, P. L. (2007). Conflicting social
motives in negotiating groups. *Journal of Personality and Social Psychology*, 93, 994–1010.

Weingart, L. R., Cronin, M. A., Houser, C. J. S., Cagan, J., and Vogel, C. (2005).
Functional diversity and conflict in cross-functional product development teams:
Considering representational gaps and task characteristics. In L. L. Neider and
C. A. Schriesheim (eds), *Understanding Teams* (pp. 89–110). Greenwich, CT: IAP.

Weingart, L. R., Hyder, E. B., and Prietula, M. J. (1996). Knowledge matters: The effect
of tactical descriptions on negotiation behavior and outcome. *Journal of Personality and
Social Psychology*, 70, 1205–1217.

Weingart, L. R., Prietula, M. J., Hyder, E., and Genovese, C. (1999). Knowledge and
the sequential processes of negotiation: A Markov chain analysis of response-in-kind.
Journal of Experimental Social Psychology, 35, 366–393.

Exercises

Personal assessment of your team conflict management style

Using the DUTCH scale (De Dreu, Evers, Beersma, Kluwer, and Nauta, 2001):

1. Use the scale below to respond to the following items as they describe how you typically approach conflict within a team. Answer in terms of your general tendencies
across a broad range of situations.

   1 = Never
   2 = Once in a while
   3 = Sometimes
   4 = Fairly often
   5 = Very frequently
   6 = Continually

When I'm involved in a team conflict, I do the following:	*Your response*
Y I give in to other team members' wishes.	
F I push my own point of view.	
P I examine issues until I find a solution that really satisfies me and my other team members.	
C I strive whenever possible towards a 50–50 compromise.	
A I avoid differences of opinion as much as possible.	
F I search for personal gains.	
P I examine ideas from different sides to find a mutually optimal solution.	
C I try to realize a middle-of-the-road solution.	
A I avoid a confrontation about our differences.	
Y I concur with the other team members.	
C I insist we all give in a little.	
F I do everything to win.	
P I work out a solution that serves my own and others' interests as much as possible.	
Y I try to accommodate the other team members.	
A I avoid a confrontation about our differences.	
C I emphasize that we have to find a compromise solution.	
Y I adapt to other team members' goals and interests.	
F I fight for a good outcome for myself.	
P I stand up for my own and others' goals and concerns.	
A I try to make differences loom less severe.	

2. Average the scores for the questions that have the same letter preceding them (A, C, F, P, Y). For example, if you filled out all 5s for Y, your average score for Y is "5". Each average represents your reliance on a specific conflict management approach.

3. Identify your dominant conflict management approach and consider the questions associated with each approach.

> A = Avoiding – you tend to avoid conflicts that occur. *Ask yourself, "Am I avoiding all conflicts (task and relationship)? How is my reliance on avoiding helping or hindering my team's performance?"*
>
> C = Compromise – the higher the score the more likely you are to compromise when faced with a conflict. While meeting in the middle may seem fair, sometimes you can miss opportunities to find creative solutions that are better than average for everyone. *Ask yourself. "When will compromise be the most or least effective way in dealing with my team's conflict?"*

F = Force – people who score high on forcing like to get their way, regardless of others' concerns. While this might be satisfying to you in the short term, it can leave other team members feeling resentful and unwilling to work with you in the future. *Ask yourself, "Under what circumstances do I tend to rely on forcing? What are the typical repercussions that I face? What alternative approaches are usually available to me?"*

P = Problem-solve – problem-solvers work hard to find solutions that meet the needs of everyone involved in the conflict. They try to satisfy others without losing sight of their own interests. *Ask yourself, "How does problem solving best promote cooperation within a team? What are the costs of using this approach?"*

Y = Yield – a yielding approach is the opposite of forcing. Yielders give in to the demands of others. This approach may end the conflict, but can leave you feeling taken advantage of. However, yielding can lead to a strategy of reciprocation, that is, "I'll give in now, but you owe me." *Ask yourself, "What are the risks of relying on yielding, especially when you consider that open discussion of alternatives and respect are critical to group success?"*

4. Break into small groups, ideally groups of people who have worked together before. Share your scores with one another. Discuss whether others see your conflict management approach as determined by this scale. What do they see as your strengths? Weaknesses?

Conflict analysis

Gather in groups of three people. Each person needs to come prepared to discuss a conflict situation from their personal work or school experience.

1. Each participant: Come prepared to discuss a conflict situation in which you are currently or were recently involved on a team at work or at school. Describe who is involved (no names necessary, just their relationship with you), what the conflict is about (describe the nature of the conflict, issues, concerns), where it occurred (context), when it occurred (how recent, how frequently), how it unfolded (actions and reactions; how people behave or typically manage the conflict).
2. Discuss the conflict situation in terms of the principles outlined in this chapter. Some possible discussion questions are outlined below.
   a. What type of conflict occurred? Task, relationship, or some combination?
   b. What was the root cause of the conflict? Was it driven by differences in personality, areas of expertise, culture, etc.?
   c. How emotional was the conflict? Were the emotions positive or negative? How did this influence the team's ability to understand and manage the conflict?
   d. Did the conflict escalate over time? Did it transform from one type to another? At what point did the team begin to address the conflict? What impact did that have on your ability to manage the conflict?
   e. Was everyone in the team equally comfortable in dealing with the conflict? If no, how did you deal with people's differing comfort levels?

   f. What approach did the team use in managing the conflict? Was it an appropriate approach? Were there alternative ways for doing so?

   g. Was the situation ripe for collaboration?

       i. Was there a focus on teamwork? Did team members feel prepared to manage the conflict that arose? Did team members trust and respect one another? Were the communication norms open?

      ii. Describe the motives of team members. What were the team members' primary motivations regarding cooperation? Were members epistemically motivated?

    iii. Did team members engage in effective conflict management behaviors?

   h. Did the conflict help or hinder the team's performance? Why and how?

       i. What role did you play in the conflict? Did you help or hinder its resolution? What were your strengths in handling the situation? What could you do to improve your ability to collaborate through conflict situations?

Part VI

LEADERSHIP

19

Use Power Effectively to Influence People

GARY YUKL

One of the most important determinants of managerial effectiveness is success in influencing people. Effective managers influence subordinates to perform the work effectively, they influence peers to provide support and assistance, and they influence superiors to provide resources and approval of necessary changes. The concept of "power" has been very useful for understanding how people are able to influence each other in organizations (Mintzberg, 1983; Pfeffer, 1981, 1992). Power is usually defined as the capacity to influence people and events (Yukl, 2006). It is a flexible concept that can be used in many different ways. For example, power has been used to explain the influence of groups on organization decisions, and the influence of one organization on another. In this chapter the focus is on the potential of one individual (called the "agent") to influence the behavior and attitudes of other individuals (called "target persons") in the same organization.

An agent will have more power over some people than over others and more influence for some types of issues than for others. Power is a dynamic variable that changes as conditions change. A person's power can increase or decrease dramatically over a relatively short period of time. Moreover, there are different types of power, and an agent may have more of some types than of others. This chapter will identify different types of individual power and describe effective ways to exercise each type.

The manner in which power is enacted usually involves influence behavior by the agent. Specific types of influence behavior are called influence tactics. This chapter will examine several influence tactics commonly used in organizations. The relative effectiveness of the various influence tactics will be described and the conditions for their successful use will be identified.

TYPES OF POWER

Behavioral scientists usually differentiate between position power and personal power. Position power is potential influence derived from one's position in the organization. This type of power is usually specified and limited by organizational policies, formal reward systems, legal constraints, and union contracts. Four specific types of position power are legitimate authority, reward power, coercive power, and information power (French and Raven, 1959; Yukl and Falbe, 1991). Personal power is potential influence derived from agent characteristics. Two specific types of personal power are expert power and referent power.

The research on power and influence is too limited to provide clear and unequivocal guidelines on the best way to exercise each type of power. Nevertheless, by drawing upon a diverse literature in the social sciences that includes research on power, leader behavior, motivation, communication, counseling, supervision, and conflict resolution, it is possible to develop some tentative guidelines. This section of the chapter will describe specific types of power and the conditions for exercising each type of power effectively.

Legitimate power

Legitimate power is derived from authority, which is the perceived right of the agent to influence specified aspects of the target person's behavior. The underlying basis for legitimate power is the agreement by members of an organization to comply with rules and legitimate requests in return for the benefits of membership (March and Simon, 1958). The conditions for continued membership may be set forth in a formal, legal contract, but the agreement to comply with legitimate authority is usually an implicit mutual understanding. Legitimate power is strengthened by an internalized value among people that it is proper to obey authority figures, show respect for the law, and follow tradition.

The amount of legitimate power reflects the chain of command and is usually much stronger in relation to subordinates than in relation to peers, superiors, or outsiders. However, even when the agent has no direct authority over a target person (e.g. a peer), the agent may have the legitimate right to make requests for necessary information, supplies, support services, technical advice, and assistance in carrying out inter-related tasks. The scope of authority for a position occupant is often specified in writing by documents (e.g. the job description, the employment contract, organization bylaws), but even when such documentation exists, there usually remains considerable ambiguity about an individual's scope of authority (Davis, 1968).

Authority is usually exercised by making a request or command orally or in writing. A polite request is more effective than an arrogant demand, because it does not emphasize a status gap or imply target dependence on the agent. Use of a polite request is especially important for people who are likely to be sensitive about status differentials and authority relationships, such as someone who is older than the agent or who is a peer rather than a direct subordinate.

Making a polite request does not imply that the agent should plead or appear apologetic about the request. To do so risks the impression that the request is not worthy or legitimate, and it may give the impression that compliance is not really expected (Sayles, 1979). A legitimate request should be made in a firm, confident manner. In an emergency situation, it is more important to be assertive than polite. A direct order by a leader in a command tone of voice is sometimes necessary to shock subordinates into immediate action in an emergency. In this type of situation, subordinates associate confident, firm direction with expertise as well as authority (Mulder, Ritsema van Eck, and de Jong, 1970). To express doubts or appear confused risks the loss of influence over subordinates.

Compliance with a request is more likely if it is perceived to be within the agent's scope of authority. A request that appears to be illegitimate is likely to be ignored or otherwise resisted, especially if the requested activity is also tedious, dangerous, or unpleasant. The issue of legitimacy is likely to be raised for unusual requests and for requests made to people over whom the agent has no direct authority. If there is any doubt about the right to make a request, its legitimacy should be verified by the agent.

Reward power

Reward power involves control over desirable resources and rewards. This type of power is greatest when the target is highly dependent on the agent for attaining the reward and cannot get it any other way. Reward power stems in part from formal authority. The authority to allocate rewards to others varies greatly across organizations and from one type of position to another within the same organization. The higher a person's position in the authority hierarchy of the organization, the more control over scarce resources the person is likely to have. Reward power over subordinates is usually much stronger than reward power over peers or superiors.

One form of reward power over subordinates is influence over their compensation, benefits, and career progress. Most managers are authorized to give pay increases, bonuses, or other economic incentives to deserving subordinates. Reward power is derived also from control over other tangible benefits such as a promotion, a better job, a better work schedule, a larger operating budget, a larger expense account, formal recognition (e.g. awards, commendations), and status symbols such as a larger office or a reserved parking space.

Reward power is also a source of influence over peers who depend on the agent for resources, funds, information, or assistance not otherwise provided by the formal authority system. Trading of favors needed to accomplish task objectives is a common form of influence among peers in organizations, and research indicates that it is important for the success of middle managers (Cohen and Bradford, 1989; Kaplan, 1984; Kotter, 1985). Access to a powerful person inside or outside the organization also provides an opportunity for an agent to seek favors for others who lack such access, thereby increasing the agent's reward power.

Upward reward power of subordinates is very limited in most organizations. Subordinates seldom have any direct influence over the reputation and career of their boss, unless the organization relies on ratings by subordinates to evaluate its managers. Nevertheless, subordinates usually have some indirect influence. If they perform well and speak favorably about the boss, his or her reputation will be enhanced (Mechanic, 1962). Occasionally subordinates also have reward power based on their ability to acquire resources outside of the formal authority system of the organization. For example, a department chairperson in a state university was able to obtain discretionary funds from grants and contracts, and these funds were used as a basis for influencing the decisions made by the college dean, whose own discretionary funds were very limited.

Reward power is most commonly exercised with an explicit or implicit promise to give the target person something under the agent's control for carrying out a request or performing a task. Compliance is most likely if the reward is something valued by the target person, and the agent is perceived as a credible source of the reward. Thus, it is essential to determine what rewards are valued by the people one wants to influence, and agent credibility should not be risked by making unrealistic promises or failing to deliver on a promise after compliance occurs.

Even when the conditions are favorable for using rewards, they are more likely to result in compliance rather than commitment. A promised reward is unlikely to motivate someone to put forth extra effort beyond what is required to complete the task. The target person may be tempted to neglect aspects of the task not included in the specification of performance criteria or aspects not easily monitored by the agent.

Rewards may result in resistance rather than compliance if used in a manipulative manner. The power to give or withhold rewards may cause resentment among people who dislike being dependent on the whims of a powerful authority figure, or who believe that the agent is manipulating them to his or her own advantage. Even when the reward is attractive, resistance may occur if the reward is seen as a bribe to get the target person to do something improper or unethical.

Coercive power

Another related source of power is control over punishments and the capacity to prevent someone from obtaining desired rewards. Compliance is motivated primarily by fear and is more likely if the agent is perceived as willing and able to punish the target person. The formal authority system of an organization usually specifies the legitimate use of punishment, which varies greatly across different types of organizations.

Coercive power is usually much greater in relation to subordinates than in relation to peers or superiors. Coercive power is derived from the authority of a manager to punish subordinates for violation of rules and policies, or failure to comply with legitimate orders and requests. Many different forms of punishment may be available, including dismissal, suspension, demotion, reassignment to a less desirable job, or a decrease in pay or benefits. However, the use of coercive power over subordinates is limited by the counterpower subordinates have over their leader. When leaders are tempted to use coercion on a large scale against followers, it undermines their authority and creates a hostile opposition seeking to restrict their power or remove them from office (Blau, 1956).

Opportunities for coercion of peers are usually very limited. A person can threaten to withhold future cooperation or complain to the superior of a peer who refuses to carry out legitimate requests. Sometimes a manager of one subunit has the authority to reject the products or plans of another subunit, and this authority also provides some coercive power. However, since mutual dependencies usually exist in lateral relations between managers of different subunits, coercion is likely to elicit retaliation and escalate into a conflict that benefits neither party.

Upward coercive power is also very limited in most organizations, but subordinates often have more of this type of counterpower than they realize. It is possible for them to damage the reputation of the boss by restricting production, sabotaging operations, initiating grievances, holding demonstrations, or making complaints to higher management (Mechanic, 1962). In organizations with elected leaders, if enough subordinates want to remove a leader from office, they usually have sufficient power to do so.

Coercive power is invoked by a threat or warning that the target person will suffer undesirable consequences for non-compliance with a request, rule, or policy. The threat may be explicit, or it may be only a hint that the person will be sorry for failing to do what the agent wants. The likelihood of compliance is greatest when the threat is perceived to be credible, and the target person strongly desires to avoid the threatened punishment. Sometimes it is necessary to establish credibility by demonstrating the ability to cause unpleasant consequences for the target person. However, even a credible threat may be unsuccessful if the target person refuses to be intimidated or believes that a way can be found to avoid compliance without being detected by the agent.

It is best to avoid using coercion except when absolutely necessary, because it is difficult to use and likely to result in undesirable side effects. Coercion often arouses anger or resentment, and it may result in retaliation. In work organizations, the most appropriate use of coercion is to deter behavior detrimental to the organization, such as illegal activities, theft, violation of safety rules, reckless acts that endanger others, and direct disobedience of legitimate requests. Coercion is not likely to result in commitment, but when used skillfully in an appropriate situation, there is a reasonably good chance that it will result in compliance.

Control over information

Access to information and control over its distribution provide another source of power in organizations. Some positions are strategically located in the communication network of an organization, and such positions can provide exclusive access to vital information and control over its distribution (Pfeffer, 1981).

Control over information makes it easier to interpret events for people in a way that serves the agent's interests. It is easier to cover up mistakes and poor decisions, or to delay their discovery. The impression of agent expertise can be heightened by exaggerated reports of successful performance. People in leadership positions often have sufficient control over the distribution of information to keep subordinates dependent and make it difficult for them to challenge the leader's decisions.

Control over the upward flow of information can be used to influence decisions made by superiors (Mechanic, 1962; Pettigrew, 1972). The agent supplies information that biases the target's perception of the problem and evaluation of alternatives. For example, a manager was able to influence the selection of a computer by systematically providing the board of directors with information that favored one option and discredited others (Pettigrew, 1972).

Information power is also available in a boundary-role position in which a person has primary responsibility for dealing with outsiders who are important for the continued prosperity and survival of the organization. For example, when consumer preferences are changing rapidly, a person who has the contacts with key customers is likely to have considerable information power in the organization.

Expert power

Expert power is perceived expertise in solving problems and performing task activities (French and Raven, 1959). This type of power can be acquired by demonstrating competence, such as by making decisions or initiating changes that prove successful, or by giving advice or making predictions that prove to be correct. Expertise is a source of power only if others are dependent on the person for advice and assistance. The more important a problem is to the target person, the greater the power derived by the agent from possessing the necessary expertise to solve it. Dependency is increased when the target person cannot easily find another source of advice besides the agent (Hickson, Hinings, Lee, Schneck, and Pennings, 1971; Patchen, 1974).

Expert power depends to a large extent on the perception of others that the agent has unique expertise to solve important problems for them. Sometimes people overestimate the agent's expertise, and the agent gains more power than is warranted. Sometimes expert power generalizes beyond the specific type of problem or task for which the person has special skills or knowledge. For example, a person who is skilled in conducting market surveys may also be considered an expert in designing new products, even though this person actually has little technical skill in product design. In the short run, perceived expertise is more important than real expertise, and some people are able to gain influence from pretending to have special expertise. However, over time, as the agent's knowledge is put to the test, target perceptions of the agent's expertise are likely to become more accurate.

When the agent has a lot of expert power and is trusted as a reliable source of information and advice, the target person may carry out a request without much explanation of the reasons for it. An example is an investor who purchases stocks recommended by a financial consultant without knowing much about the companies that issued the stocks. It is rare to possess this much expert power. In most cases, the agent must support a proposal or request by making logical arguments and presenting evidence that appears credible. Successful influence depends on the leader's credibility and persuasive communication skills in addition to technical knowledge and analytical ability. Proposals or requests should be made in a clear, confident manner, and the agent should avoid making contradictory statements or vacillating between inconsistent positions.

Expert power is based on a knowledge differential between the agent and the target person, but the very existence of such a differential can cause problems if the agent is not careful about the way expert power is exercised. An agent who flaunts his or her expertise may elicit resistance, especially if the target person is a peer or superior in the organization. In the process of presenting rational arguments, some people lecture in an arrogant, condescending manner, thereby conveying the impression that the listener is ignorant. In their efforts to sell a proposal, some people fire a steady stream of arguments, rudely interrupting any attempted replies and dismissing any objections or concerns without serious consideration. Even when the agent is acknowledged to have more expertise, the target person usually has some relevant information, ideas, and concerns that should be considered.

Referent power

Referent power is derived from the desire of others to please an agent toward whom they have strong feelings of affection, admiration, and loyalty (French and Raven, 1959). People are usually willing to do special favors for a friend, and they are more likely to carry out requests made by someone they greatly admire. The strongest form of referent power involves the influence process called personal identification. A person who identifies with an agent is usually willing to make great sacrifices to gain and maintain the agent's approval and acceptance. The target person is likely to do what the agent asks, imitate the agent's behavior, and develop attitudes similar to those expressed by the agent.

Referent power is usually greater for someone who is friendly, attractive, charming, and trustworthy. This type of power is increased by showing concern for the needs and feelings of others, demonstrating trust and respect, and treating people fairly. However, to achieve and maintain strong referent power usually requires more than just flattery, favors, and charm. Referent power ultimately depends on the agent's character and integrity. Over time, actions speak louder than words, and someone who tries to appear friendly but manipulates and exploits people will lose referent power. Integrity is demonstrated by being truthful, expressing a consistent set of values, acting in a way that is consistent with one's espoused values, taking personal risks to promote and defend important values, and carrying out promises and agreements.

Referent power is an important source of influence over subordinates, peers, and superiors, but it has limitations. A request based solely on referent power should be commensurate with the extent of the target person's loyalty and friendship toward the leader. Some things are simply too much to ask, given the nature of the relationship. When requests are extreme or made too frequently, the target person may feel exploited. The result of such behavior may be to undermine the relationship and reduce the agent's referent power.

Strong referent power will tend to increase the agent's influence over the target person even without any explicit effort by the agent to invoke this power. When there is a strong bond of love or friendship, it may be sufficient merely to ask the target person to do something. When referent power is not this strong, it may be necessary to invoke the salience of the relationship by making a personal appeal (an influence tactic described later in this chapter).

Another way to exercise referent power is through "role modeling." A person who is well liked and admired can have considerable influence over others by setting an example of proper and desirable behavior for them to imitate. When identification is strong, imitation is likely to occur even without any conscious intention by the agent. Because people also imitate undesirable behavior in someone they admire, it is important to be aware of the examples one sets.

POWER AND EFFECTIVE LEADERSHIP

Research shows that power is related to leadership effectiveness in complex ways. Effective leaders develop a considerable amount of expert and referent power, and they rely more on this personal power than on position power to influence people (Yukl, 2006). Nevertheless, some position power is usually necessary to accomplish the work. Without sufficient authority to reward competent subordinates, make necessary changes, and punish chronic troublemakers, it is difficult to develop a high-performing group or organization.

How much position and personal power is necessary will depend in part on what one seeks to accomplish. More power is needed to implement major changes in an organization, especially when there is strong opposition to change. In this difficult situation, a leader needs sufficient personal power to convince people that change is desirable, and sufficient position power to overcome the opposition and buy time to demonstrate that the proposed changes are feasible and effective.

Although some position power is needed by leaders to carry out their responsibilities, a person who has a great deal of position power may be tempted to rely on it too much instead of making an effort to develop and use expert and referent power. The notion that power corrupts is especially relevant for position power. Leaders with strong position power are more likely to perceive subordinates as objects of manipulation, devalue their worth, maintain more social distance from them, use rewards and punishments more often, and attribute the cause of subordinate achievements to the leader's power rather than to the intrinsic motivation and voluntary efforts of subordinates (Kipnis, 1974). Thus, a moderate amount of position power is probably optimal in most situations, rather than too much or too little (Yukl, 2006).

Extreme amounts of personal power can also corrupt a person. A leader with substantial expert and referent power may be tempted to act in ways that will eventually lead to failure (McClelland, 1975; Zaleznik, 1970). Surrounded by adoring supporters, a leader may begin to believe that he or she has a monopoly on wisdom and expertise. Thus, although it is desirable for a leader to develop strong personal power, it is also desirable for followers to retain some influence over key decisions. Effective leaders create relationships in which they have strong influence over subordinates but are also receptive to influence from them. These leaders consult with subordinates and encourage them to participate in making important decisions for the work unit.

EXERCISING POWER

Up to now the discussion has involved the different sources of power and how they are relevant for effective leadership. However, when describing the actual exercise of power, it is usually more meaningful to focus on specific influence attempts. The success of an influence attempt is a matter of degree, but it is helpful to differentiate among three levels of success. Commitment means the person is enthusiastic about the request and makes a maximum effort to do it effectively. Compliance means that the person is indifferent about the request and makes only a minimum effort. Resistance means the person is opposed to carrying out the request and tries to avoid doing it. Commitment is desirable for requests that require the person to take initiative in dealing with problems and to be persistent in the face of setbacks and difficulties. Compliance is often sufficient for a simple, routine type of request.

As noted earlier, a common form of influence behavior in organizations is to make a "simple request" based on legitimate power. This form of influence is most likely to be successful if the request is reasonable, it is clearly relevant for the mission of the agent's work unit, it is something the target person knows how to do, and it does not jeopardize the target person's own job performance. However, even when a simple request is perceived to be legitimate, it often results in subordinate compliance rather than commitment. When the request involves actions perceived by the target to be unpleasant, unnecessary, or detrimental, the reaction to a simple request is likely to be resistance.

Specific influence tactics are usually necessary to gain commitment for requests not initially considered by the target person to be important and feasible. Over the past quarter century, several researchers have attempted to identify distinct types of influence tactics used by individuals in organizations (e.g. Kipnis, Schmidt, and Wilkinson, 1980; Schilit and Locke, 1982; Yukl and Tracey, 1992). It is useful to differentiate among broad categories of influence tactics that have different objectives (Yukl, 2006).

Proactive influence tactics include attempts to gain compliance or commitment to a request or proposal, and specific types of proactive tactics will be described in the next section of this chapter. Most proactive tactics are also useful to resist or modify influence attempts by others. Impression management tactics involve attempts to influence how the agent is perceived by the target, and the objective may be to increase the target person's respect and appreciation of the agent. Examples include showing respect and deference, providing praise, agreeing with the target person, describing your talents and achievements, and acting in highly visible ways that indicate competence and dedication (e.g. working late, doing extra work). Finally, political tactics include attempts to influence strategic decisions about objectives, the distribution of scarce resources, and the selection of people to positions of high power and authority.

Proactive influence tactics

Research by Yukl and his colleagues (Yukl, 2006; Yukl, Seifert, and Chavez, 2008) identified 11 proactive influence tactics that are relevant for understanding effective influence in organizations. Each tactic will be explained briefly, and the conditions favoring its use will be described.

Rational persuasion. Rational persuasion involves the use of logical arguments and factual evidence that a proposal or request is important and feasible. In the most common form of rational persuasion, the agent emphasizes the potential benefits for the organization, team, or mission. This form of rational persuasion is appropriate when the target person shares the same task objectives as the agent but does not recognize that the agent's proposal is the best way to attain the objectives. On the other hand, if the agent and target person have incompatible objectives, this type of rational persuasion is unlikely to be successful for obtaining commitment or even compliance. Thus, it is useful to ensure that there are shared objectives before using this influence tactic.

An agent's technical knowledge is the source of facts and arguments used to build a persuasive case. However, in addition to facts and evidence, a persuasive case usually includes some opinions or inferences that the agent asks others to accept at face value because there is insufficient evidence to verify them. Thus, influence derived from rational persuasion is greater when the agent is perceived to be credible and trustworthy. Expert power, information power, and referent power can all enhance the effectiveness of rational persuasion. Finally, an agent needs considerable skill in persuasive speaking to present a case in a way that will have the maximum possible influence.

Apprising. Apprising is the use of information and logic to emphasize the benefits of a request or proposal for the target person as an individual. The agent may explain how a request will further the target person's career, improve the person's skills, or make the person's job easier. Unlike rational persuasion, there is not necessarily a shared objective to use as the basis for an appeal. Unlike exchange, the agent is not offering to give the target something, but is only pointing out that a proposed course of action will help get the target person something he or she wants. For apprising to be effective, the agent must be a credible source of information about potential benefits not already known to the target person.

Inspirational appeals.   An inspirational appeal is an attempt to develop enthusiasm and commitment by arousing strong emotions and linking a request or proposal to the target person's needs, values, hopes, and ideals. Some possible bases for appeal include the target person's desire to be important, to feel useful, to accomplish something worthwhile, to make an important contribution, to perform an exceptional feat, to be a member of the best team, or to participate in an exciting effort to make things better. Some ideals that may be the basis for an inspirational appeal include patriotism, loyalty, liberty, freedom, self-fulfillment, justice, fairness, equality, love, tolerance, excellence, humanitarianism, and progress. For example, employees are asked to work extra hours on a special project because it may save many lives.

Inspirational appeals vary in complexity, from a brief explanation of the ideological justification for a proposed project or change, to a major speech that articulates an appealing vision of what the organization could accomplish or become. The complexity of an inspirational appeal depends in part on the size of the task to be undertaken, the amount of effort and risk involved, and the extent to which people are asked to deviate from established, traditional ways of doing things. To formulate an appropriate appeal, the agent must have insight into the values, hopes, and fears of the person or group to be influenced. The effectiveness of an inspirational appeal also depends on the agent's communication skills, such as the ability to use vivid imagery and metaphors, manipulate symbols, and employ voice and gestures to generate enthusiasm and excitement.

Consultation.   Consultation is an attempt to increase the target person's commitment to carry a request or support a proposal by involving the person in determining how it will be done. Consultation can take a variety of forms when used as an influence tactic. For example, the agent may present a detailed policy, plan, or procedure to a target person who will be involved in implementing it to see if the person has any doubts, concerns, or suggestions about it. In the discussion that follows, which is really a form of negotiation and joint problem solving, the agent tries to find ways to modify the request so that it takes into account the target person's suggestions and concerns. In another variation of consultation, the agent presents a general strategy or objective to the target person rather than a detailed proposal and asks the person to help plan how to attain the objective or to suggest specific action steps for implementing the strategy. The suggested action steps are discussed until there is agreement by both parties. For consultation to be feasible, the target person must have at least moderate agreement with the objective that the agent wants to attain. The target person will not be very enthusiastic about suggesting ways to attain an objective that is undesirable.

Exchange tactics.   Exchange tactics involve an offer by the agent to reward the target person for doing what the agent requests. The essential condition for use of exchange tactics is control over rewards that are attractive to the person. In addition, the agent must be perceived as trustworthy enough to actually provide the promised rewards. Thus, exchange tactics are facilitated by the agent's reward power and credibility. Use of an incentive is especially appropriate when the target person is indifferent or reluctant about complying with a request. In effect, the agent offers to make it worthwhile to comply by promising to provide a reward that is desired by the target person. The reward offered by the agent may take many forms, such as recommending a pay increase or promotion for the person, sharing scarce resources with the person, helping the person do another task, providing information, providing political support on some issue or proposal, putting in a good word to help advance the person's career, and offering to share some of the benefits obtained from a project or activity. Sometimes the promise may be implicit rather than explicit. That is, the agent may suggest returning the favor in some unspecified way at a future time.

Collaboration. Collaboration involves an offer by the agent to provide necessary resources or assistance if the target person will carry out a request or approve a proposal. Examples include offering to show the target person how to do a requested task, offering to provide the equipment or technical assistance needed to perform a requested task, and offering to help the target person deal with a problem that would be caused by carrying out the request. Whereas exchange usually involves an impersonal trade of unrelated benefits, collaboration usually involves a joint effort to accomplish the same task or objective. It is a way to communicate that the agent considers the request important, and it also shows consideration for the target person's difficulties in carrying out the request. This tactic is most useful when the agent understands the obstacles faced by the target person in carrying out a request and also has sufficient expertise and resources to help the target overcome these obstacles.

Personal appeals. A personal appeal involves asking someone to do a favor based on friendship or loyalty to the agent. This tactic is one way to enact referent power, although when referent power is very strong, a personal appeal may not be necessary. If considerable effort is required to comply with a request, the target person should understand that the request is indeed important to the agent. If a request is not perceived to be important to the agent, it may be ignored or carried out with only a minimal effort. Thus, whenever appropriate, the importance of the request to the agent should be explained to the target person.

Personal appeals can take several forms. One form is to ask the target person to carry out a request or support a proposal as a personal favor. Another form is to emphasize the close relationship between agent and target before asking for something. A third form is to say that you need to ask for a favor before saying what it is. If the target person agrees, then it will be awkward to say no when the request is explained. The risk with this form of personal appeal is that the target person may feel resentment if manipulated into doing something unpleasant.

Ingratiation tactics. Ingratiation is behavior that makes a target person feel accepted and appreciated by the agent. Examples include giving compliments, showing respect, and acting especially friendly and helpful before making a request. Ingratiation can be used not only for an immediate influence attempt, but also as a longer-term strategy to improve relationships with people and gain more referent power (Liden and Mitchell, 1988; Wayne and Ferris, 1990). An especially effective form of ingratiation for a proactive influence attempt is to explain why the target person is uniquely qualified to carry out a difficult request. When ingratiation tactics are sincere, they can strengthen a friendship, increase referent power, and make a target person more willing to consider a request. However, if the target person perceives that the agent is being insincere and manipulative, then ingratiation will not increase compliance.

Legitimating tactics.   When authority is ambiguous or legitimacy is in doubt, an agent may use a legitimating tactic to establish the legitimacy of a request or command. Examples of legitimating tactics include providing evidence of prior precedent, showing consistency with organizational policies and rules, reminding the target that the request is consistent with a prior contract or agreement, and showing consistency with professional role expectations. Another legitimating tactic is to indicate that the request was approved by higher management or someone else with proper authority. Sometimes the legitimacy of a request or command can be verified by documentation such as written rules, policies, charters, contracts, plans, job descriptions, work orders, or memos from authority figures.

Pressure tactics.   Pressure tactics include threats, warnings, demands, repeated requests, and frequent checking to see if the person has complied with a request. This tactic can take many forms and can vary from being relatively hard (strongly worded threat about harsh punishment for non-compliance) to being relatively soft (a causal reminder that the deadline is approaching for a task the target person agreed to do). Sometimes when a request has been ignored, an angry complaint to the person is sufficient to invoke the possibility of unpleasant consequences and induce compliance, particularly if the person is just lazy or apathetic rather than strongly opposed to the action. Sometimes explicit warnings or threats are necessary to get compliance with legitimate requests or rules that are unpopular.

The hard pressure tactics require some coercive power over the target person, and they are more likely to result in compliance if the target person believes the agent is able and willing to carry out threats of punishment. A limitation of most pressure tactics is that they may have serious side effects. Threats and intimidation are likely to undermine working relationships and may lead to resistance, avoidance, or retaliation by the target person. For this reason, pressure tactics should not be used except as a last resort when other influence tactics have failed.

Coalition tactics.   Coalitions are an indirect type of influence tactic wherein the agent gets assistance from other people to influence the target person. The coalition partners may include peers, subordinates, superiors, or outsiders (e.g. clients and suppliers).

One form of coalition tactic is to have other people talk to the target person and express support for the agent's request or proposal. Another form of coalition tactic is for the agent to bring to a meeting someone who will help to present a proposal to the target person. A third form of coalition tactic is to use the prior endorsement of coalition partners as a basis for making a stronger appeal to the target person. The appropriate form of coalition depends on the nature of the request, the agent–target relationship, and the amount of resistance expected or encountered.

Coalition tactics are always used in combination with one or more of the direct influence tactics. For example, the agent and a coalition partner may both use rational persuasion to influence the target person. The tactics used by coalition partners are not always the same one used by the agent. For example, in a version of the "good cop–bad cop" strategy, the agent uses ingratiation and rational persuasion, and the coalition partner uses pressure.

When the agent gets assistance from a superior of the target (who may or may not also be the agent's boss), this coalition tactic is sometimes called an "upward appeal." Upward appeals are used primarily as a last resort when repeated attempts to influence the target person with other tactics are unsuccessful. The target person for an upward appeal is usually a peer, but sometimes this tactic is used to influence a subordinate or the boss. It is risky to use an upward appeal to influence the boss, because it is likely to elicit resentment. Even when used with a peer, an upward appeal may cause resentment if it is viewed as an attempt to force the peer to do what the agent wants. The resentment may undermine agent–target relations, and it can lead to covert forms of resistance by the target person.

Effectiveness of Different Influence Tactics

Research comparing influence tactics indicates that some are usually more effective than others (Falbe and Yukl, 1992; Yukl, Kim, and Falbe, 1996; Yukl and Tracey, 1992; Yukl et al., 2008). Consultation and inspirational appeals are two of the most effective tactics for influencing target commitment to carry out a request or support a proposal. Collaboration is very effective when the target person perceives that the agent's request is important but not feasible without additional resources and assistance. Rational persuasion can be very effective depending on how it is used. A strong form of rational persuasion (e.g. a detailed proposal, elaborate documentation, a convincing reply to concerns raised by the target person) is often effective, whereas a weak form of rational persuasion (e.g. a brief explanation, an assertion without supporting evidence) is much less likely to be effective.

Apprising can be effective when the request or proposal actually offers personal benefits to the target person that are sufficient to justify the time and effort to carry out the request. Exchange and ingratiation are moderately effective for influencing subordinates and peers, but these tactics are difficult to use for influencing superiors. Subordinates do not have much to exchange with bosses, and offers of exchange are unlikely to be viewed as appropriate. Compliments made to the boss just before asking for something are likely to appear insincere and manipulative. Ingratiation is more effective when used as part of a long-term strategy for improving relations with superiors rather than as a tactic for an immediate influence attempt with a superior.

Personal appeals are moderately effective for influencing a peer with whom the agent has a friendly relationship. However, this tactic is only appropriate for a limited range of requests (e.g. get assistance, get a personal favor, change a scheduled meeting or deadline), and the outcome is likely to be compliance rather than commitment. Personal appeals are seldom necessary for influencing subordinates, and they are difficult to use with bosses.

The least effective tactics for influencing target commitment are pressure and legitimating tactics. These tactics seldom result in target commitment, but they sometimes result in compliance. Nevertheless, compliance is all that is needed for some types of influence attempts (e.g. wear proper safety gear, provide requested information, turn in routine reports on time).

Coalition tactics can be effective for influencing a peer or superior to support a change or innovation. However, they are seldom effective for influencing someone to carry out an assignment or improve performance, especially when viewed as an attempt to "gang up" on the target person. Most coalition tactics are not appropriate or necessary for influencing subordinates except in special cases (e.g. asking a subordinate to move to a different position in the organization, to pursue a promotion opportunity).

The effectiveness of an attempt can be increased by using more than one type of tactic at the same time or sequentially (Falbe and Yukl, 1992; Yukl, 2006). When using tactics together in the same influence attempt, the agent should select tactics that are compatible with each other. In other words, select tactics that enhance each other's effectiveness and are easy to use together. Rational persuasion is a very flexible tactic that is usually compatible with any of the other tactics. Strong pressure tactics are not compatible with ingratiation because they weaken target feelings of friendship and loyalty, which ingratiation is intended to strengthen. When tactics are used sequentially, some types (e.g. ingratiation, consultation) are more suitable for an initial influence attempt, whereas other types (e.g. exchange, pressure) are more appropriate for a follow-up influence attempt (Yukl, Falbe, and Youn, 1993).

Even though some tactics are generally more useful than others, success is not guaranteed for any individual tactic or combination of tactics. The outcome of an influence attempt depends on other things in addition to the influence tactics that are used, including the agent's skill in using the tactics, the type of agent–target relationship, the type of the request (e.g. task related, personal), and how the request is perceived by the target person (e.g. legitimate, important, enjoyable). A tactic is more likely to be successful if the target perceives it to be a socially acceptable form of influence behavior, if the agent has sufficient position and personal power to use the tactic, if the tactic can affect target attitudes about the desirability of the request, if it is used in a skillful way, if it is used for a request that is legitimate, and if it is consistent with the target person's values and needs (Yukl and Tracey, 1992).

CASE EXAMPLES

The following case illustrates how important it is to develop an adequate power base and select an appropriate influence strategy. The provost in a large university asked each academic department with a graduate program to provide several students to participate in a new fundraising campaign. The students would telephone department alumni, describe the department's current activities and accomplishments, and then ask for donations to help support the department. Assigning students to help with fundraising does not fall within the scope of legitimate authority for department chairs, so it is necessary to ask for volunteers. These students were overloaded with academic work, and they were reluctant to perform extra tasks not directly related to this work.

Department X

The chairperson of Department X had strong referent power with the students who specialized in the graduate program associated with his department. He was a supportive, considerate teacher who interacted with students outside of the classroom and showed strong concern for them as individuals. When he met with the students, he explained why the fundraising was important to the university and how it would benefit the masters program and future students. His strong rational appeals were supplemented with inspirational appeals based on student loyalty to the program. Most of the students volunteered to participate in the fundraising effort, and they were very effective in getting donations from program alumni who had not previously contributed funds to the university.

Department Y

The chairperson of Department Y had little referent power with students who specialized in the graduate program associated with his department. He was arrogant and conceited in the classroom, he spent little time interacting with the students outside of class, and he did not develop close supportive relationships with them. At a meeting with the students to talk about the fundraising campaign, he said that the university needed more donations from alumni but did not explain how the department or the program would benefit. This weak rational persuasion was combined with pressure tactics. He demanded that the students participate and told them that they did not have any choice in the matter. The chairperson was able to pressure some of the students to agree to help with the fundraising, but discussions among the students after the meeting revealed that they resented this coercion. Several students decided to complain to the provost. As a result, the provost decided not use any of the graduate students from Department Y for the fundraising. Instead, she hired some undergraduate students and paid them an hourly wage to telephone department alumni. These undergraduate students were much less effective in getting donations from alumni.

CONCLUSION

Knowledge about power and influence tactics is useful for people who must gain cooperation and support from others to perform their job effectively. To influence people, it is essential to develop and maintain a substantial amount of expert and referent power. In addition, it is desirable to have sufficient position power to back up personal power. Position power should be exerted in a subtle, careful fashion that minimizes status differentials and avoids threats to the target person's self-esteem. People who exercise power in an arrogant and manipulative manner are likely to engender resentment and resistance.

The outcome of an influence attempt depends on what tactics are used, how skillfully they are used, and the context in which they are used. Some of the tactics require a specific type of power to be effective. For example, exchange requires reward power, hard forms of pressure require coercive power, rational persuasion requires expert power, and a personal appeal requires some referent power. Combining tactics is usually more effective for a difficult request than using a single tactic. In general, the four "core tactics" that are most useful for eliciting commitment are consultation, inspirational appeals, collaboration, and strong forms of rational persuasion. Apprising, ingratiation, or exchange can be useful supplementary tactics when combined with one or more of the core tactics. Before making an influence attempt that involves an important objective, it is essential to diagnose the situation carefully and select tactics that are mutually compatible and appropriate for the situation.

REFERENCES

Blau, P. K. (1956). *Bureaucracy in Modern Society*. New York: Random House.

Cohen, A. R., and Bradford, D. L. (1991). *Influence without Authority*. New York: John Wiley and Sons.

Davis, K. (1968). Attitudes toward the legitimacy of management efforts to influence employees. *Academy of Management Journal*, 11, 153–162.

Falbe, C. M., and Yukl, G. (1992). Consequences for managers of using single influence tactics and combinations of tactics. *Academy of Management Journal*, 35, 638–653.

French, J. R. P., and Raven, B. H. (1959). The bases of social power. In D. Cartwright (ed.), *Studies of Social Power* (pp. 150–167). Ann Arbor, MI: Institute for Social Research.

Hickson, D. J., Hinings, C. R., Lee, C. A., Schneck, R. S., and Pennings, J. M. (1971). A strategic contingencies theory of intra-organizational power. *Administrative Science Quarterly*, 16, 216–229.

Kaplan, R. E. (1984). Trade routes: The manager's network of relationships. *Organizational Dynamics*, Spring, 37–52.

Kipnis, D. (1974). *The Powerholders*. Chicago: University of Chicago Press.

Kipnis, D., Schmidt, S. M., and Wilkinson, I. (1980). Intra-organizational influence tactics: Explorations in getting one's way. *Journal of Applied Psychology*, 65, 440–452.

Kotter, J. P. (1985). *Power and Influence: Beyond Formal Authority*. New York: Free Press.

Liden, R. C., and Mitchell, T. R. (1988). Ingratiatory behaviors in organizational settings. *Academy of Management Review*, 13, 572–587.

March, J. G., and Simon, H. A. (1958). *Organizations*. New York: Wiley.

Mechanic, D. (1962). Sources of power of lower participants in complex organizations. *Administrative Science Quarterly*, 7, 349–364.

McClelland, D. C. (1975). *Power: The Inner Experience*. New York: Irvington.

Mintzberg, H. (1983). *Power In and Around Organizations*. Englewood Cliffs, NJ: Prentice Hall.

Mulder, M., Ritsema van Eck, J. R., and de Jong, R. D. (1970). An organization in crisis and noncrisis conditions. *Human Relations*, 24, 19–41.

Patchen, M. (1974). The locus and basis of influence on organizational decisions. *Organizational Behavior and Human Performance*, 11, 195–221.

Pettigrew, A. (1972). Information control as a power resource. *Sociology*, 6, 187–204.

Pfeffer, J. (1981). *Power in Organizations*. Marshfield, MA: Pittman.

Pfeffer, J. (1992). *Managing with Power: Politics and Influence in Organizations*. Boston, MA: Harvard Business School Press.

Sayles, L. R. (1979). *What Effective Managers Really Do and How They Do It*. New York: McGraw-Hill.

Schilit, W. K., and Locke, E. A. (1982). A study of upward influence in organizations. *Administrative Science Quarterly*, 27, 304–316.

Wayne, S. J., and Ferris, G. R. (1990). Influence tactics, affect, and exchange quality in supervisor–subordinate interactions: A laboratory experiment and field study. *Journal of Applied Psychology*, 75, 487–499.

Yukl, G. (2006). *Leadership in Organizations* (6th edition). Englewood Cliffs, NJ: Prentice Hall.

Yukl, G., and Falbe, C. M. (1991). The importance of different power sources in downward and lateral relations. *Journal of Applied Psychology*, 76, 416–423.

Yukl, G., Falbe, C. M., and Youn, J. Y. (1993). Patterns of influence behavior for managers. *Group and Organization Management*, 18, 5–28.

Yukl, G., Kim, H., and Falbe, C. M. (1996). Antecedents of influence outcomes. *Journal of Applied Psychology*, 81, 309–317.

Yukl, G., Seifert, C., and Chavez, C. (2008). Validation of the extended Influence Behavior Questionnaire. *Leadership Quarterly*.

Yukl, G., and Tracey, B. (1992). Consequences of influence tactics when used with subordinates, peers, and the boss. *Journal of Applied Psychology*, 77, 525–535.

Zaleznik, A. (1970). Power and politics in organizational life. *Harvard Business Review*, 48, 47–60.

EXERCISES

1. Describe a successful influence attempt made by a boss or co-worker with you during the past few months, and identify the specific influence tactics used by the person. Then describe an unsuccessful attempt by the same person or someone else in the organization to influence you, and identify the tactics used by the person. Analyze the reasons for the success or failure of the two influence attempts. Consider the agent's position and personal power, the relevance of the tactics for the situation, and your initial attitudes about the objective of the influence attempt.

2. Think about an influence attempt that you need to make or would like to make in the near future. Plan an appropriate influence strategy, taking into account your power bases, the agent–target relationship, the target's attitudes about the influence objective, and your knowledge and influence skills. Select some specific influence tactics that would be appropriate for this influence attempt and consider the best way to sequence them (e.g. initial tactics and what you would do if the initial effort is unsuccessful).

20

Lead through Vision and Values*

SHELLEY A. KIRKPATRICK

Two key leadership principles are leading through vision and leading through values. Vision statements can inspire followers to attain high levels of performance. For example, Pierre Omidyar founded eBay in order to "[make] the power of the internet available to . . . people." Another example is FedEx's vision statement of "[producing] outstanding financial returns by providing totally reliable, competitively superior, global, air–ground transportation of high priority goods and documents that require rapid, time-certain delivery."

Leaders also can motivate others through the values that they define for their organizations. Values define the acceptable means through which the vision should be attained. Grocery-chain Wegman's, for example, chooses to attain its vision as well as profitability goals through its values, which include caring about and listening to its workers, having high standards in the pursuit of excellence, making a difference in the community, and empowering employees.

In this chapter, proven principles are presented for leading through vision and values. Vision-based leadership is described first, followed by values-based leadership.

LEADING THROUGH VISION

A *vision* is a leader's statement of a desired, long-term future state for an organization (Burns, 1978; House, 1977). Although a leader may have a vision of what the organization can become over the long run, the vision will have little impact on followers unless it is communicated. The communicated vision is referred to as a *vision statement*. Most vision statements are not intended to be achieved within a given period of time; instead, they are intended to be pursued or worked toward on a daily basis over a long timeframe.

*Note: I am grateful to Selena Rezvani, Mark Leheney, and Susan Goughnour for the helpful comments and assistance in preparing this chapter.

The Importance of Vision

A key function of a leader is to inspire, or impel, others to carry out the vision statement. Employees, team members, and other stakeholders can be said to play the role of followers. Considerable evidence demonstrates that well-formed vision statements impact important outcomes, including the organization's performance, followers' performance, and followers' attitudes. Of course, not all vision statements are equally effective – even though the research evidence is supportive of the impact that a vision statement can have, the vision statement must have certain characteristics in order to be most effective (see below).

Over 50 studies have supported the relationships between communicated vision statements and desired outcomes. These studies have been conducted across a variety of samples, including students and managers who served as laboratory study participants, military combat and non-combat leaders, middle- and lower-level managers, entrepreneurs, educational leaders, national leaders, political leaders, and corporate leaders. A variety of research methods were employed in these studies, including case studies, longitudinal studies, field studies, interviews, laboratory experiments, and historical analysis of archival information.

In sum, there is strong evidence that a relationship exists between a communicated vision statement with certain characteristics and follower and organizational outcomes. Below, additional details are presented on the relationship between the vision statement and organizational and individual outcomes, followed by a description of the characteristics that comprise an effective vision statement.

Vision impacts organizational performance

A wide range of outcomes has been examined, including measures of organizational performance – business performance, stakeholder performance, and organizational change – as well as individual performance. The relationship between a communicated vision statement and the organization's performance has been supported in studies of organizations that are in competitive and entrepreneurial environments (Baum, Locke, and Kirkpatrick, 1998; Oswald, Stanwick, and LaTour, 1997). When top managers and middle managers communicate a vision statement, outcomes such as business performance and organizational stakeholder effectiveness have been positively impacted (Hart and Quinn, 1993; Howell and Avolio, 1993; Howell and Higgins, 1990). The vision statement has also been shown to have a positive impact on group, team, or division performance (Barling, Weber, and Kelloway, 1996; Bass, Avolio, Jung, and Berson, 2003; Schaubroeck, Lam, and Cha, 2007).

Further, the vision statement can play a critical role in facilitating organizational change (Coulson-Thomas, 1992; Doz and Prahalad, 1987; Larwood, Falbe, Kriger, and Meising, 1995; Roberts, 1985; Trice and Beyer, 1986). For example, the vision content examined by Larwood et al. (1995) was related to rapid change in the firms that were studied. By communicating a desired future state, the vision statement prepares the organization for change and provides a mechanism for interpreting changes as they occur. The vision statement provides a context for organizational change by providing a compelling reason for moving toward the vision.

Vision impacts individual, or follower, performance and attitudes

Follower attitudes, such as commitment to the organization and satisfaction, are positively affected by the presence of a vision statement. To isolate the effects of the vision statement on follower performance, laboratory simulations have found that a leader who communicated a vision positively affected follower performance (Howell and Frost, 1989; Kirkpatrick and Locke, 1996; Oswald, Mossholder, and Harris, 1994). Similar results were found in field studies that examined leader vision statement effects (Bono, Jackson, Foldes, Vinson, and Muros, 2007; Colbert, Kristof-Brown, Bradley, and Barrick, 2008; Niehoff, Enz, and Grover, 1990). This research supports the idea that a leader does not have to have a charismatic personality or expressive communication style in order to effectively motivate followers.

The vision statement has a positive effect on followers' attitudes. Follower attitudes that are impacted include trust in the leader, commitment to the organization, satisfaction with the task, and clarity of the task (Barling et al., 1996; Kirkpatrick and Locke, 1996; Podsakoff, MacKenzie, Moorman, and Fetter, 1990).

Effective vision statements have specific characteristics

A wide range of vision statement characteristics have been included in visionary leadership research. The following characteristics of vision statements are associated with positive outcomes, including organizational and individual performance (Baum et al., 1998):

- ◆ *Brevity.* A vision statement should be fairly succinct, which makes it easy for employees to remember as well as for managers and leaders to communicate. In two separate studies of organizational vision statements, when the leader was asked to write down his/her vision for the firm or unit, the average length of the vision statement was about 35 words, or two to three sentences (Baum et al., 1998; Kirkpatrick, Wofford, and Baum, 2002).
- ◆ *Clarity.* Because a wide variety of jobs and individuals (each with their own values, interests, personalities, skills, and so forth) exist within most organizations, it is easy for employees to obtain widely varying messages that are incongruent and inaccurate. The challenge is to create a vision statement that applies to the entire organization and its different jobs/employees while at the same time unites the organization and provides a stable, transcendent goal. Clarity often can be obtained by avoiding jargon and buzz-words and by using understandable terminology. Writing concise sentences is another way of obtaining a clear vision statement.
- ◆ *Abstractness and stability.* Vision statements are long term in nature and are meant to provide an abstract, stable picture of the organization's desired future. Abstractness means that a vision presents a general enough picture of the future that the vision can be reached in practice in many different ways. Abstractness also provides for flexibility by providing guidance to employees when they encounter novel or unforeseen situations. This characteristic is increasingly important in virtual and global work environments in which employees must make decisions. Stability implies that the vision should remain in place over the long run. The vision statement should be timeless, not requiring revision once it is achieved in practice. This is not to say that

a vision statement should never be revised or updated. When revision is necessary, it should not be because the vision has been completed but because the organization's ideal goal has changed.

◆ *Challenge.* Effective vision statements should not be too easy or too hard to carry out on a daily basis, but rather should challenge employees to live up to the vision. By describing a desirable future, the vision statement provides a future that is not easily achieved but is attainable.

◆ *Future orientation.* Effective vision statements do not describe the current state of the organization. Nor do they describe short-term desired states, such as what the organization intends to achieve this year or the following year. Instead, vision statements are long term. They describe the organization's desired end-state well into the future. Effective vision statements often describe the ongoing actions in which the organization will engage.

◆ *Desirability or ability to inspire.* An effective vision statement portrays a picture of a desirable future and, as such, is ideological in nature. By tapping into the values of the leader and followers, the vision statement should motivate and inspire them to work toward achieving it. The vision statement is a persuasive statement that draws on the values of followers. References to followers' self-worth and efficacy ("We have what it takes to achieve the vision and deserve to have the opportunity to become the best in our industry") as well as the organization's collective identities ("By working together, we can become the pre-eminent firm in our industry") are techniques that can inspire followers (Shamir, House, and Arthur, 1994).

◆ *Identification of intended products, markets, and strategy.* The vision statement should specify the products and services, markets, and strategy that it intends to pursue. It also draws a line between what the organization is willing and not willing to do to succeed (Ireland and Hitt, 1990). Vision statements are more effective when they focus follower attention on the markets to which the organization's products will be sold. How products and the market are defined will impact new or innovative products – for example, defining the company as a bicycle manufacturer will lead to different products and markets than defining the company as a producer of transportation. The strategy, or how those products will be developed or produced and sold, also may be part of the vision statement. (Nanus, 1992; Scott, Jaffe, and Tobe 1993).

Effective vision statements are unique to the organization

An effective vision statement includes references to the organization's uniqueness, such as its products/services, organizational history, market(s), customers, or geographic location. An organization that describes how it is unique has the ability to differentiate itself from its competitors and to make employees feel that they are part of something special. This enhances the collective identity among the organization's employees. Such references are likely to contain specific, vivid images that are easily remembered; leaders often communicate the organization's unique vision through storytelling of illustrative events and actions. These types of unique statements are unlikely to change significantly over time.

An exception to this principle is when the organization must change in order to survive. Organizations that have experienced crises or significant failures may need to break free from their past and can do so by using a new vision statement to put the organization on a new path. In such a case, the leader may draw comparisons between the prior history and the new future that will be created in order to build commitment to the vision.

Despite broad empirical support for visionary leadership theory, the vision formulation process is regarded as somewhat of an art form. A leader's intuition and insight into follower values, along with the organization's unique culture and environment, affect the vision that is developed and its effectiveness. One study found that an effective vision statement for a public-sector service organization may be very different from an effective vision statement for private-sector manufacturing companies (Kirkpatrick et al., 2002). Specifically, the private-sector manufacturing firms were more effective when their vision statement emphasized achievement themes, such as efficiency and excellence. In contrast, the public-sector service organizations, for whom positive stakeholder relationships are required, were more effective when themes of courtesy and customers' best interest were emphasized in the vision statement.

Note that these research findings do *not* mean that manufacturing firms should neglect customer service! Rather, the leader could employ a vision statement emphasizing efficiency, translating it into a strategy of serving customers quickly. Similarly, leaders of public-sector organizations that focus on customers may decide to pursue a culture of customer-service excellence, finding new ways to meet customers' needs with fewer resources.

Almost every organization has a vision statement. However, many vision statements do not reference unique aspects of the organization, and thus are likely to be less effective than vision statements that do. For example, many vision statements take a generic form of "Our vision is to be the best." This type of vision statement does not distinguish the company from its competitors and is unlikely to have as great an impact as the following vision statement of an architectural woodworking company that references its unique client base:

> We will be known for the striking beauty of the veneered cabinets that we will sell to the nation's most famous tenants.

Another woodworking firm emphasizes achieving quality through customer commitment and a continuous innovation process:

> To profit by being the respected leader in providing quality architectural woodwork and services to our customers through our commitment to excellence, continuous innovation, and the development of long-term relationships.

MEDIATORS OF VISION STATEMENT EFFECTIVENESS

In order to impact organizational and follower outcomes, the leader's vision statement must first have an impact on followers' motivation. Several ways in which a vision statement can affect outcomes have been researched. These mechanisms, or mediating variables, focus on the impact that the vision statement has on followers' motivation. A vision statement is more likely to lead to the desired outcomes when it inspires followers.

Mechanisms that have been identified include the following:

◆ *Goal alignment.* The vision statement serves as a long-term, general goal. Although everyday goals are typically short term and fully achievable, vision statements are long term and timeless. Thus, vision statements rely on similar motivational mechanisms, such as focusing attention, as traditional work-related goals (Locke and Latham, 1990). When individual and group goals are aligned, or consistent, performance is higher than when individual and group goals are not aligned (Crown and Rosse, 1995). Followers are likely to be committed to their goals when a vision statement is present (Piccolo and Colquitt, 2006; Arnold, Turner, Barling, Kelloway, and McKee, 2007).

◆ *Follower self-confidence.* The vision statement raises followers' self-confidence by clarifying the purpose of the organization and inspires them to help achieve the vision. Some vision statements make reference to followers' capabilities – such as talent, intelligence, or ingenuity – which, in turn, tells followers that they are qualified to achieve the vision. The vision statement can boost followers' self-confidence by emphasizing to them that they are capable of reaching a meaningful goal that will result in a better future (Shamir, House, and Arthur, 1993).

◆ *Shared meaning.* The vision statement provides a common language that followers can use to explain how their actions are effective and desirable (Shamir et al., 1994). Followers' efforts are further aligned with the vision when followers possess the same understanding as the leader regarding what it is they are to achieve. Having a shared vision that results in the same common meaning among followers can be especially important in situations when followers must make their own decisions, such as a crisis or a non-routine situation.

◆ *Perceived job characteristics.* The vision statement can reframe how followers view their jobs. Research supports the notion that followers who report working for a supervisor who displays transformational behaviors – that is, acting in an inspiring and motivational manner by communicating a vision statement, providing idealized influence, and intellectually stimulating followers – are more likely to see their jobs as more challenging and meaningful, than followers who do not report working for a supervisor who displays those behaviors (Piccolo and Colquitt, 2006; Arnold et al., 2007).

An effective vision statement impacts desired outcomes primarily due to its ability to motivate and inspire followers. However, additional mediating factors have not been identified or widely studied.

MODERATORS OF VISION STATEMENT EFFECTIVENESS

It is accepted that the situation affects leadership emergence and effectiveness (Vroom and Jago, 2007), yet little research has focused on specific contingencies that impact the effectiveness of a leader's vision statement. It is important to be aware of these contingencies because they may provide exceptions to the research findings discussed above. Two contingency factors – *organizational environment and national culture* – have been identified and are described below.

A vision statement has the unique ability to focus attention, coordinate actions, and provide guidance in novel situations. Traditional management devices, such as plans, procedure manuals, or job descriptions, may not exist in new or rapidly growing organizations, for example. Also, in today's fast-paced, global marketplace, employees may not be able to follow a traditional chain-of-command to receive guidance in a short time-frame. A highly effective vision is especially important when faced with rapidly changing environments, when specific rules may be dysfunctional due to their narrow focus and lack of adaptability, or in the early stages of the organization's lifecycle where routines are not yet in place (Yukl, 2005).

Leaders who communicate a vision in multicultural settings, be they in a multinational firm or an organization with a diverse workforce, need to consider that the values contained in the vision statement may not be as appealing or easy to discern to people from a different cultural background. In such instances, the leader must take steps to communicate an inclusive vision and allow followers time to clarify their personal values and realign them with the vision. Followers also must have the capacity to identify and be aware of their own values.

Leaders may not want to reference the organization's past periods of radical organizational change. References to those stressful periods will likely increase resistance to the vision. Similarly, aligning the vision with societal values that are inconsistent with competitiveness is not recommended. Research has shown that there are societies with a low level of performance orientation, such as some societies in Latin America (House, Hanges, Ruiz-Quintanilla et al., 1999; Javidan, Dorfman, de Luque, and House, 2006). Aligning the organization with this societal norm would hinder the international competitiveness of the organization. The leader must carefully weigh the imbalance between the values underlying the vision statement and societal norms.

The need for a high degree of participation depends on the national culture of the followers, the amount of crisis or stress in the organization, and the ability of the leader to develop a unique vision statement. In collectivistic countries, such as China, the leader's attempt to take a highly participative approach to vision formulation would be seen as disrespectful (Javidan et al., 2006). Followers in those countries expect authoritative leadership and perceive that taking their opinions into account is a sign of incompetence or weakness. Leaders in collectivistic national cultures may need either to gradually change the organization so that participation is accepted or to find other ways to gain employee buy-in of the vision statement, such as through rewards and role modeling. Similarly, followers who are confronted with an organizational crisis or stressful uncertainty tend to look for a leader to give decisive direction rather than ask for their input. Finally, many effective leaders did not arrive at the vision statement by themselves but through insights that were shared by followers.

EXCEPTIONS

Articulating the vision in a dramatic way may lead to aversion in organizations and countries which have experienced charismatic leaders who led their organization or country into a disaster (Javidan et al., 2006). In Germany, for example, a leader who uses dramatic rhetoric is likely to be viewed with suspicion due to the traumatic experience with Adolf Hitler, who communicated his vision in an extremely dramatic manner. Similarly, some national cultures do not value highly expressive behaviors. For example, in Nordic countries, which include Denmark, Sweden, Finland, and Norway, dramatic communication lies outside accepted social norms and thus is likely to lead to rejection of the leader.

IMPLEMENTING THE VISION

Even the most effective vision statement will not impact organizational or individual outcomes if the leader does not actively implement the vision statement. In addition to ensuring that the vision statement is understood, the leader must also continue to clarify it and display behavior that is consistent with it. Below are principles for effectively implementing a vision statement.

1. *Build understanding of the vision among the top management team.* The leader must consistently and repeatedly communicate the vision statement to the top management team. Ensuring that the vision statement is well understood among the top management team is essential. The leader relies heavily on the top management team to communicate the vision statement to other followers as well as find ways to implement the vision statement within their areas of responsibility. The top management team must possess a detailed understanding of the vision statement and serve as role models who display vision-consistent behaviors.

2. *Encourage a high degree of participation in the implementation of the vision statement.* Including followers in the vision implementation process ensures that the followers will be committed to the vision and, thus, it will be more likely to be carried out. Followers from all levels and functions in the organization should be included in finding new ways to carry out the vision. This is consistent with organizational image theory, which argues that the degree to which individuals identify with the organization depends on the extent to which the vision allows individuals to enhance their self-concept (Dutton, Dukerich, and Harquail, 1994). However, as noted above, leaders in collectivistic cultures may need to rely on other means to gain follower commitment to the vision.

3. *Begin by communicating the vision statement to highly influential and cooperative individuals in the organization.* The use of opinion leaders or champions in the organization is another way to gain support for carrying out the vision (Howell and Higgins, 1990). Opinion leaders may reside at all levels of the organizational hierarchy and may include middle managers and supervisors as well as employees at lower levels of the organization; they also may be stakeholders, such as union leaders (Locke, Kirkpatrick, Wheeler, Schneider, Niles, Goldstein, Welsh, and Chah, 1991). These influential individuals will not only help communicate the vision statement to other followers but will also serve as positive role models of the desired behaviors.

4. *Motivate, inspire, and teach followers to carry out the vision statement.* Motivational techniques that leaders use include setting goals that are consistent with the vision statement, rewarding them for goal achievement and/or performance, and providing individualized coaching (Bass, 1985). Effective leaders express confidence in followers' ability to achieve the vision. Visionary leaders are confident that followers can work toward the common vision. The leader's expectation of high performance has been found to result in higher performance than when poor performance is expected (Eden, 1990). Leaders inspire followers by getting them to see the world in new ways. Leaders also provide individualized consideration through teaching, mentoring, coaching, or even supporting followers during difficult times. They also promote the vision statement

by removing obstacles that prevent vision attainment – by restructuring the organization, eliminating stifling processes, and adding new processes that give the required capability.

5. *Role model behaviors that are consistent with the vision statement.* Effective leaders display behaviors that reflect the vision statement. Role modeling helps communicate the vision through action to followers (Bandura, 1986). It demonstrates that the leader is committed to the vision statement and also tells followers the behavior required to implement the vision. Followers are more likely to commit to the vision, be highly motivated, and be confident in their ability to work toward the vision when the leader serves as a role model.

6. *Use symbols, metaphors, and images that are consistent with the vision statement.* Symbols, metaphors, and images can send powerful messages (Fairhurst and Sarr, 1996). They can instantly communicate the essence of the vision statement and provoke emotional reactions more than written words. They also help anchor the vision deeply in the minds of the followers and ensure that the vision statement is passed on to future members of the organization. Although effective verbal communication skills are beneficial, the use of symbols, metaphors, and images are also powerful techniques for communicating the vision statement. Great verbal communication skills are helpful for communicating the vision, but effective leaders also use concrete examples to convey complex, abstract concepts, draw pictures, or build models to illustrate the vision (Locke et al., 1991).

LEADING THROUGH VALUES

Another key principle for effective leadership is to lead through values. Although vision statements may include values, they are not primarily value statements. Values, as noted earlier, indicate the proper means for attaining visions. By communicating and acting in accordance with a coherent set of values, the leader can influence followers to abide by the same values. In this manner, the leaders' and followers' actions are aligned with a common set of values.

The term *values* is often misunderstood. Everyone possesses certain values, which are what an individual deems important and works to acquire or retain (Peikoff, 1991). One way to lead is by specifying a set of morals (also called personal values or moral values) that the leader wants followers to abide by. Research shows that individuals can reliably identify their value hierarchies (Rokeach, 1973). That is, they can identify specific values and rank them in order of importance.

A business's values are the "organization's precepts about what is important in business and life, how business should be conducted, its view of humanity, its role in society, the way the world works, and what is to be held inviolate" (Collins and Porras, 1991). A business's values will properly include moral values (e.g., honesty, integrity), but may include other values as well such as innovation, customer service, and quality (Locke, 2004).

Both the vision and the company's values motivate action, and ideally they will work synergistically – the general goal and the means to achieve it. Both must be communicated in order to be effective.

Implementing Values

State the desired values

A leader must identify and then communicate the desired business values to which the organization will adhere. Business values should be viable, balanced, aligned with each other, and authentic (Hultman, 2005). Common and desirable business values include cooperation, honesty, integrity, change, and a more positive future, and confidence in employees' ability to achieve the vision (Conger and Kanungo, 1987; Locke and Woiceshyn, 1995; Shamir et al., 1993). In fact, these values have been shown to be universally accepted attributes of leaders across a wide range of societies (Javidan et al., 2006).

A leader who identifies and communicates a set of personal values can improve follower commitment to the organization (Den Hartog and Verburg, 1997; Dvir, Kass, and Shamir, 2004; Rowden, 2000). The leader must explain the desired personal values and take steps to gain employee buy-in to those values. For example, UK-based law firm Eversheds embarked on a campaign to identify and communicate a set of shared values, holding "have your say" sessions to discuss and gain commitment from employees. As a result, Eversheds has changed a number of key processes to implement its values of client-centered; straightforward, mutual respect, teamwork; accountability and continuous improvement (Krais and Bloomfield, 2005).

Model the desired values

Perhaps more important than stating the values, the leader must display those values in daily actions. Even in difficult circumstances, it is crucial that followers perceive the leader as acting in accordance with the stated values. A leader who is seen as acting inconsistently with stated or implied values is not likely to be as effective as a leader who "walks the talk." By role modeling the desired behaviors, the leader motivates followers to behave in the same manner and demonstrates the behaviors that should be displayed.

The leader also must act when followers fail to display the desired values. In some cases, the leader may engage in disciplinary action or even termination, while in other cases the leader may provide individualized attention or consideration to enhance the follower's understanding on the vision statement.

When a leader fails to act in accordance with stated values, the results can be disastrous. Take, for example, the case of Countrywide Financial, a home loan lender, and its top management team, who came under scrutiny by its shareholders and the financial media for not acting in accordance with its values, especially given its poor financial performance in late 2007 and early 2008. Countrywide espouses a principle-based mission of "helping individuals and families achieve and preserve the dream of home ownership" through a "high-performance and high-integrity culture." With its stock plummeting to 80% of its 2006 value and many homeowners facing foreclosure, Countrywide planned a ski trip at a Colorado Ritz-Carlton resort for 30 mortgage lenders. After receiving scrutiny that this was not reflective of a high-integrity culture, the trip was canceled, but no doubt made a bad situation even worse for Countrywide and its leadership team (Hagerty, 2008).

Some researchers claim that effective leaders must be self-sacrificial. It is not always clear what they mean by this. Sometimes it refers to the leader not taking bonus money that was earned when the leader's organization met its goals or not fulfilling his or her commitment to followers. But this would not be a sacrifice if the leader held justice as a moral value. It would be in the leader's self-interest to be fair to the followers because, if they were treated unfairly, then followers would tend to leave (Locke, 2004). Ultimately, this would hurt the organization and thus undermine the leader's effectiveness as well as undermine the leader's self-interest.

Self-sacrifice has also been referred to as the leader taking time away from family in order to help the business succeed. Many working people, including leaders, are often faced with this conflict. Choosing to work additional hours rather than spend that time with family is not a sacrifice if one passionately loves one's work and career. However, it would be a sacrifice if one disliked one's job and preferred spending those additional hours at home. Spending extra hours at work can be a sign of commitment to one's job.

A truly self-sacrificial leader would be a leader who, out of a sense of duty, worked for a company that he did not like, made a product that he did not value, worked with people that he despised and customers that he abhorred, at the expense of leading a company that truly inspired him. No business leader could be effective if motivated in this manner.

In sum, genuine leader self-sacrifice cannot be an effective role-modeling or motivational technique. In an actual business environment – where a long-term commitment and motivation on the part of the leader and followers are required – nothing less than a passionate, personal commitment on everyone's part will do.

Integrate the values into organizational systems

The desired values can be further implemented by integrating them into the organization's systems. Human resources systems, for example, should reinforce the stated business values by basing rewards and promotions on results as well as achieving those results by practicing the desired values. Other organizational systems, such as the work processes, organizational structure, and technology, should also be aligned so that they support the desired values.

For example, the Walt Disney Company has core values of imagination and wholesomeness. These values are reflected in its movies and theme parks. Disney theme parks are family oriented, and theme park employees are hired for their ability to interact with "guests." Disney's street sweepers, who are responsible for keeping the park clean, are not just hired for their skill with a broom, but also must be able to communicate with guests and work well with other team members. To give another example, Seattle-based department store Nordstrom has relied on the same core values for its entire 100 plus year history. These values include delivering outstanding customer service and striving for high individual productivity. Nordstrom's values can be observed in its commission-based compensation plan for its store clerks, its customer service policies, and its strategic focus as an up-scale department store.

The organization and its values should not change because of shifting popular opinion, competitive forces, or changes in corporate strategy. Core values should be intrinsic to the organization's business, reflected throughout the organization, at all levels, in all units, in stated policies as well as actions by leaders, managers, and employees.

CASE EXAMPLES

BB&T Bank: Living its Values

Founded in 1906, Branch Banking and Trust Company (BB&T) is currently the USA's 14th largest financial institution, with $133 billion in assets. BB&T is headquartered in Winston-Salem, North Carolina, and operates bank subsidiaries in 11 states, primarily in the Southeastern USA.

BB&T has pursued an acquisition strategy since the mid-1990s, resulting in slow and steady growth. Despite its cautious approach, BB&T consistently beats its peers in the most important measure of banking efficiency – return on assets. Despite recent downturns in the banking and lending industries, BB&T continues to steadily grow its assets and market share.

BB&T has recorded 26 consecutive years of increasing operating earnings and has demonstrated steadily increasing results for virtually every measure of success in its industry – market share, diversification of its income sources, cost control, productivity, dividend increases, and customer satisfaction and loyalty. Its growth and current market position can be attributed to its present chairman and CEO, John Allison.

Before Allison's tenure, this rural lender based in North Carolina's farm country had $5 billion in assets. After acquiring 50 banks and thrifts, 47 insurance agencies, and 14 non-bank financial services firms, as well as experiencing organic growth, BB&T's stock is up roughly 700% under Allison.

Allison first joined BB&T in 1971 after graduating from college, and he was appointed to his current position in 1994. He often sounds like a typical CEO, citing financial ratios and accounting acronyms when explaining his latest acquisition. One gets the sense the he is not your typical bank CEO when he quotes Aristotle, "We are what we repeatedly do."

Allison can speak at length about classical philosophy, providing two-and-a-half hour lectures on deductive reasoning and the value of logic in decision making. He takes a week off each year to study philosophy. He requires his senior managers to attend educational retreats and "encourages" them to read a non-banking book monthly.

Allison made philosophy a relevant science to the world of banking. He applies Ayn Rand's objectivist principles of individualism, marrying it with accountability. This is reflected in the BB&T management structure in which regional presidents are given autonomy, but it seems that every year one of them is relieved of their duties. Specific goals are set; sales reps are expected to make 10 calls daily, two of which must be in person. Branch officers are given commercial lending authority – not a generally accepted industry practice.

BB&T is clearly charting its own course through the values that Allison has identified. Its values are detailed in a 30-page manual entitled *The BB&T Philosophy*. Although Allison was the driving force behind the philosophy, he obtained support for it from BB&T's board of directors and senior managers. The philosophy (which also appears at www.bbt.com) consists of four main components:

- *BB&T Vision, Mission, and Purpose*
- *BB&T Values*
- *Concepts that Describe BB&T*
- *Strategic Objectives*

The *BB&T Vision* is "To create the best financial institution possible and to be the best of the best." The vision is further elaborated by the *Mission*, or reason for existence, which is "to make the world a better place to live by (1) helping our Clients achieve economic success and financial security, (2) creating a place where our Employees can learn, grow, and be fulfilled in their work, and (3) making the communities in which we work better places to be; thereby, optimizing the long-term return to our Shareholders, while providing a safe and sound investment." The bank's *Purpose* is summarized as "Our ultimate purpose is to create superior long-term economic rewards for our shareholders" and is explained further in detailed paragraphs explaining the importance and inter-relationships of clients, employees, communities, and shareholders.

BB&T Values form the foundation of the vision; employees are expected to display the values on a daily basis. The 10 values and a brief description of each (paraphrased from *The BB&T Philosophy*) are:

◆ Reality (fact-based): Actions must be based on the facts.
◆ Reason (objectivity): Decisions must be based on a logical reasoning process based on facts.
◆ Independent thinking: Employees are challenged to make rational decisions; creativity can only occur through independent thought.
◆ Productivity: We turn our thoughts into action to improve economic well-being, including company profitability.
◆ Honesty: We act consistently with reality; we say what we mean and mean what we say.
◆ Integrity: We act consistently, in accordance with our logically-developed principles.
◆ Justice (Fairness): Individuals are evaluated and rewarded objectively, based on their contributions toward accomplishing the mission and adhering to our values.
◆ Pride: We are proud of our accomplishments that are achieved by living our values.
◆ Self-esteem (Self-motivation): By acting in their rational self-interest and doing their work well, our employees earn positive self-esteem.
◆ Teamwork/Mutual supportiveness: Our work requires an integrated effort among outstanding individuals to accomplish important tasks.

Rather than simply listing values and expecting employees to understand how they are relevant to their job, *The BB&T Philosophy* shows how the values are applied in the company:

◆ A list of *Concepts that Describe BB&T* – client-driven, quality oriented, efficient, growing both our business and our people, continuous improvement, and objective decision making – is presented.
◆ Special attention is given to describing the BB&T management style – a participative and team-oriented process provides better information and thus results in better decisions.
◆ Attributes of an outstanding BB&T employee are described as "they believe that their lives matter and that they can accomplish something meaningful through their work."

These values served BB&T well during the recent downturn in the lending industry. Guided by its values, BB&T decided that subprime loans were not based on reality or facts but instead were irrational. These types of loans made up only .6% of BB&T's mortgage loan portfolio.

Because Allison's personal values played a strong role in formulating and articulating *The BB&T Philosophy*, there is a high degree of consistency between his personal and company values. Allison and BB&T do not pay lip service to the philosophy. They expect employees to act in accordance with the values. Those that don't lose their jobs, regardless of their title, level in the organization, or productivity. In fact, the values are reflected in BB&T's human resources system – including selection, training, performance appraisal, and promotion – as well as its strategic decisions, such as choosing to avoid exotic mortgages that resulted in losses at many of its industry competitors.

Allison firmly believes that incorporating the company's values into its decision-making process improves its chance of success. Not only are the values in the best interest of BB&T, they are also in the best interest of individual employees as well as the community which are home to BB&T banks. In the forward to the *Philosophy*, Allison sums up his views nicely, "We believe that competitive advantage is largely in the minds of our employees as represented by their capacity to turn rational ideas into action towards the accomplishment of our mission."

SOURCES

BB&T 2007 Annual Review.

Early, J. (June 20, 2007), A conversation with BB&T, The Motley Fool (www.fool.com; accessed January 11, 2008).

Vardi, N. (November 1, 2006). How does BB&T's John Allison explain his slew of bank deals? By quoting the classics. Forbes (www.forbes.com, accessed January 11, 2008).

Harrington, M. (January 8, 2008). BB&T CEO discusses philosophy, economy at luncheon. *The Business Journal of the Greater Triad Area* (triad.bizjournals.com, accessed January 11, 2008).

Roberts, R. (May 7, 2007). Allison on Strategy, Profits, and Self-Interest. The Library of Economics and Liberty, podcast and transcript available at www.econtalk.org (accessed February 7, 2008)

MidState Analytics[1]

MidState Analytics is a small, privately owned firm of 450 employees that provides specialized scientific and technical analysis to government organizations and commercial companies. Headquartered in Chicago, MidState Analytics was founded in 1975 by three graduate school colleagues. The founders are no longer active in the company but remain as major shareholders.

MidState experienced sustained, steady growth over the past decades, in part due to its ability to hire top-notch scientists in a wide range of specialty areas, such as biology, chemistry, systems engineering, physics, mathematics, and economics. A typical consulting engagement involves a cross-disciplinary team of scientists and project managers who

---

[1] This fictional case draws upon several real-life cases, but any resemblance to an actual organization or individuals is purely coincidental.

often work on-site at client locations. A company vision statement hangs on the wall in the company lobby:

> MidState Analytics provides sound, impartial scientific analysis and research in order to create safe, effective products and services.

Although no formal statement of values exists, the scientific backgrounds of MidState's employees provide them with generally accepted common values of research integrity, sharing of methodology and research findings, mentoring of more junior scientists, and treating each other with professionalism.

The company has four divisions – Consumer Products, Health, Information Systems Support, and Engineering. In early 2002, the director of the Consumer Products division, Jim Modell, brought in a new practice manager, Gabe Addison, to develop business in the toiletries and cosmetics industry. Modell and Addison knew each other from brief interactions at professional conferences. Addison's track record was impressive – author of several patents, a stint as a faculty member at the University of Massachusetts, and publications in top-notch academic journals. In his 10-year career, Addison worked at five different organizations, which, in Modell's mind, gave Addison a solid base of technical and managerial experience.

During Gabe's interviews with MidState's CEO, Gordon Levy, and the rest of the leadership team, Gabe made sure to mention his many high level contacts at potential client companies. Levy remarked, "With Gabe's high level contacts, we could easily win new clients and quickly grow our revenues."

Initial success.   Levy's impressions proved true, at first. In his first year, Addison secured four new major clients, allowing him to build a staff of about 50 scientists and technicians. Some team members transferred from within the company, while the majority were new hires. Addison's days were spent meeting with the clients and supervising the project teams who mainly worked on-site at client locations around the greater Chicago area.

A few months into one project for the NPG Corporation, Addison's staff grew concerned. After a cursory look at the team's analysis, Addison singularly authored a final report that contradicted the analysis. Karen McKnight, a senior analyst and team lead, asked Addison to take another look at their analysis. Addison snapped at her, "NPG needs to move quickly. These are the results they want." When McKnight calmly insisted that Addison take the results home to read, Addison became irate, telling her, "I have more experience than anyone else here. You need to be shown how this business works."

Downward slide.   Over the next few months, McKnight and her team experienced several similar incidents despite the fact that Addison began visiting the NPG team less frequently. When he did show up, he became incensed that the team had pressed forward in his absence. The team became increasingly frustrated and the work pace began to slow down, resulting in further reprimands from Addison for lack of productivity. Scolding McKnight in front of her team, Addison shouted, "Why are you holding team meetings? Stop meeting and get to work." Yet during his next visit, he admonished, "This project requires teamwork. How can you work together if you don't hold team meetings?"

After one particularly bad day in which Addison snapped at one of McKnight's brightest team members for "not knowing anything," McKnight called MidState colleague and close friend, Bart Thierry, who was heading up Addison's team at O'Brien Industries. Thierry and McKnight spent several hours comparing stories, only to discover that they were seeing the same behavior from Addison. Soon, all four team leads under Addison began to compare notes.

McKnight was struggling to manage both her team and Addison. Her team took long lunches and frequent sick days. Some told her that they were experiencing physical symptoms, such as headaches and nausea. McKnight knew that clients were also feeling confused, especially when they were getting one answer from Addison and another from the team.

On one occasion, Addison asked McKnight to take three team members and begin analysis for a new type of aftershave, telling her, "If you do well, I will nominate you for the MidState Researcher of the Year Award." She spent several days researching and planning the effort. When she asked usually calm and cooperative staff member Kim Harbold for assistance locating a journal article on chemical compounds, Harbold was less than helpful. At the next status meeting Harbold's unusual behavior became clear when Addison announced that he was having Harbold, not McKnight, lead the aftershave project.

In response to this slight, McKnight built up the confidence to confront Addison, not about the decision – Harbold was more than capable – but about how the decision-making process was handled. When she requested a meeting, Addison replied that he only met with staff after 6:00pm on Fridays. She canceled her usual "girls night out" to meet with Addison. Her fellow team leads expressed even more displeasure than McKnight regarding Addison's "office hours," noting their displeasure at the conflict between their family commitments and Addison's schedule. That Friday, McKnight drove to headquarters, arriving well before 6:00pm to allow time to catch up on paperwork. Finally, the appointed time came and went – Addison never showed up.

A dejected McKnight popped her head into Modell's office; she and Modell had always gotten along well, so she felt comfortable confiding in him. She explained her confusion and frustration in dealing with Addison, "I worked hard to earn my doctorate, putting myself through graduate school, and I've worked hard at MidState for over 10 years with an excellent track record, yet he makes me feel like a child."

Modell presented a balanced perspective, noting that Addison had landed some really big accounts and thus had considerable sway with the leadership team. However, Modell also told her that he had been hearing the same thing from the other team leads and that he would speak to Addison. Modell said that Addison was probably just tired and stressed. McKnight went home relieved that Modell would take some action.

Rock bottom.   That weekend, McKnight met a grad school buddy, Carlos Landy, for dinner. Landy, now a professor at the University of Massachusetts, was not surprised at all to hear what was happening. "Didn't MidState check Addison's references?" he stated, adding, "When he was on the U. Mass faculty, he routinely talked down to his graduate students and even promised the authorship on papers which he promptly 'forgot' about. One of his students, Matt Light, a really promising researcher, was often the target of Addison's outbursts. Eventually, Matt had a psychological breakdown and hasn't returned to campus since, poor guy."

The following week, McKnight called Modell to find out the result of his meeting with Addison. Modell told her, "I set up a meeting with him on Tuesday but he never showed up. There's really nothing I can do. We could never fire him because we can't replace him to keep the contracts going – no one else on our staff has the contacts that he does."

The initial contracts that Addison brought in were soon coming to an end. Projects were falling behind schedule, giving them little chance of being renewed. In his annual forecasts, Addison promised continued growth, bragging about his high level contacts, but emphasized that his "incompetent staff of inexperienced, junior analysts" made it difficult to do the work. McKnight began noticing a trend – first, one of her team members left, deciding to relocate back to his hometown. Then, Thierry's head scientist left for his "dream job" at another employer in Chicago. A few more left after that, and then a few more. Some expressed their frustration during their exit interviews, while others made no mention of Addison's behavior.

McKnight ran into Modell at headquarters one morning. "This turnover is hitting us pretty hard. I'm not sure I can take much more of Addison's outbursts, let alone handle him ignoring our analysis. Can we talk about some ways of dealing with Addison's behavior?" Modell simply shook his head, "He's the one who brought in the clients and you want me to get *him* to change?"

Ultimate impact.   Over the next year, the turnover continued and morale plummeted. Customers did not renew their contracts. Modell and the rest of the leadership team took no steps to resolve the situation. Addison's client base reduced to a handful of small contracts.

About a year later, Addison resigned after a shouting match with MidState's director of finance. McKnight took over the few remaining contracts. Over the next six months, she managed to build up the contracts into a profitable niche. She then resigned when Modell told her that she was not eligible for a promotion because Addison originally brought in the customers.

CONCLUSION

In conclusion, discernible behaviors for leading through vision and values have been shown to lead to effective outcomes. By understanding and applying these principles, leadership skills can be enhanced.

REFERENCES

Arnold, K. A., Turner, N., Barling, J., Kelloway, E. K., and McKee, M. C. (2007). Transformational leadership and psychological well-being: The mediating role of meaningful work. *Journal of Occupational Health Psychology*, 12, 193–203.

Barling, J., Weber, T., and Kelloway, E. K. (1996). Effects of transformational leadership training on attitudinal and financial outcomes: A field experiment. *Journal of Applied Psychology*, 81, 827–832.

Bandura, A. (1986). *Social Foundation of Thought and Action: A Social Cognitive Theory.* Englewood Cliffs, NJ: Prentice-Hall.

Bass, B. M. (1985). *Leadership and Performance Beyond Expectations.* New York: The Free Press.

Bass, B. M., Avolio, B. J., Jung, D. I., and Berson, Y. (2003). Predicting unit performance by assessing transformational and transactional leadership. *Journal of Applied Psychology*, 88, 207–218.

Baum, J. R., Locke, E. A., and Kirkpatrick, S. A. (1998). A longitudinal study of the relation of vision and vision communication to venture growth in entrepreneurial firms. *Journal of Applied Psychology*, 83, 43–54.

Bono, J. E., Jackson Foldes, H., Vinson, G., and Muros, J. P. (2007). Workplace emotions: The role of supervision and leadership. *Journal of Applied Psychology*, 92, 1357–1367.

Burns, J. M. (1978). *Leadership*. New York: Harper and Row.

Colbert, A. E., Kristof-Brown, A. L., Bradley, B. H., and Barrick, M. R. (2008). CEO transformational leadership: The role of goal importance congruence in top management teams. *Academy of Management Journal*, 51, 81–96.

Collins, J. C., and Porras, J. I. (1991). Organizational vision and visionary organizations. *California Management Review*, 34(1), 30–52.

Conger, J. A., and Kanungo, R. N. (1987). Toward a behavioral theory of charismatic leadership in organizational settings. *Academy of Management Review*, 12, 637–647.

Coulson-Thomas, C. (1992). Leadership and corporate transformation. *Leadership and Organizational Development Journal*, 13(4), iv–vii.

Crown, D. F., and Rosse, J. G. (1995). Yours, mine, and ours: Facilitating group productivity through the integration of individual and group goals. *Organizational Behavior and Human Decision Processes*, 64, 138–150.

Den Hartog, D. N., and Verburg, R. M. (1997). Charisma and rhetoric: Communicative techniques of international business leaders. *Leadership Quarterly*, 8, 355–391.

Doz, Y. L., and Prahalad, C. K. (1987). A process model of strategic redirection in large complex firms: The case of multinational corporations. In A. Pettigrew (ed.), *The Management of Strategic Change* (pp. 63–83). Oxford: Basil Blackwell.

Dutton, J. E., Dukerich, J. M., and Harquail, C. V. (1994). Organizational images and member identification. *Administrative Science Quarterly*, 39(2), 239–263.

Dvir, T., Kass, N., and Shamir, B. (2004). The emotional bond: Vision and organizational commitment among high-tech employees. *Journal of Organizational Change Management*, 17, 126–143.

Eden, D. (1990). *Pygmalion in Management*. Lexington, MA: Heath.

Fairhurst, G. T., and Sarr, R. A. (1996). *The Art of Framing: Managing the Language of Leadership*. San Francisco: Jossey Bass.

Hagerty, J. R. (2008). Countrywide cancels ski trip amid criticism. *Wall Street Journal Online* (January 25; accessed March 3, 2008).

Hart, S. L., and Quinn, R. E. (1993). Roles executives play: CEOs, behavioral complexity and firm performance. *Human Relations*, 46(5), 543–574.

House, R. J. (1977). A 1976 theory of charismatic leadership. In J. G. Hunt and L. L. Larson (eds), *Leadership: The Cutting Edge* (pp. 189–204). Carbondale, IL: Southern Illinois University Press.

House, R. J., Hanges, P. J., Ruiz-Quintanilla, S. A., Dorfman, P. W., Javidan, M., Dickson, M., Gupta, V. plus 170 GLOBE Country Co-Investigators (1999). Cultural influences on leadership and organizations: Project GLOBE. In J. Mobley (ed.), *Advances in Global Leadership* (Vol. 1, pp. 171–233). Greenwich/London: JAI Press.

Howell, J. M., and Avolio, B. J. (1993). Transformational leadership, transactional leadership, locus of control, and support for innovation: Key predictors of consolidated-business-unit performance. *Journal of Applied Psychology*, 78, 891–902.

Howell, J. M., and Frost, P. J. (1989). A laboratory study of charismatic leadership. *Organizational Behavior and Human Decision Processes*, 43(2), 243–269.

Howell, J. M., and Higgins, C. A. (1990). Champions of change: Identifying, understanding, and supporting champions of technological innovations. *Organizational Dynamics*, 19, 40–55

Hultman, K. (2005). Evaluating organizational values. *Organization Development Journal*, 23(4), 32–44.

Ireland, R. D. and Hitt, M. A. (1990). Achieving and maintaining strategic competitiveness in the 21st century: The role of strategic leadership. *Academy of Management Executive*, 13, 43–57.

Javidan, M., Dorfman, P. W., deLuque, M. S., and House, R. J. (2006). In the eye of the beholder: Cross cultural lessons in leadership from Project GLOBE. *Academy of Management Perspectives*, 20, 67–90.

Kirkpatrick, S. A., and Locke, E. A. (1996). Direct and indirect effects of three core charismatic leadership components on performance and attitudes. *Journal of Applied Psychology*, 81, 36–51.

Kirkpatrick, S. A., Wofford, J. C., and Baum, J. R. (2002). Measuring motive imagery contained in the vision statement. *The Leadership Quarterly*, 13, 139–150.

Krais, H., and Bloomfield, R. (2005). Making vision and values a reality at Eversheds. *Strategic Communication Management*, 9(6), 26–29.

Larwood, L., Falbe, C. M., Kriger, M. P., and Meising, P. (1995). Structure and meaning of organizational vision. *Academy of Management Journal*, 38, 740–769.

Locke, E. A. (2004). *Self-interest*. In G. Goethals, G. Sorenson, and J. Burns (eds), *Encyclopedia of Leadership* (Vol. 4). Thousand Oaks, CA: Sage.

Locke, E. A., Kirkpatrick, S., Wheeler, J. K., Schneider, J., Niles, K., Goldstein, H., Welsh, K., and Chah, D. (1991). *The Essence of Leadership: The Four Keys to Leading Successfully*. New York: Lexington Books.

Locke, E. A., and Latham, G. P. (1990). *A Theory of Goal Setting and Task Performance*. Englewood Cliffs: Prentice Hall.

Locke, E. A., and Woiceshyn, J. (1995). Why businessmen should be honest: The argument from rational egoism. *Journal of Organizational Behavior*, 16, 405–414.

Nanus, B. (1992). *Visionary Leadership: Creating a Compelling Sense of Direction for your Organization*. San Francisco: Jossey-Bass.

Niehoff, B. P., Enz, C. A., and Grover, R. A. (1990). The impact of top-management actions on employee attitudes and perceptions. *Group and Organization Studies*, 15, 337–352.

Oswald, S. L., Mossholder, K. W., and Harris, S. G. (1994). Vision salience and strategic involvement: Implications for psychological attachment to organization and job. *Strategic Management Journal*, 15, 477–489.

Oswald, S., Stanwick, P., and LaTour, M. (1997). The effect of vision, strategic planning, and cultural relationships on organizational performance: A structural approach. *International Journal of Management*, 14, 521.

Peikoff, L. (1991). *Objectivism: The Philosophy of Ayn Rand.* New York: Penguin Books (Dutton).

Piccolo, R. F., and Colquitt, J. A. (2006). Transformational leadership and job behaviors: The mediating role of core job characteristics. *Academy of Management Journal*, 49, 327–340.

Podsakoff, P. M., MacKenzie, S. B., Moorman, R. H., and Fetter, R. (1990). Transformational leader behaviors and their effects on followers' trust in leader, satisfaction, and organizational citizenship behaviors. *Leadership Quarterly*, 1, 107–142.

Roberts, N. C. (1985). Transforming leadership: A process of collective action. *Human Relations*, 38, 1023–1046.

Rokeach, M. (1973). *The Nature of Human Values.* New York: Free Press.

Rowden, R. W. (2000). The relationship between charismatic leadership behaviors and organizational commitment, *Leadership and Organization Development Journal*, 21(2), 30–35.

Schaubroeck, J., Lam, S. S. K., and Cha, S. E. (2007). Embracing transformational leadership: team values and the impact of leader behavior on team performance. *Journal of Applied Psychology*, 92, 1020–1030.

Scott, C. D., Jaffe, D. T., and Tobe, G. R. (1993). *Organizational Vision, Values and Mission: Building the Organization of Tomorrow.* Menlo Park, CA: Crisp Publications.

Shamir, B., House, R. J., and Arthur, M. B. (1993). The motivational effects of charismatic leadership: A self-concept-based theory. *Organization Science*, 4, 577–594.

Shamir, B., House, R. J., and Arthur, M. B. (1994). The rhetoric of charismatic leadership: A theoretical extension, a case study and implications for future research. *Leadership Quarterly*, 5, 25–42.

Trice, H. M., and Beyer, J. M. (1986). Charisma and its routinization in two social movement organizations. In L. L. Cummins and B. M. Staw (eds), *Research in Organizational Behavior* (Vol. 8, pp. 113–164). Greenwich, CT: JAI Press.

Vroom, V. H., and Jago, A. G. (2007). The role of situation in leadership. *American Psychologist*, 62, 17–24.

Yukl, G. (2005). *Leadership in Organizations* (6th edition). Englewood Cliffs: Prentice Hall.

EXERCISES

Write a vision statement

Congratulations, you were recently selected as the recipient of the Entrepreneurial Council for High Achievement's annual grant. You applied for the award almost a year ago, detailing your academic and professional achievements, entrepreneurial experience and aptitude, and undergoing a series of intensive interviews. Your efforts have paid off and this is your opportunity to do what you have always wanted – run your own company.

With the award comes $10 million in venture capital backing to start your own profit-making venture. The investors prefer to stay in the background and let you do what you do best, so you will be given complete autonomy to start any type of for-profit company you want. This initial round of funding could be supplemented with additional financial backing if your company does well in its early stages.

To begin your venture, you must begin by answering a series of questions about the company that you will start. It may help to put some serious thought into creating a company that provides a useful product or service.

Carefully consider these questions and write a response to each one:

1. What are you passionate about? What really peaks your interest and gets your blood flowing?
2. What product or service could your company provide that is consistent with your passion and interest?
3. How do you want others to see you and your company? When your employees are hanging out at the water cooler, what will they say about you?
4. Prepare a draft for your company's vision statement.
5. List at least 10 behaviors that you could carry out each day to live the vision.

Values comparison

The two cases, BB&T Bank and MidState Analytics, present drastically different company value systems.

1. Identify the values displayed by each company.
2. Contrast the values. How are the two companies' values different from each other?
3. What results (e.g. company performance, customer retention, motivated and committed employees, turnover, morale) have occurred at each company?
4. Which set of values is more effective? Explain why.

21

Foster Trust through Ability, Benevolence, and Integrity

Jason A. Colquitt and Sabrina C. Salam[*]

Concerns about trust are woven into many aspects of working life. Encounters with new co-workers, leaders, or followers are dominated by questions about trust, setting the tone for future interactions. As relationships develop, trust serves as a guide that paces the openness, investment, and spontaneity of the interactions between individuals at work. As individuals navigate their way through hierarchical relationships, trust influences decisions about whether to cooperate with directives at the risk of exploitation. Finally, trust takes on a renewed importance in times of organizational crisis, as it can help maintain a sense of confidence and optimism during tough times.

The academic literature defines trust as the willingness of a trustor to be vulnerable to the actions of a trustee based on positive expectations about the trustee's characteristics, behaviors, and intentions (Mayer, Davis, and Schoorman, 1995). When employees trust their supervisors, they would be prepared to grant them influence over important issues by, for example, disclosing sensitive or personal information (Mayer and Davis, 1999; Schoorman, Mayer, and Davis, 2007). Note that trust in this example is not the actual disclosing of the information; it is the psychological state that makes the employee willing to do it. The disclosing of information represents risk taking, which can be viewed as one behavioral expression of trust (Mayer et al., 1995).

The *Oxford English Dictionary* defines trust as confidence in, or reliance on, some quality or attribute of a person. A number of qualities or attributes are capable of inspiring trust in leaders. For example, research has examined attributes like competence, loyalty, concern, consistency, reliability, honesty, openness, and value congruence (Butler, 1991; Butler and Cantrell, 1984; Mayer et al., 1995). Research examines these attributes under the heading of "trustworthiness," grouping them into three distinct categories or concepts.

---

[*] Editor's note: I regret to announce that Sabrina Salam died tragically in a car accident on April 4, 2005.

One of the three concepts is *ability*. If they want their followers to trust them, leaders must know what they are talking about, meaning they must possess relevant job knowledge and skills (Mayer et al., 1995). Only then will followers be confident that the leader's ideas are worth taking seriously. Of course, ability is often domain specific (Zand, 1972). Actions that reveal an expertise in one area (e.g. running the advertisement campaign for a new product) do not necessarily signal competence in another (e.g. determining the overall strategy for the entire organization).

The other two aspects of trustworthiness are less domain specific, reflecting more on the person and character of the leader. *Benevolence* entails the degree to which a leader has a sense of goodwill toward followers, showing concern and loyalty to them for reasons that are not egocentric or solely motivated by profits (Mayer et al., 1995). One could contrast benevolent leaders with narcissistic leaders or Machiavellian leaders who simply want to "use" people as a means to their own personal ends. This facet of trustworthiness is evident in good mentor–protégé relationships, where a dyadic bond exists that goes beyond the formalized relationships reflected in an organizational chart.

Integrity, the third component, captures the degree to which a leader adheres to sound ethical and moral principles (Mayer et al., 1995). Leaders who have integrity keep their promises, exhibit consistent actions and behaviors, and adhere to values such as honesty and openness. Integrity also conveys an alignment between a leader's words and a leader's deeds (Simons, 2002). From this perspective, integrity can be gauged by asking whether leaders "do what they say they will do."

When discussing trust in leaders in organizations, what they most want to know is how to increase trust within their units. If followers do not trust leaders, they react to the leader's words with skepticism, spending time monitoring the leader, checking up on them, and creating contingency plans in the event that things go wrong (Mayer and Gavin, 2005). Such reactions amount to a "distrust tax" that can reduce the speed and efficiency of the actions, behaviors, and decisions within organizational units (Covey, 2006). In addition, a sense of distrust can undermine the communication and cooperation within the unit while increasing the potential for the kinds damaging forms of group conflict. With that in mind, this chapter focuses on using the concepts of ability, benevolence, and integrity as a means of increasing trust.

THE BENEFITS OF TRUST

Before examining our focal principle in more depth, it is useful to review the importance of trust within work units. That discussion will reveal that leaders should foster trust within their work units because it leads to many beneficial outcomes in organizational life (Colquitt, Scott, and LePine, 2007; Dirks and Ferrin, 2002). Those outcomes include:

Redefining the work relationship

The most effective work relationships involve employees who are willing to go beyond the strict definitions of their work roles (Graen and Scandura, 1987). When a leader asks a follower to "go the extra mile," the follower has to have confidence that those efforts will eventually be rewarded, despite the absence of any formalized schedule or agreement.

Followers who trust their leaders are willing to engage in those extra actions because they trust that their leader will eventually reciprocate (Blau, 1964). Put differently, they trust that their leaders will, over the long term, engage in a fair exchange relationship (see Chapter 14 of this volume for more on this issue). The end result of that trust is a work relationship built on evolving role definitions and requirements rather than bureaucratically defined lists of job duties.

Creativity and innovation

Employees face other risks in their working lives, apart from the extra-mile sorts of behaviors alluded to above. Among those risks is the decision to do their work in a creative and innovative fashion. Being innovative and creative usually entails a greater danger of making mistakes than following tradition. After all, novel ideas and solutions are not always functional, and are not always accepted by an employee's peers. Despite those dangers, followers may accept the risks involved in creativity and innovation if they trust in the leader's ability, benevolence, and integrity. When followers view a leader as trustworthy, they know he or she will not take advantage of honest mistakes in a manner that will harm the employee.

Job performance

Trust enhances employee job performance for a number of reasons. Many employees cannot perform their jobs at a truly effective level without the extra-role and risk-taking behaviors that can be fostered by trust. However, trust also impacts an employee's ability to focus on the task at hand (Mayer and Gavin, 2005). If employees are spending too much time "covering their backsides," worrying about politics, and drawing up contingency plans, they will not be able to focus enough attention on their job duties. Even if they can somehow remain focused on their jobs, the additional monitoring and backing up chores will heighten their stress level.

Communication

The amount of trust that exists between a leader and a follower affects the communication between them, including the amount of information exchange and the accuracy and efficiency of that exchange. Followers who trust their leaders will share facts and information with them more frequently, and will be less likely to be guarded or secretive in the information that is conveyed. The effectiveness of a work unit often depends on followers being willing to share "bad news" without fears of "shooting the messenger" (i.e. having the leader react punitively and destructively). Trust can enable candor, lessening the likelihood that news will be "spun" in an inaccurate manner. Indeed, the ability of trust to encourage undistorted communication and collaboration is especially important in times of organizational crisis (Zand, 1972). Furthermore, distrustful employees may even withhold good news, thinking in some way it will work to their disadvantage if others somehow claim credit for it.

Commitment to decisions

When a leader is successful in creating trust in employees, these employees are likely to be more committed to decisions developed jointly with the leader and to decisions made by the leader alone (Frost and Moussavi, 1992; Tyler and Degoey, 1996; Zand, 1972). Commitment to decisions is important in order to ensure their successful implementation. Many change programs in organizations, for example, fail because the majority of employees do not trust the motives or do not know the reasons behind them, and thus are not committed to them and do not implement the desired changes in their daily work. Employees revert to the "old way of doing things" with the only difference that they are now using, for example, more expensive tools and systems. Because trust encourages commitment to decisions, developing greater trust in the leader encourages the implementation of changes in the work unit.

Commitment to the organization

The reasons why employees leave an organization are very frequently related to their direct superiors and the trust these employees develop toward their superiors. For example, whether or not a leader follows up on promises made to the employee, whether or not a leader provides competent instruction to the employee, and whether or not a leader keeps promises are all influential in a subordinate's decision to stay with an organization. Employees may develop an emotional bond with trustworthy leaders (McAllister, 1995) or may feel a sense of obligation to remain with them to further the organization's work. Regardless of the underlying reasons, retaining such employees is critical to avoid the expense associated with turnover while protecting the knowledge and expertise of the work unit.

IMPLEMENTING THE PRINCIPLE

How can organizational leaders implement our focal principle by using ability, benevolence, and integrity to foster trust? We will describe a number of actions that flow from the top of the organization – as represented by its culture – down to the leaders themselves – particularly in terms of their traits and skills. The importance of ability, benevolence, and integrity may seem obvious, in hindsight, once leaders are told about the principle. Nevertheless, many leaders fail to act in a trustworthy fashion, either because they lack valuable aptitudes and skills, they are of poor moral character, they lack concern for the employees, or they become distracted by the challenges they face on a daily basis. Besides managing their followers, leaders need to monitor competitor movements, new product developments, government regulations, and technical and process issues in their supply chain. Because those challenges are numerous, organizations need to emphasize issues of trustworthiness throughout their management and staffing decision making.

Create a culture of trustworthiness

Organizational culture is the shared values (i.e. what is important; see Chapter 20, this volume) and beliefs (i.e. how things work) that interact with an organization's processes, structures, and control systems to create behavioral norms (i.e. how things are done around here) (Uttal, 1983). Developing and maintaining the "right" kind of organizational culture is a complex process that depends on multiple factors. The founders of an organization often set the tone for the culture, while actively managing staffing decisions so that the right people are selected and promoted over time. The leaders in an organization become the agent of that culture and therefore need to exhibit consistent actions that model the beliefs and values reflected in the culture. After all, employees look to the actions of the leader in order to understand the beliefs and values that are rewarded in the organization. If leaders' actions and words are in conflict with one another, it is likely that the actions will loom larger in the minds of followers than the words as they seek to understand the "true" culture.

There are a number of organizational activities that leaders can undertake to create a culture of trustworthiness in their organization. Probably one of the most crucial steps is to communicate and formalize the ethical principles that underlie integrity by creating fair and consistent procedures, and ensuring that adherence to those procedures is transparent to every member of the organization. This can be aided through the involvement of at least some of the affected and involved employees whenever an organization makes critical decisions, plans activities, or initiates changes. Furthermore, the decision procedures that precede and accompany any organizational changes should be communicated widely so that employees can review these procedures whenever desirable.

Additionally, during the planning and implementation of any organizational changes, employees should often have the opportunity to have a dialog with the decision makers of the organization. This includes the opportunity to voice disagreements with organizational practices and the willingness of management to listen to disagreements. That sort of exchange will give leaders the opportunity to highlight the ethical standards and business considerations that have guided the organizational change and its implementation. Without that level of two-way communication, employees may react based on mistaken impressions that undercut perceptions of trustworthiness.

A culture of trustworthiness can also be created by emphasizing competence throughout the organization. One of the first steps in such an effort is gaining a more complete and valid understanding of the knowledge, skills, abilities, and other factors that are vital to success in the various jobs in the organization. Extensive job analyses should be conducted, with the results flowing into specific and accurate job descriptions. Unfortunately, many organizations suffer from unclear roles and responsibilities, which lead to an unclear definition of job functions. Colleagues, supervisors, or employees may develop distrust towards particular individuals because they expect them to have skills in areas that are not part of their job descriptions. Every member of the organization needs to understand their own roles and responsibilities, and those of their colleagues.

Emphasizing competence within the culture also requires leaders to identify the incompetent behaviors of employees and demonstrate that such behaviors will not be tolerated or rewarded in the organization. One means of accomplishing this goal is utilizing the results of job analyses to inform the development and use of performance evaluation procedures (see Chapter 5 of this volume). That practice will ensure that leaders are knowledgeable about what it means to "do a good job" in a particular area. In cases where performance behaviors are not adequate, the organization's training and development programs need to be implemented in order to increase the right kinds of competencies (see Chapter 4 of this volume). Such programs need to be comprehensive, long term, and available to all the employees who need them. Furthermore, a process needs to be in place where the programs are continuously updated based on changes in the organization, the market, relevant technologies, consumer demands, and so forth.

Increase leader ability

Having emphasized the importance of the larger organizational culture, we now focus on the leaders themselves. A leader's trustworthiness can depend on both technical skills and general managerial competencies. Technically speaking, a leader needs to possess the competence, knowledge, and skills to perform certain actions and make certain decisions in their area of expertise. That ability is needed for followers to accept leader decisions and commit to them. Leaders therefore need extensive training in both technical and managerial skills. In addition to that training, leaders need to keep up to date with the most recent developments in their area, committing to employee development and continuous learning activities. This is something that is increasingly difficult given the high frequency of innovations and changes in any business area. Of course, leaders who are high in general intelligence will be more likely to attain and maintain high levels of technical ability (see Chapter 1, this volume).

Aside from their technical skills, however, leaders need to maintain high levels of general managerial competencies. Those competencies include being able to plan a career path with followers, setting the right kinds of goals with followers, evaluating follower performance accurately, providing coaching and development, and effectively managing conflict within the unit. Those competencies also include interpersonal skills, such as developing a knowledge and understanding of one's employees and their unique abilities. In many units, these managerial competencies have a stronger impact on unit performance than the leader's own technical skills.

Successfully managing ability levels requires leaders to show self-awareness and a realistic judgment about their strengths and weaknesses. Overestimating one's ability often results in failure, which can hamper the development of trust among followers. Thus, leaders should demonstrate to followers that they know what they do (and do not) know. It is a sign of objectivity to know when to ask for help and input in a particular task. Leaders should strive to approach the followers who possess helpful knowledge and abilities to solve a particular problem, admitting that they would not be able to accomplish this task successfully alone. This sort of participative leadership can effectively capitalize on the variations in information and competencies across followers within a work unit (see Chapter 24, this volume).

Build leader benevolence

Although followers can judge a leader's ability rather quickly and reliably, gauging a leader's benevolence requires more time and attention. One way to demonstrate benevolence is to be supportive – to show concern for follower welfare, to consider follower needs, and to help followers on work tasks when necessary (Mayer and Davis, 1999). Managerial training can emphasize the importance of leader supportiveness, and relevant personality traits could also be considered in the context of selection and placement decisions.

For example, leaders who are particularly Machiavellian or narcissistic are unlikely to engage in the kinds of behaviors needed to build a sense of benevolence.

Over time, continued demonstrations of benevolence can deepen the trust felt by a follower for a leader. Eventually, the dyad becomes characterized by a mutual investment of time and attention, and a mutual sense of fondness and respect. Role definitions become broadened, with the follower willing to "back up" the leader if necessary, or "stick his/her neck out" to support the leader (Graen and Uhl-Bien, 1995). Because it depends on frequent demonstrations of goodwill and frequent interactions between the leader and follower, this deepened sense of trust may only develop in a few select work relationships (Lewicki and Bunker, 1995; McAllister, 1995). Still, if it does develop, it can serve as a robust and long-lasting foundation for extra-role and risk-taking behaviors within those relationships.

Demonstrate leader integrity

As with benevolence, gauging a leader's integrity can be difficult for employees in the early days and weeks of a working relationship. One way for a leader to demonstrate integrity is to show full consistency between words and deeds (Simons, 2002). In simple terms, leaders need to keep their promises – to "walk the walk", not just "talk the talk." Unfortunately, a number of factors can result in a disconnect between a leader's words and deeds. For example, some leaders are too quick to revise their espoused values and aspirations in response to fads, fashions, and changes. Those tendencies can result in a sense of confusion on the part of followers, damaging leader credibility (Simons, 2002). Some leaders are also too quick to make promises they cannot keep, which further undermines credibility.

Another way for leaders to demonstrate integrity is to adhere to sound ethical principles. Although a number of principles are relevant to integrity, principles of organizational justice are particularly strong drivers of trust levels (for a review, see Colquitt, Greenberg, and Zapata-Phelan, 2005). Procedural justice, for example, encompasses a number of principles that describe how decision-making procedures should be structured (see Chapter 14 of this volume). Such procedures should be accurate, consistent, unbiased, correctable, and provide opportunities for employee voice and input. Whenever followers see a leader engage in decision making – whether in the context of a hiring decision, a performance evaluation, a conflict resolution procedure, or some other event – they can gauge adherence to these principles as evidence of trustworthiness (Lind, 2001; Tyler and Lind, 1992).

Other justice principles describe how procedures should be communicated and discussed with employees as decision making occurs (Bies and Moag, 1986). Interpersonal justice encompasses two principles – that communication should be respectful and that it should refrain from improper or prejudicial statements. Informational justice also encompasses two principles – that communications should be honest and trustful and that adequate explanations should be offered for key decisions (note that scholars have debated whether it is appropriate to classify interpersonal and informational justice as forms of "justice" per se – for more on that debate, see Locke, 2003, Bies, 2005, and Colquitt, Greenberg, and Scott, 2005). When leaders speak to followers disrespectfully or use derogatory remarks, followers will rightly question the standards and principles that guide leader behaviors. When leaders are dishonest about decision-making procedures, or remain guarded and tight-lipped about their details, followers may similarly begin to doubt or question the integrity and character of the leader.

Indeed, giving honest information may be particularly relevant to integrity because honesty is so fundamental in discussions of trustworthiness (Butler, 1991; Butler and Cantrell, 1984). Unfortunately, leaders are often reluctant to tell the truth. During times of crisis and change, business leaders are often faced with the challenge of either telling an uncomfortable truth, remaining silent, or downplaying the severity of the situation. There are plenty of other situations in which, in the short term, it may be more comfortable not to tell the truth to followers. Ultimately, however, even dishonesty that was meant to protect employee morale will eventually be exposed, undermining trustworthiness at a time when commitment to the organization is most vital. Even concerted efforts at secrecy can backfire, as employees may simply "fill in the gaps" in their understanding with there own theories about the leader's behavior. Therefore, leaders need to take steps to explain the true reasons for their decisions to those individuals affected by it, leaving less room for negative interpretations of leader behavior.

EXCEPTIONS TO THE PRINCIPLE

Are there times when increasing ability, building benevolence, and demonstrating integrity will fail to foster trust? Research has repeatedly supported the impact of the three trustworthiness aspects on employee trust (Colquitt et al., 2007). However, there are times when taking steps to increase trustworthiness will have a weaker impact on actual trust levels. Three factors comprise relevant exceptions to our focal principle.

Visibility of the leader's behavior

Increases in ability, benevolence, and integrity will only result in increases in trust when those efforts are noticed. For a follower to make an assessment of a leader's trustworthiness, the follower must be aware of and familiar with the leader's actions and decisions. Increasing the visibility of a leader's behavior is therefore necessary for the fostering of trust. The leader can ensure visibility through frequent contact and exchange of information with followers. Such contact can be face to face or through other means (e.g. telephone, memos, e-mail, etc.). However, greater face-to-face contact leads to richer and more high-quality information exchanges, which can only encourage the building of trust (Salam, 1998).

When leaders communicate face to face rather than through other means, they are able to convey information in greater detail, thereby preventing any misinterpretations by followers. Moreover, face-to-face communication allows followers to ask for immediate clarification. This, in turn, may trigger further explanations of a situation by the leader, which increases overall quality of communication. In this way, data that is relevant to ability, benevolence, and integrity can be described, discussed, and explained. Face-to-face communication also allows the leader to directly demonstrate competence in a particular task and offer shows of support, both of which makes leader trustworthiness more salient.

Personality of followers

Individuals differ in their tendency to trust others. Trust propensity is a personality trait that affects the amount of trust an individual feels towards others (Mayer et al., 1995). Individuals who are dispositionally trusting have a general belief that the words and promises of others can be relied upon. Individuals who are dispositionally suspicious are fundamentally skeptical of "human nature," doubting the trustworthiness of others as a sort of default position. Trust propensity is an important factor that affects trust early on in a relationship, before valid data on ability, benevolence, and integrity have been gathered.

Negative personal experiences, where individuals learned that trusting others can have adverse consequences, can lead to the development of a low trust propensity. Similarly, positive experiences where trust has been rewarded can lead to a high trust propensity. Early childhood experiences are particularly impactful to trust propensity, as it is believed to be one of the first personality traits to develop within individuals. National culture also has an impact, as some cultures have a higher general level of trust propensity than others. Although this trait is difficult to change, experiences over a long period of time that are incompatible with the existing disposition can lead to a modification of the trait.

An individual's trust propensity likely serves as somewhat of an anchor that binds their trust around a particular level. If a leader takes steps to increase ability, build benevolence, or demonstrate integrity, trust levels may adjust around that anchor. Still, even large increases in trustworthiness may have minimal impact on individuals who are dispositionally suspicious. Such individuals may react to such efforts with skepticism, looking for hidden motives behind leader actions or alternative explanations for the relevant changes.

Follower information processing

The development of trust depends on how the followers perceive their environment and what attributions they make based on these perceptions (Kramer, 1996). Although leaders might have an "objective" level of trustworthiness, trust depends on a personal assessment of trustworthiness by the follower. In other words, while clear and visible data about the leader's past and current actions may be available, the development of trust depends on how the follower processes and interprets this information.

There is a large stream of research studying attribution theory (Weiner, 1974). One lesson learned from this research is that cognitions and mental frameworks affect what individuals perceive and the vast amounts of information relevant to social interactions is interpreted. Theory and research on decision making also identifies how individuals differ in their "mental accounting" (Kramer, 1996). For example, how certain scenarios are framed is likely to affect the perceptions of trustworthiness in an individual. Thus, aside from influencing what the follower knows about the leader's actions, a leader can also influence how the follower processes that information by providing the appropriate framing. For example, a particular set of actions may not immediately seem consistent to an employee, until they are attuned to the common goal that those actions may have been leading towards.

CASE EXAMPLES

Below we provide real-life examples from businesses where trust has been a major issue determining the success of various endeavors. These examples illustrate how the principle explained in this chapter can be translated into real business situations. The first case illustrates factors that influence trust in interpersonal relationships while the second case illustrates factors that influence trust at an organizational level.

Moving from a functional to a product-oriented structure

The maintenance department of a large European logistics and transportation company, responsible for three products, used to be organized according to technical expertise. The department had one director. Three functional managers reported to this director, with their functions being mechanical, information technology, and hydraulics. Several technicians and operators worked within each of the functional groups. This operational structure, however, often functioned poorly in terms of cost and quality of service, so a new structure was put in place. In this new structure, teams were organized around products, rather than functions. Now the individuals reporting to the director were the expert technicians. For the first time in their career, technicians were given responsibility for an entire product line and the management of a multi-functional team.

After six months of operation, the results varied widely between the teams, with none of them functioning according to the outlined principles. The director was surprised at the high degree of operating disparity between the teams, particularly because his trust in the different team leaders was inconsistent with the actual performance of the teams. Furthermore, within the teams, the atmospheres differed from being motivated and productive to dissatisfied and demoralized. The explanation for this confusing situation lay in the different types of behaviors the team leaders exhibited toward their supervisors and subordinates – behaviors which impacted the perceived trustworthiness of the team leaders.

Product team 1 delivered the best results of all the teams. The director, however, was not happy with the leader of product team 1. As a result, he did not trust the team leader's belief that the favorable results were going to last over the long term. Product team 1's leader had no experience whatsoever in writing management reports, and therefore avoided submitting regular reports and communications to his director. That lack of management-related ability led the director to form doubts about the leader's trustworthiness. Moreover, the lack of communication itself harmed trustworthiness because the director received no information that helped him attribute the positive results of the team to the team leader's ability. Furthermore, the director interpreted the lack of communication from the leader of team 1 as a sign of low conscientiousness, harming perceptions of integrity.

Nevertheless, the members of product team 1 did develop high trust in their team leader. The leader organized many occasions for communication and information exchange within the team. Those actions fostered knowledge of one another, encouraged exchanges of helpful information, and increased the support the team members gave one another. Furthermore, the team leader did demonstrate high ability in the work content while providing team members with some decision-making power over their work. The leader also utilized fair and consistent performance evaluations and demonstrated support and concern for member needs. These actions fostered perceptions of integrity and benevolence, making the leader appear trustworthy to the team.

The performance of product team 2 was lower than that of product team 1. Nevertheless, the director trusted the leader of product team 2. In the director's opinion, it was only because of the leader that product team 2 achieved any good results at all. This situation, where the director trusted the leader of product team 2 more than the leader of product team 1, despite its lower performance, can be explained by perceptions of trustworthiness. The leader of product team 2 provided regular and detailed management reports to the director. Furthermore, the team leader frequently met with the director formally as well as informally and told him about the work of the team. The team leader told the director that the poor results of the team were due to the low performance of the operators. Often, the team leader himself had to jump in and get the operator's work done in order to compensate for their low performance. These actions painted a favorable picture of the leader's technical and managerial abilities. In addition, the leader demonstrated his integrity toward the director by honestly communicating to him the problems of the team and by being willing to exceed his responsibilities by personally assisting in the team workload.

Within product team 2, however, the atmosphere had gone sharply downhill. The operators in the team felt that the team leader unfairly provided all the bonuses to his former colleagues, namely, the mechanics in the team. This fostered conflict between the operators and the mechanics and reduced trust between the operators and the leader, and between the operators and the mechanics. The mechanics, on the other hand, felt that their team leader rightfully evaluated them more favorably than the operators and felt fairly treated. In addition, the leader spent more time coaching the mechanics than the operators, resulting in differential perceptions about the leader's benevolence. These differences created a clear division within the team. Moreover, the trust felt by only a subset of the team's members was not enough to create high performance for the team as a whole.

Product team 3 also demonstrated poor results. The results of the team were worse than those of product teams 1 and 2. Nevertheless, the director trusted the management capabilities of the leader of product team 3, revealing a further disconnect between the director's assessment of leader trustworthiness and the actual performance of the three teams. Again, however, the director's perception of the ability and integrity of the team leader can explain the favorable impressions of the leader. The leader of product team 3 had great skills in monitoring performance and in writing very detailed and informative reports. The leader was also very skilled in managing his budget, planning resources, and in setting performance goals based on this monitoring system. The director greatly appreciated this detailed information and demonstration of consistent management skills over an extended time period.

Within product team 3, however, the atmosphere was very strained. All of the members of the team were unhappy with their leader and had very low perceptions of his trustworthiness. This was clearly due to the leader's poor interpersonal, communication, and coaching skills. He avoided communication with his team members whenever he could. Furthermore, he was unable to provide valuable coaching, not only because he did not communicate with the team members, but also because he was assigned a product he had very little experience with. His members complained that the leader was a former member of the information technology team, with little experience in producing this product. The team leader was always in his office doing paperwork, preparing detailed work schedules and charts to give to management, but never spent any time with his team members to help them accomplish their jobs. These actions led to doubts about the leader's managerial abilities, while never creating the opportunity to build a sense of leader benevolence.

This case illustrates a number of principles. First, it shows the relevance of the ability, benevolence, and integrity facets of trustworthiness in driving trust levels. Second, it shows how difficult it sometimes is to judge trustworthiness. Both the director and the team members were frequently operating off different data. The trust-relevant experiences that the director could observe were different than the trust-relevant experiences that the team members could observe. The director also prioritized different aspects of ability than the team members. Taken together, these variations resulted in a disconnect in perceived trustworthiness between the director and the team members. Indeed, perceptions of trustworthiness even varied within teams, with some factions perceiving favoritism that undermined integrity whereas other factions felt that treatment was fair and just.

Managing organizational change

An international chemicals company had recently gone through the implementation of an Enterprise Resource Planning (ERP) system. The purpose of implementing this tool was to optimize the supply chain processes by having all of them based on the same kind of information technology system. Through that system, the company hoped for greater integration and a resulting increase in efficiency and productivity in its supply chain. A few months after the implementation of this tool, however, none of the desired results had been achieved. Processes were still ineffective and employees had to work with the new tools, even though they were applying their old work approaches. Overall, morale was low and employees developed greater and greater distrust in their management, doubting the success of the ERP system implementation.

Detailed interviews with employees provided insights into why this low level of trust had emerged. Employees did not understand why they had to go through this change and therefore perceived the transition as something that was imposed on them by their leadership team. This lack of perceived control made employees feel both unsupported and unfairly treated, which in turn triggered doubts about leadership's benevolence and integrity. The perception that this new system was imposed on employees was due to a lack of communication from management explaining the need for a new information technology system, and a lack of dialog with employees about the change.

The management team also neglected to inform and educate employees in how and why their roles and responsibilities had changed with this new system being in place. Management never explained to employees how the entire business process had changed and what each employee's new part in the enterprise was going to be. That lack of information, in turn, triggered perceptions that management itself did not know why it was making these changes. As a result, employees doubted the implementation capabilities of their leadership team, harming perception of the leadership team's ability.

All of these struggles were occurring in a larger context that lacked any vision or strategy for employees – something desperately needed during hard and difficult times (see Chapter 20, this volume). Furthermore, employees felt that management was "talking the talk" but not "walking the walk." In other words, there was a great deal of discussion and complaining from management about the problems that needed to be fixed, but none of this talk was followed up by action. That lack of alignment between words and deeds further clouded perceptions of the leadership team's integrity, just as management's own struggles with the new system reinforced concerns about ability.

This case further illustrates how ability, benevolence, and integrity combine to influence employees' trust in leadership. More importantly, the case reveals how the importance of trustworthiness becomes magnified in times of organizational change. Change efforts create a great deal of uncertainty and insecurity among employees, and those feelings prompt employees to take a fresh, careful, and sometimes skeptical look at their work environment (Lind, 2001). Any data that conveys questionable levels of trustworthiness will be noticed and discussed among employees, restricting their trust at precisely the time when management needs them to take risks by utilizing new methods or procedures. As a result, leaders need to take extra steps to showcase their ability, benevolence, and integrity during times of change.

CONCLUSION

Ability, benevolence, and integrity are the most critical facets of trustworthiness. They foster a sense of trust in the leader by followers. Ability reflects the knowledge, skills, and aptitudes of a leader, in both technical areas and general management competencies. Benevolence and integrity are aspects of the leader's character, and require more time and attention on the part of followers before they can be reliably judged. Benevolence reflects a desire to be considerate of the follower and can be fostered by displays of concern and support. Integrity captures an adherence to moral and ethical principles and can be fostered by aligning words with deeds and adhering to standards of organizational justice.

When ability, benevolence, and integrity do combine to increase trust levels, a number of beneficial outcomes can result. For example, followers are more likely to redefine their work relationships, understanding that they can go beyond the boundaries of their job description because they believe that their leaders will reciprocate in turn. A sense of trust also allows followers to take the risks needed to engage in creative and innovative behaviors. Job performance can benefit because employees are free to focus on the tasks at hand, as opposed to worrying about monitoring, politics, contingency plans, and "covering one's backside." High levels of trust also improve communication, as followers feel freer to share sensitive information. Finally, trust increases follower commitment to leader decisions while enhancing their desire to stay with the organization.

In order to increase trust, leaders need to take steps to increase their ability, build their benevolence, and demonstrate their integrity. Leaders can do so on a follower-by-follower basis, but can also take steps to create a culture of trustworthiness within their organizations. Although such efforts will typically result in increases in trust, there are some potential exceptions to that trend. First, leader behaviors must be sufficiently visible, otherwise followers will not be able to evaluate ability, benevolence, and integrity levels. Second, followers' trust propensities will anchor trust levels, as some followers will be more dispositionally trusting or suspicious than others. Third, follower information processing may create a disconnect between "objective" increases in trustworthiness and follower perceptions of the leader's characteristics and behaviors.

REFERENCES

Bies, R. J. (2005). Are procedural justice and interactional justice conceptually distinct? In J. Greenberg and J. A. Colquitt (eds), *The Handbook of Organizational Justice* (pp. 85–112). Mahwah, NJ: Erlbaum.

Bies, R. J., and Moag, J. F. (1986). Interactional justice: Communication criteria of fairness. In R. J. Lewicki, B. H. Sheppard, and M. H. Bazerman (eds), *Research on Negotiations in Organizations* (Vol. 1, pp. 43–55). Greenwich, CT: JAI Press.

Blau, P. M. (1964). *Exchange and Power in Social Life*. New York: Wiley.

Butler, J. K. (1991). Toward understanding and measuring conditions of trust: Evolution of a condition of trust inventory. *Journal of Management*, 17, 643–663.

Butler, J. K., Jr., and Cantrell, R. S. (1984). A behavioral decision theory approach to modeling dyadic trust in superiors and subordinates. *Psychological Reports*, 55, 19–28.

Colquitt, J. A., Greenberg, J., and Scott, B. A. (2005). Organizational justice: where do we stand? In J. Greenberg and J. A. Colquitt (eds), *The Handbook of Organizational Justice* (pp. 589–619). Mahwah, NJ: Erlbaum.

Colquitt, J. A., Greenberg, J., and Zapata-Phelan, C. P. (2005). What is organizational justice? A historical overview. In J. Greenberg and J. A. Colquitt (eds), *The Handbook of Organizational Justice* (pp. 3–56). Mahwah, NJ: Erlbaum.

Colquitt, J. A., Scott, B. A., and LePine, J. A. (2007). Trust, trustworthiness, and trust propensity: A meta-analytic test of their unique relationships with risk taking and job performance. *Journal of Applied Psychology*, 92, 909–927.

Covey, S. M. R. (2006). *The Speed of Trust: The One Thing that Changes Everything*. New York: The Free Press.

Dirks, K. T., and Ferrin, D. L. (2002). Trust in leadership: Meta-analytic findings and implications for research and practice. *Journal of Applied Psychology*, 87, 611–628.

Frost, T. F., and Moussavi, F. (1992). The relationship between leader power base and influence: The moderating role of trust. *Journal of Applied Business Research*, 8, 9–14.

Graen, G. B., and Scandura, T. (1987). Toward a psychology of dyadic organizing. In L. L. Cummings and B. M. Staw (eds), *Research in Organizational Behavior* (Vol. 9, pp. 175–208). Greenwich, CT: JAI Press.

Graen, G. B., and Uhl-Bien, M. (1995). Relationship-based approach to leadership: Development of leader–member exchange (LMX) theory of leadership over 25 years: Applying a multi-level multi-domain perspective. *Leadership Quarterly*, 6, 219–247.

Kramer, R. M. (1996). Divergent realities and convergent disappointments in the hierarchic relation: Trust and the intuitive auditor at work. In R. M. Kramer and T. R. Tyler (eds), *Trust in Organizations: Frontiers of Theory and Research* (pp. 216–245). Thousand Oaks, CA: Sage Publications.

Lewicki, R. J., and Bunker, B. B. (1995). Trust in relationships: A model of development and decline. In B. B. Banker and J. Z. Rubin (eds), *Conflict, Cooperation, and Justice* (pp. 133–173). San Francisco, CA: Jossey-Bass.

Lind, E. A. (2001). Fairness heuristic theory: justice judgments as pivotal cognitions in organizational relations. In J. Greenberg and R. Cropanzano (eds), *Advances in Organizational Justice* (pp. 56–88). Stanford, CA: Stanford University Press.

Locke, E. A. (2003). Good definitions: the epistemological foundation of scientific progress. In J. Greenberg (ed.), *Organizational Behavior: The State of the Science* (pp. 415–444). Mahwah, NJ: Lawrence Erlbaum Associates.

Mayer, R. C., and Davis, J. H. (1999). The effect of the performance appraisal system on trust for management: A field quasi-experiment. *Journal of Applied Psychology*, 84, 123–136.

Mayer, R. C., Davis, J. H., and Schoorman, F. D. (1995). An integrative model of organizational trust. *Academy of Management Review*, 20, 709–734.

Mayer, R. C., and Gavin, M. B. (2005). Trust in management and performance: Who minds the shop while the employees watch the boss? *Academy of Management Journal*, 48, 874–888.

McAllister, D. J. (1995). Affect- and cognition-based trust as foundations for interpersonal cooperation in organizations. *Academy of Management Journal*, 38, 24–59.

Salam, S. (1998). The effects of subordinate competence, leader competence, leader integrity, and technology on subordinate participation seeking, performance, satisfaction, and agreement. UMI Dissertation Information Service, Ann Arbor, Michigan.

Schoorman, F. D., Mayer, R. C., and Davis, J. H. (2007). An integrative model of organizational trust: past, present, and future. *Academy of Management Review*, 32, 344–354.

Simons, T. (2002). Behavioral integrity: the perceived alignment between managers' words and deeds as a research focus. *Organization Science*, 13, 18–35.

Tyler, T. R., and Degoey, P. (1996). Trust in organizational authorities: The influence of motive attributions on willingness to accept decisions. In R. D. Kramer and T. R. Tyler (eds), *Trust in Organizations: Frontiers of Theory and Research* (pp. 331–356). Thousand Oaks, CA: Sage Publications.

Tyler, T. R., and Lind, E. A. (1992). *A relational model of authority in groups*. In M. Snyder (ed.), *Advances in Experimental Social Psychology* (Vol. 25, pp. 115–192). New York: Academic Press.

Uttal, B. (1983). The corporate culture vultures. Fortune, October 17.

Weiner, B. (1974). *Achievement Motivation and Attribution Theory*. Morristown, NJ: General Learning Press.

Zand, D. E. (1972). Trust and managerial problem-solving. *Administrative Science Quarterly*, 17, 229–239.

Exercises

Appraising the trustworthiness of others

One valuable exercise for teaching students about trust requires them to consider how they themselves weigh information on ability, benevolence, and integrity. Students should try to think of a classmate or work colleague that fits each of the following profiles:

1. Particularly low levels of ability but seemingly acceptable levels of benevolence and integrity.
2. Particularly low levels of benevolence but seemingly acceptable levels of ability and integrity.
3. Particularly low levels of integrity but seemingly acceptable levels of ability and benevolence.

After thinking about these three classmates or colleagues, students are asked to rate how comfortable they would be turning over important duties and responsibilities to each one. Differences in that rating can then be used to explore the relative importance of the three trustworthiness facets.

Reacting to trustworthy and untrustworthy leaders

Another valuable exercise asks students to consider their experiences with trustworthy and untrustworthy leaders. Students are first asked to picture a leader that was particularly trustworthy – having a particularly strong mix of ability, benevolence, and integrity. In thinking about this leader, students should consider:

1. How did that high level of trustworthiness affect their motivation?
2. How did that high level of trustworthiness affect their tendency to take risks on the job.

Next, students should picture the opposite sort of leader – an untrustworthy leader with a particularly weak mix of ability, benevolence, and integrity. The same two questions should be considered in reference to that leader, in order to examine how trustworthiness impacts reactions to leadership.

Part VII

ORGANIZATIONAL PROCESSES

22

Design Structure to Fit Strategy

Lex Donaldson

The organizational structure should be designed to fit the organizational strategy. This is the Principle of Designing Structure to Fit Strategy – the meta-principle of effective organizational structure.

This is a broad idea. However, following from this meta-principle, there are subprinciples that turn the broad idea into useful prescriptive guidance. The principle of designing structure to fit strategy is made specific and actionable by the subprinciples. By following these subprinciples, organizations can build structures that maximize their effectiveness.

The structure of an organization is the set of relationships between its members, such as who reports to whom on the organization chart, or whether there is a "no smoking" rule. An organization coordinates the actions of its members in order to attain a goal (Scott, 1992). The strategy of an organization is its intention for the future: how it will attain its goals given its situation. The organization should adopt a structure that helps it to attain its goals, thereby promoting organizational effectiveness.

The most effective structure for an organization is one that fits its strategy (Chandler, 1962). *Strategy* determines the levels of four contingency factors: organizational size, innovation, diversification, and geographical diversity. These *contingencies*, in turn, determine the nature of the tasks that confront members of the organization. *Tasks* can themselves vary on two dimensions: uncertainty and interdependence (Donaldson, 2001). Task uncertainty and task interdependence determine the mechanisms required to coordinate effectively the tasks. These *coordination mechanisms* underlie the different types of structure that are required to fit the strategy. The causal chain is: strategy, contingencies, task, coordination mechanisms, and structure. The discussion begins by outlining the coordination mechanisms and then considers strategy, contingencies, and required structures. In closing, there are some case examples and exercises.

Coordination Mechanisms

Task uncertainty and coordination mechanisms

Each organizational member needs to know what he or she should do in order to accomplish his or her task, so that their task dovetails with that of those being performed by other members. Coordination can be attained either by rule, plan, hierarchy, or mutual agreement. Which of these coordinating mechanisms should be used depends upon the level of task uncertainty. Task uncertainty is the degree of predictability that working in a certain way will successfully accomplish the task. The coordination mechanism that is most effective is the one that fits the level of task uncertainty.

Rules state what should occur in each specified situation. A rule states that, if X occurs, then Y should be done, for example "If an employee is 15 minutes late then he or she will be fined one hour's pay." Broadly understood, rules include standard operating procedures and written instructions for performing the task. They are also present in computerization and automation, and compose the software and hardware of these systems (Blau and Schoenherr, 1971). Thus rules are really part of the programming of decisions. Any particular case is decided by a framework that pre-exists that case. This allows the decision to be made quickly, without reflection or discussion. There is no necessity for involvement by a manager, so a member may simply follow the rule. A clerk can administer the rule. Thus rules economize on managers and allow delegation to lower paid members (Blau and Schoenherr, 1971). A rule applies the same across all cases, so that rules foster consistency. This also means that rules treat every organizational member or client the same and so can be perceived as fair and equitable. However, a disadvantage of rules is that, while being a little more flexible than norms, they are still quite inflexible, in that, whenever X occurs, then Y is prescribed – even though the situation may have changed so that Y is no longer useful. Therefore, rules are appropriate where the task is low on uncertainty, so that when they were set they correctly anticipated future situations (Galbraith, 1973). Thus *rules fit low task uncertainty*.

Plans involve constructing a schedule of which member will do what and when. Plans can be flexible by updating them periodically as the situation changes. In this way, plans are appropriate where the task is less certain than for rules. Thus *plans fit quite low task uncertainty*.

Hierarchy uses managers to direct activities of their subordinates. By exercising judgment, managers achieve some flexibility in their decision making, but managerial involvement is expensive because of their relatively high compensation and benefit costs. Where task uncertainty is medium then hierarchy should be used. Thus *hierarchy fits medium task uncertainty*.

Mutual agreement means that members agree among themselves who will do what and when. It relies upon the personal commitment of the members to the goals of the organization, or at least to the accomplishment of their tasks. By participating in decisions, members have increased understanding of what is required of them and tend to be more committed. Participation, in so far as it leads to useful information exchange (see Chapter 24, this volume), tends also to increase the quality of the decision by using the experience and initiative of members, and also saves the costs of supervision (Likert, 1961). However, mutual agreement has its own costs, in that it is a time-consuming process, because members have to resolve at the start of each time period who is going to do what. Mutual agreement should be used where task uncertainty is high. High task uncertainty makes it difficult for managers to know what is best, because of their limited expertise. This tends to lead organizations to hire educated people, such as professionals, who self-manage through mutual agreement (Hage and Aiken, 1970). Thus *mutual agreement fits high task uncertainty*.

The subprinciples of task uncertainty are:

Tasks low on uncertainty should be governed by rules.
Tasks quite low on uncertainty should be governed by plans.
Tasks medium on uncertainty should be governed by hierarchy.
Tasks high on uncertainty should be governed by mutual agreement.

Task interdependence and coordination mechanisms

Task interdependence refers to whether two tasks are connected and, if so, how intensively the tasks interact. The more intensive the connection between any two tasks, the greater the coordination that is needed. To facilitate coordination, organizational subunits that are more interdependent should be placed closer together in the organizational hierarchy (Thompson, 1967). From the top of the hierarchy down, tasks are grouped according to their interdependence with one another, which defines organizational subunits at each level. At the top of the hierarchy, reporting to top management, are placed tasks that have no direct interdependence on each other, such as divisions whose products are unrelated to each other (this is termed pooled interdependence). At the next level down in the hierarchy are placed tasks that are moderately interdependent, such as where the product made by the manufacturing department becomes the input for the marketing department (this is termed sequential interdependence). At the bottom level in the hierarchy are placed tasks that are highly interdependent, such as milling and boring operations in a job shop, such that a product moves back and forth numerous times as it is fabricated (this is termed reciprocal interdependence).

The subprinciple of task interdependence is:

The greater the interdependence between tasks, the greater their coordination needs to be and so the closer they should be located in the organizational hierarchy.

Thus, the coordination mechanisms that should be used to structure an organization are set by task uncertainty and task interdependence (Birkinshaw, Nobel, and Ridderstrale, 2001). The tasks of an organization are set, in turn, by its strategy, as will now be seen. Thus strategy determines the tasks that determine the optimal structure.

STRATEGY AND CONTINGENCIES

At least five different strategies may be distinguished: differentiation, innovation, low cost, market expansion and risk reduction. Strategy affects the organization on four dimensions: size, innovation, diversification and geographical diversity. These four dimensions are known as contingency factors because high organizational performance depends on fitting the organizational structure to each of them. Size is the number of people being organized;

it relates to scale and is sought in a low-cost strategy. Innovation refers to materials, processes or outputs that are new to the organization and is sought in innovation or differentiation strategies. Diversification is producing services or products that are different from each other; the more different the services or products, the greater the diversification of the organization; it is sought in market expansion or risk reduction strategies. Geographical diversity is having different localities operate independently of each other; it is sought in market expansion or risk reduction strategies. Whenever an organization alters its strategy this tends to cause changes in one or other of the four contingency factors, that is in the levels of innovation sought or size or diversification or geographical diversity. Changes in one or other of these four contingency factors cause changes in task uncertainty or task interdependence. In this way, changes in strategy indirectly lead to changes in task uncertainty or task interdependence. Given that task uncertainty and task interdependence require particular structures, strategy ultimately drives the structural designs needed for effectiveness.

Specifically, increasing size decreases the uncertainty of many organizational tasks by making them more repetitive, leading to formalization. Increasing innovation increases task uncertainty, by requiring the solving of novel problems. Increasing innovation also increases task interdependence, because the various functional departments, such as research and manufacturing, have to interact to solve these novel problems. Increasing diversification and geographical diversity decreases task interdependence, because the different products or services or localities operate independently of each other. A consideration of each of these four contingency factors makes specific the organizational structures required to fulfill the meta-principle that structure must be designed to fit strategy.

1. *Size.*   The volume of work performed by an organization, such as the numbers of products to be produced or customers to be served, affects the number of people required to perform it and thereby the size of the organization (i.e. the number of its members) (Blau and Schoenherr, 1971). In turn, organizational size determines the appropriate levels of the structural variables of specialization, formalization, hierarchy, and decentralization.

SIZE AND SPECIALIZATION.   Tasks need to be distributed among members so that each specializes in a certain task. This is to avoid the confusion of everybody trying to do the same thing at the same time, such as serving the same customer or operating the same equipment. Specialization also has the advantage that a member can become more expert in that task by repeatedly performing it. Also, for highly specialized tasks, their simplicity allows them to be performed by members who have little education, experience, or training. This makes filling that role easier and allows lower pay. Thus the higher skill and lower cost advantages of specialization promote organizational efficiency.

The subprinciple of specialization is:

The larger size the organization, the more specialized should be the work of each member.

SIZE AND FORMALIZATION.   Increasing size means that some tasks, such as hiring employees or paying wages, are done repeatedly. Specialization also means that a member performs the same task repeatedly. Such repetition increases familiarity with the task and so reduces task uncertainty. This allows the task to be codified in rules, regulations, and standard operating procedures, which is referred to as formalization. Thus size increases formalization which promotes efficiency because of the increased programming of decisions (as discussed earlier). In contrast, an organization that fails to increase formalization as it grows in size, is relying on more costly forms of coordination, such as the managerial hierarchy and so is being inefficient.

The subprinciple of formalization is:

The larger size the organization, the more formalized it should be.

SIZE AND HIERARCHY. The height of the hierarchy is affected by the span of control, that is, the number of members who are direct subordinates of each manager. As organizational size increases, the span of control increases for a manager until it becomes too wide. At this point a new intermediary level has to be introduced into the hierarchy between the manager and his or her erstwhile direct subordinates. In this way, size leads to an increase in hierarchical levels, in order to avoid the breakdown in coordination that would occur if spans of control were too wide.

The subprinciple of hierarchical levels is:

The larger size the organization, the more hierarchical levels it should have.

SIZE AND DECENTRALIZATION. Larger size promotes decentralization. Larger number of members and customers increases the number of issues requiring managerial decision. Thus size increases organizational complexity. This complexity means that decisions cannot all be centralized, so that decentralization must increase as complexity increases. Decentralization means that some decisions are taken at levels down from the top of the hierarchy. The more decisions that are delegated and the further down the hierarchy they are delegated, the greater is the decentralization. This means that some decisions are being taken by lower-level managers who have more knowledge of the local situation, avoiding delays and also the distortions that would occur if all information had to be fed up the hierarchy for centralized decision making. Moreover, decentralization gives lower-level managers some degree of autonomy that helps involve and motivate them.

However, size increase really substitutes direct control of organizational members (i.e. centralization) by indirect control through formalization (e.g. rules) (Child, 1972). Hence, the increasing decentralization that follows from size increase is not "empowerment" which would be giving organizational members more autonomy *and* freedom from organizational constraints. Instead, in decentralization, middle- and lower-level managers gain discretion to make choices, but are limited in that, in making those choices, they must follow standard procedures and organizational policies, and the managers are subject to reporting up the line about what choices they have made (Child, 1972). For instance, a manager may hire a new employee into his or her department, but in so doing may have to fill in a form for the human resource management department, and work within an establishment of only certain positions being allowed for the department, be subject to complying with the organization's EEO policy, and have the demographics of his or her department reported annually to the organization's EEO staff unit. Thus, the manager has some choice (autonomy), but it is constrained by organizational formalization, so it is not a completely free choice (Blau and Schoenherr, 1971).

The subprinciple of decentralization is:

The larger size the organization becomes, the more it should decentralize decision making.

In sum, as an organization grows larger so it should increase its specialization, formalization, hierarchical levels, and decentralization.

2. *Innovation.* A high rate of innovation means that, within a time period, there are a large number of outputs or processes that are new to the organization. The opposite of innovation is routine operation, which leads to low task uncertainty, which, as seen, is effectively organized by rules set by the hierarchy. Also, knowledge is centralized at the top of the organizational structure, so that decisions about other, medium uncertainty tasks can be taken centrally. This kind of organizational structure, which features high formalization, centralization and psychological dependence of members on the hierarchy, is referred to as a *mechanistic structure*. Mechanistic structures are effective for routine tasks, especially low uncertainty tasks (Burns and Stalker, 1961).

In contrast, innovation requires that novel problems be solved. This often requires hiring technical experts or professionals and encouraging them to use their initiative, based upon a broad understanding of their task or the organizational mission. Such organizational members tend to coordinate through mutual agreement. Knowledge is diffused throughout the organizational structure, thus rendering ineffective a high degree of centralization. This kind of organizational structure, which features use of initiative by members, mutual agreement, decentralization and also low formalization, is referred to as an *organic structure* (Burns and Stalker, 1961). Organic structures are effective for high uncertainty, innovatory tasks.

Organizations that wish to innovate (i.e. pursue a "prospector" strategy) have higher performance if they adopt the organic structure, whereas organizations that do not and emphasize cost control (i.e. pursue a "defender" strategy) have higher performance if they adopt the mechanistic structure (Jennings and Seaman, 1994). There is a continuum of organizational structures running from highly mechanistic through to highly organic, with many organizations lying at intermediary positions. Correspondingly, organizations vary in the level of their innovativeness. The more innovative the organization wants to be, the more organic its structure has to be. For an organization to adopt the degree of "organic-ness" that fits its level of task uncertainty, its managers need to know that optimal structures are contingent, rather than there being a "one best way," i.e. a uniform structure that fits all organizations regardless of their varying contingencies (Priem and Rosenstein, 2000).

The subprinciple of innovation is:

The greater the innovation rate sought, the more organic the organizational structure should be.

Within an organization there can be variations in the level of organic-ness from department to department or section to section. These stem from variations in the uncertainty of the tasks being performed by each department. For example, manufacturing is often mechanistic, because much of its work is repetitive, whereas research is usually organic, because its work is solving novel problems (Lawrence and Lorsch, 1967). Thus, far from a homogeneous organizational culture, the organization contains divergent subcultures.

The subsubprinciple of innovation is:

The greater the task uncertainty of any organizational subunit, the more organic it should be.

Nevertheless, despite such differences between departments in the same organization, where one department is interdependent on another they must achieve coordination.

COORDINATION MECHANISMS FOR INNOVATION. Innovation affects the mechanisms that should be used to coordinate the functional departments of an organization, through the effect of innovation on task uncertainty and task interdependence.

Where the organization does not wish to innovate, then there may be no research department. The task interdependence between functions may be of the low intensity, simple, sequential kind: the sales department places an order on the manufacturing department, which makes it and passes it onto the delivery department. The coordination mechanism that is required for sequential task interdependence is planning, because there is limited task uncertainty. The uncertainty that exists mainly arises from variations in throughput volume over time. Where plans cannot be used because of more uncertainty, coordination can be achieved through use of hierarchy.

In contrast, where the organization wishes to innovate, then there will usually be a research department. The task interdependence between functions will be of the highly intensive, reciprocal kind. The research department may have an idea for a new product, but the marketing department must examine the demand and price, and the manufacturing department must examine the feasibility and costs. Therefore a discussion needs to occur back and forth between the functional departments. Because the content and interactions involved in these discussions are uncertain, planning cannot be used and hierarchy does not suffice. Each department must adjust to the other and so their coordination is ad hoc and through mutual agreement (Thompson, 1967). The discussion is made more difficult by the subcultural differences of style, language, timeframes, and values between the departments. The organization should create interfunctional teams to bring representatives of the functional departments together to facilitate cooperation. These teams may further be assisted by integrators who can act as facilitators. Inevitably, conflicts arise between the different perspectives of the functions and these should be resolved by open confrontation, that is, problem-solving discussion, rather than by using power or being evasive (Lawrence and Lorsch, 1967).

The subprinciple of interdependence is:

Where innovation is not required, interdependence between functional departments should be handled by planning through the hierarchy. Where innovation is required, interdependence between functional departments should be handled by cross-functional teams, facilitated by integrators and resolving conflict through confrontation.

3. *Diversification.* If the organization is undiversified (e.g. it produces a single product), then its tasks are interdependent – manufacturing makes what research designs – and so the main organizational subunits are functions. Thus an undiversified organization should

have a functional structure. Increasing diversification, by offering more diverse products or services, decreases the interdependence among the tasks of creating and selling each of these different outputs. If an organization is diversified, for example producing both automobiles and shoes, each of these two products is unrelated and so will have its own separate resources to design, make, and sell them. Such decreasing task interdependence reduces the amount of coordination of tasks and supervision required. These tasks that are not interdependent become the primary building blocks of the organization and so are placed at the top of the hierarchy. Thus a diversified organization should have a divisional structure. Hence diversification reduces task interdependence and so requires a shift from a functional to a divisional structure.

Divisionalization increases decentralization, so that the diversification that causes divisionalization also indirectly leads to more decentralization (in addition to that caused by size). Typically, operational decisions are decentralized to the divisions, while strategic and major financial decisions remain centralized. A division has a complete set of operating resources and functions to design, make, and sell the product or service, so that the division can act autonomously from the rest of the organization. Therefore, information processing about the product and its environment can be mainly confined within the division. This reduces the need for most of the information about the product to flow to levels above the division, thus relieving the head office of work. In essence, where there are no synergies to be extracted from the operating divisions, then the corporate head office should play a minimal role. This role is confined to work such as supervising the managers in charge of the divisions, resource allocation across divisions and managing corporate strategy (e.g. acquisitions and divestments). Thus the creation of autonomous divisions constitutes a significant increase in decentralization for the organization. Also, because the division operates independently of the other divisions, its performance can be assessed in terms of its profitability and the divisional manager rewarded on the basis of the profitability of his or her division.

The highly decentralized divisional structure, however, only fits high diversification, that is, low task interdependence. In such a case, the products or services of the divisions are unrelated, that is, they have nothing in common: materials, technologies, distribution, or customers, etc. However, many companies are only medium diversified, that is, they have related products or services (Whittington, Mayer, and Curto, 1999). The less diversified the company, that is, the more related its products or services, the greater their interdependence, that is, through sharing materials or technologies, etc. This interdependence between divisions requires coordination, so such divisions are less autonomous than in the highly diversified case (just discussed). Consequently, the corporate head office is larger, contains more operating functions, and centralizes more decisions. For example, in a company making a related set of electronics products, some technology is in common across the product divisions, so research on it is conducted in a central laboratory, swelling the number of the staff in the corporate head office (Pitts, 1976). The corporate head office should identify activities in common across the divisions and set up central functions to provide expertise to the divisions and foster distinctive corporate competences, for example a central staff group with expertise in manufacturing (Goold, Campbell, and Alexander, 1994).

Another kind of relatedness between products is the vertically integrated company, for example forest products, in which huge volumes of material pass from division to division down the value added chain. These product flows need coordinating, so that divisional autonomy on production rates is curtailed and the corporate head office contains specialists in production planning and transportation (Lorsch and Allen, 1973). In essence, in related product or service organizations, there are operating synergies to be extracted from the divisions through their coordination and this entails a more "hands-on" role for the corporate head office. Also, the managers in charge of the divisions are rewarded for their contribution to corporate profitability, not just the profitability of their division.

If a company diversifies from medium to high levels of diversification, by having products (or services) that are unrelated rather than related, it should adopt the fully decentralized type of divisional structure, with high autonomy of divisions under a small head office.

The subprinciple of diversification and divisionalization is:

As the organization increases diversification, the organization should divisionalize and use progressively more decentralization, and there should be a smaller head office with fewer operating functions, performance assessment of subunits by profits rather than costs, and rewards for divisional managers based more on the performance of their division than of the corporation.

As seen, at low levels of diversification the organization should use a functional structure, whereas at high levels of diversification the organization should use a divisional structure. However, at medium diversification there is a choice of either functional or divisional structures. Medium diversification is where there the products or services produced are related to each other in some way, such as common materials or technology or skills or customers, etc. If the organization is structured functionally then the resources are managed in an integrated way, such as by a central manufacturing department that fosters economies of scale in purchasing and manufacturing. However, the focus on products or services and their markets is blurred, which impedes innovation and customer responsiveness. Hence a functional structure should be chosen where the medium diversification organization wishes to minimize costs, such as where it faces severe price competition.

Conversely, if the medium diversification organization is structured divisionally, then there is strong focus of each division on each of its products or services and their markets. This fosters responsiveness to customers. Moreover, because each division has a complete set of functions, interaction among them is facilitated, thus boosting innovation. Responsiveness and innovation, in turn, enhance sales growth. However, the resources are scattered and duplicated across the divisions and not managed in an integrated way, so potential economies of scale in purchasing and manufacturing are sacrificed. Hence, a divisional structure should be chosen where the organization wishes to maximize innovation and sales growth. Thus there is a tradeoff, so that the medium diversification organization chooses to maximize either cost control or sales growth, while sacrificing the other.

The subprinciple of tradeoff for medium diversifiers is:

Medium diversified organizations should choose a functional structure where cost control is the main goal and a divisional structure where sales growth is the main goal.

Much organizational change today in large divisionalized corporations is reorganization of the boundaries of divisions, or "patching" (Eisenhardt and Brown, 1999), whereby units are acquired or divested by a corporation, or combined in a division or split into separate divisions (Karim, 2006). Many of these changes are compatible with the logic of building larger divisions to achieve economies of scale, or creating more tightly focused divisions to attain innovation and sales growth (Karim and Mitchell, 2000, 2004).

Furthermore, the strategy of an organization may be low-cost mass production for an existing product (or service), while simultaneously pursuing the innovation of developing and launching a new product (or service). Then the organization should adopt the "ambidexterous organization" structure (O'Reilly and Tushman, 2004). The existing mass-produced product should be run mechanistically to reap cost savings, while the new product should be run organically to maximize innovation and minimize development time. To facilitate these different substructures, they should be structurally separated, by making each a division. Greeley Hard Copy (itself a subunit of Hewlett-Packard) did so by splitting off its new, portable scanner product into a separate division from its existing flat bed scanner division (Tushman and Radov, 2000). Similarly, *USA Today* split off its new, online news service into a separate division from the existing newspaper, in order to develop the online news concept. Thus, the subprinciple that medium diversified (i.e. related products or services) companies should divisionalize to innovate, applies even if only one of the divisions is innovatory.

Some medium diversification organizations may wish to avoid the extremes of maximizing cost control or sales growth and instead may wish to compromise and have some cost control while attaining some innovation and customer responsiveness so as to attain moderate sales growth. They can retain both functional and product or service structures with equal emphasis by adopting a *matrix structure* of the functional-product or functional-project or functional-service types. Functional managers coordinate the common issues across the related products or services. A subordinate reports simultaneously to a functional manager and also to the manager in charge of a product or service. For example, the functional-project matrix of the Lockheed-Georgia Division of the Lockheed Aircraft Corporation features a manager for each function (e.g. engineering) and also a manager for each project, that is, airplane type, with subordinates reporting to both. The functional managers seek to control costs by optimizing the use of resources in an integrated way across projects, while the project managers facilitate interaction within their temporary teams (drawn from the functions), to speed innovation and to interface with their client (Corey and Star, 1971). In the contemporary era, a quite frequent type of organizational redesign in large corporations is the formation of additional teams, such as for projects, to create matrix structures or to make existing matrix structures more elaborate (Galbraith, 2001).

The subprinciple of compromise for medium diversification is:

Medium diversified organizations should choose a functional-product matrix structure where both some cost control and some sales growth is the goal.

While corporate head offices should be smaller and *less* interventionist where products (or services) are unrelated, this does not mean that they should never intervene in the divisions. On the contrary, corporate head offices can and should intervene in divisions when divisional performance is unsatisfactory. This applies not only for corporations with unrelated diversification but also for corporations with related diversification or vertical integration. When divisional performance is unsatisfactory, the corporate head office may intervene by criticizing divisional managers, cutting their budgets or bonuses, demoting or, at the extreme, firing them. The presence of a vigilant head office may provide a deterrent, so that divisional managers are "kept on their toes," without low divisional performance and sanctioning by the head office actually needing to occur (Goold et al., 1994). Corporate head offices adding value to divisions in such ways is referred to as corporate "parenting."

Other ways of corporate "parenting" include strategic planning, in which the head office discusses the details of the division's future activities (Goold et al., 1994). This is most feasible in corporations where the products (or services) are related, because the head office can become knowledgeable enough about the divisions to add value in the planning process.

Where a company is diversified, containing multiple business firms, yet the company has been unable to achieve synergies between them and has, instead, stifled their freedom, a new corporate parent may acquire the company and break it up, selling the divisions off for a higher price than paid for their combined acquisition (Sadtler, Campbell, and Koch, 1997).

For a company to successfully "parent," it should acquire firms that lack some competency that the parent has, while divesting any division that it cannot parent because it does not have a complementary competence the division lacks. Moreover, the parent should seek, over time, to develop some distinct competence that other "parenting" corporations lack, so that they are not rivals for the acquisition of the same "children" firms (Campbell, Goold, and Alexander, 1995).

4. *Geographical diversity.* Geographical diversity is another way to reduce task interdependence. Each locality has its own complete set of resources and functions to design, make, and sell its product or service in its locality, so that it operates independently of other geographical areas of the organization. In this way, diversification along geographical lines can produce autonomous divisions, similar to product or service diversification; only the divisions are defined by locality.

The subprinciple of geographical diversity is:

Where each locality operates independently of other localities then the structure should be geographical divisions.

In some multinational organizations, such as Unilever, the geographical areas operate quite autonomously, but the corporate head office sees that there are linkages made between them to share knowledge that is relevant across the world, such as new products, technologies, or advertising (Goold et al., 1994). Geographically diverse firms should reap all possible synergies between their geographical areas by creating conferences and networks for such knowledge sharing.

In some organizations their geographical diversity is at the medium level, so that there are significant differences between geographies, warranting a separate manager for each, while diversification is also medium, so that there also are significant differences between products, warranting a separate manager for each. Moreover, the activities of the products are distributed across the geographies in such a way that each product manager is coordinating his or her product across the geographies. Thus there will be both several geographical locality managers and several product managers. Each of their subordinates reports simultaneously to the managers of their geography and of their product. Hence the structure is *a geography–product, or area–product, matrix* (Davis and Lawrence, 1977). A frequently encountered example is the multinational corporation that has more than one distinct product or service, but which also produces and sells each of them in numerous different areas of the world (Galbraith and Kazanjian, 1988). For instance, geography–product matrix structures are found in German multinational corporations that have both substantial geographical and product diversity (Wolf and Egelhoff, 2002, 2007). They provide the additional information-processing capacity required to cope with these simultaneous challenges.

The subprinciple of medium geographical diversity and medium diversification is:

Where there is a medium geographical diversity and medium diversification, then the organization should have a geography–product matrix structure.

This chapter has emphasized the need to fit structure to several different aspects of strategy (size, innovation and diversification, and geographical diversity). A misfit of any of the corresponding structural dimensions (e.g. specialization, centralization) to any of these four contingencies will reduce organizational performance. Thus suboptimal organizational designs could arise from numerous sources and multiple misfits could exist in an organization (Donaldson, 2006). However, much of the reduction in performance comes in practice from only one single misfit in an organization, namely, the largest misfit, that is, the structural dimension that most misfits its contingency (Burton, Lauridsen, and Obel, 2002; Klaas, Lauridsen, and Hakonsson, 2006). Hence, if managers and consultants identify which is the greatest strategy–structure misfit in their organization, then fixing it, by adopting a fitting structure, will attain most of the potential benefit from organizational redesign. In that sense there is "low hanging fruit" waiting to be plucked. This should encourage managers and consultants to seek to fit strategy to structure. To do so, they should not be afraid to ask many questions (Goold and Campbell, 2002), so that they consider systematically each of the aspects of structure and their corresponding structural dimensions.

In some situations, there may be an industry norm about structure that would make the organization more acceptable if it adopted a structure that conformed to the norm. Where this structure fits the organization's strategy, then the benefits of acceptability add to those of operational effectiveness. Where this structure misfits the organization's strategy (Donaldson, 2008a), the loss in acceptability from not adopting the popular structure may be worth less than the benefit in operational effectiveness from fitting the structure to strategy, making the latter the more optimal choice (Donaldson, 2008b).

CASE EXAMPLES

To understand more fully how these principles work in practice, consider first a positive example and then a negative example.

Product development at Toyota

Product development is sometimes supposed to be synonymous with an organic structure. However, this presumes that the products being developed are highly innovative, based on the creation of new science or technology, so that task uncertainty is high. In contrast, at Toyota Motor Corporation product development is evolution not revolution. Thus product development involves only moderate levels of task uncertainty, so that mechanistic elements are appropriate as well as organic elements.

Toyota mass produces high-quality, reliable automobiles, yet it is mostly not a leading edge innovator. As a high-volume automobile company, it faces tough cost pressures due to global competition. Hence, new product development at Toyota seeks to create new models that are easily manufactured to tight costs and which share as much as possible across models in the range. This standardization has helped Toyota to introduce new models, and even some new products, thus "competing in time." Thus, while there is some degree of task uncertainty, it is moderate rather than high.

Each feature of the product development process at Toyota (Sobek, Liker, and Ward, 1998) can be coded as to whether it is mechanistic or organic. Toyota features strong functions both for manufacturing and product development (mechanistic). Engineers remain in one or other function for most of their careers, so that, while they are rotated, it is within one of these functions (mechanistic), not between functions. There is a lengthy process of in-company training and on-the-job experience over many years before engineers rise to the higher levels where authority is vested (mechanistic). Younger engineers are closely supervised and mentored by their superiors (mechanistic), though the style is Socratic rather than directive (organic). Ongoing cross-functional coordination is provided by meetings (organic), but the extent of these is constrained in number and scope so that engineers can get on with their work.

There is considerable use of written documents (mechanistic). There are detailed, written standards for every part of the automobile (mechanistic). These are frequently updated by the engineers. Being written, they codify the knowledge, so that it is held by the company (mechanistic), not just by the individual. Meetings often work through detailed, written checklists. Requests for changes from one section to another are written and circulated prior to meetings. The decision of the meeting is then written up to record it formally (mechanistic). These documents conform to a standard format (mechanistic). Younger engineers are coached as to how exactly to write these documents and how to conduct the meetings (mechanistic).

There is cross-functional coordination provided by a chief engineer who leads the project and stands outside the functions (organic). However, the engineers working on the project remain in their functions, subject to the authority of their functional boss (mechanistic). Hence, the project leader lacks line authority over the project and has to work by persuasion (organic). The credibility of the chief engineer rests in part on his engineering expertise and he is regarded not so much as the project manager but as the lead designer (organic). There is a considerable amount of conflict involved, so that issues are thoroughly discussed (organic), rather than being settled forcibly or evaded.

Thus there are both mechanistic as well as organic elements in the organizational structure that is used for product development at Toyota, thereby fitting its strategy.

Product divisions at Nipont

Nipont (a pseudonym for a real Japanese corporation) had a functional structure. However, as it grew and diversified the range of its product offerings, Nipont replaced the functional with a divisional structure, following the pattern of most large corporations (Rumelt, 1974). It hoped that product divisions would offer greater flexibility and speedier response to each different product market, so as to boost innovation and attain faster sales growth. In the booming markets of the time this seemed appropriate. However, shortly after the adoption of the new divisional structure the environment changed in a way that made its divisional structure inappropriate.

International events led to a dramatic rise in the cost of oil, a major raw material, so placing pressure on Nipont's costs. This was compounded by increased competition from international competitors, who "dumped" their product into the Japanese home market at marginal cost, so placing pressure on prices. Squeezed by cost and price pressures, Nipont had to bring their costs under control. Unfortunately, Nipont's divisional structure was unsuited to providing tight cost control.

The divisional structure at Nipont consisted of three product divisions: the Chemicals Division, Fibers Division, and Plastics Division. Each division operated autonomously making their own decisions. However, in strategic terms, while Nipont was a diversified company, it was a company of only medium diversification, because its products were related. There were strong links between its three main products, that is, substantial task interdependence. Fibers were the main product and were made by the Fibers Division. These are synthetic textiles that use materials made by the company, in common with the second main product, plastics, made by the Plastics Division. Much of the chemicals sold by the Chemicals Division were in fact by-products of the core processes used for the Fibers and Plastics Divisions.

Moreover, many of Nipont's production plants made more than one of these products. Two plants (Mishima and Nagoya) made products for all of the three product divisions. Other plants (Gifu and Shiga) made products for two of the product divisions. Therefore these plants were not under a unified command. The other plants each reported to their product division, so that control was split among the three product divisions. Therefore there was a lack of overall coordination of the company's production plants – despite their operations being interconnected. Thus there was no central control over manufacturing, sacrificing economies of scale. In a buoyant economy this had been a highly acceptable tradeoff for the better flexibility and innovation potential offered by organization into separate product divisions. However, it became unacceptable as the environment forced the organization towards reducing production costs. After a few years, Nipont reverted to a functional structure (Donaldson, 1979).

Given that the environments of organizations are frequently changing, this can lead them to alter their strategies, and they must then quickly change their structures in order to avoid misfit and ineffectiveness.

CONCLUSION

Managers should design their organization so that its structure fits its strategy. Strategy in turn sets the levels of four contingency variables – size, innovation, diversification, and geographical diversity – that each affects the tasks in the organization and therefore the required structure.

A small organization should use a structure that is low on specialization and formalization, and has a flat hierarchy and centralized decision making. A larger organization should use a structure that is higher on specialization and formalization, and has a taller hierarchy and more decentralized decision making.

Innovation entails more solving of novel problems and task uncertainty is higher, so that the organization should adopt a structure that relies less on rules, plans, and hierarchy (a mechanistic structure) and instead relies more on decentralization, initiative-taking, and mutual adjustment by organizational members (an organic structure). In combination, a more innovative organization should have lower levels of specialization and formalization, and higher levels of decentralization, than its size alone would require.

Innovation also increases task interdependence between the functions, which should be handled by mutual adjustment between functions, fostered by having cross-functional teams and facilitated by integrators.

Diversification of products (or services) reduces interdependence between operational units, and a divisional structure should be used, that is, product (service) divisions for product (service) diversification and geographical divisions for geographic diversity. The less relationship there is between the product (services) or geographies, the less synergy there is to extract, and so the more autonomous the divisions should be, resulting in a smaller, less interventionist corporate head office. If the products (services) are related, then a company with a strategy of sales growth should use a divisional structure, while a company with a strategy of cost control should use a functional structure, whereas a company seeking some of both sales growth and cost control should use a product (project)–functional matrix. Where the products (or services) have some inter-relationship within each geographical area, then the company should use a product (service)–geographical matrix.

By adopting the best fitting structure, the organization can realize its strategy, so that it attains its goals and achieves higher performance.

REFERENCES

Birkinshaw, J., Nobel, R., and Ridderstrale, J. (2001). Knowledge as a contingency variable: Do the characteristics of knowledge predict organization structure? *Organization Science*, 13(3), May–June, 274–289.

Blau, P. M., and Schoenherr, P. A. (1971). *The Structure of Organizations*. New York: Basic Books.

Burns, T., and Stalker, G. M. (1961). *The Management of Innovation*. London: Tavistock.

Burton, R., Lauridsen, J., and Obel, B. (2002). Return on assets loss from situational and contingency misfits. *Management Science*, 48(11), 1461–1485.

Campbell, A., Goold, M., and Alexander, M. (1995). The quest for parenting advantage. *Harvard Business Review*, March, 120–133.

Chandler, A. D. Jr., (1962). *Strategy and Structure: Chapters in the History of the Industrial Enterprise*. Cambridge, MA: MIT Press.

Child, J. (1972). Organization structure and strategies of control: A replication of the Aston study. *Administrative Science Quarterly*, 17, 163–177.

Corey, R., and Star, S. H. (1971). *Organization Strategy: A Marketing Approach*. Boston: Division of Research, Graduate School of Business Administration, Harvard University.

Davis, S. M., and Lawrence, P. R. (1977). *Matrix*. Reading, MA: Addison-Wesley.

Donaldson, L. (1979). Regaining Control at Nipont. *Journal of General Management*, 4(4), 14–30.

Donaldson, L. (2001). *The Contingency Theory of Organizations*. Sage: Thousand Oaks.

Donaldson, L. (2006). The contingency theory of organizational design: Challenges and opportunities. In R. M. Burton, B. Eriksen, D. D. Hakonsson, and C. C. Snow (eds), *Organization Design: The Evolving State-of-the-Art* (pp. 19–40). Springer.

Donaldson, L. (2008a). The conflict between contingency and institutional theories of organizational design. In R. M. Burton, B. Eriksen, D. D. Hakonsson, and C. C. Snow (eds), *New Directions in Organization Design*. Springer.

Donaldson, L. (2008b). Resolving the conflict between contingency and institutional theories of organizational design. In R. M. Burton, B. Eriksen, D. D. Hakonsson, and C. C. Snow (eds), *New Directions in Organization Design*. Springer.

Eisenhardt, K. M., and Brown, S. L. (1999). Patching: restitching business portfolios in dynamic markets. *Harvard Business Review*, 77(3), 71–82.

Galbraith, J. R. (1973). *Designing Complex Organizations*. Reading, MA: Addison-Wesley Publ. Co.

Galbraith, J. R. (2001). *Designing Organizations: An Executive Guide to Strategy, Structure, and Process*. San Francisco: Jossey-Bass.

Galbraith, J. R., and Kazanjian, R. K. (1988). Strategy, technology and emerging organizational forms. In J. Hage (ed.), *Futures of Organization: Innovating to Adapt Strategy and Human Resources to Rapid Technological Change*. MA: Lexington Books.

Goold, M., and Campbell, A. (2002). Do you have a well-designed organization? *Harvard Business Review*, March, 5–11.

Goold, M., Campbell, A., and Alexander, M. (1994). *Corporate-level Strategy: Creating Value in the Multibusiness Company*. New York: John Wiley and Sons.

Hage, J., and Aiken, M. (1970). *Social Change in Complex Organizations*. New York: Random House.

Jennings, D. F., and Seaman, S. L. (1994). High and low levels of organizational adaptation: An empirical analysis of strategy, structure and performance. *Strategic Management Journal*, 15(6), 459–475.

Karim, S. (2006). Modularity in organizational structure: The reconfiguration of internally developed and acquired business units. *Strategic Management Journal*, 27(9), 799–823.

Karim, S., and Mitchell, W. (2000). Path-dependent and path-breaking change: Reorganizing business resources following acquisitions in the U.S. medical sector, 1978–1995. *Strategic Management Journal*, 21(10–11), 1061–1081.

Karim, S., and Mitchell, W. (2004). Innovating through acquisition and internal development: A quarter-century of boundary evolution at Johnson and Johnson. *Long Range Planning*, 37, 525–547.

Klaas, P., Lauridsen, J., and Hakonsson, D. D. (2006). New developments in contingency fit theory. In R. M. Burton, B. Eriksen, D. D. Hakonsson, and C. C. Snow (eds), *Organizational Design: The Evolving State-of-the-Art*. Springer Science and Business Media.

Lawrence, P. R., and Lorsch, J. W. (1967). *Organization and Environment: Managing Differentiation and Integration*. Boston: Division of Research, Graduate School of Business Administration, Harvard University.

Likert, R. (1961). *New Patterns of Management*. New York: McGraw-Hill.

Lorsch, J. W., and Allen, S. A. (1973). *Managing Diversity and Inter-dependence: An Organizational Study of Multidivisional Firms*. Boston: Division of Research, Graduate School of Administration, Harvard University.

O'Reilly III, C. A., and Tushman, M. L. (2004). The ambidextrous organization. *Harvard Business Review*, 82(4), 74–81.

Pitts, R. A. (1976). Diversification strategies and organizational policies of large diversified firms. *Journal of Economics and Business*, 28(3), 181–188.

Priem, R. L., and Rosenstein, J. (2000). Is organization theory obvious to practitioners? A test of one established theory. *Organization Science*, 11(5), September–October, 509–524.

Rumelt, R. P. (1974). *Strategy, Structure and Economic Performance*, Boston MA: Division of Research, Graduate School of Business Administration, Harvard University.

Sadtler, D., Campbell, A., and Koch, R. (1997). *Break up!: When Large Companies are Worth More Dead than Alive*. Oxford, England: Capstone.

Scott, W. R. (1992). *Organizations: Rational, Natural and Open Systems*. 3rd edition Englewood Cliffs, N. J.: Prentice Hall.

Sobek, D. K., II, Liker, J. K., and Ward, A. C. (1998). Another look at how Toyota integrates product development. *Harvard Business Review*, 76(4), 36–49.

Thompson, J. D. (1967). *Organizations in Action*. New York: McGraw-Hill.

Tushman, M. L., and Radov, D. B. (2000). Greeley Hard Copy, Portable Scanner Initiative (A), (B) and (C). Harvard Business School Case, 9-401-003/4/5.

Whittington, R., Mayer, M., and Curto, F. (1999). Chandlerism in post-war Europe: Strategic and structural change in France, Germany and the UK, 1950–1993. *Industrial and Corporate Change*, 8(3), 519–550.

Wolf, J., and Egelhoff, W. G. (2002). Research notes and commentaries: A reexamination and extension of international strategy-structure theory. *Strategic Management Journal*, 23(2), 181–189.

Wolf, J., and Egelhoff, W. G. (2007). Strategy and structure in matrix MNCs. Paper to Academy of Management Meeting, Philadelphia, PA.

EXERCISES

Uncertainty as a contingency of organizational structure

Task uncertainty:
What is the level of uncertainty in the tasks of your organization or in the last organization you worked in? Circle the one below that best describes your organization:
Low   Medium   High

Structure:

How would you rate your organization's structure on each of the following (for each please give a score of 1 to 5 for from low to high):

Formalization	Low	_____	High
Knowledge	Diffused	_____	Top
Style	Egalitarian	_____	Hierarchical
Centralization	Low	_____	High
Total		_____	

Scores can vary from 4 = highly organic to 20 = highly mechanistic.
Is your organization more organic or more mechanistic?

Is your organization in fit between its task uncertainty and the degree to which it is mechanistic or organic – or is it in misfit? If it is in misfit, what changes to its structure would make it fit its task uncertainty?

Strategy as a contingency

Structure:

What structure does your organization have at its top level, that is, the direct reports to the CEO or MD? Which of the following structure type describes it best? Circle one of: Functional   Divisional   Matrix

Degree of diversification:

Which dimension is your organization most diversified on – product, service, customer or area? On this dimension, what is the degree of diversification that best describes your organization? Circle one of: Low   Medium   High

Fit or misfit:

Is there a fit, or a misfit, between the diversification of your organization and its structure? If there is a misfit, what structure would be a better fit?

23

Communicate Successfully by Seeking Balance

DEBORAH A. CAI AND EDWARD L. FINK

How often we hear the charge, "What we need around here is good communication"? Human communication, or the verbal and non-verbal transmission of meaning, is an aspect of everyday life that is too often taken for granted; we all do it, but how often is it done effectively? In fact, there are many misconceptions about communication in the workplace. Someone who talks louder does not necessarily know more than someone who speaks softly or who hardly talks. Someone who is more outgoing is not necessarily more competent than someone more introverted. More talk about a problem is not necessarily better. And venting does not necessarily help to resolve a conflict.

Communication is a balancing act between a sender and receiver; between talking and listening; between what is said, how it is said, and when it is said; between task and relational activities; between conveying types of trust; between using formal and informal channels; and between communicating with one's peers (if one is a newcomer) and with organizational veterans. And the balancing act varies for the level at which the communication is targeted, whether to individuals, groups or teams, departments, or the organization as a whole. This chapter examines the challenges of balancing the various needs that drive communication.

Subprinciple 1: Communication is a balancing act between senders and receivers

To communicate can include many different aspects. It can be associated with providing information, resulting in a plethora of memos, newsletters, articles, announcements, reports, and e-mails. It can mean participatory involvement, accomplished through team meetings, formal and informal discussions, negotiations, and brainstorming sessions. Or it can mean engaging employees, in the goals and purposes of the organization and in the relationships that surround them every day in the workplace.

Each approach to communication is driven by different assumptions. Some managers approach communication as a one-way barrage, sending out messages with regular frequency with the assumption that well-informed employees will be effective in what they do. Some managers approach communication as a group activity, holding regular meetings with groups of people to brainstorm, discuss, and determine directions to pursue. And some managers view colleagues and employees as both relational beings and goal oriented, involving them in a variety of ways in the various levels of deliberation and decision making that occur within the organization.

Although communication is one of those every day and all day human activities, its effectiveness can vary greatly. Just because a manager is a good talker, sends a barrage of memos and e-mails, or holds frequent meetings does not mean the manager is an effective communicator. When it comes to communicating, more is not necessarily better; it's how it is done that matters. Communication, although used throughout the day every day, is a skill like running: Most people are able to run, but only the trained athlete can competently compete.

The classic model of communication proposed by Shannon and Weaver in 1949 highlights a unidirectional mode of sending messages from sender to receiver (Shannon and Weaver, 1963). The message is encoded by the sender, sent through a channel, and decoded or interpreted by the receiver. The whole process is influenced by noise, which can be physical (e.g. aural, visual, gustatory, tactile, olfactory) as well as emotional or psychological. In other words, noise can include an ambulance siren as well as physical fatigue that can make paying attention to a message difficult. Lasswell (1948) summarized the communication process with the following statement: Who said what to whom through what channel with what effect?

More recent iterations of the process have advanced Lasswell's model of communication: Communication is not unidirectional from sender to receiver; rather, if a sender provides a message, the receiver interprets it and responds to it, even if the response is a grimace or a smile. In addition, communication often involves many parties – groups, mass audiences, readers, and message designers. While one person is speaking, another may communicate boredom or frustration or excitement just as clearly using non-verbal cues. An effective communicator pays attention to the multiple messages that are being delivered between parties as well as to the effectiveness of those messages in accomplishing the many goals of the communicators involved (Wilson and Putnam, 1990). Communication done well requires a sense of balance, between the sender and receiver of messages, between talking and listening, and between too much versus too little communication.

For example, in a recent communication training session for about 25 managers, one trainer delivered her presentation using a series of PowerPoint slides, which she scrolled through with little emotion. She held the microphone too low for it to pick up her voice, read the material verbatim off the slides, and presented the information on the assigned topic in a cursory manner. This one-way approach to communication – from presenter to audience – missed the multiple non-verbal messages being sent in the other direction by the others involved in this interaction: yawns, drooping eyelids, and glazed looks. At the end of the presentation, when the audience was asked if it had any questions, there were none, indicating that the presentation was so complete as to accomplish the training goal in its entirety, that the audience wasn't alert enough to know what to ask, or that the audience was just grateful that the presentation was over. Presentations are too often assumed to be one-way communication, yet they are much more effective when framed as interactions, even when the communication is delivered in a lecture format.

Communication, even between a speaker and a large audience, should involve a balance in the participation of both sender and receiver. Another way of saying this is that each party to the communication should play both the roles of sender and receiver. From this perspective, a manager should not be the one-way deliverer of messages to employees but should be engaged in a two-way or multiple-way exchange of messages with the team members, employees, or negotiators. A sender-only approach would be to simply send memos out to employees – one way, disappearing into the void of organizational oblivion; but a two-way, sender–receiver approach means that the effect of the memo should be assessed: Did the employees receive it, attend to it, understand it, evaluate it, and give the message sender the necessary feedback? These processes – receipt, attention, comprehension, evaluation, and feedback – are all part of communicating, but feedback is essential if the organization is to benefit from the experience, knowledge, ability, and attitudes of the organizational members. Furthermore, the implementation of any directives in the memo as the sender expects, and responses to future memos, require the complete cycle of communication, including feedback.

One of the common mistakes made about communication is that it predominantly involves talking, leading to the fallacy that the more messages sent out the more communication has occurred. Managers often make the mistake of assuming communication occurs in only one direction: "From me to you." Thus, messages are treated as if they are unidirectional, aimed outward, and rarely returning, rather than listening, watching, and responding to feedback or messages sent in return. What's more, an employee's opinions, questions, and, most importantly, criticisms are often viewed as disruptive or even a waste of time (Senge, 2006).

Subprinciple 2: Communication is a balancing act between speaking and listening

The idea that "more communication is better" needs to be reconsidered. More talk may help, but more talk is not sufficient to improve communication, and at times, more talk can even be detrimental to problem solving. It is not enough for an athlete to say, "I need to run more" or "I need to play more tennis" or "I need to swim more." Whatever the sport, the athlete improves through a planned program that includes targeted improvement across needed skills, good nutrition, and careful attention to prevent injuries. At times, too much activity, especially when done wrong, can cause more injury than benefit. In the same way, too much talk can actually hurt the communication process rather than help it. More talk is not sufficient; more effective communication is what is needed.

Communication involves both talking and listening, neither of which is as simple as it sounds. But here's a good place to start: *To talk effectively depends on the ability to listen effectively.* And the balance between the two should be that some talking should be balanced with a lot more listening.

Listening has been significantly associated with perceptions of communication competence in the workplace (Haas and Arnold, 1995) and has been shown to contribute to promotion and advancement within organizations (Sypher, Bostrom, and Seibert, 1989; Sypher and Zorn, 1986). It is one of the most important abilities for employees and employers (Wolvin and Coakley, 1992). Listening involves both accuracy and support (Cooper and Husband, 1993), seeking input and suggestions, willingness to put one's own thoughts aside, empathy, willingness to respond to others' questions and suggestions, and willingness to ask questions of others and seek their response to those questions. Listening behaviors include not interrupting as well as acknowledging others' comments with both verbal and non-verbal responses. And most of all, listening takes time, an ability to remember the content of the conversation, and a willingness to act on what was heard (Halone and Pecchioni, 2001). At times listening may require ensuring that there is sufficient time to listen and consider suggestions and options rather than coming up with an immediate plan of action.

Generic listening responses include nodding and backchanneling (e.g. giving vocal responses such as *mmhmm*, *yeah*, or *go on*), whereas specific listening behaviors include leaning forward to punctuate a point the other has made, adjusting one's posture to mirror the other person's physical position, or providing responses that signal specific acknowledgment of the other person's points such as found in empathic listening (Pasupathi, Stallworth, and Murdoch, 1998). The empathic listener summarizes the emotions expressed by the speaker. In addressing how to communicate effectively during crises, Donohue (1992) has provided the *Four R* method for effective listening:

1. *Receive* the other's comments without interruption and don't get defensive.
2. *Repeat* the person's comments as objectively as possible.
3. *Request* the other's proposed ways of dealing with the problem.
4. *Review* the options and decide on the best approach. (p. 41)

This approach focuses on allowing others to work through their emotions (see Chapter 8), helping them move to considering viable options, and respecting their conclusions before issuing or pushing one's own views of the matter. Effective listening requires the balance of putting one's own views aside long enough to really comprehend what others are saying and then determining the messages that will be most appropriate and effective based on this information.

Subprinciple 3: Communication is a balancing act among what is said (content), how it is said (manner), and when it is said (time)

Too often communicators emphasize only the verbal aspects of messages – the words with which the message is expressed – without attending to supporting cues, such as paralinguistic features, the role of pauses, and the value of silence. Communication is much more than just the content of the message, or *what* is said.

Manner. An effective communicator adapts not only the message but the delivery to what is known about the other party. Not only is it important to attend to how messages are communicated to others through one's tone of voice or supportive cues, but hearing through the paralanguage of others is also needed. Paralanguage consists of the vocal elements and vocalization that modifies verbal communication by expressing emotion through tone of voice, speech rate, and other audible sounds, such as hisses, *uh huh*, tongue clicking, and *shhh*. The paralanguage associated with how a thought is expressed can be as important as the words that are used to express the thought. If one is inattentive to how one comes across, a speaker may sound frustrated or angry or apathetic when communicating simply because the speaker is tired, in a hurry, or is having difficulty hearing over background noises. Communication over the telephone is especially challenging to the use of paralinguistic cues: Laughter must be communicated aurally − with sound − not just with a smile, because the person on the other end cannot see a smile over the phone; low or monotone voices can come across as unfriendly or uninterested when no facial cues are available to suggest otherwise.

Misunderstandings and conflict often occur between people more because of how something is said rather than because of what is said. Furthermore, national, ethnic, and regional differences in paralanguage can result in misinterpretation of someone's meaning simply because of the tone of voice or the pace at which a person speaks. For example, for Korean men, slower speech rate is considered more competent, whereas for American men, faster speech is perceived as more competent (Lee and Boster, 1992). For Arabs and Greeks, louder speech indicates strength whereas soft speech indicates frailty; for Filipinos and Thai, a soft tone of voice is considered more competent and respectful than a loud tone of voice. Japanese, Austrians, and Americans tend to use louder speech whereas Swedes, Norwegians, and Dutch use more relaxed speech patterns (Ngai, 2000). Native Japanese and Spanish speakers were found to misjudge emotion communicated in spoken English, misinterpreting anger and hate as indicating nervousness and depression (Graham, Hamblin, and Feldstein, 2001).

Many examples are available to illustrate the importance of attending to paralinguistic features of communicating (see Chapter 33 on cultural differences). The Chinese language, for example, tends to be spoken with a bit louder tone of voice and a more clipped articulation than English. To a native English speaker, this louder and clipped vocalization can sound angry. In addition, Chinese culture uses fewer polite forms than most Americans are used to, such as *please* and *thank you*. In Chinese, polite forms are reserved to "give face" within relationships that need to be nurtured and preserved (see Brown and Levinson, 1987). As a result, to a native English speaker, a native Chinese speaker can sound pushy or upset when speaking English. A phrase such as "Please, have a seat" may be expressed as "Sit here," which seems impolite to the English speaker, especially when, as mentioned, it is clipped and louder than the English speaker is used to. Although the meaning of "Please, have a seat" means the same to the English speaker that "Sit here" means to the Chinese speaker, the paralanguage along with the lack of the polite form, *please*, results in the Chinese speaker being perceived to be unfriendly and curt by the English speaker. Especially in a diverse workplace, in which diversity can include gender, ethnicity, and cultural and even regional differences, effective communication includes realizing that the delivery of the message may have as much to do with how a message is understood as the verbal content of the message.

Time. Because discussions of communication generally center on what is said and how it is said, the effects of silence, pauses, and timing are often overlooked. Silence can have both negative and positive effects on communication, depending on how it is used and how attentive people are to its use. Some people are silent because of personality or because of cultural norms: Japanese and Finns prefer silence because it is an opportunity to learn and a protection of privacy, whereas excessive talking is viewed as indicating arrogance. Americans, French, and Italians value thinking out loud and expressive communication to share ideas and gain the confidence of the listener (Lewis, 1999). As a result, brainstorming – the process of quickly emitting ideas, whether good or bad, to encourage people to be creative in coming up with new ideas – is a process that is not comfortable for people from cultures in which being wrong creates a loss of face or in which only leaders are expected to provide direction. A brainstorming session, or similar group discussions, may leave a person who is reticent, due to culture or personality, out of the discussion, even when the person has good ideas to contribute. Team members, and especially team leaders, may find that the reticent individual has much to offer to the discussion when given the opportunity to express ideas in a different setting. Thus, such individuals need to be encouraged to give their input during the meeting or they need to be talked to one on one outside of the meeting if their input, which may be very valuable, is to be obtained. (Technology can be used to facilitate communication without the threat posed by face-to-face interaction; see Chapter 32.)

A more subtle influence of silence is the use of conversational pauses. Ford and Thompson (1996) found that a pause of 0.3 seconds was noticeable in conversation, and pauses of as little as 0.13 seconds have been found to have psychological relevance to listeners (Hieke, Kowal, and O'Connell, 1983). In a study of conversational patterns, people who paused before responding, especially when they then responded with *um* after pausing, were judged to be less honest and less comfortable with the topic of discussion (Fox Tree, 2002). A pause of only half a second is likely to be interpreted as meaning that the speaker is giving up his or her turn to speak (Wennerstrom and Siegel, 2003).

Pauses can be helpful or harmful depending on their use within conversation and the national, ethnic, or regional meanings attached to them. A person who pauses longer, waiting for his or her chance to speak, may be left out of the conversation and may even be perceived as uninterested or as having nothing to contribute, when what is actually happening is that the pattern of conversation simply leaves that person out. Gender and regional differences as well as non-native English speech patterns can result in longer or shorter pauses than those used in standard spoken English. When a question has been asked, people from some cultures wait longer than half a second to answer, which could shut them out of the conversation in most American business meetings. Similarly, women in the US are often socialized to wait for a speaker to stop speaking, signaled by a brief pause, before taking their turn to speak, whereas men tend to begin speaking at the very end of someone else's sentence, picking up the turn to speak just before the other person has finished. This pattern can leave women out of an ongoing discussion with men if the women don't adjust their speech patterns or if turn-taking is not enforced, as it is, for example, by parliamentary procedure (Robert, Robert, Evans, Honemann, and Balch, 2000).

In contrast, Ngai (2000) found that Ethiopian and Tanzanian negotiators, once they began to talk, often continued talking for five to 15 minutes without giving up their turn to speak; when others tried to break into the conversation the negotiators from these countries continued to speak over them. But Ngai also found that Ethiopians used long, dead silences to communicate displeasure or show disagreement.

The use of filled pauses – *uh*, *er*, *ah*, and *um*, for example – gives a communicator time to think and reflects the range of word choices that a speaker has (Schachter, Christenfeld,

Ravina, and Bilous, 1991). Thus, speakers who are searching for what to say resort to filled pauses, which should be noticeable to the audience. Some communication topics give the speaker fewer word choice options, and therefore the speaker will emit filled pauses at a low rate (Schachter et al., 1991). Schachter et al. (1991) found that those lecturing on the natural sciences emitted filled pauses at lower rate than did those lecturing on the social sciences, who, in turn, emitted filled pauses at a lower rate (but not significantly lower) than did those lecturing on the humanities. Thus, if a speaker emits filled pauses at a relatively high rate, the listener may either attribute that to the speaker's lack of expertise on the topic or to the topic's not being very "factual."

So differences in pauses can leave someone out of the conversation unintentionally and lead to misattributions about the quality and quantity of one's contributions to the group. To address this issue, a good communicator will not only listen to the person talking but also watch to see who is not talking and find ways to involve those people who appear to be less responsive to the conversation (see case example "Managing the babbler," below).

But pauses can also be helpful in communicating. Long pauses can be used strategically to put pressure on another person to respond to a question or to concede an offer. Because even a half-second pause means something to listeners, Americans find pauses that exceed more than a few brief seconds to be uncomfortable. Thus, creating a long pause puts pressure on the other person to fill the pause. Teachers use this tactic to pressure students to respond to their questions, but teachers must be taught to wait, to count to 15 seconds, before restating the question or providing an answer. Similarly, trained negotiators use this tactic to pressure an opponent to give in. The one who breaks the silence is often the one who concedes. In a study conducted by the first author, participants from Taiwan and the US engaged in negotiation, and a repeated pattern was observed: An American participant would make an offer; the participant from Taiwan would look down at his or her profit sheet to consider the offer; a long pause would ensue, during which time the Taiwan participant was thinking. Inevitably, the American would make a conceding offer before the Taiwan participant could respond to the initial offer. The Americans couldn't wait through the extended pause, taking the pause as a rejection of the offer. In fact, the pause could have been an opportunity for both parties to think through their options.

Communication involves a balance between knowing when to speak, when to listen, when to let others speak, and when to wait. And waiting can sometimes take hours, days, or even longer. When emotions are intense or the path of decision is unclear, waiting a period of time, to let emotions cool or to gather more information about interests and options, can be a worthwhile investment of time. Rather than continuing to meet in an attempt to force a decision, allowing interested parties to consider information provided in an initial meeting and to think through options made or new options may result in a more reasoned decision, one that the parties are more willing to accept and agree to.

Technology affects the pace, structure, and ambiguity of communication. For example, e-mail and text messaging encourage brief messages, "point-for-point statements and rebuttals" (Kolb, 1966, as cited in Rice and Gattiker, 2001, p. 561), and, due to the absence of paralinguistic and other non-verbal cues, misunderstandings especially with regard to the emotional tone and intent of the sender. Emoticons, such as ☺ and ☹, developed in part to deal with this problem. Furthermore, these high-tech high-text methods of communicating generally lack the formal structure of, for example, a formal meeting or business letter, and the norms for these forms of communication within and between organizations are just being developed: Does one begin an e-mail as if it is a letter or as if it is a telephone call or as if it is a face-to-face conversation? Conversations, even business conversation, typically have a playful element prior to termination; does one engage in non-serious communication with a business associate via e-mail, and if so, how? In addition, because these communications are asynchronous, it is often hard to interpret a non-response: Is the other party angry or busy or consulting others or considering and weighing options or merely engaging in other activities rather than responding? Strategic non-responses, such as seeming unavailable when actually available, are easier to pull off with technology because it is harder to find out the communicative availability of the other party when one is at a distance. Finally, initiating these high-tech high-text communications when angry is frequently disastrous: When the "send" key is clicked, there is no recourse.

More communication is not better when emotions are high, not if the communication is no longer effective at sharing information or if the greater amount of communication may lead to damaging relationships. Sometimes delaying the communication and then approaching the issues from a different direction, such as by one-on-one discussions, providing summaries of the variety of interests covered in the initial meeting, and allowing emotions to subside, is a more effective approach. Then returning to communicate about the issues at another time can generate a fresh look at the problems at hand, one that can be successful in part because tempers have cooled and new ideas have come to the forefront (see case example "The team dissent over hiring," below).

Subprinciple 4: Communication is a balancing act between task and relational activities

For an organization, there are several balancing acts that are notable. Most importantly, there is a balancing act between the task and relational (socio-emotional) functions to which the organizational leadership must attend. According to Bernard, "the survival of any organization depends on its ability to solve two problems: the achievement of the purposes for which the organization was formed, and the satisfaction of the more immediate needs of the members of the organization" (Slater, 1955, p. 308).

A communication may convey information about the task at hand (related to "the purposes for which the organization was formed," for example deciding whom to hire), relationship information (related to "the satisfaction of the more immediate needs of the members of the organization," for example how solid the friendship is between group members), or both. And communication is the medium by which these activities are accomplished. An example of task and relational activity phases over time is found in phone and hallway conversations: However task-focused a conversation is, it will often end with a joke or some other unserious remark that brings the conversation to a close.

Early coding schemes differentiated task from relational communications (Bales, 1950). Communications that are positive and socio-emotional are those that show solidarity, tension release, and agreement; those that are task related are those that give or ask for suggestions, opinions, or orientations; and those that are negative and socio-emotional are those that show disagreement, tension, or antagonism. When we communicate over time, we go through phases when either task or relational communication predominates. In addition to this over-time specialization, groups tend to have individuals who generally focus on task matters and others who focus on relational matters.

The differentiation of task and relational leadership in an organization is sometimes captured in the formal organizational roles. Managers are, generally speaking, supposed to focus on organizational success, as, for example, determined by sales, productivity, and corporate image. Some organizations overlay this management structure with counselors, ombudspersons, and human relations staff, whose function is to solve problems associated with inappropriate communication, animosities, and cliques in the workplace. Modern organizations have HR departments to deal with relational issues, although the "bottom line" may still be the implicit underlying consideration.

In organizational groups or teams, there is likely to be a differentiation between both the relative amounts that group members communicate and the orientation of their communications between tasks and relationships. As for the first, there is evidence that sheer talking helps create a leadership hierarchy (Mullen, Salas, and Driskell, 1989; Stein and Heller, 1983; but cf. Pavitt, Whitchurch, Siple, and Petersen, 1997). Talking more helps make one a group leader (for better or for worse). On the other hand, there is some evidence that leaders specialize in task activities or in relational activities (Slater, 1955; cf. Lewis, 1972). Burke (1968) stated that "inequality of participation [by group members] in task activities leads to the emergence of separate specialized task and social-emotional roles [when task activity is low in legitimacy]" (p. 404). Thus, the amount of communication along with the balance of specialization in task activities versus relational activities helps to create the group's hierarchical structure.

This hierarchical structure has important implications for the way that antagonisms and disagreements are created and transform the group. A relationship has been found between the amount that the group's task leader exceeds others in task performance and the amount that the low-status group member is scapegoated, at least in groups whose activities are low in legitimation (i.e. the acceptability of the tasks to the group members; see Burke, 1969). Further, if the task leader does not support the low-status member, scapegoating the low-status member increases (Gallagher and Burke, 1974). In other words, group members are likely to be antagonistic and disagree with the low-status group member, rather than show solidarity toward or agree with this person, when the task leader is performing admirably and doesn't support the low-status group member.

Consistent with these ideas, a simulation found that the most effective five-member group had members with different roles, including a social organizer and a democratic task leader (Hare and Hare, 2001). Furthermore, in student groups, "the nature and frequency of the leader's communication," among other things, affected the quality of what the group produced (Harper and Askling, 1980, p. 6). In this study, the leaders of successful groups communicated more about task than about socio-emotional matters and were perceived as communicating more than others. Finally, scapegoating undermines group effectiveness, because it lessens the involvement and productivity of the person scapegoated, takes the time and energy of group members to "excommunicate" a group member rather than integrate the member in the group, and in most bureaucratic organizations it takes additional time and energy if the scapegoated member is to be dismissed: Typically, the leader must repeatedly (1) document the failures of this individual, (2) document the attempts to improve this individual's performance, (3) sanction this individual, and (4) document the acknowledgments by the scapegoated individual of these documents and meetings related to them. Although these activities may be necessary if a member is not

competent or is particularly disruptive to the group, these activities are usually quite costly
to the group and to the organization.

Thus, several balancing acts are needed:

◆ Leaders may wish to democratize group meetings by encouraging greater communication by all group members, but doing so may undermine the leader's role
as a leader. Therefore, the leader must realize that equality of communication by
group members is not realistic and is ultimately inefficient, but promoting task-
related communication generates support for the leader and efficiency in the group.
◆ Leaders may concentrate on task-related activities, but they also should be aware
that relational concerns require time and effort. Therefore, leaders may designate
another person to give these concerns their necessary attention, and they should not
minimize the importance of maintaining morale and preventing scapegoating.
◆ Joking and other unserious activities may appear to reduce task activity, but at various times they may be necessary for the group's communicative health. Therefore,
the leader must recognize this need for playful communication, especially as groups
complete their scheduled work time; they should not view these activities merely
as diversions from work; and they may need to provide organizational resources –
release time, space, and funds – for these activities.
◆ If task activities are not viewed as acceptable, or if support for the low-status group
member is not communicated, group members may resort to scapegoating, which is
an unproductive and divisive activity. Therefore, a leader needs to persuade group
members that its tasks are legitimate and needs to avoid undermining any low-status
(but potentially valuable) group members, which, in the long term, builds a more
effective group. These ideas also suggest that reprimands be private whenever possible; otherwise group members may either scapegoat the individual who has been
reprimanded or, if that individual can form a coalition with other group members,
the coalition can undermine the leader.

Subprinciple 5: Communication is a balancing act between learning from formal versus informal channels

The process of becoming integrated into an organization also requires a balancing act.
On entering an organization, a new employee is expected to be successful in handling
a new job, which requires acquiring new knowledge and becoming acclimated to new
expectations, decision-making processes, and relationships. Furthermore, these "novelties"
take place in an environment that is new to the recruit or novice. Socialization is the process through which an employee comes to understand the knowledge, values, norms, and
behaviors needed to participate as a member of the organization (Van Maanen, 1975; see
also Jablin, 2001). These aspects – organizational knowledge, values, norms, and behaviors – must be learned, and they are learned through communication (see Chapter 20), via
formal as well as informal channels. Furthermore, the formal and informal channels both
provide information, which is sometimes reinforcing, sometimes independent, and sometimes contradictory. So there is a balancing act between learning about the organization
through formal policy documents, hierarchies, and plans, and adhering to them, versus
utilizing informal interactions and organizational norms to generate one's organizational

conduct and understanding. Both the formal and informal structures and norms are necessary to learn, and successful newcomers' behavior is a synthesis of these normative systems.

Informal channels are typically replete with stories – narratives that are presumed to tell the "real" version of what's what (Mumby, 1987) – and gossip. Gossip, even if ultimately wrong, mean spirited or innocuous, is a means to acquire influence by selectively sharing information, and information is power. Biological anthropologist Robin Dunbar (1996) hypothesized that gossip provides the same "positive strokes" that grooming does among other primates. In addition to gossip, much of the novice's organizational learning involves listening to and interacting with third parties, vicarious learning (i.e. being influenced, often unconsciously, by what happens to others), and surveillance (purposeful observation). One sees who talks with whom, who is formally rewarded or punished, who is informally derogated or praised, who has broad freedom of action and who does not, who has formal or informal influence over others, and who knows how and with whom to connect to get the job done. As Mechanic (1962) has shown, often lower-status people – an office manager who handles files, or, more humorously, company clerk (and bugler) Corporal Walter "Radar" O'Reilly in *M*A*S*H* (Hornberger and Gelbart, 1972–1983) – control access to people, information, and the flow of information (see Katz and Kahn, 1966).

People who learn and adopt the organization's values develop strong interaction skills, become competent communicators within the organization, are generally more satisfied in their work, identify more closely with those with whom they work, and become more integrated into the organization's communication networks. This integration results in greater accessibility to information and facilitates further integration. But the hard part of the socialization process is not to put too much stock in the informal network, nor to put too much stock in the formal one. And it should be noted that there are ethical limits on organizational commitment: Some organizations may not be worth one's commitment (see Chapter 20).

Subprinciple 6: Communication is a balancing act between learning from newcomers versus veterans

If a person is new to an organization, with whom does that person talk? On the one hand, the organizational veterans presumably know how the organization works; after all, they have already been integrated, with varying degrees of success, into the organization. On the other hand, these veterans may appear (and often are) unapproachable – they might want to distance themselves from the newcomer because of an "anti-fraternization" ethos – and they might even delight in some small degree of hazing the newcomer. There may be a veteran who serves as a mentor, but even if this were the case the interaction of mentor and newcomer may be limited and too "official," that is, too closely tied to formal communication channels and the information that it provides. On the other hand, one's peers may be quite approachable, but they may lack the requisite knowledge that the novice needs. Furthermore, being seen as too closely tied to other novices may give the appearance of being too loosely connected to the organization. If the newcomer uses peers for social support, how is the newcomer to "learn the ropes"? Interacting with veterans to acquire organizational knowledge may have the inadvertent effect of looking like a brownnoser, and no one wants to be characterized in this way. Hence, another communication balancing act.

There is evidence about how this balancing act works. Fink and Chen (1995) studied a university's faculty members. They divided their sample into three groups based on the number of years that each person had been a faculty on that campus: 17 or more years ("HI tenure"), five to 16 years ("MI tenure"), and less than five years ("LO tenure"). Comparing the high- versus the low-tenure groups, the high-tenure group was found to be significantly more homogeneous with regard to university-related beliefs and attitudes. Furthermore, members of each tenure group spent significantly more time communicating with their own group members than with members of the other group. The higher net amount of communication within the HI tenure group was thought to explain why its members were more homogeneous than the LO tenure group was.

The effect of this communication pattern to relative veterans versus to relative novices was clear: An individual's attitudes and beliefs become more similar to the group with whom he or she has greater communication. The balancing act for novices involves having greater communication with their peers but sufficient communication with their seniors so as to accelerate their integration into the organization. Integration into the organization makes newcomers more effective organizational members, and the more that newcomers communicate with veterans, the faster their integration into the organization.

Finally, it should be noted that communication with non-peers has a special informational advantage when one is seeking ties that go beyond one's immediate organizational "neighborhood." Granovetter (1973, 1995) has shown that one's peers are likely to want to be of help, but they are likely to have the same base of information that one already has. On the other hand, those with whom one is less associated – in Granovetter's terms, those who are *weak ties* – are likely to have information that one doesn't have. So, for purposes of connecting to those outside one's immediate communication network, such as for getting a job, one might turn to those with whom one is weakly attached. Granovetter (1973, 1983, 1995) has shown that these weak ties are associated with the diffusion of ideas and fashion as well as finding out about job opportunities; his 1983 essay clarifies the weak-tie hypothesis and its relevance to a broad array of studies. The communicative balance discussed here is between the support but ignorance of those who are close and the inaccessibility but knowledge of those who are communicatively far.

Subprinciple 7: Communication is a balancing act between types of trust

It should be obvious that communication affects the trust people have for each other (see Chapter 21). At the negotiation table trust can make or break a deal; trust between parties allows the negotiators to focus on the instrumental issues, whereas low trust can redirect the negotiators' attention to psychological and emotional issues. Lulofs (1993) showed that the level of trust between people affects the level of uncertainty they have interacting with each other, which in turn affects the goals they are likely to pursue during their interaction, which then affects their likelihood of using power strategies: When parties have low trust, they are more likely to use defensive power strategies that exacerbate conflict rather than constructive problem-solving strategies.

Trust is often described in unidimensional terms; Pruitt and Carnevale (1993), for example, defined trust as an expectation that the other person will cooperate in the future. But trust is a multidimensional concept, so communication with co-workers must entail a balance between four different types of trust (Cai and Hung, 2005), each of which affects different perceptions about the communicator (see Chapter 21 for a more detailed discussion of trust). The first dimension, *competence*, has to do with conveying to others that they can trust in the abilities and capabilities of the communicator. In the case of a manager, the competence of the manager affects the perceptions employees and colleagues have of the manager's ability to deliver promises, accomplish goals, and lead effectively. Low competence on the part of the manager can quickly lead to distrust on the part of the employees and result in lack of attention on the part of those receiving the manager's messages. Similarly, perceptions that an employee lacks competence can have negative consequences on gaining increased responsibilities, promotion, and raises. Communicating competence requires that a person understands what is expected for the roles that one plays, as an employee, a negotiator, or a manager; further, the individual must understand how these expectations are shaped by the culture of the specific organization. The individual needs to be able to enact those expectations when they communicate.

The second dimension of trust is *integrity*, which is the expectation that a communicator will adhere to high ethical and moral standards A manager may be competent in her job performance, but if she lacks a moral compass, acting without clear principles for determining fairness and discipline or without attention to organizational policies designed to protect and uphold rights of employees, distrust will quickly ensue. Communicating integrity involves articulating the fair and reasonable principles that guide judgments and actions.

Dependability (or what is also referred to as conscientiousness, see Chapter 2) is the third dimension of trust: knowing that a person can be counted on to do what he says he will do. When a job needs to be done, the best person for the job is one who is both competent to do the job as well as dependable to get the job done (and, of course, will do so with integrity).

The last dimension of trust is *benevolence*: communicating that the other person's best interest is kept in mind. This dimension involves letting people know that they are important, that their goals and needs have value, that their ideas are heard and considered, and that the communicator can be trusted to act on their behalf. However, communicating this aspect of trust requires careful attention to that fine balance of attending to the job and attending to the people doing the job. A manager cannot act with too much integrity, but communicating too much benevolence can undermine the working relationship that the manager maintains with the employees, especially if benevolence is not balanced with competence and dependability. And too much benevolence on the part of employees may be perceived as weakness or may result in a manager taking advantage of employees who communicate too much goodwill. By all means, communicate benevolence but do so with attention to the requirements of the organizational roles one must play.

Communicating trust, in all its dimensions, involves a balance between taking into account both who you are as the sender of the message and with whom you are communicating. One size does not fit all when it comes to communicating trust. Messages must be tailored with the recipient in mind and adjusted based on the feedback the recipient communicates in return. Credentials, which communicate competence, only go so far. The most competent employee who is not dependable may soon be left out of decision making. And a manager who acts only as a sender of messages is likely to find that his or her communication is not reaching those meant to receive the message or the message has but a limited effect.

Case Examples

Managing the babbler

Sally works with a group of managers that meet regularly for planning meetings. She has come to view the meetings as a waste of time because it seems nothing ever gets done. One person in particular is the source of the problem; in private, Sally refers to this person as a *babbler*: someone who jumps into the conversation before anyone else has a chance to speak, dominates the discussion, expresses strong opinions on every issue that arises, and speaks far too long to say what could have been said in a sentence or two.

Given the economic challenges the company is facing, some important issues are coming up in the next meeting. This meeting is especially important because it will require the managers to work through some tough decisions over issues such as whether to replace some of the old initiatives with new ones and whether layoffs will be necessary. Sally feels strongly that this meeting is not one in which one person should dominate the discussion. A variety of perspectives need to be heard, and there needs to be an opportunity to debate the issues and listen to options to come to a joint agreement about where the company is headed. Sally's afraid that this process of discussion won't happen with the *babbler* on board.

1. Suppose Sally were the group leader: In that role what could Sally do to address her concerns?
2. Suppose Sally were a relative newcomer to the organization. In that role what could Sally do to address her concerns?
3. As a group, what could be done to manage the communication for better decision making before the meeting? During the meeting? After the meeting?
4. Review the balancing acts that are discussed above. What types of communication need to be balanced in this situation? How should they be balanced?

The team dissent over hiring

In recent months, Kampen Company has hired several people to fill important positions. Not only has the competition for the jobs been fierce, but conflicts that have arisen over whom to hire have been fierce within the organization. In one recent situation, the team in charge of hiring consisted of seven team members plus a team leader. Although the person to be hired will be a member of the team as a whole, some of the team members will work more closely with this person than others. Having narrowed the choices down to three candidates, the team was split in its decision as to whom to hire, and strong emotions drove the discussion. Group A, which consisted of the three team members who would work the most closely with the new hire, felt strongly that the first candidate was clearly the most qualified, that the second candidate met the basic job requirements, and that the third candidate was not at all qualified. Because they would work closest with the new hire, Group A believed strongly that its preference should carry the most weight in the hiring decision.

Group B, which consisted of four team members, saw the situation quite differently. These four people all agreed that the third candidate was the best person for the job and should be hired because this candidate not only met the job requirements but also brought much needed diversity to the team overall.

During the meeting in which the team was to discuss whom to hire, a long and heated discussion unfolded. The team leader tried to maintain a civil discussion, but managing the group's emotions and keeping the communication from becoming too heated was a challenge. Group A felt that it was being treated unfairly and was being dominated by the rest of the team members, who they believed did not fully understand the requirements of the position. As a result, Group A felt disrespected and distrustful of Group B's motives. The discussion continued to disintegrate.

In the final analysis, the team leader had the authority to hire whomever the leader considered to be the best candidate for the job. But the team leader faced several challenges. One challenge was to be responsive to the interests of all the team members. Another challenge was to hire the best person for the job. A third challenge was to somehow prevent the divisive rift that seemed to be emerging on the team. And a fourth challenge was to support diversity in hiring.

In an effort to be responsive to the interests of the team members and to end the long and heated discussion, the team leader called for a vote. As was predictable, Group B outvoted Group A, and the third candidate won the vote. Also predictable was that, although Group B "won," everyone walked out of the room feeling angry and betrayed by some members of the team.

So now the team leader had a new dilemma. The team leader agreed with Group A that the first candidate was a much stronger candidate than the third candidate, who was the least qualified for the position. The leader must consider whether to rely on majority rule and hire the person who won the vote or to exert authority and hire according to her judgment. In addition, the leader must consider the ramifications of these choices.

In the end, the team leader did neither. First, the team leader delayed hiring for a week to give the process the time that was needed for tempers to cool and to give the team leader a chance to talk with people one on one about their preferences. Second, based on individual discussions with each team member, the leader wrote up a list of several issues that seemed to be central to various team members in making the hiring decision, putting in writing the objective interests and then circulating this list of concerns to the members of the team. Third, after time had passed, tempers had cooled, and everyone had time to consider the scope of interests that influenced the hiring decision, the team leader called another meeting to discuss once again whom to hire. This time the team members assessed the three candidates based on the list of interests that had been provided. Discussion ensued, resulting in a reconsideration of all the candidates. In the end, rather than polarizing around two candidates, the reassessment resulted in all of the team members realizing that candidate two, who had been largely overlooked because of previous polarization around candidates one and three, met the interests of everyone on the team. When a new vote was taken, candidate two received nearly unanimous support. This time the team leader's decision of whom to hire was clear. Candidate two was given the offer and, after some negotiating, accepted the job.

Several principles arise from this case:

1. Preserving relationships in the long run is better than reaching a decision in the short run if the short-term decision is at the cost of sacrificing relationships.

2. Majority rule is not always the best rule for team decisions.
3. When group communication falls apart, sometimes talking one on one may be more effective than trying to force discussion and a decision within a group setting that is over-run by strong emotions.
4. Finding ways to move away from emotionally charged communication to focus on interests can redirect the discussion to what matters most, but sometimes it takes effort and creativity to find ways to redirect the communication.
5. Buying time to make a decision can be a very good investment.

Discuss these five principles and relate them to the seven communication subprinciples discussed in this chapter. Are the five principles new ones, or are they the same as or corollaries of the seven principles in the chapter?

CONCLUSION

This chapter has focused on several balancing acts that a successful communicator must manage. Aristotle, and many others, has written about *seeking the golden mean* by avoiding both deficiency and excess. For communication, one must balance

- the needs of senders and receivers;
- the requirements of speaking and listening;
- the content, manner, and time of communicating;
- the different phases and roles associated with task and relational activities;
- the resources provided by use of formal and informal channels;
- the costs and benefits of learning from newcomers versus veterans;
- the value that different types of trust have for the communicator.

Of course, there are other balancing acts that are not discussed here; for example, Eisenberg and Goodall (2004) subtitle their book on organizational communication "balancing creativity and constraint." But if a communicator within an organization can balance the seven aspects of communication discussed here, that communicator will indeed have achieved the golden mean of effective communication.

REFERENCES

Bales, R. F. (1950). *Interaction Process Analysis*. Cambridge, MA: Harvard University Press.

Brown, P., and Levinson, S. C. (1987). *Politeness: Some Universals in Language Usage*. New York: Cambridge University.

Burke, P. J. (1968). Role differentiation and the legitimation of task activity. *Sociometry*, 31, 404–411.

Burke, P. J. (1969). Scapegoating: An alternative to role differentiation. *Sociometry*, 32, 159–168.

Cai, D. A., and Hung, C. J. F. (2005). Whom do you trust? A cross-cultural comparison. In G. Cheney and G. A. Barnett (eds), *International and Multicultural Organizational Communication* (pp. 73–104). Cresskill, NJ: Hampton Press.

Cooper, L., and Husband, R. (1993). Developing a model of organizational listening competency. *Journal of the International Listening Association*, 7, 6–34.

Donohue, W. A. (with Kolt, R.) (1992). *Managing Interpersonal Conflict*. Newbury Park, CA: Sage.

Dunbar, R. (1996). *Grooming, Gossip, and the Evolution of Language*. Cambridge, MA: Harvard University.

Eisenberg, E. M., and Goodall, H. L., Jr. (2004). *Organizational Communication: Balancing Creativity and Constraint* (4th edition). Boston: Bedford/St. Martin's.

Fink, E. L., and Chen, S.-S. (1995). A Galileo analysis of organizational climate. *Human Communication Research*, 21, 494–521.

Ford, C., and Thompson, S. (1996). Interactional units in conversation: Syntactic, intonational, and pragmatic resources for the management of turns. In E. Ochs, E. Schegloff, and S. Thompson (eds), *Interaction and Grammar* (pp. 134–184). Cambridge, England: Cambridge University Press.

Fox Tree, J. E. (2002). Interpreting pauses and ums at turn exchanges. *Discourse Processes*, 34, 37–55.

Gallagher, J., and Burke, P. J. (1974). Scapegoating and leader behavior. *Social Forces*, 52, 481–488.

Graham, C. R., Hamblin, A. W., and Feldstein, S. (2001). Recognition of emotion in English voices by speakers of Japanese, Spanish and English. *IRAL: International Review of Applied Linguistics in Language Teaching*, 39, 19–37.

Granovetter, M. S. (1973). The strength of weak ties. *American Journal of Sociology*, 78, 1360–1380.

Granovetter, M. S. (1983). The strength of weak ties: A network theory revisited. *Sociological Theory*, 1, 201–233.

Granovetter, M. S. (1995). *Getting a Job: A Study of Contacts and Careers* (2nd edition). Chicago: University of Chicago Press.

Haas, J. W., and Arnold, C. L. (1995). An examination of the role of listening in judgments of communication competence in co-workers. *Journal of Business Communication*, 32, 123–139.

Halone, K. K., and Pecchioni, L. L. (2001). Relational listening: A grounded theoretical model. *Communication Reports*, 14, 59–71.

Hare, S. E., and Hare, A. P. (2001). Role repertoires of members in an effective small group: a simulation. *International Journal of Action Methods*, 54, 91–105.

Harper, N. L., and Askling, L. E. (1980). Group communication and quality of task solution in a media production organization. *Communication Monographs*, 47, 77–100.

Hieke, A., Kowal, S., and O'Connell, M. (1983). The trouble with "articulatory" pauses. *Language and Speech*, 26, 203–214.

Hornberger, H. R. (creator), and Gelbart, L. (developer) (1972–1983). *M*A*S*H* (television series). Los Angeles, CA: Twentieth Century Fox Television.

Jablin, F. M. (2001). Organizational entry, assimilation and disengagement/exit. In F. M. Jablin and L. L. Putnam (eds), *The New Handbook of Organizational Communication: Advances in Theory, Research, and Methods* (pp. 732–818). Thousand Oaks, CA: Sage.

Katz, D., and Kahn, R. L. (1966). Communication: the flow of information. In *The Social Psychology of Organizations* (pp. 223–258). New York: John Wiley and Sons.

Lasswell, H. D. (1948). The structure and function of communication in society. In L. Bryson (ed.), *The Communication of Ideas* (pp. 37–51). New York: Harper and Brothers.

Lee, H. O., and Boster, F. J. (1992). Collectivism–individualism in perceptions of speech rate: A cross-cultural comparison. *Journal of Cross-Cultural Psychology*, 23, 377–388.

Lewis, G. H. (1972). Role differentiation. *American Sociological Review*, 37, 424–434.

Lewis, R. D. (1999). *When Cultures Collide: Managing Successfully Across Cultures*. London: Nicholas Brealey Publishers.

Lulofs, R. S. (1993). *Conflict: From Theory to Action*. Scottsdale, AZ: Gorsuch Scarisbrick.

Mechanic, D. (1962). Sources of power of lower participants in complex organizations. *Administrative Science Quarterly*, 7, 349–369.

Mullen, B., Salas, E., and Driskell, J. E. (1989). Salience, motivation, and artifact as contributions to the relation between participation rate and leadership. *Journal of Experimental Social Psychology*, 25, 545–559.

Mumby, D. K. (1987). The political function of narrative in organizations. *Communication Monographs*, 54, 113–127.

Ngai, P. B.-Y. (2000). Nonverbal communicative behavior in intercultural negotiations: Insights and applications based on findings from Ethiopia, Tanzania, Hong Kong, and the China mainland. *World Communication*, 29(4), 5–35.

Pasupathi, M., Stallworth, L. M., and Murdoch, K. (1998). How what we tell becomes what we know: Listener effects on speakers' long-term memory for events. *Discourse Processes*, 26, 1–25.

Pavitt, C., Whitchurch, G. G., Siple, H., and Petersen, N. (1997). Communication and emergent group leadership: Does content count? *Communication Research Reports*, 14, 470–480.

Pruitt, D. G., and Carnevale, P. J. (1993). *Negotiation in Social Conflict*. Pacific Grove, CA: Brooks/Cole.

Rice, R. E., and Gattiker, U. E. (2001). New media and organizational structuring. In F. M. Jablin and L. L. Putnam (eds), *The New Handbook of Organizational Communication: Advances in Theory, Research, and Methods* (pp. 544–581). Thousand Oaks, CA: Sage Publications.

Robert, S. C., Robert, III, H. M., Evans, W. J., Honemann, D. H., and Balch, T. J. (2000). *Robert's Rules of Order Newly Revised* (10th edition). New York: Da Capo Press.

Schachter, S., Christenfeld, N., Ravina, B., and Bilous, F. (1991). Speech disfluency and the structure of knowledge. *Journal of Personality and Social Psychology*, 60, 362–367.

Senge, P. M. (2006). *The Fifth Discipline: The Art and Practice of the Learning Organization*. New York: Doubleday.

Shannon, C. E., and Weaver, W. (1963). *The Mathematical Theory of Communication*. Urbana: University of Illinois Press.

Slater, P. E. (1955). Role differentiation in small groups. *American Sociological Review*, 20, 300–310.

Stein, R. T., and Heller, T. (1983). The relationship of participation rates to leadership status: A meta-analysis. In H. H. Blumberg, A. P. Hare, V. Kent, and M. Davies (eds), *Small Groups and Social Interaction* (Vol. 1, pp. 401–406). Chichester, England: John Wiley and Sons.

Sypher, B. D., Bostrom, R. N., and Seibert, J. H. (1989). Listening, communication abilities, and success at work. *Journal of Business Communication*, 26, 293–303.

Sypher, B. D., and Zorn, T. E. (1986). Communication-related abilities and upward mobility: a longitudinal investigation. *Human Communication Research*, 12, 420–431.

Van Maanen, J. (1975). Breaking in: Socialization to work. In R. Dubin (ed.), *Handbook of Work, Organization and Society* (pp. 67–120). Chicago: Rand McNally.

Wennerstrom, A., and Siegel, A. F. (2003). Keeping the floor in multiparty conversations: Intonation, syntax, and pause. *Discourse Processes*, 36, 77–107.

Wilson, S. R., and Putnam, L. L. (1990). Interaction goals in negotiation. In J. A. Anderson (ed.), *Communication Yearbook* 13 (pp. 374–406). Newbury Park, CA: Sage.

Wolvin, A., and Coakley, C. G. (1992). *Listening* (4th edition). New York: McGraw-Hill.

EXERCISES

Take-home exercise – sociograms

Communication is both the substance and the medium for information flow. To learn how information flows, we need to gather data on communication behavior, in particular, who speaks to whom about what. A *sociogram* is a diagram in which people are points or circles and lines represent types of relationships between the people.

1. Keep a journal of everyone whom you spoke to for one day at work. Write down to whom you spoke (individuals or groups), for how long, about what topics, and the type of relationship you have with those persons.
2. Group these people together according to the reason you interacted with them; for example, people you work with on a particular project are grouped together, people who are in particular departments are grouped together, clients are grouped together, and so on.
3. Draw a sociogram (or network) that connects these people or groups of people (use no more than 10 people or groups) to you and to each other. Use thicker lines to denote strong relationships, thinner lines to denote weaker but important relationships, and dotted lines to denote relationships with people that are both weak and not important to you.
4. Now redraw the sociogram to illustrate the amount of time you talked with these people. Use thicker lines to denote more minutes, thinner lines to denote fewer minutes, and dotted lines to denote very brief conversations.
5. Compare the two sociograms. What do these illustrations tell you about whom you communicate with, why, and for how long? Do these sociograms suggest ways you may improve your communication with others?

In-class exercise – effect of trust on communication

Describe a recent dispute that you had with another person *where the trust between you and the other person was either very high or very low.* Describe the relationship between you and the other party, why there was high or low trust between you, and what happened in the dispute?

1. Did the level of trust you had with the other person affect the way you communicated with the other person and the outcome of the dispute? In what ways? Which of the four aspects of trust were involved?
2. If the level of trust had been the opposite of what it was, how do you think your communication would have been affected? Do you think the outcome would have been different (in other words, if there was high trust, what do you think would have happened if trust had been very low, or vice versa)?
3. What do you conclude about the influence of trust on how you communicate? How can knowledge about trust help you communicate more effectively in the future?

24

Use Participation to Share Information and Distribute Knowledge

John A. Wagner III

Participation is a process in which decision making, problem solving, action planning, or similar activities are shared and performed jointly by hierarchical superiors and their subordinates. To participate, superiors and subordinates work together to identify alternatives, consider preferences, and finalize judgments. Defined in this manner, participation differs from direction, in which superiors follow autocratic procedures and act alone (Wagner, 1982). Participation also differs from consultation, in which superiors ask subordinates for their inputs and opinions but then weigh alternatives and make a final choice on their own (Vroom and Yetton, 1973). Less obviously, perhaps, participation differs from delegation, in which superiors remove themselves and cede complete authority to their subordinates. Whereas participation requires that outcomes reflect needs and interests shared across hierarchical levels, delegation is more likely to allow subordinates the autonomy to act in accordance with personal desires (Leana, 1987).

Social theorists have long suggested that participation influences human behavior by (1) involving participants directly in ongoing processes, thereby securing their commitment to participatory outcomes through the "sense of ownership" stimulated by their personal involvement, or by (2) providing participants the opportunity to exchange and collect information, and to become more fully informed and knowledgeable about ongoing activities and participatory results (e.g. Pateman, 1970). Organizational researchers have similarly speculated that participation might influence behavior in organizations through two distinct mechanisms, one termed *motivational* and the other *cognitive* (Bartlem and Locke, 1981; Locke and Schweiger, 1979; Miller and Monge, 1986; Schweiger and Leana, 1986; Wagner, Leana, Locke, and Schweiger, 1997). Research on the two mechanisms sheds light on each mechanism's ability to predict and explain likely outcomes of participatory processes, and thus holds important implications for the management of organizational behavior.

PARTICIPATION DOES NOT ALWAYS MOTIVATE, AND THE
LACK OF IT DOES NOT ALWAYS DEMOTIVATE

The motivational mechanism is thought to affect behavior in organizations through the heightened sense of personal commitment to or acceptance of participatory outcomes that comes from having a say in participatory processes and a part in shaping the outcomes of those processes. According to this explanation, participation stimulates a sense of commitment that motivates participants to support and implement participatory resolutions. Behavior is motivated and satisfaction is experienced as participants strive to see their resolutions through to completion.

Research on the motivational mechanism extends back to a series of studies conducted, during the 1920s and 1930s, at Western Electric's Hawthorne Plant, located near Chicago, Illinois. In reviewing analyses of the effects of factors such as factory lighting, incentive payment, and supportive supervision on workforce satisfaction and performance, Hawthorne researchers noticed a pattern of results that seemed to indicate that workers were influenced by social conditions – specifically, by desires to satisfy needs for companionship and support at work – and that such conditions might have strong motivational effects. This led them to suggest that participatory involvement, in providing the opportunity to satisfy social needs, might motivate increased task performance and stimulate greater acceptance of organizational policies (Roethlisberger and Dickson, 1939).

Following up on this speculation, Coch and French (1948) performed a study of textile pieceworkers that appeared to indicate that workers would accept changes in job practices more readily if involved in the design and implementation of those practices. The authors identified participatory processes as effective in encouraging acceptance of and commitment to changed standards and procedures. They also characterized participation as a potentially powerful method of reducing personal frustration and aggression attributable to resistance to change.

Subsequent analyses of the motivational effects of participation focused increasing attention on *participation defined as a process of influence sharing*, and on the heightened personal commitment thought to accompany the redistribution and equalizing of influence and authority in organizations. Theorists identified participatory processes as likely to have strong positive effects on workforce morale and satisfaction, feelings of involvement and commitment, and employee motivation and performance (e.g. Anderson, 1959; Dickson, 1981; McMahon, 1976; Patchen, 1964). Research first seemed to support this assertion (Fox, 1957; McCurdy and Eber, 1953; Pennington, Haravey, and Bass, 1958; Vroom, 1960), but as further evidence amassed, it became apparent that participation's motivational effects were neither as strong nor as generalizable as originally proposed. Some studies reported zero or near-zero relationships between participation and motivation, commitment, or performance (Alutto and Belasco, 1972; Castore and Murnighan, 1978; Ivancevich, 1977; Jenkins and Lawler, 1981; Rosenbaum and Rosenbaum, 1971), and others reported evidence of negative relationships between participation and the same outcome variables (Gibb, 1951; Green and Taber, 1980; Latham and Saari, 1979).

In the wake of these conflicting findings, Wagner and Gooding (1987) used a statistical technique called meta-analysis to aggregate the results of 70 published studies of participation, in order to estimate the strength of participation's general effects. After removing the effects of a troubling research artifact, percept–percept inflation (Crampton and

Wagner, 1994), Wagner and Gooding discovered that participation correlated, on average, .11 with performance, .11 with satisfaction, and .10 with acceptance (i.e. commitment). Although a subsequent reanalysis of Wagner and Gooding's data appeared to contradict their findings (Erez, Bloom, and Wells, 1996), an additional analysis showed the contradictory interpretation to be invalid (Wagner and LePine, 1999). Other studies have produced findings similar to and supportive of Wagner and Gooding's results (e.g. Locke, Feren, McCaleb, Shaw, and Denny, 1980; Wagner, 1994). After considering the available evidence, Locke, Alavi, and Wagner (1997) concluded that participation's likely correlations with performance and satisfaction are both on the order of .11. Changing levels of participation (i.e. from direction to participation) therefore explain only about 1% of the concurrent change in performance or satisfaction. This conclusion offers little general support for the use of participation as a motivational technique in the workplace.

Exceptions: when is participation most likely to motivate?

Despite documenting participation's limitation, in general, as a motivational tool, Wagner and Gooding (1987) also discovered situational conditions under which participation might have more substantial effects. In particular, their analysis suggested that *participation is more likely to be related to employee satisfaction when participation takes place in smaller groups* – typically, groups of 12 or fewer members. Implied by this finding is the possibility that participants are unable to develop a sense of personal connection to or ownership of participatory outcomes in larger group settings, due perhaps to the fact that many people share in the creation of those outcomes, and thus each participant fails to derive satisfaction from participatory processes or results. In small groups, however, participation and satisfaction are correlated at the level of .25 on average, indicating that about 6% of the change in satisfaction can be attributed to participation's effects. The size of this relationship suggests that group size is an important situational condition and that participation in small groups has limited, but nonetheless noteworthy, utility as a practical means of stimulating workplace satisfaction.

Wagner and Gooding (1987) also reported that *differences in task complexity have effects on the strength of relationships between participation and both satisfaction and acceptance*. In each relationship, the effect is stronger when tasks are less complex, meaning more behaviorally routine and less cognitively demanding. Suggested is the possibility that participation can be used to enrich – make more challenging – otherwise oversimplified work. Participation's relationship with satisfaction is again somewhat modest, with an average correlation of .26 revealed in the presence of simple tasks, but its relationship with acceptance is more substantial, as evidenced by an average correlation of .32 under simple task conditions. Indicated by the latter finding is a fairly strong enrichment effect, in which increasing participation by individuals who otherwise perform simple tasks explains just over 10% of the corresponding increase in acceptance of the results of participatory processes.

PRIMARY CAUSAL MECHANISM: PARTICIPATION DISSEMINATES INFORMATION

In contrast to the motivational mechanism's definition of participation as a process of influence sharing, within the framework of the cognitive mechanism the focus is on *participation defined as a process of information sharing*. From this perspective, participation's effects on organizational behavior are thought to be a function of the increased knowledge and deeper understanding afforded by participatory information sharing. Researchers have proposed that participatory information sharing might influence participant behaviors in several ways, for example: (1) knowing how to do a job increases the opportunity to do the job productively (Lawler and Hackman, 1969; Scheflen, Lawler, and Hackman, 1971); (2) understanding how a job fits into the larger picture of workgroup interdependence and organizational mission enables effective adjustment to changing work conditions (Ledford and Lawler, 1994; Williams, 1982); (3) sharing knowledge and insights encourages common understanding and greater cooperation (Dickson, 1981; Marrow and French, 1946); and (4) being able to access and make use of the collective information of an organization's membership increases the likelihood of successful organizational innovation and creativity (Stewart, 1997; Tannenbaum, 1968).

Research on the cognitive mechanism has sought to determine whether participation does, in fact, promote information sharing, and whether such sharing can have beneficial consequences for the performance of individuals, groups, or organizations. In one study, Latham, Winters, and Locke (1994) allowed some subjects in a laboratory experiment to share and discuss strategies for attaining assigned goals on a class scheduling task, but prohibited other subjects from participating in similar discussions. Results of the experiment indicated that individuals who participated in strategy discussions formed better task strategies, felt more able to succeed in the task, and performed better on the task than did subjects barred from participation. Moreover, differences in strategy quality were found to explain much of the effect of participation on performance, indicating that participation improved performance by helping participants discover better performance strategies – a cognitive rather than motivational effect.

In another study, Scully, Kirkpatrick, and Locke (1995) manipulated the knowledge held by supervisors and subordinates in two-person laboratory groups. In one third of the groups in the study, supervisors had the correct information needed to do their tasks, in one third they had incorrect information, and in one third they had no information whatsoever; subordinates were also split in thirds and assigned the same three levels of information; and half of the groups engaged in participatory information sharing while the other half did not. Results indicated that participation alone had no effect on subjects' performance, but that participation had beneficial effects on performance if the subordinate had correct information and the supervisor had none. In addition, performance suffered if the supervisor lacked correct information or if either or both members of a pair had incorrect information.

In a third study, Quigley and colleagues (2007) distributed knowledge differentially within dyads of laboratory partners, then examined motivational factors expected to influence the degree of knowledge sharing between partners and the effects of this sharing on partner performance. Among the results of this study is the finding that group-oriented incentives motivated sharing more than did individualized incentives, especially when norms between partners supported knowledge exchange, and that knowledge sharing enhanced partner performance, especially when high self-efficacy and trust in dyad partner led to the development of difficult self-set performance goals. These results suggest that participation might exert an indirect motivational effect by encouraging knowledge sharing within groups or teams. An effect of this sort differs from the direct motivational effects assessed in prior participation research and described above, and appears worthy of further consideration.

In sum, these studies and others like them indicate that participatory processes can be used to share or redistribute information, and that such redistribution can have positive effects on performance when it provides otherwise uninformed individuals with ready access to requisite knowledge and insights (Bartlem and Locke, 1981; Bass, Valenzi, Farrow, and Solomon, 1975; Lowin, 1968; Tsai, 2001). Also highlighted are motivational boundary conditions that influence the strength and utility of these effects. Supported is the principle that participation will be beneficial when some individuals possess or can discover pertinent information and use participatory processes to disseminate it to others (Durham, Knight, and Locke, 1997).

MODERATORS: WHEN IS PARTICIPATION MOST ABLE TO INFORM?

In addition to confirming participation's effectiveness in distributing information, Scully, Kirkpatrick, and Locke (1995) also provided evidence of an important situational condition – information impactedness, or the degree to which information is *differentially* distributed among people – that appears able to determine whether participation will improve participant cognition and performance. Participation's effects appear stronger in instances where information is impacted, that is, in the possession of some but not all individuals, since participatory information exchange allows participants to break down information disparities and increase the extent to which knowledge is shared and generally accessible. Conversely, participation's effects are weaker when information is already available to all, since additional information sharing is unnecessary and consumes resources more profitably devoted to other activities (Latham and Yukl, 1975; Bass and Valenzi, 1974; Williams, 1982).

Beyond the effects of impactedness, speculation and the results of prior research suggest several additional situational conditions that might also affect the workings of the cognitive mechanism. One of these, *interdependence*, concerns the degree to which participants must work together to perform and succeed. Under conditions of low interdependence, individuals, groups, or organizations can perform successfully by working alone, while under conditions of high interdependence, individuals, groups, or organizations must work together to succeed. Differences in interdependence exert situational influence on participation's efficacy by affecting the amount of information required to coordinate ongoing relationships. While individuals performing independent tasks need not exchange much information to do their work, individuals performing interdependent tasks must share a great deal of information, including messages about what has been done, what must be done next, what adjustments need to be made in response to changing conditions, and so forth. To the extent that this information flow must be ongoing, that is, occurring as coordination problems emerge (as opposed to taking place on an occasional basis or through a supervisory intermediary), participatory "mutual adjustment" contributes to successful coordination and enhanced performance (Durham et al., 1997; Lawler, 1982; Sashkin, 1976).

Another situational condition, *complexity*, also appears likely to exert contingency effects on relationships between participation and performance. Complexity reflects the degree to which a task, objective, or situation is understandable, with low complexity referring to conditions that are simple and readily understood, and high complexity alluding to conditions that are complicated or intricate and therefore difficult to interpret and comprehend. Successful performance in the presence of lower complexity is possible without additional information or insight. However, success under conditions of higher complexity requires access to the additional information needed to render the complex understandable. To the degree that participatory information exchange is able to provide such access, participation may produce little benefit when combined with low complexity but should provide appreciable benefit when paired with high complexity (e.g. Anderson, 1959; Singer, 1974). Note that this pattern is exactly opposite the configuration of effects revealed in research on the motivational mechanism, described earlier, wherein participatory enrichment improved performance on simple tasks.

Finally, the situational condition of change concerns *the extent to which tasks, group conditions, and organizational contexts are stable, consistent, and predictable*, under conditions of low change, versus dynamic, variable, and unpredictable, in situations of high change. In the presence of low change, success can be achieved by following familiar procedures, without modifying customary ways of doing things. In contrast, high amounts of change require that variability first be sensed, and that modifications then be made to existing plans and processes to match them to the demands of changing conditions. Such sensing and modification normally require information about the nature of change and the state of changed conditions. To the extent that such information is available to some but not necessarily all participants, participation can facilitate information dissemination and lead to successful adaptation and continued productivity (e.g. Abdel-Halim, 1983; Jermier and Berkes, 1979; Koch and Fox, 1978; Schuler, 1976).

IMPLEMENTATION: STRUCTURING PARTICIPATION CAN MAKE IT MORE EFFECTIVE

In thinking about participation, the first picture to come to mind is often that of a group of participants, seated casually around a table and engaged in spontaneous conversation. In fact, much research on participatory processes uses a physical arrangement that closely resembles this configuration. However, studies on group processes have indicated that grouping people together and asking them to suggest ideas and state opinions in front of others can stifle input into ongoing discussions. In particular, when personal statements are readily attributable to individual participants, ideas and opinions that might be considered even the least bit controversial may remain unstated (e.g. Diehl and Stroebe, 1987).

To deal with this problem, researchers have suggested structuring group discussion sessions so that innovation or judgment is done individually and discussion occurs only to clarify the interpretation of information and brainstorm additional alternatives. Using the *Nominal Group Technique (NGT)*, for instance, a group of individuals convenes around a table with a session coordinator and receives a description of the problem to be dealt with or issue to be addressed. Next, working alone, each participant writes down whatever ideas come to mind. The coordinator then asks each participant to share his or her ideas and writes them on a public display. Subsequently, participants discuss each other's ideas to clarify and expand on them, and then evaluate them as a group. Finally, participants rank the ideas privately, and the idea that ranks the highest among the participants is chosen as the group's final recommendation (Moore, 1987).

As an alternative to using discussion structuring such as the NGT, Locke et al. (1997) suggested that emerging information technologies – specifically groupware technologies – might be used to improve the effectiveness of participatory information exchange. For example, an *electronic meeting support system* can be used in a room of participants to display each individual's comments – typed in on personal computer terminals – anonymously on a projected screen. This manner of computer-mediated communication reduces the reluctance that participants might have to present unfavorable information or state controversial opinions. As a result, more information and information of higher quality can be exchanged among participants, and participants report more satisfaction with participatory processes and outcomes (Alavi, 1993; Alavi and Palmer, 2000; see also Chapter 32, this volume).

In addition, *videoconferencing* can be used to bring together participants from several different sites. Although anonymity may be lost, participation is able to nullify some of the negative effects of physical separation and encourage information sharing across great distances. Asynchronous approaches can also be used to structure participatory information exchange without the requirement of simultaneous presence. For instance, website bulletin boards and chat rooms can be set up for groups of participants, allowing them to share information and disseminate knowledge without requiring that everyone be available at the same time. Corporate e-mail systems can also be used to channel and catalog information exchanged among participants separated by both time and distance. Using such procedures, the prototypical face-to-face group is replaced by technological mediation (Locke et al., 1997).

CASE EXAMPLES

Volvo

To illustrate some of the costs and benefits of encouraging participation in the workplace, consider the differing experiences of Volvo and Toyota. Well known as a Swedish producer of cars, trucks, and marine engines, Volvo's automotive operations were hailed, during the 1970s and 1980s, as among the foremost examples of progressive industrial participation (e.g. Jenkins, 1976). Assembly employees often worked in groups as direct participants in personnel decision making (what group members to hire, reward, or fire), job design procedures (how to accomplish the group's work, how to divide and assign this work as individualized tasks, when to rotate among task assignments), and similar activities. Employees also elected worker representatives to serve on management committees charged with such tasks as insuring workplace health and safety, establishing corporate environmental policies, overseeing training programs, and assessing proposed product innovations. In addition, an employee representative sat on Volvo's corporate board of directors. Finally, newer plants at sites including Kalimar and Skovde were designed and built to support team-based manufacturing and, at the same time, reduce hierarchical distinctions between managers and workers by placing open management offices on the shop floor, providing central cafeterias to be used by all employees, and creating "small workshop" areas wherein individual teams could produce complete subassemblies without substantial outside intervention.

By the middle 1970s, Volvo's labor costs had grown to become among the highest in the automotive industry (Gyllenhammar, 1977). Although some of this expense could be attributed to the cost of complying with Sweden's social welfare regulations then in effect, as much as a 15% falloff in productivity appeared due to the redirection of workforce energy away from shop floor production and toward participatory interaction (Swedish Employers' Confederation, 1975). As long as Volvo was able to command premium prices for its cars, due to the high perceived quality and durability of its products, the company was able to offset production costs and compete in the world marketplace. However, with the introduction of such Japanese lines as Lexus, Infiniti, and Acura, Volvo's position as a quality leader deteriorated and the company's ability to offset its high internal costs declined.

Initially, Volvo attempted to meet market challenges by implementing cost control measures that included shutting down most major operations at Kalimar, Skovde, and other newer plants, and cutting back on participatory programming in its older locations. By 1994, however, rumors within the automotive industry suggested that Volvo was seeking a friendly merger to stave off bankruptcy or dissolution (Taylor, 1994). After considering several possible partners, in early 1999 Volvo sold its automotive business to the Ford Motor Company. In 2008, after several failed attempts to cut costs and create profitable operations, Ford put Volvo up for sale with the hope of recouping enough money to offset the costs of a decade of inefficiency.

Toyota

As Volvo's market position declined during the late 1970s and 1980s, the position of Toyota, another automotive manufacturer, improved dramatically. Toyota typifies the approach used in Japanese-based companies of that era to organize shop floor operations and structure managerial affairs. Its production facilities were set up as traditional assembly line operations, and written, standardized instructions regulated most production processes (Shingo, 1981). Centralized, directive, and sometimes secretive management practices controlled company operations (Sethi, Namiki, and Swanson, 1984). In contrast to Volvo's attempts to involve workers in all phases of corporate management, Toyota's higher-level managers reserved the prerogative to lead the company without significant input from below.

Within this general structure, however, such practices as Quality Circles and *ringi* decision making introduced a degree of participation into the shop floor and lower managerial ranks. Quality Circles consist of groups of operative employees that meet with their immediate supervisors on a regular basis, typically every week or two, for an hour or two at a time to discuss problems with production scheduling, product quality, shop floor safety, and so forth. Circle participants work together to suggest solutions and improvements, which are then sent up the management hierarchy for further study and possible adoption (Ferris and Wagner, 1985). *Ringi* decision making is a system in which proposed decisions are circulated among management subordinates and their hierarchical superiors for deliberation and approval. Often, proposals are originated by senior managers and sent through the subordinate ranks for further refinement, although on occasion junior managers initiate the process with proposals of their own that are sent upward for approval (Cole, 1971).

In contrast to Volvo's experience, Toyota was able to control production costs and, at the same time, produce cars perceived by consumers to be of high quality and reasonable price. In an age of oil embargoes and environmental concerns, the company produced small, fuel efficient cars that came to dominate the North American market. In the 1980s, Toyota introduced larger cars and later, the Lexus line of luxury automobiles. The company also expanded its production facilities worldwide and branched into the Scion line of affordable small cars. All the while, efforts to control costs and improve quality allowed Toyota to gain increasing market share at home and abroad. During the first quarter of 2008, Toyota's sales figures surpassed those of General Motors, up to that time the largest automotive company in the world. Toyota's management worried about becoming too successful and growing complacent in the highly competitive auto industry of the 21st century.

In comparing Volvo's situation with Toyota's, there are obvious differences in the scope of participation implemented in the two companies, since at Volvo participatory processes were central to corporate governance while at Toyota they played an ancillary role. This difference alone seems to explain Toyota's greater relative efficiency as a producer of automobiles, since the same kinds of resources that were consumed in participation at Volvo were expended in production at Toyota. Yet, beneath this conspicuous difference lies a deeper explanation, originating in differences in the primary reasons why participation was enacted within the two firms to begin with.

At Volvo, participation was seen mainly as a way of restoring the ability of otherwise routinized manufacturing tasks to satisfy human needs, encourage commitment to the company and its products, and motivate attendance and successful performance (Aguren, Bredbacka, Hansson, Ihregren, and Karllson, 1985; Nicol, 1975). The fact that participation could encourage information exchange was acknowledged by Volvo's management, but this exchange was thought to be valuable more for the commitment and motivation that would be aroused for the increased understanding or cognitive gain that might also occur (Gyllenhammar, 1977). Volvo's approach was clearly designed to activate participation's motivational mechanism.

At Toyota, in contrast, participation was used to redistribute information that would otherwise remain buried on the shop floor or hidden among lower-level managers (Dore, 1973). Motivation at Toyota, as in other large firms in Japan, was presumed by management to come from a combination of deference to authority and cultural collectivism that tied each employee's welfare to the well-being of the employer. Such "Japanese management" practices as lifetime employment and seniority-based pay were used to remind employees of the permanence of their relationship with their employer and of the importance of working hard to bring honor to their company and its management (Wagner, 1982). The primary aim of participation was consistent – and at Toyota remains consistent to the present day – with the cognitive mechanism's focus on information sharing and improved understanding.

As suggested by Toyota's experiences, participation can serve as an effective method of managing information and distributing knowledge. Although all of Toyota's achievements in the world marketplace cannot be attributed to the effects of participation alone, in facilitating the redistribution of information and sharing of knowledge among employees participation has contributed significantly to the company's continuing success.

Conclusion

Individual studies of participation's motivational effects have sometimes reported evidence of positive effects, leading researchers and practitioners alike to advocate the use of participation as a source of workplace motivation and employee satisfaction (e.g. Cotton, 1993; Gyllenhammar, 1977; Petersen and Hillkirk, 1991). However, more generalizable evidence suggests that participation's usefulness as a motivational tool is often quite limited. Only in small groups or in combination with simple tasks is participation likely to have appreciable effects, and even then only on the outcomes of satisfaction or acceptance. Managers facing problems with workforce motivation are better advised to look for solutions in such practices as goal setting, job redesign, and incentive payment.

Although the collection of studies performed specifically to assess the cognitive mechanism is considerably smaller than the stream of research conducted on the motivational mechanism, a stronger case can be made for using participation to influence performance through its effects on the distribution of information among subordinates and their hierarchical superiors. Especially when information is unevenly distributed and the work being performed incorporates significant interdependence, complexity, or change, participation should yield substantial increases in participant knowledge and insight which, in turn, should enhance performance and effectiveness in the workplace. Structuring participatory sessions specifically to encourage the exchange of information should have additional positive effects. Managers seeking ways to improve the distribution of information and knowledge are well advised to consider participatory processes

References

Abdel-Halim, A. A. (1983). Effects of task and personality characteristics on subordinate responses to participative decision making. *Academy of Management Journal*, 26, 477–484.

Aguren, S., Bredbacka, C., Hansson, R., Ihregren, K., and Karlsson, K. G. (1985). *Volvo Kalimar Revisited: Ten Years of Experience*. Stockholm: Efficiency and Participation Development Council.

Alavi, M. (1993). An assessment of electronic meeting systems in a corporation setting. *Information and Management*, 25, 175–182.

Alavi, M., and Palmer, J. (2000). Use information technology as a catalyst for organizational change. In E. A. Locke (ed.), *The Blackwell Handbook of Principles of Organizational Behavior* (pp. 404–417). Oxford, UK: Blackwell Publishers Ltd.

Alutto, J. A., and Belasco, J. (1972). A typology for participation in organizational decision making. *Administrative Science Quarterly*, 17, 117–125.

Anderson, R. C. (1959). Learning in discussions: a resume of authoritarian-democratic studies. *Harvard Education Review*, 29, 210–215.

Bartlem, C. S., and Locke, E. A. (1981). The Coch and French study: A critique and reinterpretation. *Human Relations*, 34, 555–566.

Bass, B. M., and Valenzi, E. R. (1974). Contingent aspects of effective management styles. In J. G. Hunt and L. L. Larson (eds), *Contingency Approaches to Leadership* (pp. 75–123). Carbondale, IL: Southern Illinois University Press.

Bass, B. M., Valenzi, E. R., Farrow, D. L., and Solomon, R. J. (1975). Managerial styles associated with organizational, task, personal, and interpersonal contingencies. *Journal of Applied Psychology*, 66, 720–729.

Castore, C. H., and Murnighan, J. K. (1978). Determinants of support for group decision. *Organizational Behavior and Human Performance*, 22, 75–92.

Coch, L., and French, J. R. P., Jr. (1948). Overcoming resistance to change. *Human Relations*, 1, 512–532.

Cole, R. E. (1971). *Japanese Blue Collar*. Berkeley, CA: University of California Press.

Cotton, J. L. (1993). *Employee Involvement: Methods for Improving Performance and Work Attitudes*. Newbury Park, CA: Sage.

Crampton, S. M., and Wagner, J. A., III (1994). Percept–percept inflation in microorganizational research: An investigation of prevalence and effect. *Journal of Applied Psychology*, 79, 67–76.

Dickson, J. W. (1981). Participation as a means of organizational control. *Journal of Management Studies*, 18, 159–176.

Diehl, M., and Stroebe, W. (1987). Productivity loss in brainstorming groups: Toward the solution of a riddle. *Journal of Personality and Social Psychology*, 53, 497–509.

Dore, R. (1973). *British Factory, Japanese Factory*. Berkeley, CA: University of California Press.

Durham, C. C., Knight, D., and Locke, E. A. (1997). Effects of leader role, team-set goal difficulty, efficacy, and tactics on team effectiveness. *Organizational Behavior and Human Decision Processes*, 72, 203–231.

Erez, A., Bloom, M. C., and Wells, M. T. (1996). Random rather than fixed effects models in meta-analysis: Implications for situational specificity and validity generalization. *Personnel Psychology*, 49, 275–306.

Ferris, G. R., and Wagner, J. A., III (1985). Quality circles in the United States: A conceptual reevaluation. *Journal of Applied Behavioral Science*, 21, 155–167.

Fox, W. M. (1957). Group reaction to two types of conference leadership. *Human Relations*, 10, 279–289.

Gibb, C. A. (1951). An experimental approach to the study of leadership. *Occupational Psychology*, 25, 233–248.

Green, S. G., and Taber, T. D. (1980). The effects of three social decision schemes on decision group processes. *Organizational Behavior and Human Performance*, 25, 97–106.

Gyllenhammar, P. G. (1977). *People at Work*. Reading, MA: Addison-Wesley.

Ivancevich, J. M. (1977). Different goal setting treatments and their effects on performance and job satisfaction. *Academy of Management Journal*, 20, 406–419.

Jenkins, D. (1976). *Job Power*. Garden City, NY: Doubleday.

Jenkins, G. D., and Lawler, E. E., III (1981). Impact of employee participation on pay plan development. *Organizational Behavior and Human Performance*, 28, 111–128.

Jermier, J. M., and Berkes, L. J. (1979). Leader behavior in a police command bureaucracy: A closer look at the quasi-military model. *Administrative Science Quarterly*, 24, 1–23.

Koch, J. L., and Fox, C. L. (1978). The industrial relations setting, organizational forces, and the form and content of worker participation. *Academy of Management Review*, 3, 572–583.

Latham, G. P., and Saari, L. M. (1979). Importance of supportive relationships in goal setting. *Journal of Applied Psychology*, 64, 151–156.

Latham, G. P., and Yukl, G. A. (1975). Assigned versus participative goal setting with educated and uneducated woods workers. *Journal of Applied Psychology*, 60, 299–302.

Latham, G. P., Winters, D., and Locke, E. A. (1994). Cognitive and motivational effects of participation: A mediator study. *Journal of Organizational Behavior*, 15, 49–63.

Lawler, E. E., III (1982). Increasing worker involvement to enhance organizational effectiveness. In P. S. Goodman (ed.), *Change in Organizations: New Perspectives on Theory, Research, and Practice* (pp. 33–70). San Francisco, CA: Jossey-Bass.

Lawler, E. E., III, and Hackman, J. R. (1969). Impact of employee participation in the development of pay incentive plans: A field experiment. *Journal of Applied Psychology*, 53, 467–471.

Leana, C. P. (1987). Power relinquishment versus power sharing: Theoretical clarification and empirical comparison of delegation and participation. *Journal of Applied Psychology*, 72, 228–233.

Ledford, G. E., Jr., and Lawler, E. E., III (1994). Research on employee participation: Beating a dead horse. *Academy of Management Review*, 19, 633–636.

Locke, E. A., Alavi, M., and Wagner, J. A. III (1997). Participation in decision making: An information exchange perspective. In G. R. Ferris (ed.), *Research in Personnel and Human Resources Management*, 15, 293–331. Greenwich, CT: JAI Press.

Locke, E. A., Feren, D. B., McCaleb, V. M., Shaw, K. N., and Denny, A. T. (1980). The relative effectiveness of four methods of motivating employee performance. In K. D. Duncan, M. M. Gruneberg, and D. Wallis (eds), *Changes in Working Life* (pp. 363–388). London, UK: John Wiley and Sons.

Locke, E. A., and Schweiger, D. M. (1979). Participation in decision making: one more look. In B. M. Staw (ed.), *New Directions in Organizational Behavior* (Vol. 1, pp. 265–339). Greenwich, CT: JAI Press Inc.

Lowin, A. (1968). Participative decision making: A model, literature critique, and prescription for research. *Organizational Behavior and Human Performance*, 3, 68–106.

Marrow, A. J., and French, J. R. P., Jr. (1946). A case of employee participation in a nonunion shop. *Journal of Social Issues*, 2, 29–34.

McCurdy, H. G., and Eber, H. W. (1953). Democratic vs. authoritarian: A further investigation of group problem-solving. *Journal of Personality*, 22, 258–269.

McMahon, J. T. (1976). Participative and power-equalized organizational systems: An empirical investigation and theoretical integration. *Human Relations*, 29, 203–214.

Miller, K. I. and Monge, P. R. (1986). Participation, satisfaction, and productivity: A meta-analytic review. *Academy of Management Journal*, 29, 727–753.

Moore, C. M. (1987). *Group Techniques for Idea Building*. Beverly Hills, CA: Sage.

Nicol, G. (1975). *Volvo*. London, UK: William Luscombe Publisher Limited.

Patchen, M. (1964). Participation in decision making and motivation: What is the relation? *Personnel Administrator*, 27, 24–31.

Pateman, C. (1970). *Participation and Democratic Theory*. London, UK: Cambridge University Press.

Pennington, D. F., Haravey, F., and Bass, B. M. (1958). Some effects of decision and discussion on coalescence, change, and effectiveness. *Journal of Applied Psychology*, 42, 404–408.

Petersen, D. E., and Hillkirk, J. (1991). *A Better Idea: Redefining the Way Americans Work*. Boston, MA: Houghton-Mifflin.

Quigley, N. R., Tesluk, P. E., Locke, E. A., and Bartol, K. M. (2007). A multilevel investigation of the motivational mechanisms underlying knowledge sharing and performance. *Organization Science*, 18, 71–88.

Roethlisberger, F. J., and Dickson, W. J. (1939). *Management and Morale*. Cambridge, MA: Harvard University Press.

Rosenbaum, L. L., and Rosenbaum, W. (1971). Morale and productivity consequences of group leadership style, stress, and type of task. *Journal of Applied Psychology*, 55, 343–348.

Sashkin, M. (1976). Changing toward participative management approaches: A model and methods. *Academy of Management Review*, 1, 75–86.

Scheflen, K. C., Lawler, E. E., III and Hackman, J. R. (1971). Long-term impact of employee participation in the development of pay incentive plans: A field experiment revisited. *Journal of Applied Psychology*, 55, 182–186.

Schuler, R. S. (1976). Participation with supervisor and subordinate authoritarianism: A path–goal theory reconciliation. *Administrative Science Quarterly*, 21, 320–325.

Schweiger, D. M., and Leana, C. R. (1986). Participation in decision making. In E. A. Locke (ed.), *Generalizing from Laboratory to Field Settings* (pp. 147–166). Lexington, MA: Lexington Books.

Scully, J. A., Kirkpatrick, S. A., and Locke, E. A. (1995). Locus of knowledge as a determinant of the effects of participation on performance, affect, and perceptions. *Organizational Behavior and Human Decision Processes*, 61, 276–288.

Sethi, S. P., Namiki, N., and Swanson, C. L. (1984). *The False Promise of the Japanese Miracle*. Marshfield, MA: Pitman.

Shingo, S. (1981). *Study of "Toyota" Production System from Industrial Engineering Viewpoint*. Tokyo: Japan Management Association.

Singer, J. N. (1974). Participative decision making about work: An overdue look at variables which mediate its effects. *Sociology of Work and Occupations*, 1, 347–371.

Stewart, T. A. (1997). *Intellectual Capital: The New Wealth of Organizations*. New York: Currency Doubleday.

Swedish Employers' Confederation (1975). *Job Reform in Sweden*. Stockholm: Swedish Employers' Confederation.

Tannenbaum, A. S. (1968). *Control in Organizations*. New York: McGraw Hill.

Tsai, W. (2001). Knowledge transfer in intraorganizational networks: Effects of network position and absorptive capacity on business unit innovation and performance. *Academy of Management Journal*, 44, 996–1004.

Taylor, A., III (1994). New ideas from Europe's automakers: managing the crisis at Volvo. *Fortune*, December 12, 168.

Vroom, V. H. (1960). *Some Personality Determinants of the Effects of Participation*. Englewood Cliffs, NJ: Prentice Hall.

Vroom, V. H., and Yetton, P. W. (1973). *Leadership and Decision-making*. Pittsburgh, PA: University of Pittsburgh Press.

Wagner, J. A., III (1982). Individualism, collectivism, and the control of organization. Unpublished dissertation, University of Illinois, Department of Business Administration, Urbana-Champaign IL.

Wagner, J. A., III (1994). Participation's effects on performance and satisfaction: A reconsideration of research evidence. *Academy of Management Review*, 19, 312–330.

Wagner, J. A., III and Gooding, R. Z. (1987). Shared influence and organizational behavior: A meta-analysis of situational variables expected to moderate participation–outcome relationships. *Academy of Management Journal*, 30, 524–541.

Wagner, J. A., III, Leana, C. R., Locke, E. A., and Schweiger, D. A. (1997). Cognitive and motivational frameworks in research on participation: A meta-analysis of effects. *Journal of Organizational Behavior*, 18, 49–65.

Wagner, J. A., III and LePine, J. A. (1999). Participation's effects on performance and satisfaction: Additional evidence from U.S. research. *Psychological Reports*, 84, 719–725.

Williams, T. A. (1982). A participative design for dispersed employees in turbulent environments. *Human Relations*, 35, 1043–1058.

EXERCISES

Demonstrating the effectiveness of participation as a method of sharing information

Materials: Index cards and pen or pencil.

Preparation: Form teams of six members and select one member to serve as leader. For each team, prepare a deck of eight cards as follows:

Facts [each one on a card with the card number (1, 2, 3, 4, 5, 6, 7, or 8) on the back]:

1. Provider B offers low prices with proven technology but never finishes a job on time or without bugs.
2. Provider C does very good work with proven technology but is typically quite expensive.
3. Provider D is going to offer new yet inexpensive technology in its bid. Only two other companies have used it but have no complaints. The system worked and was on time.
4. Provider E has never been late on a project and its prices are reasonable but almost always its systems take two weeks to work seamlessly.
5. Company A headquarters is adamant about the project being completed on time and that it work perfectly within two days.
6. The company (A) has been barely profitable in the last two years and headquarters is very cost conscious.
7. Blank.
8. Blank.

Procedure: The team of one leader plus five members work for company A. Company A headquarters wants to install a new telephone system and has delegated the project to the team. The team is looking at bids from competing companies (B, C, D, and E) for the telephone system. Each team member and the leader have spent several months doing research related to the decision (different people have worked on different things). The project leader makes the final decision. Complete each of the following three trials.

Trial 1. The leader gets cards 1, 2, and 5. Team members get 3, 4, and 6–8. The leader makes the decision without talking to the members. The decision is recorded without further discussion.

Trial 2. Distribute the cards as in Trial 1. The leader can talk to *one* member about what is on the member's card. A blank card allows another choice. The leader then makes the decision. The decision is recorded without further discussion.

Trial 3 (Suggested time for this part: about 10 minutes).   Cards 1 to 6 are randomly distributed, one per person (cards 7 and 8 are not used in this trial). There is full discussion, allowing all members (including the leader) to report the contents of their cards and fully argue their views. Then the leader makes the final decision. The decision is recorded.

Questions for discussion:

1. Which trial yielded the best decision? Why?
2. What happens when leaders do not seek information from followers, as in Trial 1? Knowing this, why do you think that leaders do not often seek information from their followers?
3. Why do subordinates sometimes choose not to speak up even when they have relevant information?
4. In light of what you have learned in this exercise, what can be done in organizations to ensure the distribution of knowledge and information?

[Teaching note: The best choice is Provider D. B is too unreliable. C is too expensive. E is almost never on time. By design, Trial 3 is supposed to yield the correct decision without fail.]

Choosing the most appropriate process

Form groups of 4–6 members and talk about the following in small-group discussions, then report the results of these discussions back to the entire class in a large-group discussion:

1. Thinking about where you work, describe an instance in which top-down processes were used to make a major decision. How quickly was the decision made? Was it the right decision? How well was the decision accepted by those individuals it affected?
2. Next, describe an instance in which participatory processes were used to make a major decision. How quickly was the decision made? Was it the right decision? How well was the decision accepted by those individuals it affected?
3. Finally, describe an instance where delegation was used to make a major decision. How quickly was the decision made? Was it the right decision? How well was the decision accepted by those individuals it affected?
4. Based on your answers to Questions 1–3, when are each of the three decision-making processes – top-down, participatory, delegation – likely to be most effective? When will each be least effective? What do your answers have to say about the strengths and limitations of participation as a decision-making process?

25

Broaden the Decision Frame to Make Effective Decisions

RICHARD P. LARRICK

No decision process can guarantee a perfect outcome. Humans are not omniscient. There is some uncertainty in both what we know and in what can be controlled. For example, as a company contemplates a set of project investments, organizational decision makers are making a number of judgments about both the nature of the projects – the quality of the personnel involved, the size of an untapped market, the reliability of a new product design – and the nature of the future – changes in demand or changes in the economy over time.

In light of this uncertainty, what characterizes an effective decision? This chapter will argue that a major barrier to good decisions is overly narrow views of a decision, or *narrow frames*, which pretend that knowledge is complete. The principle for effectively dealing with narrow representations is to follow a process that broadens the decision frame. A broad decision frame takes into account (1) multiple objectives – not just the most salient one at the moment; (2) multiple alternatives – not just the first option that lands on the table; and (3) multiple outcomes that could arise in the near and long term – not just the expected state of the world.

Both the psychological and organizational literatures have identified many tendencies that produce narrow decision representations (Bazerman and Moore, 2009; Miller, 2008). Over the decades, these processes have gone by a variety of technical names that include "functional fixedness," "satisficing," "selective perception," "concreteness," "anchoring," "availability," "confirmation bias," "predecisional distortion," "framing," "accessibility," and "focalism." Recent theoretical work on decision making has placed these tendencies in a more general framework (Kahneman, 2003; Stanovich, 1999; see also Arkes, 1991; Kahneman and Lovallo, 1993), arguing that the mind is wired with many "System 1" processes that are intuitive, fast, and automatic, with more deliberate and conscious processes ("System 2") attempting to monitor and correct these intuitive processes. I will not review all of these intuitive, automatic tendencies but will instead focus on their consequences for decision representations – overly narrow views of objectives, alternatives, and future states of the world. I will then consider a set of tools for broadening the decision frame, including formal tools of decision making, but also many informal practices that range from organizational rules of thumb ("the Five Whys") to tapping the "Wisdom of Crowds." I will consider limitations and exceptions to broadening the decision frame before closing with a few illustrative cases of narrow and broad frames.

THE CAUSES AND PITFALLS OF NARROW DECISION FRAMES

In 1772, Benjamin Franklin gave the following advice to Joseph Priestley on how to make a difficult decision he was facing:

> In the affair of so much importance to you, wherein you ask my advice, I cannot, for want of sufficient premises, advise you what to determine, but if you please I will tell you how. When these difficult cases occur, they are difficult, chiefly because while we have them under consideration, all the reasons pro and con are not present to mind at the same time; but sometimes one set present themselves, and at other times another, the first being out of sight. Hence the various purposes or inclinations that alternatively prevail, and the uncertainty that perplexes us. To get over this, my way is to divide half a sheet of paper into two columns; writing over the one Pro, and over the other Con. Then, during three or four days consideration, I put down under the different heads short hints of the different motives, that at different times occur to me, for or against the measure. When I have thus got them all together in one view, I endeavor to estimate their respective weights; and where I find two, one on each side, that seem equal, I strike out the two . . . And, though the weights or reasons cannot be taken with the precision of algebraic quantities . . . I have found great advantage from this kind of equation, in what may be called moral or prudential algebra. (Isaacson, 2003, p. 236)

There are two interesting insights in this passage. First, it sketches a formal if simple decision process that has been frequently celebrated as an early model of more sophisticated decision techniques (Dawes and Corrigan, 1974; Hammond, Keeney, and Raiffa, 1997). It lays out a rough version of what would now be called "cost–benefit analysis." The 20th century has witnessed the birth and maturation of many heirs to Franklin's simple technique across a range of fields, including economics, statistics, and business disciplines such as operations research. Over the past few decades, each era's most popular organizational "best practice" (Total Quality Management, Six Sigma) has tried to spread formal decision frameworks to a broad organizational base. In this chapter, I will give some examples of formal decision techniques to illustrate the principle of "broadening the decision frame" without attempting to be exhaustive (or exhausting).

A second, more subtle insight in Franklin's passage is his explanation for why he conducts his "prudential algebra" over "three or four days." In his words, decisions are difficult because "all the reasons pro and con are not present to mind at the same time; but sometimes one set present themselves, and at other times another, the first being out of sight. Hence the various purposes or inclinations that alternatively prevail, and the uncertainty that perplexes us." A key psychological insight in this passage is at the heart of why decisions makers need broad decision frames: the initial representation of a decision is often incomplete. In Franklin's view, all the relevant motives and reasons are not immediately salient, but come into view over time. Recent cognitive psychology on memory (Anderson and Spellman, 1995) and inference (Sanbonmatsu, Posavac, Kardes, and

Mantel, 1998) suggest the source of the problem: decision makers get "stuck" in one way of thinking about a situation and cannot easily generate and entertain new thoughts. Yet, even as their thinking gets stuck, decision makers are confident that their understanding is complete and their resulting judgments are accurate (Soll and Klayman, 2004). Three illustrations of "narrow frames" follow. This section closes with a description of how the social environment will often reinforce narrow individual frames.

Narrow view of the future

When people are asked to make predictions about future events, they typically have an overly narrow view of what could happen. For example, imagine a company that is weighing a series of investments that each hinge on future inflation. The company relies on internal experts to provide a forecast. One form of narrowness occurs when decision makers accept a point estimate – a single "best guess" number – and act on that number. Point estimates fail to capture the range of outcomes that could result. But a second manifestation of narrowness can occur even when forecasters try to give a range of plausible outcomes. The resulting picture of the future is too narrow. Decades of laboratory research on overconfidence (see Buehler, Griffin, and Ross, 2002 and Soll and Klayman, 2004 for reviews) has shown that people overestimate the predictability of the future, and these results have held up well in field settings. For example, recent research has shown that when corporate financial experts are asked to give a range of values that has an 80% chance of capturing some future economic variable, the experts give a range that captures the true outcome less than 40% of the time (Ben-David, Harvey, and Graham, 2007). The "truth" is a regular surprise.

Although people make a good faith attempt to use evidence to form an accurate expectation about the future, they focus too much on evidence that is consistent with a single scenario (often an extension of the status quo), and fail to imagine the wider range of possible scenarios that could happen. This is potentially costly to the extent that a wider, more accurate range would dictate pursuing a different, better course of action. For example, an unexpectedly high or low inflation rate might change the valuation of different project investments. Moreover, anticipating the full range of possible future outcomes can lead decision makers to develop a contingency plan that can best meet the opportunities and challenges of different circumstances.

Narrow set of objectives

People often pursue a narrow list of objectives in their decisions. For example, in hiring new employees, managers will typically focus on the goals of finding someone with technical ability, appropriate training, and at the right salary, as they should. But a variety of other objectives might also matter to the hiring decision, such as a new hire's leadership potential, ability to work in teams, or ability to shift to new tasks later. Similarly, in evaluating new product lines, senior-level managers will no doubt focus on profitability; however, they might also wish to consider less obvious objectives, such as diversification of product lines, development of new organizational capabilities, and development opportunities for personnel.

Where does the process of weighing objectives go wrong? One problem is that individuals evaluate choice options without considering their objectives at all (effectively "shooting from the hip"). Even when decision makers generate specific objectives, however, the list is typically incomplete. Often the most salient or easily measured objectives block consideration of other objectives.

In a recent article, Bond, Carlson, and Keeney (2008) provided a compelling empirical demonstration that people generate a narrow set of objectives. In one study, Bond et al. had MBA students generate objectives for a highly self-relevant decision: the things they cared about in choosing an internship. They found that students listed about seven objectives on average and felt satisfied that they had covered everything important. However, when they were then presented with both their own objectives along with a list of objectives generated by others, the students tended to find another seven objectives that were as important as the ones they had generated on their own. Left to their own devices, students had spontaneously generated about half of the objectives that they themselves acknowledged to be most relevant for one of the most important decisions of their life.

In business decisions, this narrow search for objectives is compounded by other organizational and social factors (Cronin and Weingart, 2007). Differences in training, experience, and function lead individuals to focus on only a subset of the objectives that are relevant to a decision from an *organizational* perspective (e.g. product costs, development time, materials, features, service support, etc.). Organizational mechanisms, such as cross-functional teams or job rotations, are designed precisely to ensure that decisions are made with a broader set of objectives.

Narrow set of alternatives

As a final example, people often consider an overly narrow set of choice alternatives. The alternatives might be narrow in number (e.g. considering only one job candidate) or narrow in scope (e.g. considering only job candidates with an accounting degree). One reason for a narrow consideration of choice options is due to organizational dynamics: a new hire or a new project may be suggested at a meeting without any prior consideration of objectives or options, and is then considered in isolation.

A more subtle form of narrowness, however, arises from individual cognitive processes. Research on creativity has shown that once one approach to solving a problem is generated, it is hard to generate new approaches (Chrysikou and Weisberg, 2005). Similarly, research in marketing has shown that thinking of one brand for a consumer good can actually block thinking of other brands (Alba and Chattopadhyay, 1986). By extension, organizational decisions that involve generating a range of options (e.g. job candidates, solutions to a manufacturing problem, etc.) are likely to suffer from the same "functional fixedness" once initial alternatives are generated. However, just as with objectives, decision makers do not recognize their limited ability to generate alternatives. Research has found that decision makers report being satisfied that they have generated a broad and complete set of choice alternatives even when they fail to generate many relevant options (Gettys, Pliske, Manning, and Casey, 1987).

The compounding influence of the social environment

In all of the foregoing examples, the basic cause of narrow framing in individuals is cognitive: associative memory processes lead people to start with a set of assumptions and then recruit evidence in a way that is consistent with the initial view. There is no compensating psychological tendency to spontaneously search broadly for a differing mix of objectives, alternatives, and scenarios. In part, failure to search further is a product of minimizing effort; but the more subtle obstacle is that the information that comes to mind seems complete and coherent, reducing the feeling of uncertainty that would prompt further search.

These individual cognitive tendencies are only part of the story. These individual factors then tend to be reinforced through social and organizational processes. Common training, common experiences, and frequent interaction all have the effect of leading to shared views on problems (Cronin and Weingart, 2007). Although shared views can be beneficial because they facilitate communication and coordination of efforts, they can be harmful when they perpetuate narrow perspectives on a decision problem. For example, marketers who are trained at the same school and work at the same firm on the same product at the same time will undoubtedly develop expertise, but it is an expertise that will be largely overlapping. Through training, experience, and discussion, they will tend to think about problems in the same way – which product features are best, which markets are most promising, which form of media to emphasize, which analysis to follow, etc. To the degree that the group members possess a particular insight, that insight will be shared. However, to the degree that the group members possess blindspots in their thinking, they too will be shared. Ironically, a like-minded group is a poor source for new objectives, alternatives, and future scenarios, but more confident in its ability – the consistency of perspective across colleagues leads each individual to feel validated and confident in his or her view of decisions.

Network sociologists have made similar arguments about how social structure limits diversity of perspective. They argue that dense network structures – in which clusters of people frequently interact – lead to overlapping individual perspectives on problems (Burt, 1992). Empirical research has shown that decision makers who depend on dense networks alone perform more poorly than those who are connected to non-redundant knowledge from outside that dense network (see Chapter 16).

Other organizational and social processes reinforce narrow frames because they discourage independence and dissent. A group that starts a brainstorming session without first asking each member to generate his or her own views on a problem risks having a specific view emerge early in the discussion that then frames everyone's view of the problem. Finally, even when there are divergent, independent perspectives, they may not be expressed if the group environment focuses on harmony – or conformity to a boss's opinion – over debate (see Chapters 17 and 18). In sum, although narrow representations may occur at the individual level for basic cognitive reasons, they are often compounded by the social environment. People surrounded by like-minded peers, who follow poor group processes, or who are located in dense networks will tend to share the same narrow frame.

TECHNIQUES FOR BROADENING THE DECISION FRAME

Formal techniques

This section reviews three representative formal techniques for broadening the frame. Although not exhaustive, the three techniques have been chosen for their applicability to many common decisions.

Considering multiple attributes and alternatives.   Choosing among alternatives is typically difficult because there is no alternative that is superior on all dimensions. Instead, one has to forego an alternative that may be superior on a less important dimension to gain superiority on more important dimensions. Multiattribute choice techniques prescribe that you think through a wide range of objectives you care about and the attributes that would predict achieving those objectives.

To make this problem concrete, imagine a prototypical organizational hiring process. A set of candidates has applied and your unit has information on each candidate (degree, past work experience, letters of recommendation, and so on). You also have a set of objectives in mind in the hiring process: you need to hire someone who has strong accounting training but who can also manage a team and can, with time, move into a leadership role. The information you have on each candidate defines the attribute levels for a given candidate (accounting degree versus marketing degree; five years of managing others versus three years of managing others). These attribute levels help you evaluate how well each candidate can meet an objective. If a person's attribute level for accounting experience consists entirely of "prior experience with spreadsheets," that person does not fare well on an important attribute.

With this information in hand, you can evaluate each candidate on the level they demonstrate for each attribute. With luck, someone has strong levels on all attributes. More likely, however, one alternative will be strong on some but not all attributes. The decision maker must then make tradeoffs and decide whether accounting skills are more or less important than team skills. This last step is essentially a "weighting" step – how important are the differences between candidates on each attribute to achieving your objectives? It should be noted that attributes need not be quantitative or objective – if there is an important subjective dimension, such as collegiality, this can be assessed and weighed in the decision.

This very general form of a choice process, anticipated by Franklin's quote, is the raw structure for a host of decision-making techniques. The basic structure is to break a problem down into alternatives and attributes and think about the importance of the attributes. The actual application of the method can take a variety of forms. When there is a large set of data that allows one to connect the attributes of past alternatives to subsequent success and failure, one can statistically regress outcomes on attributes to see which attributes are important in predicting success. The attribute weights in this case are derived statistically and can be applied in subsequent decisions – with a few caveats. The method does assume that the predictive value of attributes is reasonably stable and that one is predicting to other cases "inside the range" of what has been observed in the past. Various crises in the 1990s and 2000s, such as the failure at Long Term Capital Management and the subprime mortgage credit crisis, have illustrated problems of predicting "outside the range" of what was observed in the past (often compounded by other problems created by misaligned incentives and insufficient monitoring).

When there are no past data, there are decision analytic techniques for putting weights on attributes (see Clemen and Reilly, 2004; Hammond, Keeney, and Raiffa, 1997, for a user-friendly starting point). Some of these processes are "top down" – one consciously weighs the importance of tradeoffs across attributes – and some are "bottom up" – one simply ranks a set of alternatives that differ across attributes and captures the implicit weights one is giving to each attribute (this technique is known as "conjoint analysis" in marketing). It can be quite useful to use both steps to see whether the head ("top down") and gut ("bottom up") agree. If they do not agree, it can help identify a missing objective or force one to reconsider weights on attributes.

Once a multiattribute analysis is done, it can help inform subsequent decisions. And, in some cases, it can serve as a formula for future decisions that could replace individual discretion. When would this be desirable? First, a good deal of research in psychology has shown that when decision makers make a series of choices intuitively – without an explicit formula – decision makers make less consistent and accurate choices. By looking at alternatives case by case, decision makers inconsistently apply weights across cases (Arkes, 2003) and over-react to fleeting bits of information about specific alternatives (echoing Franklin's insight about the vagaries of "what comes to mind"). Second, basic issues of fairness can actually support the use of formulas over individual choice. For example, when mortgage decisions are left to individual loan officers, various prejudices can influence their judgments; even if they have no prejudices, officers can still create procedurally unfair outcomes if they weight the same attributes differently for different potential customers. These inconsistencies may be even more damaging in promotion and raise decisions inside an organization, since the shadow of the future is longer between employee and company, and friends share private information. A formula can be an organizational tool for ensuring neutrality and consistency in decisions (Arkes, 2003).

The multiattribute choice process broadens the decision frame by making explicit the need to consider multiple objectives, multiple attributes that help you achieve the objectives, and multiple alternatives. It directly avoids the trap of paying attention to only one objective or alternative. By making tradeoffs salient, it prevents decision makers from being surprised later when unattractive aspects of an alternative become apparent ("this person is good with numbers but lousy with people – what do we do now?"). By paying attention to all attributes, good and bad, early in the decision process, steps can be taken to mitigate weaknesses. It may be easier to give someone relevant management experience on the job than to teach them accounting (or vice versa), and a plan can be made accordingly. Finally, by calling attention to the good and bad early on, it can lead decision makers to be more creative – to acknowledge that there is no superior alternative at this point, and to explore in new ways (or with more investment) for an alternative that *is* strong on all relevant attributes. A clear understanding of multiple objectives creates a necessity that becomes the mother of invention.

Assessing and weighing future states of the world.   A second formal technique for broadening the frame is thinking through the range and likelihood of different uncontrollable events that could influence the outcome of a decision. A course of action that is attractive under one state of the world (e.g. demand for our product stays strong) could be disastrous under another state of the world (e.g. demand declines). The first step in assessing risk is to generate the range of possible scenarios that could arise in the future that influence achieving your objectives. With such an understanding, one can then assess both the likelihood of each scenario and how it would affect the outcomes attached to each alternative under consideration. Finally, one can generate new, contingent ways of responding to each scenario (Schoemaker, 2004).

To continue the hiring decision example, a company may be facing an increase in demand for a product at the moment, but needs to anticipate the need for work over various periods of time (a quarter, a year, etc.). Decisions about hiring for a current increase in demand depend on how controllable decisions (e.g. opening a new market) and uncontrollable factors (e.g. changes in demand) affect long-term needs. Uncontrollable factors, such as a change in demand, require that the company assess the range of plausible changes in demand and attach probabilities to each change. This picture of the uncertain future can then be used to calculate the "expected value" of various hiring options for dealing with a current increase in demand, such as paying overtime to current employees, hiring temps, or hiring new permanent employees. Flexibility in reducing staff is valuable if there is a significant risk of a decline in demand over the long term; adding well-trained, permanent employees is more valuable if there is a strong likelihood of continued demand.

Risk assessment broadens the decision frame by forcing the decision maker to imagine a range of scenarios, think through their likelihoods, and assess their impact on the value of different choice alternatives. It overcomes a basic habit of planning for one future state of the world. Often the envisioned future is a rosy one (Buehler et al., 2002), which is especially likely for people who are pushing a specific plan or course of action, but it can also be a gloomy one that leads decision makers to be unprepared for unexpected opportunities. Having assessed scenarios, likelihoods, and outcomes, one can then formally calculate "expected values" that weight outcomes by their likelihoods. One can also assess whether an alternative could lead to a wide range of good and bad outcomes and decide whether one would prefer a safer alternative that has a smaller range of highs and lows (technically, an alternative that has lower variance). Most importantly from a decision-making perspective, anticipating future scenarios allows one to make contingent plans – to create alternatives that have known decision points at which a planned new course of action would be pursued.

Using "all four cells" to make accurate predictions. The final formal tool is the simplest: do the right checks to see whether an attribute predicts an outcome. Consider one more example related to predicting job performance. Many years ago, *Management Focus Magazine* reported a research study claiming that pet ownership as a child predicted future success as a leader. How did the researchers reach this conclusion? They surveyed 74 Fortune 500 CEOs and found that 94% had owned a dog, cat, or both as a child. In interviews, the CEOs observed that "pet ownership had helped them to develop many of the positive character traits that make good managers today, including responsibility, empathy, respect for other living beings, generosity, and good communication skills." (One is tempted to ask whether "communication skills" include beg, sit, and heel. . . .) Should pet ownership be an attribute in hiring decisions?

A little reflection reveals two shortcomings with this study. First, the study is looking at only two cells in a four cell table. Specifically, it is examining the presence or absence of pet ownership among CEOs. The remaining two cells of interest are the presence or absence of pet ownership among *non*-CEOs. If most people have a dog or cat at some point in their childhood, then we have not learned much from the 94% figure among CEOs. This is a classic problem of sampling on the dependent variable, and there are many famous examples. For example, the research underlying *In Search of Excellence* in the 1980s looked at a sample of successful firms to uncover their common practices, such as "management by walking around." One danger with this "two cell" method is that it invites imbuing ordinary activities with special qualities. Until all four cells are examined, one cannot even tell if there is a relationship between the attribute and the outcome. (For example, managers may also be walking around unsuccessful companies, but there it is called "micromanaging.") In the extreme, we can observe that all CEOs brush their teeth and all successful companies have buildings, but we have not learned anything about predicting success. (See also Denrell, 2003, for how managers draw poor conclusions from "survivors" in risky environments.)

The second shortcoming of the pet study is that, even if CEOs show a higher rate of childhood pet ownership, this may not be the causal factor in their success (despite enhanced communication skills, etc.). Families that have other characteristics that lead to success in business – money, educational opportunities, job opportunities, and social networks – may be more likely to own pets. This is a classic problem of interpreting correlation as causation.

The business press and our day-to-day decisions often rely on casual observation that "sees" a relationship based on only two cells. GE seems to produce a large number of managers who go on to run other companies. Should other companies copy their system for training and promoting leaders? It is also the case that GE produces a staggeringly large number of non-CEOs as well. The key question in evaluating their ability to train and promote is whether they produce at a higher rate given their employee base. In using attributes in a decision, one must broaden the decision frame by checking all four cells in a covariation table to see if there is a relationship, and then, if there is, asking what additional factors might be serving as causes of the relationship.

Barriers to adopting quantitative techniques.   Highly quantitative versions of the techniques described above are, in theory, already present in many organizations. These techniques have been taught in business and engineering schools for years. They have also been part of the major management movements of the past two decades. For example, both Total Quality Management (TQM) and Six Sigma have major components that focus on risk assessment, causal analysis, and processes for weighing attributes and alternatives.

However, the everyday organizational reaction to using formal, quantitative techniques is quite mixed (Zbaracki, 1998). Employees are cynical when such techniques are proposed in new programs because they are often introduced by outsiders or from above. The mathematical nature of the techniques appeals to some employees, but requires extensive training for many employees. Once learned, the techniques are time consuming to use. And, finally, these formal techniques face a classic problem described in the diffusion of innovation literature: the benefits of adoption are not easily demonstrated. Thus there is a tendency for the formal, quantitative aspects of these practices to wither in the process of adoption (Zbaracki, 1998).

The major benefits of the practices described above do not depend on rigorous quantification but on attempting to follow the general process. The more important factor in broadening the frame is to strive for a complete representation of the decision problem. Breadth is accomplished by thinking about attributes, alternatives, tradeoffs, and scenarios. Because extensive quantification in decision making can be offputting to many organizational decision makers, I next consider informal techniques that also preserve the benefits of broadening the frame with even less formality.

Informal techniques

Heath, Larrick, and Klayman (1998) have proposed that many of the most effective decision techniques that are actually used in organizations are less formal than the abstract, quantitative techniques described in economics and statistics. Instead, these informal decision techniques, which they called "cognitive repairs," fix narrow frames by being simple, specific, home-grown, and social. This section briefly describes several of these informal practices.

Informal techniques for broadening the search for information.   Some simple techniques force decision makers to search for more information without directing decision makers to specific information. For example, one basic technique that has proven to help a variety of decision shortcomings is to "consider an alternative" to the current conclusion (Hirt and Markman, 1995). The technique simply requires a person to ask "why might my favorite answer be wrong?" This question can be applied to a range of decision problems. If a future scenario seems likely, one can ask why it might not happen. If a single best alternative has been proposed, one can ask how other options might be better. If pets seem to predict being a CEO, one can ask whether they also predict not being a CEO. This is one of the few informal techniques that has proven to have broad utility (summarized in Larrick, 2004; see also Herzog and Hertwig, 2009; Kray and Galinsky, 2003).

A second simple technique for broadening search is the "Five Whys" which has been a regular component of TQM and Six Sigma. The process is simply one of starting with a problem, asking why, and then following up each answer with an additional why. The goal is to go beyond a superficial, narrow understanding of a situation to a deeper understanding. For example, the Five Whys can be used to identify a decision maker's basic objectives. In a hiring decision, one can ask: Why do we need someone with an accounting degree? Because the person needs to have a good understanding of the financials. Why does the person need a good understanding of the financials? Because he or she will have primary responsibility for cutting costs. Why is the emphasis on cutting costs? There has been no revenue growth in recent years. And so on. The result of asking Five Whys will be more fundamental objectives that could be pursued through a wider variety of attributes than initially considered. It can reveal that an accounting degree is not the only way to address the fundamental objectives, allowing one to consider alternatives that are strong on other attributes to be considered. Of course, like any informal technique, the Five Whys is coarse and can go wrong: one can easily ask why owning pets would make one a better CEO and talk oneself into an elaborate (false) theory of communication skills.

Informal techniques for using a broader set of attributes and alternatives in decisions.   A second class of informal techniques overcomes narrow frames by requiring decision makers to use checklists for gathering information and evaluating alternatives. For example, one bank's commercial loan department required that officers evaluate potential customers on the "5 Cs" – Collateral, Capacity, Capital, Conditions, and Character (Heath et al., 1998). Although necessarily imprecise, specifying these attributes helps officers avoid over-reacting to one favorable or unfavorable piece information as they assess a given loan candidate. Similarly, recent research in medicine has shown that what should be habitual decisions for doctors can also be helped by checklists. For example, a simple five-point hygiene checklist helped reduce infection rates at Johns Hopkins hospital from 11% to 0% (Gawande, 2007). Similar protocols have proved useful in diagnosis by encouraging doctors to systematically consider a wider range of symptoms and disease scenarios (Heath et al., 1998). Checklists, of course, are not perfect. They are likely to provoke resistance from users at first, since they seem controlling. They will be more acceptable if they are home-grown or inherited from experts. Moreover, checklists are only as good as the validity of the items on the checklist and run the risk of omitting important considerations. The bet one makes with a checklist is that individuals with narrow frames would omit even more of the important considerations.

Informal techniques for broadening diversity of perspective. A final set of informal techniques takes advantage of the fact that combining multiple narrow frames can create a broad, complete understanding of a decision. Specifically, if the independent perspectives of multiple people are pooled together, the resulting knowledge is broader and more complete than the view of any one person. However, the benefit of drawing on multiple people is highly contingent on tapping a set of people who hold diverse perspectives initially and then following procedures that preserve it.

Consider a technique used in TQM, known as a *Kokai watch* (Walton, 1990), that involved assembling a team to evaluate a current procedure and look for improvements. The team was deliberately assembled with "non-experts" – people who were managers or employees in another department and not expert in the domain they were studying. The logic of using non-experts is that those wrapped up in a routine cannot step back to question the process; people with fresh eyes, however, can reason by analogy to a broader set of knowledge and experience. In general, decisions that involve diagnosing problems and generating new alternatives can benefit by having non-experts provide fresh eyes. In a similar vein, Motorola would compose cross-functional teams for new product designs to ensure diversity of perspective (on objectives, attributes, alternatives, future scenarios, etc.), but would then break up the team at the end of an assignment (Heath et al., 1998). One could argue that once a team meshes – and especially if it is successful – it should be preserved for the next assignment. Motorola, however, recognized that even cross-functional teams can come to share a common perspective on decisions that could limit the objectives and alternatives in subsequent assignments. By mixing teams, there was a constant tension created by different perspectives coming into contact.

The value of using groups (see Chapters 15–18) to broaden frames has received increasing recognition in recent years, and was popularized as the "wisdom of crowds" in a book with that title (Surowiecki, 2004). The main factors that make a crowd wise are diversity and independence. Unfortunately, classic brainstorming can undermine independence of thought to the extent that early suggestions can entrain everyone's subsequent ideas. Thus, the best group techniques preserve initial differences in perspective by having individuals think about a problem alone (this stage is often called a "nominal" group), but then pool the information so that others can react to it. Empirical research shows that nominal groups will generate a much broader set of objectives and alternatives than any individual can (Bond et al., 2008; Gettys et al., 1987). If desired, one can use the frequency of naming specific objectives and alternatives as a "vote" for their importance, with the caveat that truly creative ideas will tend to be rare ones.

Nominal groups are also superior to individuals in estimating unknown, uncertain outcomes. Each person's glimpse of the unknown is imperfect. However, when a large number of such imperfect estimates are averaged together, extreme errors cancel out, and the resulting group average will be closer to the truth than the answer of the average individual (this holds whenever the extremes in the group bracket the truth), which is a common pattern (Larrick, Mannes, and Soll, 2009). By way of illustration, the *Wall Street Journal* publishes twice-yearly economic forecasts from 50 professional economists. These data are useful for seeing the range of outcomes they think are possible (providing a sense of possible future scenarios); moreover, the mean estimate tends to be more accurate than the majority of judges in the panel. Although the *WSJ* routinely celebrates which economist "wins" in a given six month period after the fact, there is no reliable way to pick a single expert a priori that can beat the group average over time (Larrick et al., 2008). Averaging judgments is also helpful in quantifying subjective attributes in a multiattribute choice process: one can ask multiple interviewers to rate different job candidates on collegiality and use their average judgment for each candidate in a decision.

Although brainstorming is the prototype for group techniques, many hybrid group processes are possible with the advent of new forms of electronic communication (Chapter 32). Organizations are finding increasing ways to tap the wisdom of their own employees, customers, and partners in events like innovation jams and prediction markets. These can be efficient (even fun) ways for organizations to aggregate hundreds of narrow individual frames to broaden the decision frames of individual decision makers higher in the organization.

Groups, of course, can talk themselves into poor decisions that they then hold with high confidence because of the perceived widespread support of the conclusion. To prevent conformity pressures and groupthink, it is essential that groups encourage diversity of perspective, independence of thinking, and a willingness to express dissent (Chapters 15 to 18).

Limitations to Broadening the Frame

This chapter has argued for taking a broad view of objectives, attributes, alternatives, and scenarios in making decisions. This picture of effective decision making is consistent with a large body of theoretical and empirical work. However, there are potential limitations to using the principle. This section considers two possible challenges to the principle of broadening the frame. The first challenge is practical considerations about implementation. The second challenge is recent proposals to rely on quick, automatic, intuitive processes; in short, to "blink" rather than think.

Practical limits on broad frames.   There are several practical limitations to broadening the frame:

◆ Elaborate techniques, such as multiattribute choice processes, are time consuming, and risk "analysis paralysis." (How do you know when you have reviewed enough attributes and alternatives?) As decisions become more complex, decision makers often rely on simplifying processes to make the task manageable (Payne, Bettman, and Johnson, 1993). Recent research has found that too much choice can lead decision makers to avoid making a choice at all. The diminishing marginal benefit of considering more attributes and alternatives needs to be balanced against the potential cost of overwhelming people with information. Traditionally, decision makers suffered from too little information. It may be the case that technology is able to capture so much information that selecting alternatives and attributes – rather than seeking them – is the greater challenge.

◆ Recommendations that involve soliciting objectives and alternatives from many different parties risk introducing conflict, politics, and negotiation. However, even in a politically charged environment, an awareness of objectives and alternatives can lead to better decisions through negotiation – specifically, good decisions can be made if each party sacrifices unimportant attributes to gain more desirable attributes. And participation at least has one silver lining. Broad participation in generating objectives, alternatives, and scenarios will tend to increase commitment to a final decision, especially if the process of collecting and weighing information is seen as procedurally fair.

◆ More comprehensive processes may increase confidence and satisfaction with a decision, but, if the processes make obvious stark tradeoffs, they may dampen satisfaction with a final decision.

Blinking rather than thinking.   In his book *Blink*, the *New Yorker* writer Malcolm Gladwell (2005) popularized the notion that sometimes very quick decisions are highly accurate. This idea has also received serious academic attention in recent years, perhaps as a bit of a backlash to the rational, deliberate models that had been studied in earlier work. Three major academic claims in the spirit of *Blink* seem to challenge the "broaden the frame" principle.

The first claim is that many decisions can be made better and more quickly by focusing on a single attribute or predictor and then incorporating additional information only if that first piece is inconclusive (a strategy termed "Take the Best," or TTB, Gigerenzer and Goldstein, 1999). If TTB were generally effective, it would directly undermine the prescription to use a broad frame. Many studies have shown that TTB is effective – specifically, it works well in situations when one attribute is much more important than other attributes, and it works well when the most important attribute is obvious. The problem with these demonstrations, however, is that they are selective. One of the main difficulties in decision making is the uncertainty around identifying the most important attributes and in knowing how much weight to place on them. Empirical research shows that people have a hard time learning which attributes are most important (or predictive). If there is error in identifying the most important attribute, TTB performs much less well than broad strategies that use multiple attributes (Hogarth and Karelaia, 2007; Payne et al., 1993). The case for TTB also has other weaknesses, such as testing it only with attributes that have two levels. In short, using multiple attributes or multiple predictors is a better strategy when information is known with uncertainty.

A second claim that challenges the principle of broaden the frame is that many expert decisions are done quickly and automatically, without extensive weighing of options. Expert decision making has been studied in a number of domains, ranging from tasks such as chess to firefighting. Research by Klein and colleagues (Lipshitz, Klein, Orsaanu, and Salas, 2001) makes a convincing case that experts do process information differently than novices. Specifically, experts have a wide array of experience in their particular task that allows them to quickly recognize a situation and retrieve an effective course of action. The main question for organizational decision making is what conditions support the development of these skills? First, it should be noted that the skills of experts are domain specific – chess masters and firefighters do not develop general decision-making skills that apply to new domains, but only to their own. Second, experts are able to develop skills because they face a very favorable environment for learning – an environment in which a person can experience a broad but recurring set of situations and see the immediate, unambiguous results of his or her actions (Hogarth, 2001). If situations were constantly novel, or feedback were ambiguous or delayed, it would be very difficult to learn how to react effectively – and "experts" in many judgment domains make predictions that are no better than those of novices (Camerer and Johnson, 1991; Tetlock, 2005).

Moreover, it is not quite accurate to say that experts use narrow frames; it is more accurate to describe them as quickly taking in relevant attributes and automatically generating alternatives. These automatic responses are based on broad experience that is quite costly to gain. Research indicates that expertise takes about 10 years of hard, conscious practice to develop (Ericsson, Krampe, and Tesch-Römer 1993). Finally, despite the ability to rapidly recognize situations, it is interesting to note that chess experts make a fast initial assessment but then broaden the frame by weighing different alternative actions and anticipating a range of possible scenarios that might follow (Makridakis, Hogarth, and Gaba, 2009).

A third claim that challenges the principle of broaden the frame is the proposal that "unconscious" decision making is superior to "conscious" decision making (Dijksterhuis, Bos, Nordgren, and van Baaren, 2006). In these studies, people were presented with four apartments that differed on 12 attributes, creating 48 pieces of information. Participants saw each piece of information once, in random order; the information was then taken away and decision makers were either told to think about the decision for four minutes or asked to complete a filler task for four minutes. All participants then reported a decision. The filler-task group was more likely than the deliberation group to select the apartment that was superior on more attributes. This paradigm, however, has not stood up well to additional empirical tests. First, deliberating for four minutes on a fairly simple decision is an unusual task; when decision makers are allowed to "self-pace" their decision (which is often relatively quick), they perform as well as the "unconscious" decision makers. Second, when the task is changed so that the magnitude of the differences between alternatives on some attributes is quite large, conscious decision making correctly favors the better option – in this case, an option that has fewer positive attributes but that has a higher expected value (Payne, Samper, Bettman, and Luce, 2008). The Dijksterhuis paradigm also has practical weaknesses. First, it is not a pure instantiation of unconscious decision making – it involved a great deal of conscious consideration of both alternatives and attributes prior to the unconscious decision process. Second, the paradigm does not pass a day-to-day plausibility test – if attribute and alternative information is both available to a decision maker and unfamiliar, why would the person not be able to examine the information as he or she made a decision?

A more compelling argument against deliberation was made in research by Wilson and colleagues (Wilson, Lisle, Schooler, Hodges, Kaaren, and LaFleur, 1993). In this study, student participants listed reasons as they chose a poster for their dorm or apartment; a control group chose a poster without any deliberation. Three weeks later, the group that listed reasons was less happy with their poster than the "gut reaction" group. The authors argue that articulating pros and cons for the poster decision is a poor strategy because the important attributes are hard to articulate (the beauty and style of a poster), leading decision makers to focus on less important but easier to articulate attributes (the color, size, or subject). This is a fair critique of broadening the frame – if broadening the frame brings in irrelevant attributes that distract decision makers from relevant attributes, it will hurt decisions. As I mentioned in the section on multiattribute choice, however, subjective dimensions are fair game for inclusion in the choice process. It would be reasonable when choosing a poster to capture a gut reaction in addition to reasons pro and con and weigh them against each other if they are in conflict. Recent research has started to examine the benefits of combining intuitive and analytic judgments (much like averaging judgments in a crowd) because each type of judgment can compensate for weaknesses in the other.

In popularizing the idea of "blinking," Gladwell himself does not take a clear stand on when it makes sense to blink and when it makes sense to think. He describes how many intuitive processes, such as stereotyping, are inaccurate and harmful. It is also interesting to note that many of his examples of successful blinking support the principle of broadening the frame. For example, Gladwell reviews John Gottman's startling research on couples. Gottman is able to watch short videotaped segments of couples interacting early in their relationship and predict whether they will stay together over subsequent years. Moreover, he has identified a handful of specific cues, or attributes, that predict whether couples will stay together (when they have a disagreement, for example, do they show a lack of respect for each other?). As amazing as these results are, however, they are not compelling illustrations of blinking over thinking. First, untrained observers cannot watch the brief clips and make accurate predictions – in this case, fast, automatic, intuitive processing fails. Second, trained observers can make accurate predictions, but they only know what to look for because cues and outcomes were carefully measured for decades in Gottman's lab. Large regression models were then performed on the data to identify which cues or attributes were most predictive. Regression is the quintessential multiattribute choice technique.

CASE EXAMPLES

In this section, we consider two cases that illustrate varying degrees of narrow and broad frames. The first case, the *Challenger* space shuttle analysis, is an infamous example of a narrow frame for checking information. The second case, Seagate, illustrates how individuals often hold narrow objectives, but an organizational process of gathering objectives can broaden the final decision frame.

The Challenger launch decision

After years of glory striving for and reaching the moon, the National Aeronautic and Space Administration (NASA) found itself in the early 1980s slipping from the national limelight. To slip from the limelight meant not only to lose glory, but also to lose stature when requesting funding in each year's federal budget. NASA had made space travel more economical with the creation of the reusable space shuttle in the late 1970s and had flown over 20 successful missions by 1986. However, orbital flights did not attract the attention of lunar missions and sporadic delays had diluted the interest of NASA's remaining audience. In the early 1980s, NASA decided to send a civilian into space – a teacher named Krista McAuliffe – to help recapture the imagination of teachers and school children.

Even while NASA was having success with the space shuttle it was discovering problems with the shuttle design. Engineers from the firm that designed the shuttle's fuel boosters, Morton-Thiokol, had gathered data on various physical problems observed after shuttle flights. In particular, they noted that large rubber gaskets known as O-rings frequently showed wear and signs of "blow-by" (escaped exhaust). These O-rings played a critical role in containing the burning fuel in the shuttle boosters. By the early 1980s, the engineers had suspicions that temperature was related to O-ring problems. (It was later recognized that cold temperatures made the rubber of the O-rings brittle, thereby preventing them from sealing.) As they approached the February 1986 *Challenger* launch, engineers were concerned that the below-freezing launch temperature was *far* below that of any previous launch. The engineers raised their concerns with NASA administrators, but they gathered and presented data in a piecemeal fashion which blocked the ability to see any overall picture.

As importantly, all of the data the engineers presented were focused on past problem flights, seven in number, which had occurred at a wide range of temperatures and provided a murky picture. To quantify it, four problem flights had occurred when temperatures were below 65 degrees; three had occurred when temperatures were above 65 degrees. NASA administrators decided that staying on schedule was more important than acting cautiously based on such ambiguous evidence. However, as Tufte (1997) notes in his retrospective analysis, the evidence was not ambiguous – it was incomplete. (And, to be fair, the engineers also did not have access to all the temperature data.) Tufte notes that "the flights without damage provide the statistical leverage necessary to understand the effects of temperature . . . and no single chart contained data on both in relation to each other" (pp. 44–45). In other words, to see all four cells in the *Challenger* example, one needs to know how many past flights were flown *without* damage at warm and cold temperatures. The answer: 17 flights had been flown at temperatures above 65 degrees with no problems; no flights were flown at temperatures below 65 degrees without a problem. Using all 24 historical cases, the conditional probability of a problem was 15% above 65 degrees and 100% below 65 degrees. (These results hold for alternative cuts of the data: problems arose on 41% of flights flown at temperatures below 75 degrees (7/17 cases) compared to 0% for flights above 75 degrees (0/7 cases).)

The *Challenger* incident has become the most famous example of a failure to broaden the frame when assessing a relationship. It shows why it is not enough to look at the relationship between a variable of interest, temperature, and one outcome, failure. One must also look at the relationship between temperature and success. The combined data – all four cells – supported the suspicion of a link between temperature and O-ring failure and made a convincing case for caution when the temperature was below freezing.

Defining objectives at Seagate

In the early 1990s, Seagate Technology was the largest manufacturer of disk drives in the world. It had recently acquired a dozen companies and was working to create a single, integrated company from the disparate parts. Ralph Keeney was approached to help the company identify a comprehensive set of objectives that would help Seagate define its mission (Bond et al., 2008). Keeney started by meeting with each high-level executive separately. In each discussion, he asked the executive to identify "any objectives, hopes, desires, aspirations, or plans (s)he had for the new organization" (p. 65). This open-ended questioning was followed by more tailored questioning that helped respondents consider objectives that he or she touched on only lightly. Keeney then summarized the objectives and sent the summary to each respondent to see if they accurately represented his or her views. Obviously, the future of the firm was an important issue to each of the executives.

Executives committed a substantial amount of time to the task and had a chance to reflect on their answers.

By pooling the objectives together, Keeney identified eight overarching objectives ("contribute customer value," "help employees achieve satisfaction," and so on) with 39 specific objectives tied to meeting the larger objectives ("increase customer productivity," "provide opportunities for career growth," and so on). On average, each individual executive mentioned five of the eight overarching objectives, and 14 of the 39 specific objectives. When the entire set of objectives was organized and presented to senior management, there was a consensus that the aggregate list was what Seagate wanted to achieve. Only one individual had close to half the overall picture.

The Seagate example illustrates how individuals tend to have an incomplete representation of firm objectives. As importantly, it shows one example of a process for broadening the frame – anoint a specific individual to gather information (in this case, a neutral outsider trained in eliciting information). However other processes could substitute for hiring a consultant. A trusted inside member could play the same role. Or electronic mechanisms (see Chapter 32), such as a jam or bulletin board, could be used to gather insights over a period of time. All of these mechanisms will lead to a more complete representation of objectives that should guide both company and, at times, department-level decisions.

CONCLUSION

This chapter has focused on narrow frames as a general problem in decision making. It has not focused on enumerating the many specific biases that have been identified through research, such as honoring sunk costs, forming probability judgments based on what is available in memory, and treating gains and losses differently (interested readers should see Bazerman and Moore, 2009, for a useful review of these specific biases). These specific biases are important and worth knowing about. Most of them, such as "availability," are examples of how fast, automatic cognitive processes yield an incomplete cognitive representation. The premise of this chapter is that the fundamental problem in decision making is accepting such incomplete representations as complete.

The prescription to decision makers therefore is to use processes that broaden the frame for important decisions. By incorporating more complete information, broad frames will, on average, be more accurate than narrow frames. In the spirit of the chapter's principle, however, I must acknowledge that future research may identify predictable contingencies when narrow frames – rapid, intuitive, simple representations – are more accurate than broad frames. The bet based on current evidence is on broad frames. Future research will broaden the frame of our understanding.

REFERENCES

Alba, J. W., and Chattopadhyay, A. (1986). Salience effects in brand recall. *Journal of Marketing Research*, 23, 363–369.

Anderson, M. C., and Spellman, B. A. (1995). On the status of inhibitory mechanisms in cognition: Memory retrieval as a model case. *Psychological Review*, 102, 68–100.

Arkes, H. R. (1991). Costs and benefits of judgment errors: Implications for debiasing. *Psychological Bulletin*, 110, 486–498.

Arkes, H. R. (2003). The nonuse of psychological research at two federal agencies. *Psychological Science*, 14, 1–6.

Bazerman, M. H., and Moore, D. A. (2009). *Judgment in Managerial Decision Making*. Wiley.

Ben-David, I., Harvey, C. R., and Graham, J. R. (2007). *Managerial Overconfidence and Corporate Policies*. American Financial Association, Chicago, November.

Bond, S. D., Carlson, K. A., and Keeney, R. L. (2008). Generating objectives: Can decision makers articulate what they want? *Management Science*, 54, 56–70.

Buehler, R., Griffin, D., and Ross, M. (2002). Inside the planning fallacy: The causes and consequences of optimistic time predictions. In T. Gilovich, D. Griffin, and D. Kahneman (eds), *Heuristics and Biases: The Psychology of Intuitive Judgment* (pp. 250–270). Cambridge: Cambridge University Press.

Burt, R. S. (1992). *Structural Holes: The Social Structure of Competition*. Cambridge, MA: Harvard University Press.

Camerer, C. F., and Johnson, E. J. (1991). The process–performance paradox in expert judgment: How can experts know so much and predict so badly? In K. A. Ericsson and J. Smith (eds), *Towards a General Theory of Expertise: Prospects and Limits* (pp. 195–217). New York: Cambridge Press.

Chrysikou, E. G., and Weisberg, R. W. (2005). Following the wrong footsteps: Fixation effects of pictorial examples in a design problem-solving task. *Journal of Experimental Psychology: Learning, Memory, and Cognition*, 31, 1134–1148.

Clemen, R. T., and Reilly, T. (2004). *Making Hard Decisions*. Boston: South-Western College Publishing.

Cronin, M. A., and Weingart, L. R. (2007). Representational gaps, information processing, and conflict in functionally diverse teams. *Academy of Management Review*, 32, 761–773.

Dawes, R. M., and Corrigan, B. (1974). Linear models in decision making. *Psychological Bulletin*, 81, 95–106.

Denrell, J. (2003). Vicarious learning, under-sampling of failure, and the myths of management. *Organization Science*, 14, 227–243.

Dijksterhuis, A., Bos, M. W., Nordgren, L. F., and van Baaren, R. B. (2006). On making the right choice: the deliberation-without-attention effect. *Science*, 311, 1005–1007.

Ericsson, K. A., Krampe, R. T., and Tesch-Römer, C. (1993). The role of deliberate practice in the acquisition of expert performance. *Psychological Review*, 100, 363–406.

Gawande, A. (2007). The checklist. *The New Yorker* (December 10).

Gettys, C. F., Pliske, R. M., Manning, C., and Casey, J. T. (1987). An evaluation of human act generation performance. *Organizational Behavior and Human Decision Processes*, 39, 23–51.

Gigerenzer, G., and Goldstein, D. G. (1999). Betting on one good reason: The take the best heuristic. In G. Gigerenzer, P. M. Todd, and the ABC Research Group (eds), *Simple Heuristics that Make us Smart* (pp. 75–95). New York: Oxford University Press.

Gladwell, M. (2005). *Blink: The Power of Thinking without Thinking*. New York: Little, Brown and Company.

Hammond, J. S., Keeney, R. L., and Raiffa, H. (1997). *Smart Choices: A Practical Guide to Making Better Life Decisions*. New York: Broadway Books.

Heath, C., Larrick, R. P., and Klayman, J. (1998). Cognitive repairs: How organizations compensate for the shortcomings of individual learners. *Research in Organizational Behavior*, 20, 1–37.

Herzog, S. M., and Hertwig, R. (2009). The wisdom of many in one mind. *Psychological Science*, 20, 231–237.

Hirt, E. R., and Markman, K. D. (1995). Multiple explanation: A consider-an-alternative strategy for debiasing judgment. *Journal of Personality and Social Psychology*, 69, 1069–1086.

Hogarth, R. M. (2001). *Educating Intuition*. Chicago: University of Chicago.

Hogarth, R. M., and Karelaia, N. (2007). Heuristic and linear models of judgment. Matching rules and environments. *Psychological Review*, 114, 733–758.

Isaacson, W. (2003). *A Benjamin Franklin Reader*. New York: Simon & Schuster.

Kahneman, D. (2003). A perspective on judgment and choice: Mapping bounded rationality. *American Psychologist*, 58, 697–720.

Kahneman, D., and Lovallo, D. (1993). Timid choices and bold forecasts: A cognitive perspective on risk taking. *Management Science*, 39, 17–31.

Kray, L. J., and Galinsky, A. D. (2003). The debiasing effect of counterfactual mindsets: Increasing the search for disconfirmatory information in groups. *Organizational Bahavior and Human Decision Processes*, 91, 61–81.

Larrick, R. P. (2004). Debiasing. In D. J. Koehler and N. Harvey (eds), *The Blackwell Handbook of Judgment and Decision Making* (pp. 316–337). Malden, MA: Blackwell.

Larrick, R. P., Mannes, A. E., and Soll, J. B. (2009). The wisdom of small crowds. Unpublished manuscript: Duke University.

Lipshitz, R., Klein, G., Orsaanu, J., and Salas, E. (2001). Focus article: Taking stock of naturalistic decision making. *Journal of Behavioral Decision Making*, 14, 331–352.

Makridakis, S., Hogarth, R., and Gaba, A. (2009). *Dance with Chance: Making Luck Work for You*. Oxford: Oneworld Publications.

Miller, C. C. (2008). Decisional comprehensiveness and firm performance: Towards a more complete understanding. *Journal of Behavioral Decision Making*, 21, 598–620.

Payne, J. W., Bettman, J. R., and Johnson, E. J. (1993). *The Adaptive Decision Maker*. Cambridge: Cambridge University Press.

Payne, J. W., Samper, A., Bettman, J. R., and Luce, M. F. (2008). Boundary conditions on unconscious thought in complex decision making. *Psychological Science*, 119, 1118–1123.

Sanbonmatsu, D. M., Posavac, S. S., Kardes, F. R., and Mantel, S. P. (1998). Selective hypothesis testing. *Psychonomic Bulletin and Review*, 5, 197–220.

Schoemaker, P. J. H. (2004). Forecasting and scenario planning: The challenges of uncertainty and complexity. In D. J. Koehler and N. Harvey (eds), *Blackwell Handbook of Judgment and Decision Making* (pp. 274–296). Malden, MA: Blackwell.

Soll, J. B., and Klayman, J. (2004). Overconfidence in interval estimates. *Journal of Experimental Psychology: Learning, Memory, and Cognition*, 30, 299–314.

Stanovich, K. E. (1999) *Who is Rational? Studies of Individual Differences in Reasoning*. Mahwah, NJ: Erlbaum.

Surowiecki, J. (2004). *The Wisdom of Crowds: Why the Many are Smarter than the Few and How Collective Wisdom Shapes Business, Economies, Societies, and Nations*. New York: Doubleday.

Tetlock, P. E. (2005). *Expert Political Judgment: How Good is It? How Can We Know?* Princeton, NJ: Princeton.

Tufte, E. R. (1997). *Visual Explanations: Images and Quantities, Evidence and Narrative*. Cheshire, CT: Graphics Press.

Walton, M. (1990). *Deming Management at Work*. New York: Putnam.

Wilson, T. D., Lisle, D. J., Schooler, J. W., Hodges, S. D., Kaaren, K. J., and La Fleur, S. J. (1993). Introspecting about reasons can reduce post-choice satisfaction. *Personality and Social Psychology Bulletin*, 19, 331–339.

Zbaracki, M. J. (1998). The rhetoric and reality of total quality management. *Administrative Science Quarterly*, 43, 602–636.

EXERCISES

Generating alternative causes

Have a group of participants think about the following scenario: "The Delta Corporation is in trouble. One of its best products, the portable z-phone, is not selling well even while related products from Apple and other companies are selling very well."

Divide the participants into groups of about five. First, have each person work alone to list all the reasons why the product might not be selling. Then have each group combine ideas from all members (discarding those they think are preposterous). Count how many more ideas the group as a whole had as compared to each individual member, including the best member. If there is time, see if the groups combined did better than any one group. Further, there could be a discussion of what actions to take on each of the ideas presented.

Generating objectives

This exercise is modeled after research conducted by Bond et al. (2008). In this exercise, participants are asked to generate objectives for an important decision. If this is conducted in a group, try to identify a decision of common interest and importance. For example, ask participants "What objectives are relevant to you when buying a house?" (Depending on the audience, other topics might include business unit objectives, choosing a major, or choosing a job.)

Have participants independently generate a list of objectives. Then break them into teams to compare lists of objectives. If you wish to conduct a formal exercise, you can have a note-taker list all of the objectives for each team, which will involve grouping and eliminating redundant objectives. Have participants assess the completeness of their own list of objectives – were there important objectives generated by other group members that they overlooked? Expand the conversation by having participants discuss how a list of objectives could be used as a decision tool in an organization.

26

Stimulate Creativity by Fueling Passion

Teresa M. Amabile and Colin M. Fisher

People will be most creative when they feel motivated primarily by the interest, enjoyment, satisfaction, and challenge of the work itself – and not by external pressures. This is the "Intrinsic Motivation Principle of Creativity" (Amabile, 1996), and it suggests that the social environment, particularly the presence or absence of external pressures in that environment, can influence creativity by influencing people's passion for their work. Managers can influence the level of creativity in their organizations by establishing work environments that support passion for the work.

Intrinsic motivation is the motivation to do work because it is interesting, engaging, or positively challenging. In its highest form, it is called passion and can lead to complete absorption in the work (Csikszentmihalyi, 1990). The elements that make up intrinsic motivation include a sense of *self-determination* in doing the work (rather than a sense of being a pawn of someone else), a feeling that *one's skills are being both fully utilized* and further developed, and *positive feelings about the work*, which may be akin to positive affect or positive emotion (e.g. deCharms, 1968; Deci, Koestner, and Ryan, 1999; Deci and Ryan, 1985; Lepper and Greene, 1978).

A considerable body of research over the past 35 years (conducted with both children and adults) has demonstrated that *external pressures* in the work environment, also called extrinsic motivators, can *decrease* intrinsic motivation and, as a result, can decrease creativity. Most of this research has been experimental, demonstrating that reduced intrinsic motivation and reduced creativity can be caused by each of several different extrinsic factors, including: expected external evaluation (Amabile, 1979; Amabile, Goldfarb, and Brackfield, 1990; Hennessey, 1989), surveillance (Amabile et al., 1990), contracted-for reward (Amabile, Hennessey, and Grossman, 1986; Hennessey, 1989; Kruglanski, Friedman, and Zeevi, 1971); competition with peers (Amabile, 1982, 1987); and constrained choice in how to do one's work (Amabile and Gitomer, 1984; Koestner, Ryan, Bernieri, and Holt, 1984). Each of these factors causes lower levels of intrinsic motivation and creativity. In fact, one experiment demonstrated that simply thinking about extrinsic motivators led to temporarily lower levels of creativity in adults (Amabile, 1985).

Non-experimental research in organizational settings has largely supported these findings. This research suggests that there is indeed a link between intrinsic motivation and creativity (e.g. Amabile, Hill, Hennessey, and Tighe, 1994; Dewett, 2007; Shin and Zhou, 2003) and that extrinsic constraints in the work environment operate as killers of intrinsic motivation and creativity at work. This research also suggests, however, that certain other work environment factors operate as stimulants and supports of intrinsic motivation and creativity (e.g. Amabile, Conti, Coon, Lazenby, and Herron, 1996; Amabile and Gryskiewicz, 1987; Andrews and Farris, 1967; Pelz and Andrews, 1976; Stahl and Koser, 1978). Interestingly, although constraints on how to do one's work can undermine intrinsic motivation and creativity in organizations, *clear ultimate goals* for the work can support intrinsic motivation by providing a structure for focusing creative efforts (e.g. Shalley, 1995). Moreover, as we explain below, certain forms of reward can be beneficial for both intrinsic motivation and creativity in organizations.

Before effects of the work environment on the passion for creativity can be fully understood, it is important to define the basic concepts. Creativity within an organization is the production of novel, appropriate ideas by individuals or small groups. Those ideas can appear in any organizational activity, and are not limited to the domains usually considered to be "creative" (such as R&D, marketing, and strategy formulation). Innovation is the successful implementation of creative ideas by an organization. Notice that ideas cannot be merely new to be considered creative; they must be somehow appropriate to the problem or task at hand. Notice also that it is possible to have many creative contributions – that is, a great deal of creative behavior by individual employees or teams – without having any significant innovation within an organization. This outcome will arise if the new ideas are not communicated or developed effectively within the organization. However, it is not possible to have much innovation in an organization without considerable creativity.

Contrary to popular notions that creativity is the sole province of a few rare geniuses, creativity appears across most levels of human ability. Reviews of the literature suggest that, at low levels of intelligence, creativity is relatively low. However, at higher levels of intelligence (from slightly above average up to genius levels), all levels of creativity are found. In other words, the variability in creativity is much greater for higher levels of intelligence than for lower levels of intelligence (e.g. Stein, 1968; Wallach, 1971).

This suggests a continuum of creativity from the simplest "garden variety" ideas for small improvements to the highest levels of creative achievement in any field. Certainly, products at the highest levels of creativity appear to be qualitatively different from products at the lower levels; it seems odd to compare the invention of the microcomputer with an incrementally improved microcomputer processor. However, the underlying processes do appear to be the same. A useful analogy comes from work in dynamic systems, which has shown that the different gaits of a horse on a treadmill (walking, trotting, cantering, and galloping) appear to be qualitatively different activities. Yet these qualitatively different outcomes arise from gradual quantitative increases in the underlying system: the speed of the treadmill and the energy output of the horse. Similarly, it is quite possible that the most astonishing human accomplishments come about by people doing more, and better, work than goes into the more ordinary instances of creativity in everyday life.

Contextual Factors: Features of the Work Environment

Several specific features of the work environment can influence intrinsic motivation and creativity. *Challenge*, a sense of having to work hard on personally important, enriched, and meaningful tasks, appears to be crucial (see Chapter 6, this volume). *Autonomy*, a sense of freedom in how to carry out one's work, also plays a significant role (see Chapter 11, this volume). *Workgroup supports* include feelings of mutual support for ideas, constructive feedback on ideas, and shared commitment to the work within a team; they also include a broad *diversity of skills* and backgrounds within the team. Diversity of skills and backgrounds can even mean including individuals lacking "standard" areas of expertise. *Supervisory encouragement* includes setting clear strategic goals for a project (while allowing the operational autonomy that is important for creativity), encouraging open communication and collaboration within the team, giving useful, positive feedback on ideas, and supporting the workgroup within the organization (see Chapter 15, this volume). *Organizational encouragement* is the sense that top management encourages, supports, and recognizes creative work (even when that work might not ultimately lead to a successful product), that there are mechanisms for fairly considering new ideas, and that the entire organization collaborates and cooperates to develop new ideas. *Organizational impediments* can have negative effects on intrinsic motivation and creativity; these include political problems within an organization, extremely negative criticism of new ideas, and an emphasis on maintaining the status quo.

All of these features have been identified through research within organizations (e.g. Amabile, Schatzel, Moneta and Kramer, 2004; Amabile and Gryskiewicz, 1987; Andrews and Farris, 1967; Carson and Carson, 1993; Leonard and Swap, 1999; Oldham and Cummings, 1996; Pelz and Andrews, 1976; Stahl and Koser, 1978; Tierney and Farmer, 2002; Zhou, 1998, 2003). One study that used a validated instrument to assess the work environment (Amabile, 1995), and obtained outcome measures from independent expert assessments of creativity, demonstrated that these work environment factors distinguished organizational teams producing highly creative work from those whose work was disappointingly uncreative (Amabile et al., 1996).

Note that two of the contextual features that relate to creativity stem from the nature of the work and how it is presented to an individual. A sense of positive challenge arises from the person's perception that the work uses and develops a set of important skills to accomplish an important goal. A sense of freedom arises from the extent to which the person has control over and discretion in carrying out the work. Because these features capture several aspects of the job characteristics model (Hackman and Oldham, 1980), job design must be considered an important part of the context for creativity.

Supervisors and group leaders play a key role in creating a suitable work environment for creativity. For example, recent studies have found *supervisory support* linked with higher creativity (Amabile et al., 2004), but more controlling supervisory behavior linked with lower creativity (Zhou, 2003). Another study found that even dissatisfied employees' creativity can be enhanced through a work environment in which they are supported and encouraged to share their views (Zhou and George, 2001). Creating such an environment can have benefits beyond stimulating creativity; one study found that workers who have appropriate support and autonomy to do challenging, creative work tend to be more satisfied and intend to stay longer with their organizations (Shalley, Gilson, and Blum, 2000).

DETERMINING FACTORS

The creative process is generally conceived as composed of four basic stages: problem definition or problem finding, when people try to understand or articulate the specific problem to be solved; preparation, when they gather potentially relevant information from a number of sources; idea-generation, when they try to come up with interesting candidate ideas among which to select; and validation/communication, when the final idea is worked through and communicated to others (Amabile, 1996). These stages may occur iteratively or non-linearly over time, or in a more immediate and improvisational fashion (Fisher and Amabile, 2008). *Intrinsic motivation appears to have its strongest influence in the problem-definition and idea-generation stages.* Both of these stages require particularly flexible thinking and deep involvement in the problem. It appears that intrinsic motivation fosters just this sort of thinking process. One study discovered that people who were more intrinsically motivated toward doing work in a particular domain (verbal activities or problem solving) produced work that was independently judged as more creative (Ruscio, Whitney, and Amabile, 1998). Moreover, people who were intrinsically motivated were more likely to engage in exploratory, set-breaking behaviors while they were working on the task; that is, they were more likely to take novel, flexible approaches to the activity as they were trying to figure out how to tackle it. And intrinsically motivated people were more likely to concentrate on the activity, becoming deeply involved cognitively in it. Importantly, involvement mediated the effect of intrinsic motivation on creativity; in other words, intrinsic motivation appeared to influence creativity primarily because it influenced depth of involvement in the task.

Thus, the creative process can be thought of as a maze that the problem solver has to navigate; getting out of the maze is analogous to finding a satisfactory solution to the problem. Following a familiar, straightforward path for solving problems of that type does indeed lead to an exit. However, such approaches to problems are unlikely to yield creative solutions. In order to discover those more creative solutions – those other ways out of the maze – it is necessary to deviate from the familiar, and to take the risk of running into a dead end. If people are *primarily* extrinsically motivated, they are motivated by something outside of the maze – by a reward or a deadline set by someone else, for example. Under these work environment circumstances, they are unlikely to get very involved in the problem itself or do much exploration for a new solution. But if people are primarily intrinsically motivated – if they have a basic interest in the task and if their work environment allows them to retain that intrinsic focus – they enjoy the process of exploring for one of those more creative solutions.

Some research *suggests a connection between positive affect, intrinsic motivation, and creativity.* Experiments demonstrating a negative impact of extrinsic constraint on intrinsic motivation and creativity generally reveal that people not working under extrinsic constraint feel better about the experience and about the work that they have done (e.g. Amabile, 1979; Amabile et al., 1986). Moreover, in addition to experimental evidence that induced positive affect produces more flexible thinking (e.g. Isen, Daubman, and Nowicki, 1987), there is evidence inside organizations. A recent field study of the daily experiences of workers in seven companies found that the level of positive mood on a given day predicted creativity that day as well as the next day (taking the next day's mood into account) (Amabile, Barsade, Mueller, and Staw, 2005). This suggests that positive work environments might influence intrinsic motivation in part by influencing how happy people feel about their work.

Certainly, the work environment's impact on motivation is not the only determinant of creativity. To stimulate creative productivity, managers should not only *engineer supportive work environments* (Amabile et al., 2004), they should also *select for employees who demonstrate high levels of each of the individual components of creativity* (see Amabile, 1983, 1996), and they should help to develop those components. The first component is *expertise*, or skill in the domain where the person will be working. This expertise is a function of the person's talent in the domain, as well as formal and informal education and experience. Not surprisingly, research has shown that, all else being equal, people are more creative if they have more education and experience in a field (McDermid, 1965; Scott and Bruce, 1994). The second component is a set of creativity-relevant processes stemming from the person's personality, cognitive style, and working style. In general, *people produce more creative work if they are oriented toward risk-taking and independence, if they know how to take new perspectives on problems and question basic assumptions, if they have a high tolerance for ambiguity, and if they work hard by energetically and persistently pursuing the problems they are trying to solve* (MacKinnon, 1965; Feist, 1999). The third component is *intrinsic motivation*. Although – as discussed above – intrinsic motivation can be influenced positively or negatively by extrinsic constraints in the work environment, people do differ from each other in their baseline levels of intrinsic and extrinsic motivation. Research has shown that there are stable individual differences in people's basic intrinsic motivation toward work (which can be broken down into challenge motivation and enjoyment motivation) and their basic extrinsic motivation toward work (which can be broken down into recognition motivation and compensation motivation) (Amabile et al., 1994). These basic intrinsic and extrinsic motivational orientations are more or less orthogonal, however; it is possible for people to be high on both intrinsic and extrinsic motives, high on neither, or high on only one. Recent research supports the importance of individual employees' intrinsic motivation orientation to their creativity at work (Munoz-Doyague, Gonzalez-Alvarez, and Nieto, 2008).

A person's creativity skill (the second creativity component) can interact with features of the work context to influence the level of creative output (Shalley, Zhou, and Oldham, 2004). One study demonstrated that technical employees were most likely to produce patent disclosures and receive high ratings on creativity from their supervisors if they not only scored high on a test of individual creative personality, but also if they had both complex jobs and non-controlling, supportive supervisors (Oldham and Cummings, 1996).

Further, for individuals to aggregate their knowledge and skills to create creative products in a group, *several group processes are necessary*. For instance, one study showed that, although the three individual creativity components were important in predicting individual differences, group creativity was an aggregate of each individual's creativity only when the group engaged in certain behaviors. These behaviors, termed "team creativity-relevant processes," included such activities as *effective communication, providing feedback during group tasks*, and *addressing conflict when it occurs* (Taggar, 2002). Another study also showed that, in cross-functional teams, freedom to express doubts and effective management of disagreements was associated with higher levels of creativity (Lovelace, Shapiro, and Weingart, 2001) (see Chapter 18, this volume).

EXCEPTIONS TO THE BASIC PRINCIPLE

The research evidence overwhelmingly points to the importance of intrinsic motivation for creativity. However, under some circumstances, certain forms of extrinsic motivation may support intrinsic motivation and creativity – or at least not undermine it (Amabile, 1993).

This "motivational synergy" is most likely to occur when people start out highly intrinsically motivated to do their work, and when the extrinsic motivators are limited primarily to the stages of the creative process that involve the preparation to generate ideas or the validation and communication of the final idea. *Synergistic effects are unlikely when people feel that the extrinsic motivator – say, a reward – is being used to control their behavior.* Synergistic effects are likely, however, when people feel that the reward confirms their competence and the value of their work, or enables them to do work that they were already interested in doing. There is considerable evidence that such "informational" and "enabling" rewards can have powerfully positive effects on intrinsic motivation (see Deci and Ryan, 1985).

In addition, *three specific features of the social work environment require qualification: competition, time pressure, and resources.* First, competition appears to have different effects on creativity depending on the locus of the competition (Amabile, 1982, 1987; Amabile and Gryskiewicz, 1987). When people are competing with peers (peers with whom they might ideally be sharing information), their creativity seems to be dampened. However, when they are competing with outside groups or organizations, creativity may be stimulated. Second, time pressure appears to have somewhat paradoxical effects although, overall, there appears to be a somewhat negative impact of time pressure on organizational creativity (Amabile and Gryskiewicz, 1987; Amabile et al., 1996; Amabile, Hadley, and Kramer, 2002). Research suggests that, when time pressure is unavoidable, the type of time pressure matters (Amabile et al., 2002). If people's time is fragmented by a large number of demands unrelated to centrally important problems (the most common form of time pressure in organizations), creativity suffers. On the other hand, if people believe that there is a real urgency to solve the problem, because their unit, their organization, or the world has a clear need for a swift resolution, they may be spurred on to higher levels of creativity by that time pressure – as long as they are protected from unrelated interruptions and allowed to focus on the central problem (a set of conditions that is relatively rare in organizations). The effects of time pressure on creativity, though, require ongoing research; one recent study found that, for certain employees and under certain conditions, a moderate degree of time pressure appears to be optimal for creative performance (Baer and Oldham, 2006). Third, the availability of tangible and intangible resources for projects has somewhat complex effects (Amabile and Gryskiewicz, 1987; Amabile et al., 1996). Although, in general, an insufficiency of resources is associated with lower levels of creativity, there may be a threshold effect. That is, although it is rare to find high levels of creativity when resources are extremely scarce, adding resources above a sufficient level may not add to creativity.

Although the vast majority of studies on contextual effects on creativity have focused on the social work environment rather than the physical work environment, there is a small body of research suggesting that *the physical environment may play a role.* Specifically, it appears that people who work in densely crowded spaces that provide little protection from unwanted intrusions exhibit lower levels of creativity than those who work in more protected spaces (Aiello, DeRisi, Epstein, and Karlin, 1977; Alencar and Bruno-Faria, 1997). Nonetheless, the weight of research evidence suggests that the social environment is a more powerful influence than the physical one.

IMPLEMENTATION

Managers can directly affect employee's intrinsic motivation and creativity by the ways in which they construct assignments, teams, and work environments. The research suggests that it is important *to select people not only on the basis of their skills but also on the basis of their interests*. People should be matched to projects that will effectively use their best skills and tap into their strongest passions. Teams should be formed so that, as long as they have some common language for discussing the problem at hand, the *team members represent a diversity of backgrounds and perspectives. Team leaders and direct supervisors should clearly communicate overall strategic goals for a project, but allow the individuals working on the problem to make decisions about how to accomplish those goals.* Supervisors and peers should be genuinely open to new ideas, but should also give constructively challenging feedback on those ideas. *Top-level managers should clearly communicate their desire for creative ideas throughout the organization*, recognizing such ideas when they occur, and rewarding creative work with additional resources that will enable people to do work that excites them. In general, creativity should be rewarded in ways that convey information about the sort of performance the organization values most highly. Moreover, there should be *mechanisms to foster idea-sharing* and general communication about work across the organization, as well as mechanisms for containing turf battles and political problems. Finally, *sufficient resources* should be provided for creative projects, and there should be a *careful examination of timeframes* and an avoidance of extremely tight or arbitrary deadlines where possible.

Some specific tools can be useful for fostering creativity in organizations. Techniques for creative thinking, such as the Creative Problem Solving (CPS) process, appear to increase the fluency, flexibility, and originality of people's thinking to some extent (e.g. Puccio, Firestien, Coyle, and Masucci, 2006). The paper-and-pencil instrument KEYS: Assessing the Climate for Creativity can diagnose an organization's work environment stimulants and obstacles to creativity (Amabile, 1995; Amabile, Burnside, and Gryskiewicz, 1999). And an "innovation office" within a company can serve as a mechanism for improving the care and attention given to new ideas. However, setting up an innovation office, or hiring consultants to "teach" creativity skills or conduct a work environment assessment, will most likely backfire unless such actions are accompanied by a deep management commitment to understanding and improving the context for creativity for the long term.

Case Examples[1]

Karpenter vs. O'Reilly

As Dwight Walton, the CEO of Karpenter Corporation, looked out across the manicured lawns of his company's sprawling suburban campus, he wondered whether there was a problem in his largest division – Karpenter Indoor Living and Home Maintenance (ILHM). Karpenter was one of the dominant names in power tools and appliances – its products appeared in nearly 80% of American homes – and was among the most highly

---

[1] Karpenter and O'Reilly are pseudonyms for two real companies we studied. Over the course of several months, we collected daily diary entries from teams doing creative work in seven organizations. Names and facts about the companies, teams, projects, and individuals are somewhat disguised to protect confidentiality. The character of Heather Shaw and the vignette presented here are fictional; however, they represent the general findings of our study.

regarded companies in the world. Much of Karpenter's success came from ILHM, which had created and managed the products that accounted for a healthy portion of the company's revenue. Cross-functional teams within this division were responsible for all aspects of a particular product line (e.g. power tools, food preparation equipment) and were composed of members from R&D, marketing, manufacturing, and finance. Along with maintaining their current product offerings, these teams were responsible for designing and developing many of the new Karpenter products.

Despite Karpenter's long-running success, Walton was concerned that this year's profits looked less certain. Moreover, the stream of creative products from ILHM had slowed considerably and a few key employees had left in recent months. He began to wonder what was causing these problems; ILHM teams had been successful for many years by leveraging diverse perspectives from across the company and using well the high degree of autonomy they had traditionally had in running their product lines.

Fortuitously, Walton's next meeting was with Heather Shaw – an outside consultant, who had collected data about the daily work experiences of ILHM teams, as well as teams from six other organizations. During his last meeting with Shaw, Walton had asked her to see if there was anything she had found that might help explain the drop in creative productivity. As he cleared away the papers from his prior meeting, he wondered if Shaw could tell him anything useful.

In her presentation, Shaw began by telling Walton that the ILHM teams had the lowest ratings of intrinsic motivation of any teams she had studied, explaining intrinsic motivation and its link to creativity.

"How can that be?" interrupted Walton. "These teams have autonomy, exciting challenges, and support for their work – all the things that they told me in b-school should increase intrinsic motivation."

"Yes, those things do help – when they are experienced that way by your employees," Shaw answered. "But, it looks as if your people don't feel that they have a real say in how to do their work and have trouble getting other units and their supervisors to support their ideas and decisions."

Shaw then explained that, despite the teams' nominal autonomy, divisional management often made decisions without consulting or informing the team. Without naming specific individuals or divulging any details about the confidential diary data that the divisional team members had sent her for a period of time, she described the ways in which intrinsic motivation was systematically being stifled. The diaries that Shaw had analyzed contained powerful information about how things had changed since a new ILHM management team had come on board a year earlier. As one team member recounted:

> Once again, Dean [divisional VP of R&D] has struck. Without informing ANYONE on the team, he has the CAD department redesigning one of our products. The team doesn't even know if we want to work on this project at all this year. (Theoretically, we have control of our capital budget and we have much higher priorities, with much greater potential to improve the bottom line, than this project) . . . So, the team is responsible for the outcome of our business, but someone else is making the decisions that seal our fate. And, not only are they making these decisions, but we have to find out by accident because they don't have the common courtesy to inform us of what they are doing. Just f--king wonderful!!

"You may have told these teams that they have autonomy over decisions about what to work on," Shaw continued. "But, in practice, your people aren't experiencing it that way. Making decisions for a supposedly autonomous team will decrease the team's perceptions of ownership of their work, and, thus, intrinsic motivation. Failing to consult or even inform them only lowers motivation further, by arousing anger and frustration, and leading to perceptions that they are not valued by the organization."

As Walton listened stoically, Shaw began to explain how organizational and supervisory supports for the teams' initiatives were also lacking. She gave several examples of times when a team created a new product but had trouble coordinating with other parts of the organization. Not only were requests for help from central departments, such as manufacturing, not granted, but again, the team was not informed about decisions that affected their products. As described in a team member's diary:

> We have been working very hard to get production running, so we can fill a huge order that has a very tight deadline. Yesterday, production was up and running, and everyone breathed a sigh of relief. But, when we came in this morning, we found out (again by accident, because no one made the effort to tell us) that Manufacturing had shut down production and was refusing to start back up until all the packaging arrived. The packaging was due today, and they had an empty warehouse to stage the parts until it got there. But, without asking/threatening/informing anyone on the team, they just did what they damn well pleased. By the way, they definitely knew this was a hot order, but they just shrugged their shoulders and said it wouldn't be their fault if the order didn't ship. Where in the hell are the common goals, communication and sharing, and teamwork that top management claim they are fostering in this organization?? I'm sure not seeing much evidence.

Shaw told Walton that there were several specific instances showing a lack of organizational support for team innovative efforts, and she described the general nature of those instances.

Further, team members within ILHM felt they received mixed messages from leadership – including their team leaders, division leaders, and even top corporate leaders, about innovation priorities:

> Had meetings with Steve (team leader), Allen (finance person on the team), and Beth (product development head for the team), to discuss how to reposition our proposal for a new hand-held mixer. This project has taken over 1 year to develop, mainly because the division's Management Team [MT] continually asked for more analysis, and R&D was slow in developing a reasonable technology to create a soft grip handle. Finally, the team rallied to present a viable project which the MT approved, only to have the COO say he wants a hard grip handle [instead,] at a $5 lower retail. Steve waffles back and forth. Allen is very helpful in running the financials and giving meaningful discussion on the subject. Beth is contrary on most points – really doesn't seem to care one way or the other. Very frustrating project, getting little support from Corporate, MT, or key team members other than myself and Allen. Yet, all agree that the competitive situation is becoming desperate – especially since Boltmann [a key competitor] has just come out with yet another new hand-held mixer. I'm still trying to catch up to their last new mixer – UGH! Result was that Allen and I have prepared yet another proposal to show the MT tomorrow, but I need to get Steve to buy in; not sure which way he will go.

Because of problems coordinating and communicating with the rest of the organization and mixed messages about what to work on, this team ultimately failed to come up with a new product to successfully challenge Boltmann's competitive position.

"The people you need to come up with creative ideas are having trouble coordinating and communicating with other parts of the organization, which leads to trouble even within the teams; this means they devote a lot of energy to this, rather than developing products. Also, they don't feel respected or supported in their work and ideas," Shaw said. "I think you need to address these issues in order to increase the intrinsic motivation that is so essential to creativity."

"So, there are people who don't like their bosses and get frustrated by the reality of working in a big organization," muttered Walton. "You show me a place that doesn't have problems like that . . ."

"Actually," said Shaw, "that's exactly what I'd like to do."

Shaw proceeded to tell Walton about another company she had studied (without divulging its identity) – O'Reilly Coated Materials. O'Reilly was considered an innovative leader in the coated and laminated fabrics industry. Its core products included industrial goods, such as awnings, canopies, tents, and military supplies, and consumer products, such as luggage, toys, and sports equipment. O'Reilly was just coming off another strong fiscal year. The motor behind this impressive performance was O'Reilly Central Research (OCR), which was composed of teams of scientists and technicians responsible for creating the new products and innovations to keep the company healthy.

Protecting the confidentiality of the O'Reilly company, teams, projects, and individuals, Shaw used her analysis of the OCR diaries to tell Walton of specific factors supporting intrinsic motivation and creativity there. In contrast to the reports about feeling disrespected, unsupported, and micro-managed at ILHM, OCR teams reported norms of cooperation and support across the organization. As one OCR team member reported:

> Met with a number of contributors to the project – people in the Research Analyses group [at OCR] who have helped tremendously, although they are not officially team members – to get them to present their contributions at the project review. Meetings went well and I am glad that they will get a chance to show their contribution to the success [of this project].

Supervisory support was also commonly mentioned by the OCR team members. One wrote:

> Our VP/Director of R&D shared what he reported to the CEO, about OCR's very significant contribution to the business of the Corporation this past [fiscal] year. This makes us all feel very good and look forward to an even better year next year.

Another team member wrote:

> The Gate review [project review by upper management, to decide whether to move on to next stage] and the meetings with the Technical Directors of the divisions went very well. They are completely supportive of all aspects of the project and were thrilled by the progress the team has made over the last few months. I could not have asked for anything more!!

"In your ILHM teams, the diary entries I analyzed often focused on the many obstacles and setbacks people had to overcome," Shaw explained. "At this other company, most of the entries described small steps forward in the work, or things in the work environment that enabled people to make those steps forward. Those teams had considerable autonomy, and were always consulted about possible modifications in project priorities." Walton nodded and shifted uncomfortably in his chair. "Your ILHM team members also reported a lot of criticism and negative feedback, almost never reporting praise," she continued. "This was another point of contrast between the companies."

"I think that the work environment here – the factors that are external to the creative work itself – are interfering with your teams' creativity by undermining their intrinsic motivation. It doesn't have to be that way, though. This other company's teams rated their mood, their work environment, and their intrinsic motivation much higher than your teams did. Not surprisingly, their creative productivity was a lot higher, too. The differences can't be explained away by individual personalities or skill levels; our measures of those don't show much difference between the two companies."

"Although I've mentioned that some of the other company's diaries expressed positive emotions, it's really interesting that most of that company's diary entries did not express any emotion at all, but instead talked about the work itself. In contrast, your ILHM teams wrote extensively about their frustrations with the work environment created by superiors and other parts of the organization. Regardless of how that came to be, you don't want these people thinking about their frustrations when you need them to focus on making great new products – you want them thinking about the products."

As their meeting ended, Walton thanked Shaw for her work and saw her out. Despite the report, Walton couldn't shake the feeling that the comments from his workers were little more than whining at the realities of organizational life. "If my ILHM teams worked harder and smarter," he thought, "they'd get the results we need. On the other hand, maybe there are some things I could change to make it easier for them to focus on the creative work I need them to do. . . . ."

Epilogue: As in our fictitious vignette, the real Karpenter top management team was shocked to find out how frequently their team members experienced negative emotions, how low their intrinsic motivation was, and the degree to which the team members perceived management as overcontrolling, overly critical of new ideas, indecisive, and generally unsupportive. All of these measures were far more positive at O'Reilly. So were measures of creativity. Co-workers at Karpenter rated each other's creative contributions so low that the averages had almost no overlap with the high co-worker ratings at O'Reilly. However, even in the face of this evidence, Karpenter's top management believed the company's work environment to be fundamentally healthy, with a suitable climate for improved creativity.

A year after our study ended, the poor motivation and low creativity exhibited by Karpenter's ILHM employees caught up with the company; profits dropped dramatically. A year later, Karpenter was taken over by a large conglomerate and eventually ceased to exist. O'Reilly, on the other hand, continues as a healthy, profitable firm.

Conclusion

People do their most creative work when they are passionate about what they are doing. Such high levels of intrinsic motivation are influenced both by a person's basic interest in a particular kind of work and by the work environment surrounding the person. Managers can support creative productivity by matching people to projects on the basis of interest as well as skill, by using rewards that recognize competence and support further involvement in the work, and by establishing a work environment across the organization – from the level of top management to the level of workgroups – that removes the barriers and enhances the supports to active, collaborative, intrinsic involvement in the work.

In establishing that work environment, managers should strive first to remove micromanagement of creative work and limit excessive time pressure, particularly time pressure when workdays are marked by fragmented demands unrelated to the organization's most important creative work. They should also take steps to calm political problems that play out on the battlefield of creativity, resulting in excessive criticism of new ideas and an emphasis on maintaining the status quo. Managers can enhance supports for intrinsic involvement in the work by giving people tasks that are meaningful to them and that positively challenge their skills. Middle-level managers should form workgroups that combine diverse perspectives and talents, and then facilitate the members of those groups to work collaboratively as they both support and constructively challenge each other's ideas. Low-level managers – immediate supervisors – should set clear overall goals for projects, but give people as much operational autonomy as possible; they should also serve as champions for creative projects in the organization. Top organizational leaders can provide encouragement and support for creative work in a number of ways, including the establishment of well-coordinated mechanisms for developing new ideas and systems for recognizing and rewarding creative efforts. Perhaps most importantly, the passion for creativity can be stimulated by an open flow of ideas across an organization in which people feel safe to give honest, constructive feedback on someone else's brainchild – and to fearlessly share their own.

REFERENCES

Aiello, J. R., DeRisi, D. T., Epstein, Y. M., and Karlin, R. A. (1977). Crowding and the role of interpersonal distance preference. *Sociometry*, 40, 271–282.

Alencar, E. M., and Bruno-Faria, M. F. (1997). Characteristics of an organizational environment which stimulate and inhibit creativity. *Journal of Creative Behavior*, 31, 271–281.

Amabile, T. M. (1979). Effects of external evaluation on artistic creativity. *Journal of Personality and Social Psychology*, 37, 221–233.

Amabile, T. M. (1982). Children's artistic creativity: detrimental effects of competition in a field setting. *Personality and Social Psychology Bulletin*, 8, 573–578.

Amabile, T. M. (1983). Social psychology of creativity: A componential conceptualization. *Journal of Personality and Social Psychology*, 45, 357–377.

Amabile, T. M. (1985). Motivation and creativity: effects of motivational orientation on creative writers. *Journal of Personality and Social Psychology*, 48, 393–399.

Amabile, T. M. (1987). The motivation to be creative. In S. Isaksen (ed.), *Frontiers of Creativity Research: Beyond the Basics*. Buffalo, NY: Bearly Limited.

Amabile, T. M. (1993). Motivational synergy: toward new conceptualizations of intrinsic and extrinsic motivation in the workplace. *Human Resource Management Review*, 3, 185–201.

Amabile, T. M. (1995). *KEYS: Assessing the Climate for Creativity.* Greensboro, NC: Center for Creative Leadership.

Amabile, T. M. (1996). *Creativity in Context.* Boulder, CO: Westview Press.

Amabile, T. M., Barsade, S. G., Mueller, J. S., and Staw, B. M. (2005). Affect and creativity at work. *Administrative Science Quarterly*, 50, 367–403.

Amabile, T. M., Burnside, R., and Gryskiewicz, S. S. (1999). *User's Manual for KEYS: Assessing the Climate for Creativity.* Greensboro, NC: Center for Creative Leadership.

Amabile, T. M., Conti, R., Coon, H., Lazenby, J., and Herron, M. (1996). Assessing the work environment for creativity. *Academy of Management Journal*, 39, 1154–1184.

Amabile, T. M., and Gitomer, J. (1984). Children's artistic creativity: Effects of choice in task materials. *Personality and Social Psychology Bulletin*, 10, 209–215.

Amabile, T. M., Goldfarb, P., and Brackfield, S. C. (1990). Social influences on creativity: Evaluation, coaction, and surveillance. *Creativity Research Journal*, 3, 6–21.

Amabile, T. M., and Gryskiewicz, S. S. (1987). Creativity in the R&D laboratory. Technical Report Number 30. Greensboro, NC: Center for Creative Leadership.

Amabile, T. M., Hadley, C. N., and Kramer, S. J. (2002). Creativity under the gun. *Harvard Business Review*, August, 52–61.

Amabile, T. M., Hennessey, B. A., and Grossman, B. S. (1986). Social influences on creativity: the effects of contracted-for reward. *Journal of Personality and Social Psychology*, 50, 14–23.

Amabile, T. M., Hill, K. G., Hennessey, B. A., and Tighe, E. M. (1994). The Work Preference Inventory: Assessing intrinsic and extrinsic motivational orientations. *Journal of Personality and Social Psychology*, 66, 950–967.

Amabile, T. M., Schatzel, E. A., Moneta, G. B., and Kramer, S. J. (2004). Leader behaviors and the work environment for creativity: Perceived leader support. *The Leadership Quarterly*, 15, 5–32.

Andrews, F. M., and Farris, G. F. (1967). Supervisory practices and innovation in scientific teams. *Personnel Psychology*, 20, 497–515.

Baer, M., and Oldham, G. R. (2006). The curvilinear relation between experienced creative time pressure and creativity: Moderating effects of openness to experience and support for creativity. *Journal of Applied Psychology*, 9, 963–970.

Carson, P. P., and Carson, K. D. (1993). Managing creativity enhancement through goal-setting and feedback. *Journal of Creative Behavior*, 27, 36–45.

Csikszentmihalyi, M. (1990). *Flow: The Psychology of Optimal Experience.* New York: Harper Perennial.

deCharms, R. (1968). *Personal Causation.* New York: Academic Press.

Deci, E. L., Koestner, R., and Ryan, R. M. (1999). A meta-analytic review of experiments examining the effects of extrinsic rewards on intrinsic motivation. *Psychological Bulletin*, 125, 627–668.

Deci, E. L., and Ryan, R. M. (1985). *Intrinsic Motivation and Self-determination in Human Behavior.* New York: Plenum.

Dewett, T. (2007). Linking intrinsic motivation, risk taking, and employee creativity in an R&D environment. *R&D Management*, 37, 197–208.

Feist, G. J. (1999). The influence of personality on artistic and scientific creativity. In R. Sternberg (ed.), *Handbook of Creativity* (pp. 273–296). Cambridge, UK: Cambridge University Press.

Fisher, C. M. and Amabile, T. M. (2008). Creativity, improvisation, and organizations. In T. Rickards, M. Runco, and S. Moger (eds), *Routledge Companion to Creativity*. Taylor and Francis: London.

Hackman, J. R., and Oldham, G. R. (1980). *Work Redesign*. Reading, MA: Addison-Wesley.

Hennessey, B. A. (1989). The effect of extrinsic constraints on children's creativity while using a computer. *Creativity Research Journal*, 2, 151–168.

Isen, A. M., Daubman, K. A., and Nowicki, G. P. (1987). Positive affect facilitates creative problem solving. *Journal of Personality and Social Psychology*, 52, 1122–1131.

Koestner, R., Ryan, R., Bernieri, F., and Holt, K. (1984). Setting limits on children's behavior: The differential effects of controlling vs. informational styles on intrinsic motivation and creativity. *Journal of Personality*, 52, 233–248.

Kruglanski, A. W., Friedman, I., and Zeevi, G. (1971). The effects of extrinsic incentive on some qualitative aspects of task performance. *Journal of Personality*, 39, 606–617.

Leonard, D. A., and Swap, W. C. (1999). *When Sparks Fly*. Boston: Harvard Business School Press.

Lepper, M., and Greene, D. (1978). Overjustification research and beyond: Toward a means-end analysis of intrinsic and extrinsic motivation. In M. Lepper and D. Greene (eds), *The Hidden Costs of Reward*. New Jersey: Lawrence Erlbaum Associates.

Lovelace, K., Shapiro, D. L., and Weingart, L. R. (2001). Maximizing cross-functional new product teams' innovativeness and constraint adherence: A conflict communications perspective. *Academy of Management Journal*, 44, 779–793.

MacKinnon, D. W. (1965). Personality and the realization of creative potential. *American Psychologist*, 20, 273–281.

McDermid, C. D. (1965). Some correlates of creativity in engineering personnel. *Journal of Applied Psychology*, 49, 14–19.

Munoz-Doyague, M. F., Gonzalez-Alvarez, N., and Nieto, M. (2008). An examination of individual factors and employees' creativity: The case of Spain. *Creativity Research Journal*, 20, 21–33.

Oldham, G. R., and Cummings, A. (1996). Employee creativity: Personal and contextual factors at work. *Academy of Management Journal*, 39, 607–634.

Pelz, D. C., and Andrews, F. M. (1976). *Scientists in Organizations* (2nd edition). New York: Wiley.

Puccio, G. J., Firestien, R. L., Coyle, C., and Masucci, C. (2006). A review of the effectiveness of CPS training: A focus on workplace issues. *Creativity and Innovation Management*, 15, 19–33.

Ruscio, J., Whitney, D. M., and Amabile, T. M. (1998). Looking inside the fishbowl of creativity: Verbal and behavioral predictors of creative performance. *Creativity Research Journal*, 11, 243–263.

Scott, S. G., and Bruce, R. A. (1994). Determinants of innovative behavior: A path model of individual innovation in the workplace. *Academy of Management Journal*, 37, 580–607.

Shalley, C. E. (1995). Effects of coaction, expected evaluation, and goal setting on creativity and productivity. *Academy of Management Journal*, 38, 483–503.

Shalley, C. E., Gilson, L. L., and Blum, T. C. (2000). Matching creativity requirements and the work environment: Effects on satisfaction and intentions to leave. *Academy of Management Journal*, 43, 215–223.

Shalley, C. E., Zhou, J., and Oldham, G. R. (2004). Effects of personal and contextual characteristics on creativity: Where should we go from here? *Journal of Management*, 30, 933–958.

Shin, S., and Zhou, J. (2003). Transformational leadership, conservation, and creativity: Evidence from Korea. *Academy of Management Journal*, 46, 703–714.

Stahl, M. J., and Koser, M. C. (1978). Weighted productivity in R&D: Some associated individual and organizational variables. *IEEE Transactions on Engineering Management*, 25, 20–24.

Stein, M. I. (1968). Creativity. In E. F. Borgatta and W. W. Lambert (eds), *Handbook of Personality Theory and Research*. Chicago: Rand McNally.

Taggar, S. (2002). Individual creativity and group ability to utilize individual creative resources: a multilevel model. *Academy of Management Journal*, 45, 315–330.

Tierney, P., and Farmer, S. M. (2002). Creative self-efficacy: Potential antecedents and relationship to creative performance. *Academy of Management Journal*, 45, 1137–1148.

Wallach, M. A. (1971). *The Creativity–Intelligence Distinction*. New York: General Learning Press.

Zhou, J. (1998). Feedback valence, feedback style, task autonomy, and achievement orientation: Interactive effects on creative performance. *Journal of Applied Psychology*, 83, 261–276.

Zhou, J. (2003). When the presence of creative coworkers is related to creativity: Role of supervisor close monitoring, developmental feedback, and creative personality. *Journal of Applied Psychology*, 88, 413–422.

Zhou, J., and George, J. M. (2001). When job dissatisfaction leads to creativity: Encouraging the expression of voice. *Academy of Management Journal*, 44, 682–696.

EXERCISES

"Scribbles"

To illustrate in real time a few "creativity killers" – environmental factors that undermine creativity by lowering intrinsic motivation – you will instruct students to make a creative drawing out of a scribble under tight time pressure, surveillance, constraint, peer competition, and unclear/meaningless goals, with external evaluation looming. This exercise takes 15–30 minutes and is best used at the very beginning of a workshop/class on creativity.

To run this exercise, first tell the class that they are going to take a short test of their individual creativity. Emphasize the word "test" during the instructions, and continue to remind them that their test will be evaluated – judged by their classmates according to a procedure that you will explain after the test. Tell them that this test is used for assessing artistic creativity, but is also a good indicator of their overall levels of creativity. Make sure that all class members have a blank sheet of paper and a pen or pencil. Have students draw a single, large scribble or squiggle on their page and then stop. Then, have students exchange their papers with another person near them and put their names on the new paper (which has someone else's scribble). Tell the class they will have two minutes to make a creative drawing based on this scribble and give it a creative title. Then give the signal for them to start. As students make their drawings, move throughout the room and look at students' drawings. In reality, give students somewhat less than two minutes (perhaps 90 seconds), and announce how much time is remaining every 30 seconds when there is one minute left. When there are 30 seconds remaining, remind students to give their drawing a creative title. Count down the last 10 seconds aloud. Then say, "Stop!

Pencils down!" and have all students pass in their drawings. There is likely to be much nervous laughter among students during the exercise, and it is fine for you to maintain a pleasant demeanor. When drawings are being passed in, begin to make the atmosphere truly light and fun by inviting students to glance at the drawings as they go by.

After you have the drawings, begin by assuring students that their creations will not actually be judged, and that the reason for the exercise was to give everyone the same shared experience of trying to be creative on the same thing at the same point in time. Then debrief the class on their experience of creating something that was supposed to represent their true creativity, asking them to focus on any factors that made it difficult to be creative. Record their comments on the blackboard in three columns corresponding to the three creativity components. After taking comments for a few minutes (ideally waiting until the major work environment impediments have been mentioned), label these columns "task expertise," "creative thinking skills," and "work environment→intrinsic motivation." Emphasize that this task was not really a test of creativity, but a demonstration of what happens to intrinsic motivation and creativity when people are told to "be creative" in a work environment full of extrinsic constraints and extrinsic motivators. The debriefing should include a brief explanation of intrinsic motivation and the other two components of creativity, extrinsic constraints/motivators, and the intrinsic motivation principle of creativity. For an additional element of fun at the end of the class or workshop, spread out the drawings on an empty table for an informal "art show."

Your ideal work environment

The purpose of this exercise is to allow students to think about the sort of organizational work environment that they should seek (or create) for their future career moves, if they wish to optimize their own opportunities for creative work. It takes about 30–45 minutes, depending on how much time you allocate for discussion.

In this exercise, students will rate how important various aspects of their work environment are for their own personal creativity. For that reason, the exercise is most appropriate after you have taught them about how various aspects of the work environment can facilitate or impede creativity. Begin the exercise by asking them to reflect for a few moments on their prior work experiences (or school-work experiences, if they have not yet held jobs). They should try to recall, in detail, one or two instances in which they did truly creative work, and think about the work environment surrounding them in those instances. Then they should recall, in detail, one or two instances in which their creativity was blocked, and think about the work environment surrounding them in those instances.

Next, tell them that they will generalize from these instances (and others like them) to the future work environments that might best support their own creativity. On a sheet of paper (ideally, a form that you have prepared for them in advance), have students privately indicate whether they would like to HAVE or AVOID the following features of the work environment. Then, they should indicate whether each of those features is VERY IMPORTANT to them, SOMEWHAT IMPORTANT to them, or LESS IMPORTANT to them. Remind them that they will likely have to make tradeoffs, that it is unrealistic to rate everything as VERY IMPORTANT. This first part of the exercise (remembering specific instances and then completing the form individually) generally takes about 15 minutes.

1. *Freedom* in deciding what work to do or how to do it.
2. A sense of *challenge* in your work – working hard on challenging or important projects.
3. Sufficient *resources* – including funds, materials, and information – to accomplish the work.
4. *Supervisory encouragement* from a good work model who sets goals appropriately, supports the workgroup, values individual contributions, and shows confidence in the workgroup.
5. *Workgroup supports* from people who are diversely skilled, communicate well, are open to new ideas, constructively challenge each other's work, trust and help each other, and feel committed to the work they are doing.
6. *Organizational encouragement* that promotes the fair, constructive judgment of ideas, rewards and recognizes people for creative work, helps foster an active flow of new ideas, and maintains a shared vision of what the organization is trying to do.
7. *Organizational impediments*, including internal political problems, harsh criticism of new ideas, destructive internal competition, an avoidance of risk, and an overemphasis on the status quo.
8. *Workload pressure*, such as extreme time pressures, unrealistic expectations for productivity, or distractions from creative work.

After students have indicated whether they would like to HAVE or AVOID each feature of the work environment, and how important the features are to them, have them brainstorm (in pairs or small groups) ways in which they can find or create their ideal work environments. Have them consider the following questions: What sorts of companies and industries should you look for? What sorts of companies and industries should you avoid? What can you do to proactively create your ideal work environment? If there is time, you may wish to continue with a whole-group discussion in which students share some of the insights they developed through the individual exercise and the small-group discussions. This exercise will help students identify those few key features that deserve most of their attention as they look for jobs or think about establishing their own work environments.

27

Manage Stress at Work through Preventive and Proactive Coping

Tabea Reuter and Ralf Schwarzer

Coping with stress at work can be defined as an effort by a person or an organization to manage and overcome demands and critical events that pose a challenge, threat, harm, or loss to that person and that person's functioning or to the organization as a whole. Coping can occur as a response to an event or in anticipation of upcoming demands, but it can also involve a proactive approach to self-imposed goals and challenges.

Coping with stress is considered as one of the top skills inherent in effective managers. In samples recruited from business, educational, health care, and state government organizations, 402 highly effective managers were identified by peers and superiors. Interviews revealed that coping was second on a list of 10 key skills attributed to managers. The management of time and stress was beneficial to the organization because the leaders were role models for employees. Moreover, the executives themselves benefited from successful coping in terms of performance and health (Whetton and Cameron, 1993). This underscores the importance of coping in the workplace. A host of research conducted during the last three decades has found that poor adjustment to demanding or adverse work environments can lead to illness, in particular to high blood pressure and cardiovascular disease (Kasl, 1996; Marmot, Bosma, Hemingway, Brunner, and Stansfeld, 1997; Siegrist, 1996; Theorell and Karasek, 1996; Weidner, Boughal, Conner, Pieper, and Mendell, 1997).

This chapter outlines an approach to coping that makes a distinction between four perspectives, namely reactive coping, anticipatory coping, preventive coping, and proactive coping. This distinction is based on time-related stress appraisals and on the perceived certainty of critical events or demands. Reactive coping refers to harm or loss experienced in the past, whereas anticipatory coping pertains to inevitable threats in the near future. Preventive coping refers to uncertain threats in the distant future, and proactive coping involves future challenges that are seen as self-promoting.

In addition to this approach, numerous ways of coping are presented, and their use at the level of organizations and at the level of individuals is discussed. To begin with, the nature of stress at work will be described.

STRESS AT WORK

The experience of stress

The workplace provides numerous sources of stress. The job itself might involve difficult and demanding tasks that tax or exceed the coping resources of the employee. The role of an individual within the organization might be ambiguous or might even be the cause of frequent conflicts. Relationships at work could entail friction and impair functioning or motivation. Career development might be restricted or echo a constant struggle for acknowledgment. The organizational climate might reflect a battleground for competition. Further, it is possible that all of these examples are aggravated by non-work factors that interact with job stress. Adverse conditions are one of the factors that constitute or set the stage for experiencing stress, such as working shifts, long hours, place of work, work overload, frequent travel, speed of change, and new technology. Often-cited stressors are job insecurity, friction with bosses, subordinates, or colleagues, and role conflict or ambiguity (Cartwright and Cooper, 1997; Quick, Quick, Nelson, and Hurrell, 1997).

Surveys have found a "growing epidemic of stress" (Quick et al., 1997). This does not necessarily indicate that people experience more stress now than they did earlier in their lives, or more stress than earlier generations. Instead, it may signify greater public awareness of the stress phenomenon and the existence of a handy label for a common feeling. Research on the prevalence of stress is difficult because the term is not clearly defined. In the public health literature, and likewise in industrial and organizational psychology, a distinction is sometimes made between "objective stress," also called stressor, and "subjective stress," also called strain or distress. The former is used in research as an independent variable, and the latter as a dependent variable. However, in mainstream psychology, stimulus-based and response-based definitions have become less prevalent. Instead, transactional conceptions are widely accepted, in which stress is understood as a complex process, rather than as a descriptive variable or as a single explanatory concept.

Cognitive-transactional theory of stress

Cognitive-transactional theory defines stress as a particular relationship between the person and the environment that is appraised by the person as taxing or exceeding his or her resources and endangering his or her well-being. Lazarus (1991) conceives stress as an active, unfolding process that is composed of causal antecedents, mediating processes, and effects. *Antecedents* are person variables, such as commitments or beliefs, and environmental variables, such as demands or situational constraints. *Mediating processes* refer to coping and appraisals of demands and resources. Experiencing stress and coping bring about both immediate *effects*, such as affect or physiological changes, and long-term effects concerning psychological well-being, somatic health, and social functioning (see Figure 27.1).

Cognitive appraisals comprise two simultaneous processes, namely primary (demand) appraisals and secondary (resource) appraisals. The terms primary and secondary appraisals have been often misunderstood as reflecting a temporal order which was not meant by Lazarus (personal communication). Therefore, demand and resource appraisals are better terms. Appraisal outcomes are divided into the categories challenge, threat, and harm/loss. First, *demand appraisal* refers to one's evaluation of a situation or event as a potential hazard.

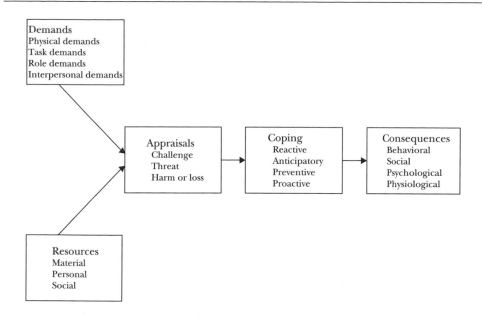

FIGURE 27.1 A process model of stress and coping

Second, *resource appraisals* refer to one's available coping options for dealing with the demands at hand. The individual evaluates his or her competence, social support, and material or other resources that can help to readapt to the circumstances and to reestablish an equilibrium between the person and the environment. Hobfoll (1989) has expanded stress and coping theory with respect to the conservation of resources as the main human motive in the struggle with stressful encounters.

Three outcome categories occur as a result of demand and resource appraisals: a situation is appraised as challenging when it mobilizes physical and mental activity and involvement. In the evaluation of *challenge*, a person may see an opportunity to prove oneself, anticipating gain, mastery, or personal growth from the venture. The situation is experienced as pleasant, exciting, and interesting, and the person feels ardent and confident in being able to meet the demands. *Threat* occurs when the individual perceives danger, anticipating physical injuries or blows to one's self-esteem. In the experience of *harm/loss*, some damage has already occurred. This can be the injury or loss of valued persons, important objects, self-worth, or social standing.

Assessment of stress

The main practical problem with transactional theories of stress is that there is no good way of measuring stress as a process. Therefore, all common procedures to assess stress are either stimulus based, pointing at critical events and demands, or response based, pointing at symptoms and feelings experienced. Some procedures measure the frequency or intensity of stressors, while others measure individual distress (strain). An example for a *stimulus-based* instrument is Spielberger's (1994) Job Stress Survey (JSS). It includes 30 items that describe stressors typically experienced by managerial, professional, and clerical employees. The respondents first rate the severity (intensity) of 30 job stressors (such as excessive paperwork, poorly motivated co-workers). Next, they rate the same list once more on a frequency scale. The two ratings result in scores that can be interpreted as state and trait job stress. Other instruments deal with critical events at the workplace, hassles and uplifts, and the work environment in general.

Response-based measures are available that entail symptoms, emotions, arousal, illness, burnout, and behavioral changes. Job burnout, however, cannot be equated to stress, but has to be seen as a long-term consequence of stress (Klusmann, Kunter, Trautwein, Lüdtke, and Baumert, 2008; Maslach, Schaufeli, and Leiter, 2001; Schaufeli, and Bakker, 2004). The Maslach Burnout Inventory (MBI) is the standard measure in this field (Maslach, Jackson, and Leiter, 1996). Using measures for burnout, symptoms, mental disorder, or illness to tap the concept of "stress" is questionable and misleading because individual changes in these variables occur only at later stages of a stress episode. Thus, stress is confounded with its consequences. Any use of stress inventories involves a particular definition of stress that is not always made transparent and may not even reflect the researcher's theory.

In any case, no matter whether stimulus-based or response-based measures are used, individuals respond to them with their coping resources in mind. The transactional perspective entails the relationship between demands and resources, which is viewed as causing the resulting emotional response.

COPING WITH STRESS AT WORK

Consequences of poor adjustment to stress at work

Stress is inevitable, but the degree of stress can be modified in two ways: by changing the environment and by changing the individual. If coping attempts are unsuccessful, adverse consequences will result. Job performance may decline and job satisfaction fade, burnout symptoms emerge or accidents happen. Further, social relationships at work may become tense, or mental and physical health could deteriorate, leading to sleep problems and substance abuse, etc. Poor adjustment to demanding or adverse work environments can lead to a number of health conditions, in particular high blood pressure and cardiovascular disease. The study of coping at the workplace has often been reduced to only a few variables, such as demands, control, decision latitude, social support, and opportunities for relaxation and exercise. The literature on occupational health has documented an array of findings where these variables were examined in relation to demand factors and population characteristics. Adverse health outcomes have been demonstrated most often (Kasl, 1996; Marmot et al., 1997; Siegrist, 1996; Theorell and Karasek, 1996; Weidner et al., 1997). Successful individual adjustment to stress at work depends partly on resources and partly on the nature of the stress episode.

In the following section, coping resources are described, then dimensions and perspectives of coping are examined that help to gain a better understanding of the psychological meaning of coping.

Antecedents of stress and coping: demands and resources

To characterize *demands* or situational stressors, Lazarus (1991) describes formal properties, such as novelty, event uncertainty, ambiguity, and temporal aspects of stressful conditions. For example, demands that are difficult, ambiguous, unexpected, unprepared, or are very time consuming under time pressure, are more likely to induce threat than easy tasks that can be prepared for thoroughly and solved at a convenient pace without time constraints. The work environment can be evaluated with respect to the stakes inherent in a given situation. For example, demanding social situations imply interpersonal threat, the danger of physical injury is perceived as physical threat, and anticipated failures endangering self-worth indicate ego threat. Lazarus additionally distinguishes between task-specific stress, including cognitive demands and other formal task properties, and failure-induced stress, including evaluation aspects such as social feedback, valence of goal, possibilities of failure, or actual failure. Large and unfavorable task conditions combined with failure-inducing situational cues are likely to provoke stress.

Personal resources refer to the internal coping options that are available in a particular stressful encounter. Competence and skills have to match the work demands. Individuals who are affluent, healthy, capable, and optimistic are resourceful, and, thus, they are less vulnerable toward stress at work. Social competence, empathy, and assertiveness might be necessary to deal with specific interpersonal demands. It is crucial to feel competent to handle a stressful situation. But actual competence is not a sufficient prerequisite. If the individual underestimates his or her potential for action, no adaptive strategies will be developed. Therefore, perceived competence is crucial. This has been labeled "perceived self-efficacy" or "optimistic self-beliefs" by Bandura (see Chapter 10, this volume). Perceived self-efficacy or optimism (as a state) are seen as a prerequisite for coping with all kinds of stress, such as job loss, demotion, promotion, or work overload (Schwarzer and Luszczynska, 2007). Job-specific self-efficacy has been studied (for example, teacher self-efficacy, Schwarzer and Hallum, 2008).

Social resources refer to the external coping options that are available to an individual in a certain stressful encounter. Social integration reflects the individual's embeddedness in a network of social interactions, mutual assistance, attachment, and obligations. Social support reflects the actual or perceived coping assistance in critical situations (see review in Schwarzer and Knoll, 2007). Social support has been defined in various ways, for example as a resource provided by others, coping assistance, or an exchange of resources "perceived by the provider or the recipient to be intended to enhance the well-being of the recipient" (Shumaker and Brownell, 1984, p. 13). Several types of social support have been investigated, for instance instrumental, for example, assist with a problem, tangible help such as goods, informational help such as advice, and emotional support such as giving reassurance, among others.

Dimensions of coping

Many attempts have been made to reduce the universe of possible coping responses to a parsimonious set of coping dimensions. Some researchers have come up with two basic distinctions, that is, instrumental, attentive, vigilant, or confrontative coping, as opposed to avoidant, palliative, and emotional coping (for an overview see Schwarzer and Schwarzer, 1996). A related approach has been put forward by Lazarus (1991), who *separates problem-focused* from *emotion-focused* coping, or by Locke (2005), who distinguishes between action-focused and emotion-focused coping. Another conceptual distinction has been suggested between *assimilative* and *accommodative* coping, whereby the former aims at modifying the environment and the latter at modifying oneself (Brandtstädter, 1992). This pair has also been coined "*mastery* versus *meaning*" (Taylor, 1983) or "*primary control* versus *secondary control*" (Rothbaum, Weisz, and Snyder, 1982). These coping preferences may occur in a certain time order when, for example, individuals first try to alter the demands that are at stake, and, after failing, turn inwards to reinterpret their plight and find subjective meaning in it.

Four coping perspectives in terms of timing and certainty

Work demands can be continuous or changing. They can reflect an ongoing harmful encounter, or they can exist in the near or distant future, creating a threat to someone who feels incapable of matching the upcoming demands with the coping resources at hand. Critical events at the workplace may have occurred in the past, leading to layoff, demotion, or adverse restrictions. In light of the complexity of stressful episodes, coping cannot be reduced to either relaxation or fight-and-flight responses. Coping depends, among other factors, on the time perspective of the demands and the subjective certainty of the events. Reactive coping refers to harm or loss experienced in the past, whereas anticipatory coping pertains to inevitable threats in the near future. Preventive coping refers to uncertain threats in the distant future, whereas proactive coping involves future challenges that are seen as self-promoting (see Figure 27.2).

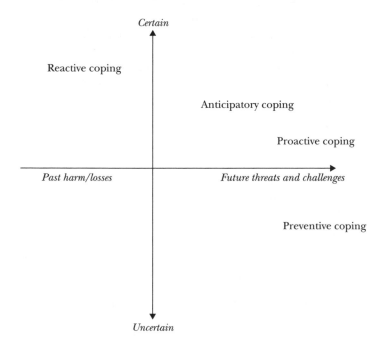

FIGURE 27.2 Four coping perspectives

Reactive coping. Reactive coping can be defined as an effort to deal with a stressful encounter that is ongoing or that has already happened, or with the aim to compensate for or to accept harm or loss. Examples for loss or harm are job loss, failing a job interview, having an accident at work, being criticized by the boss, or having been demoted. All of these events happened in the past with absolute certainty; thus, the individual who needs to cope has to either compensate for loss or alleviate harm. Another option is to readjust the goals or to search for meaning to reconceptualize one's life (Locke, 2002, 2005). Reactive coping may be problem focused, emotion focused, or social-relations focused. For coping with loss or harm, individuals have to be resilient. Since they aim at compensation or recovery, they need "recovery self-efficacy," a particular optimistic belief in their capability to overcome setbacks (Schwarzer, 2008).

Anticipatory coping. Anticipatory coping can be defined as an effort to deal with imminent threat. In anticipatory coping, individuals face a critical event that is certain to occur in the near future. Examples are speaking in public, a confrontation at a business meeting, a job interview, adapting to a new job, increased workload, promotion, retirement, downsizing, etc. There is a risk that the upcoming event may cause harm or loss later on, and the person has to manage this perceived risk. The situation is appraised as an imminent threat. The function of coping may lie in preparatory actions, for example practicing speaking to an audience or solving the actual problem at hand through taking actions, such as increasing effort, getting help, or investing other resources. Another function may lie in feeling good in spite of the risk. For example, one could reframe the situation as less threatening, distract oneself, or gain reassurance from others. Thus, anticipatory coping can also be understood as the management of known risks, which includes investing one's resources to prevent or combat the stressor. One of the resources is specific "coping self-efficacy." This is the optimistic belief of being able to cope successfully with the particular situation.

Preventive coping. Preventive coping can be defined as an effort to build up general resistance resources that result in less strain in the future (minimizing severity of impact), less severe consequences of stress, should it occur, and less likely onset of stressful events in the first place. In preventive coping, individuals face the risk of a critical event that may or may not occur in the distant future. Examples are job loss, forced retirement, physical impairment, disaster, or poverty. The individual plans for the occurrence of such non-normative life events that are potentially threatening. Again, coping equals risk management, but here one has to manage various unknown risks in the distant future. The outlook creates anxiety sufficient to stimulate a broad range of coping behaviors. Since all kinds of harm or loss could materialize one day, the individual builds up general resistance resources, accumulating wealth, insurance, social bonds, and skills (as in the case of anticipatory coping), "just in case." Skill development is a major coping process that helps to prevent undesirable outcomes. General "coping self-efficacy" is a prerequisite to plan and successfully initiate multifarious preventive actions that help build up resistance against threatening non-normative life events in the distant future.

Proactive coping. Proactive coping can be defined as an effort to build up general resources that facilitate promotion toward challenging goals and personal growth (Locke, 2002, 2005). In proactive coping, people have a vision. They see risks, demands, and opportunities in the far future, but they do not appraise these as threats, harm, or loss. Rather, they perceive difficult situations as challenges. Coping becomes goal management instead of risk management (Locke and Latham, 2002, 2006). Individuals are not reactive, but proactive in the sense that they initiate a constructive path of action and create opportunities for growth. The proactive individual strives for improvement of life or work and builds up resources that assure progress and quality of functioning. Proactively creating better work conditions and higher performance levels is experienced as an opportunity to render life meaningful or to find purpose in life. Instead of strain, the individual experiences productive arousal and vital energy along with perceived self-efficacy.

Preventive and proactive coping are partly manifested in the same kinds of overt behaviors as skill development, resource accumulation, and long-term planning. However, the motivation can emanate either from threat appraisal or from challenge appraisal, which makes a difference. Worry levels are high in the former and low in the latter. Proactive individuals are motivated to meet challenges and commit themselves to personal quality standards. Self-regulatory goal management includes an ambitious manner of goal setting and tenacious goal pursuit (Locke and Latham, 2002, 2006; see Chapter 9, this volume). Goal pursuit requires "action self-efficacy," an optimistic belief that one is capable of initiating difficult courses of action. The role of beliefs in self-regulatory goal attainment has been spelled out in more detail in the Health Action Process Approach (Lippke and Ziegelmann, 2008; Reuter, Ziegelmann, Wiedemann, and Lippke, 2008; Schwarzer, 2008; Schwarzer and Luszczynska, 2008).

The distinction between these four perspectives on coping is highly useful because it shifts the focus from mere responses to negative events toward a broader range of risk and goal management. The latter includes the active creation of opportunities and the positive experience of challenge, in particular in the work domain. Aspinwall and Taylor (1997) have described a proactive coping theory that is similar, but not identical, to the present one. Schwarzer and Taubert (2002) have made psychometric discriminations between preventive and proactive coping. The Proactive Coping Scale can be downloaded from the web (Greenglass, Schwarzer, and Taubert, 1999).

WAYS OF COPING

Coping at the level of organizations: designing healthy workplaces

When an unexpected event happens, such as a strike or a company takeover, an organization has to cope in a reactive manner. Reducing harm or compensating for loss is required, and the way this is done depends largely on the particular nature of the stress episode. When such events are imminent and certain, anticipatory coping is required. The adequate way of coping is highly idiosyncratic. Preventive coping is called for when no specific events are envisioned, but a more general threat in the distant future comes into view. Such events could be the dangers of economic decline, potential mergers or downsizing, revised governmental employee health regulations, aging workforce, new technology, etc. When visions or challenges and a perceived potential for growth or mastery prevail, proactive coping is initiated. The latter two perspectives entail about the same set of innovations. In the literature, this is usually discussed as "primary prevention" or "organizational prevention" (Quick et al., 1997), which includes modifying work demands and improving relationships at work.

Physical settings can be redesigned to minimize distressful effects of the physical work environment, such as noise, heat, and crowding. The creation of pleasant and suitable offices or workshops, enriched by cafeterias and fitness centers, can elevate job satisfaction, job safety, and mental health, which indirectly may improve performance and loyalty. *Job redesign* is aimed at changing task demands, for example by partitioning the workload, job rotation, job enlargement, job enrichment, building teams, opening feedback channels, etc. (cf. Judge, this volume). *Flexible work schedules* can help to enhance the employee's control and discretion and allow for a better time management and integration of work and non-work demands (cf. Balzer, this volume). *Participative management and delegation* expand the amount of autonomy at work by disseminating information, decentralizing decision making, and involving subordinates in a variety of work arrangements. When a boss promotes trust (see Chapter 21, this volume) with the employees, tension and conflict are reduced, and awareness of partnership may arise. The empowerment approach has a similar focus (see Chapter 11, this volume). *Career development* is another method of preventive or proactive coping to improve an estimable portfolio of skills and talents. A set of career paths must be made transparent, and various opportunities for promotion need to be created to motivate employees to set goals for themselves and strive for these goals. This needs to be enriched by an effective feedback and reward system. Self-assessment must be encouraged, and opportunities constantly need to be analyzed (Lawler, 1994).

Organizational prevention is also directed at interpersonal demands placed on individuals at the workplace (Quick et al., 1997). *Role analysis* is aimed at making a person's role within an organization transparent. Clarifying one's role profile in comparison to the profiles of others may help to reduce tension, misperceptions, and conflict. Roles are defined as a set of expectations (by boss, peers, and subordinates) toward a particular position holder. If roles are misperceived, "role stress" will emerge. Thus, role analysis and correction of perceptions constitute a way of preventive coping. *Goal setting* in itself can be regarded as a method of preventive coping in order to avoid miscomprehension about one's responsibilities and expected task performance (Locke, 2005). Negotiating proximal and distal work goals includes an agreement between supervisor and subordinate or team about the conditions under which they should be attained and the criteria that apply for their evaluation (Chapter 9, this volume). *Team building* is a preventive coping method that aims at the establishment of cohesive and effective work groups that perform at a higher level than isolated individuals, partly because they resolve interpersonal conflicts and develop a cohesive spirit (Peterson, Park, and Sweeney, 2008). *Social support* reflects broad-range prevention and intervention at all levels. The term denotes a coping resource as well as an interpersonal coping process, depending on the point in time within a defined stress episode. Social support is generally seen as a buffer against the impact of stress – although, empirically, main effects occur more frequently than statistical interactions (Greenglass, Fiksenbaum, and Eaton, 2006; Schwarzer and Knoll, 2007). As a buffer, social support can be part of reactive coping after the event has struck. As a preventive and proactive coping strategy, social network building equals the institution of a convoy that accompanies and protects the individual throughout the life course when times get rough.

Stress in organizations is related to their culture and leadership, organizational structures, and developments. Proactive leaders have transformed stressed corporations into healthy ones, and restructuring has created relatively stress-free work environments, as has been documented for Southwest Airlines, Chaparral Steel Company, Xerox Corporation, Johnson and Johnson, or, as a negative example, Eastern Airlines (Quick et al., 1997).

CASE EXAMPLES

Preventive coping at the level of organizations: improving the employability of an aging workforce

The following example demonstrates how an organization may cope with the demographic changes of its workforce in a preventive as well as a proactive manner. The Deutsche Bahn AG, Germany's national railway company, employs approximately 200,000 employees, of whom about 30% are 50 years and older. By 2015, this number is expected to double to an estimated 60%. Whereas such a demographic change is often seen as a threat to organizational functioning, the view and strategies taken by the company's human resources department is more differentiated in that it counteracts risks and values opportunities. The risks inherent in an aging work staff are faced by preventive coping strategies and, at the same time, the opportunities seized with proactive measures. Risks of the aging workforce include diminishing health and physical functioning as well as outdated qualifications. The human resources department set up an agenda for maintaining the employability of their workforce. At the organizational level, this refers to the capability to realize potential through sustainable employment. Such preventive coping strategies include comprehensive health-promotion strategies, job rotation, job enlargement, job enrichment, and technological advances to minimize physical strain.

The other side of the coin of an increasing percentage of older employees is to value their judgments and competence, along with their sense of responsibility and ability to gauge complex situations. These resources of older employees that are highly correlated with professional experience are coined "demographic return." Comprehending these advantages can be viewed as proactive coping strategies that encompass age-mixed teams, individual tandem solutions, and systematic job selection. In the face of rapidly changing macroeconomic demands, preventive and proactive coping behavior at the organizational level allows organizations to develop their potential for growth.

At the school level, teacher stress and burnout can be prevented and mitigated by making them healthier workplaces. Based on his work in schools in Israel, Friedman (1999) suggests tackling the sources of stress by reducing the degree of polarization in the classroom and the number of pupils per class and by changing teachers' work schedules. To treat the symptoms of stress at the school level, he suggests creating a supportive atmosphere, open channels of communication, involving teachers in decision making, and developing an open and positive organizational climate.

Coping at the individual level within organizations

At the individual level, Friedman (1999) suggests tackling the sources of stress by training teachers to cope with stressful situations, instructing them about the causes of burnout, and developing and improving their abilities in problem solving, conflict resolution, and leadership. To treat the symptoms of stress, he suggests in-service training, holidays, support and assistance groups, and workshops.

Some general theoretical comments on individual coping have to be added here, based on the distinction between reactive, anticipatory, preventive, and proactive coping. If a person fails to meet a work goal, is rejected by colleagues, has a conflict with the boss, suffers from repetitive stress injury, or loses a contract or the job itself, *reactive coping* takes place because the demands or events are appraised as ongoing or as prior harm or loss. A range of mental and behavioral coping options are at the individual's disposal, depending on the available resources, preferences, and nature of the stress episode. Relaxation is a commonplace recommendation to alleviate negative emotions or arousal, although it does not contribute much to solve the underlying problem. Cognitive restructuring helps to see the world with different eyes. Instrumental action may solve the problem at hand. As noted earlier, the distinctions have been made between problem-focused and emotion-focused coping (Lazarus, 1991). Social relations coping (Hobfoll, 1989) has been added as a third dimension. Mobilizing support and talking with others are suggestions to cope with adversity. The experience of harm or loss calls for compensatory efforts (mastery) or search for meaning and flexible goal adjustment (Locke, 2002). There is no basic rule or rank order of good and bad coping strategies that apply to harm or loss situations. The individual adapts in an idiosyncratic manner to the situation and evaluates the coping efforts retrospectively as having been more or less successful, which may not correspond with the evaluation of onlookers. If someone fails to adapt, social support needs to be mobilized from outside, and psychological counseling, therapy, traumatic event debriefing, or even medical care may become necessary.

If someone faces a critical event in the near future, such as a public presentation, job interview, medical procedure, or corporate decision about redundancy of jobs – in other words, situations that are appraised as threatening – this stress episode requires *anticipatory coping*. The range of coping options is the same as before. Increased effort to master the situation is adaptive only if the situation is under personal control (interview, presentation), whereas situations under external control (medical procedure, corporate decision) require mainly emotional and cognitive efforts (e.g. relaxation, reappraisal).

An individual who faces increasing work challenges or job volatility in the distant future, such as downsizing, mergers, demotion, promotion, entrepreneurship, is better off to choose either *preventive coping* strategies (in the case of threat appraisal) or *proactive coping* strategies (in the case of challenge appraisal). The long-term accumulation of general resistance resources includes behavioral, social, and cognitive strategies. Coping with one's work demands, for example, comprises setting priorities, avoiding overload, delegating tasks, acquiring social support, planning, and having good time management (Quick et al., 1997), and, above all, always improving one's skills and developing new ones. Managing one's lifestyle is directed at a healthy balance between work, family, and leisure (Schaer, Bodenmann, and Klink, 2008, and Chapter 31). Workaholics do not maintain such a balance because they are trying to use work to alleviate self-doubt that is not caused by work problems, and they hardly find refuge anywhere. Work stress can spill over into non-work settings, and vice versa, which places a particular burden on women and dual-career couples (Greenglass, 2002). Protecting life domains from daily hassles is an important aspect of self-regulation. Some companies grant their employees extra time for revitalization and personal growth, for example by funding sabbaticals. Healthy nutrition and physical exercise are other lifestyle ingredients that bear a protective shield against the experience of stress.

Stress management programs are usually not implemented by corporations as stand-alone programs, but rather as part of more comprehensive *health promotion strategies* that also aim at preventive nutrition, physical exercise, smoking cessation, preventing use of alcohol and drugs, and others. IBM, Control Data Corporation, Illinois Bell, New York Telephone Company, B. F. Goodrich Tire, Citicorp, Johnson and Johnson, and Dupont are among the companies cited frequently that have established high-quality health-promotion programs for their employees (see also Quick et al., 1997).

The cognitive way of coping includes stress reappraisal, internal dialog, constructive self-talk, search for meaning, or optimistic explanatory style, among others. Individuals can develop a more positive view of stressful situations, which may facilitate all kinds of coping. Reinterpreting a threat into a challenge transforms preventive coping into proactive coping. The following case study, inspired by Covey (1989), demonstrates how proactive coping behavior may enlarge an individual's range of control at the workplace.

Proactive coping at the individual level within organizations: dealing with an authoritarian leader

The president of the organization in which Mr. X is employed is known for his authoritarian leadership style. Even though his executives view the president as being a dynamic and talented person, they feel restricted and alienated by his style of management, which consists of orders and creates an atmosphere of dictatorship. Unlike the other colleagues, who cope with the situation by criticizing and complaining about the conditions, Mr. X tries to compensate for the weak management by trying to enlarge his range of control. When assigned to a task, he acts proactively by anticipating the president's needs. He provides not only requested information on an issue, but also an analysis and recommendations on how to deal with the issue. Eventually, he wins the president's trust. Instead of receiving orders, he is asked for his opinion. This example illustrates how proactively taking the initiative may not only increase one's decision latitude, but also how an obstacle may be turned into a positive experience.

Proactive coping at the individual level within organizations: gain control by developing hardiness

Habitual mindsets that reflect a constructive approach to life are inherent in the concepts of perceived self-efficacy (Chapter 10, this volume), learned optimism (Seligman, 1991), and hardiness (Maddi, 1998). By improving such mindsets, employees can be empowered to take charge of upcoming challenges in the workplace and to gain more control over their lives. In other words, they develop resources as a prerequisite for preventive and proactive coping. The hardiness concept has been applied frequently to prevent and mitigate stress at work. It comprises the attitudes of commitment, control, and challenge. The goal of interventions, for example, as those conducted by the Hardiness Institute, lies in the promotion of these attitudes. Initially, participants respond to the HardiSurvey that assesses these three components and allows one to gauge how much work stress a person experiences. Clients then undergo the 16 hour HardiTraining course, consisting of exercises on how to cope with stress, relax, seek social support, eat right, and work out (Maddi, Kahn, and Maddi, 1998). With a group of 54 managers, hardiness training was compared to relaxation training and to a social support control condition. The first group reported less strain and illness and higher job satisfaction. Thus, hardiness is seen as stimulating effective functioning and protecting wellness under stressful conditions.

Proactive coping at the individual level within organizations: learned optimism training

An example of a program at the individual level within organizations is "learned optimism training" which was conducted at Metropolitan Life Insurance Company (Seligman, 1991; Seligman and Schulman, 1986). Learned optimism is a proxy for a particular explanatory style that can be acquired to improve one's interpretation of stressful events in general or specifically at work. A diagnostic measure, the Attributional Style Questionnaire (ASQ), was developed, which ranks individuals on an optimism/pessimism scale. One prediction of this measure concerns job performance, for example successfully selling life insurance. Insurance agents with high scores on the ASQ invest more effort and are more persistent in "cold calling" of customers and attain better sales commissions than low scorers. By using this diagnostic instrument to select personnel, Metropolitan Life has saved millions of dollars. Many companies now use such scales in order to identify applicants who possess more than just drive and talent, namely, the optimism necessary for success as well. Based on Seligman's theory and his assessment procedure, a training program has been developed to teach employees cognitive coping with stress. Participants with chronic negative thoughts learn to talk to themselves in a constructive manner. If something goes wrong, pessimists tend to have hopeless thoughts ("I always screw up," "I'll never get it right"), that is, internal, stable, and global attributions of negative events. They learn to transform these thoughts into external, variable, or specific attributions, such as "Things didn't go well today, but I learned a lot from the experience." Workshop participants learn to listen to their own internal dialog and to dispute their chronic negative thoughts and come up with a more balanced view of themselves, the world, and the future. The four day course is administered by Foresight, Inc., at Falls Church, Virginia. Unlike other courses for sales agents, which teach what to say to clients, this course teaches what to say to oneself when the client says no. Thus, it represents a cognitive coping training to reduce stress when facing interpersonal demands. The most typical exercise is to identify adverse events, the corresponding subjective belief, and the most likely subsequent emotions and behaviors. Then, after recognizing one's explanatory style, the participants learn to dispute their thoughts. They are asked to make the revised explanatory style a new habit to supplant their usual automatic pessimistic explanations. In psychotherapy, this is known as cognitive restructuring. This principle has turned out to be a powerful coping strategy that facilitates job performance, job satisfaction, and health.

In sum, the examples have demonstrated the broad scope of coping in organizations and have pointed to the direction in which interventions could go to facilitate more preventive and proactive coping. Coping is a set of mental and physical behaviors, whereas perceived self-efficacy, hardiness, optimism, etc., are social-cognitive concepts that may provide the backdrop for improved coping. As such, they can be regarded as moderators of the stress–coping relationship. Those who harbor high levels of resourceful mindsets are better off when it comes to transforming a demanding situation. Emotional or impulsive ways of coping are not compatible with preventive and proactive coping because the latter are based on reason (Locke, 2005).

Conclusion

Coping with stress is a normal and necessary experience in daily life. At the workplace, it gains particular importance because it is related not only to individual career goals, health, and satisfaction, but also to organizational success and social relations. To understand coping, a number of analytical dimensions, perspectives, theoretical models, and approaches have been suggested. In the present chapter, a new distinction between reactive, anticipatory, preventive, and proactive coping has been put forward because these coping perspectives have unique value for stress at the workplace, including the positive side of stress. Interventions have to be tailored to these perspectives. Events that are appraised as harm or loss require different coping interventions than those that are appraised as threats or challenges. The current view connects coping theory with action theory and sets the stage for integrative programs at the organizational and individual level. It is in line with the contemporary trend toward a "positive psychology" (Peterson et al., 2008; Seligman, 2008).

References

Aspinwall, L. G., and Taylor, S. E. (1997). A stitch in time: Self-regulation and proactive coping. *Psychological Bulletin*, 121, 417–436.

Brandtstädter, J. (1992). Personal control over development: Implications of self-efficacy. In R. Schwarzer (ed.), *Self Efficacy: Thought Control of Action* (pp. 127–145). Washington, DC: Hemisphere.

Cartwright, S., and Cooper, C. L. (1997). *Managing Workplace Stress*. Thousand Oaks, CA: Sage.

Covey, S. R. (1989). *The 7 Habits of Highly Effective People: Restoring the Character Ethic*. New York: Simon and Schuster.

Friedman, I. A. (1999). Turning over schools into a healthier workplace: Bridging between professional self-efficacy and professional demands. In R. Vandenberghe and A. M. Huberman (eds), *Understanding and Preventing Teacher Burnout* (pp. 166–175). Cambridge, UK: Cambridge University Press.

Greenglass, E. (2002). Proactive coping. In E. Frydenberg (ed.), *Beyond Coping: Meeting Goals, Vision, and Challenges* (pp. 37–62). London: Oxford University Press.

Greenglass, E., Schwarzer, R., and Taubert, S. (1999). The Proactive Coping Inventory (PCI): A multidimensional research instrument. (Online publication.) Available at: http://www.ralfschwarzer.de.

Greenglass, E., Fiksenbaum, L., and Eaton, J. (2006). The relationship between coping, social support, functional disability and depression in the elderly. *Anxiety, Stress and Coping*, 19(1), 15–31.

Hobfoll, S. E. (1989). Conservation of resources: A new attempt at conceptualizing stress. *American Psychologist*, 44(3), 513–524.

Kasl, S. V. (1996). The influence of the work environment on cardiovascular health: A historical, conceptual, and methodological perspective. *Journal of Occupational Health Psychology*, 1(1), 42–56.

Klusmann, U., Kunter, M., Trautwein, U., Lüdtke, O., and Baumert, J. (2008). Engagement and emotional exhaustion in teachers. Does the school context make a difference? *Applied Psychology: An International Review. Special Issue: Health and Well-being*, 57, 127–151.

Lawler, E. E., III (1994). From job-based to competency-based organizations. *Journal of Organizational Behavior*, 15, 3–16.

Lazarus, R. S. (1991). *Emotion and Adaptation*. London: Oxford University Press.

Lippke, S., and Ziegelmann, J. P. (2008). Theory-based health behavior change: Developing, testing and applying theories for evidence-based interventions. *Applied Psychology: International Review*, 57, 698–716.

Locke, E. A. (2002). Setting goals for life and happiness. In C. R. Snyder and S. Lopez (eds), *Handbook of Positive Psychology* (pp. 299–312). Oxford, UK: Oxford University Press.

Locke, E. A. (2005). Coping with stress through reason. In A. Antoniou and C. Cooper (eds), *Research Companion to Organizational Health Psychology*, 188–197. Cheltenham, UK: Elgar.

Locke, E. A., and Latham, G. P. (2002). Building a practically useful theory of goal setting and task motivation: A 35-year odyssey. *American Psychologist*, 57, 705–717.

Locke, E. A., and Latham, G. P. (2006). New directions in goal-setting theory. *Current Directions in Psychological Science*, 15, 265–268.

Maddi, S. R. (1998). Creating meaning through making decisions. In P. T. P. Wong, P. S. Fry et al. (eds), *The Human Quest for Meaning: A Handbook of Psychological Research and Clinical Applications* (pp. 3–26). Mahwah, NJ: Erlbaum.

Maddi, S. R., Kahn, S., and Maddi, K. L. (1998). The effectiveness of hardiness training. *Consulting Psychology Journal*, 50, 78–86.

Marmot, M. G., Bosma, H., Hemingway, H., Brunner, E., and Stansfeld, S. (1997). Contribution of job control and other risk factors to social variations in coronary heart disease incidence. *Lancet*, 350, 235–239.

Maslach, C., Jackson, S. E., and Leiter, M. P. (1996). *Maslach Burnout Inventory Manual* (3rd edition). Palo Alto, CA: Consulting Psychologists Press.

Maslach, C., Schaufeli, W. B., and Leiter, M. P. (2001). Job burnout. *Annual Review of Psychology*, 52, 397–422.

Peterson, C., Park, N., and Sweeney, P. J. (2008). Group well-being: Morale from a positive psychology perspective. *Applied Psychology: An International Review. Special Issue: Health and Well-being*, 57, 19–36.

Quick, J. C., Quick, J. D., Nelson, D. L., and Hurrell, J. J., Jr. (1997). *Preventive Stress Management in Organizations*. Washington, DC: APA.

Reuter, T., Ziegelmann, J. P., Wiedemann, A. U., and Lippke, S. (2008). Dietary planning as a mediator of the intention–behavior relation: An experimental-causal-chain design. *Applied Psychology: An International Review. Special Issue: Health and Well-being*, 57, 194–297.

Rothbaum, F., Weisz, J. R., and Snyder, S. (1982). Changing the world and changing the self: A two-process model of perceived control. *Journal of Personality and Social Psychology*, 42, 5–37.

Schaer, M., Bodenmann, G., and Klink, T. (2008). Balancing work and relationship: Couples coping enhancement training (CCET) in the workplace. *Applied Psychology: An International Review. Special Issue: Health and Well-being*, 57, 71–89.

Schaufeli, W. B., and Bakker, A. B. (2004). Job demands, job resources and their relationship with burnout and engagement: A multi-sample study. *Journal of Organizational Behavior*, 25, 293–315.

Schwarzer, R. (2008). Modeling health behavior change: How to predict and modify the adoption and maintenance of health behaviors. *Applied Psychology*, 57(1), 1–29.

Schwarzer, R., and Hallum, S. (2008). Perceived teacher self-efficacy as a predictor of job stress and burnout: Mediation analyses. *Applied Psychology: An International Review. Special Issue: Health and Well-being*, 57, 152–171.

Schwarzer, R., and Knoll, N. (2007). Functional roles of social support within the stress and coping process: A theoretical and empirical overview. *International Journal of Psychology*, 42(4), 243–252.

Schwarzer, R., and Luszczynska, A. (2007). Self-efficacy. In M. Gerrard and K. D. McCaul (eds), *Health Behavior Constructs: Theory, Measurement, and Research*. National Cancer Institute Website: http://cancercontrol.cancer.gov/constructs.

Schwarzer, R., and Luszczynska, A. (2008). How to overcome health-compromising behaviors: The health action process approach. *European Psychologist*, 2, 141–151.

Schwarzer, R., and Schwarzer, C. (1996). A critical survey of coping instruments. In M. Zeidner and N. S. Endler (eds), *Handbook of Coping: Theory, Research and Applications* (pp. 107–132). New York: Wiley.

Schwarzer, R., and Taubert, S. (2002). Tenacious goal pursuits and striving toward personal growth: Proactive coping. In E. Frydenberg (ed.), *Beyond Coping: Meeting Goals, Visions and Challenges* (pp. 19–35). London: Oxford University Press.

Seligman, M. E. P. (1991). *Learned Optimism*. New York: Knopf.

Seligman, M. E. P. (2008). Positive health. *Applied Psychology: An International Review. Special Issue: Health and Well-being*, 57, 3–18.

Seligman, M. E. P., and Schulman, P. (1986). Explanatory style as a predictor of productivity and quitting among life insurance sales agents. *Journal of Personality and Social Psychology*, 50(4), 832–838.

Shumaker, S. A., and Brownell, A. (1984). Toward a theory of social support: Closing conceptual gaps. *Journal of Social Issues*, 40, 11–36.

Siegrist, J. (1996). Adverse health effects of high-effort/low-reward conditions. *Journal of Occupational Health Psychology*, 1, 27–41.

Spielberger, C. D. (1994). *Professional Manual for the Job Stress Survey (JSS)*. Odessa, FL: Psychological Assessment Resources.

Taylor, S. E. (1983). Adjustment to threatening events: A theory of cognitive adaptation. *American Psychologist*, 38, 1161–1173.

Theorell, T., and Karasek, R. (1996). Current issues relating to psychosocial job strain and cardiovascular disease research. *Journal of Occupational Health Psychology*, 1(1), 9–26.

Weidner, G., Boughal, T., Connor, S. L., Pieper, C., and Mendell, N. R. (1997). Relationship of job strain to standard coronary risk factors and psychological characteristics in women and men of the Family Heart study. *Health Psychology*, 16(3), 239–247.

Whetton, D. A., and Cameron, K. S. (1993). *Developing Management Skills: Managing Stress*. New York: HarperCollins.

Exercises

Coping behaviors

In your classroom or work group, you may share each other's experience with proactive coping behaviors, and, thus, provide and find role models for future situations. In the following you find the proactive coping subscale of the Proactive Coping Inventory (PCI) by Greenglass, Schwarzer, and Taubert (1999). The statements deal with reactions you may have to various situations. Indicate how true each of these statements is depending on how you feel about the situation. Do this by responding to one of the four statements "not at all true," "barely true," "somewhat true," or "completely true."

1. "I am a 'take charge' person."
2. "I try to let things work out on their own." (−)
3. "After attaining a goal, I look for another, more challenging one."
4. "I like challenges and beating the odds."
5. "I visualize my dreams and try to achieve them."
6. "Despite numerous setbacks, I usually succeed in getting what I want."
7. "I try to pinpoint what I need to succeed."
8. "I always try to find a way to work around obstacles; nothing really stops me."
9. "I often see myself failing so I don't get my hopes up too high." (−)
10. "When I apply for a position, I imagine myself filling it."
11. "I turn obstacles into positive experiences."
12. "If someone tells me I can't do something, you can be sure I will do it."
13. "When I experience a problem, I take the initiative in resolving it."
14. "When I have a problem, I usually see myself in a no-win situation." (−)

Complete the assignments and then, in small groups of four to five individuals, compare your own answers with those of your colleagues. Choose a statement on which you responded "completely true" (statements marked with a (−) demand reverse coding) as a positive example for proactive coping and one statement as a negative example ("not at all" or "completely true" for (−) statements) and share your experience by illustrating a situation in which you responded in the way it is described in the statements.

Personal coping experiences

Identify a situation you encountered in the past where you behaved in a reactive manner (e.g. reacting toward criticism, working on a project with a colleague who is permanently late). Review the situation in the context of your range of control and potential alternate pathways. How could you have responded? Take several moments and create the experience vividly in your mind. Share your experience with your classmates/colleagues and discuss further ways of coping with challenging situations.

28

Manage Conflict through Negotiation and Mediation

M. Susan Taylor and Ashley Fielbig

Managers' often find that their formal authority falls far short of their responsibilities and their success is dependent on the actions of others outside the chain of command. Though people in this predicament may yearn for more control, there is often no practical way to follow the textbook advice to match authority with responsibility. "Indirect management" is the name we give this increasingly important phenomenon of concentrated responsibility but shared authority and resources. It calls for a very different approach from traditional line management. (Lax and Sebenius, 1986)

Managers function in an increasingly complex world where competition is intense and global for virtually all product or service lines. Their revenue generating initiatives require cross-unit cooperation and coordination. In addition, the structural parameters or procedural precedents that might assist in the implementation of revenue generating initiatives are often absent or inconsistent. Furthermore, teams of employees who require and demand substantial self-determination in order to perform their jobs effectively, increasingly staff manager's work units. Factors such as scarce resources, ambiguous lines of authority, conflicting goals, and high levels of interdependence generate a perfect set of conditions for conflict in the managerial job.

What exactly is meant by the term conflict? Conflict is the process that occurs when one party perceives that another has frustrated or is about to frustrate one or more of its goals or "interests" as they are often referred to in the applied negotiations literature (Fisher, Uri, and Patten, 1981; Thomas, 1976). In which aspects of a manager's job might we expect conflict to emerge? Both research and experience show us that conflict frequently occurs across many aspects of managers' jobs, for example in interactions with their own managers, dealings with peers or associates, discussions with the employees they manage, and in their need or desire to "shore up" their formal authority in the organization. Therefore, managers face and must attempt to resolve conflict on virtually a daily basis. Perhaps not surprising then, Fred Luthans and his colleagues have found that managing conflict between employees ranked 5th on a list of 12 managerial activities found to be most important to managerial effectiveness (Luthans et al., 1988).

This chapter focuses on the manager's role as conflict resolver. It is based on the meta-principle that negotiation and mediation processes, when used appropriately, enhance managers' effectiveness in resolving many of the conflicts that confront them at work. Although written from a normative perspective that is based on research findings, the chapter also explores descriptive information concerning what is known about the ways managers tend to deal with conflict.

HOW MANAGERS ATTEMPT TO RESOLVE CONFLICTS

Past research has identified three ways in which conflicts or disputes may be resolved: (1) interests, (2) rights, and (3) power (Ury, Brett, and Goldberg, 1988). First, parties may seek to reconcile conflicts by finding solutions that will appeal to the most important interests of most of those involved in the dispute. Ury et al.'s second way to settle disputes is focused on "rights". In this method, managers determine whose "rights" they want to satisfy, through the assessment of some independent standard. The standard must be legitimate for all involved. Examples of such standards include contracts, or even socially accepted norms such as reciprocity and precedence, or existing guidelines created by the organization to resolve such disputes. The third approach towards conflict resolution focuses on power. Parties may attempt to resolve conflicts according to who is more powerful, or influential in the organization. Power can be defined as the ability to force through ordering or suggesting the other party to do things he/she would not otherwise do. Unfortunately, however, as Ury et al. (1988) observes, power differentials are generally difficult to reconcile without a costly "test of wills."

Fortunately, the work of Ury et al. (1988) also provides some assistance in assessing the effectiveness of conflict resolution methods.

THE RELATIVE EFFECTIVENESS OF RESOLUTION METHODS

One method of assessing the effectiveness of different conflict resolution methods is to consider the "costs of disputing." Costs of disputing include: (1) various transaction expenses, including those that are economic, psychological, and time based; (2) parties' satisfaction with the fairness of the outcomes and of the resolution process in general; (3) the effect of the resolution on the parties' relationship, particularly on their ability to work together on a day-to-day basis; and finally (4) the likelihood of conflict recurrence, either between the two parties or between one of them and another party. Once assessing method effectiveness vis-à-vis these four criteria, Ury et al. (1988, p. 15) concluded that: "in general reconciling interests is less costly than determining whose rights are more clearly supported by the contract or precedent, which in turn is less costly than determining who is more powerful," a process likely to result in the drawn-out battle of wills mentioned earlier. However, rights and power may sometimes be used to enhance the effectiveness of interest reconciliation by setting boundaries around what will be determined through the reconciliation of interests. Thus, a sales manager might well use his or her legitimate power (see Chapter 19) to establish monetary limits on the size of the account that sales representatives involved in a dispute about account ownership might resolve through negotiation or to develop a process determining the percentage of revenues that particular divisions might lay claim to when revenues exceed 10 million. Overall, evidence seems to support the relative effectiveness of reconciling parties' interests as an appropriate conflict resolution method for managers. This conclusion brings us to the topic of negotiation.

Negotiation as a Managerial Tool for Reconciling Interests

Negotiation is a frequently applied technique for reconciling interests. It may be extremely useful to managers when their perceived or actual interests are directly in conflict with interests of others in the workplace. Others include managers' employees, their bosses, and those outside their chain of command, for example the support staff charged with the operations of various management systems in the organization, for example budget, human resources, etc. As Lax and Sebenius (1986, p. 2) have noted, "Negotiation is a useful skill for important occasions, but it also lies at the core of the manager's job. Managers' negotiate not only to win contracts but also to guide enterprises in the face of change."

Negotiation is defined as "the situation where parties, with some apparent conflict, seek to do better through jointly decided action than they could do otherwise" (Lax and Sebenius, 1986, p. 12). There are essentially two types of negotiation: (1) distributive or win/lose and (2) collaborative or win/win. The body of research on the nature and effects of negotiation is quite substantial. Because collaborative negotiation is best used in situations: (1) where a long-term, rather than a short-term relationship exists, or is envisioned between parties; (2) when those involved share important values or principles that shape their goals in the negotiation; and (3) where there are a number of different issues at stake, such that the likelihood of creating a situation of joint gain is higher, we strongly argue that this type of negotiation is better than distributive in resolving the kinds of conflict in which managers are frequently involved. Thus, in this chapter, we provide a number of principles about the nature of collaborative negotiation and also generate several recommendations for enhancing managers' negotiation effectiveness.

Negotiation principles and recommendations

Which negotiating styles of behavior tend to enable managers to "do better through joint action?" Work by Fisher, Ury, and Patten (Fisher, Ury, and Patten, 1991) at the Harvard Negotiation School have found that higher joint gains frequently result from *collaborative negotiation* focused on achieving the interests of both parties. Principles of collaborative negotiation include:

1. Parties' should engage in a candid and open exchange of information about both their interests.
2. Each party should intend to satisfy the other's interests to some degree such that the focal party's (the manager's) interests are satisfied to the greatest extent and the other party's interests are satisfied at least to an acceptable degree.
3. Both parties should be *creative* in identifying many possible options that might satisfy the other party's interests.
4. Parties should rely on external standards, facts, or criteria to resolve disputes over the value of various options (e.g. the use of the Blue Book to determine used car values).

5. Parties should identify and try to enhance a "BATNA," the best alternative to a negotiated solution, in order to enhance their ability to "do better through nego-tiating," than through other methods, because they will not be forced to accept an undesirable offer simply to reach agreement. Thus the key idea of a BATNA is to have a very strong alternative that you can move to if your existing partner does not meet your important interests or goals. During negotiation, parties should communi-cate with one another in ways that enhance their relationship by focusing on resolv-ing the issues, rather than singling out one another for disdain and contempt (see also Chapter 18), and working hard to improve their relationship so that negotiation is easier for subsequent conflicts; at the very least, the communication used in nego-tiation should not worsen the relationship.

Recommendations for negotiating collaboratively

1. Take stock of your own interests to make sure you understand and can prioritize them. What is it you want out of this negotiation? Prioritize your interests so you will be ready to make some tradeoffs if necessary. Set higher goals for what you would like to walk away with – research shows they tend to yield higher gains.
2. Begin the bargaining with a positive overture, perhaps by making a small concession – then reciprocate the other party's concessions but not at the cost of abandoning your own.
3. Look beneath the other party's behavioral tactics (bluffing, silence) and try to deter-mine his or her strategy. Even threats and power plays can be intended to guide you toward a mutually acceptable agreement. Be sensitive to this and follow it if it is beneficial to your interests.
4. Do not allow accountability to your constituents (e.g. your manager or your employ-ees) or surveillance by them to spawn highly aggressive competitive bargaining; it often spirals quickly out of control, making joint gains impossible.
5. If you have power (whether greater expertise, legitimate, referent, etc.), in a nego-tiation, use it – with specific demands, mild threats, and persuasion – to guide the other party toward an agreement (see also Chapter 19).
6. Be open to accepting third party assistance to reach agreement (more on this below).
7. Attend to the negotiation environment. Be aware that your behavior and power as well as that of the other party are altered by it. Opponents who come from environ-ments of scarce resources are often rewarded for highly competitive and aggres-sive bargaining. Anticipate this and strive to protect your interests (Wall and Blum, 1991).
8. Negotiation tends to be more efficient (faster, more likely to reach agreement) and more likely to yield agreements in the interests of both parties (collaborative nego-tiations) when they have positive working relationships. Thus, strive to develop a positive working relationship with your negotiation partner. Design situations in which you both depend on one another for help across a number of issues and opportunities for action. When working relationships are already strained, suggest problem-solving workshops to improve them before beginning the negotiations.
9. Teams of negotiators often respond more competitively than do individuals. Be alert to the possibility that when teams are involved, contentious behavior is more likely to

spiral and escalate the conflict. Also internal conflict within a team will lower the likelihood of reaching agreement between the two parties. Strive to minimize within team conflict before between-group negotiations start (Chapter 18). Try to align the thinking on your own team before starting. Note that you may have to use coercive power to obtain compliance from members who are less attached to the group, while conciliation techniques – explanation, reciprocal favors, concessions – often work for members with a greater sense of group commitment (see again Chapter 19).

10. Compared to face-to-face negotiations, e-negotiations (computer mediated) generate: (a) more multi-issue offers, (b) less rapport in the relationship, (c) mixed findings on the creation of joint gain, meaning some studies show better results with face-to-face negotiations and some show no difference between face-to-face and e-negotiations, and (d) more equal gains for both parties. However, by enhancing e-negotiations with schmoozing, such as brief personal disclosure and short telephone calls prior to negotiations, negotiators are able to decrease the use of aggressive strategies that reduce their outcomes. In addition, schmoozing tends to: (a) increase cooperation, trust, and relationship quality; (b) improve joint outcomes; and (c) reduce the likelihood of impasse (Thompson and Nadler, 2002).

THIRD PARTY ROLES: THE MANAGER AS MEDIATOR

Not only do managers have to resolve conflicts where they are directly involved as a participating party, but they often have to resolve it when they are indirectly involved and affected, for example the case where two employees from the manager's work group are engaged in a dispute. How do managers respond in these situations? Research by Sheppard (1984) indicates that they choose one of four third party modes of conflict resolution based on four criteria: (1) efficiency: whether the action taken will resolve the conflict with a minimal amount of resources, for example their time, employees' time, expense, etc.; (2) effectiveness: whether the action will insure the conflict is solved well and remains solved (see Chapter 23) – for example, using a mode of resolution that involves listening to all parties' views, and then brainstorming an appropriate solution minimizes the re-emergence of the conflict; (3) participant satisfaction: whether the action will insure that parties are satisfied with the outcome – one way joint satisfaction is achieved is by letting both parties present their views and then inventing a solution that satisfies both of them; (4) fairness: whether the action will solve the dispute in a way that the parties believe is fair according to some external standard. Research has shown that when choosing which actions to take, managers typically weight efficiency and effectiveness higher than the other criteria. Furthermore, research shows emphasizing efficiency and effectiveness encourages managers to attempt to take control of the conflict situation, a situation we examine below that suboptimizes potential outcomes to the parties themselves and their organization.

Sheppard (1984) proposed a four-fold classification system for the modes in which third parties, such as managers, may intervene in conflicts. His system is based on high and low levels of procedural and outcome control by the third party (the manager in our case) and is supported by at least two studies. The classification system and study results are shown below:

1. **Inquisitorial Intervention** (High process control/high outcome control) – in this mode, managers actively control the discussion between parties, frequently directing what is said, and they control the outcome by inventing and enforcing a

solution that they believe will meet both parties' needs, much like an inquisitor or benevolent parent. Sheppard and his colleagues (Sheppard, 1984; Lewicki and Sheppard, 1985) found that the managers tend to use this method of intervention most frequently.

2. **Adversarial Intervention/Judge** (Low process control/high outcome control) – in this mode, a manager decides how the conflict will be resolved and enforces the resolution if needed. However, the manager does not try to actively control the process. Rather he or she allows the parties to determine how they wish to present information about the conflict, listens to the information presented and then makes a decision. This style was the second most frequent used by managers.

3. **Avoiders, Delegators, Impetus Providers/Motivating** (Low process control, low outcome control) – for this mode, a manager may totally ignore the conflict, delegate it to others such as human resources or lower level managers to resolve or try to motivate the parties themselves to resolve it by asking, "What is going on here?" and then signaling the parties that strong punishment will be forthcoming if they don't solve their own dispute. This was the third most common mode of third party intervention.

4. **Mediation** (High process control/low outcome control – in this mode a manager controls the process through which parties reveal information about their conflict but does not attempt to control the decision concerning how the conflict will be resolved. Mediation was virtually unused by the mangers studied.

What then are the effects of these different interventions?

EFFECTS OF DIFFERENT INTERVENTION MODES

Research on the effects of mode usage indicates that a greater reliance on the mediator mode of conflict resolution is likely to enhance managers' effectiveness the most in resolving third party conflicts. Managers' use of a particular mode has important implications, not only for the content of the resolution obtained, but also for the disputing parties' perceptions of the fairness of the outcome and the procedure used.

The bottom line is that those managers who use the mediator mode tended to produce compromise outcomes that incorporate at least some of each party's interests, while those who used other modes, for example questioning parties, opposing their perspectives of the conflict, threatening to resolve it unilaterally if they did not, etc., tended to produce outcomes favoring one of the conflicting parties over the other (Karambayya and Brett, 1989). Not surprisingly, employees were more satisfied when their interests were either favored in the outcome, or when they experienced a compromise outcome. Further, those who experienced the mediator mode of third party resolution tended to perceive that the conflict outcome, resolution process, and mediator were fairer than did those who experienced the other three modes of inquisitor, judge, or the combined avoiding/delegating/providing impetus mode. Parties' fairness perceptions are important (see Chapters 14 and 21) because they have been shown to impact the effectiveness of conflict resolution, that is, to strengthen the relationship between parties, and aid in preventing a recurrence of the conflict (Karambayya, Brett, and Lytle, 1992). Therefore, even though managers show a tendency to resolve conflict in ways that allow them greater control over the outcome implemented, such as inquisitor or judge, these are *not* the best approaches. Instead, using these modes increases the risk that managers will produce solutions that undermine the relationship between parties. This tends to erode the conflict resolution and to prevent the parties themselves from working together effectively to resolve their own conflicts in the future.

WHY MANAGERS FAIL TO USE THE MEDIATION MODE

Why do managers use modes of conflict resolution other than mediation, even though, as discussed above, they tend to be suboptimal. Modes that provide managers with greater control over the outcome of the conflict, such as inquisitor and judge, are more likely to be used in cases where time pressures for settlement are severe and the settlement will have broad implications for the resolution of other disputes in the work unit or organization. Other factors increasing managers' tendency to take greater control of outcome of the dispute include: whether the manager will have to interact with disputing parties again in the future (if yes, the manager will assume greater control); whether the manager possesses formal authority over the conflicting parties (i.e. their own employees rather than peers – if yes, the manager will assume greater control); and the amount of experience a manager has supervising employees – less experienced managers assume greater control (Lewicki and Sheppard, 1985; Karambayya et al., 1992).

Two other overarching explanations for managers' tendency to suboptimize conflict resolution in cases where they are the third party only indirectly involved are, first, that they tend to attribute the cause of the conflict to parties' personality dysfunctions, rather than to differing goals or interests, and then assume it is their job to intervene in conflicts quickly and directly. These factors are likely to discourage the manager's use of a mediating style for conflict resolution (Kolb, 1986; Kolb and Sheppard, 1985). Finally, managers are unlikely to rely on mediation to resolve third party conflict because they lack the basic behavioral skills to do so. Thus, we discuss the types of mediation behaviors that managers may use and which works best, when.

TYPES OF MEDIATION BEHAVIOR

Research has confirmed three types of mediator behavior – diagnostic (formerly called reflexive by the researchers, Kressel and Pruitt, 1985), contextual, and substantive interventions. However, it is important to note prior to discussing these that employees' reactions to managers' attempts to mediate conflicts at work tend to be more positive when the disputing individuals are allowed some time to resolve the conflict on their own, without mediation. Quick intervention in a conflict between employees by a manager attempting to mediate is likely to violate the employees' sense of due process, their perceptions of fairness, and, subsequently, the longevity and effectiveness of any agreement reached (Conlon and Fasolo, 1990).

That being said, the following types of mediation interventions are applicable at different points in the mediation episode; thus a mediator might use all of them in a single mediation or simply one or two, based on his or her judgment that the parties require more or less assistance in resolving their own dispute. We begin with "Diagnostic" mediation interventions as they tend to be used first in a mediation episode.

Diagnostic interventions occur early in the mediation process and involve the manager's attempt to become familiar with the conflict between the parties, bond with them, and establish ground rules for parties' behavior that will prevent the conflict from escalating until the manager understands it better. The manager then attempts to diagnose the nature of the conflict and the types of tactics that are likely to result in agreement. Although it is commonly accepted that mediators must be neutral and disinterested in the conflicts of the parties they assist, mediator neutrality does not appear to be as important as previously believed. Many times mediators are chosen because of their relationship with one party (e.g. labor mediation). Thus, they are able to influence the conflict because they have an interest in the way it is resolved.

Contextual interventions consist of managers' attempts to impact the process through which the two parties interact with one another to discuss, negotiate, and resolve their conflict. It does not address the content of the conflict resolution but instead focuses on issues such as climate, structure, conflict within each party's team, etc. At the most basic level, contextual interventions are intended to encourage parties to persist in their efforts to resolve the conflict, help them to engage in problem solving and get them to the point of developing their own solution. Thus, this type of intervention may address issues of poor communication, facilitate effective discussion sessions that diffuse anger and keep parties focused on the problem that faces them, and perhaps even establish joint fact finding so that both parties will accept the results.

Substantive interventions concern how the mediator deals directly with the issues in conflict between the parties. These behaviors tend to occur later during the mediation process and include the exploration of potential compromises, the suggestion of possible agreements, and assistance in evaluating the pros and cons of various proposals.

In general, research (Lim and Carnevale, 1990) indicates that all three types of intervention are effective with one exception. At *very* high levels of conflict, only the diagnostic intervention remains effective, probably because it helps build trust between the mediator and parties and provides both with a better understanding of the nature of the conflict. However, at very high levels of conflict, both contextual and substantive interventions tend to decrease parties' likelihood of reaching agreement, probably because the parties view them as attempts to undermine their key interests.

In addition, there are active versus passive approaches that underlie the three interventions discussed above (Lim and Carnevale, 1990). These approaches refer to the mediators' level of assertiveness or forcefulness in enacting any of the three types of interventions. Mediators often exert considerable pressure on the parties to agree to specific proposals, particularly in cases where the mediator's own interests or values are involved, he or she feels pressure to avoid the high costs of litigation, or very high levels of tension or hostility exist between parties. In general, research indicates that an assertive mediator approach is positively associated with the incidence of settlement rather than a stalemate. Thus, mediators should tend to use all three interventions in an assertive, rather than passive manner.

Summary: Third Party Conflict Resolution and Mediation Principles and Recommendations

Below is a summary of several principles from managers' use of third party conflict resolution modes at work:

1. When managers choose to mediate the dispute between parties at work, employees or peers, many favorable results occur from the mediator approach. They include high, shared perceptions of fairness in the process, an acceptance of a proposed settlement, and a settlement that reflects the interests of both parties. In addition, parties' fairness perceptions positively affect the nature of their relationship with the mediator, and decrease the likelihood that conflict will recur.

2. Nevertheless, managers show strong tendencies to question parties about the causes of the conflict, to challenge their approaches to resolving it, and to unilaterally decide the dispute if parties can't resolve it themselves – all behaviors that deliver poorer results than does well-implemented mediation.

3. Managers' tendencies to unilaterally solve disputes between employees increase when time is scarce, the conflict has implications for the rest of their unit or for the organization, and disputing parties will not have to work together in the future.

Thus, we recommend that managers interested in pursuing a mediation mode of conflict resolution should act assertively and use:

1. Diagnostic interventions that increase each party's trust of the manager's fairness, also increase the likelihood of the manager's identifying the underlying causes of the conflict, and his or her display of behaviors most likely to result in settlement.

2. Contextual interventions that facilitate communication between parties, help to diffuse anger and other intense emotions, assist in identifying the most important issues of dispute, provide for the systematic discussion of issues and incremental agreement, and develop a joint, unbiased process for locating information needed to resolve the conflict.

3. Substantive interventions that propose solutions to the conflict that may have escaped the attention of the parties while also assuring them that the choice of solutions will be left up to them.

4. Contextual and substantive interventions to first address the within-group conflict when it is internal to the organization within groups of employees.

Exceptions to the Recommendations

There are notable exceptions to the recommendations provided within this chapter for enhancing the effectiveness of managers' negotiation and mediation skills. For negotiations, the recommendations are limited to parties who rationally seek out solutions that will enhance and maintain their own interests. When conflicting parties act irrationally by showing little concern for important interests, earlier recommendations provided in the negotiation section of this chapter are unlikely to prove effective. Irrational behavior could be inspired by intense anger or latent hostility, drug or alcohol abuse, psychosis, or constraints placed on the party by their constituents. An example of negotiating with an irrational party is provided in the case illustration below and the sequel that follows. In a similar vein, when negotiators hold different principles about what constitutes fairness in negotiation procedures and outcomes, prior negotiation recommendations made in this chapter are unlikely to result in agreements. Such differences may result from past negotiation experiences that were quite distributive, i.e. win–lose of differences in equity sensitivity. In any event, when differences in definitions of fairness vary between parties, they often become hostile and rigid, and are unwilling to concede any option that is acceptable to the other; thus no agreement is reached and a stalemate generally occurs as well as a decrease in the quality of the relationship (Pruitt, Pierce, Zubeck, McGillicuddy, and Welton, 1991).

In the case of the manager as mediator, it is important to realize that most types of mediation behavior tend to be more effective under moderate levels of conflict, rather than extremely high or low levels. At very high or very low levels of conflict, the probability that either contextual or substantive mediation interventions will lead to an agreement diminishes rapidly (Kressel and Pruitt, 1985). Similarly, very low levels of conflict also tend to weaken the positive settlement effects of mediation interventions. Mediation is likely to result in cooperation and agreement by the involved parties only when they are motivated by sufficiently high levels of conflict to bargain and resolve their conflict (Wall and Blum, 1990). Finally, employees are likely to react more positively to managers' mediation attempts when they are first allowed some time to resolve the conflict on their own. Quick intervention by a manager attempting mediation is likely to violate the employees' sense of due process and their perceptions of fairness. Subsequently, it is also likely to affect the longevity and effectiveness of any agreement reached (Conlon and Fasolo, 1990). Having examined some possible exceptions or boundary conditions to mediation we further illustrate the application of the concepts through the use of a case study and its sequel several years later.

CASE EXAMPLES

Negotiating with irrational folks: the case of Jay Leno's agent

An excellent illustration of what happens when rational managers attempt to negotiate conflicts with irrational parties is provided in the book *The Late Show*. *The Late Show* discusses the David Letterman and Jay Leno battle for late night TV. According to the author, Bill Carter (1994), this negotiation was highly influenced by the persona of Leno's long-time agent, Helen Kushnick. It was Helen who helped Jay, not initially liked or favored by NBC *Tonight Show* host Johnny Carson, attain an edge over Carson's preferred choice, David Letterman. Realizing that NBC affiliate stations would have considerable influence in any decision about a new host for the *Tonight Show*, Kushnick convinced Jay to conduct several cross-country tours where he appeared live on many NBC affiliates and devoted considerable time to building rapport with their owners and managers. The support of the NBC affiliates, as well NBC executives' belief that Jay's personality and style of comedy were better suited to a long-term run on NBC's *Tonight Show* than were David Letterman's, ultimately clinched the deal for him. On May 16, 1991, Leno signed a lucrative agreement making him host of the *Tonight Show* on the departure of Johnny Carson. This contract also named Helen Kushnick as the executive producer on the show.

An understanding of the negotiations that unfold below requires some background on Helen Kushnick's negotiation style, personality, and relationship with Jay Leno. Helen's style was one of extreme contending. She had experienced much sadness during her adult life including the death of one of her twins. Her only son died while still an infant as the result of an AIDs infected blood transfusion. In 1989, shortly after her son's death, her husband died from colon cancer. Furthermore, Helen was ill with breast cancer and was undergoing chemotherapy at the time of the negotiations. On his deathbed, Jerry Kushnick, Helen's husband, asked Jay Leno to take care of his wife and his 11-year-old daughter. Jay consented and then publicly repeated his promise at the funeral. According to her close associates, Helen's style never faltered in the face of these overwhelming obstacles, it just became more intense. Carter noted, "She didn't become beaten or bowed; she just became more determined, more driven, more ferociously focused than ever before" (Carter, 1994, p. 171). Angered by Johnny Carson's rejection of Jay, Helen secretly started a rumor that NBC was going to drop Carson for Jay. This rumor caused incredible tension between the network and Carson for a period of time before his retirement.

Once Jay Leno took over as *Tonight Show* host in 1991, NBC executives were surprised to find that he appeared stiff and uncomfortable in the host slot. He was without the spontaneity and humor that had consistently characterized his guest spots. Many attributed this change in style to Helen's influence on the show as executive producer. Angered by Carson's rejection of Jay and his refusal to invite Jay to appear on any of the final shows before his retirement, Helen repeatedly rejected NBC executives' request that Jay make a complimentary statement about Carson and his career on Jay's first show. The absence of such a statement was conspicuously noted in all the press given to Jay's opening and a source of embarrassment to him and to NBC. Helen went on to attempt to choreograph Jay's movements on the set, making them appear stiff, formal, and affected. She placed the blue-collar comic in expensive designer suits, and erupted in a tirade of name-calling and endless criticism of anyone who tried to question these changes. Soon her attacks extended to Jay himself; she publicly and privately belittled him and attacked his comedy and his intelligence. Jay never responded to the attacks or even appeared embarrassed by them. However, many on the *Tonight Show* felt that the effects of Helen's attacks were apparent in Jay's shaky appearance on the set, particularly during the opening monolog. Further, Helen undertook a bloodletting campaign to protect Jay from the competition by blacklisting the signing of any guests who appeared on Arsenio Hall's show. Disliking Jerry Seinfeld, one of Jay's closest friends, she denied Seinfeld's request to use the *Tonight Show* set. She further denied the scheduling of a surprise guest appearance by Jay on Seinfeld's own show. She even blacklisted Seinfeld himself, the host of one of NBC's most popular shows, from the *Tonight Show* until NBC executive Warren Littlefield personally intervened.

Time and time again during this period, Helen ignored the pleas of NBC executives to tone down her "Winner Take All" approach. Her approach was belittling the network's image and its long-term relationships with distinguished guests. However, Helen refused, and actually intensified her destructive activities. She was confident that her hold on Leno would prevent NBC from ever firing her. She believed if she was fired Jay would leave the show as well. At first she was right. Ignoring NBC's multiple requests that Helen be fired,

Jay instead asked the network to write out a list of what was acceptable for Helen to do and not do. Shortly afterward in the middle of a meeting, the executives and Jay watched as Helen's form morphed from cool, controlled, and rational into a lotus form accompanied with screaming and rocking. Warren Littlefield, the President of NBC, then told Leno that she was totally out of control and had to go. Still, Jay was reluctant to cut the 17-year bond between them. Leno refused to assure Littlefield that he would show up for work if Helen were fired. Finally, Jay learned that Helen had started the rumor that NBC would replace Carson with Leno. This was a rumor he had personally denied starting, even when speaking to Johnny Carson himself. His support for Helen began to crumble. He signaled Littlefield that he would do the show, with or without Kushnick.

On Monday morning when Helen arrived for work, the network handed her a letter of dismissal. Still, Jay refused to support the action, issuing press releases that he supported Ms. Kushnick. He hoped to duck the conflict until after that day's show was taped, but Helen confronted him in his dressing room. She was raging and screaming so loud that she could be heard throughout the set. When these tactics failed to work, she came at Leno with emotion, arguing that he had to quit the *Tonight Show* for Sarah, her daughter's sake. At this point, even Jay had had enough. He broke a glass cover on his desk to stop the tirade, refused to quit, and went on to display a dazzling performance on that night's show. Helen stormed off the studio lot shortly after the filming began, leaving Jay's direction in the hands of others. As soon as she left, NBC barred her from the set, posting little photos of her at all the studio gates.

Helen Kushnick's behavior provides a perfect illustration of the way in which irrational negotiators use threats and intimidation to obtain their own way and ignore even courteous entreaties from the other party to maintain a long and valued relationship. Clearly unable to see the impact of her behavior on the interests the network held supreme, Helen simply grew more and more confident that she could do whatever she pleased. She believed because she held power over Jay Leno, the network star, she could do whatever she wanted regardless of no matter how negatively it impacted her long-term interests or those of the network. Time and time again, she chose to satisfy short-term emotional needs, rather than preserve the long-term interests and relationship at stake. As shown here, neither collaborative win–win nor contending win–lose approaches tend to work with irrational negotiators. Instead, a party caught up in this kind of exchange is generally better off to find a strong BATNA (meaning the "Best Alternative to a Negotiated Agreement," see Negotiation Principles), or satisfying alternative, and exit the relationship without agreement.

Sequel: Jay Leno's own upcoming departure from NBC

Fast-forward 16 years after Jay Leno's succession to Johnny Carson in 1992. We find an incredibly successful comedian whose own upcoming succession by Conan O'Brien in 2009 appears right on target. Jay exemplifies the same workaholic he has been throughout his reign. However, he apparently learned a great deal from his own gut-wrenching ascension to the primer NBC *Tonight* talk show host at the expense of David Letterman, who subsequently went to CBS where his current contract expires in 2010. In 2001, however, when Jay's late night coworker, Conan O'Brien, expressed his desire to work at an earlier hour, Jay was at one of the many highpoints in his ratings and career. What might have evolved into another fistfight negotiation that took no prisoners at NBC instead was easily averted with a deal that focused on the needs and interests of both parties. Jay got a contract for another five years after promising to step down in time to make way for Conan in 2009. While Conan, despite his eagerness, agreed to sit tight in his late night position for another half decade in exchange for a guaranteed two-year stint at the prime NBC *Tonight Show* spot. By all accounts, this friendly, collaborative agreement was largely due to the graciousness and hard-earned negotiation insights of Jay himself. He was heard to remark that during his earlier battle with Letterman for the *Tonight* slot, "A lot of good friendships were permanently damaged." "Quite frankly, I don't want to see anybody go through that again" (Sheppard, 2004). In fact Jay termed the new deal "the world's easiest negotiation" and followed with "I like what I do. They were very generous." In fact, Leno neither sought nor received an ownership stake in the show, even though Letterman and Carson have/had partial ownership. Instead, he cited his loyalty to Jack Welch, then CEO of General Electric, parent company to NBC, commenting, "I'm a handshake guy. I work for Jack. He was loyal to me, and I am to him" (Carter, 2001).

As the transition date, expected to be May 2009, approaches, Jay Leno at 58 is at the top of his game. He's the reigning champion of late night television and continues to report that he is leaving NBC as promised. However, Leno has given no indication that he will do anything but continue to be a comedian, stating, "What I do is tell jokes at 11:30 at night." Meanwhile senior executives at ABC, Fox, and Sony Studios have begun to circle Leno, making discrete, but highly lucrative, bids that will allow Leno to do what he does and enjoys best. His attorney, Kenneth Ziffren, states, "Jay, will of course, honor his contract obligations to NBC." "Jay isn't talking to anyone about anything and won't be until it's contractually proper" (Carter, 2008).

Jay Leno remains one classy, incredibly talented comedian who learned the pitfalls of irrational negotiations the hard way from his bulldozer agent Helen Kusnick. As a result he is now an expert negotiator in his own right. We can certainly expect that his next deal will be a very profitable one, yet one also centered on his primary interest, "telling jokes at 11:30 at night."

References

Carter, B. (1994). *The Late Shift*. NY: Hyperion Press.

Carter, B. (2001). Leno signs for 5 year of 'Tonight'. *New York Times*, January 11.

Carter, B. (2008). Suiters are set to say to Leno, long live the king. *New York Times*, February 27, Late Edition.

Conlon, D. E., and Fasolo, P. M. (1990). Influence of speed of third-party intervention and outcome on negotiator and constituencies fairness judgments. *Academy of Management Journal*, 33, 833–846.

Fisher, R., Ury, W., and Patten, B. (1991). *Getting to Yes*. NY: Penguin Books.

Karambayya, R., and Brett, J. M. (1989). Managers handling disputes. *Academy of Management Journal*, 32, 6897–6704.

Karambayya, R., Brett, J. M., and Lytle, A. (1992). Effects of formal authority and experience on third party roles, outcomes and perceptions of fairness. *Academy of Management Journal*, 35, 426–438.

Kolb, D. (1986). Who are organizational third parties and what do they do? In Bazerman, M. A., Lewicki, R. A., and Sheppard, B. H. (eds), *Research on Negotiations in Organizations*, vol 1, JAI: Greenwich CT, 207–228.

Kolb, D., and Sheppard, B. (1985). Do managers mediate or even arbitrate? *Negotiation Journal*, 1, 379–388.

Kressel, K., and Pruitt, D. G. (1985). Themes in the mediation of social conflict. *Journal of Social Issues*, 41, 179–198.

Lax, D. A., and Sebenius, J. K. (1986). *The Manager as Negotiator*. NY: Free Press.

Lewicki, R. J., and Sheppard, B. H. (1985). Choosing how to intervene. *Journal of Occupational Behavior*, 6, 49–64.

Lim, R. G., and Carnevale, P.J. (1990). Contingencies in the mediation of disputes. *Journal of Personality and Social Psychology*, 58, 259–272.

Luthans, F., Hodgetts, R., and Rosenkrantz, L. (1988). *Real Managers*. New York: Harper Row.

Pruitt, D. G., Pierce, R. S., Zubeck, J. M., McGillicuddy, N. B., Welton, G. L. (1991). Determinants of short-term and long-term success in mediation. In Sorchel, S. and Simpson, J. A. (eds), *Conflict Between People and Peoples*. Chicago: Nelson Hall.

Sheppard, B. H. (1984). Third party conflict intervention: A procedural framework. In *Research in Organizational Behavior*, 6, JAI Press, 141–190.

Sheppard, B. H. (2004). Tonight without a fight. *Broadcasting and Cable*, October 4, p. 32.

Thomas, K. (1976). Conflict and conflict management. In M. D. Dunnette's *Handbook of Industrial/Organizational Psychology* (pp. 889–935). Chicago: Rand McNally.

Thompson, L., and Nadler, J. (2002). Negotiating via information technology: Theory and application. *Journal of Social Issues*, 58, 109–124.

Ury, W. L., Brett, J. M., and Goldberg, S. J. (1988). *Getting Disputes Resolved*. San Francisco: Jossey-Bass.

Wall, J. A., and Blum, M. W. (1991). Negotiations. *Journal of Management*, 17, 273–303.

EXERCISES

Negotiating an apartment rental in a college town: an exercise stressing the principles of and recommendations for collaborative negotiation

Introduction. This scenario asks you to adopt a collaborative negotiation style and start to work negotiating your first off-campus apartment. To simplify things for first-time role players, the negotiation involves one main issue – the price of renting/leasing an apartment. The negotiation has two roles: (a) the owner landlord and (b) the student who is a potential renter. You will be negotiating the cost of monthly rent as well as terms of benefits/services for the lease. There is additional information you can use to leverage your negotiation and obtain the best deal for your role. However, it is important that you use your confidential role information to determine how attractive various offers made by your partner are to you.

Background information. You are negotiating the terms of a lease for an unfurnished, one bedroom, and one bathroom apartment. The lease comes with three benefits/services free, while the other benefits/services are allowed at an additional negotiated price. The landlord must allow three benefits/services to be included free of charge. The landlord is allowed to deny any service/benefit. The landlord decides if a security deposit is necessary. You must negotiate your lease combination as well as the monthly rent payments. The city of College Park lists the monthly rent of comparable apartments as averaging $650.

Below is a list of possible benefits/services:

◆ Parking privileges for tenants and guests
◆ Safety: alarm system installed
◆ Safety: insurance for anything stolen
◆ Rodents, insects: exterminator fees
◆ Air conditioning and heating
◆ Allowance of pets on premise/in apartment
◆ Maintenance problems: agree to fix maintenance problems (negotiable) within a timely (negotiable) manner
◆ Furniture: apartment comes furnished
◆ Utilities: gas and electric bundle
◆ Utilities: water and basic cable and internet (not wireless) bundle

Role A:

Student renter. The tenant is currently a student at the University of Maryland and is looking for an apartment to live in the College Park area. The university is going through a housing shortage and has decided to "kick" all upper classmen off campus. You don't have a car, and need a place to live. Since you don't have a car, this landlord's apartment would be ideal. The landlord apartments are the only ones within 5 minute walking distance of the university. However, there are other apartments a little bit further. The maximum you can afford is $900/month. You want to get the most benefits/services for the least amount of money.

Role B:

Landlord: You want to lease your apartment out for the highest price with the least amount of benefits/services. Each service requires additional money from you to pay the workers. The university housing shortage has created a demand in off-campus housing. In addition, the economy isn't doing well. The competition is steep from the surrounding landlords, so you want to ensure you lease out your apartment. Furthermore, you need to establish a long-term relationship with the renter. You want to utilize the renter as a resource to network future business opportunities. In addition, you want good relations with the renter to ensure future stay. You must negotiate with the renter to determine the appropriate set of benefits/services that will satisfy the student's needs in order to secure the desired amount of profit for yourself.

Negotiating a Spring Break vacation: an exercise stressing both collaborative negotiation principles and recommendations and third party mediation

Part A

Introduction. Part A of this exercise is a negotiation whereby a college student and a travel agent attempt to come to terms on the price and services associated with a Spring Break trip to Acapulco, Mexico. The Spring Break trip includes a party package. You will be negotiating the cost of the Spring Break trip as well as what components will be involved in the Spring Break trip package. There is additional information you can use to leverage your negotiation and to compromise the best deal for your role. However, how closely one matches their roles utility is what will determine how well you did in comparison to the other groups.

Roles: Student and travel agent.

Background information. All trip options include roundtrip fare and hotel stay fare in prices. You will negotiate the length and price of the trip. In addition, you will negotiate the options for the party package combination. The party package must include three options. One option is free (determined through negotiation which one) while the others are available at a negotiable cost. All prices listed are the suggested price and are negotiable. The travel agent has the right to change any price at their discretion.

Basic information:

	Length of trip	
	5 days	*7 days*
Cost	$800	$1,000
Money due at time of booking	$400	$500

Party package information: Based on negotiation; one option is free and any other two options for list price (must have three; can have more)

Other things to consider:

♦ Taxi fare (not all clubs are within walking distance)
♦ Passport (need to renew?)
♦ Doesn't include tourist activities (i.e. jet skiing, parasailing, bungee jumping, cliff diving)
♦ Phone card – phone coverage might not reach into Mexico
♦ Travel protection – can be provided for an additional $68

Role A:

Student: You want to party on Spring Break. Your parents agreed to pay $1000 of your Spring Break vacation. This is money you have upfront. You have saved $300 of your own money, which is available to you upfront as well. You are able to earn an additional $350 before your Spring Break trip. This money will not be available to you until the week before the trip. Your main motivation is to party hard for the least amount of money. You will need to bargain to get the best components out of the package deal. You will highlight the

		Cost	Condition 1	Condition 2	Condition 3	Condition 4	Condition 5
Option 1	Open bar; free drinks at hotel everyday	$150	Need to tip the bartender	Can't bring drinks onto the beach; must stay at hotel pool			
Option 2	VIP Entrance into clubs every night		VIP entrance is instant; regular entrance average wait time for entry 1 hour	Free drinks all night; without VIP pass drinks average $6/drink	Need to tip the bartender to get service	VIP entrance is only for the club specified for that night (different club each night); can't choose which night you get to go to each club	Includes entrance into VIP concert (Fergie, DJ Scribbles, Fat Joe) at club; net worth $100
	5 night option 7 night option	$300 $450					
Option 3	VIP Admittance into day parties	$220	Include admittance into: foam party, booze cruise, beach Olympics, and beach BBQ	Free drinks while at events	Entrance on the day is $30; and drinks without pass are $6/drink		
Option 4	Food vouchers for 7 days	$140	Applicable at certain restaurants only	Modified menu options	Modified portion size	Guaranteed safe; no threat of Montezuma's revenge (intestinal sickness from drinking/eating food prepared in infected water)	Get two a day; can only be used at specified times. Options include: breakfast, lunch, dinner and late night

limitations or drawbacks of the options as well as allude to additional costs not included in the package option deals to get the best price. You want to ensure you have the most opportunities to enjoy yourself as possible. In addition, you can always book with another travel agent.

Role B:

Travel agent: The economy isn't doing well and your salary depends on your ability to fill a plane for Spring Break. You want to book your student's trip at the highest cost. For each trip booked .01% of the total cost of that booked trip is deducted off your next vacation. You want to book the trip quickly in order to maximize the amount of clients you can book. You also want to maintain good relationships with your clients in order to build a network of future clients through the student. Thus you want a happy client who will tell their friends to book with you as well. The more people that book through you, the more money you receive off your next trip. Your main motivation is to emphasize the most expensive options of the party package. You will highlight the benefits of each option and try to convince the student they need all options for the best Spring Break experience. You want to book the student the most expensive trip you can, in a timely manner. You have the power to change the list price for any of the options if doing so aides in your negotiation.

Part B – Mediating a settlement between student and travel agent after a failure to agree

Introduction.   Part B assumes that two days before Spring Break, the student and the travel agent are still unable to reach a mutually satisfying agreement over the Spring Break trip, leaving the student with no vacation options. As a last course of action, the student contacts his/her father, a talented manager in the computer industry and asks for help. The father, an experienced manager who has recently read Chapter 28 agrees to mediate the dispute in order to try to help the parties reach agreement. Please assume the mediator role in this exercise and use the principles and recommendations for third party mediation. Your interests are simply to help your son or daughter settle on an affordable and enjoyable vacation without putting the travel agent at a disadvantage, to strengthen your own mediation skills through practice and to teach both parties something about the value of effectively implemented mediation in resolving conflicts between two parties.

Joint discussion questions for the above exercises

1. What kind of negotiation did you use in the exercises, distributive – win/lose or collaborative – win/win? Why did you choose this type?
2. Which negotiation principles did you rely on most heavily? Why? How well did they work?
3. Did you reach an agreement with your partner? What were the terms? How satisfied were you both with the agreement and what effect do you believe it will have on your ability to work together on a deal again?
4. What was the outcome of the mediation exercise? Why did this outcome occur?

5. Did the mediator assertively apply diagnostic, contextual and substantive interventions during the mediation attempt? What, if any, effect did these behavioral interventions have?
6. What might the mediator have done differently to enhance the likelihood of settlement between the parties?
7. Did any boundary conditions exist that negatively affected the impact of the mediation interventions? Please explain.

29

Sustain Organizational Performance through Continuous Learning, Change and Realignment

Michael Beer

We are living in a world in which the only constant is change. Companies must respond to rapid changes in markets and technology if they are to survive and prosper. Senior executives must, in turn, lead a process of change that develops employee dissatisfaction with the status quo and realigns the organization as a total system with new business realities.

Consider the case of Apple Computer (Beer and Gibbs, 1990). Founded by Steve Jobs and Steve Wozniak in a garage in Silicon Valley in 1977, the company was the first to develop and produce a personal computer. The Apple II, and its successor the Macintosh, led the industry in technology, design, and user friendliness. In 1980 the company had virtually 100% of the market. It had grown 100% a year and was among the fastest growing companies in the world. In 1990 its revenues reached $5.5 billion and employment reached 14,500. By 1997, however, the company's market share was down to 3% and its revenues and number of employees were shrinking. It was also losing money and had lost the race to dominate the personal computer market to Dell, Compaq, and IBM.

Apple's dominance in the computer market declined despite the fact that in 1983 John Scully, at the time President of PepsiCo, was brought in as Apple's new CEO to enable the company to cope with new competitive realities. As we shall see throughout this chapter, Scully failed to lead an organizational learning and change process from which he and his top team could learn about barriers to organizational and leadership effectiveness. His task was to mobilize energy for change among senior executives by creating dissatisfaction with the status quo and then develop a new organization – structure, systems, people, processes, and culture – needed to compete in the volatile computer industry. Such changes would have enabled Apple to develop organizational capabilities and behaviors it did not possess. Though the company had talented and creative technical people it lacked several essential organizational capabilities associated with success in uncertain and rapidly changing environments (Lawrence and Lorsch, 1967; Kotter and Heskett, 1992; Lawler, 1997; Miles and Snow, 1978). They are:[1]

◆ *Coordination* between functions, businesses and geographic regions around businesses and/or customers is essential for speed of response to customer needs and a cost-effective operation. Apple's individualistic culture and lack of cross-functional teams made coordination between marketing, sales and research and development difficult. Consequently, the company failed to recognize and respond to a rapidly growing business market that demanded new and lower cost products.

◆ *Commitment* to customer needs and an economically successful business is essential for any enterprise. Without that commitment employee's interests are not aligned with the purpose of business. Apple's people were committed to technical innovation not meeting customer needs in a changing market. This blinded them to the possibility that a less elegant and lower cost technical solution being introduced by competitors (low cost PCs with a DOS operating system) might succeed.

◆ *Competence* in the activities most critical to success, as well as in management and leadership, are essential. Some companies rely on selling or distribution for success. Others on merchandising. Still others may rely on technical skills in research and development, the capability that made Apple a success in its early years. But without effective leadership and management, firms like Apple cannot mobilize technical and functional competencies into a coordinated effort and results. That was certainly true of Apple Computer. As a result of its rapid growth Apple's technically excellent people were promoted to key positions, but they lacked leadership and management skills to develop the coordination Apple desperately needed to succeed.

◆ *Honest conversations* that enable people at all levels to voice their views and concerns are essential in an uncertain and rapidly changing environment. They enable an airing of differences and lead to a resolution of conflicting views. This in turn ensures good decisions. For this trust and skills in dialog are needed. Top management must communicate to lower level its intended direction and lower levels must feel free to communicate to top management if they believe the direction is flawed or organizational barriers exist to successful implementation. At Apple lower level managers that saw the need for lower cost computers were ignored. Similarly, differences between key functions – at Apple research and development (R&D) and marketing – were never discussed in a way that would enable R&D to understand threats marketing perceived.

◆ *Creativity* and *innovation* in both technical and administrative matters are essential for a business to retain its competitive edge. Apple succeeded largely on the basis of its creativity and innovation in technology. But it lacked the capacity to innovate and change its approaches to organizing and managing people, something that was essential if it was going to succeed in a changing marketplace.

---

[1] The term behavior incorporates the description of actual behaviors as well as the description of attitudes and skills that are proxies for behavior.

Leading organizational change is about defining a new strategic direction for the business and realigning its structure, management processes, systems, people skills, and culture so that needed organizational capabilities required to implement the new direction emerge. Of course, implementing the new direction typically also leads to redefinition of direction as the organization learns through the process of implementation what works and what doesn't work. That is why the behaviors above, particularly open communication and creativity, are so essential to the capacity of the organization to adapt and renew itself. The effectiveness of an effort to lead change should be judged by the extent to which it develops the five Cs – the organizational capabilities listed above – *and* the extent to which it develops the capacity of the organization to renew itself in the future.

The story of Apple illustrates the tendency of all organizations to stop learning and changing in the face of success. Why does this happen to organizations? What are the essential principles of organizational change that leaders in John Scully's position should follow if they are to overcome the natural tendency of organizations to maintain the status quo.

BASIC FACTS ABOUT ORGANIZATIONAL BEHAVIOR AND CHANGE

This section presents basic facts managers must understand about organizational behavior and change if they are to succeed in the difficult task of leading change. They explain why organizations resist change and what is needed to change them (Beer, Eisenstat, and Spector, 1990; Katz and Kahn, 1978; Pfeffer, 1997; Schein, 1990).

Organizations are complex open systems

A variety of organizational facets – structure, human resource policies, management processes, values and skills of people, and the leadership behavior of top management – conspire to produce an organization's distinctive pattern of behavior. These facets are interdependent and are continuously engaged in a process of mutual adaptation to achieve "fit" or congruence with the organization's chosen strategy (Lawrence and Lorsch, 1967). By an open system we mean that the organization is subject to influence by the external environment, largely through the influence of markets, society and/or the larger corporate organization (if the organization is a subunit of a larger corporation).

Figure 29.1 illustrates the key dimensions that must fit together – be aligned – for an organization to be effective. It suggests that organizational behavior is shaped by four forces – the organization's environment and the emergent strategic task the organization must manage to succeed, the organization's design, the people selected and promoted, and the behavior of leaders and their top team. Organizations naturally evolve toward an equilibrium state in which these elements fit tightly. In the short term, fit leads to organizational effectiveness. The organization has developed certain behaviors required for its success and has developed leadership behavior, structures, and systems to cause these behaviors consistently. When the environment changes and places new demands on the organization, leaders must realign the organization to fit new circumstances.

Implicit in this formulation is a contingency perspective. It holds that the best way to organize and manage people depends on the nature of the situation and strategy (Lawrence and Lorsch, 1967; Miles and Snow, 1978). We know for example that the optimal structure

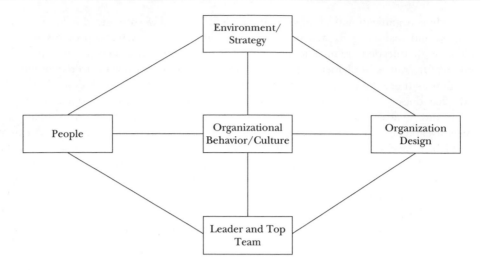

FIGURE 29.1 Organizational alignment model

of an organization depends on the nature of the environment and strategy (Miles and Snow, 1978; Nadler and Tushman, 1988). At the same time there is growing evidence that sustainable advantage depends on organizing and managing people around a set of values and principles including the use of teams, collaboration, symbolic egalitarianism, training and development for employees, and open communication (Pfeffer, 1998; Beer, 2009). The five Cs listed above reflect these findings. The implication is that the change process itself must be aligned with these principles if they are to become embedded in the organization.

ORGANIZATIONAL ALIGNMENT DEVELOPS A DISTINCTIVE AND PERSISTENT CULTURE

Culture is defined as the assumptions, beliefs, values, and resultant behavior leaders invent or discover to solve problems in the external and internal environment. It is what these leaders teach new members as the correct way of perceiving, thinking, and acting to solve problems (Schein, 1985). The tendency of managers to attract, select, and promote people based on how similar they are to those already in the organization increases the strength of the culture (Schneider, 1994). Under the leadership of its founder Steve Jobs, Apple Computer attracted, selected, and promoted employees who were individualistic and committed to elegant technology. This created a strong culture that demanded conformity to these values of and eschewed more pragmatic business considerations.

That companies develop a persistent culture and have difficulty in adapting is evident in the low survival rate of companies (Miller, 1990; Foster and Kaplan, 2001). A substantial number of the Fortune 500 companies 20 years ago – Gulf Oil, Digital Equipment, International Harvester, Scott Paper, US Steel, and Westinghouse – no longer exist.

Organizations vary in the strength of their culture, however. Moreover, subcultures typically exist in various parts and subunits of the organization. Organization change involves confronting the persistent pattern of behavior that is blocking the organization from higher performance, diagnosing its consequences, and identifying the underlying assumptions and values that have created it. That process must go on at the corporate level as well as in multiple businesses and operating units, each with a different strategic task and subculture.

Organizational behavior is resistant to change

Fundamental organizational change calls into question existing patterns of management – the authority, decision rights, and values of existing managers and departments. When a changing environment threatens an organization's capacity to survive, top management is challenged to redefine how it will compete. It must define new objectives and a new strategic task. It should not be surprising that making these changes is painful. Key members of the organization will experience psychological and sometimes material losses (Beer, 1991). Their power and status may diminish. Past relationships may be disrupted. New skills may be required threatening employees' sense of competence and self-esteem as well as their careers and job security. The perception of these potential losses leads to resistance. For example, research and development – the technical function at Apple computer – stood to lose some of its influence in designing products if Apple were to compete more aggressively in selling personal computers to the business market. Consequently, careers, self-esteem, and the very sense of identity and meaning technical people derived from work were also threatened.

All human beings employ emotional and cognitive processes to defend themselves against threat (Argyris and Schon, 1996). Moreover, people make sense of past behavior by forming beliefs that rationalize them and by escalating commitment to them. These common human characteristics prevent managers from learning that their actual behavior – their theory in action – is inconsistent with their stated aspiration – their espoused theory. These human characteristics cause organizational policies, management practices, and leadership behavior and style to persist in the face of new realities unless skills and norms of inquiry and constructive conflict resolution are developed (Argyris and Schon, 1996). All attempts to change organizations must overcome defensiveness of individuals and groups, cause learning to occur, or result in the replacement of individuals not capable of learning. Effective change efforts attempt to maximize the amount of learning and minimize the need for replacement. This enables the organization to retain the wealth of company-specific knowledge about customers, products, and technology and retain commitment that is otherwise lost when key people are replaced.

Substantial evidence exists that many efforts to change organizations do not succeed in making a fundamental transformation in organizational culture (Beer et al., 1990; Schaffer, 1988; Hall, Rosenthal, and Wade, 1993). They produce only superficial change due to the fact that underlying assumptions and beliefs about the business and how it should be managed are not confronted. These change efforts are characterized by wave after wave of programs – education and training initiatives for all employees, continuous changes in structure, the development of mission and value statements, or initiatives such as re-engineering and total quality management.

Consider a large industrial enterprise whose financial performance lagged the industry. Management felt that the cause was the ineffectiveness of its managers. With the help of a new senior human resource, executives hired from a company known for its best human resource practices launched a four week management education program in an effort to change the company. The program's faculty was world class and the content highly relevant including a module on competition and strategy, organizational effectiveness, leadership, and interpersonal skills. The last module of the program involved participants working on analyzing and making recommendations to top management about an important corporate problem. Participants were so enthusiastic about the potential of the program for changing the company that they asked top management to go through the program. They were certain that if the company was to adopt the ways of thinking and doing embedded in the program the corporation would regain its competitive edge. Top management agreed to go through the program. Despite the enthusiasm of all parties involved in the program (faculty, students, and top management) three years later top management and managers who went through the program indicated in interviews and surveys that very little change had occurred in the company's pattern of management.

John Scully's efforts to change Apple Computer also suffered from programmatic change, thereby delaying a dialog about the real underlying problems. During a five-year period, Scully changed the organization's structure four times but coordination between marketing, sales, and R&D and communication between top management and lower levels did not improve, nor did Apple's performance live up to expectations.

Programs fail because the top management team has delegated the task for change to a staff group or consultants. In this way, they avoid the difficult task of confronting the underlying causes of the problems faced by the firm. These are often connected to their own and other managers' assumptions and beliefs about the nature of the business and the best means for organizing and managing people. It is far easier for a CEO to obtain agreement from key people to a program or initiative than it is to breach defenses that block learning about deeper underlying problems. These require leadership – the hard work of confronting problems and developing commitment to change and making difficult decisions about people who will not or cannot change. It should come as no surprise that the capacity to confront conflict has been found to be associated with a firm's ability to succeed in highly uncertain and turbulent environments where the rate of change has to be rapid and continuous (Lawrence and Lorsch, 1967).

FORCES FOR ORGANIZATIONAL CHANGE: DISSATISFACTION AND LEADERSHIP

Given the natural tendency of all management to defend the past and resist change, it has been observed that change does not seem to occur unless a sense of urgency exists among the organization's leaders (Kotter, 1997, 2008). This does not typically occur unless they become highly dissatisfied with the status quo (Beer, 1991). Dissatisfaction with the status quo arises naturally as a result of problems that threaten the firm's performance and even survival. Financial losses, a long and protracted decline in stock price, shrinking market share, loss of a major customer, high employee turnover, or a union strike are all forces that can bring management to a realization that change is needed. The more severe the crisis the higher the dissatisfaction with the status quo and the more energy will be released to take action. And it takes enormous amounts of human energy to confront entrenched assumptions and practices.

Severe problems may not be enough, however. As we saw in the case of Apple Computer, management was able to ignore dramatic changes in their markets and a shrinking market share. The missing ingredient was leadership (Beer, 1991; Kotter, 1997). John Scully was unable to mobilize the commitment to change of key people, particularly his top team. He lacked the courage to engage people in a dialog about historic assumptions, practices, and norms of behavior. Change leaders, it has been found, possess the capacity to confront difficult issues. Indeed, companies that succeed in transforming themselves appear to do so as a result of changes in their top team (Virany, Tushman, and Romanelli, 1992). Leaders, typically new leaders, develop a top management team that is like minded about the need for and the direction of change (Beer and Eisenstat, 1996). A united and effective top team results in improvements in coordination and thereby consistent action across all parts of the organization. Without this, lower level employees perceive an inconsistency between the new direction espoused by top management and their actual behavior. This raises doubts about top management's commitment and makes it unlikely that commitment to change at lower levels will develop.

Consistency between means and ends

There is great variation in the consistency between change ends and means chosen by leaders. To the extent that means contradict the values and practices leaders intend to embed in the future organizational state, people question management's true commitment to the values and practices they espouse. Trust between leaders and lower level people declines. Lowered trust makes it more difficult for leaders to engage people and mobilize commitment to change.

Leaders who intend to develop high performance organizations characterized by the behavior and practices discussed above (good coordination and teamwork, high creativity, open communication, high commitment, and good interpersonal and leadership skills) are not successful unless they *involve people in the change process* (Beer et al., 1990). Contradictions between words and deeds are inevitable, of course, in any complex organizational change process. But a strong bias towards involvement appears to be necessary. Just as importantly, *management's willingness and skills in encouraging lower levels to raise issues of inconsistency* between their (management's) words and their actions builds the trust and partnership with lower levels that high performance organizations typically embody.

How to Lead Change: Seven Steps for Successful Change

The dynamics of organizational behavior and change discussed above translate into *seven steps* a general manager must take to lead change in his or her organization. These steps assume that the leader is dissatisfied with the status quo and feels that change is needed to cope with new competitive realities. Effective leaders are always on the lookout for a discontinuity in the organization's environment, says Andrew Grove, CEO of Intel. His book, *Only the Paranoid Survive* (Grove, 1996), captures well the need for constant vigilance.

Unfortunately, incumbent top managers are often slow to recognize the need for change and/or are too timid in confronting managers and workers below them with the need for change. Under these circumstances change cannot take place until the leader is replaced. The price of not being vigilant can be seen in statistics for Fortune 500 CEO tenure. Average CEO tenure in 2008 is 3.2 years versus 10.5 years in 1990. Leaders who are not dissatisfied with the status quo are removed by boards of directors so significant organizational change can occur. Even new managers, however, can fail to manage change if they do not understand and/or are unskillful in leading change. As a new CEO John Scully had nine years to change Apple Computer. He failed because he did not take the steps outlined below.

1. Mobilize energy for change

Energy for change must be mobilized in the top management team as well as in key managers at lower levels. It is mobilized by creating dissatisfaction with the status quo as was noted above. The following three actions can mobilize energy for change (Beer, 1991).

- ◆ *Demanding improved performance and behavior* – Leaders can energize organizational members by articulating demanding goals and standards for behavior. When Jack Welch took over General Electric in the early 1980s he told all business unit managers that they had to get their business units to be number 1 or 2 in their industries or the business would be sold. Stan Mahalik, Executive Vice President for Manufacturing at Goodyear Tire and Rubber, energized his 100 plant managers around the world to change their operations by demanding that unless their tires met certain quality standards they would become scrap. This energized them to search for new technology and management approaches. Percy Barnevik, CEO of ABB, articulated new performance goals and behavioral standards at a worldwide meeting of the top 500 executives in the company within weeks after a merger that formed the new company. With regard to behavior, taking action even if it is wrong, he said, is better than not taking action at all.
- ◆ *Exposing the top team and employees to feedback* – A general manager who is dissatisfied with the status quo has come by this view through awareness of low quality, high cost, poor profits, dissatisfied customers, or unhappy shareholders. Exposing managers and workers to this information through presentations as well as direct experience is a powerful way to unleash energy for change. When Louis Gerstner took over IBM after it had fallen on hard times in the early 1990s he asked all top executives to visit at least one customer a month. These visits gave them new insights into what was happening in the industry and how IBM needed to respond. Likewise, staff groups in corporations have been energized to become more effective when they have been exposed to feedback from line organizations they serve. Manufacturing plant managers faced with a resistant workforce and union have taken workers and union leaders on trips to see customers, displayed competitive products in the lobby of the building, and informed employees about the plant's financial performance through presentations and display of information on bulletin boards.
- ◆ *Exposing employees to model organizations* – Exposing managers and lower levels to radically different practices in other companies or within the same company can unleash energy. This has been referred to as benchmarking best practice. A visit to an innovative team-based manufacturing plant unleashed energy in managers,

workers, and union leaders to transform Navigation Products, their business unit, to a similar model of management, one that promised to improve coordination across functions, build trust, and improve communication (Beer et al., 1990). In the early 1980s the automobile companies sent managers by the hundreds to Japan to learn about manufacturing methods that gave Japanese manufacturers a significant edge in quality, though in this instance what they learned failed to be translated into change rapidly enough given the state of the automobile industry in 2008.

2. Develop a new compelling direction – strategy and values

Feedback and information is not enough. A new direction must be developed. To develop this direction, change leaders orchestrate a series of discussions in their management team to develop an understanding of what this information means for change in the company's direction. Exactly how successful is the organization being in its product or service offering? Why is it not successful? How committed are people? How effective is the organization? What is the implication for the future survival and success of the organization? What should be the new objectives and strategy? What should be the guiding values of the organization? What are the implied priorities? Discussing these questions in the light of the feedback and data to which managers have been exposed can lead to a new understanding and sense of urgency.

Jerry Simpson, general manager of Navigation Products, held a series of meetings with his top team that led them to defining new and ambitious goals for the business and a new direction (Beer et al., 1990). A study of 25 business units undergoing change found that units that had changed the most were more likely than lagging units to have established a clear and broadly understood link between business problems and the need for change (Beer et al., 1990). Making the link is what makes the new direction compelling to members of the organization. It is quite important for leaders to involve the whole top team in the formulation of the new objectives and strategy. And, it is important for that top team to involve other key managers in discussing and critiquing their new strategy. This builds the commitment needed to implement the new direction.

Moreover, the general manager or CEO can use the work of developing a new direction to develop their top team's effectiveness. Research shows that effective strategy formulation and implementation depends on top team effectiveness (Eisenhardt, 1989; Beer and Eisenstat, 2000). Team effectiveness is developed through encouraging new behavior, coaching, and if needed replacement of those key executives who do not play a constructive role in the team and/or do not become committed to the new direction.

3. Identify organizational barriers to implementing the new direction

Often the resistance to change is at the highest levels of the company (Miller, 1990; Finkelstein, 2003). Hierarchy insulates top management teams from the effects of their behavior and policies. Exposing top management to feedback about what employees perceive as barriers to implementing a new strategy further creates dissatisfaction and identifies what changes in organization and behavior are needed to implement the new strategy. John Scully began his belated and ultimately unsuccessful effort to change Apple Computer after an attitude survey showed strong negative sentiments in the company about the lack of strategic clarity and problems with top management's leadership.

Eisenstat and I (Beer and Eisenstat, 2000) asked top teams, as part of a planned effort to develop an organization capable of strategy implementation, to appoint a taskforce of eight of their best employees. Taskforce members interviewed organizational members one or two levels below the top about barriers to strategy implementation. The taskforce then fed back its findings to top teams using a carefully crafted process that enabled the taskforce to be honest and management to be non-defensive (Beer and Eisenstat, 2004). Six barriers were consistently identified across many organizations and, not surprisingly, they obverse the principles for an aligned organization and the change principles discussed in this chapter. The barriers were:

- Unclear strategy and conflicting priorities;
- An ineffective top team;
- A general manager who was either too autocratic or too laissez-faire (not confronting problems);
- Poor coordination;
- Poor vertical communication;
- Inadequate leadership and management and its development at lower levels.

Because these barriers were known to everyone but were not discussible we called them the "silent killers." Like hypertension, they can cause an organizational heart attack – organizational failures in implementing strategy. Until a commitment is developed by top teams to overcome the fundamental management problems represented by the silent killers it is unlikely that a new strategic direction can be implemented or the organization aligned with that strategy. Many change initiatives fail because underlying management problems are not confronted and overcome. Change leaders should, therefore, make an effort to collect data about barriers perceived by lower levels so plans for change can incorporate their voice about leadership and organizational problems. Efforts to change organizations without this step lead to cynicism and low commitment. Of course, this requires top managers to be open to learning about their own role in the organization's performance problems. If this does not happen, as it often does not, a new general manager or CEO will be appointed when the silent killers and their consequences begin to affect performance in a significant way.

4. Develop a vision of how the business will be organized for success

Having heard the voice of lower level employees regarding barriers to achieving the new strategic direction, the top team must work together to fashion a vision of the organization's future state (see Chapter 20, this volume). They will have to envision how the elements in the organizational model presented in Figure 29.1 will need to change to enable a change in organizational behavior. The following questions will have to be answered:

- How should the organization be redesigned to ensure the appropriate coordination between value creating activities that must work together to implement the strategic task defined in step 2 above? Redesign of the organization will include changes in structure, systems, and planning process. These changes are intended to change roles, responsibilities, and relationships so that the new strategy can be implemented. For example, business, customer or product and project teams may be created; change from a decentralized divisional structure to a matrix structure may be necessary; the number of hierarchical layers may be reduced; the size and role of corporate staff may change.

◆ How will the top team's own leadership behavior change to enable the new organization to function effectively? These changes may include modification in the CEO's style and/or changes in the frequency and focus of top management meetings and work. For example, the CEO of Becton Dickinson received feedback from an employee taskforce that he too closely supervised the corporate strategic planning process and that there were too many meetings. He responded by delegating more responsibility to his sector presidents and changing the focus and content of his top team's management work (Beer and Williamson, 1991).

◆ What changes in people's skills will be needed to ensure that the new organization works effectively? Changes in human resource policies and practices will be needed to ensure that the right people with the right skills occupy the new roles designated by the reorganization.

5. Communicate and involve people in implementation

The new organizational vision has to be communicated to the whole organization. People in the organization should be told why a new strategy is needed and how the new organizational arrangements will help shape new behavior and better performance. Articulating the links between new competitive realities and the new organization will enable people to commit to the changes.

Consider what Don Rogers, the general manager of the Electronic Products, a Division at Allentown Materials Corporation, did in this regard (Beer, 1998a). Rogers' top team had just decided to implement cross-functional new product development teams to enhance product development success, a strategic imperative for them to compete in their industry. Rogers and his whole top team visited 13 locations over a two-month period to communicate with every salaried employee how the new organization would work and why they were adopting it. The why included telling all employees about competitive problems that led to change and organizational barriers that had been uncovered through a survey and diagnosis of the division, including problems people perceived in Rogers' own leadership. Communication was two-way. After Rogers and his team presented their change plan, employees met in small groups to discuss what they heard. They then assembled to raise questions and challenge management. A *dialog* between top and bottom is essential for top management to learn about potential problems they will encounter in implementation so that they can make changes in their action plans accordingly. And that dialog must be continuous and ongoing for change to succeed.

6. Support behavior change

After the new organization is implemented, employees, particularly those whose roles and responsibilities have been most impacted by the organizational changes, will need support to develop needed skills and attitudes. This is often done through consultants who coach individuals and teams. It can also be done through training and education programs.

In the Electronic Products division mentioned above, consultants sat in on all team meetings for the first six months and coached the teams and their leaders in how to work in these new unfamiliar arrangements. Moreover, consultants brought together key managers in pairs of departments whose relationships were blocking coordination and facilitated a discussion that led to improvements. The purpose was to change behavior and skills within teams, thereby increasing the probability of their success.

7. Monitor progress and make further changes

Organizational change is an action learning process. As the new organizational arrangements are enacted, much is learned about how to modify structure, systems, policies and practices, and behavior to achieve intended results. Top and lower level managers discover how to carry out their new roles and responsibilities and gain insights into how their own styles and skills need to be changed. Those who cannot adapt decide to leave on their own or are asked to leave. As time goes on the organization begins to function more effectively and this is translated into better performance. Because the business environment and strategy are constantly changing, survival requires organizations to recycle these seven steps periodically so that the organization can be realigned with new realities.

ORCHESTRATING CORPORATE-WIDE STRATEGIC CHANGE

A large organization is typically made up of many interdependent subunits, each a business unit, and regional and country organizations or operating units such as manufacturing plants, stores, and offices. Leading the organization through the seven steps discussed above is the responsibility of unit leaders at every level. Corporate-wide change requires top management to play two roles (Beer, 1980; Ghoshal and Bartlett, 2000). They must *lead a change process within the top management unit*. This process would define how the corporate whole will coordinate the activities of the corporation's many subunits to achieve the wider purpose of the corporation. But that is not enough. Corporate leaders must also *orchestrate a process which encourages leaders in each of the corporation's subunits to lead their own seven step learning and organizational alignment process* (Beer and Eisenstat, 1996). Innovations in organizing and managing will occur from such a process and it is top management's role to orchestrate the diffusion of managerial innovations in leading units through conferences, visits to leading edge units and, most importantly, through the transfer of successful leaders from leading edge to lagging units (Beer et al., 1990).

Where should corporate-wide change start? Sometimes subunit change comes about naturally at the periphery, in businesses units, manufacturing facilities, or stores far from headquarters. Often these are subunits offering quite different products or services from the parent. It is in these units that managers are faced with different competitive demands and/or have the freedom to innovate and lead change. Under these circumstances changes are only adopted by other organizational subunits if top management actively works to move the innovations and the managers who led them to other parts of the large company (Beer et al., 1990; Walton, 1987).

Clearly, corporate-wide change will occur much more quickly if top management has conviction that change is needed. Top management's role is to encourage, even demand, that managers of independent business units, manufacturing plants, retail stores, or country organizations (in global companies) lead change in their units (Beer et al., 1990; Ghoshal and Bartlett, 2000). Jack Welch who led General Electric through a major transformation in the 1980s and 1990s *required* key managers to employ a process that required leaders to listen to key people about barriers to effectiveness, to assess their root causes and realign it for greater effectiveness (Ulrich, Kerr, and Ashkenas, 2002). Top management's role is not to drive change through corporate staff and consultant-led programs. As discussed earlier these will fail to mobilize energy and leadership at the unit level needed for change to succeed. Moreover, corporate programs prevent top management from discovering who of their subunit managers are able to lead the seven step organizational learning and change process, an indicator of their leadership potential.

CASE EXAMPLES

I will first summarize briefly the case of Apple Computer used throughout this chapter to illustrate an unsuccessful effort to lead change. I then review two successful change efforts.

Apple Computer: a case of failure

John Scully did not restore Apple to its former dominant market position. He was unable to develop sufficient dissatisfaction with the status quo to produce the energy needed for change. He never created a top team capable of agreeing on Apple's new strategic direction. As late as 1988, he appointed to a key top management position an executive whose strategic vision was diametrically opposite to the one that Apple had to take to cope with new competitive realities. His inclination to avoid conflict prevented him from confronting key strategic and organizational issues. And he never led a change process that enabled his top team to discover and discuss the silent killers that blocked them from realigning their organization with their intention to succeed in selling Apple's offering to the business market, one quite different from the education market where they had been successful. Consequently, shareholders, customers, and employees failed to derive the value (stock price, lower cost products, and career opportunities, respectively) that a successful enterprise would otherwise have yielded. Apple's success in the late 1990s to the present under the leadership of CEO Steve Jobs represents a new strategic era enabled by a "new" CEO (Jobs was actually Apple's founder and first CEO but was replaced by Scully). After Scully's departure, Jobs articulated a new strategy and successfully aligned the organization with it.

Hewlett Packard's Santa Rosa Systems Division (HP/SRSD): successful unit level change

The Hewlett Packard Santa Rosa Systems Division is a case of successful change at the business unit level but failure by HP's top management to spread innovation to other units (Beer and Rogers, 1997). In 1992, HP/SRSD was formed to manage and grow a new measurement systems business for HP. By 1994, the division was experiencing many problems and its performance did not meet top management's expectations. There were numerous reasons for this. The division had organized itself and was being managed in a manner similar to HP's traditional test and measurement divisions. Yet the systems business was significantly different, particularly with respect to the need to customize systems. The mismatch between the traditional approach to organizing and managing and the demands of a very different business environment and strategy created many tensions between functions and between the top team and the remainder of the organization.

Data collected by a taskforce of the division's best employees revealed that the six silent killers described above were blocking organizational effectiveness. Employees perceived the general manager's style was laissez faire. He was not engaging his top team in a discussion of conflicting strategies and priorities perceived by lower levels. Consequently, coordination between several functions essential for successful execution of two interdependent strategies was not occurring. Section managers who had been assigned to lead cross-functional teams were ineffective in gaining consensus in their teams in part because they lacked experience and skills needed to lead teams and in part because they lacked formal authority. And, while everyone in the division knew of these problems and complained about them to each other in private conversations, they did not give voice to their frustrations to the top team. The division manager and his staff were also aware of tensions and knew the division was failing but without feedback from lower levels they did not quite understand the urgency for change that lower level managers felt.

With the encouragement of his human resource executive, the division manager hired an external consultant, who, using a process called the Strategic Fitness Process (Beer and Eisenstat, 2004), helped the top team go through the seven step change process. This enabled these issues to be surfaced for discussion and diagnosis. As a result the top team identified their own ineffectiveness as a team, the general manager's style, and the ineffectiveness of cross-functional teams in coordinating functional departments as the root cause of poor performance. In that same meeting they agreed to reorganize the division as a matrix structure in order to facilitate coordination, defined new roles for key people and teams in the new structure, and defined a new role for the top team, one that would fit the new structure, and created new ground rules for how the top team should operate and how decisions would be made.

Data collected a year later by the same taskforce and an employee survey showed significant improvement, though some issues persisted. Sales had tripled and profits went up 250%. While the division's management attributed some of the improvements in the division's performance to an upturn in the market they served, they felt that they would not have been able to take advantage of market demand without the changes in organizing and managing they had made. The division manager and his team also decided to lead the seven step task alignment process once a year as a way of fostering continuous change. Five years later HP's top management felt that SRSD, which had lagged its sister divisions in performance and effectiveness, was now a model to which others divisions could look. Division management had successfully led change and innovated when they adopted the Strategic Fitness Process for fast change.

ASDA: successful corporate-wide strategic change

ASDA, a UK grocery chain, offers an example of excellent top management leadership of strategic change (Beer and Weber, 1998b). With the company £1.5 billion in debt and near bankruptcy, Archie Norman was appointed as CEO to turn round the company. Upon arriving in December of 1991, he met with his top team and quickly resolved to make changes in its membership. He also announced that while he did not have any pre-conceived ideas about what the problems were or how to solve them, he would insist on debate and transparency. He also announced that a "renewal store" would be identified where managers would be given license to innovate in the retail proposition, the physical space, and in the way people were organized and managed. He promptly began an assessment of the company's situation by making unannounced visits to many of the company's 200 stores. There he talked to lower level workers and store management asking them to tell him about barriers to company performance. They quickly informed him that for years headquarters, particularly the trading (purchasing) department, had not been listening to stores about what products the stores thought would sell.

Within months he began to reshape the way the top team worked together and the way the trading department at corporate headquarters communicated with and incorporated store views into their buying decisions. He told everyone that stores were to be "loved" and listened to. He established multiple mechanisms for communication between headquarters and the stores, and between store management and customers and employees. Within nine months a totally new approach to retailing and organizing and managing a store was created in the "renewal store" by the store manager and his top team working with a corporate cross-functional team. Sales increased immediately, as did morale. Over a six-year period virtually every store in the company had gone through the renewal process. Sales and profits not only improved, but also improved at a faster rate than its competitors. By 1998 the stock price had multiplied eight-fold.

The success of the renewal program – the heart of the change effort – rested on top management's recognition that it had to spread innovation in the first renewal store to all 200 stores. What enabled this to happen was top management's decision to withhold financial resources for a given store's renewal until its management had exhibited the behavior and values of teamwork, delegation, and communication top management thought were critical to store performance. It also became clear to store managers that their career success was now dependent on leading a renewal process in their own store. A "Driving Test" – an assessment of the extent to which each store's management had turned barriers like the "silent killers" into organizational and managerial strengths – was employed to assess a store's senior team's readiness to lead change. In stores where this did not happen quickly enough they replaced the store manager. Six years after the change effort began over 50% of store managers had been replaced with leaders who would and could lead store renewal.

EXCEPTIONS: HOW UNIVERSAL ARE THESE CHANGE GUIDELINES?

So long as the objectives of organizational change are the development of organizational capabilities for sustained competitive advantage over time, the principles and guidelines offered in this chapter hold. If, however, the objective is to enhance shareholder value quickly without regard to developing organizational capability for the long term, the guidelines for change proposed in the chapter do not apply. Management that wants to obtain short-term improvements in stock price are much more likely to succeed by drastic restructuring, cost reductions, and layoffs. Considerable evidence exists that such steps enhance the stock price of companies in the short term, but do not create alignment and sustained high commitment and high performance (Cascio, 2002). This is precisely what Al Dunlap did in just a few years as CEO of Scott Paper. What was not downsized was sold. The company no longer exists today.

There are, of course, many instances where top management wants to build organizational capability for the long term but the company's performance is so poor that drastic steps have to be taken to reduce cost in the short run. Under these circumstances there are two options (Beer and Nohria, 2000). The first option is to phase the change process so that restructuring (selling businesses that could not be turned around), productivity improvements, cost reduction, and layoffs come first, followed by the action steps outlined in this chapter. That is what Jack Welch did at General Electric with great success. The second option is to press forward with both cost reduction and layoffs while also following the guidelines in this chapter for a change process that builds organizational capability. There is evidence that such a dual strategy, cost reduction, and investment in building organizational capability can lead to successful change (Beer et al., 1990; Beer and Nohria, 2000). Companies that emphasized cost reduction at the expense of the steps described here did not successfully change their culture.

Embedded in the change process recommended here is an assumption that leaders value excellence, people, involvement, teamwork, and learning, including learning about themselves. Autocratic, controlling, and defensive leaders are unlikely to be able to implement the seven step change and alignment process. These steps require a commitment to building organizational capability, organizational learning, and to empowering leaders throughout the organization to lead change in their subunits. The somewhat slower pace of capability building change demands that leaders buy time by managing expectations of capital markets. Again, the case of ASDA described above is an excellent example of what can be done in this regard. By telling financial markets that they would not see major improvements in performance for three years, CEO Norman bought the time he needed to begin to rebuild organizational capabilities.

CONCLUSION

Organizations are complex systems normally resistant to change. Multiple facets of the organization – its design, its leadership, and its people – become tightly aligned with the historic strategy of the organization. This tight alignment leads to a distinctive and persistent pattern of behavior resistant to change. Resistance is caused by fear that change will result in losses of power, status, esteem, and position. Fear leads to defensiveness and the inability to consider new alternatives and to learn about what has to change.

Organizational change is motivated when leaders use environmental pressures, poor performance, or the prospect of poor performance to develop dissatisfaction with the status quo. When people realize that the organization's future is endangered, energy for change is released. Successful change managers lead a process that approximates the seven steps described in this chapter. They mobilize energy for change, develop a new compelling direction, identify organizational barriers to implementing the new strategy, develop a vision of how the organization will operate in the future, communicate the vision and involve people, support behavior change through coaching, and recycle learning and change to monitor progress and make new changes whenever the business faces new strategic inflections.

In large multi-unit corporations the responsibility for change lies with leaders at every level, not just with corporate top management. Top management's responsibility is to demand that unit managers lead change consistent with the competitive task faced by their unit. They then spread change to all parts of the larger organization through transfer of managers from leading edge to lagging units. They must also lead change in the top management unit. Change can start anywhere, but will be slow to spread unless top management creates a context that encourages change in subunits.

The capacity to lead an organization through change is increasingly important as the pace of competition and change increases. Effective change leadership enhances organizational performance, economic value, and organizational effectiveness needed in the long run. Managers who do not recognize the need for change or lack skills to lead it will ultimately be replaced as the performance of their organization lags expectations.

REFERENCES

Argyris, C., and Schon, D. A. (1996). *Organizational Learning II: Theory, Method and Practice*. Reading, MA: Addison-Wesley.

Beer, M. (1980). *Organization Change and Development: A Systems View*. Santa Monica, CA: Goodyear.

Beer, M. (1991). *Leading Change*. Boston, MA: Harvard Business School Note, Harvard Business School Press.

Beer, M. (2009). *Building High Commitment and High Performance Organizations*. San Francisco, CA: Jossey-Bass.

Beer, M., and Eisenstat, R. (2000). The silent killers of strategy implementation and learning. *Sloan Management Review*, 41(4), 29–40.

Beer, M., and Eisenstat, R. (2004). How to have an honest conversation about your strategy. *Harvard Business Review*, November.

Beer, M., and Gibbs, M. (1990). *Apple Computer (Abridged): Corporate Strategy and Culture*. Boston, MA: Harvard Business School Case, Harvard Business School Press.

Beer, M., and Williamson, A. (1991). *Becton Dickinson: Corporate Strategy and Culture*. Boston, MA: Harvard Business School Case, Harvard Business School Press.

Beer, M., and Eisenstat, R. (1996). Developing an organization capable of strategy implementation and learning. *Human Relations* 49, 597–619.

Beer, M., and Rogers, G. A. (1997). *Hewlett Packard's Santa Rosa Systems Division*. Harvard Boston, MA: Business School Case, Harvard Business School Press.

Beer, M., and Weber, J. (1998a). *Allentown Materials Corporation: The Electronic Products Division (B)*. Boston, MA: Harvard Business School Case, Harvard Business School Press.

Beer, M., and Weber, J. (1998b). *ASDA (A) (A1) (B) (C)*. Boston, MA: Harvard Business School Case, Harvard Business School Press.

Beer, M., and Nohria, N. (eds) (2000). *Breaking the Code of Change*. Boston, MA: Harvard Business School Press.

Beer, M., Eisenstat, R., and Spector, B. (1990). *The Critical Path to Corporate Renewal*. Boston, MA: Harvard Business School Press.

Cascio, W. F. (2002). *Responsible Restructuring: Creative and Profitable Alternatives to Layoffs*. San Francisco: Berrett-Koehler Publishers, Inc.

Eisenhardt, K. M. (1989). Making Fast Strategic Decisions in High Velocity Environments. *Academy of Management Journal*, 32, 543–576.

Finkelstein, S. (2003). *Why Smart Executives Fail*. London: Portfolio.

Foster, R., and Kaplan, S. (2001). *Creative Destruction: Why Companies that are Built to Last Underperform the Market – And How to Transform Them*. New York: Doubleday.

Ghoshal, S., and Bartlett, C. A. (2000). Building behavioral context; a blueprint for corporate renewal, to appear in M. Beer and N. Nohria (eds), *Breaking the Code of Change*. Boston, MA: Harvard Business School Press.

Grove, A. (1996). *Only the Paranoid Survive*. New York, NY: Doubleday.

Hall, G., Rosenthal, J., and Wade, J. (1993). How to make reengineering really work. *Harvard Business Review*, Nov.–Dec.

Katz, D., and Kahn, R. L. (1978). *The Social Psychology of Organizations*. Hoboken, NJ: John Wiley & Sons, Inc.

Kotter, J. (1997). *Leading Change*. Boston, MA: Harvard Business School Press.

Kotter, J. (2008). *A Sense of Urgency*. Boston, MA: Harvard Business School Press.

Kotter, J., and Heskett, J. (1992). *Corporate Culture and Organizational Performance*. New York, NY: The Free Press.

Lawler, E., III (1997). *The New Logic of Organizations*. San Francisco, CA: Jossey-Bass.

Lawrence, P. R., and Lorsch, J. W. (1967). *Organization and Environment*. Boston, MA: Division of Research, Graduate School of Business Administration, Harvard University.

Miles, R. E., and Snow, C. C. (1978). *Organizational Strategy, Structure and Process*. New York: McGraw Hill.

Miller, D. (1990). *The Icarus Paradox: How Exceptional Companies Bring About Their Own Downfall*. New York: Harper Business.

Nadler, D., and Tushman, M. L. (1988). *Strategic Organizational Design*. Homewood, IL: Scott Foresman.

Pfeffer, J. (1997). *New Directions for Organization Theory*. New York, NY: Oxford University Press.

Pfeffer, J. (1998). *The Human Equation*. Boston, MA: Harvard Business School Press.

Schaffer, R. H. (1988). *The Breakthrough Strategy: Using Short Term Successes to Build the High Performance Organization*. Cambridge, MA: Ballinger.

Schein, E. (1985). *Organizational Culture and Leadership*. San Francisco, CA: Jossey-Bass.

Schein, E. H. (1990). Organizational culture. *American Psychologist*, 45, 109–119.

Schneider, B. (1994). The people make the place. *Personnel Psychology*, 40, 437–454.

Ulrich, D., Kerr, S., and Ashkenas, R. (2002). *GE Work-Out: How to Implement GE's Revolutionary Method for Busting Bureaucracy and Attacking Organizational Problems – Fast*. New York: McGraw-Hill.

Virany, B., Tushman, M., and Romanelli, E. (1992). Executive succession and organization outcomes in turbulent environments: An organization learning approach. *Organizational Science*, 3, 72–91.

Walton, R. E. (1987). *Innovating to Compete: Lessons for Diffusing and Managing Change in the Workplace*. San Francisco: Jossey-Bass.

Exercises

Assess the alignment of your MBA program and diagnose reasons for misalignment

1. Instructor leads a discussion of what students expect to obtain from the MBA education.
2. A consensus-strategic statement which represents three or less primary goals of students is crafted (30 minutes).
3. The goals will serve as the strategy statement for the remainder of the exercise.
4. The class is divides into trios.
5. Each trio is assigned the following task:
   a. Students interview each other about shortfalls they see in achieving student aspirations for the MBA program and the barriers they see to their achievement (30 minutes).
   b. Groups diagnose the root causes for the success or failure of the MBA program in achieving strategic goals (45 minutes).
6. Groups report their findings.

Develop a change plan that will align the MBA program with strategic goals articulated in the first exercise

1. Class is divided into trios.
2. Groups discuss success or failure of change efforts each person experienced in their previous job. Each student presents a success or failure and ties it to the principles discussed in this chapter (30 minutes).
3. Each group decides on what must change in the MBA program in order to achieve strategic goals developed in the first exercise (30 minutes).
4. Each group arrives at barriers to change they anticipate (20 minutes).
5. Each group develops recommendations for a change strategy the dean should employ (30 minutes).
6. Group reports: what are the barriers to change and their implications for leading change in the MBA program (30 minutes)?
7. Instructor leads a discussion of reports.

Part VIII

ENTREPRENEURSHIP

30

Gain Entrepreneurship Success through Swiftness and Experimentation

J. ROBERT BAUM

THE PRINCIPLES

Entrepreneurs face higher uncertainty, risk, and barriers to market entry than established businesses. Risk is high because entrepreneurs typically introduce new products, new processes, and/or new business models. Little market information is available, and products or processes may be untested. However, the reward for being first to serve a market niche or for establishing a learning site in new market territory can be astounding. Sergey Brin, Larry Page, Steven Jobs, Oprah Winfrey, Bill Gates, and Michael Dell survived resource shortages, failed products, skeptics, and production challenges to make a positive difference for all of us – and for themselves. They did it, in part, through rapid introduction and continuous improvement of new products, services, and business types. Thus, I explain and promote two key entrepreneurship principles: *gain entrepreneurship success through swiftness and experimentation*.

Swiftness and experimentation are demonstrated predictors of venture success (Baum and Bird, in press). In 1996, Sergy Brin and Larry Page, founders of Google, needed computing capacity to continue experimentation with their latest search engine. Instead of waiting to acquire enough money to purchase a large server, they quickly moved through an eight iteration experiment and found a way to link multiple borrowed servers together to create a network of inexpensive PCs. This pattern of swiftness through rapid experimentation was repeated as they: (1) acquired a terabyte of discs and built their own computers in their dorm room, (2) negotiated with their first $100,000 investor for only five minutes, and (3) " . . . in short order, . . . introduced improved posting, post removal, and threading of the 500 million-plus messages exchanged . . ." (pp. 5 of 22: www.google.com/corporate/history.html).

Obviously, Google's founders were skilled programmers with good ideas, but this is not sufficient to build a successful new business. I focus on successful exploitation of good ideas. Over time, successful entrepreneurs modify their initial vision, initial plans, and products to fit their improved understanding of the market. In this chapter, I prescribe swiftness and experimentation as the best way to adapt to shifting market demands; swiftness and experimentation involve intense initial market monitoring, rapid variation, fast reintroduction, and follow-up monitoring. Swift entrepreneurial action is apparent when entrepreneurs move from step to step during their problem solving and opportunity taking without delay between steps and with fast paced thinking and action. Swift actors reach conclusions and accomplishments surprisingly fast.

As shown in the Figure 30.1, I review the important factors that affect swiftness and experimentation and focus on four that have demonstrated significant relationships with successful entrepreneurial behavior and subsequent venture success: creativity, tenacity, entrepreneurial self-efficacy, and goal setting. I elaborate the explanation of entrepreneurial self-efficacy by explaining the two types of experience that have the greatest impact on improved entrepreneurial self-efficacy, and I describe ways to enhance creativity, goal setting, swiftness, and experimentation.

I begin with a review of the importance of entrepreneurship and explain what scholars mean when they refer to "entrepreneur" and "entrepreneurship." I follow with an explanation of the unique and extremely important context that surrounds entrepreneurial behavior. The context helps us understand the types of factors that enable and motivate entrepreneurs to enact successful behaviors such as swiftness and experimentation. I describe swiftness and experimentation and explore factors that increase thinking and

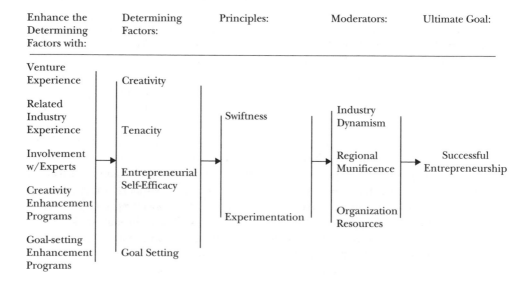

FIGURE 30.1 Gain entrepreneurship success through swiftness and experimentation

acting speed and inspire an effective and continuous search for improved products, processes, and business models.

THE IMPORTANCE OF ENTREPRENEURSHIP

Successful entrepreneurship is important because it creates wealth through conversion of technological and organizational innovation into valued products and services (Schumpeter, 1934). It also motivates established competitors to improve their products and processes. The Organization for Economic Cooperation and Development (OECD) stated that "Entrepreneurship is central to the functioning of market economies." The US Small Business Administration went even further to declare, " . . . the crucial barometer of economic freedom and well-being is the continued creation of new and small firms in all sectors of the economy by all segments of society."

Brin, Page, Jobs, Winfrey, Gates, and Dell are "ideal type" entrepreneurs; they built large well-known organizations that have enhanced our lives. Their companies are big now, but once they were only small new ventures. Indeed, most founders establish ventures that continue as small businesses for life. But even these new permanently small businesses are a major economic force. Taken together, US firms with fewer than 500 employees account for 51% of private sector output, employ 51% of private sector workers, and constitute 99% of all employers.

In summary, those who found and operate new successful ventures and new small businesses are important in terms of their impact upon absolute GNP and employment and their *potential* for social and economic impact. Indeed, entrepreneurship through establishment of new independent businesses was so successful in the US during the 1980s and 1990s in creating new jobs that it overcame the elimination of over 5 million jobs in established big business (Kirchhoff, 1997). On the other hand, over 50% of new ventures fail within five years in the US (Aldrich, 1999); thus, it is important to understand the factors that influence new venture creation and growth.

ENTREPRENEURS AND ENTREPRENEURSHIP DESCRIBED

Hundreds of conceptions – "entrepreneur," "entrepreneurship," and "entrepreneurial" – exist. These include "successful small businesspersons," "retired founders," "failed founders," and "managers." To avoid confusion about what I mean by entrepreneur and to avoid a discussion about "who is an entrepreneur," I focus on early stage entrepreneurs who intend to make a significant difference in people's lives – entrepreneurs with big dreams and high potential. No studies that included the solitary self-employed or small business managers were used. The people who start these high potential high growth companies are involved in a process of discovery, evaluation, and exploitation of opportunities that will introduce new products, services, processes, ways of organizing, or markets" (Venkataraman, 1997).

There are many indicators of venture success (entrepreneur's personal satisfaction, rates of commercialized innovation, rates of improvement in market efficiency, etc.); however, venture growth is the best general indicator of entrepreneurship success because venture growth reflects personal and market gains (Kirzner, 1985). Venture growth is a measurable and well-understood entrepreneurship goal. Covin and Slevin (1997) explain that venture growth is the essence of entrepreneurship.

The entrepreneurship process begins with exploration for ideas and proceeds through opportunity evaluation and recognition to start-up. Start-up is followed by emergence (revenues and employees), and, finally, early stage growth. Although the principles described in this chapter apply in all venture stages, the research findings that I draw upon are based upon studies of early stage companies that were founded with plans for major growth. Early stage growth was taken as the best predictor of ultimate success. Experimentation and swiftness are also important during exploration, opportunity recognition and evaluation, start-up, and emergence. Furthermore, the conclusions that are drawn herein about behaviours that impact venture success may also apply to ambitious managers everywhere.

The entrepreneurship context

Entrepreneurs face extreme situations because their work involves disruptive change. They create new markets where none existed and enter established markets with new products. Sometimes they displace other companies and employees, so their gains may create losses for others. Obviously, aggressive competitive challengers may appear. Little or no information is usually available to guide entrepreneurs' expectations about new marketing and organizational outcomes, and products may be introduced with limited market trials in attempts to stay ahead of competitors. Unless intellectual property is protected, competitive advantages may be temporary as competitors with valuable substitutes emerge.

Few entrepreneurs have sufficient financial resources to acquire complete facilities, process systems, equipment, and professional talent; and few can support start-up losses alone. The financing challenge is heightened in rapidly growing new ventures as investment demands accelerate and cash dwindles. Entrepreneurs are frequently forced to accept capital from financiers who negotiate from aggressive and powerful positions and who minimize their investors' risk by setting high goals for the entrepreneurs and offering just-in-time cash. Thus, entrepreneurs who manage high potential start-ups with outside financing confront a threatening array of continuous demands for high performance, and they experience a continuous and stressful sense of urgency as they worry about survival (Smith and Smith, 2000).

Thus, starting, running, and making a successful business is usually a very difficult undertaking. There are many tasks involved. For example, formulating the basic vision, finding investors, hiring competent people, finding a suitable location, making the product, finding customers, building a sales force, beating out competitors, dealing with lawsuits and government regulations, and overcoming setbacks at every phase.

In summary, high growth entrepreneurs function in the midst of high uncertainty, urgency, surprise, complexity, personal risk, and resource scarcity (Baum, Frese, Baron, and Katz, 2006; Smith and Smith, 2000). High speed continuous improvements are required to replace continuous erosion of competitive advantages (Baum et al., 2006; Eisenhardt, 1989). High uncertainty increases the value of fast decision making and fast action, and minimal resources drive entrepreneurs to experiment with vigilant monitoring and continuous adaptation to gain and maintain competitive advantages. Entrepreneurship is not a career for the fainthearted.

SWIFTNESS – PRINCIPLE 1

Swiftness is beneficial for high growth entrepreneurs because they gain little by waiting. High growth entrepreneurs face new or immature markets with scant existing information, so the only way to get market information is through entry. Market acceptance or rejection is full of important information, and it speeds the search for the right products, services, markets, and organization forms ahead of competitors.

So the principle offered here is based on the simple question, "Why wait for certainty when it does not exist when you start something new?" Why not act quickly to uncover potential markets? Taken together, it is not surprising that experienced entrepreneurs advise, "Just start, move quickly, and watch the unfolding action for answers and opportunities" (Jones, 1993, p. 110).

In other words, early action can generate information, dynamic learning, and knowledge ahead of rivals. Unexpected opportunities sometimes emerge but only if action is started. Swiftness increases the number of trials that can be attempted within time and resource constraints, thereby providing more information and narrowed confidence intervals.

Swiftness has appeared as a prescription and organizational competency in studies of product development projects (Eisenhardt and Tabrizi, 1995), global competition (Stalk and Hout, 1990), and successful competitive actions (Ferrier, Smith, and Grimm, 1999). Fast decisions, which lead to swiftness, have related positively with firm performance in new industries (Eisenhardt, 1989) and in new ventures in mature industries (Baum and Wally, 2003).

EXPERIMENTATION – PRINCIPLE 2

"Experimentation" involves repeatedly conducting trials or tests to discover something that is not known. It involves *continuous searches for betterment with repeated goal-driven revision* (Thomke, 2003). Particularly, in the new venture context, experimentation appears as actions toward goals that will involve new (or better) products, services, processes, or organizations. Experimentation connotes use of a conceptual model and controls across the trials in contrast with "trial and error" which reflects a more random set of variables for each trial. Both experimentation and trial and error suggest repeated cycles of action with monitoring and revision or reformulation.

Other concepts are related to experimentation, and understanding their characteristics may help us grasp the meaning and usefulness of experimentation for entrepreneurs. For example, improvisation is extemporaneous composition and execution of novel actions (Miner, Bassoff, and Moorman, 2001). Monitoring and revision are not included in conceptions of improvisation; however, follow-up is implicit because improvisation is short-term, real-time learning.

"Bricolage" is similar to improvisation but with resources strictly limited to those that are "available" (Baker, Miner, and Eesley, 2003). Some studies of improvisation have focused on resource conditions, suggesting that improvisation occurs only with resources in hand (e.g. in the style of improv theatre); however, most do not imply resource constraints. "Flexibility" and "adaptation" are more general "change behaviors" that are triggered by changed "situations."

The entire set of change behaviors is most useful for information gathering, learning, resource conservation, and opportunity taking when follow-up involves close monitoring of responses from markets, employees, and stakeholders. It is important to control the unfolding action and reformulation or revision so that the experimenting entrepreneur can know which, among many possible variations, is working and which are not working.

Experimentation is useful for high growth entrepreneurs, because it reveals information about potential markets where no markets exist. Experimentation reveals customer reactions to disruptive product, service, and business model introductions in existing markets (Bhide, 2000, p. 60), and it may enable recovery from poor past decisions or missed opportunities. Experimentation exposes competitors' "barriers to entry" and guides the rapid changes that are required (Smith and Smith, 2000); it may also expose opportunities to build new products or offer new services. Thus, the fast-moving unresolved markets that entrepreneurs face and their inability to get "hard" information to guide foresight require experimentation.

Recent research about entrepreneurs indicates that successful entrepreneurs are comfortable enacting changes to cope with processes, products, or markets that do not meet their goals (Baum and Bird, in press). Miner et al. (2001) and Hmieleski and Corbett (2006) found that entrepreneurial behaviors related to experimentation (improvisation and trial and error) are used by entrepreneurs to deal successfully with their changing urgent situations, and Eisenhart (1989) observed "unintended trial actions" among the successful entrepreneurs whom she studied. Thus, past research findings and evaluation of the HGEs' situation point to the value of experimentation for new venture growth.

DETERMINING FACTORS

There are many important factors that inspire and enable swiftness and experimentation. I focus on creativity, tenacity, self-efficacy, and goal setting as primary predictors because each has been consistently important across entrepreneurship studies.

Creativity

Creativity is intellectual inventiveness. It is the ability to generate high quality novel ideas that meet the needs of a task or context. Those who have high creativity challenge the status quo and seek alternative ways to solve problems and gain advantage from opportunities. Creativity is a stereotypical trait of entrepreneurs, the movers and shakers behind creative destruction (Schumpeter, 1934). Those entrepreneurs who do not have creativity must look elsewhere for innovations by partnering with an inventor or developer through licensing or joint venturing. Of course, some entrepreneurs simply copy the basic ideas of others, like discount retailer Sam Walton, and express their creativity through innovative execution of the idea.

High growth entrepreneurs need creativity to commercialize their products and service their customers successfully because creativity enables option generation. Those who are creative enough to envision multiple novel paths to get their products to market and who are sufficiently creative to envision the multiple outcomes from each path are advantaged because they can conduct multiple market experiments. Similarly, high creativity speeds the conception and description of variant paths which may speed market trials. Thus, creativity may enable entrepreneurs who are more creative to avoid delays as they search for options.

Sometimes, option generation is urgent. Surprise barriers to success emerge, and high creativity entrepreneurs are better able to quickly see novel ways to solution. For example, in Sam Walton's early years, he was surprised at the ability of competitors to retain their customers – even though they charged more for their goods than he charged. In a flash of creativity – and action over two days – he conceived, designed, selected, and began work on his first store. It was to be located in a small community where existing competition was weak, and it was supposed to be very large with broad and deep stocks of general merchandise and with costs so low that customers would travel from a large region to shop (Huey and Walton, 1992).

I have discussed the importance of creativity for option generation during market entry. Entrepreneurs also need creativity during the idea-getting and opportunity recognition stages, but I have not focused on these stages. Nevertheless, entrepreneurs who can quickly envision a whole set of market options and outcomes have a competitive advantage at all stages.

Tenacity

Tenacity, or perseverance, is a trait that involves sustaining goal-directed action and energy even when faced with obstacles. Tenacious people do not give up when things go wrong.

Tenacity has been identified consistently as an archetypical entrepreneurship trait because the business start-up process involves confrontation of formidable barriers to market entry. Research points to one trait above others that sets the successful apart from failures. They did not give up when things went wrong. They were tenacious (Gartner, Gatewood, and Shaver, 1991).

Tenacity is important for high growth entrepreneurs because they must be able to conduct extensive, even continuous, experiments. They must persist with their search for options and solutions and continue market monitoring after they institute trials. Monitoring must persist following revision of products and services.

Nearly all entrepreneurs at some point in their careers confront difficult obstacles (e.g. barriers to entry) or have setbacks (e.g. a product that does not work as planned, cost overruns). Some will even fail completely (and have to start over). If making a new business succeed or making an existing business grow were easy, then almost anyone would be able to do it. But, only a relatively small number of people are successful entrepreneurs. Shaver and Scott (1991) note that successful entrepreneurs pick themselves up after failure, in part because they attribute failure to bad luck or insufficient effort on their part. They assume that if they work harder, they will succeed. In a study of 217 inventors, those who had a higher adversity quotient (able to recover from bad news) founded more businesses (Markman, Balkin, and Baron, 2002). Baum, Locke, and Smith (2001) found that the trait of tenacity contributed to venture growth even with a six-year time lag between the measurement of the trait and subsequent performance.

There are many examples of tenacity among entrepreneurs. FedEx was on the verge of bankruptcy for three years until Fred Smith made it work. Mary Kay Ash staggered through the death of two husbands, the failure of her first beauty show, and a disastrous sales decline before making her beauty products company a huge international success. It took Bill Gates and Microsoft seven years to develop a viable Windows operating system.

Sam Walton failed with a drug chain, a home improvement center, two hypermarts, and some disastrous store openings, but he made it big in the end with Wal-Mart's magnet stores in low competition locations.

It can be asked: where does a successful entrepreneur draw the line between productive tenacity and foolish persistence (Locke, 2000)? Sometimes it is hard to tell until after the fact, especially in the case of an entirely new product, but one common type of foolish persistence is to stick to a strategy that worked in the past, even in the face of mounting evidence that the competitive environment is radically changing. Consider Henry Ford's refusal to abandon the Model T – which had been a best selling car for 19 years – in the face of threats from General Motors. By the time Ford developed new models, GM had snatched away Ford's position as the number one car company in the world – a position which Ford never regained. One guideline then is that an entrepreneur should keep close tabs on the outside world when deciding whether or not to retain or abandon a strategy or product. If the product is totally new, the entrepreneur has to decide if there is enough cash flow to keep the project going (Locke and Baum, 2007).

In summary, tenacity is important for experimentation and venture success because entrepreneurs who hold stubbornly to their goals and who hate to give up increase their chances of finding the solution for a market need. Baum et al. (2001) found that tenacity was the most powerful trait predictor of new venture growth.

Entrepreneurial self-efficacy

It is not enough for entrepreneurs to be creative and tenacious; they must also be confident that they have everything that they need to perform a task. Confidence is reflected in "self-efficacy," the belief or degree of confidence that someone has the ability to successfully perform a task (see Chapter 10, this volume). Bandura (1997) and a subsequent meta analyses by Judge and Bono (2001) point to the central role of self-efficacy in causing high performance through its impact on motivation; Stajkovic and Luthans (1998) explained that self-efficacy enhances focus, direction, persistence, and intensity of action.

Without self-efficacy, little will happen. I point to high self-efficacy as a factor that enhances experimentation and swiftness because both behaviors will only occur when entrepreneurs are sufficiently confident that they can move quickly and successfully. When entrepreneurs have confidence, they can, with sufficient trials, find market acceptance.

Entrepreneurship researchers have quantitative evidence that general self-efficacy predicts new venture creation (Markman et al., 2002) and venture growth (Baum and Locke, 2004). Chandler and Jansen (1992) found a significant relationship between general self-confidence (measured to yield self-efficacy) and early stage venture performance.

Self-confidence specifically about entrepreneurship was studied by Chen, Green, and Crick (1998). The authors defined entrepreneurial self-efficacy (ESE) as "the strength of a person's belief that he or she is capable of successfully performing the various roles and tasks of entrepreneurship." It consisted of five factors: innovation, risk taking, marketing, management, and financial control. Higher ESE distinguished entrepreneurs from managers.

Similarly, higher ESE predicted higher "experimentation" and higher "swiftness" in a recent empirical study (Baum and Bird, in press). Thus, I employ it here as an important factor that impacts the principle studied: *gain entrepreneurship success through swiftness and experimentation.*

Goal setting

Goal-setting theory (Locke and Latham, 2002) has shown that specific, difficult goals lead consistently to higher performance than vague and/or easy goals. Goal setting works most effectively when people are committed to their goals and have feedback regarding their progress in relation to their goals (see Chapter 9, this volume).

No other theory of motivation has deeper or broader empirical support at the individual, group, and unit level (Landy and Becker, 1987; Locke and Latham, 1990, 2002). Entrepreneurship theorists cite goals as an important factor in venture growth (Covin and Slevin, 1997) and new venture survival (Carsrud and Krueger, 1995). An empirical study of the effects of entrepreneurs' characteristics found that goals had a direct effect on firm growth over six years (Baum and Locke, 2004). In another study Tracy, Locke, and Renard (1999) found significant relationships between the financial, growth, and innovation goals of entrepreneurs in the printing business and corresponding performance measures obtained two years later.

I employ goal setting here as a predictor of entrepreneurs' swiftness and experimentation because goals help motivate people to use suitable task strategies or to search for suitable strategies, if they lack the knowledge they need. Swiftness and experimentation are suitable strategies for the entrepreneurship context wherein uncertainty is high because new markets and products are untested. Sufficient information is not available to reduce uncertainty about market performance or financial returns, so those who set specific, difficult growth goals choose strategies and related behaviors that yield more information faster.

CEO goal setting is an ideal practice in new ventures because CEOs in small firms have relatively direct control over the actions that lead to goal accomplishment. In larger more established firms, there are more layers and most work is delegated. Furthermore, firm strategies in large organizations may be more complex than those in smaller companies and, thus, more prone to error. Complex strategies are also less easily and less rapidly changed when problems occur and decision makers may not have the knowledge required to achieve the goals. In summary, entrepreneurial goal setting in the new venture setting provides a potent competitive advantage, compared with the effects in larger established companies, because it directly inspires the entrepreneur's swiftness and experimentation.

MODERATING FACTORS

There are many organization characteristics (e.g. structure and size) and external conditions (e.g. industry, economic conditions, and zeitgeist) that impact successful new venture creation (Baum et al., 2001; Rauch and Frese, 2000). I point particularly to industry dynamism, regional munificence, and organization resources because in multiple research studies they have interacted most strongly with entrepreneurs' behavior to affect venture success (Baum and Wally, 2003; Covin and Slevin, 1997).

Industry dynamism

Dynamism (instability or turbulence) refers to the level of environmental *predictability*; it is manifested in the variance in the rate of market and industry change and the level of uncertainty about forces that are beyond the control of individual businesses. Dynamism creates competitive advantages for entrepreneurs because new ventures are typically more nimble (responsive) than big companies. In contrast, dynamic markets challenge large cumbersome companies when product revision is required – and product revision is almost always a characteristic of dynamic industries. Indeed, Eisenhardt (1989) and Judge and Miller (1991) found that fast-paced settings with rapid changes in demand and discontinuous outcomes motivated fast decision making and action and yielded profits for those who were able to respond. Thus, dynamism enhances (moderate positively) the effects of swiftness and experimentation.

Many dynamic markets are caused by new technologies (Eisenhardt and Tabrizi, 1995), and many high growth entrepreneurs are leading technology innovators. Although some second-movers gain competitive advantage by quickly copying the first mover, most technology entrepreneurs count first-mover advantages as more important for success (Ferrier et al., 1999). Thus, technology entrepreneurs need to master fast decision making and swiftness to capture fleeting advantages. Furthermore, if information is scarce, resource-poor entrepreneurs are not disadvantaged because rich established competitors cannot gain information by outspending the upstarts.

In contrast, dynamism has been cited as a challenge for entrepreneurs because it increases the difficulty of understanding supplier and customer markets (Priem, Rasheed, and Kotulic, 1995). Valuation of strategic options is difficult because there are many options with low probabilities, and risk is high because sufficient resources are required to sustain firms during the downside of large operating variances (Bourgeois, 1980). Nevertheless, most entrepreneurs claim that they can beat larger established companies in dynamic markets (Eisenhart and Tabrizi, 1995).

Some have suggested that swift is not better, and this may be true in some cases; however, in dynamic situations, Eisenhardt (1989) found that fast decision makers were also more comprehensive and more successful. Some unsuccessful entrepreneurs lurch quickly from one bad idea to another, so I emphasize that decisions, even when swift, should be based on reason and reality. Decisions should be the result of thought, not change for the sake of change.

Regional munificence

Regional munificence (capacity) refers to the local environment's support for organizational growth. In established industries, it is manifested in high industry sales growth (Dess and Beard, 1984). Munificent environments provide a reserve against competitive and environmental threats through availability of sufficient financing, intellectual support from institutions, and developed human resource markets. Both new ventures and larger competitors benefit from environmental munificence. For example, the availability of financing and skilled labor is good for both.

However, one can argue that munificent environments diminish the value of new ventures' experimental behavior, causing a negative interaction between experimentation and entrepreneurship success. To explain, a benefit of experimentation is that minimal financial resources are applied in each trial. Most new high growth ventures cannot obtain sufficient financial support, so experimentation is a mandate. However, if the region is rich in financial resources it may be better for a new venture to gain market information by financing entrance to multiple markets with multiple products simultaneously. Despite conflicting theories about the effects of munificence, Baum and Bird (in press) found that regional munificence enhanced the interaction between rapid change behaviors and new venture growth in the graphics industry.

In light of the competing effects of munificence, I suggest that entrepreneurs evaluate the region and the nature of competition in the industry to be clear about the value of experimentation in high munificence regions.

Organization resources

Whereas dynamism and munificence are industry forces that have different effects when they interact with entrepreneurial behavior, high organization resources are almost always beneficial (Baum and Bird, in press; Smith and Smith, 2000). In short, the greater the internal resources of a venture, the greater the benefit from positive entrepreneurial behavior. For example, rich organization resources such as financing and human resources enable higher growth without money worries and enable management growth without hiring challenges. For example, after Sam Walton saved sufficient money from his first six years of operations, he was able to experiment more freely with different practices and promotions (Huey and Walton, 1992). When these worked in his experimental store, he replicated the practice in his two other stores. A well-financed venture is nearly always better off than its poor cousin. Similarly, a well-staffed venture is nearly always better off than an understaffed venture (Stevenson, 1985). Nevertheless, there is anecdotal evidence of negative effects of excess resources. For example, IBM had many programmers and Microsoft had few when they worked jointly, but the Microsoft programmers were more effective than the IBM programmers because they worked more efficiently and designed with cost minimization in mind.

Industry forces and organizational forces are important, but entrepreneurship is fundamentally personal. It takes *human* vision, intention, and work to conceive and convert business ideas to successful products and services. Through their thinking and action, entrepreneurs themselves integrate human and financial resources to organize, produce, and market products and services that yield value for customers and workers. According to venture financiers, entrepreneurs' personal characteristics (individual differences) are the most important factors for business success – even more important than the business idea or industry setting (Shepherd, 1999; Zopounidis, 1994). Thus, external forces amplify the effects of entrepreneurial behavior, but good entrepreneurial behavior is a first order condition.

IMPLEMENTATION

High levels of creativity, tenacity, entrepreneurial self-efficacy, and goal setting enable and motivate swiftness and experimentation which, in turn, yield high venture growth. But, how can an entrepreneur – or wannabe entrepreneur – gain creativity, tenacity, self-efficacy, and goal setting? I explore the possibilities and offer suggestions. This brief treatment of learning opportunities points to the importance of venture and industry experience, as well as the value of building relationships with expert models. It also suggests that creativity-building and goal-setting educational programs may enhance one's creativity and inclination to set effective goals.

I address the value of venture and industry experience primarily for improvement of entrepreneurial self-efficacy; however, relevant experience can also expose wannabe entrepreneurs to leaders/entrepreneurs who are models of tenacious behavior and goal setting. Ideally, wannabe entrepreneurs should work for a new venture or entrepreneurial company, and they should focus on the pace and process of product and service development. Those fortunate enough to work with an entrepreneur in the industry of their choice may also gain from industry creativity programs and cultures. Indeed, consider the proliferation of successful new ventures in communities such as Silicon Valley and the Boston technology crescent. Concentrated industry communities offer relevant opportunities for learning from others, and this condition should figure in career choice.

Improving your creativity

Creativity is often described as a trait – a human characteristic that is inherent and stable. However, hundreds of psychology professionals promote their creativity education programs at company sponsored seminars and trade shows based upon evidence that creativity has been enhanced with training (Runco, Plucker, and Lim, 2000). Most professionals employ group exercises involving analogies, brainstorming, cross-fertilization, devil's advocacy, lateral thinking, or vertical thinking. I think that most wannabe entrepreneurs should engage with these programs because they offer hope for improving personal creativity. Some lessons learned in group sessions can translate to solitary thinking, and solitary thinking is the mode for entrepreneurs. In particular, a focus on the creative process and practices such as divergent thinking appear to improve creativity in high uncertainty settings (Mumford, Supinski, Baughman, Constanza, and Threlfall, 1997).

Relevant experience enhances creative processes such as brainstorming (even at a personal level). For example, Angel Johnson Organics (AJO), an early marketer of organic foods, was unsuccessful in placing products in established supermarkets. A creative AJO marketing manager who had worked for Honest Tea, a sugar-free iced tea manufacturer, noticed the success that Honest Tea had in health-oriented institutions such as gymnasiums and hospital facilities. After a brainstorming session with her sales, marketing, and operations staff, she developed a refrigerated display cabinet that enabled the successful introduction of her organic fruit and vegetable products to health-oriented institutions. Success led to a joint venture with Honest Tea and subsequent placement of AJO *and* Honest Tea products in established supermarkets. Thus, I prescribe industry experience to enhance creative thinking processes that focus on generating product and marketing options.

Improving your tenacity

Tenacity is a trait, a predisposition. It is far more difficult to change traits such as tenacity or perseverance through training or experience than to change behavior. (Of course, behavior itself is hard to change.) However, extended exposure to successful others who are tenacious may raise a person's intention to be more tenacious (Bhide, 2000). Also, motivation through goal setting, external rewards, and punishment may inspire tenacity (Locke and Latham, 1990). Locke and Latham also explain that self-efficacy, which can be acquired, may increase tenacity.

Improving your entrepreneurial self-efficacy

Self-efficacy reflects past experience and attainment, but more importantly, the conclusion one has drawn about one's capacity for performance attainment from past experiences. Entrepreneurs can improve their entrepreneurial self-efficacy by gaining relevant experience.

Often entrepreneurial self-efficacy is developed from childhood experiences in which one undertakes independent projects (e.g. running a paper route, building a computer and selling it), masters difficulties, and succeeds. Confidence may also stem from one's awareness of one's own cognitive abilities.

Entrepreneurs' most valuable experiences are related to time spent starting a new company or with others who start new companies. The new venture situation is dominated by newness; however, all is not totally new. Some decision processes, resource aggregation activities, customer fulfillment conditions, and market characteristics appear and reappear. Through prior venture experience, entrepreneurs' mental structures about new venture processes are continuously used, revised, and reused. Indeed, multiple entrepreneurship researchers have found significant positive relationships between "habitual" or repeat entrepreneurs and venture start-up and growth (Davidsson and Honig, 2002).

The second important type of experience for developing entrepreneurial self-efficacy is industry experience. Herron and Robinson (1993) posit that industry knowledge and related industry networks are important assets in specifying the new venture's need for resources, finding those resources, selecting partners, and structuring more flexible resource contracts. Herron and Robinson (1993) found that 15% of new venture performance variance was accounted for in terms of the entrepreneur's technical industry experience. Financiers also point to specific career experience as most important for predicting entrepreneurs' job performance. Indeed, venture capitalists note that industry and technology experience, when related with the products, processes, or business models proposed for financing, are among the most important personal characteristics of the entrepreneur (Smith and Smith, 2000).

Improving your goal setting

Chapter 9 of this volume explains that personal and employee performance can be improved through goal setting. Goal setting motivates entrepreneurial behavior, so it improves the pace of action and the rate of experimentation in new ventures. Those who aspire to venture success should devote their time, money, and other resources to personal and organizational goal setting.

In the early growth stages of a new venture, goal setting may be highly personal. The solitary entrepreneur who maintains a timeline with goals will have an important tool for personal motivation and for attraction of financial and human resources. Such a formal written timeline should include benchmarks such as: complete prototype, obtain patent or copyright, sell first unit, employ operations manager, attain $300,000 annual revenue rate, cash breakeven, profitable, etc. As the venture team is formed, the goals/timeline should be formalized, communicated, and updated to include team members' views about important indicators of success and the appropriate levels of the indicators.

It is important to develop compensation schemes that motivate team members on the basis of performance goals. These may include cash awards, stock options, and non-cash rewards. Incentive practices are addressed in Chapter 12 of this volume. In particular, goal-based pay for performance, including the entrepreneur's own compensation, is important. As the organization develops, the range of goals should be expanded to include product improvement (pace of innovation and level of product and market experimentation), product quality, and market penetration. Similarly, the range of goal-based rewards should be expanded to include recognition and increased non-cash benefits, and regular team/employee sessions should address employee knowledge about goals and associated rewards.

Again, wannabe entrepreneurs may gain knowledge about goal setting through relevant venture and industry experience. *Management by objective (MBO)* seminars are based in goal theory, and they offer guidance about the types of goals and rewards that are most effective. I recommend exposure to these programs and emphasize that specific challenging goals are effective for personal and venture success through all levels of the new venture and through all stages of new venture creation.

Note that early MBO programs failed because managers set their own goals and were judged only on goal success, so they set easy goals to be sure of personal success while their firms often failed. To prevent this, goals below the CEO level must be assigned and/or stretch (very hard) goals should be encouraged with the proviso that goal failure will not be punished as long as the manager has made a creative effort to improve. At GE, Jack Welch set minimum goals which were mandatory and also stretch goals which were meant to encourage innovation but did not have to be met on a regular basis.

EXCEPTIONS

Swiftness is usually better than slow action because more work is accomplished, more value is added, and learning opportunities appear in advance of competitor's learning. However, even high growth entrepreneurs have periods when urgency is not great – when sufficient time and resources are available for a thorough and comprehensive information search and analysis, and swiftness is not important. So it may be all right to pause, but realize that downtime can be used (1) to gain advance learning about how to find the needed explicit information or (2) to find the best way to conduct the evaluation of new ideas.

CASE EXAMPLES

Lad and Hooker Beer

Brothers Hans and Heinrich Stolzfus experimented with beer making when they were teenagers. Despite their parents' concern and complaints, they secretly brewed small batches and sold it to friends. Their circle of friends grew, and their passion for beer making was carried to UCLA in 1996. Hans was admitted to the Liberal Arts program and Heinrich entered the Business School. The brothers set up a small propane brew pot in their dorm room and sold ice cold home brew privately to their classmates. Their beer was good and within one semester their volume had grown beyond their wildest dreams. At the end of 1998, the brothers were brewing a keg a day and the activity attracted unwanted institutional attention.

Hans moved quickly to rent a garage in Culver City and began to brew larger quantities. He successfully obtained a license to make and distribute limited quantities of the home brew. Hans entered the brothers' beer in the Great American Beer Festival and won a gold medal. Upon graduation, Heinrich joined his brother. Heinrich believed that they could expand the operation, so they borrowed $100,000 through an SBA loan guaranteed by their parents. The beer began to attract public attention because the brothers established a social mission connection. They donated $2 to California's Safe Driver Foundation for every keg sold. This experiment worked well. Newspaper and TV publicity followed, and demand increased dramatically.

In 2003 on a Monday morning, the owner of a Coors distributorship explained that the Coors company now allowed their distributors to carry a limited number of craft beers. The owner had been impressed with the progress of Lad and Hooker beer and liked the relation with the Safe Driver Foundation. He explained that he wanted to distribute Lad and Hooker beer. Quickly, in two days, the three settled on terms of the potential deal. The brothers would have to sign an exclusivity agreement and a contract that described volume-sensitive returns for the brothers (the brothers' share of revenues increased as volume increased). The distributorship owner explained that the brothers would have to develop a dark and light Lad and Hooker beer. If they agreed and if they established a relationship with a reputable brewer, the distributor would carry their accounts payable with a charge of 1% of the average balance every month. The distributor insisted that the brewer would have to match the brothers' quality and satisfy demand. The distributor insisted that when the contract rolled over, he must have a right of first refusal to match any competing arrangement that the brothers found. Overall, the arrangement was sufficient for the brothers to begin development and explore expanded markets. Importantly, the brand was protected for the brothers.

On Wednesday, a wealthy friend, also taken with the product and interested in the social mission, offered to finance the brothers' expansion in return for 51% of the stock of the business. Uncertainty about whether the brothers should continue to do everything themselves, partner with the distributor, or take their angel friend's offer caused debates and two sleepless nights. However, they decided that they must act quickly to grow the business because another craft brewer had begun to make contributions to a regional charity.

On Saturday morning, the brothers agreed to the distributors' arrangement for one year, and asked their friend to "hold" his offer for a year. As the arrangement developed with the Coors distributor, Hans began to experiment with dark and light beer formulae and Heinrich set about to find a brewer who could brew for them and who would let Hans and Heinrich control the formula. Both initiatives moved quickly and successfully.

In 2004, the arrangement with the distributor was renewed for five years and the brothers' beer continued to dominate the regional craft beer market. Their competitor never grew and it faded from the market. Hans and Heinrich expanded their product to Oregon and Washington State and reported profits of $890,000 in 2007 with 100% of the stock in their hands. Between 2004 and 2008, Lad and Hooker beer was packaged in bottles and cans. An innovative Christmas 12-pack with the social mission contribution emblazoned on the package became a best seller for the distributor and the brothers. However, along the way experiments with bar and restaurant distribution failed. Experiments with contributions to Mothers Against Drunk Driving failed to attract sufficient attention in the region, and a buyout discussion with the distributor failed (the brothers proposed that they purchase the distributorship, and the distributor countered with an offer to buy Lad and Hooker).

Currently, Hans and Heinrich continue with the Coors distributor, but they are evaluating the possibility of establishing their own distribution network, developing Lad and Hooker soda, and development of a Brew Pub featuring Lad and Hooker beer.

Staub's Famous Draft and Grub

In 1960, Marlan Staub's family had operated a Coors distributorship in Philadelphia, PA. Coors beer was not pasteurized in the 1960s, and it was shipped in refrigerated trucks to Pennsylvania and sold at a premium. Selling shipped beer at a premium was against Coors policy, but the alternative for Coors was to fight a growing black market for their fine Colorado beers. Over 30 years, Coors and the family business profited with little apparent change. Marlan worked in the family business before it closed in 1996. Folks said that Coors lost its special attraction in the region, and that Staub Beer Distributors was slow to find alternative products. Staub Beer Distributors continued to pay the family members exceptional salaries, even as the volume fell in the early 1990s. The cash drain made it impossible to field an aggressive sales force or to promote Coors beer at the levels demanded by Coors. The family business closed in 1996.

Marlan liked beer and he needed to do something to support his young family. He had desperately tried to find financing for the family business in its dying days, so he had local "angel financing" connections. He decided to lean on the two things that he knew about: beer and financing.

Marlan read two books about beer making and decided that he could do it. In addition, his exposure to Coors plant tours for their distributors gave him confidence to start his own beer operation, so he decided to open a brew pub in Reading, PA, and make and sell Staub's Famous Draft and Grub.

Marlan figured that he would need $1 million to purchase a used craft beer still and to begin operations in a vacant factory building in Reading. Three months after he decided to brew and open the brew pub, Marlan found a great deal on a used 100% copper still and purchased it for $115,000, which left him with $25,000 in savings. He made a minimum down payment ($5000) on the factory building and received a contract that required no principle payments for a year. Marlan spent three months placing the copper still in the building, and planning the space for the restaurant. During this period, Marlan received publicity from an admiring newspaper, his family, and the public for his entrepreneurial vision. Many were thrilled that an old industrial building would be restored.

Eight months after conception, Marlan employed a friend to develop the first beer, a hearty dark beer, and he paid him $70,000 per year plus a promise of a share of the company. Again, he drew upon his dwindling savings.

Marlan spent five more months designing the renovations for the building. He finally asked contractors to bid on the renovation 14 months after the initial purchase (at the 12th month, the bank reluctantly extended the principal free mortgage period). Unfortunately, renovation costs and the cost of restaurant fixtures were finally quoted at $1.4 million. The plumbing cost for the still exceeded estimates by $40,000. Marlan told local reporters that the renovation delays were temporary.

Four months later, at the 17th month, Marlan had finally prepared advertising and brochures that he planned to use to raise $1.5 million from community angels. Several history buffs agreed to give Marlan $300,000 for convertible stock in the new company, and two beer loving angels came forward with an additional $158,000. After an extended period of soul-searching, which involved using angel money to pay the factory building mortgage, Marlan decided to move forward with a partial renovation. It was two whole years after his decision to open before Marlan awarded a contract for a partial renovation of the factory building for $400,000. He employed his friend, the brew master, to guide the renovation. His hope was that evidence of construction would inspire investors to come forward who had not responded to the initial offering. Meanwhile he had not been doing much experimenting with the beer itself. Unfortunately, Marlan failed to make new contacts for financing and the contractor ended up suing Marlan for late payment 16 months after the plan to open a brew pub occurred. The contractor now owns the building and its contents: a still, 110 bar stools, 16 old tables, and a grand opening poster advertisement with a box of unsent fundraising brochures. The endless delays, all of which cost a great deal of money, doomed the business to failure.

CONCLUSION

This chapter promotes swiftness and experimentation as entrepreneurial behaviors that contribute to new venture success. Entrepreneurship occurs in the midst of uncertainty, risk, and competitive barriers that are associated with new market entry with new products, processes, and business models. Swiftness and experimentation are sensible responses because they produce market feedback where little information exists. Information can guide revision of market offerings – even revision of market and business model choices to yield attractive profitable offerings.

Creativity, tenacity, self-efficacy, and goal setting are among the factors that enable swiftness and experimentation, which has been confirmed in entrepreneurship research. The factors that contribute to the focal entrepreneurial behaviors, presented here as principles of entrepreneurship, are enhanced with industry and venture experience, as well as learning from expert models and creativity and goal-setting enhancement programs.

REFERENCES

Aldrich, H. E. (1999). *Organizations evolving*. London: Sage.

Baker, T., Miner, A., and Eesley, D. (2003). Improvising firms: Bricolage, account giving, and improvisational competency in the founding process. *Research Policy*, 32, 255–276.

Bandura, A. (1997). *Self-efficacy: The Exercise of Control*. New York: Freeman.

Baum, J. R., and Bird, B. J. (in press). The successful intelligence of high growth entrepreneurs: links to new venture growth. *Organization Science*.

Baum, J. R., and Locke, E. A. (2004). The relationship of entrepreneurial traits, skill, and motivation to subsequent venture growth. *Journal of Applied Psychology*, 89(4), 587–598.

Baum, J. R., and Wally, S. (2003). Strategic decision-making speed and firm performance. *Strategic Management Journal*, 24, 1107–1129.

Baum, J. R., Locke, E. A., and Smith, K. G. (2001). A multidimensional model of venture growth. *Academy of Management Journal*, 44(2), 292–303.

Baum, J. R., Frese, M., Baron, R., and Katz, J. A. (2006). Entrepreneurship as an area of psychology: An introduction. In J. R. Baum, M. Frese, and R. Baron (eds), *The Psychology of Entrepreneurship* (pp. 1–18). New York: Erlbaum.

Bhide, A. V. (2000). *The Origin and Evolution of New Businesses*. New York: Oxford University Press.

Bourgeois, L. J. (1980). Strategy and environment: A conceptual integration. *Academy of Management Review*, 5, 25–39.

Carsrud, A. L., and Krueger, N. F., Jr. (1995). Entrepreneurship and social psychology: Behavioral technology for the new venture initiation process. In J. A. Katz and R. H. Brockhaus, Sr. (eds), *Advances in Entrepreneurship, Firm Emergence, and Growth* (pp. 73–96). Greenwich, CT: JAI Press.

Chandler, G. N., and Jansen, E. (1992). The founder's self-assessed competence and venture performance. *Journal of Business Venturing*, 7, 223–236.

Chen, C. C., Greene, P. G., and Crick, A. (1998). Does entrepreneurial self-efficacy distinguish entrepreneurs from managers? *Journal of Business Venturing*, 13, 395–316.

Covin, J. G., and Slevin, D. P. (1997). High growth transitions: theoretical perspectives and suggested directions. In D. L. Sexton and R. W. Smilor (eds), *Entrepreneurship 2000* (pp. 99–126). Chicago: Upstart.

Davidsson, P., and Honig, B. (2002). The role of social and human capital among nascent entrepreneurs. *Journal of Business Venturing*, 18, 301–331.

Dess, G. D., and Beard, D. W. (1984). Dimensions of organizational task environments. *Administrative Science Quarterly*, 30, 52–73.

Eisenhardt, K. M. (1989). Making fast strategic decisions in high velocity environments. *Academy of Management Journal*, 32, 543–576.

Eisenhardt, K. M., and Tabrizi, B. N. (1995). Accelerating adaptive processes: Product innovation in the global computer industry. *Administrative Science Quarterly*, 40(1), 84–110.

Ferrier, W. J., Smith, K. G., and Grimm, C. M. (1999). The role of competitive action in market share erosion and industry dethronement: A study of industry leaders and challengers. *Academy of Management Journal*, 42(4), 372–388.

Gartner, W. B., Gatewood, E., and Shaver, K. G. (1991). Reasons for starting a business: Not-so-simple answers to simple questions. In G. E. Hills and R. W. Lafarge (eds), *Research at the Marketing/Entrepreneurship Interface* (pp. 90–101). Chicago, IL: Office of Entrepreneurial Studies, University of Illinois at Chicago.

Herron, L. A., and Robinson, R. B., Jr. (1993). A structural model of the effects of entrepreneurial characteristics on venture performance. *Journal of Business Venturing*, 8, 281–294.

Hmieleski, K. M., and Corbett, A. C. (2006). Proclivity for improvisation as a predictor of entrepreneurial intentions. *Journal of Small Business Management*, 41(1), 45–63.

Huey, J., and Walton, S. (1992). *Sam Walton: Made in America – My Story*. Garden City, New York: Doubleday.

Jones, J. W. (1993). *High Speed Management: Time-based Strategies for Managers and Organizations*. San Francisco: Jossey Bass.

Judge, T. A., and Bono, J. E. (2001). The relationship of core self-evaluations traits – self-esteem, generalized self-efficacy, locus of control, and emotional stability – with job satisfaction and job performance: a meta-analysis. *Journal of Applied Psychology*, 86(1), 80–92.

Judge, W. Q. and Miller, A. (1991). Antecedents and outcomes of decision speed in different environmental contexts. *Academy of Management Journal*, 34, 449–463.

Kirchhoff, B. (1997). Entrepreneurship economics. In W. B. Bygrave (ed.), *The Portable MBA in Entrepreneurship*. New York: Wiley.

Kirzner, I. M. (1985). *Discovery and the Capitalist Process*. Chicago: The University of Chicago Press.

Landy, F. J., and Becker, W. S. (1987). Motivation theory reconsidered. In L. L. Cummings and B. M. Staw (eds), *Research in Organizational Behavior*, 9, 1–38. Greenwich, CT: JAI Press.

Locke, E. A. (2000). *The Prime Movers: Traits of the Great wealth Creators*. New York: AMACOM.

Locke, E. A., and Baum, J. R. (2007). Entrepreneurial motivation. In J. R. Baum, M. Frese, and R. Baron (eds), *The Psychology of Entrepreneurship* (pp. 93–112). New York: Erlbaum.

Locke, E. A., and Latham, G. P. (1990). *A Theory of Goal Setting and Task Performance*. Englewood Cliffs, NJ: Prentice Hall.

Locke, E. A., and Latham, G. P. (2002). Building a practically useful theory of goal setting and task motivation: A 35-year odyssey. *American Psychologist*, 57, 705–717.

Markman, G. D., Balkin, D. B., and Baron, R. A. (2002). Inventors and new venture formation: The effects of general self-efficacy and regretful thinking. *Entrepreneurship Theory and Practice*, Winter, 149–165.

Miner, A. S., Bassoff, P., and Moorman, C. (2001). Organizational improvisation and learning: A field study. *Administrative Science Quarterly*, 46, 304–337.

Mumford, M., Supinski, E. P., Baughman, W. A., Constanza, D. P., and Threlfall, K. V. (1997). Process-based measures of creative problem-solving skills: Overall Prediction. *Creativity Research Journal*, 10(6), 73–85.

Priem, R. L., Rasheed, A. M. A., and Kotulic, A. G. (1995). Rationality in strategic decision processes, environmental dynamism and firm performance. *Journal of Management*, 21, 913–929.

Rauch, A., and Frese, M. (2000). Psychological approaches to entrepreneurial success: A general model and an overview of findings. In C. L. Cooper and I. T. Robertson (eds), *International Review of Industrial and Organizational Psychology*, 15, 101–142. New York: John Wiley and Sons, Ltd.

Runco, M. A., Plucker, J. A., and Lim, W. (2000). Development and psychometric integrity of a measure of ideation behavior. *Creativity Research Journal*, 13, 391–398.

Schumpeter, J. A. (1934). *The Theory of Economic Development*. Cambridge, MA: Harvard University Press.

Shaver, K. G., and Scott, L. R. (1991). Person, process, choice: The psychology of new venture creation. *Entrepreneurship Theory and Practice*, Winter, 23–45.

Shepherd, D. A. (1999). Venture capitalists' assessment of new venture survival. *Management Science*, 45(5), 621–632.

Smith, K. S., and Smith, R. L. (2000). *Entrepreneurial Finance*. New York: Wiley.

Stajkovic, A. D., and Luthans, F. (1998). Self-efficacy and work related performance: A meta analysis. *Psychology Bulletin*, 124, 240–261.

Stalk, G., and Hout, T. M. (1990). *Competing against Time: How Time-based Competition is Reshaping Global Markets*. New York: Free Press.

Stevenson, H. H. (1985). A new paradigm for entrepreneurial management. In J. J. Kao and H. H Stevenson (eds), *Entrepreneurship: What it is and How to Teach it*. Boston: Harvard Business School Press.

Thomke, S. H. (2003). *Experimentation Matters*. Boston: Harvard Business School Press.

Tracy, K., Locke, E. A., and Renard, M. (1999). Conscious goal setting vs. subconscious motives: Longitudinal and concurrent effects on the performance of entrepreneurial firms. Paper presented at the Academy of Management Conference.

Venkataraman, S. (1997). The distinctive domain of entrepreneurship research: An editor's perspective. In J. Katz and R. Brockhaus (eds), *Advances in Entrepreneurship, Firm Emergence, and Growth* (pp. 119–138). Greenwich, CT: JAI Press.

Zopounidis, C. (1994). Venture capital modeling: Evaluation criteria for the appraisal of investments. *The Financier*, 1(2), 54–64.

EXERCISES

Venture change

In most successful ventures, the product, processes, or business model that ultimately finds market acceptance and profitability are some variation of the original market entry. Choose an example and write a short history (two paragraphs) of the changes that have occurred. Identify the period from market entry to today and point to evidence of swiftness and experimentation.

If you do not have an idea yourself, you could write about laptop computers, the automobile, or mobile telephones. If you can, indicate which of the original entrants survived.

Business venture idea

Divide into groups of 3–6 people. Come up with an idea for a new business venture, and assume that you have $2 million in financing. If your new venture idea could be copied, how fast would you have to move to introduce your first product? How fast would you need to expand from your local market? Assuming everything does not go as planned, what types of experiments could you try to see if some variant on your original idea might work?

Part IX

WORK, FAMILY, TECHNOLOGY, AND CULTURE

31

Achieve Work–Family Balance through Individual and Organizational Strategies

Boris B. Baltes and Malissa A. Clark

As the average workweek is steadily increasing in the USA, along with the number of dual-earner households, many workers today find themselves struggling to balance their work and family lives. Indeed, a recent poll by the Equal Opportunities Commission found that nearly three out of five adults believe it is harder now for working parents to balance work and family life than it was 30 years ago. Because of concerns such as this, both organizations and researchers have become increasingly focused on a better understanding of what helps employees to balance their work and family lives. To date, most of the focus has been on how organizational initiatives (e.g. flextime) can help individuals manage these two goals but recent research has begun to realize the importance of individual level strategies in achieving this balance. The guiding principle of this chapter is that both individual and organizational strategies are necessary if employees are to achieve work–family balance and that the use of individual strategies can often be affected by organizational level factors. In the present chapter, we present a definition of work–family balance, followed by a discussion of the organizational and individual strategies that can help one to achieve balance.

Work–Family Balance (Conflict)

Work–family conflict can be defined as "a form of interrole conflict in which the role pressures from the work and family domains are mutually incompatible in some respect" (Greenhaus and Beutell, 1985, p. 77). Individuals may feel conflict because their work life is interfering with their family life, termed work interfering with family (WIF) conflict, or they may feel conflict because their family life is interfering with their work life, termed family interfering with work (FIW) conflict (Frone, Russell, and Cooper, 1997). Work–family balance is a newer term, but basically can be understood as a person achieving a low level of work–family conflict.

It should also be pointed out that researchers and practitioners have recently begun to focus on the positive aspects of participating in multiple life roles. Perhaps this shift was partially influenced by the ideas put forth by proponents of positive psychology or perhaps this shift was due to a realization that some individuals were finding ways to thrive in multiple life roles. In either case, research in the work–family domain has begun also to focus on the concept of work-family facilitation (often referred to as enrichment, or positive spillover). In the present chapter, however, we will focus solely on work–family balance.

What causes conflict between work and family roles?

In the work domain, significant relationships between levels of WIF conflict and a myriad of variables have been found (for a comprehensive review of antecedents of WFC, see Byron, 2005). Not surprisingly, a key variable is time. Both the number of hours worked and the amount of overtime worked have been linked to increased work–family conflict. Furthermore, having heavy workloads and responsibilities in one's job can increase an individual's stress, which can then carry over to his or her family life. Various shift schedules have also been linked to WIF conflict. For example, working second or third shifts can cause increased WIF conflict because these schedules often make it difficult to arrange childcare or attend children's events that are often scheduled around the typical work shift (i.e. first shift).

Another factor that can increase an individual's level of WIF conflict is a lack of job autonomy, presumably because having freedom to adjust one's job responsibilities can lessen the extent to which work interferes with the demands of family. In addition to autonomy, job type can have an impact on WIF conflict, as some jobs (e.g. lawyer, doctor) require long hours and are less flexible than other jobs. Having a supportive supervisor has been shown to reduce the extent to which work can interfere with family life, because not only can supervisors provide instrumental aid to their employees, which can reduce workload and work stress, but they can also provide emotional support and advice. Conversely, a lack of supervisor support has been found to increase work–family conflict.

In the family domain, positive linkages have been found between WIF conflict and/or FIW conflict and marital status, size, and the developmental stage of family. Family stressors (i.e. parental workload, extent of children's misbehavior, lack of spousal support, and degree of tension in the marital relationship) and family involvement have been shown to increase the extent to which family can interfere with work. For example, if individuals have many family responsibilities (e.g. picking children up from school, cooking dinner) and they do not get support from their spouse, such family stress could drain individuals both mentally and physically, thereby leaving less energy that can be devoted to their work. Both the number and age of children play a role in the level of FIW conflict experienced by parents. Past research has demonstrated that the number of children individuals have impacts their ability to accommodate family responsibilities with work demands. Additionally, younger children typically require more care and thus more resources from their caregivers, which results in greater conflict between work and family. More recently, eldercare has become a topic of interest since an ever-increasing number of employees are also dealing with this issue which can contribute to FIW conflict. Individuals can benefit from various forms of social support, as negative relationships have been found between WIF conflict and spousal and family support and between FIW conflict and spousal and family support.

In sum, there are a number of antecedents that cause work–family conflict. However, these can all be categorized as either work (job) or family stressors. Furthermore, it should be apparent that any strategy to achieve work–family balance must be targeted at reducing these stressors. Indeed, organizational initiatives aimed at reducing such stressors have been attempted with varying levels of success; the next section will address such initiatives.

ORGANIZATIONAL STRATEGIES

Organizational initiatives intended to help employees balance their work and family lives are becoming increasingly popular. These initiatives include implementing flexible work hours (flextime), allowing telecommuting, compressed workweeks, offering on-site childcare, and implementing part-time schedules and job sharing. Research has shown that these initiatives can reduce employees' work–family conflict and increase their family satisfaction. For example, in a 2000 study by the Boston College Center for Work and Family, which surveyed over 1300 employees and 150 managers in six companies, flexible work arrangements had a positive impact on productivity, employees' quality of work, and employee retention. We believe that with careful implementation and a supportive organizational culture, these initiatives have the potential to increase employees' work–family balance. We will discuss each of these organizational initiatives and their benefits and potential drawbacks in more detail below, and will conclude with a discussion of how an organization's culture can help or impede an organization's effort to increase their employee's work–family balance.

Flextime. To date, the most widely used organizational initiative to help workers balance their work and family lives is flextime, or flexible workweeks. Flextime involves setting a band of time where all employees are required to be in the office (typically from 9 or 10 A.M. until 2 or 3 P.M.), but employees have the discretion as to exactly what time they will arrive and leave work outside that band of time. An obvious benefit of a flexible workweek is that employees can start or end their day earlier or later, depending on their other non-work obligations and needs at that time. Thus, if employees have an outside obligation in the afternoon on a particular day (e.g. doctor's appointment, child's sporting event) they can simply arrive at work earlier in the morning, which allows them to leave earlier in the afternoon. According to a Families and Work Institute national study, 68% of companies allow at least some employees to periodically change starting and quitting times (although only 34% of companies allowed employees to do this on a daily basis), and the percentage of companies offering flextime has increased from 1998 to 2005. This national study also found that flextime was offered more frequently in smaller companies (50–99 employees) than larger companies (1000+ employees). Also, according to a large-scale study of over 30,000 government employees, approximately 41% of employees surveyed utilize flextime (Saltzstein, Ting, and Saltzstein, 2001).

Overall, research has shown that flextime is associated with many individual as well as organizational benefits. Several studies have found that flextime is associated with positive attitudinal outcomes. For example, flextime has been associated with greater employee loyalty to the organization, and greater employee job satisfaction (Baltes, Briggs, Huff, Wright, and Neuman, 1999). Additionally, employees who have greater control over their work hours have also reported reduced work–family conflict. In addition to these attitudinal outcomes, research has linked flextime to various organizational outcomes, such as increased productivity and reduced turnover.

There is some evidence that all forms of flextime are not created equal, however. For example, researchers have found that some flexible schedules offered by organizations allow for very little flexibility, and that the number of hours in which an employee actually works may increase with a flexible schedule. In fact, one study of Canadian employees found that the percentage of employees working 50+ hours doubled or sometimes tripled in the presence of flexible work arrangements (Comfort, Johnson, and Wallace, 2003). In the Boston College Center for Work and Family's 2000 study, researchers made a distinction between traditional flextime and daily flextime. Whereas traditional flextime involves employees choosing their start and end times, which must include certain core hours, daily flextime is a working schedule in which employees are allowed to vary their work hours on a daily basis. The researchers at the Center for Work and Family found that employees using daily flextime were more satisfied with their jobs, lives, and more productive than employees using traditional flextime.

Compressed workweeks.   Compressed workweeks are used in a broad range of industries, including manufacturing, health care, food service, government, the airline industry, and law enforcement (Harrington and Hall, 2007). With a compressed workweek, the workweek is shortened to fewer than five days by having employees work longer hours on the days they do work. There are many different variations of a compressed workweek, but the most typical is to have full-time employees (i.e. 40 hour workweek) work four 10-hour days per week instead of five eight-hour days per week. According to the Families and Work Institute's study, 39% of companies allow at least some employees to work a compressed workweek schedule, and the number of companies offering compressed workweeks has increased since 1998.

As with many of the family-friendly policies we discuss, there are pros and cons to implementing a compressed workweek in an organization. Among the benefits are that compressed workweeks have been shown to decrease work–family conflict, stress, and fatigue, as well as increase work satisfaction and positive attitudes about the effect of work schedules on one's family and social life. In addition to these attitudinal benefits, compressed workweeks have been shown to reduce employee absenteeism and increase productivity.

Compressed workweeks can be problematic for some employees, however; specifically, for those employees who have time-specific responsibilities (e.g. picking up a child from school). Indeed, Saltzstein et al. (2001) found that mothers with an unemployed spouse (who can presumably help with childcare or eldercare obligations) experienced significantly more satisfaction with their work–family balance as a result of a compressed workweek, whereas unmarried mothers experienced significantly *less* satisfaction with work–family balance. This finding illustrates that compressed workweeks may only benefit employees when they have someone to assist in their time-specific responsibilities. In the case of childcare, most daycare facilities close at 6 P.M., which can make it difficult for employees who do not have outside assistance to find childcare on the days they work extended hours.

Telecommuting.   Telecommuting is generally defined as working from home or off-site for all or part of the workweek, made possible by advances in telecommunication and information technology. According to the 2005 Families and Work study of employers, 31% of companies allowed some of its employees to work from home or off-site on a regular basis. However, telecommuting is not suitable for all jobs, or all people. Telecommuting is most often used in jobs that rely heavily on phones, the internet/computers, and other technology devices, where face-to-face time with other employees or customers is not as essential, and where constant supervision is not necessary. Further, researchers have identified several personality traits and skills that differentiate employees suitable for telecommuting from those who would struggle with such a work arrangement. Examples include self-motivation, time management and organizational skills, trustworthiness, comfort with solitude, strong communication skills, independence, and confidence.

Like flextime and compressed workweeks, there are pros and cons to telecommuting. From an employee's perspective, telecommuting can have many advantages, including the cost savings on gas, reduced time spent commuting to work, greater autonomy, and greater flexibility of the work schedule. From an organization's perspective, telecommuting can increase employee productivity, lower employee absenteeism, and reduce overhead costs. Research has shown telecommuting to have a positive impact on employees, in that telecommuting has been linked to greater work–family balance than traditional occupations, more perceived control over one's work and family roles, higher performance ratings, and reduced depression rates.

Conversely, telecommuting can pose challenges to employees and organizations alike. Employees may feel isolated from their co-workers, or have difficulty separating their work and family roles, while organizations may have difficulty monitoring employees as well as fostering team synergy. Indeed, research has linked telecommuting to increased work–family conflict, increased spillover from work to family, and higher depression rates. Kossek, Lautsch, and Eaton (2006) point out that telecommuting may lead to increased work–family conflict because the border between the work and family domains is more permeable if one is working at home. To resolve this, some employees have developed routines to help solidify the role boundaries between work and family, such as putting on work clothes, reading the business section of the newspaper, or saying goodbye to the family before stepping into the home office.

On-site childcare. Another recent trend within organizations is to provide a daycare facility on-site. Providing an on-site childcare facility has the potential to increase work–family balance for employees with children, presumably because employees do not have to travel to drop off and pick up their children, and they can visit their children at various times in the workday (e.g. during their lunch hour), thus helping parents to feel close to their children even while at work. Although a recent study found that the usage of employer-provided childcare is relatively low, those using such services have reported more positive attitudes towards managing their work and family responsibilities and were less likely to experience problems with daycare. On-site childcare has also been found to result in positive organizational outcomes, such as increased organizational loyalty, and reduced absenteeism and turnover. A potential unintended outcome for on-site childcare is that there may be a backlash, or "frustration effect," from workers who are not able to take advantage of such a policy, either because they do not have children, are on the waitlist, or cannot afford such services.

Part-time and job sharing. Another type of organizational policy aimed at helping employees balance their work and family involves reducing the total number of hours employees work per week. This can be accomplished either by reducing the number of hours an employee works from full-time to part-time, or by dividing up the responsibility of one full-time position among two employees (i.e. job sharing). Many organizations currently use these policies, with 53% allowing employees to switch from full-time to part-time and 46% allowing employees to share jobs (Bond, Galinsky, Kim, and Brownfield, 2005). Research has shown that employees who reduced their hours to part-time experienced greater life satisfaction, increased work–family balance, felt less stressed, and reported better relationships with their children.

However, part-time work may not be a feasible alternative for certain occupations (e.g. lawyer, doctor) thus limiting its usefulness. Job sharing is also only suitable for some positions, mostly ones that require long workweeks (greater than 40 hours/week) or jobs that cannot be easily reduced to part-time positions. If the employees sharing a particular position are able to coordinate and work well together, job sharing can be a great option for employees. For example, if one employee has an unexpected family situation, he/she can work out an arrangement with his/her job sharing partner to cover this time lost. Understandably, there are some potential disadvantages that come with sharing a job with another person, particularly if one of the partners is not carrying his/her share of the workload, or there are communication breakdowns. Additionally, sometimes the job performance of each individual employee is not easily distinguished, which can be problematic if individuals make unequal contributions.

MEDIATORS/MODERATORS OF ORGANIZATIONAL STRATEGIES

In order for organizational strategies/initiatives to help employees balance their work and family lives, the employees first need to (1) use the policies that are offered to them and (2) perceive that the organization is fully supportive of the use of such policies. For example, if the organization offers on-site childcare, but charges so much for these services that only the top executives in the company can afford such a service, then it will not be effective in helping most of the organization's employees manage their work and family (a point we discuss below in one of our case studies). Second, employees will not take advantage of such policies if they perceive negative ramifications may come from utilizing such a policy. For example, if an organization offers telecommuting but employees believe that if they take advantage of such a policy their manager will think negatively of their work ethic, which may subsequently impact their potential for promotions or pay raises, then they will not take advantage of such a policy. Indeed, Allen (2001) points out that offering family-friendly policies may not be sufficient; rather it is the *perception* that the organization is family supportive that mediates the relationship between the family-friendly policies available and positive outcomes. Perceptions of a family-supportive environment are an individual level variable that reflects individual perceptions and can vary widely within an organization. Family-friendly culture on the other hand is an organizational level variable that should reflect "reality" and assumes that agreement exists between employees on how family-friendly the culture actually is. Family-friendly culture has been found to act as a moderator. Specifically, we believe that family-friendly policies will have a greater impact on facilitating work–family balance in organizations with a family-friendly culture than those with a culture that does not support its policies. Indeed, Thompson, Beauvais, and

Lyness (1999) found that a supportive work–family culture was related to employees' use of work–family benefits, and both the availability of such policies and a supportive work culture predicted lower work–family conflict. Taking the organization's family-friendly climate into account may explain why some prior organizational initiatives did not work, as it may be difficult to fully take advantage of such family-friendly policies if the climate does not support it.

In sum, while some organizational initiatives have been successful at increasing work–family balance, it appears that many factors such as individual perceptions as well as organizational level culture play a role in their success. Simply implementing organizational policies such as flextime or telecommuting is not enough; the organization must ensure that its culture is supportive of such policies as well.

HOW TO IMPLEMENT ORGANIZATIONAL STRATEGIES

From our discussion, we hope it is clear that organizations cannot simply implement one or more family-friendly policies, sit back, and watch the employees thrive. On the contrary, an organization must ensure that its leaders fully support and embrace such a policy and make efforts to change the company culture if it is currently not supportive of such endeavors.

Additionally, we believe that even effectively implemented organizational initiatives are only half of the equation. That is, employees should realize that organizational policies aimed at reducing their employees' work–family balance are not one-size-fits-all solutions. Instead, employees must take the initiative and evaluate their particular work and family stressors and how they are working to cope with them. Effective management of work and family roles takes efforts by both the organization and the individual. Thus, the following section will discuss how employees can take steps to improve their work–family balance through various individual strategies.

INDIVIDUAL STRATEGIES

Over the past 15 years a relatively small but increasing amount of research has examined the role of the individual in reducing their work–family conflict (i.e. achieving work–family balance). For example, it has been found that women who possessed self-control skills were less stressed by handling multiple roles than were women who did not possess these skills. Furthermore, qualitative research studies have also shown that both dual-career men and women use certain coping strategies more during stages of their lifecycles which included more stressful situations (i.e. young children at home). For instance, Becker and Moen (1999) found that many dual-earner couples engaged in what they called scaling back strategies (i.e. reducing and restructuring a couple's commitment to paid work). While early research on individual strategies lacked a cohesive framework, this recently changed with the introduction of a meta-theory entitled Selection, Optimization, and Compensation (SOC).

Selection, optimization, and compensation

SOC was originally developed as a lifespan model to explain successful adaptation to the loss of resources due to aging through adjustments in the use and allocation of resources

(Baltes and Baltes, 1990; Baltes, 1997). It is based on the underlying assumption that limited internal and external resources (e.g. mental capacity, time, social support) require people to make choices regarding the allocation of those resources. These limitations of resources necessitate the use of several processes: selection, optimization, and compensation.

Selection is divided into two categories, elective selection and loss-based selection. The primary focus of both types of selection is on *choosing goals*. Specifically, one always has a limited amount of resources and selection is needed to focus on a subset of possible goals. Elective selection involves choosing from among positive options. Loss-based selection occurs when an individual is pressured to change or abandon certain goals (or change one's goal hierarchy) by the loss of some internal or external resource.

Optimization and compensation pertain to the means for attaining goals. Optimization refers to the acquisition of and refinement in the use of resources to achieve selected goals. General categories of optimization include persistence, practice, learning of new skills, modeling of successful others, as well as the scheduling of time.

Compensation occurs when lost resources (or those anticipated to be lost, for example time) are replaced by new ones in order to sustain progress towards one's existing goals. The use of external aids (e.g. the internet) or help from others (e.g. childcare) are examples of compensatory behaviors.

As stated previously, work–family conflict occurs when both are important goals and an individual's time and energy resources are limited. Since the theory of SOC hypothesizes (and research supports) that, when faced with the limitation of resources (e.g. time, energy), those who use SOC strategies are more likely to maximize gains and minimize losses, it is plausible to assume that individuals who use SOC behaviors will be more successful at dealing with the competing roles of work and family. For example, after the birth of a child, an individual could engage in loss-based selection and choose to focus on a more limited number of work goals (e.g. no longer focus on organizational networking) and/ or family goals (only focus on the immediate and not extended family) given that their resources have become more limited. Further, an individual could engage in optimization and decide what individual skills (e.g. organizational, technological) could be acquired or improved to help insure successful goal completion. For example, if an employee has decided that successfully leading/managing her workgroup is a goal she will pursue then she can decide to take a leadership training program to enhance her skills. By enhancing her skills she should more efficiently achieve the same level of productivity allowing more time for family commitments. Finally, individuals can engage in compensation by maintaining their prior productivity (even though they may have to work less because of family commitments) through the use of delegation. They could attempt to give more responsibility to subordinates to decrease their actual workload but maintain overall productivity.

Research has now demonstrated that the use of these SOC strategies are related to lower amounts of job and family stressors and thereby lower amounts of WFC. For example, the results from a study by Baltes and Heydens-Gahir (2003) show that employees who reported using SOC strategies at work and/or at home also reported lower amounts of job and family stressors, and subsequently work–family conflict.

Qualitative, interview-based research has provided us with some specific examples of SOC that employees report using.

Examples of selection strategies in both the work and family domain included:

"I prioritize my workload."

"I say no to other projects because I don't have the time."

"(We) sit down as a family and say ok this is what we want to do, this is our five year plan, and this is our five month plan. You have to prioritize!"

Examples of optimization in both domains included:

"I try to find the best way to do it, or the fastest way to complete home or job tasks."

"I increase my efficiency by eating my lunch at my desk while I continue to work."

"I have increased my listening skills so as to better understand my family."

"I reevaluate what didn't work to make sure I do things more efficiently the next time."

"I keep a calendar of when things are due."

Examples of compensation in both domains included:

"I try to empower more people to do more things; I try to delegate more."

"I try to share (the workload) between different individuals so that it's not all put on me to complete tasks."

"I verbalize to my boss that I need help."

"We give the kids more responsibility at home."

"I hired a part-time housekeeper."

Additional research appears to indicate that, given one's selected goals, the strategy of optimization seems to be the most effective in reducing work and family stressors. Of course, the exact way individuals choose to engage in SOC strategies is open to much variability. While the use of the SOC model as a framework has demonstrated that at a broad (or general) level the reported use of SOC strategies is related to lower work family conflict, what is still needed is more research that generates an exhaustive list of specific behaviors that might be used in the future as part of a training program for employees.

MODERATORS OF INDIVIDUAL STRATEGIES

Research has suggested two major types of possible moderators with respect to individual level strategies. First, one can have variables that act as moderators with respect to the potential efficacy or even the possibility of using any of the SOC strategies. For instance, the presence of training programs that allows an employee to optimize (i.e. become more efficient at work tasks) would probably moderate the effect that optimization strategies might have. Specifically, attempts at optimization might be more effective if the organization offered training programs. Another example of this type of moderator would be job type. For example, some research suggests that use of SOC strategies is affected quite a bit by job type/level. A manager may have much more flexibility when it comes to prioritizing his/her workload (i.e. elective selection) than a clerical employee has. Thus, even if a clerical worker would choose to engage in elective selection they do not have the autonomy to do so. Finally, socio-economic level could act as a moderator with respect to the use of compensation strategies.

For instance, wealthier families would be able to engage in compensatory behaviors such as the use of daycare and/or household help much easier than poorer families.

A second set of moderators of any of the SOC strategies are those variables that could affect the demand on one's resources or the supply of one's resources. These types of variables would make the use of individual level strategies more important to achieving work–family balance. That is, it is most likely that employees in the most demanding situations can benefit the most. To date, we are aware of only one study that had theorized and examined these types of potential moderators of individual level strategies (Young, Baltes, and Pratt, 2007). This study examined SOC-type strategies and theorized that SOC strategies should be most effective for the individuals who have the most demands on their resources. Several factors that impact the amount of resources demanded of, or resources available to, an individual with respect to the domains of work and family were tested as potential moderators. Furthermore, the study found that the age of a participant's youngest child at home, family support, the number of family-friendly policies offered by the organization, supervisor support, and participant age moderated the work (family) SOC–job (family) stressor relationship. For example, as the age of the youngest child in the house decreased (it has been found that younger children put more resource demands on parents) the use of SOC strategies became much more effective/useful. In sum, it appears as though these individual level strategies are very important for achieving work–life balance especially for the employees who are in the most demanding situations.

How to Implement Individual Strategies

Implementation of individual strategies is obviously in the hands of each employee. However, we hope it has become clear that organizational level factors may influence the extent to which SOC behaviors can be undertaken by employees and potentially also the extent to which these behaviors/strategies are effective. For example, an individual attempting to optimize through the use of new skills training will have a harder time if the organization does not offer or support the use of training programs.

Case Examples

First Tennessee Bank

First Tennessee Bank has earned top ratings when it comes to being a family-friendly company by both *Business Week* and *Working Mother*. First Tennessee offers a wide variety of family-friendly programs, including flextime, telecommuting, on-site childcare or vouchers, job sharing, prime-time schedules (reduced hours with benefits), and adoption benefits. In addition, First Tennessee was one of the only companies surveyed by *Business Week* that have actually measured the effect of work–family strategies on profits. However, perhaps even more impressive is that family friendliness is ingrained in both culture and business strategy. Realizing that family issues do affect business results, executives have integrated issues pertaining to balancing work and family into job design, work processes, and organizational structures. Company executives have made strides to show workers that the company is serious in their endeavors to help employees balance their work and family lives. To ensure that the work–family policies are working smoothly and that employees are satisfied with them, First Tennessee has created the First Power Council, which is comprised of high level executives and currently chaired by the HR manager. The First Power Council meets quarterly to go over employee satisfaction surveys and to discuss any matters (work–family related and otherwise) of concern to the employees. John Daniel, HR manager at First Tennessee, views the work–family benefits offered to employees as a win–win: "I often get more productivity from the people we offer work–family benefits to than the average person because they are so appreciative of the flexibility the program allows. In sum, offering work–family benefits is a great way to attract and retain the right people."

First Tennessee Bank provides a great example of how a supportive culture can enhance the effectiveness of family-friendly policies. Regardless of how many benefits are offered to employees, if only a select few are able/allowed to use them, or if the company culture still does not support the use of such policies on a regular basis, then employees will not feel the benefits of such programs.

XYZ Company

The top management at XYZ Company (a fictional but representative company) has recently implemented several work–family policies in response to employee satisfaction surveys that indicated many employees were concerned about balancing their work and families. After consideration of which policies would work best for their particular company, executives decided to offer flextime and part-time work to employees. Despite their good intentions and initial excitement for these work–family programs, recent events at the company suggest that the top management did not follow through to ensure that these work–family policies were being properly implemented.

Since the implementation of the two work–family policies, several employees have filed complaints that they have been denied the opportunity to use them. Several employees were denied flextime because their supervisor reportedly stated that their particular job within the company required that they be there during normal operating hours to deal with clients. Other supervisors reportedly denied part-time work because, in their opinion, it was an "all or nothing" position – either the employee commits to full-time work, or they will find someone who will commit to full-time. Some complaints were filed because managers did offer flextime or part-time work, but only when the employees agreed to a lesser pay or a lower level position. Upon investigation of these instances, top management discovered that some supervisors were strongly opposed to such policies because they feared this would decrease the productivity of their work group.

According to recent focus groups held with XYZ employees, once employees learned of these grievances regarding the flextime and part-time work options offered to employees, employees began to fear that taking advantage of such policies would in fact limit their ability to move up within the organization. These fears were not entirely unwarranted, as there have been at least two documented instances of an employee being demoted or transferred to a less desirable position within two months of requesting either the flextime or part-time work option from his/her supervisor. Although the supervisors in these two instances deny such a link, the focus group discussions revealed that many employees believe otherwise.

In sum, although XYZ Company had intended to help employees balance their work and family by offering flexible benefits, these policies are not having the intended consequences. First, because top management have not clearly conveyed to company supervisors that these work–family policies should be encouraged, and every attempt should be made to accommodate employees who wish to take advantage of them, some supervisors have been reluctant to grant these flexible arrangements to their subordinates for fear that they would decrease their work group productivity. Thus, in many ways, these work–family policies failed in their attempt to help employees balance their work and family, because either the employees have been denied such benefits or the employees were reluctant to ask for such an arrangement for fear of demotion or other work-related consequences. Most importantly, at XYZ Company, the implementation of the work–family policies has actually caused more damage than benefit. Specifically, since the flextime and part-time work policies have been implemented, recent employee satisfaction surveys have shown a decrease in job satisfaction and organizational commitment. Moreover, turnover has increased from 20% to 28% since flextime and part-time work were first offered to employees. Thus, not only have these work–family policies failed to help improve employees' work–family balance, they have actually *lowered* (based on the employee surveys mentioned above) employee satisfaction and commitment to the organization. Company XYZ is a prime example of just how important it is that all company employees, as well as the company culture, is supportive of such policies. The bottom line is this: if you are going to offer work–family policies to employees, you have got to do it right.

REFERENCES

Allen, T. D. (2001). Family supportive work environments: The role of organizational perceptions. *Journal of Vocational Behavior*, 58, 414–435.

Baltes, P. B. (1997). On the incomplete architecture of human ontogeny: Selection, optimization, and compensation as foundation of developmental theory. *American Psychologist*, 52(4), 366–380.

Baltes, P. B., and Baltes, M. M. (eds). (1990). *Successful Aging: Perspectives from the Behavioral Sciences*. Cambridge, MA: Cambridge University Press.

Baltes, B. B., Briggs, T. E., Huff, J. W., Wright, J. A., and Neuman, G. A. (1999). Flexible and compressed workweek schedules: A meta-analysis of their effects on work-related criteria. *Journal of Applied Psychology*, 84, 496–513.

Baltes, B. B., and Heydens-Gahir, H. A. (2003). Reduction of work–family conflict through the use of selection, optimization, and compensation behaviors. *Journal of Applied Psychology*, 88, 1005–1018.

Becker, P. E., and Moen, P. (1999). Scaling back: Dual earner couples' work–family strategies. *Journal of Marriage and the Family*, 61, 995–1007.

Bond, J. T., Galinsky, E., Kim, S. S., and Brownfield, E. (2005). *The 2005 National Study of Employers*. New York: Families and Work Institute.

Byron, K. (2005). A meta-analytic review of work–family conflict and its antecedents. *Journal of Vocational Behavior*, 67, 169–198.

Comfort, D., Johnson, K., and Wallace, D. (2003). Part-time work and family-friendly practices in Canadian workplaces. *Human Resources Development Canada*, 6, 1–78.

Frone, M. R., Russell, M., and Cooper, M. L. (1997). Relation of work–family conflict to health outcomes: A four-year longitudinal study of employed parents. *Journal of Occupational and Organizational Psychology*, 70, 325–335.

Greenhaus, J. H., and Beutell, N. J. (1985). Sources of conflict between work and family roles. *Academy of Management Review*, 10, 76–88.

Harrington, B., and Hall, D. T. (2007). *Career management and work-life integration: using self-assessment to navigate contemporary careers*. Thousand Oaks, CA: Sage Publications.

Kossek, E. E., Lautsch, B. A., and Eaton, S. C. (2006). Telecommuting, control, and boundary management: Correlates of policy use and practice, job control, and work-family effectiveness. *Journal of Vocational Behavior*, 68, 347–367.

Saltzstein, A. L., Ting, Y., and Saltzstein, G. H. (2001). Work–family balance and job satisfaction: The impact of family-friendly policies on attitudes of federal government employees. *Public Administration Review*, 61, 452–467.

Thompson, C., Beauvais, L. L., and Lyness, K. S. (1999). When work–family benefits are not enough: The influence of work–family culture on benefit utilization, organizational attachment, and work–family conflict. *Journal of Vocational Behavior*, 54, 392–415.

Young, L. M., Baltes, B. B., and Pratt, A. (2007). Using selection, optimization, and compensation to reduce job/family stressors: Effective when it matters. *Journal of Business and Psychology*, 18, 1–29.

EXERCISES

Designing and implementing family-friendly policies from the top down

Students may work individually or in groups, and they are to assume the role of CEO of a large electronics manufacturer. The company has 150 employees – of which 75 are manufacturing, 30 are support staff (accounting, administrative), 30 are sales representatives and account managers, and 15 are high-level executives. The company is 50% males, average age of 35. The shareholders recently decided they want the organization to become more family friendly, and wishes to implement a family-friendly policy, but they can't decide on the best one, how it should be implemented, and who should be allowed to use it (i.e. should everyone in the company be able to use the policy, or a select group of employees?). As CEO, he/she must come to decisions on several points:

◆ Which policy or policies will you be implementing (e.g. flextime, compressed work-weeks, job sharing)?
◆ Who should be allowed to use the particular policy/policies? Will it cause problems if everyone is not treated the same?
◆ Finally, how can you ensure the organizational culture is going to support the policy?

Generating individual strategies / behaviors

Judy is a HR manager with a full-time position at a large beverage company. She has a significant other who also has a full-time position and two small children (both of whom are in daycare). Given that her job as a manager is not always limited to a 9 to 5 schedule (e.g. sometimes she needs to work late or take work home) combined with the fact that her children are involved in quite a few activities (e.g. soccer, swimming) she finds it very difficult to successfully fulfill both her roles as a manager and as a parent/spouse. She often finds that her work interferes with her family (e.g. needs to work late which causes her to miss or cancel family activities) but also that her family role interferes with her work (e.g. cannot meet deadlines partly due to family responsibilities that do not let her complete work at home). Students may work individually or in groups and they are to try to identify behaviors/strategies that Judy could use to try to better balance her work and family life.

32

Use Information Technology for Organizational Change

Maryam Alavi and Youngjin Yoo

The information age is upon us. With a few clicks of a mouse button, we can instantly access everything from current stock prices to video clips of current movies, with millions of bytes of information in between. Like the steam engine helped enable the transition into the industrial age, information technologies are fueling the transition into the information age.

The phrase information technologies (IT) refers to computer and communication technologies (both hardware and software) used to process, store, retrieve, and transmit information in electronic form. Today, information technologies are pervasive in industrialized nations and are changing the way we work and live with an accelerating pace. According to Forrester Research, it was estimated that there would be over 1 billion personal computers (PCs) in the world by the end of 2008 and the number is expected to double by 2015. While it will have taken 27 years to reach the first billion PCs in the world, it will take only seven years to reach the next billion (Champan, 2007). When we consider new forms of computing devices such as the mobile phone, the number is even more overwhelming. Consider the following. According to a report by Reuters (November 29, 2007), there were over 3.3 billion mobile phone subscribers in the world in November 2007, which is the half of the world population. Furthermore, there are 50 countries in the world that have more mobile phones than people. One can presume this dramatic penetration of IT will only accelerate over the coming decade. According to *Computerworld*, the average spending on information technologies in the USA by various industries grew to 6.4% in 2008 from 3% in 1993.

Why do firms invest so heavily in IT? What are the organizational impact and outcomes of IT? What positive changes can be expected and realized from IT applications in organizational settings? These questions have been of great interest to both researchers and practitioners in the field of information systems (IS) over the last 40 years. It is expected that the study of the organizational impact and benefits of IT will increase in popularity and importance due to the increasing dependence of global commerce on IT as well as the steady introduction of new information technologies with new capabilities.

Dramatic and rapid developments in information technology have brought fundamental changes in the strategic landscape. Companies can no longer rest on the success of yester-years. Instead, they constantly need to look out for emerging new technologies that might make their core products and strategies obsolete overnight. Many companies that used to dominate their own market have seen their key products quickly becoming obsolete due to these disruptive technologies. We will summarize some of the key technological trends that underpin these fundamental changes. We then discuss four different ways to use IT as a catalyst of organizational change in an information age.

EMERGING TECHNOLOGIES

Ever since organizations started using large mainframe computers for their back-office auto-mation in the 1950s, the development of new technologies have created new opportunities to change organizations. The introduction of PCs, the development of network technology, and the emergence of the internet as a viable platform of commerce activities all signifi-cantly influenced organizations. Now, the introduction of ubiquitous computing, fueled by the advancements in mobile technology and miniaturization of computing chips, is poised to revolutionize organizational computing one more time. Below we will summarize some of the key technological trends that will influence the way organizations perform.

Miniaturization of computing resources

One important driver behind the current development of ubiquitous computing is minia-turization of various computing resources. The computing power of microprocessors has been doubled roughly every 18 months. Such dramatic improvements in computing power have enabled companies to reduce the size of chips dramatically. As a result, we can embed computing powers into tools and equipment, and even physical environments to create intelligent tools and intelligent environments. Such intelligent environments and tools can recognize the changing context and render appropriate computing services to meet the needs.

Broadband network

Another important development in technology is the rapid penetration of broadband net-work. Over the last decade, the bandwidth of communication network has been doubled every 6–9 months. Not long ago, 28.8 kbps dial-up connection was considered a luxury. ISDN, T1, and T3 connections were available only at selected organizations. Today, through the use of DSL, cable modem, fiber optics, and satellite, increasingly large band-widths in communication network are available.

The emergence of the internet as a communication backbone

In the past, organizations had to maintain two different types of communication net-work: voice and data. Recent developments in network and digital signal technologies, however, made it possible to exchange rich multimedia data over the internet network without losing the quality of services. Consequently, individuals can conduct voice and video conferencing over the internet. A key development in the internet is the development of a new internet protocol, called IP V6 (internet protocol version 6). An important significance of IP V6 is the large number of unique IP addresses that can be assigned. Theoretically, the new addressing scheme allows up to 3.4×10^{38} unique addresses. This can be translated into approximately 5×10^{28} for each of the 6.5 billion people alive in 2006. It will be more than enough to assign a unique IP address for everyone on earth and many of the objects that they possess, not to mention their computers. This opens up unlimited possibilities of connecting various tools and equipment to the network, which in turn opens up many novel business opportunities.

Wireless technology

In the past, users had to go to a specific location in order to use computers. Increasingly, however, computing services will follow users when and where they are needed. This is due to the explosive growth and developments in wireless communication technologies and mobile handheld devices. The speed of current wireless technologies easily exceeds the speed limit of fixed line internet connection of just a few years ago. Furthermore, the development of global positioning systems (GPS), sensors, and RFID (radio frequency identification) which can be embedded into small devices enables completely new ways of organizing resources.

Mobile devices

The increasing miniaturization of computing resources and increasing mobility gave birth to various small handheld devices that can perform powerful computing services. Various mobile devices, including mobile phones, PDAs (Personal Digital Assistants), Blackberries and portable media devices (e.g. iPods), provide convenient mobility with increasing computing powers to the mobile users. These devices increasingly liberate users from the *past limitations* of space and time so that they can use computers anywhere and anytime.

Organizational implications of technology trends

The aforementioned developments in various areas in information technology can be summarized in three characteristics: mobility, digital convergence, and mass scale. First, computing services have become increasing mobile, following where users are and providing services when it makes most sense. At the same time, we will see increasing convergence toward digital signals. For example, so-called "triple-play" (combining broadband internet, phone, and TV services) or "quadruple-play" (adding mobile internet) has resulted from rapid digital convergence in media content, storage, and distribution mechanisms which have created major disruptions in media and communication industries. By utilizing the quickly converging digital platforms, companies in these industries can and must explore new media products and services that combine, for example, internet services and mobile communications.

While the technological developments reviewed in this section are breathtaking and impressive, managers need to think about how to leverage such new technological capabilities for their organizations. They need to constantly ask the question "Do we deliberately harness the technology innovations?" The developments in IT as reviewed here have created new sets of opportunities to improve efficiency, transform the way they are organized, disrupt competitive dynamics, and invent new business opportunities. Yet, organizations must act deliberately in order to leverage these new capabilities (Zammuto, Griffith, Majchrzak, Dougherty, and Faraj, 2007). New technological capabilities cannot be simply plugged into an existing organizational structure. Instead, organizations need to revisit long-held rules and assumptions (Yoo, Boland, and Lyytinen, 2006).

FOUR WAYS IT CAN CHANGE ORGANIZATIONS

Studies of various forms of IT systems and applications in organizational settings (Boland, Lyytinen, and Yoo, 2007; Harris and Katz, 1991; Keen, 1991) have established that IT use in organizations can lead to four major categories of changes. These categories consist of:

1. *gaining large-scale efficiencies* in business processes and transactions (Brynjolfsson, 1994; Davenport, 1993; Hitt and Brynjolfsson, 1996),
2. *enhancing communication*, information access, decision making and knowledge sharing (Alavi and Leidner, 2001; Jarvenpaa and Leidner, 1999; Kanawattanachai and Yoo, 2007; Lipnack and Stamps, 2000; Majchrzak, Rice, Malhotra, King, and Ba, 2000),
3. *changing the basis of competition and industry structure* to a firm's advantage (Pavlou and El-Sawy, 2006; Porter and Millar, 1985; Sambamurthy, Bharadwaj, and Grover, 2003; Sambamurthy and Zmud, 2000), and
4. *exploiting new business models* (Malone, 2004; Tapscott and Williams, 2006; Yoo, 2008; Yoo et al., 2006).

These categories are not mutually exclusive and a particular firm can realize various changes simultaneously through the effective use of various IT capabilities. Now, we will discuss these four impacts of IT in more detail.

Gaining large-scale operational efficiencies

The use of information technologies for transaction processing systems and enterprise resource planning systems can greatly enhance the operational efficiency of organizational processes. The development of advanced information technologies (such as service-oriented architecture and data warehouse) enabled the development of enterprise-wide integration across different business functions. For example, enterprise resource planning (ERP) is a highly integrated set of software modules designed to handle the most common business function transactions including general ledger accounting, accounts payable, accounts receivable, inventory management, order management, and human resources. At the heart of an ERP system is a single common database that collects data from and feeds data into all the software modules comprising the system. When an information item is changed in one of the software modules, related information is automatically updated in all other modules. By integrating information, streamlining data flow, and updating information across an entire business in a real-time mode, ERP systems can lead to dramatic productivity and speed gains in operations. Consider the efficiency gains at IBM's Storage Systems division after the deployment of an ERP system. The division reduced the time required for repricing its products from five days to five minutes and the time required to complete a credit check from 20 minutes to three seconds (Davenport, 1998). Once Fujitsu Microelectronics implemented an ERP system, it was able to close its financial books in four days (compared to eight days prior to the ERP system) and reduce order-filling time from 18 days to two days.

Continuing developments of communication and network technology further accelerate the trend toward tight integration in other areas. For example, in a healthcare setting, an integrated electronic medical record (EMR) system can be an integral tool in reducing the cost of healthcare service. Through the use of a centralized database, redundant and inconsistent data entry for the same patient can be minimized. Vital information about the patient can be easily shared between doctors, hospitals, insurance companies, and drug stores, dramatically reducing the time and effort it normally takes.

Enhance decision making and communication

Decision making and communication constitute two core organizational processes. Complex and challenging demands are placed on these two core processes in the current and emergent business environments, particularly due to globalization and the increased volatility of business and competitive environments.

Globalization has dispersed the operation of large firms across time and geography, increasing the need for effective and efficient ways to communicate across distance. Change in business and competitive environments in and of itself is not new (see Chapter 29, this volume). After all, it has been said that change is the only constant. However, the *rate* of change in today's economy has greatly increased, making it a major force to contend with. The rapid rate of change increases decision-making complexity in several ways. An increase in fluctuations and uncertainty in the decision environment requires more sophisticated analysis for developing, evaluating, and selecting alternatives. An increase in the uncertainty and complexity of decision tasks further increases the information processing requirements of the decision maker. Larger volumes of information from various sources need to be assembled and organized more frequently. And finally, the rapid rate of change combined with the increased complexity in analysis and information requirements in decision environments increases the time pressure on decision makers. It is simple to see that the traditional approaches to organizational decision making (manual analysis and information management) and communication (face-to-face and same place, same time modes of interaction) are insufficient. Information technologies such as decision support systems and group support systems provide powerful capabilities in meeting the decision-making and communication demands of modern organizations.

The decision support system (DSS) concept was first articulated by Gorry and Scott Morton (1971) as an interactive computer-based system that enables decision makers to use data and analytical models to solve unstructured problems. The objective of decision support systems is not to replace the decision maker but to support and augment his/her judgment and experience in order to improve decision-making effectiveness. Recent developments in database technology further enable decision makers to analyze large-scale complex datasets with multidimensional decision-making criteria (Turban, Aronson, and Liang, 2006). These emerging DSS tools take advantage of sophisticated artificial intelligence and multidimensional statistical techniques to detect hidden patterns and associations. Furthermore, powerful visualization tools enable decision makers to analyze the data from many different angles (Dillon and Information Management Forum, 1998). Leading companies like Wal-Mart have been very successful in utilizing the huge volume of transaction databases to gain new insights into customer behaviors. Organizations can deepen their relationship with customers by leveraging better insight on customers' behavior (Cooper, Watson, Wixom, and Goodhue, 2000). In information systems literature, several researchers have articulated and investigated the relationship between DSS and organizational decision-making processes and outcomes. For example, Leidner and Elam (1995) in their study involving 91 users of decision support systems in 22 organizations found that the use of DSS led to better decision-making outcomes as well as enhanced user mental models. Thus, the information access and analytical capabilities offered by DSS can bring about changes and improvements in decision-making processes and outcomes.

Information technologies, with their vast capacity for creating, transmitting, and storing messages, can also play a key role in the support of communication and collaboration processes in organizations. An early effort to use information technology to support organizational communication and collaboration processes led to the development of group support systems (GSS). More specifically, GSS refers to a range of computer- and communication-based capabilities designed to support work group interaction processes in order to enhance the performance of groups in organizational settings (Jessup and Valacich, 1993; Nunamaker, Dennis, Valacich, Vogel, and George, 1991). Dominant forms of early GSS tools include electronic mail and computer conferencing systems, videoconferencing, and electronic meeting systems.

There has been a major growth in the application of group support systems in organizations over the past decade. Consider the following examples and changes resulting from applications of group support systems. Boeing experienced a return on investment of 681% with an approximately $100,000 investment (Briggs, 2004). Andersen Consulting uses a Lotus Notes software system as a corporate backbone for the support of its knowledge sharing (Yoo and Torrey, 2002). Notes is deployed to over 10,000 people worldwide and is actively used for a variety of group functions, including e-mail, project management, and information exchange and capture.

Early GSS research literature (Benbasat and Lim, 1993; Dennis, Wixom, and Vandeberg, 2001; DeSanctis and Poole, 1994; Pinsonneault and Kraemer, 1989) point out that, in general, three types of value-added organizational change can be expected from group support system applications. These include: (1) reducing the effects of time and distance barriers that constrain face-to-face interactions and communication, (2) enhancing the timeliness, range, depth, and format of the information available to organizational members, and (3) improving performance and effectiveness by reducing group process losses (e.g. evaluation apprehension) through more efficient and structured group interaction processes.

The continuing development of communication technology has enabled the emergence of virtual teams as a viable form of organizing and coordinating group works (Jarvenpaa, Knoll, and Leidner, 1998; Jarvenpaa and Leidner, 1999; Lipnack and Stamps, 2000; Piccoli, Powell, and Ives, 2004; Powell, Piccoli, and Ives, 2004). A virtual team is a temporary, geographically dispersed, culturally diverse, and electronically communicating work group (Jarvenpaa and Leidner, 1999). Faced with global competitions and increased need to draw on a more diverse pool of talents, organizations routinely use virtual teams. Leading firms like Intel, Hewlett-Packard, and IBM rely on global virtual teams for their engineering tasks (Lipnack and Stamps, 2000). These organizations use a barrage of communication tools including electronic mail, intranet sites, groupware, and desktop video-conferencing to support these virtual teams. In many cases, virtual teams allow individuals to collaborate without permanently relocating, thus providing significant cost savings and productivity gains (Malhotra, Majchrzak, Carman, and Lott, 2001). Over time, virtual teams have become a pervasive and permanent reality of leading organizations.

Virtual teams present unique challenges to management, however. Some of these are old and familiar management challenges of managing diverse teams, only in the context of computer-mediated communications. Yet, at the same time, virtual teams present unique management problems that stem from the fact that virtual teams are explicitly socio-technical entities. Over the last decade, a large body of literature on virtual teams has emerged (Powell, Piccoli, and Ives, 2004; Wiesenfeld, Raguram, and Garud, 1999). Trust (see Chapter 21) (Jarvenpaa et al., 1998; Jarvenpaa and Leidner, 1999; Kanawattanachai and Yoo, 2002), leadership (see Chapter 15) (Kristof, Brown, Simps, and Smith, 1995; Pearce, Yoo, and Alavi, 2003; Yoo and Alavi, 2004), group composition (see Chapter 16) (Jarvenpaa et al., 1998), culture (Jarvenpaa and Leidner, 1999; Massey, Montoya-Weiss, Hung, and Ramesh, 2001), conflict (see Chapters 17 and 18) (Iacono and Weisband, 1997), the appropriation of communication technology (Majchrzak et al., 2000), and transactive memory (Cramton, 2001; Kanawattanachai and Yoo, 2007) are among a few of the factors that have been identified as drivers of the success and failure of virtual teams. These studies show that while virtual teams indeed face similar challenges that face-to-face teams have faced in the past, in many cases, the nature of those challenges are quite unique and different.

Virtual teams often rely on electronic communication media as primary means to communicate. These electronic media have different material characteristics that afford different communication capabilities to teams, which in turn afford different social dynamics in the teams (Fulk and DeSanctis, 1995; Zammuto et al., 2007). For example, Kanawattanachai and Yoo (2002, 2007) found that in virtual teams early communication plays a much more critical role than their counters in a face-to-face setting, as the early communication affects the emergence of swift trust and transactive memory systems – meta-knowledge of knowing who knows what. These early trust and transactive memory systems in virtual teams act more like a set of hypotheses that need to be validated and sustained later through teams' actual interactions. This non-experience-based, hypothetical nature of trust and transactive memory systems in virtual teams are formed entirely through early communications via electronic media among team members.

In summary, information technologies in the form of decision support systems and group support systems can play a major transformational role in organizations through their impact on the key organizational processes of decision making and communication. Future developments in this area will depend not only on technological advances but also on our understanding of and open-mindedness toward their applications and the resulting changes.

Change the competition and industry structure to your firm's advantage

Information technology offers organizations opportunities to change the competitive landscape by more effectively defining the dimensions of competition. The information and knowledge intensity (Porter and Millar, 1985; Palmer and Griffith, 1998) of products and services has become an important element in defining competitive advantage. Information intensity includes the amount of information that goes into the development of the product or the service, the amount of information required by consumers to utilize the product, and the amount of information required across the value chain to develop and deliver the product or service. Firms have redefined the basis of competition by providing additional information regarding their products or in extending the information content. Recent developments of ubiquitous computing technologies provide new ways of embedding information and knowledge into products and services; such actions can fundamentally disrupt the existing competitive dynamics.

Consider the case of Progressive Auto Insurance that opened up new competitive opportunity to leverage its knowledge on customer behaviors. It conducted an experimental program in Texas using advanced telecommunication technologies that included GPS and wireless communication tools. Progressive Insurance installed special equipment to the customers' automobiles that were enrolled into a special program. The equipment recorded the customer's driving pattern (time and location) and uploaded the information to the company's data center at the end of each month. By combining the real driving records from customers with its massive database of past history, Progressive Insurance was then able to customize the insurance premium for each customer for the next month. Customers who drove more safely got big discounts, while customers who drove dangerously saw higher premiums. This model offers a serious disruption to the auto insurance industry given its cost structure. The profit margin of an insurance company is the difference between the insurance premium it receives from the customers and the incurred loss to cover the accidents. The Progressive Insurance program attracted a pool of low-risk customers from its competitors and drove out high-risk customers to them. This shift gave significant competitive advantage to Progressive Insurance.

The most significant change in industry structure came from the emergence of the Internet as a means of conducting viable commerce transactions. The Internet caused fundamental restructuring of highly fragmented industries through disintermediation. Two perfect examples are the travel industry and the office products delivery industry. Traditionally, the travel industry involved numerous independent travel agents presenting travel options of providers such as airlines, hotels, and rental cars presented to the business and leisure traveler. The advent of the Internet has significantly changed the industry structure, with providers providing services directly to customers via Internet sites. This disintermediation of the travel agents is a major structural change for the industry.

Supply chain management has been a critical area for the use of information technologies to change the competitive dimensions. The early implementation of electronic data interchange (EDI) in which supply chain partners exchange data on sales trends, inventory replenishment, and in-store space allocation and management has been replaced with B2B Internet commerce. Improvements in supply chain efficiencies have led to several significant competitive advantages for firms such as Wal-Mart and Dell, including improved bargaining power over suppliers, reduced inventory costs, and enhanced in-store space management.

Finally, some organizations use advanced IT in order to fundamentally reshape inter-firm relationships. Shared database, interconnected IT-enabled business processes, and digitized tools can change the nature of interfirm relationships. Architecture, engineering and construction (AEC), the world largest industry, is experiencing a fundamental reshaping of interfirm relationships. The traditional practice of an AEC project begins with an architect working with a client to create a set of paper drawings and detailed specifications, which indicate the intention and form of what is to be built. The architect's drawings leave it to the contractors and subcontractors to determine an appropriate method of constructing the building. Contractors take the architect's drawings and use them as a basis for creating their own "shop drawings" which show how they intend to fabricate and install their part of the building. In preparing their shop drawings, contractors ask architects questions by submitting RFIs (requests for information) or RFCs (requests for clarification). In this traditional contractual context, architects and contractors need to be collaborative, yet often maintain adversarial relationships, maintaining an arm's-length relationship and sharing minimally required information.

Recently, however, firms in the AEC industry began forming much more collaborative relationships among each other based on Building Information Management (BIM) systems (Berente, Srinivasan, Lyytinen, and Yoo, 2008; Boland et al., 2007). Such collaborations are based on information transparency and co-creation using a shared BIM platform. With BIM systems, contractors do not create their own shop drawings based on archi-tectural drawings. Instead, there is a central repository of data and model, with layers of information that is created and consumed by different parties involved in the project. In a typical AEC project, design conflicts between different trades are often found at the field site, which cause delay and budget overrun. With BIM systems, such design conflicts are detected during the design stage and negotiated much earlier in the process, saving time and money. A communication pattern which used to be linear and sequential in the past now has become more dynamic and reciprocal using a centralized BIM platform. AEC firms that use these technologies have become more competitive with their improved efficiency and their ability to build more challenging projects (Berente et al., 2008).

The use of IT to change competitive dynamics often involves identifying opportunities for greater use of information in (1) the supply chain, (2) the description of the product or its use, or (3) the after-sales support or service dimension. Industry structures can be changed when the use of information technologies can (1) aggregate previously fragmented markets, (2) replace existing channels at lower cost or improved convenience, (3) more effectively bundle products and services, or (4) fundamentally alter interfirm relationships.

Exploit new business models

The speed, scope, and ubiquity of information technologies offer the opportunity to exploit entirely new business models in a variety of industries. The opportunity for firms to enhance customer relationships by offering 24/7 (24 hours a day, 7 days a week) access to purchasing, product information, and service offers an enhanced model for customer convenience and connection. This capability has influenced both Internet-based retailers as well as traditional retailers in the provision of customer convenience (Palmer, 1997).

The Internet has dramatically increased the marketing activities available to many organizations. While the Internet has helped organizations to gain efficiency, to improve communication and decision making, and to create new competitive dynamics, its most important impact was the creation of new business models. Take the most well-known Amazon.com as an example. The basic idea of using the Internet to sell millions of books on the Internet without relying on any type of physical direct interactions with the customers was a novel idea at the time it was first introduced. Other online companies such as eBay.com and Priceline.com also leveraged the Internet in order to implement a unique and novel business model. In the case of eBay, it uses a large community of passionate buyers and sellers, combined with an auction pricing model, to radically outsource procurement, pricing, sales and fulfillment of products that are sold (Malone, 2004). In the case of Priceline.com, it uses a unique "reverse auction" model so that sellers will bid for the price set by potential buyers in travel-related products. In these cases, the Internet provides these organizations an opportunity to present information regarding their products and services to both customers and suppliers. With the potential to reach global markets with product and service information as well as the ability to provide user interaction with the website, these companies were able to tap into so-called "long-tail" markets that were not practical in the past (Anderson, 2006).

The Internet also opens up the possibility of "open innovation" (von Hippel, 2005a, 2005b). Consider the examples of Linux and Apache software, two of the most popular and reliable software systems that run the Internet. Tens of thousands of volunteer programmers around the world worked together to build these software systems with minimum hierarchical control (O'Reilly, 1999; von Hippel and von Krogh, 2003). Open source developers use electronic communication and coordination tools in order to maintain a sense of social community and to coordinate their actions (Stewart and Gosain, 2006). This allows them to organize and source globally distributed programming knowledge and skills into exceptionally complex software products. The success of open forms of digital innovation is not limited to software. Companies like General Electric and Procter and Gamble have now started to turn to Internet-based innovation communities to find new ideas and solutions (Chesbrough, Vanhaverbeke, and West., 2006; von Hippel, 2005a). Such open innovation represents a novel business model for many organizations that are looking for new avenues for innovations.

Recently, companies like General Motors, IBM, and Sears began experimenting with Internet-based virtual reality. Emerging platforms like Second Life™ provide relatively scalable and inexpensive platforms to create virtual reality. Unlike conventional virtual reality technology that required expensive specialized hardware, software and facility, the new generation of virtual reality technologies use the Internet to reach millions of users. Furthermore, compared to conventional websites, these virtual reality platforms provide a much more engaging user interface. Individual users can create their own avatar which can navigate through the three-dimensional terrain in the virtual world. These avatars mimic human behaviors creating more intimate social context for interactions. Leveraging such a rich user interface, some companies like IBM are using virtual reality to add social dimensions to its global operations. Other organizations use virtual reality to introduce and/or experiment their new product ideas. For example, many consumer goods manufacturers are using virtual reality to let consumers experience their products virtually, even before those products are introduced to the real world market.

Finally, embedding of software-enabled capability into products and services enables organizations to invent new products and services (Yoo, Boland, and Lyytinen, 2008).

Many products that used to be non-digital are now increasingly composed of fully digital components, enabling the products to interact with other local digital devices, or to use the Internet to control behaviors or learn about the environment in which they operate. This offers organizations a way to differentiate customer or user experience. For example, the widespread availability of GPS (Global Positioning Systems) functions in digital cameras and mobile phones, when combined with comprehensive digital maps and sensors in surrounding buildings, cars or clothing, can spur a stream of novel services and products that will connect previously unconnected experiences and create a new "virtual" physical world. By embedding digital RFID chips into running shoes, Nike and Apple were able to integrate the iPod into running shoes, creating a novel product that never existed before.

In summary, the development of IT offers four different ways to invent new business models: (1) organizations can use the Internet to reach out to "long-tail" markets; (2) organizations can draw on the power of crowds by employing open innovations; (3) organizations can leverage increasingly powerful virtual reality; and (4) organizations can invent novel products and services by embedding software-enabled capabilities into products and services.

BEWARE OF IT IMPLEMENTATION ISSUES

Considering the prevalence of IT applications and the large and growing investments in them in modern organizations, one might expect a consistently positive set of outcomes associated with IT initiatives. This, however, is not always the case. Both research and practice have shown that due to implementation failures, IT may not lead to the planned or expected organizational changes described above. One form of implementation failure involves the cancellation of an IT project before the completion and installation of the system. For example, in 1995, 31% of large IT projects were canceled in US companies prior to their completion for an estimated total cost of $81 billion (Robey and Boudreau, 1999).

Another form of IT implementation failure involves situations in which the IT system is completed and installed, but the targeted organizational users resist the system, or do not use it in the intended way. An interesting example is provided by Robey and Boudreau (1999) and involves a system originally described by Kraut, Dumais, and Koch (1989). One of the goals of the system, a computerized record-keeping system, was to enhance the operational efficiency of the organization by reducing the opportunities for social interactions among employees during working hours. After the system installation, although the employees were more isolated, they "invented" a new and unintended way of using the system for social interactions. They used a memo field designed for capturing customer comments for passing messages back and forth among themselves, undermining the expected organizational efficiency gains from the IT system.

Thus, the successful implementation of IT systems is a prerequisite for realizing the planned and expected changes associated with these systems. The researchers in the information systems field have identified several factors that seem to contribute to the implementation success of IT systems. These factors *include top management support* and *commitment, user involvement in the planning and design of the IT system, and user training in the use of IT* (Alavi and Joachimsthaler, 1992; Lucas, Ginzberg, and Schultz, 1991). Top management support and IT commitment are prerequisites for the success of all forms of organizational change initiative, including IT-centered change. This is partly due to the need for top management support and commitment for garnering organizational resources required for IT implementation. Furthermore, top management support is shown to influence the level of individual user personal stake in the IT implementation success (Lucas et al., 1991). The strength of the relationships between user involvement and training and IT implementation success was established through the meta-analysis study of Alavi and Joachimsthaler (1992). This finding is consistent with the views presented in normative models of organizational change (e.g. Kolb and Frohman, 1970) and the diffusion of the innovation model (Cooper and Zmud, 1990) of IT implementation. These models highlight the importance of involvement and training as the means to create a favorable and accepting environment in which to bring about the IT-centered change.

Other researchers investigating IT implementation issues have suggested that the above-mentioned factors seem to be necessary, but not sufficient conditions for the success of large-scale IT implementations (Markus and Robey, 1988; Robey and Boudreau, 1999). According to these researchers, organizational change associated with large-scale IT applications is complex and should be analyzed at different levels including individual, group, and departmental as well as organizational and strategic levels. Consider the enterprise resource planning (ERP) systems described earlier in the chapter. At the operational level, these systems can lead to highly integrated, coordinated, and efficient core operational processes. These benefits are achieved by imposing generic and streamlined workflow logic encoded in the software on the organization. This impact at the operational level may restrict the latitude of authority at the individual worker level. On the other hand, the standardization of workflow and information items across departments may empower cross-functional teamwork in the organization. At the same time, the company's move toward generic and standardized processes may have a negative impact on the competitive positioning of the firm, if customized processes are a source of competitive advantage in the firm. For example, Dell Computer found that its ERP implementation would not fit its new, decentralized management model (Davenport, 1998).

In summary, to enhance the success of IT implementation and to realize the desired organizational changes, IT impacts should be considered and planned for at multiple levels of analysis *simultaneously*. Failure to do so may lead to negative and unexpected consequences.

CASE STUDIES

Implementing ERP systems at NASA

NASA was established in 1958 with the passage of the National Aeronautics and Space Act. It succeeded the National Advisory Committee for Aeronautics (NACA) by adding the development of space technology and inherited three major research laboratories – Langley and Ames aeronautical laboratories and Lewis Flight Propulsion Laboratory – along with two smaller test facilities. Soon after, other centers and facilities were added. Currently, there is one central headquarters and 10 field centers for research and spaceflight control (including the Jet Propulsion Laboratory which is managed by Caltech under a contract arrangement) around the USA.

From the beginning, each center was established in order to meet unique challenges in fulfilling the mission of the Agency. Over time, each center established its own unique competencies, culture, organizational structure, and technical infrastructures. The centers' unique technical capabilities and foci of their research and development have served the Agency's ambitious purpose of pursuing complex human and robotic space exploration projects. Centers have established worldwide reputations in their own unique areas for their technical excellence. Over time, however, this has resulted in "stove-piped" information systems and organizational processes at each center and for different functional needs. Each functional area built their legacy systems in order to meet their idiosyncratic needs. Furthermore, similar capabilities and knowledge resources were established in different centers, resulting in redundant investment. Different administrative and organizational procedures have made it difficult for the individuals within NASA to identify knowledge resources and capabilities distributed throughout the Agency. Even if they identify the potentially useful knowledge resources, differences in organizational rules, accounting standards, and information technology have made it difficult to collaborate across the center boundaries. As documented in a Columbia Accident Investigation Board (CAIB) report, the lack of integrated information systems and organizational practices caused major challenges in coordination and control across the Agency.

To address these challenges, NASA began working on an integrated financial management system in 1987 after the GAO found that NASA's accounting and financial information systems "constitute a material weakness of the Agency." The attempt to design and implement an agency-wide integrated system, officially named NASA Accounting and Financial Information Systems (NAFIS), failed after eight years and more than $90 million. After the failure of the NAFIS project, NASA decided to implement a "commercial off-the-shelf" (COTS) software system. In 1995, NASA officially launched the first iteration of the IFMP and hired KMPG Peat Marwick to customize a system that they had implemented elsewhere and implement it. Yet, NASA and KPMG agreed to cease the work in early 2000 as KPMG continued to fail to meet the major milestones.

In February 2000, NASA started its third attempt to integrate its financial management systems. NASA established an Integrated Financial Management Program (IFMP) and decided to implement the industry-leading product SAP and hired Andersen Consulting and IBM as the technical implementation and change agent consulting firms, respectively. NASA appointed new leadership of the project in February 2000 and redesigned the project. Marshall Space Center was selected as the lead center where most technical implementation teams are based, and Glenn Research Center was chosen as the first phase site. The vision of the IFMP program is to build a modern, leading edge business system that will provide the management information needed for mission success, meet the information needs of internal and external customers, support compliance with external regulatory guidance, and promote standardization and integration of business processes and systems across NASA. Specifically, the IFMP aims at delivering five business objectives:

- ◆ Provide timely, consistent and reliable information for management decisions;
- ◆ Improve NASA's accountability and enable full cost management;
- ◆ Achieve efficiencies and operate effectively;
- ◆ Exchange information with customers and stakeholders;
- ◆ Attract and retain a world-class workforce.

The first wave implementation of the SAP Core Financial Module at Glenn went live in October 2002. The rest of the Agency went live with financial core in fall of 2003. Although the system officially went live in October 2002 at Glenn, there were continuing training, minor upgrades, and fixes throughout the duration of the data collection. Subsequently, NASA implemented budget formulation, an updated version of financial core, project management, and asset management modules. Currently, the project is combined with the e-government initiatives.

Initial implementation of SAP, however, was marred with technical and organizational challenges. Scientists and engineers at NASA were frustrated with the new system as its complexity quickly overwhelmed them. Given NASA's unique mission and organizational structure, many NASA employees found that SAP does not provide adequate reports and lacks flexibility in managing large complex projects. Furthermore, despite the implementation of SAP, PricewaterhouseCoopers, the agency's auditor, issued a disclaimed opinion on NASA's 2003 financial statements. PricewaterhouseCoopers complained that NASA couldn't adequately document more than $565 billion in year-end adjustments to the financial statement accounts, which NASA delivered to the auditors two months late. Because of "the lack of a sufficient audit trail to support that its financial statements are presented fairly," concluded the auditors, "it was not possible to complete further audit procedures on NASA's September 30, 2003 financial statements within the reporting deadline established by [the Office of Management and Budget]."

NASA says blame for the financial mayhem falls squarely on IFMP. NASA's CFO, Gwendolyn Brown, says the conversion to the new system caused problems with the audit. In particular, she blames the difficulty the agency had converting the historical financial data from 10 legacy systems – some written in COBOL – into the new system, and reconciling the two versions for its year-end reports. Brown says that despite the difficulties with both the June 30 quarterly financial statement preparation and the year-end close, the system is up and running, and she has confidence in the accuracy of the Agency's financial reporting going forward. "It is working," says Brown, who was confirmed as CFO in November 2003, "and we are moving forward to ensure that we're ready to go to the moon, to Mars, and beyond, financially."

Large-scale IT-enabled organizational change at Federal Express

Federal Express, located in Memphis, Tennessee, is one of the leading logistic integrators in the world and is famous for its commitment to timely delivery and customer service. It is currently the world's largest express transportation company and part of the Federal Express Corporation. Federal Express has annual revenues of US$15 billion dollars and 138,000 employees. It operates over 650 airplanes and employs over 45,000 courier vehicles worldwide. It handles approximately 3.5 million packages per day but during peak times the number of packages flowing through the system is significantly greater. The company offers over 40 different types of delivery services and has over 200 different delivery services. Combined with thousands of different routing possibilities and fluctuating seasonal volumes, the package handling system is enormously complex.

Federal Express has utilized information technology to gain large-scale efficiencies in business processes and transactions, enhance communication, expand information access and decision making, change the basis of competition and industry structure to its advantage, and constantly exploit new business models. Because Federal Express operates in an industry with low profit margins and intense price competition, the company is very sensitive to the costs incurred due to incorrect information, poor coordination, or inappropriate incentives. Therefore, its use of information technology in the deployment of its core operations has always been aggressive. Federal Express has always been an industry leader in adopting new technological solutions.

As technology continues to develop, Federal Express is trying to transform itself once again. Utilizing an increasingly powerful communication network, Federal Express is constantly trying to push its intelligence toward the edge of the organization. The PowerPad solution is Federal Express's next generation computer support for courier tasks and work processes. It replaces and expands their current courier support technology that employs the DADS (Digitally Assisted Dispatching System) and the SuperTracker handheld computer that operates on an analog wireless network. The new PowerPad platform integrates a specially built and designed handheld computer, a Bluetooth enabled Personal Area Network (PAN) solution – which integrates DADS, a printer (called ASTRA), a smartphone (running broadband wireless), a barcode scanner, and associated technologies (called Electronic SuperTracker) – and a headset unit.

PowerPad is expected to influence couriers' operations on their customer premises, while driving in the van, and also during their stay in the pick-up centers (stations). Federal Express envisions that the introduction of the PowerPad technology will accomplish the following: (1) reduce the time couriers need to perform package handling tasks; (2) enable couriers to carry out expanded operations at the customers' premises; (3) reduce dependency on manual tasks and other system entities during pick-up; and (4) reduce duplicate data entry. The new system minimizes the couriers' need to return to their van during any pick-up or delivery operation and gives near instantaneous connectivity, which allows the completion of any initiated transaction on the spot. It enables almost real-time planning of routes and load schedules across the whole Federal Express network. The systems also embed much of the operational knowledge and intelligence required to allocate picked packages to correct service categories, thereby reducing routine and data capture errors, while also providing better feedback to customers about how their packages will be handled. The PowerPad system is expected also to improve the couriers' mobility and service within their routes by offering them nearly instantaneous and transparent access to different information services at the station level (or higher), including communications with other couriers. The system is also useful for other information sharing purposes such as distributing and maintaining delivery guidelines, providing remote support for exceptional situations, and so on.

The PowerPad system is a typical example of a new set of emerging applications that draw upon multiple ubiquitous computing concepts and technologies that help embed computing intelligence with a mobile workforce. All major logistic firms are currently rolling out similar applications. Associated "location-aware" ubiquitous computing systems will eventually become standard in organizations providing transportation, maintenance, and support services. More generally, these systems can be expected to have a major impact on the everyday tasks of a distributed workforce as they will be able in the future to integrate flexibly with other ubiquitous computing technologies such as voice-activated tasks, wearable components in uniforms, radio technologies that enable "smart" environments and packages, or Bluetooth-enabled glasses or heads-up screens.

Finally, multiple external networks provide an opportunity for Federal Express to enhance the logistics chain as well as its customer relationships, changing the nature of competition within the online delivery industry. Federal Express integrated its data systems with those of its customers. Allowing customers to track packages not only reduced internal costs to Federal Express, but more importantly linked the Federal Express database to those of its customers. This linkage allowed Federal Express customers to better serve their own clients, increasing customer loyalty and reducing the likelihood of switching to another provider (Goldman, Nagel, and Preiss, 1995). This use of the Internet resulted in improved customer satisfaction and involvement, while reducing costs through the elimination of call centers. In addition, Federal Express information technology capabilities include a knowledge base of expertise in shipping, customs brokerage, and governmental regulations, which supports the globalization of their business and is value added information for Federal Express customers.

Over time, Federal Express has extended its expertise in information technology applications to position itself as a logistics integrator. This new business model goes beyond that of package delivery to develop warehousing, notification, tracking, and packaging technology for its customers. This enhanced business model also includes multiple new revenue streams from each of the value adding activities. This model is particularly attractive given the development of Internet-based selling of physical products requiring full logistics support. An example is the Federal Express alliance with Laura Ashley. Under this agreement, Federal Express took over the warehouse and distribution activities. This provides a global distribution network for Laura Ashley and firmly established Federal Express as a logistics provider.

CONCLUSION

Information technology can serve as a significant catalyst for organizational change. The impact of information technology can improve operating efficiencies across the organization, improve the communication and decision-making processes, fundamentally alter competitive dynamics, and invent new business models. Emerging information technologies in particular offer radically different new products and services.

Implementation of technology continues to be a challenge for all companies. In the past, organizations saw technology implementation as a discrete occasional task, only occuring during the time when the organization installed new technology or upgraded the existing technology. However, in the current organizational environments where the technology development cycle has been radically reduced and the impact of information technology in organizations is far more pervasive, organizations cannot treat technology implementation as discrete periodic challenges any more. Furthermore, the impact of success and failure of information technology is often felt far beyond the boundary of an organization's information systems department.

The tremendous potential for improvements through information technology is only fully realized when existing organizational processes, incentives, and culture are reflected in the implementation process. Successful use of information technology involves strong organizational commitment and a clear identification of the role information technology will play.

REFERENCES

Alavi, M., and Joachimsthaler, E. A. (1992). Revisting DSS implementation: A meta-analysis of the literature and suggestions for researchers. *MIS Quarterly*, 95–116.

Alavi, M., and Leidner, D. E. (2001). Knowledge management and knowledge management systems: Conceptual foundations and research issues. *MIS Quarterly*, 25(1), 107–136.

Anderson, C. (2006). *The Long Tail: Why the Future of Business is Selling Less of More.* Hyperion: New York.

Benbasat, I., and Lim, L. (1993). The effects of group, task, context, and technology variables on the usefulness of group support systems: A meta-analysis of experimental studies. *Small Group Research*, 24(4), 430–462.

Berente, N., Srinivasan, N., Lyytinen, K., and Yoo, Y. (2008). Design principles for IT in doubly distributed design networks. The Twenty Ninth International Conference on Information Systems, Paris.

Boland, R. J., Lyytinen, K., and Yoo, Y. (2007). Wakes of innovation in project networks: The case of digital 3-D representations in architecture, engineering and construction. *Organization Science*, 18(4), 631–647.

Briggs, R. O. (2004). On theory-driven design of collaboration technology and process. In G.-J. de Vreede, L. A. Guerrero, and G. M. Raventos (eds), *Groupware: Design, Implementation and Use*, pp. 1–15. Springer Berlin: Heidelberg.

Brynjolfsson, E. (1994). Information assets, technology, and organization. *Management Science*, 40(12), December, 1645–1662.

Champan, S. (2007). PC numbers set to hit to 1 billion. *TechWorld*.

Chesbrough, H., Vanhaverbeke, W., and West, J. (2006). *Open Innovation: Researching a New Paradigm.* Oxford University Press: New York.

Cooper, B. L., Watson, H. J., Wixom, B. H., and Goodhue, D. L. (2000). Data warehousing supports corporate strategy at First American Corporation. *MIS Quarterly*, 24(4), 547–568.

Cooper, R. B., and Zmud, R. W. (1990). Information technology implementation research: A technological diffusion approach. *Management Science*, 36(2), 123–139.

Davenport, T. (1998). Putting the enterprise into the enterprise systems. *Harvard Business Review*, 121–131.

Davenport, T. H. (1993). *Process Innovation: Re-engineering Work Through Information Technology.* Harvard Business School Press: Boston.

Dennis, A. R., Wixom, B. H., and Vandeberg, R. J. (2001). Understanding fit and appropriation effects in group support systems via meta-analysis. *MIS Quarterly*, 25(2), 167–194.

DeSanctis, G., and Poole, M. S. (1994). Capturing the complexity in advanced technology use: Adaptive structuration theory. *Organization Science*, 5(2), May, 121–147.

Dillon, P. M., and Information Management Forum (1998). *Data Mining: Transforming Business Data into Competitive Advantage and Intellectual Capital*, pp. ii, 49. Information Management Forum: Atlanta, GA.

Fulk, J., and DeSanctis, G. (1995). Electronic communication and changing organizational forms. *Organization Science*, 6(4), 337–349.

Goldman, S., Nagel, R., and Preiss, K. (1995). *Agile Competitors and Virtual Organizations: Strategies for Enriching the Customer.* Van Nostrand Reinhold: New York.

Gorry, G. A., and Scott Morton, M. S. (1971). A framework for management information systems. *Sloan Management Review*, 13(1), 55–70.

Harris, S. E., and Katz, J. L. (1991). Firm size and the information technology investment intensity of life insurers. *MIS Quarterly*, 15(3), 333–352.

Hitt, L. M., and Brynjolfsson, E. (1996). Productivity, business profitability, and consumer surplus: Three different measures of information technology value. *MIS Quarterly*, 20(2), 121–142.

Iacono, C. S., and Weisband, S. (1997). Developing trust in virtual teams. HICSS-30 Conference, Hawaii, pp. 412–420.

Jarvenpaa, S. L., Knoll, K., and Leidner, D. E. (1998). Is anybody out there? The implications of trust in global virtual teams. *Journal of Management Information Systems*, 14(4), 29–64.

Jarvenpaa, S. L., and Leidner, D. E. (1999). Communication and trust in global virtual team. *Organization Science*, 10(6), 791–865.

Jessup, L., and Valacich, J. S. (1993). *Group Support Systems: New Perspective*. Macmillan Publishing Company: New York, NY.

Kanawattanachai, P., and Yoo, Y. (2002). Dynamics of trust in virtual teams. *Journal of Strategic Information Systems*, 11(3–4), 187–213.

Kanawattanachai, P., and Yoo, Y. (2007). The impact of knowledge coordination on virtual team performance over time. *MIS Quarterly*, 31(4), 783–808.

Keen, P. G. W. (1991). *Shaping the Future: Business Design through Information Technology*, p. 264. Harvard Business School Press.

Kolb, D. A., and Frohman, A. L. (1970). An organizational development approach to consulting. *Sloan Management Review*, 12(1), 51–66.

Kraut, R. E., Dumais, R. S., and Koch, S. (1989). Computerisation, productivity, and quality of work-life. *Communications of the ACM*, 32, 220–238.

Kristof, A. L., Brown, K. G., Simps, H. P., and Smith, K. A. (1995). The virtual team: A case study and inductive model. In M. M. Beyerlein, D. A. Johnson, and S. T. Beyerlein (eds), *Advances in Interdisciplinary Studies of Work Teams*, pp. 229–253. Jossey-Bass Publishers: San Francisco.

Leidner, D. E., and Elam, J. J. (1995). The impact of executive information systems on organizational design, intelligence, and decision making. *Organization Science*, 6(6), 645–664.

Lipnack, J., and Stamps, J. (2000). *Virtual Teams: People Working Across Boundaries with Technology* (2nd edition). Wiley, New York.

Lucas, H. C., Ginzberg, M. J., and Schultz, R. L. (1991). *Information Systems Implementation: Testing a Structural Model* Ablex Publishing: Norwood, NJ.

Majchrzak, A., Rice, R. E., Malhotra, A., King, N., and Ba, S. (2000). Technology adaptation: The case of computer-supported inter-organizational virtual team. *MIS Quarterly*, 24(4), 569–600.

Malhotra, A., Majchrzak, A., Carman, R., and Lott, V. (2001). Radical innovation without collocation: A case study at Boeing-Rocketdyne. *MIS Quarterly*, 25(2), 229–250.

Malone, T. W. (2004). *The Future of Work: How the New Order of Business Will Shape Your Organization, Your Management Style, and Your Life*. Harvard Business School Publishing: Boston, MA.

Markus, M. L., and Robey, D. (1988). Information technology and organizational change: casual structure in theory and research. *Management Science*, 34(5), 583–598.

Massey, A. P., Montoya-Weiss, M. M., Hung, C., and Ramesh, V. (2001). Cultural perceptions of task-technology fit. *Communications of the ACM*, 44(12), 83–84.

Nunamaker, J. F., Dennis, A. R., Valacich, J. S., Vogel, D. R., and George, J. F. (1991). Electronic meeting systems to support group work. *Communications of the ACM*, 34(7), 40–61.

O'Reilly, T. (1999). Lessons learned from open source software development. *Communications of the ACM*, 42(4), 33–37.

Palmer, J. W. (1997). Electronic commerce in retailing: Differences across retailing formats. *The Information Society*, 13(1), 97–108.

Palmer, J. W., and Griffith, D. A. (1998). An emerging model of web site design for marketing. *Communications of the ACM*, March, 41(3), 44–52.

Pavlou, P. A., and El-Sawy, O. A. (2006). From IT leveraging competence to competitive advantage in turbulent environments: The case of new product development. *Information Systems Research*, 17(3), 198–227.

Pearce, C., Yoo, Y., and Alavi, M. (2003). Leadership in virtual teams: the relative influence of vertical vs. shared leadership in virtual teams. In R. Riggion and S. S. Orr (eds), *Improving Leadership in Nonprofit Organizations*, pp. 180–204. Jossey-Bass: San Francisco, CA.

Piccoli, G., Powell, A., and Ives, B. (2004). Virtual teams: Team control structures, internal processes, and team effectiveness. *Information Technology and People*, 17(4), 359–379.

Pinsonneault, A., and Kraemer., K. (1989). The impact of technological support of groups: An assessment of the empirical research. *Decision Support Systems*, 5, 197–216.

Porter, M. E., and Millar, V. E. (1985). How information gives you competitive advantage. *Harvard Business Review*, 64(4), 149–160.

Powell, A., Piccoli, G., and Ives, B. (2004). Virtual teams: A review of current literature and directions for future research. *Data Base Advances*.

Robey, D., and Boudreau, M. -C. (1999). Accounting for the contradictory organizational consequences of information technology: Theoretical directions and methodological implications. *Information Systems Research*, 10(2), 167–185.

Sambamurthy, V., Bharadwaj, A., and Grover, V. (2003). Shaping agility through digital options: Reconceptualizing the role of information technology in contemporary firms. *MIS Quarterly*, 27(2), 237–264.

Sambamurthy, V., and Zmud, R.W. (2000). The organizing logic for an enterprise's IT activities in the digital era – a prognosis of practice and a call for research. *Information Systems Research*, 11(2), 105–114.

Stewart, K., and Gosain, S. (2006). The impact of ideology on effectiveness in open source software development teams. *MIS Quarterly*, 30(2), 291–314.

Tapscott, D., and Williams, A. D. (2006). *Wikinomics: How Mass Collaboration Changes Everything*. Penguin Group: New York.

Turban, E., Aronson, J. E., and Liang, T. -P. (2006). *Decision Support and Business Intelligence Systems* (8th edition). Prentice-Hall: New York.

von Hippel, E. (2005a). *Democratizing Innovation*. MIT Press: Cambridge, MA.

von Hippel, E. (2005b). Open source software projects as user innovation networks – no manufacturer required. In J. Feller, B. Fitzegeral, S. Hissam, and K. Lakhani (eds), *Perspectives on Free and Open Source Software*. MIT Press, Cambridge.

von Hippel, E., and von Krogh, G. (2003). Open source software and the "private-collective" innovation model: Issues for organization science. *Organization Science*, 14(2), 208–223.

Wiesenfeld, B. M., Raguram, S., and Garud, R. (1999). Communication patterns as determinants of organizational identification in a virtual organization. *Organization Science*, 10(6), 777–790.

Yoo, Y. (2008). Mobilizing knowledge in a Yu-Gi-Oh! world. In I. Becerra-Fernandez and D. Leidner (eds), *Knowledge Management: An Evolutionary View*. M. E. Sharpe: New York.

Yoo, Y., and Alavi, M. (2004). Emergent leadership in virtual teams: what do emergent leaders do? *Information and Organization*, 14(1), 27–58.

Yoo, Y., Boland, R. J., and Lyytinen, K. (2006). From organization design to organization designing. *Organization Science*, 17(2), 215–229.

Yoo, Y., Boland, R. J., and Lyytinen, K. (2008). Distributed Innovation in classes of network. The 41st Hawaiian International Conference on Systems Science, IEEE, Big Island, Hawaii.

Yoo, Y., and Torrey, B. (2002). National cultures and knowledge management in a global learning organization: a case study. In N. Bontis and C. W. Choo (eds), *The Strategic Management of Intellectual Capital and Organizational Knowledge: A Collection of Readings*, pp. 421–434. Oxford University Press: New York.

Zammuto, R., Griffith, T. L., Majchrzak, A., Dougherty, D. J., and Faraj, S. (2007). Information technology and the changing fabric of organization. *Organization Science*, 18(5), 749–762.

EXERCISES

Discuss risk factors associated with large-scale IT implementation and develop an effective mitigation plan (30 min)

1. Discuss the organizational and institutional background of NASA. Have students study NASA's history ahead of time. Alternatively, you can give a short lecture on NASA's history and organizational structure. (5 min)
2. Identify various risk factors in implementing ERP at NASA.
   (a) Divide the class into groups of four. Have students identify technical, organizational, cultural, and institutional risks associated with ERP implementation. (10 min)
   (b) Groups report their findings. Using a board, develop a comprehensive list of risk factors for large-scale IT projects in organizations. (5 min)
3. For each major risk factor identified, discuss effective risk mitigation strategies. (10 min)

Discuss potential benefits of large-scale IT implementation based on the Federal Express case (30 min)

1. Discuss Federal Express's competitive strategy and some of the key threats and opportunities. (10 min)
2. Discuss the future potential of PowerPack.
   (a) Have students develop a concrete business scenario where Federal Express can engage in a new strategic alliance with its mobile computing platform in small groups. (10 min)
   (b) Have groups report back. As groups make their presentations, explore pros and cons of their ideas. (10 min)

33

Make Management Practice Fit National Cultures and the Global Culture

Miriam Erez

This chapter focuses on the interface between cultures that takes place in the global work context. This change in focus is driven by the changes in the work environment, as more and more people around the world work for multinational and global organizations that cross geographical zones and cultural borders.

Organizational behavior principles should take into consideration the context in which they are implemented and specifically the work context that is shifting from local to global. This global context is characterized by economic interdependence across countries, a free flow of capital, and goods, knowledge and labor moving across national and geographical borders (Erez and Shokef, 2008; Govindarajan and Gupta, 2001). It is not very difficult to understand why Thomas Friedman used the metaphor of the "World is Flat" as the title of his recent book, in which he reviewed the factors that are flattening the global business environment, including historical, technological, and communication issues (Friedman, 2005).

Yet, is the world really flat and are managers developing identical or nearly identical principles for managing organizations and people around the world? The answer, as reported both by practitioners and researchers, is "no." Cross-cultural differences in values, norms, and accepted modes of behaviors still exist and they differ across cultures.

The next question is, therefore, how do managers cope with the paradox of operating in the globally flat business world and at the same time, also manage culturally diverse employees working in culturally diverse subsidiaries and business units? The aim of this chapter is to answer this question by providing some principles to serve as guidelines for managers in navigating between the macro level of the global, flat culture and the uneven level of diverse national cultures lying underneath.

From Local to Global Work Contexts

For many years, the dominant theories of organizational behavior were mostly Western/ American, generated and validated on Western samples of managers and employees, working in Western organizations.

In the late 1980s, the fierce competition between Japan and the USA called attention to cultural issues. During this period, articles in business papers reflected fear of Japan, attempting to understand how Japan was growing, why it was dangerous, and what could be done about the supposed threat to Western hegemony (Smith, 1990). Over the years, an increasing number of American managers found themselves negotiating with the Japanese, marketing their products in Japan, offering services to foreign customers, and managing operations outside their home countries. As a result, the popularity of guidebooks on how to do business with the Japanese and other foreign countries grew. The demand for such books testified to the fact that managers recognized their lack of knowledge and competence in managing across cultural borders.

By the late 1990s, the competition between companies situated in different cultures turned from conflict to cooperation in the form of international mergers and acquisitions, joint ventures, and business alliances. A wedding ceremony becomes a common metaphor for international mergers, with a question mark overhanging these unions: will they last, or unravel?

Cooperation rather than competition requires a better understanding of one's international partner. It is not enough to merely know of one's collaborator but rather the need

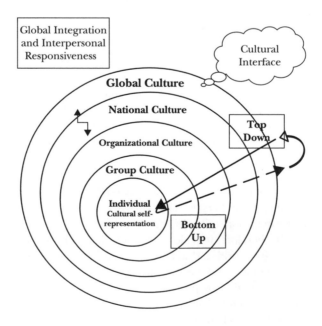

FIGURE 33.1 A multi-level model of culture (based on Erez and Gati, 2004)

for understanding cross-cultural differences and similarities is becoming increasingly crucial for effective international partnerships and their managers.

However, recognizing and accepting cultural diversity is necessary, but not sufficient for operating across cultural borders. What is needed is a shared meaning system that enables players in the global work context to communicate and understand each other, so there is a basis for collaboration and coordination (Gelfand, Erez, and Aycan, 2007). This shared meaning system reflects the emergence of a global work culture. The global work culture has emerged as the most macro level of culture which subsumes the national, organizational, group, and individual levels of cultural values nested within each other, portraying a multi-level model of culture (Erez and Gati, 2004), as shown in Model 1, Figure 33.1.

THE GLOBAL WORK CULTURE

Social scientists drew attention to the dissemination of three socio-cultural values around the world: *rationalization, professionalization* and *actorhood* (Drori, Jang, and Meyer, 2006). Rationalization pertains to systemization, standardization, and routinization of actions. Rationalization facilitates comparability across cultures, as evident by the global rating systems of economic, educational, and government institutions. Comparability enhances global competition across all institutional domains. Organizations compete for their relative ranking: business companies, as well as national educational systems, universities, business schools, legal systems, etc. make every effort to be ranked at the top of their respective world list. Furthermore, rationalization enforces universal criteria for professionalism, pertaining to universal knowledge, and expertise that are necessary for becoming a certified professional and a member of local professional organizations, recognized by international professional organizations. Finally, globalization also diffuses the value of actorhood, which champions the proactive individual, with the capacity and motivation for taking a proactive stand and control over him/herself. This value has been globally disseminated by educating for democracy around the world. Such global values provide the infrastructure for the development of a global organizational culture, common to all organizations operating in the global work context.

Values are instrumental for adaptation to and/or changing one's environment. The global work environment is known to be geographically dispersed and culturally diverse, highly competitive, dynamic, and uncertain. Paradoxically, while this global environment emerges beyond national cultures it also consists of diverse cultures representing the multiple subsidiaries and business units of the global organization. Unlike managers operating in local organizations, nested within one culture, managers of global organizations operate in a complex environment, where they need to safeguard the global integration of the companies' operations; on the other hand, alongside this global integration, they must maintain local responsiveness to their diverse subsidiaries and business units, nested within diverse local cultures. The global context determines the principles that should guide managers operating in the global work context. Below is a set of subprinciples for the global manager, as summarized in Figure 33.2.

As evident, the core principle relates to the interplay between global integration and local responsiveness (Kostova and Roth, 2002).

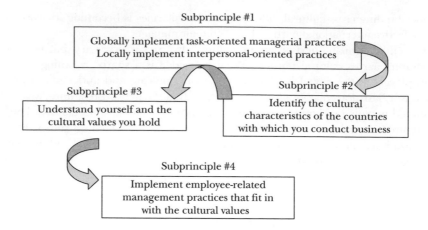

FIGURE 33.2 The four principles of global management

The first subprinciple: Globally implement task-oriented managerial practices and locally implement interpersonal-oriented practices

Research has demonstrated that managers should differentiate between two groups of values and practices: those pertaining to the execution of tasks and operations, and those pertaining to interpersonal relationships with employees, peers, superiors, and customers (Berson, Erez, and Adler, 2004; Erez and Shokef, 2008).

Task-oriented practices enable managers to cope with the highly competitive global work environment, where the competition is on market share, customers, new products, and prices. To cope with such demands, managers of multinational and global organizations should uniformly share the values of competitive performance orientation and customer orientation. They should agree on the importance of their task-related managerial roles of planning and coordination, and initiating changes and innovation, wherever on the globe they manage business units.

On the other hand, interpersonal practices pertain to the relationship between managers and subordinates, peers, superiors, and customers. These relationships should be tuned to the diverse local cultural values and norms. Therefore, interpersonal practices should be loosely implemented, respecting the diverse local cultural values. To maintain the fit between interpersonal-related management practices and local cultures, managers need to identify the variations in cultural values.

The second subprinciple: Identify the cultural characteristics of the countries with which you conduct business

Managers and employees in different cultures bring to their workplace their cultures' behavior codes and norms. These norms and cultural values shape the organizational processes and managerial practices. Therefore, different managerial practices, in particular the relational ones, are implemented in different parts of the world within the same global organization. For example, in individualistic cultures, such as that of the USA, the selection procedure of new employees is based on his or her personal records. In collectivistic cultures, such as that of Mexico, recommendations by family members, who already work for the company, serve as an important criterion for selecting new employees. In the USA, promotion to higher managerial levels is based on personal achievements, as they appear in an employee's performance appraisal records. However, in collectivistic and hierarchical cultures such as Japan, seniority plays a major role in promotion decisions. Payment based on results constitutes a greater part of Americans' compensation packages compared to those in Europe. In European countries, flat salaries are more common than in the USA. The compensation package of American managers includes a large portion of stock options, whereas this is less common for local European and Far Eastern managers. Explicit feedback on performance is highly valued in Western countries, whereas in the Far East implicit feedback is the norm, and explicit feedback is not acceptable. Explicit feedback, if negative, violates the important value of face saving; if positive, it violates the important value of collectivism and the sense of being part of the group rather than being unique and different than others.

There are so many different codes of behavior and variations of management practices that relate to employees and interpersonal relationships that they cannot all be described in the "how to" books. Managers, therefore, should recognize the key cultural values that determine which practices will be positively evaluated by employees, enhancing their sense of self-worth and well-being, and consequently motivating them to stretch their goals (see Chapter 9, this volume) and improve their performance (Erez and Earley, 1993). Managerial approaches that are at odds with prevailing cultural values are unlikely to be effective. Since cultures differ in the values they endorse, people from these cultures often interpret the same managerial practices quite differently than a manager coming in from the "outside" would expect. Identifying the core cultural values will enable managers to fit their management practices to cultural context.

Culture can be defined as a shared meaning (value) system (Schwartz, 1992; Shweder and LeVine, 1984). In metaphorical terms, culture is the software of the mind (Hofstede, 1991). Culture shapes the core values and norms of its members. These values are transmitted from one generation to another through social learning processes of modeling and observation, as well as through the effects of individual actions (Bandura, 1986). Homogeneous societies form tight cultures, and their norms and values, are closely shared by most members of the society. Societies consisting of subgroups with dissimilar norms and values form loose cultures (Triandis, 1989; Gelfand, Nishii, and Raver, 2006).

Cultures differ in their content components. The two values that depict most of the variance among cultures are: collectivism versus individualism, and power distance.

Individualism–collectivism signifies the level of inter-relatedness among members of one culture (Hofstede, 1991, 2001; Brewer and Chen, 2007). Collectivism means preferring to work in teams, subordinating personal goals to group goals, being concerned about the group integrity, and having an intense emotional attachment to the in-group. In contrast, individualism emphasizes personal autonomy and independence, adherence to personal goals, and less concern and emotional attachment to the in-groups (Triandis, Bontempo, Vilareal, Masaaki, and Lucca, 1988). The USA, Australia, and England are highly individualistic cultures, whereas South America, Pakistan, Korea, Japan, and Taiwan are highly collectivistic.

Power distance reflects the level of equality in the society. High power distance means low equality in the society and a clear power structure in organizations. Employees in such cultures know their place in the organizational hierarchy, and there are clear status symbols that differentiate between employees of different organizational levels. On the other hand, in low power distance cultures, employees feel free to disagree with their superiors and to express their ideas openly. Malaysia, the Philippines, Arab countries, India and some of the South American countries are known for their high level of power distance. In contrast, Israel, Scandinavia, and New Zealand are known for their low levels of power distance. Recently, a group of more than 80 researchers, headed by Robert House from the Wharton School, joined together to conduct the *Globe Study* in 60 different countries. (House, Hanges, Javidan, Dorfman, and Gupta, 2004). This study assessed differences and similarities in cultural and organizational values, as well as in preferences for leadership characteristics. Table 33.1 depicts the cultural values of collectivism and power distance in a sample of eight countries that includes the USA, England, West Germany, East Germany, Russia, Finland, Japan, and Israel.

The results demonstrate that in this sample, East Germany and Russia are the countries with the highest level of power distance, and Israel is the most egalitarian country. Similarly, the USA is the most individualistic culture, and Japan and Russia have the most collectivistic cultures.

Three additional values that help differentiate cultures are: uncertainty avoidance, masculinity/femininity, and future time orientation.

Uncertainty avoidance reflects the extent to which members of the society feel threatened by uncertain or unknown situations. High levels of uncertainty lead to anxiety. Organizations that seek to avoid uncertainty have formal rules and regulations, clear task definitions, and low tolerance for deviation from their rules and norms. In opposition, organizations with a high tolerance for uncertainty are less formal, more flexible, and allow for higher levels of heterogeneity in norms and behavior. Cultures with high levels of uncertainty avoidance are: Switzerland, Sweden, and Singapore; cultures with low levels of uncertainty avoidance are Greece, Venezuela, and Russia.

Masculine versus feminine cultures – the former pertains to societies in which social gender roles are clearly defined (i.e. men are supposed to be assertive, tough, and focused on material

Table 33.1   Differences in cultural values across selected countries (based on House et al., 2004)

	Collectivism		Power distance		Uncertainty avoidance	
England	4.08	(C)*	5.15	(B)	4.65	(B)
USA	4.25	(C)	4.88	(B)	4.15	(B)
Israel	4.7	(B)	4.73	(C)	4.01	(C)
Germany (W)	4.02	(C)	5.25	(B)	5.22	(A)
Germany (E)	4.52	(B)	5.54	(A)	5.16	(A)
Russia	5.63	(A)	5.52	(A)	2.88	(D)
Finland	4.07	(C)	4.89	(B)	5.02	(A)
China	5.8	(A)	5.04	(B)	4.94	(A)
Japan	4.63	(A)	5.11	(B)	4.07	(C)

*Different letters mean statistically significant differences between the numbers.

success, whereas women are supposed to be more modest, tender, and concerned with the quality of life). Femininity pertains to societies in which social gender roles overlap (i.e. both men and women are concerned with the quality of life; Hofstede, 1991). Kuwait and South Korea are classified as the most masculine country. The most feminine cultures are Hungary, Denmark and Sweden.

Future time orientation reflects the extent to which the culture focuses on long-term planning and outcomes, and on the delay of gratification. The most future oriented countries are Singapore, Malaysia, Switzerland and the Netherlands.

Employees internalize the respective cultural values and use them to evaluate the meaning of different managerial and motivational approaches as either opportunities or threats. For example, differential reward systems would be positively viewed by employees in individualistic cultures, and team-based incentives would be appreciated by employees in collectivistic cultures.

People in different cultures internalize the prevalent cultural values of their society. Therefore, they differ in the meaning they ascribe to a particular managerial approach. To further understand what motivates employees in other cultures, and how they interpret the meaning of various managerial practices, managers should first develop self-awareness and understanding of their own motives and values (see Chapter 8).

The third subprinciple: Understand yourself and the cultural values you hold

The self is shaped by the choices one makes and by the shared understanding within a particular culture of what it means to be human (Cushman, 1990; Markus and Kitayama, 1991). People develop self-knowledge through introspection (Chapter 8), direct experience and evaluations provided by significant others.

People strive to have positive self-perceptions and to experience self-worth and well-being. They do their utmost to fulfill the motives of enhancement, efficacy, and consistency. Self-enhancement is the experience of a positive cognitive and affective state of self-worth and well-being; self-efficacy (Chapter 10) is the conviction that one is competent and efficacious in relation to specific tasks; self-consistency is the desire to sense and experience coherence and continuity.

People monitor and evaluate the extent to which their behavior leads to the fulfillment of the three motives and the degree to which the work setting offers opportunities for such behaviors (Bandura, 1986; Markus and Wurf, 1987).

The self and self-motives are shaped by one's choices and one's cultural values and they set the standards and criteria for self-evaluation. These criteria vary across individuals and cultures and, consequently, result in different self-conceptions. Individualistic cultures support the *independent self*, who attends to personal criteria and standards for evaluating the meaning of certain management practices as enhancing or inhibiting opportunities for self-worth and well-being (Triandis, 1989; Markus and Kitayama, 1991). On the other hand, collectivistic cultures support the *interdependent self*, who internalizes the criteria and standards advocated by one's reference groups. One common measure of the independent and interdependent selves is the Twenty Statement Test, which asks a person to write 20 statements starting with the words "I am . . ." People with a strong independent self use individual characteristics, such as: "I am smart" or "I am tall," more frequently than those who rank high on the interdependent self scale. The latter use attributes that reflect their relationships with others, such as: "I am a father," "I am a member of the ABC organization," etc.

Managerial and motivational practices that satisfy self-motives of the independent self would be different than those satisfying the interdependent self. For example, self-enhancement driven by the independent self motivates individuals toward personal accomplishment. The independent self evaluates positively managerial practices that provide opportunities for individual success. People driven by the interdependent self, on the other hand, experience enhancement when they contribute to the group's success because their self definition is in terms of their relationship to others. This does not mean that independent people cannot work in groups but it would be out of self-interest rather than duty. Similarly, self-efficacy is salient for people with a strong independent self, whereas collective efficacy, or the perceptions of the group as competent, is important for the interdependent self. Finally, self-consistency of the independent self is interpreted in reference to the individual's personal history. Conversely, the interdependent self evaluates the level of collective consistency in line with the collective history of the group to which one belongs.

The self constitutes the link between the macro level of culture and managerial practices, and the micro level of employee behavior. Employees use their cultural values as criteria for evaluating the potential contribution of various management practices to the fulfillment of their self-derived motives (Erez and Earley, 1993).

Managers who are aware of their own cultural values and motives are more amenable to developing an understanding of other people's values and motives. Once they identify the cultural characteristics of people from other cultures, they can more easily follow how employees in foreign cultures would react to various managerial approaches.

However, employees working in the global work context belong not only to their local national culture, but also to their global organizational culture. The social identity theory (Tajfel, 1981) proposes that individuals develop a sense of belongingness to the group that is meaningful to them. Extrapolating, we can say that individuals working in the global work context develop a dual identity – a local identity, which reflects their sense of belongingness to their local cultures, and a global identity, reflecting their sense of belongingness to their global work culture. People may hold multiple identities and they apply the relevant identity to the context. When they communicate with others in the global work context, their global identity and sense of belongingness to the global organization become dominant, regardless of their location and national culture. On the other hand, when they relate to others in their local organizational unit, their local identity becomes dominant and they expect to be treated according to the norms of their local culture. Thus, successful managers working in the global work context should be able to recognize the dominant facet of the other person's self identity, whether it is the global or the local self-identity and relate to the dominant facet accordingly.

The fourth subprinciple: Implement employee-related management practices that fit in with the cultural values

Managerial practices represent certain ideological or philosophical frameworks. For example, individual-based differential reward systems and flat salary or team-based reward systems reflect different values. The former represents cultural values of individualism and the importance of personal achievement, whereas flat salary or team-based rewards represent cultural values of collectivism, where productivity is often measured on the team level and compensation is based on team performance. Top-down communication systems represent high power distance cultures, whereas a two-way communication system represents low power distance cultures.

Formal rules and regulations and extensive written documentation represent high uncertainty avoidance, whereas flexibility, risk taking, and low levels of formality represent low uncertainty avoidance. Long-term investment in R&D represents future time orientation, whereas short-term goals and balance sheets reported every quarter represent a short-term orientation. Finally, the high percentage of women in socially oriented professions rather than in engineering and sciences, and their low representation at the top managerial levels, represent masculine rather than feminine cultures.

Very often, consultants and practitioners serve as agents of certain managerial techniques. They advise management how to implement these techniques, following success achieved in other places, while overlooking the cultural and ideological meaning of such techniques. For example, the CEO of one steel company in Israel, who came to the company after many years of military service, was known for his authoritarian leadership style. He visited the steel industry in Japan and was very impressed with the participative management approach and the quality control circles he saw. Upon his return to Israel he called in all his senior managers, told them about his visit, and instructed them that "from now on, you are going to implement participative management in the organization." Obviously, his style of dictating to his subordinates was not a good model for participative management.

The three principles – understanding the cultural values, knowing your motives and values, and understanding the values reflected by various managerial approaches – should serve managers when selecting and implementing managerial practices. These principles enable the fit between people-oriented management practices and local cultural values.

Matching Management Practices to Cultural Variations

Management practices represent the way things are done in the organization: The way managers delegate authority, allocate rewards, make decisions, and design jobs.

Figure 33.3 depicts the differences in management practices between collectivistic versus individualistic cultures, in combination with high versus low power distance.

The following section elaborates on the implementation of goals and feedback, reward allocation, participation in decision making and empowerment, and quality improvement systems in different cultures.

Goals and feedback

One major responsibility of managers is to set goals and motivate their employees to achieving them. There are different ways to set goals – either by assigning them or by involving employees in making the decision about them – and different ways to realize them. In some cases, employees can be empowered to set their own work goals. Employees

High	**Top-Down – Group** Assigned Group Goals Group Feedback Face Saving – error prevention Team based bonus – high differential	**Top-Down – Individual** Assigned Individuals Goals – Individual Feedback Be successful – promotion Individual based bonus – high differential
Low	**Lateral – Group** Participative Group Goal setting Team reflexivity – Feedback Face Saving/harmony – Error prevention Team based bonus – low differential	**Lateral – Individual** Empowering personal goal setting 360-degree personal feedback Risk taking/uniqueness – promotion towards new opportunities and new records Individual based bonus – low differential
	Collectivism	**Individualism**

(Power Distance — vertical axis label, from High to Low)

FIGURE 33.3 Fit interpersonal management practices with local cultures

in Western cultures are more intrinsically motivated when they are involved in setting the goals rather than when goals are externally set for them. Empowerment is considered to be a strong motivational approach in Western cultures. This is not the case in India and the Far East. In these high power distance cultures, employees expect their boss to set goals for them and they are highly motivated to accomplish externally set goals. In fact, managers who empower their employees to set goals are considered to be weak and they often lose the respect of their subordinates.

Employees in Asian countries, where there is high collectivism and high power distance, are often more strongly motivated to avoid errors and failures than they are motivated to win and be the first one. This may be because of the fear of authority should they fail, and because of fear of failing the group to which a person belongs, as his/her personal failure is attributed to the entire group. Therefore, employees in the Far East are likely to set moderate rather than difficult goals, to reduce the risk of failure.

The motivations to avoid failure and to save face have implications for what is deemed the acceptable form of feedback. Feedback is considered to be a strong motivational factor in Western cultures, in particular when it is provided at the individual level. Yet, in countries such as Japan, feedback takes a different form. Explicit individual feedback threatens the individual's status in the team. It violates the important value of face saving, causing a person to feel shame. For this reason, implicit and impersonal feedback, oriented to the collective rather than to the individual, is considered to be the norm. Consequently, Western managers operating in the Far East should recognize such cultural differences and adjust their feedback to their employees to the local culture.

Reward allocation

A key issue is how to allocate rewards in order to enhance motivation. If you are an American manager, you most likely implement the principle of equity. Indeed, in most individualistic cultures, the rule of individual merit serves as the criterion for reward allocation. Employees receive rewards based on their individual contribution to goal attainment. Implementing rewards for performance requires the setting of criteria and standards for performance and an appraisal system for evaluating employees according to these criteria.

Payment-by-results dominates individualistic cultures such as the USA, England, and Australia. In collectivistic cultures payment-by-results may violate group harmony. Furthermore, it threatens the organizational hierarchy, as the most effective employee may not necessarily be the most senior and respected one. In that case, seniority plays an important role in the reward structure. Furthermore, when the work design is for teams, as is often the case, the reward differential is team based.

Managers in different cultures value different work components when evaluating their employees. Western managers evaluate employees mostly on the basis of performance effectiveness. Yet, Chinese managers put less emphasis on work performance as a criterion for rewards, compared with American managers. Rather, they consider the quality of interpersonal relationships to be more important for work than Americans (Zhou and Martocchio, 2001).

Rewarding for performance is less acceptable in collectivistic cultures and mainly when it is public. Chinese managers use the rule of equality more often than Americans mainly with respect to in-group members. However, for out-group allocation, equality is used when the allocation is public, to maintain face saving, while in-group favoritism often takes place when allocation is done privately. Similarly, Koreans, as opposed to Americans, perceive allocators who use equality rather than the merit rule more favorably. Swedish people use equality more frequently than Americans. The Swedish educational system discourages competition in favor of cooperation and teamwork.

In addition, the Swedish view the idea of need more positively than do Americans. The need rule is most highly preferred in India and in other collectivistic cultures, particularly when needs become visible (Murphy-Berman, Berman, Singh, Pachauri, and Kumar, 1984).

The above findings lead to the conclusion that the application of an inappropriate distribution rule may engender feelings of injustice, mitigating employees' motivation. Therefore, knowledge about cross-cultural differences with regard to preferences of allocation rules is vital for managers who operate outside their home country.

Teamwork and multicultural, virtual teams

Teams have different meanings in individualistic versus collectivistic cultures. Metaphors of teams in Puerto Rico and the Philippines, two collectivistic countries, are often in relational terms such as family and community. On the other hand, Americans use metaphors involving sport teams, reflecting an instrumental approach to teams as the means of accomplishing certain outcomes (Gibson and Zellmer-Bruhn, 2001).

Team work and tasks of high interdependence among team members prevail in collectivistic cultures. Yet, individualists prefer to be personally responsible for their job and to get personal recognition for their performance outcomes. Individualists are intrinsically motivated when empowered by their managers and when given the autonomy to craft their jobs to fit their personal resources. In contrast, collectivists are empowered when participating in the team decision-making process and when their team voice is being heard.

Work autonomy, whether at the individual or the team level, is not acceptable in high power distance cultures. Yet, in low power distance cultures, such as that of Israel, employees react negatively to goals that are assigned to them, as compared to employees who were allowed to participate in goal setting (Erez and Earley, 1987). Social loafing as observed by group performance loss is more prevalent among individualists who do not share responsibility and prefer to take a free ride, mainly when their individual contribution to the team cannot be identified. In contrast, social loafing was not observed in group-oriented cultures, such as China and Israel, providing the team members had a specific goal to acheive (Earley, 1989; Erez and Somech, 1996). In individualistic cultures, social loafing disappears when team members' contribution can be identified and when they are held personally accountable and responsible for the group outcomes (Weldon and Gargano, 1988).

Recent developments in communication technology have supported a relatively new form of virtual-multicultural teams (see Chapters 15 and 32). Such teams collaborate on joint projects while their members are located in different geographical zones and cultural environments.

Managing multicultural, virtual teams requires first and foremost the creation of a shared understanding among the team members. This is done by cultivating the global work values to be shared by all team members, and by creating a team identity that strengthens the sense of belongingness to and identification with the team.

Case Examples

Personal dilemma in an international acquisition

David A. is the CEO of Diamob, a young Israeli start-up in the medical instrument industry that develops high-resolution ultrasound diagnostics equipment on mobile computers. Diamob has just been acquired by a large US-based multinational company – Medica. Right after the acquisition there were rumors that Medica was going to transfer the new technology to other existing departments, closing Diamob Israel. The small group of 40 engineers and scientists was in a state of high ambiguity and each one of them had to decide what to do next. There were two options: to leave the company and search for another job, or to stay as a group and negotiate with Medica to let Diamob grow to a self-sustained profit unit.

David A. – Diamob CEO – knew that he could easily get a job in another company. Yet, if he quit, it would probably lead to the end of Diamob. David was a personal friend of most of the other engineers in Diamob. Many of them served together in the Israeli Defence Force and have remained friends since then. David was proud to see that in the first month after the acquisition the group stayed together and no one left in search of a new job even though their job security was at risk.

David gathered together the unit managers to discuss their future strategy. After long hours of discussions they developed a business plan that justified their continuous growth as a sustainable profit unit. David had to meet with Jeff S. – CEO Medica – and present to him the new Diamob business plan.

The meeting took place in an airport hotel on the East Coast. David's voice represented the voice of all his 40 engineers and he was very determined to succeed in getting Jeff to support the new business plan. Jeff listened to David and said: "listen, David, you are a very small group. We acquired Diamob because of your technology innovation and your initiative to develop the new product. We plan to recruit a small number of key experts from Diamob to Medica by offering them a high salary and then close Diamob, letting all other members go. You are the first one we want to hire. Your salary will be equal to the top executives in Medica, with a nice package of bonuses and stock options. You and the few people we hire will have to move to the US. Israel has a very small market and there is no reason for us to keep the site there.

David reflected upon what he just heard. From a personal point of view he had an opportunity to grow, to open up his horizon and scope and to get promoted in a large MNC. His salary and compensation package was going to be much higher than the present one. He would be able to support his family easily without any financial worries. On the other hand, it would mean that he would be separated from his colleagues, they would be losing their jobs and their dream to develop the small start-up company into a large profit organization would not materialize.

What is David's reply going to be? To answer this question, please take into consideration the cultural values of Israel, as summarized in Table 33.1.

What do you think David's reply would be if he were an American, working in the US and getting an offer from a European MNC?

Take into consideration the tension between global integration and local responsiveness and elaborate on how this tension is going to influence David's decision.

Cultural differences between employees and their manager

Red Algae is a Japanese company located in Eilat, a tourist town on the Red Sea, the south point of Israel. The location, the water and the temperature are most suitable for growing Red Algae, which is considered to be a very healthy food supplement consisting of high percentages of beta-carotene.

The company grows the Red Algae in Eilat, produces it as a food supplement pill in Japan, and sells it in the global market. The patent for Red Algae was written by life science researchers at the Weizmann Science Institute in Israel. The climate and type of soil in Eilat are considered by scientists to be most suitable for this purpose. The founder of the company and the top management team are all Japanese, but the chief scientist and the employees are all Israelis. The profit gain on the raw material grown in Israel is not that high. Most of the profit is being made on the food supplement pills. The Israeli inventor who has the technological patent is interested in making a joint venture with the Japanese company and to produce the pill in Israel. However, the Japanese headquarters strongly objects to it. In their view, Israeli employees do not strictly follow the rules, they like to improvise and they do not pay enough attention to detail. They are good in idea generation and innovation, but not in the careful, error-free implementation.

Mr. Takashi was appointed the Israel site manager. He oversees the process of growing the Red Algae in a special outdoor farm. The process is highly automatic and for this reason, the number of employees is relatively small, about 35, including Dan, the chief scientist. Mr. Takashi learned the production process with the help of Dan. He carefully read all the existing literature on growing Red Algae, including the patent of the Weizmann Institute. He, then, developed a set of procedures that should be carefully followed by the employees, to assure the high quality of the Red Algae.

Mr. Takashi wanted to implement Japanese management procedures. He expected all employees to appear on time, early in the day, to get together for the morning meeting to get updated about special problems and to align expectations. However, he has difficulties controlling the Israeli employees. First, they do not arrive at the same time in the morning. For this reason, he cannot properly hold the morning meeting. Second, they hardly follow the rules that he set for them. Some of them take a break during working hours to complete some family duties they have outside the workplace. Then, they stay late on their own, to compensate for the time taken, rather than working in close coordination with all other employees. Furthermore, employees are careless with respect to documenting their activities, as he requested. He often worries that the lack of standardization and documentation will result in a big disaster – the Red Algae will not grow to the quality and size needed. It often gets to critical points when he does not know how to cope with unexpected situations. These are exactly the moments when the Israeli employees become very alert, full of energy and resourcefulness, and they manage to improvise, rather than going by the book to resolve the problem.

Mr. Takashi keeps saying to his Israeli employees: "Please, do what you are required to do, please follow the rules very accurately. If you do this you will not have to improvise. I gave you specific guidelines. Simply follow them. Why argue with me all the time that there is a better way to do things. If I give you instructions, you need to follow them without any arguments."

Mr. Takashi feels that he does not properly manage the site and does not want to fail. Therefore, he asks his board to send him back to Japan. The Red Algae site in Israel now operates without the CEO.

Answer the following questions:

1. Should the company replace the Japanese manager with a local manager?
2. What are the main differences between Japanese and Israeli cultures?
3. Do you see these cultural differences as an advantage or a disadvantage to the company?
4. How can managers turn a potential disadvantage of cultural diversity into an advantage?
5. Think of culturally diverse teams. How can you bring people from diverse cultural backgrounds to work, communicate, and collaborate with each other effectively?

CONCLUSION

Global managers in the third millennium operate across cultural borders and geographical zones. They need to cope with the complexity of the global work environment, which consists of both the macro level of the global culture and the level of diverse national cultures nested underneath it. The core principle is, therefore, one of maintaining a global integration of one unified organization, but in parallel, understanding the cultural values and norms of the diverse workforce and relating to employees in each cultural setting according to their codes of behavior.

Global integration should take place with respect to the task-oriented managerial roles and values. These values should be homogeneously adopted across all subsidiaries and business units to allow communication and coordination of all organizational activities towards organizational goal accomplishment.

Nonetheless, local responsiveness should be implemented, mainly with respect to interpersonal relationships. Sensitivity to others begins with self-knowledge. Managers who learn about their own motives and cultural values recognize how such values shape the motives for coming to work, the desire to achieve goals, identification with the organization, and adaptation to the changing requirements. Managers who are aware of the meaning of their own self-worth and well-being can be sensitive to others' values and they are aware of the meaning of respecting these values for a person's sense of self-worth and well-being. Recognizing the diverse cultural environment should guide managers in selecting and implementing management practices that best fit the cultural values of employees in the business units they manage. While there are potentially many different practices that managers can implement, cultural values, once acknowledged, should serve as criteria for selecting and implementing the most effective management practices.

REFERENCES

Bandura, A. (1986). *Social Foundations of Thoughts and Action: A Social Cognitive Theory.* Englewood Cliffs, NJ: Prentice-Hall.

Berson, Y., Erez, M., and Adler, S. (2004). Reflections of organizational identity and national culture on managerial roles in a multinational corporation. *Academy of Management Best Paper Proceedings*, Q1–Q6.

Brewer, M. B., and Chen, Y. (2007). Where (who) are collectives in collectivism? Toward conceptual clarification of individualism and collectivism. *Annual Review of Psychology*, 114(1), 133–151.

Cushman, P. (1990). Why the self is empty? Towards a historically situated psychology. *American Psychologist*, 45, 599–611.

Drori, G. S., Jang, Y. S., and Meyer, J. W. 2006. Sources of Rationalized Governance: Cross-National Longitudinal Analyses, 1985–2002. *Administrative Science Quarterly*, 51, 205–229.

Earley, P. C. (1989). Social loafing and collectivism: a comparison of United States and the People's Republic of China. *Administrative Science Quarterly*, 34, 565–581.

Erez, M., and Earley, P. C. (1987). Comparative analysis of goal-setting strategies across cultures. *Journal of Applied Psychology*, 72, 658–665.

Erez, M., and Earley, P. C. (1993). *Culture, Self-Identity, and Work.* NY: Oxford University Press.

Erez, M., and Gati, E. (2004). A dynamic, multi-level model of culture: from the micro-level of the individual to the macro-level of a global culture. *Applied Psychology: An International Review*, 53, 583–598.

Erez, M., and Shokef, E. (2008). The culture of global organizations. In P. Smith, M. Peterson and D. Thomas (eds), *The Handbook of Cross-Cultural Management Research* (pp. 285–300). Thousdand Oaks, CA: Sage Publications, Inc.

Erez, M., and Somech, A. (1996). Group performance loss: The rule of the exception. *Academy of Management Journal*, 39, 1513–1537.

Friedman, L. T. (2005). *The World is Flat: A Brief History of the Twenty-first Century*. New York: Farrar, Straus and Giroux.

Gelfand, M., Erez, M., and Aycan, Z. (2007). Cross-cultural organizational behavior. *Annual Review of Psychology*, 58, 479–514.

Gelfand, M. J., Nishii, L. H., and Raver, J. L. (2006). On the nature and importance of cultural tightness-looseness. *Journal of Applied Psychology*, 91(6), 1225–1244.

Gibson, C. B., and Zellmer-Bruhn, M. E. (2001). Metaphors and meaning: An inter-cultural analysis of the concept of teamwork. *Administrative Science Quarterly*, 46(2), 274–306.

Govindarajan, V., and Gupta, A. K. (2001). *The Quest for Global Dominance*. San Francisco, CA: Jossey-Bass.

Hofstede, G. (1991). *Cultures and Organizations: Software of the Mind*. New York: McGraw-Hill.

Hofstede, G. (2001). Cultures consequences: Comparing values, behaviors, institutions and organizations across nations. Thousand Oaks, CA: Sage.

House, R., Hanges, P. J., Javidan, M., Dorfman, P. W., Gupta, V. (2004). *Culture, Leadership, and Organizations: The GLOBE Study of 62 Societies*. Thousand Oaks, CA: Sage.

Kostova, T., and Roth, K. (2002). Adoption of organizational practice by subsidiaries of multinational corporations: Institutional and relational effects. *Academy of Management Journal*, 45, 215–233.

Markus, H. R., and Kitayama, S. (1991). Culture and the self: Implications for cognition, emotion, and motivation. *Psychological Review*, 98, 224–253.

Markus, H. R., and Wurf, E. (1987). The dynamic self-concept: A social psychological perspective. *Annual Review of Psychology*, 38, 299–337.

Murphy-Berman, V., Berman, J., Singh, P., Pachuri, A., and Kumar, P. (1984). Factors affecting allocation to needy and meritorious recipients: A cross-cultural comparison. *Journal of Personality and Social Psychology*, 46, 1267–1272.

Schwartz, S. H. (1992). Universals in the content and structure of values: Theoretical advances and empirical tests in 20 countries. In M. Zanna (Ed.), *Advances in Experimental Social Psychology* (Vol. 25, pp. 1–65). Orlando, FL: Academic Press.

Shweder, R., and LeVine, R. (1984). *Culture Theory*. NY: Cambridge University Press.

Smith, L. (1990). Fear and loathing of Japan *Fortune*, No. 26, February, pp. 50–60.

Tajfel, H. (1981). Human groups and social categories: studies in social psychology. Cambridge: Cambridge University Press.

Triandis, H. C. (1989). The self and social behavior differing cultural contexts. *Psychological Review*, 96, 506–520.

Triandis, H. C., Bontempo, R., Vilareal, M. J., Masaaki, A., and Lucca, N. (1988). Individualism and collectivism: cross-cultural perspectives on self-ingroup relationships. *Journal of Personality and Social Psychology*, 54, 328–338.

Weldon, E., and Gargano, G. M. (1988). Cognitive loafing: The effects of accountability and shared responsibility on cognitive effort. *Personality and Social Psychology Bulletin*, 14, 159–171.

Zhou, J., and Martocchio, J. J. (2001). Chinese and American managers' compensation award decisions: A comparative policy-capturing study. *Personnel Psychology*, 54(1), 115–145.

Exercises[*]

The MCT project – bonus allocation

You are the global HR manager in a big multinational company that provides programming services. The company received a big project from a new global Chinese customer. The estimated time for accomplishing the project was one year.

A multicultural team (MCT) from a few subsidiaries was nominated to complete the mission. The virtual MCT consisted of five employees who worked on this project, which was estimated to bring revenues of about $2,000,000. However, the customer needed to have the project completed within nine months due to some changes in the market.

You talked with the team and promised them a bonus if they meet the new deadline. The team members stayed long hours and put in a lot of effort. As a result of the extra time and effort, the team was able to make it on time.

You have $100,000 to allocate as a bonus to the five group members. You have the following information about the five employees:

Person A: American nationality. He was the team leader. Put in a lot of effort and extra time to accomplish the project. He is very young (26 years old), single, individualist, and a promising manager.

Person B: German nationality. Did his best to get the project done within nine months and stayed extra hours at work, despite the fact that he is a single parent with two young children.

Person C: Mexican nationality. She is an excellent team member, very helpful to the other members. She badly needs more money to cover extra medical expenses for her parents.

Person D: Chinese nationality. He is a very influential person in his community. His social network helped the company to get this project. He spends a great deal of time socializing with employees of the customer Chinese company during the project.

Person E: Indian nationality. She is a specialist. She has the specialized knowledge necessary to do the work. Her contribution was crucial to the project and accounted for about 30% of the total time saving.

Distribute the $100,000 among the five team members. Indicate the percentage allocated to each member, the amount of money allocated to each member, and why. Specify the reasons for your decision.

---

[*]I would like to thank my doctoral student Alon Lisak for his contribution to preparing the exercises.

Person	%	Amount	Why
A			
B			
C			
D			
E			
TOTAL			

Getting to know the host culture

Practice target
Develop an awareness of cultural differences and identify the underlying cultural values of observed behaviors.

Instructions

1. Four volunteers leave the classroom for a few minutes.
2. The remaining students receive the following instructions: When your friends return to class, you will act as employees from a foreign country. When you answer their questions, you must follow these rules:
   (a) You refer to "We" and not to "I." You do not respond to very personal questions concerning your personal opinion, feelings, etc. You look at your classmates, trying to get their agreement to what you say. *(Individualism–Collectivism)*
   (b) You answer only when they use your family name, or another gesture of respect (e.g. Mr., Dr.). You also respond with gestures of respect. *(Power distance)*
   (c) When a woman is being asked, the man sitting next to her will reply instead. *(Masculinity–femininity)*
   (d) Your answer should not be factual or evidence based. Rather, you should respond in vague and ambiguous terms. (For example, "it will be all right"; "people say . . .," "we'll give it a try . . .," etc.). *(Uncertainty avoidance)*
   (e) You avoid conflicts and disagreements. *(Harmony)*
3. Please call back the volunteers and say: "Your multinational organization sent you as expatriates to work on a project which runs in a foreign country. This is your first day in the new site. You want to establish relationships with the local employees. Employees in your host country have different cultural values and rules than the ones you have. Your objective is to discover these rules. You can ask your foreign employees any question you like."
4. Let the class play the game for 15 minutes.
5. Discussion: At the end of the exercise you ask your class to interpret the rules in terms of Hofstede's cultural dimensions (1991, 2001). Identify differences between the host country and the expatriates. Ask the class to reflect upon the process of discovering the rules of behaviors and their underlying values. In addition, ask the participants to say how they felt about each other, what frustrated them, whether they were able to relate to each other and whether they believe they could successfully work together.

Index